Henry Kamen is Reader in History at the University of Warwick. He is the author of numerous articles in learned and other journals, and his published books, several of which have been translated into various foreign languages, include *The Spanish Inquisition, The Rise of Toleration, The War of Succession in Spain 1700-15,* and *A Concise History of Spain.* He has also published an English translation of Boris Pasternak's *In the Interlude: Poems 1945-1960.*

Cover picture: Fighting in a village by
Pieter Breughel.
(courtesy of Bulloz)

I

Also in this series and available in Cardinal

HISTORY OF CIVILISATION

THE IRON CENTURY

Social Change in
Europe 1550-1660

Henry Kamen

III

CARDINAL revised edition published in 1976
by Sphere Books Ltd
30/32 Gray's Inn Road, London WC1X 8JL

First published in Great Britain by
Weidenfeld & Nicholson Ltd 1971
Copyright (C) Henry Kamen 1971

Set and Printed by
The Guernsey Press Co., Ltd.,
Guernsey, Channel Islands.

CONTENTS

LIST OF ILLUSTRATIONS

ACKNOWLEDGMENTS

The author and publishers would like to thank the following for supplying, or for giving permission to reproduce, the photographs in this volume: Ashmolean Museum, Oxford, plate 34; Bibliothèque Nationale, Paris, plate 16; British Museum, plates 5, 22, 23, 28; Bulloz, plate 13; Country Life, plate 11; Foto-mas, Barcelona, plate 30; John Freeman, plate 29; Germanisches Nationalmuseum, Nuremburg, plates 17, 29; Mansell Collection, plates 10, 14, 16, 19; Mary Evans Picture Library, plates 4, 7, 21; Musée Royaux des Beaux Arts, plate 6; Museo del Prado, Madrid, plates 3, 33; National Gallery, plate 27; Osterreichische Nationalbibliothek, Vienna, plates, 2, 15, 36; Press-Photo Agency, Warsaw, plate 9; Radio Times Hulton Picture Library, plates 1, 8, 18, 20, 21, 24, 25, 26, 32, 35; Rijksmuseum, Amsterdam, plate 13; Roger Viollet, Paris, plate 12; Soprintendenza alle Gallerie e alle Opere d'Arte della Campania, Naples, plate 31.

FIGURES

This is the Iron Age, wherein iniquitie hath the upper hande, and all conditions and estates of men seeke to live by their wittes, and he is counted the wisest that hath the deepest insight into the getting of gaines.

ROBERT GREENE, *Defence of Conny Catching* (1592).

Happy the age, happy those centuries which the ancients called the age of gold: not because gold, so much adored in this Iron Age, was then easily obtained, but because those two words, *thine* and *mine*, were unknown to the people living in that holy age, when all things were in common.

GERVANTES, *Don Quijote de la Mancha* (1605).

Je ne veux rien prononcer sur les moeurs du siecle ous nous sommes. Je peux bien assurer seulement qu'il n'est des meilleurs, estant un Siecle de Fer.

ROBERT MENTET DE SALMONET,
Historie des troubles de la Grande-Bretagne (1649).

For Nicholas and Jeffrey.

Many thanks go to my publishers, who have shown considerable patience in waiting for me to produce this book: though I must say in my defence that some of the blame for the delay belongs to my two infant sons who appear in the dedication. Dr Michael Mallet, Dr Henry Cohn and Professor Hugh Trevor-Roper were kind enough to look through parts of the text, and I am extremely grateful for their comments and criticisms. My wife typed most of the text and saved me from several errors.

FOREWORD

This is not a comprehensive survey of the period 1550-1660. I have chosen to concentrate on social change and the fate of the lower classes, and to set these subjects against the background of economic and political history. Sections I, II and IV therefore share some unity of theme. Section III is more idiosyncratic, the emphasis being on the Counter Reformation (rather than on Protestantism) and on those aspects, such as toleration and Utopianism, which seldom make a showing in general surveys. Readers will find virtually nothing here on art, culture or science, and even the section on religion is clearly fragmentary. Before the critics accuse me of ignorance or distortion, I hasten to make two points. In the first place, this book is an essay in quantitative social history, in the material infrastructure of life rather than the cultural superstructure. The social history of culture has barely begun to be written, and this essay is not the place to make the attempt. Secondly, I believe that art, culture and science are so important that for this exciting period they deserve a special volume, rather than a few hasty references in what is already a fairly large book. *The Iron Century* in other words, makes no claim to represent the total reality of the century of the Counter Reformation,

It will be seen that my treatment of themes has been uneven, and topics such as refugees and witchcraft have been given an inordinate amount of attention. I have, in effect, deliberately expanded those sections where the availability of evidence and the interest (though not necessarily the importance) of the subject seemed to justify it. In this respect the lengthy Chapter 10, on popular rebellions, represents an effort to communicate to the reader all the available literature on the subject, and in a sense may be considered the key chapter in the book.

The unevenness and imbalance are part of the plan of the work, since I have aimed to set out arguments and to develop lines of enquiry rather than merely to provide a text-book exposition. Readers who prefer a more conventional approach have enough books to choose from: mine is not meant to add to their number. I have chosen to write of an Iron Century and an Iron Age because this is how contemporaries thought of it, and it is time that we looked again at the past through their eyes rather than through the eyes of those modern writers who see only the gilt glittering on the surface.

Substantial parts of the volume are based on original research, but I have decided not to complicate the presentation by adding footnotes or a list of primary sources. For this I crave the forgiveness of scholars.

University of Warwick

Foreword to the Second Edition

I have taken the opportunity of this new edition, to revise several passages and to correct errors that have been pointed out to me by reviewers and colleagues, particularly by Dr Henry Cohn, Mr Bob Knecht, Professor John Elliott and Professor Andrew Lossky. A discussion of some implications of the phrase 'an Iron Century' is given in my article 'Golden age, iron age: a conflict of concepts in the Renaissance', in the autumn 1974 issue of *The Journal of Medieval and Renaissance Studies*.

H.K.

I

STRUCTURES

1 THE DIMENSIONS OF LIFE

The world is small: I mean that it is not as large as people say it is.
CHRISTOPHER COLUMBUS (in 1503)

. . . and the life of man, solitary, poor, nasty, brutish, and short.
THOMAS HOBBS. Leviathan (1651)

By the middle of the sixteenth century, Europe had begun to expand into every corner of the world, and Europeans were threatening the security of the most advanced civilisations of the globe. Inevitably this vigorous expansion brought with it a shift in the perspectives of everyday life at home, as trade brought new goods into the home market, and commercial activity began to exploit the riches of newly acquired overseas possessions. It was not only the outside world that was changing. At home the whole outlook of Europeans had been overturned by the revolutionary events of the Reformation. The period that concerns us here, the century after the Reformation, still seethed with the problems and conflicts raised by the split in Christendom. So profound are the changes of the post-Reformation era that many historians continue to look on the religious, economic and political events of the time as being revolutionary in character. But it is important to notice also that in its turn the revolutionary tide produced a reaction which checked and altered the momentum of change. This tension between ebb and flow, between stagnation and advance, that characterises the age, will be described here in terms of a 'crisis': one that occurred specifically towards the middle of the seventeenth century.

When speaking of a 'crisis', we are principally describing the dialectic of change, but we are also relating it specifically to the immensely important developments of the period. Thinking men at the time were certainly aware of changes in every branch of social activity, whether in the diminishing value of the money in their pockets, or in the growing number of unemployed in the towns, or in the growing intensity of ideological conflict and the

3

havoc created by years of incessant war. On every side the pattern of existence was being rapidly transformed, and it is to examine the significance of this that we now turn.

SPACE

How big was the European world of 1550? Here we have some evidence of the great transformation that had come over Europe. The traders, adventurers and explorers of the Atlantic seaboard had immeasurably extended the horizons of a late sixteenth-century European. The brief and fragmentary mediaeval contacts between Europe and Asia were replaced in the Renaissance epoch by direct, extensive and profitable contacts between the traders of Europe and the Asian monarchies. While Portugal was reaping a rich harvest from the spice trade in the East Indies, the Spaniards in America had begun to consolidate an empire which in territory and in mineral wealth exceeded that of every other European power.

Between the Portuguese and Spanish enterprises there had always been bitter rivalry, which asserted itself not only in an exclusive control of their respective empires, but also in the control of information. Before about 1550 the Portuguese exercised strict control over the circulation of printed literature concerning their territories in Asia, in order to preserve the security that surrounded their monopoly of the spice trade. The Spaniards were not so secretive, partly because there seemed less danger of foreign intrusion into America, partly because the controversies surrounding the methods of conquest required public airing, otherwise, as the contemporary historian Antonio de Herrera said, 'the reputation of Spain would fall rapidly, for foreign and enemy nations would say that small credence could be placed in the words of her rulers, since their subjects were not allowed to speak freely'. The desire to curtail information, a desire common to most states at this time, crumbled before a growing curiosity on the part of the public, and increased activity on the part of the printing press.

After 1550, Europe was flooded by literature on the overseas territories opened up by the explorer and trader. The collections of the Venetian scholar Gian Battista Ramusio, whose three-volume *Delle navigazioni e viaggi* began to appear in 1550, and of Richard Hakluyt, whose *Principall Navigations, Voiages and Discoveries of the English nation* first came out in 1589, were typical of the best in travel accounts. Their publication was both symptom and cause of a curiosity about the outside world, and an acceptance of the colonial destiny, that confirmed Europe's will to expansion. In these accounts the literate public, and through them the non-reading public, could acquaint themselves with realities far removed from the fabulous and fantastic compilations, descriptions of bisexual monstrosities and dog-headed men, with which their fathers had been regaled.

Travel and exploration were only the first stage in Europe's discovery of the outside world. The sharp contrast in attitudes between the early and the late sixteenth century is testimony to this. In the early period the sense of wonder was still paramount in the reports of European travellers. Many realised with a sense of shock that Asia and America frequently outdid any marvels that Europe might offer. Antonio Pigafetta, who sailed with Magellan in 1522 on the first European circumnavigation of the globe, claimed to have heard that the Emperor of China was 'the greatest in all the world'. Cortés, writing to his own emperor after his entry into Tenochtitlán in 1519, claimed soberly of Moteczuma's palaces that 'there is not their like in all Spain'. The great temple, he said, was one 'whose size and magnificence no human tongue could describe', and the city itself he called 'the most beautiful thing in the world'. Recalling in his old age the splendours of Mexico, Bernal Díaz said that even the market place was such that 'some of our soldiers who had been in many parts of the world, in Constantinople, in Rome, and all over Italy, said that they had never seen a market so well laid out, so large, so orderly, and so full of people'.

In the course of the sixteenth century this awareness of Europe's unpretentious part in world civilisation was superseded by a new, more aggressive attitude. Confident in his own superiority of technology and weapons, the European moved forward almost effortlessly into the colonial epoch. The result was an all too easy assumption of moral and civil destiny-to-rule. The commercial enterprise of the Portuguese and the English, no less than the more ruthless imperialism of the Spaniards and the Dutch, were alike infused by this attitude. In part, it sprang from a purely religious conviction that the Faith must be taken to the heathen. In this respect the most remarkable achievements were those of men like St Francis Xavier, whose global vision took him to Goa, Malabar, Malacca, Japan and the Chinese coast; and of Fray Toribio de Motolinía, who in 1524 landed in Mexico with eleven other Franciscans to begin the first large-scale

5

evangelisation ever undertaken by Christians outside Europe. In part it sprang also from an assumption of inherent racial superiority. 'How can we doubt', wrote the Spanish humanist Juan Ginés de Sepúlveda in 1547, 'that these people—so uncivilised, so barbaric, contaminated with so many impieties and obscenities—have been justly conquered by such an excellent, pious and most just king, and by a nation so humane and so excelling in every kind of virtue?' His attitude to the American natives, the attitude of a theoretician with no direct personal knowledge of America, may be set beside the creed of a man who did have extensive personal knowledge of his country's colonial possessions. This was the seventeenth-century Dutchman, Jan Pieterz Coen, creator of the Dutch empire in the East Indies. 'May not a man in Europe', he asked a critic of his policies, 'do what he likes with his cattle? Even so does the master here do with his men, for these with all that belongs to them are as much the property of the master as are brute beasts in the Netherlands.'

What we are stating extremely briefly here—the fact that European awareness of the outside world was moving from exploration to colonialism—may best be illustrated by looking at the power of Spain. By the 1580s Spain had established the largest empire on the face of the earth. The European world-space had been extended to fill the globe. Dominant in Europe, supreme in the Iberian peninsula, heir to the Portuguese empire abroad, master of America and conqueror of the Philippines, Spain typified the new vigour of Europe. The soul of a Spaniard could not fail to show some pride in this universal monarchy. 'All has now been traversed and all is known', cried the historian Francisco López de Gómara in 1552. The frontiers open to the spreading of the Faith were now boundless, proclaimed a writer in 1588: 'there is no Peru so far removed, no China, no island so secret, no torrid zone so glowing with heat, no Arctic or Antarctic Circle so wintry and frozen, that God's hand cannot reach'. And in tune with this confidence came the new and growing tradition of dominance, as stated firmly in 1590 by the Jesuit historian José de Acosta when, applauding the possession by Spain of America, he affirmed that this was entirely 'in accordance with the desire of Providence that certain kingdoms rule others'.

The enlargement of space was not confined only to the world-vision of statesmen, propagandists and traders. For the first time, extraordinary opportunities for movement were offered to the ordinary people of Europe. Within their own countries,

6

Europeans were capable of regular internal migration, so that they were not confined for life to a limited space in which they were fated both to be born and to die. Beyond this, however, they were now offered the dazzling prospect of emigration to the new lands across the Atlantic. It was the Spaniards who led the way to America, but in the early seventeenth century the English also emigrated in large numbers. Which of them could resist the appeal of the continent where, wrote an English propagandist, the 'fertilitie of soyle, insinuation of seas, multiplicitie of rivers, safetie of ports, healthfulnesse of air, opportunitie of habitations, hopes in present, hopes of future, worlds of varietie in that diversified world; do quicken our minds to apprehend what our tongues do declare and fill both with arguments of divine praise'?

DISTANCE

Not the least amazing feature of the expansion of Europe was the conquest of distance. A casual look at the map, at the distances covered by the ships trading to Asia round the Cape, the voyages made by the English settlers to North America, the territory traversed by Francis Xavier or by Pizarro, might lead to the suspicion that technological progress had made it all possible, and had reduced the space-time ratio. Yet, for all the revolutionary progress in nautical science, time was barely attacked. Ships and land vehicles had to wait as before on wind and weather, and the endurance of man alone was a decisive factor in the conquest of distance. Even the best transport was subject to the caprice of the elements: why else should the norm of the overland postal service between Lisbon and Danzig at the end of the sixteenth century vary from fifty-three to one hundred and thirty-two days?

Within Europe the conquest of distance was relatively easy, if uncertain. Water, horse or coach were the three means of travel, and their efficiency varied. Over long distances the sea was beyond all doubt the quickest method of communication, but over smaller, overland areas the horse was certainly faster and more reliable, making it the obvious basis for the nascent postal services of Europe. An elementary distinction must be made between postal distance and human distance, for the post would clearly be despatched at speeds that the ordinary traveller could not or would not wish to attain. For all that, the postal transmissions were certainly helping to make the European space smaller, both by making news available more rapidly and by making swift travel more habitual. The publication of news is a useful guide to the time-distance between cities. A Haarlem gazette of 9 January 1627, for example, included dispatches from Linz dated 12 December, from Venice dated 18 December, from Paris dated 21 December, and from Berlin dated 22 December. Allowing for the delay before publication, this gives some idea of the speed at which news could travel. Figure 1, overleaf, shows the various speeds at which news travelled between Venice and other European cities in the early sixteenth century.

Thanks to the uncertainty of conditions, it is difficult to specify what the normal time-distance between any two points would have been. For the late sixteenth century, it seems that the post-horse between, for example, Augsburg and Ulm normally took one day, while the distance from Augsburg to Marseilles, with appropriate stops, was covered in fourteen days. From Antwerp at the same period the post to Amsterdam normally took between three and nine days, while to Danzig the time was anything between twenty-four and thirty-five days. At a later date, an English regulation of 1637 specified that post-letters were to travel in summer at seven miles an hour and in winter at six. Little progress appears to have been made in this direction, since we find that in 1666 the average speed of letters from Plymouth, Chester and York to London was not more than four miles an hour. To turn from this almost leisurely pace to the New World in the sixteenth century comes as something of a shock. There the Inca postal system attained speeds unequalled until the invention of the internal combustion engine. The Inca roads had regular stages at which runners were posted, and all messages were run by them. The average speed they attained was in the region of one hundred and fifty miles a day. The distance from Lima to Cuzco by runner took mail three days, whereas a post-horse in the seventeenth century doing the same distance took about twelve days. So efficient was the delivery that the Inca used to have fresh fish run up from the coast to Cuzco, a distance of some three hundred and fifty miles, in two days.

Despite the uncertain and dilatory progress of com-munications, Europeans were gradually being put within reasonable distance of each other. Outside Europe, the vastness of distance required measurement more in terms of endurance than of time (and the Inca postal service may well be put in this category). Those who could conquer these spaces were truly heroic, like Columbus, who informed Queen Isabella in 1503 that

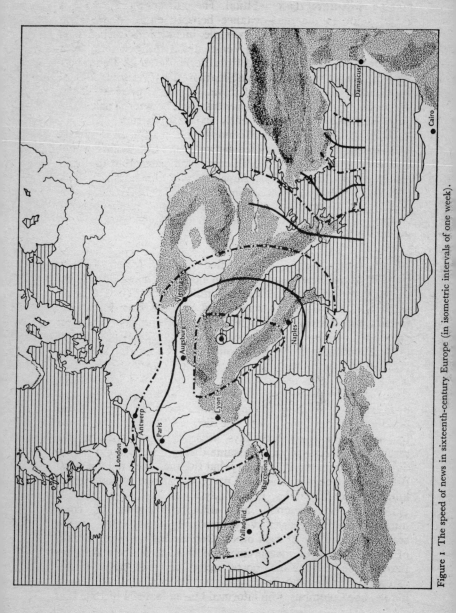

Figure 1 The speed of news in sixteenth-century Europe (in isometric intervals of one week).

9

'the world is small: I mean that it is not as large as people say it is'. Few others would have agreed with the words of the admiral. The prodigious feat of Magellan and Sebastián del Cano, in an expedition which set out from Seville with five ships in September 1519 and returned in September 1522 with only one vessel containing fifteen men, after having sailed around the world, was proof of the high cost exacted by any attempt to make the world smaller. When Francis Drake made the same voyage fifty-five years later, the difficulties were still prohibitive: he had five ships when he set sail from Plymouth in December 1577, and only one when he returned just under three years later, in September 1580. The long absence is deceptive, for in all voyages of the time far longer periods were spent in harbour than at sea, but the sea was still a formidable distance. The ships of the American passage, the *carrera de Indias*, took on the average seventy-five days to cross the Atlantic from Seville to Vera Cruz, and one hundred and thirty days to cross in the reverse direction, about a fortnight of the latter period being spent in Havana waiting for the fleet to assemble. The entire period of absence, however, including the stay in Vera Cruz, would mean that a ship leaving Seville in July one year did not normally return before October in the subsequent year. America was still, then, a distant country, and those who ventured to it had to undergo all the rigours of the passage. When the *Mayflower* left Plymouth in September 1620 on its sixty-five day journey across the ocean, its passengers could hardly suspect the heavy price they were to pay for their venture. Only five of the full complement of one hundred and forty-nine passengers and crew died on the crossing, but the sufferings of the voyage led directly to an epidemic that killed off half their number in America.

To note these individual sea voyages is hardly enough to describe the fortitude with which European adventurers and pilgrims overcame the problem of distance, particularly in Central and South America. What other race but the Spanish, asked the historian Cieza de León, could have penetrated 'through such rugged lands, such dense forests, such great mountains and deserts, and over such broad rivers'? We can reply that the Russians in Siberia, the Puritans in New England, the Dutch and Portuguese in Africa and Asia, were each in their own way, and often with methods that few would approve, bringing the outside world closer to Europe and thereby conquering the great gulf imposed by time and space.

Only to the imperialist did distance seem constantly insuperable. From 1870 the British could govern India almost effortlessly through the telegraph, but in the sixteenth century Philip II remained gravely embarrassed by the slowness of communication with his administrators. 'I have not heard anything from the king about the affairs of the Netherlands since 20 November last', complained the governor of that region, Luis de Requeséns, from Antwerp on 24 February 1575. A delay in communication of this magnitude—three months—would certainly have had serious consequences if it occurred too often. The tragedy is that it occurred all too often in the vain attempt made by Madrid to keep direct and efficient control over America. Insistence by the Spanish authorities that they control the essential business of the Indies meant that many decisions would only be referred to the peninsula. Given the distance involved, and the time allowed for deliberation in Madrid, a reply would take a year, or more commonly two years, to reach America. Administrators in America could likewise make delays to serve their own purposes. When Charles V, for example, wrote to Cortés in June 1523 with orders to respect the freedom of the Indians, Cortés did not reply until October 1524, which meant that it was not until 1525 that the emperor learnt of Cortés's unwillingness to carry out his orders! Between delays in decision and delays in expedition the machinery of absolutist government inevitably dwindled in efficiency.

TIME

To the administrators, as to the generals, and those who governed human affairs, time remained supremely important. So important was it in 1560 for Philip II's ambassador in France to get an urgent message through to Toledo, and have a reply brought to him at Chartres, that he paid the enormous sum of three hundred and fifty-eight ducats (well above the entirely yearly salary of a university professor) for the service. Businessmen also had an investment in time. Any delay in the payment of bills of exchange, in the arrival of the galleons, in the shipment of perishable cargo, might spell ruin. Yet when all the evidence for the urgent demands of these men of the world is considered, there can be little doubt that they were only a minority group. Time had not yet become what it now is in an industrial age, a pacemaker. On the contrary, there were few activities that needed to be measured against a stopwatch, so that the age appears to move at a casual and unconscionably slow pace, regulated only by the movements of the sun, the cycle of the seasons, and an occasional clock.

Clocks, like the precise regulation of time, were a relative novelty in 1550. The population still took its division of the hours and minutes from the Church. The day was measured by liturgical hours, church bells tolled the passing of its constituent units, and smaller divisions of time were commonly expressed in terms of *Aves* or *Paternosters*. In such a culture civil time and ecclesiastical time were inseparable, and it was one of the virtues of the post-Reformation era that it helped to distinguish between the two. Protestantism liberated time from its clerical dress, and clocks came in to secularise it completely. By the end of the sixteenth century the clock industry was booming, particularly when the clockmakers from Catholic countries fled as refugees to Protestant states. In 1515 there were no clockmakers in Geneva, after 1550 they came as refugees from France, and by 1600 the city had twenty-five to thirty master clockmakers and an unknown number of apprentices. England too had to wait for its watch industry until the immigrants came at the end of the sixteenth century. In the strongly mathematical universe that scientists and intellectuals invented for themselves in the early seventeenth century, clocks played an essential part. In contrast to the genial, unmeasured pace of earlier decades, in contrast to Gargantua's protest, 'I never rule myself by time!', the seventeenth century began the remorseless subjection of humanity to the clock. It was Kepler, the great astronomer, who looked upon the universe and pronounced it 'similar to a clock', Boyle who considered it 'a great piece of clockwork'. The march of the clock was advanced further in 1657 when Huyghens presented to the Estates of Holland a clock whose measurement of time was precisely controlled by the perfectly balanced swings of a pendulum.

Despite these scientific advances, the European world remained essentially independent of any attempt to rationalise time. Clocks and watches were the preserve of a minority. The working population still ruled itself by the hours of daylight, by the bells and by the seasons. It was usual to work only by daylight, so that a winter working day was usually shorter than a summer working day by at least two hours, and wages were consequently less. In sixteenth-century Antwerp, for example, building workers had a seven-hour day in winter but a twelve-hour day in summer; winter wages were one-fifth lower than in summer. Concepts like 'daylight' and 'from sunrise to sunset' were habitually written into regulations for work, but could seldom have been literally enforced. Only a very few trades had their hours of work laid down precisely, regardless of daylight: thus in 1571 the printers of Lyon complained because their working day was scheduled to begin at 2 am and did not end until about 8 pm.

For most workers, especially those on the land, imprecision of time took strict discipline out of work. Rest from labours was officially recognised and encouraged. Sunday was normally a day of rest, but so too in many places was Monday taken as an unofficial rest day. In addition the feast days of the Church continued to loom large. In the diocese of Paris at the beginning of the seventeenth century, for example, there were fifty-nine obligatory religious holidays, which together with the Sundays made up well over 100 days a year. As La Fontaine commented later in the century, ' *on nous ruine en fêtes* '. But this system was not necessarily as harmful as it may seem, for, particularly in the mainly agricultural economy of the time, there was not always enough work to employ people intensively throughout the week, so that holidays provided an alternative to what might otherwise have passed for days of unemployment. All classes, and not merely the leisured section of the population, accepted this casual attitude to the utilisation of time. It was a programme imposed by an age ignorant of industrial capitalism, an age of slow communications and long distances, an age in which the dominant agrarian economy waited more on the tardy seasons than on the clock. Small wonder then that there should be revolt when the old and well-tried order was replaced by a new calendar. In France the king in 1563 decreed that instead of the previous system by which the year was dated from Easter to Easter, the whole country should henceforward start the year on 1 January. There was strong opposition and the Parlement of Paris refused to register the edict until January 1567, so that the year 1566 in France was only eight months seventeen days long. A definitive international reform of the calendar did not come until 1582, when Pope Gregory XIII formulated a new year from which he had abolished ten days. This time the opposition came from the majority of Protestant countries, which chose to ignore the papal reform and to lag ten days behind the rest of Europe.

POPULATION STRUCTURES

What was the place of man in the Europe of this century? Perhaps the most obvious feature is that the time allotted to the average man was short in comparison with modern life expectation. Fewer children than now lived to grow old, and more adults than now died young. The situation would differ according to environment and social class, but on the whole it was a society (and, since the research so far done has been limited in area, we must say a western European society) in which the balance was heavily tilted in favour of youth, simply because the possibility of a ripe old age had been foreshortened.

One way of looking at the brevity of life is to consider what the average life expectancy at birth might have been. Evidence is most readily available for privileged and easily measurable minorities such as the aristocracy. A survey of the ruling families of western Europe over the whole seventeenth century suggests that the average male expectation of life at birth was twenty-eight years, and the female expectation thirty-four years. In the English peerage over the century 1575-1674 the average male expectation at birth was thirty-two years, the average female 34·8 years (figures which can be compared with the period 1900-24, when the life expectation of a male peer was sixty, of a female seventy years). Similarly, a study of nineteen of Geneva's leading bourgeois families shows that in the half-century 1600-49 the male child at birth could expect to live to thirty, the female to thirty-five years. By modern standards these figures are staggering, yet it is worth remembering that it is the privileged, those most likely to be protected against hunger and disease, who are represented here. The lot of the poorer people, for whom records are more difficult to come by, was certainly and indescribably worse. A study covering 3,700 children of all classes born in Paris at the end of the seventeenth century, for instance, arrives at an overall life expectancy of twenty-three years, a figure which begins to come closer to the condition of the mass of the population.

The picture seems bad enough when compared with a life expectancy of over sixty years for a modern British male child, but it becomes immeasurably worse when we look at the recorded child mortality of the time. The figures show that life expectancy was lowered principally by the very high death rate during infancy and childhood. In sixteenth-century Castile the mortality was notably high: in the rural areas round the city of Valladolid, in the villages of Simancas, Cabezón and Cigales, it appears that between forty and fifty per cent of all children died before their seventh year; while in the neighbouring city of Palencia as many as sixty-eight per cent of those born between 1576 and 1600 died before the age of seven. Comparable figures can be obtained for France. Generalising from the data available for the parish of Crulai in Normandy and the area round the cities of Beauvais and Amiens, we can say that nearly twenty-five per cent of all children born in the north of France in the seventeenth century died during their first year of life, and that a possible average of fifty per cent of all babies failed to reach the age of twenty. This can be illustrated in detail from the Auneuil district of Beauvais, where over the period 1656-1735 out of one thousand live births there were only seven hundred and twelve survivors of both sexes at the end of the first year. At the end of five years there were five hundred and sixty-seven survivors, five hundred and twenty-nine at the end of ten, and four hundred and eighty-nine at the end of twenty. This indicates a levelling out of the incidence of mortality, and a rise in the rate of life expectancy after the years of infancy. The example of the Capdebosc family in the Condomois (France) is instructive. Jean Dudrot de Capdebosc married Margaride de Mouille on 19 May 1560. They had ten children, of whom five died before their tenth year. Odet, the eldest son, married Marie de la Crompe in 1595: of their eight children five did not reach their tenth year. Jean, the eldest, married twice. Jeanne, his first wife, had two children, one of whom died at nine years, the other at five weeks. Marie, the second wife, had thirteen children in the twenty-one years 1623-45. Of them six died in infancy, one was killed in war, two became nuns. Of the thirty-three children born to this prolific family during the century, only six founded a family. The principal reason: infant mortality.

The knowledge that life would be short, and that only a relatively small proportion of the population would survive into old age, must have made the quality of life differ appreciably from that of modern Europe. Without a large complement of aged people, the Europe of 1600 was predominantly a youthful one, a pre-industrial society in which natural forces conspired to keep life cruelly short. Children and young people must have been everywhere more in evidence than the aged. In Germany in 1538 we find Sebastian Franck complaining that 'the whole of Germany is teeming with children'. That this was not mere imagination is suggested by the calculation of the English demographer Gregory King in 1695 that over forty-five per cent of the people of England and Wales were children. Elsewhere in Europe the picture was similar. In four parishes of Cologne in 1574, thirty-five per cent of the people were children below the age of fifteen; in six districts of Jena in 1640 the proportion was an average thirty-eight per cent; while Leiden in 1622 seems to have had somewhere near forty-seven per cent. The predominant age group in society was therefore a surprisingly young one. Gregory King's figures for England put the average age of the population at about twenty-seven years, a calculation that is supported by other evidence. England was not exceptional in this low average. In Geneva in the period 1561-1600 the average age of the population was as low as twenty-three, and only in the years 1601-1700 did it rise to 27·5 years. This unusual age structure in society may be made clearer by comparing some figures. In the table opposite, some data for modern England are set beside figures for the earlier period.

Age group	Venice 1610-20	England and Wales 1695 (King)	Elbogen circle (Bohemia) late 17th century	England and Wales 1958
		in percentages of the population		
0 to 9	18.5	27.6	26	14.8
10 to 9	18.2	20.2	20	14.2
20 to 9	15.4	15.5	18	13.8
30 to 9	15.7	11.7	14	14.1
40 to 9	11.0	8.4	9	13.9
50 to 9	8.3	5.8	] 13	13.2
60+	12.9	10.7		16.9

If the dominant age group was young, it may be presumed that marriages occurred even earlier than they do now. Such an assumption, which at one time used to be made on the basis of literary evidence, can no longer be held. The carefully considered evidence of demographic historians now shows that, contrary to the earlier impression, people in fact tended to marry at a reasonably mature age, and that this was equally true of both urban and rural areas. The reasons for this are not entirely clear. It may be that, as in some modern communities, the partners delayed until they could achieve economic independence from their relatives; or it may be that late marriage was a conscious way of restricting the size of one's family. A few years could make quite a lot of difference. As one historian has observed, 'an average age at first marriage for women of, say, twenty-four might well produce two more children than marriages contracted at an average age of, say, twenty-nine'. Whatever the reasons, the available figures speak for themselves. The admittedly limited data obtained from an analysis of the Genevan bourgeoisie shows that in the late sixteenth century (1550-99) the girls tended to marry on the average at about twenty-two years, the men at about twenty-seven; by the early seventeenth century (1600-49) this had risen to nearly twenty-five for the girls, twenty-nine for the men. In Old Castile in the sixteenth century the ages were somewhat lower: girls married at about twenty, men at about twenty-five. None of these figures is representative enough to allow us to generalise about common practice: the Genevan ages apply to a small, perhaps untypical, class; the Castilian ages to a solid rural community.

When we get to the seventeenth century, however, we find the pattern largely unchanged. In the diocese of Canterbury between 1619 and 1660, out of a total of over one thousand recorded first marriages the mean age of brides was 23·9, of grooms 26·8 years. In the country parish of Colyton in Devon in the late sixteenth and early seventeenth centuries the average age at first marriage of both men and women was about twenty-seven years. The marriage habits of the English nobility differed from these figures only in that noblewomen tended to marry younger. While the age of noblemen at first marriage varied from about twenty-five years in 1560 to nearly twenty-seven in 1660, noblewomen in 1560 married at just over twenty years and in 1660 at just under twenty-two. The data for Crulai, Beauvais and Amiens in France give the same sort of conclusion for the mid-seventeenth century. Here the girls tended to marry at between twenty-four and twenty-five years, the men at twenty-seven or over.

When we consider the life expectancy of the period, these marriage ages seem to be late rather than early, and it would appear that the average couple could look forward to a relatively short married life. At Basel in the 1660s, for example, the average length of a marriage was just over twenty years. As a consequence of this and of high mortality, the unity of the family often had to be maintained by a second or even a third marriage. The upper classes were more in a position to afford this than anyone else. In the Genevan group, in 1550-99, out of every hundred marriages among men, seventy-four were for the first time and twenty-six were re-marriages. The English nobility also had a high re-marriage rate. In the period 1575-1674 as many as 21·8 per cent of those nobles of either sex who had married once, married again. Looking at a wider social spectrum than those privileged classes, we still find a very similar pattern, as in Amsterdam in 1600, where there were twenty-one re-marriages for every hundred first marriages among the population.

The relative brevity of married life, and the very high infant mortality, meant that the balance of birth over death was very precariously maintained. It only needed a disaster—say a war or an epidemic—to tilt the balance heavily in favour of death. Even without such disasters, in normal conditions in the early seventeenth century something like two live births were necessary to produce every adult human. Enormous importance must therefore be attached to the fertility rate at this period. For present purposes it is simplest to look at the size of the average western European family. One contrast with the modern condition stands out immediately. In twentieth-century Europe the economically privileged classes and nations tend to have small families, and the poorer communities tend to have large ones. In sixteenth- and seventeenth-century Europe, on the other hand, precisely the opposite held good: poorer people tended to have fewer children, while those high up the social scale had more. In sixteenth-century Old Castile, a study of the village of Villabáñez shows that families on the average seldom had more than four children. In seventeenth-century France and England the same sort of size was maintained in small towns and rural communities, the average number of children in France being just over four per family. A census of the city of Norwich in the late sixteenth century suggests a figure of 2·3 as the average number of children in a family from the poor sectors of the population (as against 4·2 children among the wealthy burgesses). From evidence like this about the size of families and households it can be seen that the Europe of this time was far from having the large families usually associated with underprivileged pre-industrial communities.

It is not until we turn to the privileged sector of the population, the rich bourgeoise and the nobility, that we find it possible for parents to afford numerous children. The English aristocracy seem to have been fairly restrained in this respect, since over the century 1575-1674 they averaged five children per family. This moderate pattern was upset only seldom by the heroic few, such as the first Earl Ferrers (1650-1717), who had thirty bastards and twenty-seven legitimate children to his credit. It is when we come to the flourishing bourgeoisie of Geneva that we meet fairly large families as the rule rather than the exception. Here in the late sixteenth century we find that of families where the wife had married before the age of twenty, no less than forty-two per cent had nine to eleven children, and eleven per cent had over fifteen. Over the whole period 1550-1649 the average number of children in a family depended on the wife's age at marriage, as follows:

Age at marriage:	under 20	20-24	25-29	30-39
Children:	9.67	7.37	4.85	2.29

The imbalance in size of families between different sectors of the population causes little discussion in an age like ours where birth control is a common practice. The clear difference between the number of live births in rich and poor families in the sixteenth century, however, suggests that some form of birth control was also practised then. The poor could not afford many children, and resorted to means of control. One of the biggest social problems that St Vincent de Paul had to deal with in France, for example, was the number of abandoned babies, *enfants trouvés*, who could be found anywhere, in town or country, deliberately exposed to die, or neglected because no food could be found. More difficult to trace than this sort of practice was the actual prevention of conception. This was probably not widespread, and the full weight of Church disapproval lay against it, but evidence suggests that on certain occasions—during a famine, for example—a severe fall in the birth rate could be attributed not only to unusual mortality but also to some voluntary limitation. Even in normal times, as a study of the parish of Colyton in the early seventeenth century has shown, there is no doubt that limitation of births was undertaken, though the actual means used remains obscure.

The best documented cases of birth control refer not to the rural population so much as to people in the cities, middle-class people, and above all the court. Prostitutes, of course, had to be adept at contraception, but there were others. A French writer, Henri Estienne, refers in a 1566 work to women who utilise 'preservatives that prevent them becoming pregnant'; and another Frenchman of the period, Pierre de Bourdeille, quotes the case of a servant-maid who, on being upbraided by her master for becoming pregnant, claimed that it would not have happened

19

'if I had been as well instructed as most of my friends'. By the seventeenth century, according to a confessor's manual published in Paris in 1671, priests were instructed to enquire in the confessional whether the faithful had 'employed means to prevent generation', and whether 'women during their pregnancy had taken a drink or some other concoction to prevent conception'. Other evidence can be quoted along the same lines, such as the well-known anxiety of Madame de Sévigné over her daughter becoming pregnant too often. Hints of information like this make it certain that contraception was practised by both men and women in the early modern period. The interesting development, however, doubly so since it seems to take place at the same time as a slowing down in population growth towards the middle of the seventeenth century, is the rise among the upper classes of a prejudice against too many offspring. In England this attitude led to the publication in 1695 of a book called *Populaidias, or a Discourse concerning the having many children in which the prejudices against having a numerous offspring are removed, and the objections answered.* The author condemns those who 'nowadays are much wiser or much worse than in earlier generations they were; who are afraid of what they so much wished for; who look upon the fruitfulness of wives to be less eligible than their barrenness; and had rather their families should be none, than large'. Limitation of births because of moral pressures (the fear of illegitimacy) and poverty had been common; limitation in those circles where poverty and starvation was unknown was a novel trend, a move towards the standards and values of the modern age.

POPULATION TRENDS

What were the growth trends in population in the century 1550-1660? Was the expanding Europe of the post-Renaissance era also expanding in terms of population? It is possible to arrive at some kind of general answer to these questions, but the lack of accurate data makes a detailed survey difficult. Statesmen of the time were often conscious of the importance of population figures, particularly for military and tax purposes, but took little care to collect information methodically, and appear to have been easily satisfied with imperfect or contradictory returns to tax censuses and recruiting assessments. Fragmentary records of births, marriages and deaths were kept in several countries prior to the Reformation. But even after such registrations became compulsory—in England after 1653 (the registration of baptisms had been ordered as early as 1538), in Catholic countries after the Council of Trent—it was rare to find a parish clergyman conscientious enough to keep his records up to date. The demands made on the Catholic clergy alone were daunting: as many as five different registers were supposed to be kept up to date by each priest. Both officials and clergy were unable to live up to the demands of their superiors, with the result that population estimates were bound to remain imprecise.

For a global survey it may be most convenient to look first at the population of some cities, towns and selected areas; after this, it should be possible to sketch in the general European trend. Europe by 1660 was still predominantly a rural, pre-industrial society. The countryside dominated life: its open spaces, punctuated here and there by settlements, gave the traveller a feeling of immense loneliness. Very little change occurred in overall population densities over this period. At one end of Europe, in Russia and the Ukraine, the population had a density of five inhabitants per square kilometre. The largest area of dense population in Europe was north Italy, which at the end of the sixteenth century had something like forty-four inhabitants per square kilometre, but the most densely populated area was in fact the Netherlands, with about fifty inhabitants. A very general picture of the distribution of population density in Europe is given in the map at Figure 2. Rough calculations for various countries suggest that France at the end of the sixteenth century had a density of about thirty-four inhabitants per square kilometre, central Germany one of from eighteen to twenty-three inhabitants, and Castile one of 18·2 inhabitants. As the map shows, more people lived in the west. As one went farther east the towns disappeared and the spaces opened up.

Despite these spaces, the towns everywhere were growing, particularly in response to the demands of commercial enterprise. The most outstanding example of this is Antwerp, which had attained a population level of about one hundred thousand by 1568, an improvement of about fifty per cent within a generation. A majority of the large cities of the time owed their growth principally, but not exclusively, to trade. Seville apparently reached one hundred and fifty thousand by 1588, Amsterdam one hundred thousand by the beginning of the seventeenth century. The growth of some of the principal cities in Europe is illustrated in Figure 3.

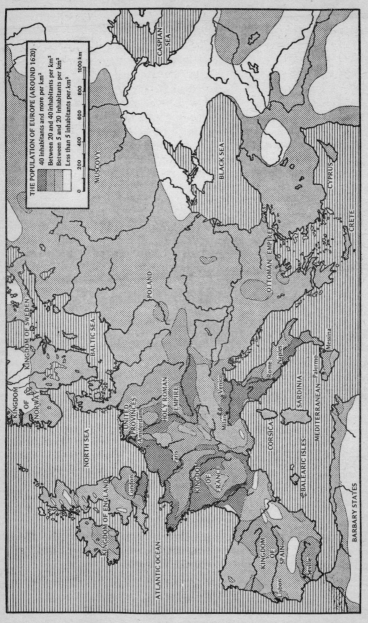

THE POPULATION OF EUROPE (AROUND 1620)

▨ 40 inhabitants and more per km²
▥ Between 20 and 40 inhabitants per km²
▤ Between 5 and 20 inhabitants per km²
☐ Less than 5 inhabitants per km²

0 200 400 600 800 1000 km

Figure 2 The density of population in seventeenth-century Europe.

22

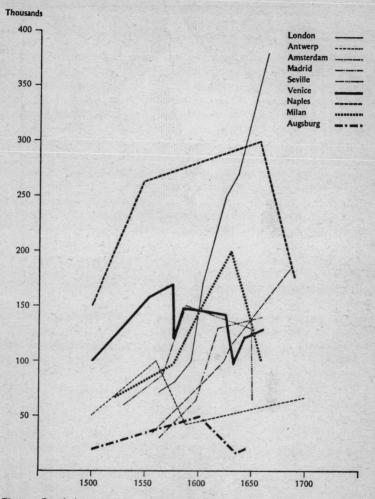

Thousands

Legend	
London	————
Antwerp	--------
Amsterdam	—·—·—
Madrid	—··—··
Seville	·········
Venice	■■■■■■
Naples	--------
Milan	·········
Augsburg	—·—·—

Figure 3 Population growth in some European cities.

The cities in Figure 3 were not chosen exclusively because of their large size. The largest cities, with a population in about 1600 exceeding one hundred thousand people were as follows:

over 100,000: Amsterdam, Antwerp, Lisbon, London, Messina, Milan, Palermo, Seville, Venice.

over 200,000: Naples, Paris.

The growth of urban centres is not of course an infallible guide to general population trends, since the factors governing the life of a city differed significantly from those applicable to country areas. We should look, then, at a few select regions to see if there is any recognisable pattern. All the information that we have suggests that the late sixteenth century witnessed a striking increase in population. Evidence for rural areas, from which the growth of the cities is deliberately excluded, provides support for this. In France the baptismal records of the village of La Chapelle-des-Fougerets (Ile-et-Vilaine) point to a population increase of fifty per cent between 1520 and 1610, and records from parishes in Brittany apparently point the same way. In Spain, a study of the rural area round Valladolid in Old Castile confirms this trend. The village of Tudela de Duero increased from three hundred and twenty-three to five hundred and eighty-seven households between 1530 and 1593, a rise of 81·7 per cent, while the village of Cigales increased by fifty-three per cent between 1530 and 1591. In Italy the picture is the same. Between 1545 and 1595 the kingdom of Naples (excluding the city itself) increased by twenty-six per cent from an estimated 422,080 people to 540,090 people. In Switzerland the territory of Zurich (again excluding the city) is estimated to have increased its population by about forty-five per cent between 1529 and 1585. Norway—to move further north—grew from 246,000 people in 1520 to 359,000 in 1590, an increase of forty-six per cent in seventy years.

The increase in population of both countryside and cities seems to have gathered force particularly in the early years of the sixteenth century, and to have slowed down after the beginning of the seventeenth. While it lasted it had momentous consequences, for it supplied the necessary momentum to economic and political change. The causes of the population increase are not yet clear, but the effects are fairly well known. The sudden consciousness, justified or not, of overcrowding, the restless movement of migratory populations, the settlement of overseas territories, are all in some way connected with demographic expansion. So too are the rise in European prices because of increased demand, the pressure on utilisation of the land, and the crisis in the exploitation of labour and the settlement of wages. We can say with some certainty that a period of rising population such as this was one of adaptation and change, and more outstandingly one of expansion in every branch of human activity.

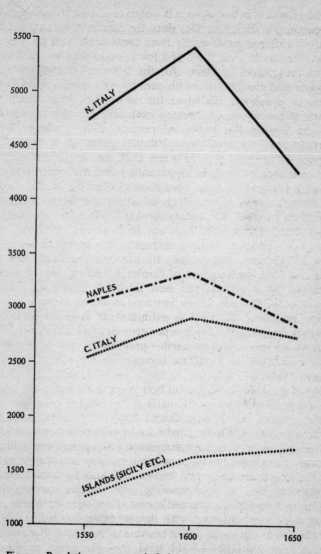

Figure 4 Population movements in Italy.

The expansionist trend in population was reversed in the early seventeenth century. In Castile the turning point came fairly early, just before 1600. Here, as in some other regions, notably Italy, the downward movement was aggravated by severe epidemics. Although the whole of Europe was victim to the ravages of mortality, the Mediterranean area seems to have suffered the worst. From the early seventeenth century we can see a general ebb in the vigour of demographic growth in the south. To illustrate this, Figure 4 gives a diagram of the general trend in Italian population.

Although epidemics played a major part in this contraction, any satisfactory explanation must take account of other factors which will be discussed below. In contrast to the Mediterranean area, there were only mild reverses in north and northwest Europe, and some regions even registered advances in population. The crisis in demographic growth thus had two main aspects: a general reverse after the beginning of the seventeenth century, and a pronounced contrast between the north and the south of Europe. In political terms the second aspect can be seen as the passing of leadership from the Mediterranean, Catholic powers to the Protestant states of the north. The population of England and Wales, to take one northern country, grew fairly steadily, and without decisive checks, throughout the seventeenth century. The peak growth period appears to have come in the first three decades of the 1600s. Over a wider period, the increase from 1500 to 1600 has been put at forty per cent, and from 1600 to 1700 at twenty-five per cent. The United Provinces, and particularly Holland, likewise expanded significantly over the whole century 1550-1660. In part this was due to the influx of refugees from the Spanish Netherlands and elsewhere, but there was also a natural increase, notably in the towns. This unimpeded growth of the two chief maritime powers was to have a powerful effect on the history of Europe. The Dutch were held up as a model of industry and populousness: 'they swarm with people as beehives with bees', wrote an English pamphleteer in 1677.

The maritime states apart, over most of Europe the population advance of the late sixteenth century was reversed in the course of the early seventeenth. Where epidemics alone were not the cause, wars could be blamed. By the mid-seventeenth century the multiplication and intensity of subsistence crises, wars and epidemics had established a general pattern of population decline. This contraction was not the least important feature of the general crisis of the century. Complaints of depopulation in Spain were a standard item in memoranda to the Spanish crown, but by the 1650s Spain was not the only sufferer. France had been ravaged by the Thirty Years War and by the Frondes, Poland and western Muscovy by the Swedes and by the Ukrainian revolts, Sweden had spent its manpower on the battlefields of Germany, and the Empire itself was to become a byword for all that a country could suffer short of total annihilation.

POPULATION CHECKS

The one great reality of life was death, readily accepted because always unavoidable, omnipresent not only in the ordinary course of living but also in the whole environment of the time: in the teaching and imagery of religion; in art, poetry and drama; in popular entertainment and public celebrations. The hand of death seemed all the more inevitable since it could not be controlled. Of the three scourges bewailed by the Litany — *a peste, fame et bello, libera nos Domine* — the first two could be considered only as natural cataclysms, though already there were suggestions that public policy could remedy their worst effects. The scale of infant mortality and the short span of life suggests that most households were familiar with the consequences of death through unlooked-for causes. Mortality came with ruthless regularity, so much so that even periods of population expansion or of civil peace were not necessarily free from serious loss of life.

EPIDEMICS

The first, and perhaps most serious, cause of untimely death was the epidemic. Since these were seldom continental in extent, it may help us to list the principal occasions when they occurred and the main areas known to have been affected:

1563-4 :	London, Barcelona, Hamburg, Bohemia
1575-8 :	Northern Italy, London, Bremen, Belgium
1580 :	Paris, Marseille, England
1595-9 :	Spain, England, Germany
1625 :	England, Germany, Palermo
1630 :	Northern Italy, Bavaria, Saxony, Danzig, Montpellier
1635-6 :	Holland, England, Germany
1655-6 :	Holland, Naples, Rome, Genoa
1664-5 :	London, Amsterdam

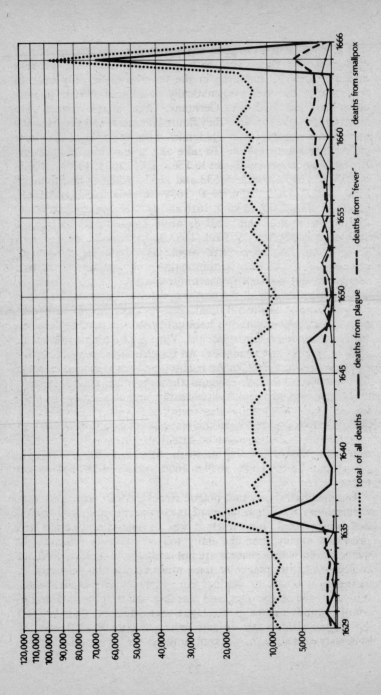

120,000
110,000
100,000
90,000
80,000
70,000
60,000
50,000
40,000
30,000
20,000
10,000
5,000

1629   1635   1640   1645   1650   1655   1660   1666

······· total of all deaths   ——— deaths from plague   - - - deaths from "fever"   ·······×······· deaths from smallpox

It is impossible to impose any pattern on the appearance of epidemics, for they came with great frequency but at very irregular periods, and even in the list above the only ones to devastate a wide area systematically were those of 1630 in northern Italy and 1635-6 in Germany. Great urban centres were naturally the places where they flourished most, and the data for some cities suggests that epidemics were the rule of life here rather than the exception. To take only a few cities at random, Bremen had severe epidemics in 1565, 1566, 1568, 1575-7, 1581-6, 1597-8, 1610-12, 1626, 1633 and 1653-7; Danzig had them in 1564, 1601-2, 1620, 1624, 1630, 1639-40, 1653, 1657, and 1661; Seville in 1571, 1582, 1595-9, 1616 and 1648-9; Amiens in 1582-4, 1596-8, 1619, 1627 and 1631-8; while London had its biggest outbreaks in 1563-4, 1577-83, 1592-3, 1603, 1625, 1636-7 and 1665. These dates show little regularity. The cities come from varying areas, but even within national boundaries there was seldom a rigid pattern to the outbreaks.

Why was mortality of this sort so common a feature of life? It is certain that not all the outbreaks can be attributed to 'plague', even though contemporaries habitually used the word to describe any particularly virulent epidemic. We can also blame influenza, typhus, typhoid and smallpox. An English observer in 1558, for example, reported that 'in the beginning of this year died many of the wealthiest men all England through, of a strange fever'. Historians have since tended to identify 'fevers' such as this with one or other of the diseases mentioned, principally with influenza. By distinguishing in this way between the several types of complaint, it becomes easier to explain the reasons for the high death-rate. Figure 5, which shows the three main types of disease prevalent in London from 1629 to 1666, will make an explanation easier.

The diagram shows that plague struck seldom, and then with unusual ferocity. The savagery of its attacks caused it to be feared and remembered, but clearly it was in numerical terms a less persistent enemy than the daily toll of common diseases. In outbreaks for which records are not available, it is often difficult to decide whether plague or some other disease was responsible. Generally it is safe to say that the epidemics with highest mortality were the plague ones, and that they tended to be confined to towns. London's three great plague years illustrate this. In 1603 the plague victims were seventy-seven per cent of all deaths, in 1625 they were sixty-five per cent, while in 1665 the total of deaths was eight times that in a normal year, and the number of plague deaths was seventy per cent of the total.

It is not always easy to estimate what proportion of the population was lost in this way, but something like one-eighth was a minimum. The three London plagues just mentioned were of this dimension. The outbreaks in Amsterdam in 1624, 1636, 1655 and 1664 are estimated to have removed respectively one-ninth, one-seventh, one-eighth and one-sixth of the population. For an analysis of the impact on a small community, we can take the town of Uelzen in Lower Saxony. Here the plague of 1566 carried off twenty-three per cent of the population of 1,180, and another outbreak in 1597 carried off thirty-three per cent of a population numbering 1,540. The high death-rate for plague may be contrasted with a dysentery epidemic in the same town in 1599, which carried off only about fourteen per cent. In large cities, thanks to overcrowding and extremely unhygienic conditions, the rate could be very much higher. Santander in Spain was virtually wiped off the map in 1599, losing two thousand five hundred of its three thousand inhabitants. Italian examples are particularly striking. Venice from July 1575 to July 1576 lost 46,721 of its population of about 170,000, a proportion of twenty-seven per cent; Mantua in 1630 lost nearly seventy per cent of a population of some thirty thousand; and both Naples and Genoa lost nearly half their population in the plague of 1656.

What was peculiarly horrible about the plague was that there appeared to be no defence against it. In so far as it was understood to be transmitted through human agents, isolation was the surest insurance. During the 1563 plague in England, Queen Elizabeth ordered Windsor to be sealed off from London, and, we are informed by the annalist Stow, 'a gallows was set up in the market-place of Windsor to hang all such as should come there from London'. Isolation of humans, however, was no protection against the flea-infected rat, which was eventually recognised to be the principal carrier of the disease. The speed at which an epidemic could develop, thanks to this carrier, is shown by Figure 6, which illustrates the progress of the 1563-6 outbreak from its origins in the Middle East and its first European foothold in Bohemia.

The early eighteenth century saw the last appearance of the disease. London's 1665 outbreak was the last in England. There was a further epidemic in Spain in the late 1670s, and then severe outbreaks in the Baltic and in Provence in the early years of the

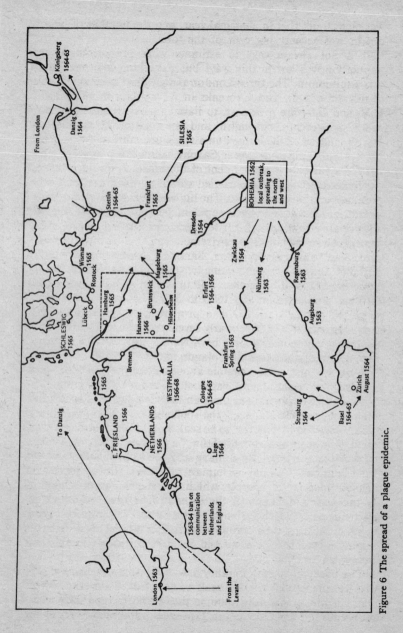

Figure 6 The spread of a plague epidemic.

Königsberg
1564–65

From London

Danzig
1564

SILESIA
1565

Stettin
1564–65

Frankfurt
1565

BOHEMIA 1562
local outbreak,
spreading to
the north
and west

Dresden
1564

Magdeburg
1565

Zwickau
1564

Wismar
1565

Rostock

Hamburg
1565

Brunswick

Hildesheim

Erfurt
1564–1566

Nürnberg
1563

Regensburg
1563

Lübeck

Hanover
1566

Augsburg
1563

SCHLESWIG
1565

Bremen

Frankfurt
Spring 1563

1565

WESTPHALIA
1566–68

Cologne
1564–65

Strasburg
1564

Zürich
August 1564

Basel
1564–65

To Danzig

E. FRIESLAND
1566

NETHERLANDS
1566

Liège
1564

1563–64 ban on
communication
between
Netherlands
and England

London 1563

From the
Levant

next century. The epidemic at Messina in 1743 ended the reign of plague in Europe.

The social effects of plague have been imperfectly studied, but there can be no doubt that it discriminated among its victims. Thriving on filthy conditions, it struck first and foremost at the lowest classes in the towns. An analysis of the incidence of plague in Amiens has shown that the wealthier parts of the city were invariably spared during an outbreak, and it was the poorest quarters that were most hit. The same is true of London, where the Mortality Bills show the epidemics taking their origin in the poorest suburbs. When an epidemic struck Lyon in 1628 a contemporary comforted himself with the thought that 'only seven or eight persons of quality died, and five or six hundred of lower condition'. The pattern was a familiar one. We find a bourgeois of Toulouse observing in his journal of 1561: 'The contagion only ever hits the poor people . . . God by his grace will have it so. The rich protect themselves against it.' The low mortality among the rich and the upper classes may to some extent be explained by the fact that it was they, the guardians of the state, who were the first to take refuge in flight. When the plague hit Bilbao in the early autumn of 1598, says one report, 'only the totally impoverished remained' in the city. The bourgeoisie moved to other towns, the nobility to their country estates. Some of the rich who remained did so in the conviction that the plague was discriminatory and that they were largely immune. The banker Fabio Nelli, writing from Valladolid in July 1599, in a week when nearly a thousand people had died of the plague, observed that since only nine senior officials of the municipality had died, 'I don't intend to move from here... almost nobody of consideration has died.' Figures available for Venice just before and after the epidemic of 1630 give added proof that it was the common people who suffered principally, since their numbers as a proportion of the total population fell from 88·7 per cent to 85·4 per cent, while the proportion of nobles and bourgeois rose from 11·3 to 14·6 per cent. The result of this situation was aggravation of social tensions and class hatred. With the evidence plain before their eyes, the upper classes considered that the plague had been caused and spread by the poor. Their contempt for the unprivileged was matched on the other side by a bitter resentment that those who had never lacked material comforts should also be spared the vengeance of the scourge. In these circumstances, times of epidemic became potentially times of class violence.

Poverty and poor nutrition were the two principal features of the victims of any epidemic, and the same was true of plague. Examples from Spain in the crippling epidemic of 1599 illustrate this. Of the eighty victims of plague in Burgos on 22 April, 'from those who had food to eat only seven persons died'. In the town of Santo Tomé del Puerto, only five of the two hundred and five dead on 26 April were adequately fed. Of the three hundred who died in Aranda de Duero on 11 May, only two were well-off. In Sepúlveda on 26 April 'all those who have died in this town and its region were very poor and lacked all sustenance'. The connection between poverty and epidemics could hardly have failed to attract the attention of public authorities, who made some attempt to improve conditions of hygiene in towns and cities. It is doubtful, however, if any of the measures taken by municipalities were really effective. If the plague receded it was because of purely natural causes connected with the life-history of the rat. The fact that typhus, smallpox and other diseases went on from strength to strength shows how much remained to be fought for in the struggle for the preservation of life.

One important aspect of the social crisis precipitated by an epidemic is worth noting. In the absence of public authorities who deserted their posts as soon as an outbreak occurred, the citizens resorted to direct popular control. In Bilbao in 1598 and 1599 all major decisions were sanctioned by a general assembly of the citizens meeting in the church of St John. In several other towns the participation of citizens in government was enlarged so as to enable control measures to be taken more effectively. Emergency situations bred emergency measures, even concessions to democracy. Sometimes these concessions were inevitable: in Santander a popular riot occurred in January 1597 when the mayor deserted the town because of the plague, and thereafter a general assembly of the citizens was called for any important decisions.

FAMINE

A regular and adequate supply of food was essential for life, but how could this be maintained if nature itself was hostile? 'This year', a Spanish correspondent wrote home from Naples in 1606, 'God has seen fit to visit this realm and Sicily and other parts of Italy with a ruinous harvest, and the one here is said to be the worst one for forty years.' Typically, the report was an exaggeration, for there had been an even severer famine only ten years previously; but inevitably every crisis seemed to be worse than its predecessor, and the number of years when there was a serious lack of food supplies was regular enough to have an adverse cumulative effect. The incidence of crises must be put in perspective. Famines, in the sense of great natural disasters, were infrequent: far more significant was the constant threat of starvation from the common, daily inability to obtain enough food.

The availability of food was affected in several ways: by the weather above all else, then by factors such as demand from a large population, good land exploitation, ease of transport and the presence of war. Any or all of these could have a devastating effect on the price of supplies. The case of Rome in the sixteenth century illustrates most of the factors. Threatened for long periods by bandits, with communications repeatedly cut, grain supplies could not always get through to the city. When the bandits had been eliminated, the utilisation of the land con-tinued to affect supplies, for an enormous area that had pre-viously grown grain had over a period of years been turned from tillage to pasture. Another Italian city, Naples, illustrates the effect that the rapid growth of its population had on the amount of food required. The city suffered six crisis years of want, of *carestie,* between 1560 and 1600—in 1560, 1565, 1570, 1584, 1585 and 1591. Such subsistence crises were not necessarily caused by major harvest failures. They produced famine none the less, since no provision had been made to supply the swollen population.

The possibility of starvation, then, depended on a great number of interdependent factors and not on the weather alone. In an era of poor communications, and in countries where customs barriers even separated one province from another, it was possible for one of two contiguous regions to starve while the other fed comfortably. The extreme variation in prices between different regions in the same country is proof of this. The search for profit, and administrative inadequacy, both bear witness to the fact that man-made famines are no innovation of modern capitalism. But in the final analysis it was the hand of God that mattered. Harvest failures aggravated the already severe situation brought about by incompetent officials and grain speculators.

Two great famines—those of 1594-7 and 1659-62—had a particularly disastrous impact on Europe in this century. The years 1594-7 over most of Europe were years of excessive rain and bad harvests, resulting in a steep rise in the price of the little grain that could be obtained. In Spain, Italy and Germany in particular the disaster coincided with heavy mortality brought on by widespread epidemics of plague. Discontent and unrest led to large-scale peasant revolts and urban insurrections as far afield as France, Austria, Finland and Lithuania. In England there were unsuccessful attempts at armed uprisings. In the face of this discontent, the English government drew up a new Poor Law in 1597 to deal with the widespread poverty and distress. Death became commonplace in those years. The authorities at Bristol undertook relief measures whereby, they claimed with satisfaction, 'the poor of our city were all relieved and kept from starving or rising'. Newcastle was not so fortunate. An entry in the town accounts reads: 'October 1597. Paid for the charge of buringe 16 poore folkes who died for wante in the strettes 6s. 8d.' The whole of the north of England suffered acute famine in 1597. On the continent conditions were similar. A contemporary diarist reported that in Aix-en-Provence in 1597 when 'the clergy of the church of Saint-Esprit were giving bread to succour the poor, of whom there were over twelve hundred, six or seven of them died, including little girls and a woman'.

The depression of 1659-62 was politically far more significant, since it created crisis conditions that in many countries eased the way for a transition to absolute monarchy. In London, riots and popular discontent helped to make the return to power of the Stuart monarchy more acceptable to the ruling classes. The harvest failure of 1661 helped to present the young Louis XIV to his people as a beneficent ruler. Colbert tells us that the new king 'not only distributed grain to individuals and communities in Paris and around, but even ordered thirty and forty thousand pounds of bread to be given out daily'. The need of the people was extreme. In the countryside, reported an eye-witness, 'the pasturage of wolves has become the food of Christians, for when they find horses, asses and other dead animals they feed off the rotting flesh'. 'In the thirty-two years that I have practised medicine in this province', reported a doctor in Blois, 'I have seen nothing to approach the desolation throughout the countryside. The famine there is so great that the peasants go without bi ad and throw themselves on to carrion. As soon as a horse or other animal dies, they eat it.'

The reality of famine is undeniable, but its distribution more controversial. There were certainly some regions that were spared the horrors resulting from poor harvests. Towns in Spain, Italy and elsewhere had municipal grain stores which they turned to in cases of necessity; towns in Germany, the Netherlands and England were fairly conscientious in their resort to poor relief. But the very practice of grain storage was itself evidence of a situation where the security of supplies had become an obsession because of the constant threat of a food crisis.

Not all the people starved. 'Nothing new here', reported a Rome newsletter in February 1558, 'except that people are dying of hunger.' The same newsletter then went on to describe a great banquet given by the pope at which the chief wonders were 'statues made of sugar carrying real torches'. The contrast was glaring, and deliberate. The rich were sometimes touched by the plague, but almost never by hunger. It is rare to find reports such as the one from Geneva in 1628 that 'several people of substance who refuse to beg are suffering greatly from the lack of bread'. In Dijon in the great famine of 1694 the number of deaths in the wealthy parish of Notre Dame was ninety-nine, in the poor parish of St Philibert two hundred and sixty-six. Famine was not a companion to the rich. We learn from the Fugger newsletters that in 1587, a year of severe grain scarcity through most of Europe, one of the leading nobles of Prague, William of Rožmberk, had a wedding feast at which thirty-six deer, twelve tons of venison, thirty-six boars, one thousand two hundred and ninety hares, two hundred and seventy-two pheasants, seventy-five oxen, seven hundred and sixty-four sheep, two hundred and twenty-one lambs, thirty-two fattened pigs, one hundred and sixty young sows and much else, was eaten and drunk.

Among the lower classes, mortality was as a rule higher among the rural proletariat than in the towns, for while the townspeople could beg for relief the peasants had to find sustenance from their own inhospitable environment. When the soil had no grain to offer them they tended to turn to carrion, roots, bark, straw and vermin, as they certainly did in France at this time. Of the famine in 1637 in Franche Comté a contemporary recorded that 'posterity will not believe it: people lived off the plants in gardens and fields; they even sought out the carcasses of dead animals. The roads were paved with people . . . Finally it came to cannibalism.' It requires considerable courage to reject all the stories given by contemporaries of this last and most horrifying phenomenon.

The difficulty in isolating numerically those deaths attributable to famine alone can give rise to doubts whether starvation was really so close a companion of our ancestors. It is certainly true that the records speak more often in terms of disease, fever or other causes. Yet the possibility remains that early death and susceptibility to disease were provoked by a low level of nourishment that had grave results during subsistence crises. It may be correct to say that death from hunger was rare in normal conditions, but it is not easy to define what 'normal conditions' were in a society that suffered so frequently from crises of one sort or another. The common people were under no illusions about their susceptibility to starvation, and the regularity of bread riots in towns illustrates their refusal to accept their fate with resignation. In 1628 one of the pastors in Geneva explained to his congregation that the current food crisis (which was to last up to 1631) was brought upon them by their sinfulness. His audience was infuriated by this suggestion.

> The people, who had been suffering for a very long time on a meagre diet, were outraged by this and left the church in great dissatisfaction, saying that they were more in need of consolation than of accusations . . .; that they were very well aware of the true state of things; and that the pastor had no idea of the misery of the great number who passed whole days and weeks in their homes without a few loaves of bread; and that they had to go without that which others fattened themselves upon.

Undernourishment was common in Geneva in both normal and abnormal times. In January 1630, during a grave subsistence crisis, silk-workers were earning only two *sols* a day, whereas the cost of bread was five *sols* a pound and two pounds was the minimum required for a reasonable daily diet. In these circumstances the city Council had to order the payment of supplementary wages. In 1655, a normal year with normal prices, when bread was five *sols* a pound, and cheese and meat seven *sols*, a carpenter's daily wages were about twenty-two *sols*. This could barely have sufficed to support a family, yet carpenters were by no means the bottom layer of the urban working class.

Some information about the level of subsistence may be obtained by examining whether the land produced enough food for its population; and by analysing the daily diet of the working population.

The inadequacy or otherwise of food production can be

determined on an elementary level merely by looking at the pattern of overseas trade. The entry of Baltic wheat into the Mediterranean in the late sixteenth century was a clear sign that the southern countries could not feed their peoples, and that a considerable surplus existed in the north. It was because of this great demand for grain that the estates of the east European gentry prospered. This example, however, gives us no guarantee that the east European peasantry fed better than their Italian counterparts. It has even been argued very plausibly that the production and export of grain depressed the standard of living of the Polish peasants. Evidence of a more statistical sort is required in order to establish a relationship between food production and the likelihood of starvation. The case of the Netherlands (before the partition into Holland and Belgium) is a useful one. It has been calculated that in the sixteenth century the minimum average consumption of bread here required about two hundred kilos of grain per person per year. This would involve consumption of four hundred million kilos for the whole of the Netherlands. Since the average return from the land was something like six hundred kilos a hectare per annum, the whole of the territory of the Netherlands would have been needed in order to supply the population adequately. This land was not available, so that even slight variations in weather and output affected prices severely, and the Netherlands was obliged to import grain regularly. On a smaller scale than the national, peasant communities and individual peasants often lived very close to subsistence level, since the land they possessed did not suffice to supply all their needs. In an age when the vast majority of the population was peasantry, the land they tilled was fragmented more and more in order to give each peasant the basis for life. Such fragmentation, aggravated by the growth in population of the sixteenth century, served in practice to destroy the self-sufficiency of the rural classes. The village of Lespignan in Languedoc gives us evidence of this. In 1492 the great majority of the peasant proprietors were able to produce a surplus which they sold in order to buy goods, so putting themselves above the minimum level of independence. By 1607, the majority were having to buy grain in order to feed themselves, and had to support their families by finding work elsewhere. Such a community was easy prey to starvation years. Yet the process of fragmentation of peasant holdings went on in this area and elsewhere. In Beauvaisis this led to a situation where as many as nine-tenths of the peasant population were not economically independent and could not guarantee to feed their families adequately under all circumstances. As Goubert observes, 'the peasant who aspired to a state of economic independence had to farm a minimum of 12 hectares (nearly thirty acres) in years of plenty, and 27 hectares (65 acres) in years of shortage'. Yet in the seventeenth century less than one-tenth of the peasants here owned twenty-seven or more hectares. The majority inevitably knew starvation during periods of agrarian crisis.

No analysis of diet for this period has failed to be controversial, since it is extremely difficult to agree upon a criterion for the level of nourishment. It is relatively easy to find out what food people ate, more complex to determine the health value of the food. Goubert argues that it is beyond dispute that the majority of the peasants of the Beauvaisis suffered from almost continuous undernourishment, on the grounds that meat was almost totally absent from the diet, fruit equally rare, and vegetables usually of poor quality, so that the staple was bread, soup, gruel, peas and beans. In other areas for which we have information, however, the food was more varied than this. Bread, vegetables, butter, cheese and meat figured in the diet of a worker in Antwerp in the sixteenth century, and it has been estimated that this gave each worker the food value of something like two thousand calories a day. This can be compared with the figure of just under three thousand calories which the FAO laid down in 1957 as being the minimum necessary to proper nourishment. The disparity is not large, particularly in view of the fact that most of the world's present population live well below this norm. Can it be said, however, that the Antwerp worker was undernourished? A modern historian of the city of Valladolid suggests the figure of 1,580 calories as the value of the diet of the average citizen in the sixteenth century, but also concludes that such a level was perfectly adequate for the time. A study of peasant diet on the Polish royal estates in the late sixteenth century, on the other hand, arrives at a daily average of about 3,500 calories. Such substantial variations in estimates clearly make it impossible to arrive at any exact conclusion. The only indisputable fact is that the vast mass of the people lived perilously close to a level of food consumption that threatened their very existence.

WAR

All other scourges could be, and were, subsumed in war. 'It has been impossible to collect any taxes', runs a report from Lorraine in the 1630s, 'because of the wars that have hit most of the villages, which are deserted through the flight of some of the inhabitants and the death of others from disease or from sickness arising out of starvation.' Epidemics and famine were a natural consequence of the depredations of the soldiery: in this period there is every possibility that they killed more than the military campaigns themselves did. It is consequently rather misleading to look on the era as one of limited warfare. It is true that armies were relatively small, that mass mobilisation did not exist, and that weapons were not outrageously lethal. Yet countries that suffered war underwent such severe damage to both economy and people that no attempt should be made to minimise the scale of destruction. Even the fact that deaths in battle tended to be moderate needs to be set in perspective, for there certainly were occasions when zeal exceeded all bounds. Perhaps the worst atrocities in the seventeenth century were committed by the English. The genocide they practised on the Irish people led, in the years 1641-52, if we may trust the figures of Sir William Petty, to the diminution of their number by some five hundred and four thousand.

Laments against war were universal. 'When shall we see an end to these men of war?' was the cry of a villager in a French dialogue of the mid-seventeenth century. It required the evils of the Thirty Years War to bring the European population to an understanding of the horrors involved, and it is no coincidence that the drawings of Callot should take their origins in the same situation that led to St Vincent de Paul's apostolate in Picardy. Among the many anti-war books to emerge from the 1640s, Grimmelshausen's *Simplicissimus* (1668) takes pride of place, with its unmitigated denunciation of the soldiery, its depiction of the carnage in the battle at Wittstock, and its attack on the *Merodebrüder*, the straggling soldiers to whom much of the plundering in the war was attributed.

The overall effect of a war on population is difficult to estimate. It is not enough to count deaths; one also has to take account of refugees and emigration, of a possible fall in the number of males and in the level of fertility. The four short case histories that follow will give us some idea of the impact of war in the period 1550-1660.

France undoubtedly suffered badly from the half-century (1559-98) of conflict known as the Wars of Religion. We are not concerned here with the serious effects on trade and industry, but only with the loss of life. Quite apart from the great atrocities, such as the massacre of St Bartholomew's, which cost more than three thousand Protestant lives in Paris and about twenty thousand in the whole of France, substantial losses of population occurred in many regions. In Burgundy the 1590s had constant bad weather and harvests, ending in the great famine of 1597. War certainly aggravated this situation: we find the *bailliage* of Auxerrois in 1597, for instance, with as many as 864 of its houses destroyed and 1,144 abandoned to the enemy. It is only when we move from individual cases like this to a more general perspective that the depressing picture seems to change. In Burgundy itself, it has been shown that the figure for births and marriages increased regularly during the wars, with a decrease only in the 1590s, when factors other than war were particularly operative. For other regions, a survey of parish registers suggests that the earlier period of the wars, up to the 1580s, coincided with the great population expansion of the sixteenth century, and did not check it to any appreciable extent. Annual baptism figures for the village of Souvigny (Loir-et-Cher) show a rise from twenty-three baptisms in the early century to thirty-seven in the 1580s and about thirty in the 1590s. Similarly Saint-Erblon (Ille-et-Vilaine) had an annual thirty-four baptisms before and forty-one during the wars. When there were serious reverses, they could generally be traced to crisis and epidemic years. The limited evidence at hand makes it possible to say that France shared in the demographic expansion of the period, and that the wars had much less effect on the civil population than has commonly been thought. These observations do not, of course, take into account the consequences for other sectors of the economy.

At roughly the same time the Netherlands were going through a war of their own. The long war for Dutch independence, known in Holland as the Eighty Years War (1568-1648), split the country into a northern section (the United Provinces) and a southern (under Spanish rule). In the early years the north suffered substantially, but from the end of the sixteenth century it was the south that took the brunt of the war. A number of factors combined to produce totally disastrous effects on the south, and though they resulted not so much in loss of life as in emigration they can reasonably be discussed here. The collapse of the country was to some extent a consequence of the collapse of Antwerp, which suffered from the blockade of the Scheldt after 1572 and from the rebellion of Spanish troops—the Spanish

Fury—in 1576. From 1580 onwards a severe crisis developed in Belgian territory as the economy ground to a halt. In 1581 the linen industries of Courtrai and Oudenarde collapsed. In 1582 the Duke of Anjou's troops sacked several industrial towns. In the autumn of 1581 nothing could be sown in the fields round Brussels because of the war. Mercenaries murdered farmers, farms were destroyed, fields were left untilled. In 1585 wolves attacked people in the vicinity of Ghent. It was in that year too that the Scheldt was firmly closed by the Dutch. Villages were levelled to the ground. Near Ghent one area of cultivation dropped from 4,726 to 377 hectares. There was widespread famine, particularly in 1586. In most villages of Brabant the population by 1586 had dropped to between twenty-five and fifty per cent of what it had been before 1575. In Louvain the number of inhabited houses fell from 3,299 in 1526 to 1,658 by the end of the sixteenth century. In 1604 the Estates of Flanders claimed that 'the voice of the poor peasant cries out to God'. 'Trade has almost totally ceased', reported the Duke of Saxony when he visited Antwerp in 1613. 'Where once crowds of merchants thronged, one now sees only a few Spaniards pacing the streets.' This depression did not hit all the southern provinces equally. The northerly parts, populated by Flemings, suffered worst; the southern, Walloon, section saw some recovery, particularly around Liège. But the outbreak of war in 1621, after the expiry of the Twelve Years Truce between Spain and the United Provinces, brought further calamities. Death and distress confirmed the dramatic drop in the population of the southern Netherlands. 'I have come to Amsterdam where I now am', reported a priest in 1627, 'and find all the towns as full of people as those held by Spain are empty.'

These disastrous wars of the sixteenth century coincided to some extent with a period of demographic expansion, so that there appears to have been no serious check to birth and fertility rates. It is when we come to the wars of the mid-seventeenth century that a different picture begins to form. Whatever their actual effect in different areas, these wars mark the critical turning point. From the early seventeenth century a demographic recession takes effect, and the wars accentuate the trend. In France the population reverses were closely associated with the Fronde. The campaigns of 1648-53 occurred mainly in the north of France, and in particular around Paris. Contemporaries leave us in no doubt about the horrifying effect they had on law, order,

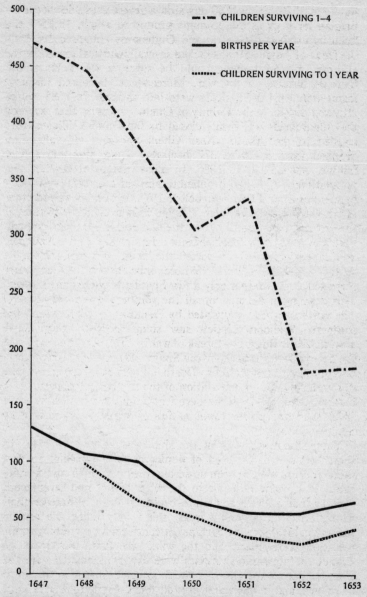

Figure 7 War and the birth-rate in the Fronde (St Lambert des Levées, Anjou).

life and property. Angélique Arnauld, writing in 1649, speaks of 'the frightful state of this poor countryside; all is pillaged, ploughing has ceased, there are no horses, everything is stolen, the peasants are driven to sleeping in the woods'. A report on the area around Paris, drawn up in 1652 for the ecclesiastical authorities, speaks of 'villages and hamlets deserted and bereft of clergy, streets infected by stinking carrion and dead bodies lying exposed, houses without doors or windows, everything reduced to cesspools and stables, and above all the sick and dying, with no bread, meat, medicine, fire, beds, linen or covering, and no priest, doctor, surgeon or anyone to comfort them'. It has been estimated that the population loss caused by the Fronde was in the region of twenty per cent. In the five years of the war, in other words, a village would have lost about one-fifth of its people. Within this period, to take one well-documented example, the parish of Saint-Lambert-des-Levées (population three thousand) lost six hundred and fifty-three lives, this figure representing the excess of deaths over births. The cumulative effect that such mortality had on the birth rate is shown by Figure 7. The diagram illustrates concisely and effectively how a protracted war could threaten human survival.

Events in Germany offer yet more evidence of war as a killer. The long controversy over the effects of the Thirty Years War on German population has now been largely resolved, thanks to the detailed surveys of hundreds of localities affected by the conflict. The death and destruction was extensive; even worse, it was prolonged. When all allowance is made for the exaggeration and propaganda of stories about the horrors of the war, there is still no reason to discount the reality of devastation, plague, famine and sheer barbarism of the soldiery. The Rhineland, fought for by the troops of every nation in Europe, was reduced to ruins. 'From Cologne hither' (to Frankfurt), reported the English ambassador in 1635, 'all the towns, villages and castles be battered, pillaged and burnt.' 'I am leading my men', claimed the Bavarian general Johann von Werth when crossing the Rhineland in 1637, 'through a country where many thousands of men have died of hunger and not a living soul can be seen for many miles along the way.' The actual measurable loss of population is so great as to be incredible. In the county of Lippe, to take a region only moderately hit by the war, the population fell by thirty-five per cent from 40,220 to 26,000 between 1618 and 1648. In the district of Lautern in the Rhineland, a more severely devastated region, of a total of sixty-two towns thirty were deserted in 1656, and a population of four thousand two hundred (excluding the chief town Kaiserslautern) had sunk to about five hundred. Going beyond individual examples, Figure 8 gives some idea of the loss of population in Germany as a whole.

The general conclusion to be drawn from this diagram is that over the German lands as a whole the urban centres lost one-third of their population and the rural areas lost about forty per cent. The losses varied from under ten per cent in Lower Saxony to over fifty per cent in Württemberg and Pomerania. These figures must be treated with caution, for 'loss' is an ambiguous term. We know, for instance, that there was an enormous refugee population, and that a good proportion of them returned after several years to their homes. A 'loss of population', then, does not necessarily imply death, and it may be more correct to talk of a 'displacement of population'.

Incomplete registers of births and deaths, and high mortality caused by epidemics, make it virtually impossible to arrive at a death rate attributable solely to the war. Estimates can be made for casualties in battles and sieges, but these are invariably

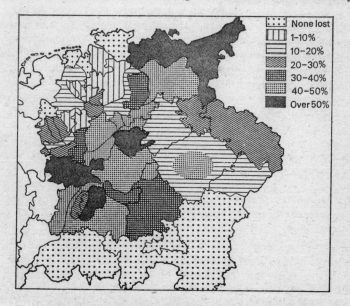

Figure 8 The impact of the Thirty Years' War on German population.

dwarfed by the deaths attributed to 'plague'. This does not mean that the war can be absolved from responsibility, for though epidemics were a regular phenomenon the outbreaks during the war in Germany were very closely related to the movement of troops, and pestilence invariably flourished in the wake of armies.

To cite an interminable list of figures for deaths does not by itself prove the serious impact of the war. As the contemporary writer John Graunt observed of London after the Great Plague of 1665, a natural corrective often operates in order to remedy the ravages of disaster: marriages increase, immigrants augment the population, and the birth-rate exceeds its normal pre-disaster level. A corrective of this sort might compensate for a serious demographic reverse, and so not lead to any fundamental change in the overall trend. Unfortunately there is little evidence of this happening in Germany (and even in England the response of the village of Colyton to the plague of 1646 shows no compensatory rise in births after that disaster year). The Thirty Years War had hit the most vital sections of the people. A fall in the level of nutrition and public health may well have affected fertility. The result was that in many towns the birth-rate fell below its pre-war level, in Stuttgart by forty-eight per cent, in Augsburg by forty-two per cent, in Nuremberg by thirty-six per cent. Though newssheets of the time may frequently have exaggerated the sufferings of the Germans, this is no reason to doubt the extremely serious impact of the war on the lives of the people. In a particularly bad year one pastor who had stuck at his post through many disasters gave way to his despair by signing a letter, 'Given at my castle of misery, Stelzen, 1633'. In him we may personify the epoch of disaster that overtook the German people through war.

POPULATION AND THE GENERAL CRISIS

We have already observed that the population increase of the sixteenth century was checked in the course of the seventeenth, but it should be made clear that the reversal of the trend was not everywhere of the same intensity. The contraction was most severe in the Mediterranean countries, but barely perceptible in the north. It is true that evidence from some village communities of England suggests that population growth ceased in the years around 1620, but the national trend, supported by the unimpeded growth of the great ports and towns, was towards moderate expansion. The same can be said of the other northern powers. Whatever the pattern in specific localities may have been, the long-term tendency in rising nations such as Holland and Russia was still towards growth. While the whole of Europe seems to have shared in the expansion of the sixteenth century, therefore, in the early seventeenth century a levelling off in the rate of growth occurred in the northern countries. It was not until the wars of the mid-century, in the German lands and in Poland, that this decelerated growth was replaced by a sudden and brutal check to the numbers of the population.

In the south of Europe, on the other hand, the decline was steep and extremely serious. In many cases we can date the reversal to specific disasters: in Castile to the epidemic of 1599, in Italy to the subsistence crises of the 1590s, and the demographic catastrophes of 1630 and 1656. Many southern cities did continue to expand in size, but often this reflected not growth so much as a depopulation of the countryside by an impoverished peasantry seeking a living in the towns.

The great demographic advances of the sixteenth century had had momentous consequences, which we have referred to only very briefly above. No less momentous were the consequences of a fall in population. Both economic growth and military power were affected, so much so that in Spain the commentators on economic affairs—the *arbitristas*—became obsessed with the problem of manpower. The economic consequences involved a reduction in the labour force, decreased output, and falling demand. In military terms, the paucity of soldiers bred a growing desire to save the country's remaining sons from foreign battlefields, and above all from the Netherlands, 'that graveyard of Spaniards' as a late seventeenth-century writer was to call it. It is instructive to see what forms the obsession with manpower took. Clerical celibacy became a prime target for attack, the view being that men should procreate in order to serve their country. In his *Memorial,* published at Valladolid in 1600, Martín González de Cellórigo went so far as to demand that slaves be imported on a massive scale in order to make up for the diminishing labour force. Cellórigo was also among those who strongly opposed the view, then gaining popularity, that the Moriscos be expelled: with labour so short, he argued, such a move was unjustified. All commentators agreed that emigration to America should be limited. The policies of both Church and State were called in question in an effort to find a solution to the phenomenon of decreasing numbers.

It was this enormous gap between the actual and the ideal,

between the population decay that really existed and the unrealisable desire to remedy it, that contributed to the crisis of the seventeenth century. Moreover, the abruptness of natural disaster was too great for any government ever to attempt a remedy. As Professor Cipolla has observed of Italy,

> if one admits that it would have been impossible for Italy to keep her ancient sources of revenue or to find new ones, then a long slow decline of her total population might have been a solution for the economic problems of the seventeenth century. But a drastic and rapid fall in population, provoked by plague, had the effect of raising wages and putting Italian exports in an even more difficult position.

While it led to tension within the country, the crisis in population also led to imbalance between countries. The loss of vitality in the Mediterranean area meant that in the course of the 1600s the initiative, in economic and military terms, passed to the countries of the Baltic and of the north Atlantic. As Italian interests shrank and the Spaniards drew in on themselves, others took up the task of extending the sway of European man over the world.

2 CHANGE AND DECAY

It has been the general policy to send out from these kingdoms men who hate work and who are of rebellious disposition and spirit, and who are more anxious to get rich quickly than to settle in the country.

LÓPEZ DE VELASCO. *Descripción universal de las Indias* (1574)

The people are increased and ground for ploughs doth want, corn and all other victual is scant . . . and dear . . .

ALDERMAN BOX to Lord Burghley (1576)

In the decades preceding 1550 much had changed in the European world, in the horizons opened up towards America and Asia, but also at home in the balance between states and between religions. The apparently fixed order of the past, in which men had lived and moved within a unified Christendom, within a circumscribed community and a specified social function, was now collapsing. The reality of change had been commented upon by writers on affairs of state as well as by literary figures, and they were quite capable of citing evidence to confirm their impressions. Most periods of history witness some degree of alteration in the relationships between men and the social classes to which they belong. Why then should this age appear to be unusual in the extent of change? To take one witness, we may quote William Harrison, in his *Description of England* (1577):

There are old men yet dwelling in the village where I remain, which have noted three things to be marvellously altered in England within their sound remembrance; and other three things (that) are too much increased. One is the multitude of chimneys lately erected . . .; the second is the great (although not general) amendment of lodging . . .; the third thing . . . is the exchange of vessel, as of wooden platters into pewter, and wooden spoons into silver or tin. And as they commend these, so they speak also of three things that are grown to be very grievous unto them, to wit the enhancing of rents . . .; the daily oppression of copyholders . . .; (and) usury, a trade brought in by the Jews, now perfectly practised almost by every Christian, and so commonly that he is accounted but for a fool that does lend his money for nothing.

Three changes for the better, then, and three for the worse. Chimneys had been and would continue to be a sign of affluence, for they meant better ventilation. By 'amendment of lodging' Harrison meant that people now actually had mattresses and pillows where they had previously used only straw. They were, moreover, eating off better quality utensils. Living, sleeping and eating had therefore tended to improve. On the other hand, money had become scarce and rents prohibitive: the cost of living had risen all round and the landlord was knocking constantly at the door. This was change at the level of the common people. But even at the higher level, among the nobles, Harrison had changes to report. Nor was he alone in his commentary on the new developments. A contemporary, Thomas Wilson, said of great men's fortunes in his *The State of England* (1600) that 'I find great alterations almost every year, so mutable are worldly things and worldly men's affairs'.

It is difficult to speak in a general way about the developments touched on by Harrison or Wilson, since the mechanics of change necessarily differed from country to country. Instead of attempting to survey the whole spectrum, we shall look at two interrelated factors which contributed powerfully to make the Europe of 1660 different from that of 1550. The first of these two fundamental causes of change is demographic expansion, the second is the price revolution.

DEMOGRAPHIC CHANGE

We have already seen that the pressure of population growth occurred mainly in the sixteenth century. The consequences of this expansion were far-reaching. Commentators began for the first time to complain of overpopulation. As early as 1518 Ulrich von Hutten had claimed that 'there is a dearth of provisions and Germany is overcrowded'; while in that same year a commission of Jeronimite friars in Spain appealed to Cardinal Cisneros to 'let His Highness (i.e. Ferdinand) order the surplus population of these realms to go and colonise' America. By the end of the century the complaints were even more common, but they were for the most part being made by propagandists with a cause to plead. Opponents of vagabondage, defenders of the peasantry, promoters of emigration, were among those who argued in this way. 'An infinite number of people has multiplied in this realm'. wrote Bodin about France in 1568. A few years before, in 1561, the Venetian ambassador had given a similar opinion: 'France is full of people . . . every spot is occupied to capacity'. 'England, where no room remains, her dwellers to bestow', was how Sir John Hawkins commented on the reasons for emigration. In Germany in 1538 Sebastian Franck described the country as being 'full of people', and a preacher in 1600 recalled 'the great number of houses that have been built within living memory'. So great was the pressure on space in Swabia, we are assured by a chronicler writing in 1550, that 'there was not a corner, even in the wildest woods and the highest mountains, that was not occupied'. 'The people are increased and ground for ploughs doth want', complained an English writer in 1576. 'This main business', wrote Sir William Vaughan, one of the first settlers in America, in 1623, 'is to be promoted in regard of the general populousness of Great Britain.' The Germans, like other continental nations, could expand inland, and did so. The English, however, had no alternative but the sea, and like other maritime nations fled abroad from the real or imagined pressure of population at home.

Within a generation the fears of overpopulation were reversed and complaints of depopulation had taken their place, above all in Spain. Over and above the exaggerations about too many people, there was the reality that men were more on the move than ever, and it may have been the volume of movement (in particular towards the towns) that gave the impression of a swollen population. This geographical mobility, movement from place to place, was usually a balanced one and did not have severe repercussions. As examples of this we can point to those rural communities in Elizabethan England where the population, far from being fixed from the cradle to the grave in one spot, experienced a high rate of turnover. A survey of the muster rolls for militia in the district of Godalming (Surrey), for instance, shows that between the years 1575 and 1583 somewhere in the region of fifty per cent of the personnel answering the musters had changed and had presumably moved somewhere else. Similarly, an analysis of the tax rolls in Northamptonshire shows that in some areas from forty to sixty per cent of the non-freeholders disappeared between the years 1597 and 1628, as well as about twenty-seven per cent of the freeholders. The search for work, for better opportunities, perhaps even for a wife, may have contributed to this high turnover. In Dorset, reports that 'some of our welthie men and merchauntes be gone from us' suggest a move to the thriving capital of business and fortune, London.

A seventeenth-century example is provided by the village of Clayworth (Nottinghamshire) where a survey of the surnames of residents suggests that between 1676 and 1688 as many as thirty-seven per cent seem to have moved. Nearby in Cogenhoe (Bedfordshire) the turnover from 1618 to 1628, out of a total population of one hundred and eighty, was about fifty-two per cent. It has been calculated for eighteen villages in Nottinghamshire, that only sixteen per cent of the surnames existing in 1544 could be found in 1641. If the evidence here is reliable, it means that many village communities, at least in the more accessible lowland areas, were far from being static and isolated units. They took part actively in the everyday life of the country. It is not enough, of course, simply to show that men moved, for they may have moved no farther than the next parish. Fragmentary evidence from Sussex in the seventeenth century does indeed suggest that most people on the move went no more distant than this, and that few ventured more than twenty miles from their place of origin.

Rural emigrants also contributed to the other notable phenomenon of internal migration in this period, the growth of urban centres. We have seen that cities continued to expand, often despite the fact that severe epidemics tended to focus on them. There is little doubt that much of the demographic loss experienced on these occasions was made up by an influx from the countryside, with the result that the city too, like the village, had a substantial turnover of population. A London clergyman at the end of the sixteenth century claimed that every twelve years or so 'the most part of the parish changeth, as I by experience know, some going and some coming'. Employment was most readily found in the cities and ports, resulting inevitably in the influx of thousands of men when need impelled them.

We have dwelt so far on examples from rural England, with its free village communities and its relative freedom from wars. Little effort is required to see that disruption of this way of life could lead to massive internal migration. Inflation, enclosures and rising rents could and did drive rural labourers from home; heavy taxation and the depredations of war could and did, in France as elsewhere, lead to depopulation of villages. The ever-swelling army of poor and vagabonds became a commonplace in every country in Europe. When these are added to the considerable force of seasonal workers, landless peasants and drifting soldiery, the picture that emerges is not one of a static rural community but of one in the process of change and dissolution. A century and a half of change in the countryside is illustrated by the villages around the town of Ratzeburg (near Hamburg), where an analysis of two hundred and fifty-six peasant households between 1444 and 1618 shows that thirteen per cent were immigrants, ten per cent were natives of the region, eighteen per cent had changed their residence once, seventeen per cent twice, sixteen per cent three times, ten per cent four times, fourteen per cent five to seven times, and four per cent over eight times (the figures have been rounded and so exceed one hundred per cent). The evidence from changing family names, which we have quoted in the case of England, is also applicable to Germany. Three towns in Brandenburg show the apparently high rate of turnover in population. In Beeskow, only fifteen per cent of the surnames existing in 1518 could be found in 1652. In Freienwalde between 1652 and 1704 only four family names survived. In Driesen between 1591 and 1718 no more than nine per cent of the names were unchanged. All this confirms the existence of a remarkable degree of mobility in western Europe among workers on the land. A word of caution must be added here. Peasants who held land of their own, or who could not expect to find a more favourable tenancy elsewhere, were of course less likely to be mobile. Historians therefore continue quite correctly to stress that the predominant feature of the European countryside was stability rather than change. For our purposes, however, it is the small signs of change that are significant. Of the thousands of people befriended in the hospital at Montpellier in the years 1696-9, only a minority—some 544— did not belong to the region. Of this minority, over eighty per cent were rural workers from the north of France, among them a good number of Irish, drifting south in search of seasonal employment. In this combination of internal and international migration we get a fair picture of the growth of movement in the countryside.

The search for employment was clearly the principal reason for population mobility, and though this mobility may have increased during this period we must be careful not to date it only to these years, since even in the mediaeval community there was often a high turnover of residents. Some professions seem to have made it a rule to move about. This happened in France, for instance, where apprentices were encouraged to train in different towns, and we have the case of Jean de La Mothe, a sixteenth-century cordwainer, who left his home town of Tours at the age of sixteen and ended up in Dijon four years later, after having trained in thirteen different localities. The question of employment and mobility leads us to ask two questions: how far did people go to find work, and what proportion of the towns and cities consisted of migrants from rural areas?

We have already seen that in seventeenth-century Sussex people did not tend to move more than twenty miles away. The same holds for Sheffield in the seventeenth century; figures for cutlers who went there to take up their apprenticeship show that of those outside a five-mile radius over seventy per cent came from less than twenty miles away. While this sort of distance was very much a norm, we must distinguish carefully between the distances that different professions and social classes would have to travel. The available evidence suggests that migrants of good standing (the sort, for example, who could easily gain citizenship rights in European towns) did not move very far, possibly because their skills made them more acceptable, whereas the lower and less skilled levels of the working population often had to move farther, and in greater numbers, in order to find employment. Of nearly four thousand outsiders who came to Frankfurt in the fifteenth century and obtained citizenship, seventy-six per cent came from within a radius of seventy-five kilometres (forty-six miles). Of 2,800 locksmiths, however, who came in the fifteenth and early sixteenth centuries to train and work, as many as fifty-six per cent came from over one hundred and fifty kilometres (ninety-three miles) away. Figures for the city of Zurich in 1637 give a similar pattern. Where only four per cent of new citizens here came from Germany and abroad, thirty-three per cent of immigrant apprentice workers did.

Some of the factors we have been looking at can be illustrated in the useful case of the town of Weissenburg in seventeenth-century Bavaria. A study of all population movements into and out of the town gives the following results. Of those who merely travelled through the town, a majority—fifty-eight per cent—came from less than twenty kilometres (twelve miles) away; but many—nearly twenty per cent—had travelled from sixty to three hundred kilometres. Of immigrants into the town, by far the greater number—seventy-three per cent—came from within a radius of forty kilometres (twenty-five miles). Nearly two-thirds of these immigrants were women; only when the distance exceeded forty kilometres did the men begin to form the majority. People who left the town permanently tended to go a bit farther—forty-three per cent went up to forty kilometres, and another thirty-two per cent went up to a hundred kilometres. Once again, women formed the majority of these. Analysis of the male working class shows that day-labourers *(Tagelohner)* were the majority among those coming from under twenty kilometres, while artisans and skilled workers tended to come from greater distances.

The countryside contributed a high proportion of population to the towns, but in addition to this phenomenon we have the fact that some towns also contributed to the growth of others. The rural contribution is so obvious that it needs little emphasis, even though the numerical evidence is hard to find. The general rule to be followed is that if immigrants came from nearby they were almost certainly rural, whereas if they came from farther away the likelihood of them being townsmen increased. Given the relatively small radius of movement in Europe at this time, most towns inevitably increased at the expense of the countryside. More interesting a phenomenon than this is the way in which some towns robbed each other of population. In areas with a high density of urban settlement, in Italy and in the Netherlands above all, movement could be predominantly inter-urban; and when crisis years occurred, as in the Netherlands in the sixteenth-century revolt, whole towns were on the move. Within towns, then, there could be and was substantial mobility. The London clergyman we have already quoted would have found his evidence readily corroborated by an example from the European mainland, where as many as one-sixth of the population of the city of Cologne seem to have changed their domicile in the half a dozen years between 1568 and 1574.

People moved because they needed to work, to marry, to make a fortune. Geographical and occupational mobility went hand in hand. As at all times emigrants in this period wished to better themselves, and many did. It is perhaps no accident that 1605 saw the appearance of the Dick Whittington legend in the form of a play licensed in that year called *The History of Richard Whittington*. In the play a penniless youth comes to London to make his fortune, and succeeds in a spectacular way. Most penniless migrants of this type were frowned upon by the authorities, who tried to deport them to their original parish as vagabonds; but some may well have earned success. The legend illustrates another aspect of mobility, namely that one could move into an entirely strange social environment and yet rise to the top of the ladder and become Lord Mayor of London, regardless of one's class origins. An artisan, trader or yeoman could transplant himself, start anew, and rise to become a great man. The process of transplantation was limitless, and the most fruitful ground for expansion was the overseas territories. At home there were bound to be practical limits to the possibilities of class transference. The guild system, for instance, was a powerful barrier to an independent artisan hoping to make his way in the world and to improve his status through his own efforts. It was not until the battle with privileged corporations was joined that the voice of the small man could be heard. For those who could not make their way in the world they knew, there was always the frontier, the West.

WESTWARD EMIGRATION

In the mid-sixteenth century attempts were made to expand the European frontier east and south, as well as west. Success in the first two was extremely limited. The Russians had no difficulty in crossing the Urals, but their penetration of Siberia did not involve any significant movement of population. On the contrary, even as late as 1650 the outposts in Siberia were manned by no more than about ten thousand men, and these were not settlers so much as mercenary troops and Cossacks employed by the tsar. The hero and pioneer of the eastern frontier was Yermak, the famous brigand turned mercenary soldier, who went to Siberia in 1582. The decades after him saw no heroes, only the remorseless push forward of troop-detachments and fur merchants. The southern land frontier was even less promising for Europeans, since the whole of the eastern and southern Mediterranean lay in the hands of the Muslim powers. Perhaps the most obvious hero to single out here is Yermak's contemporary Sebastian, king of Portugal, who like the Russian perished in an attempt to extend the frontier. Marching out to Morocco in 1578 at the head of an army, the king was overwhelmed by Moorish forces at the battle of Alcazar-Kebir. It was only in the western lands across the Atlantic that emigrants found it possible to venture without needing the protection of a large army, and it was there as a consequence that the colonists flooded.

Richard Hakluyt, the great English promoter of travel and colonisation, urged as one of his principal reasons for emigration the fact that 'wee are growen more populous than ever heretofore', and that people 'can hardly lyve one by another, nay rather they are readie to eate upp one another'. John Winthrop had a similar argument in 1629: 'When then should we stand striving here for places of habitation (where many are spending as much labour and coste to recover or keepe sometimes an acre or two of land, as would produce them many and as good or better in another countrie) and in the mean time suffer a whole continent . . . to be waste without any improvement?'

Whatever the argument's validity, it seems to have had an appeal. The westward movement of people led to the colonisation of America, and it was here that the process of change was most remarkable and the social benefits the most revolutionary. The methods used by the two leading nations in this upsurge, England and Spain, were so different that we must look at them briefly.

England's population overspill began at the Irish Sea. The conquest of Ireland enriched thousands of English soldiers and settlers, dispossessed and degraded the Irish people, and drove a great part of the nation into exile. Most prominent of all those to profit from this agony, and for our purposes most typical of the process of social change, was Richard Boyle, an impecunious adventurer who landed in Ireland in 1588, accumulated for himself a rapid fortune by means of corruption, fraud and marriage, and ended up as a Privy Councillor, Earl of Cork, and one of the wealthiest men in England. Boyle's career showed what fortunes could be won across the sea by men of humble birth. Beyond Ireland, and therefore even farther beyond the restricting values of English society, lay America, where a society in every respect opposite to the colonialist regime of Ireland was being created by English settlers. The distinctive social feature of the New England emigrants was their economic status rather than their religion. Consisting for the most part of small yeoman farmers and lesser traders, they were content to till their own soil and trade their own produce. As a self-sufficient community, they were from the beginning very close to being a one-class society, with the normal chain of command and obedience, but without any landlord or noble class above them or any depressed labour force below. There were several exceptions to this in the early days, notably in Virginia and the crown colonies, but the dominant trend, even in the proprietary colonies, was socially democratic and politically oligarchic. The attraction, then, was not so much the winning of great wealth, which could be won only through agriculture or through conscientious trading, as the winning of emancipation from the class barriers of Stuart England.

The liberty sought by the emigrants to America was complete.

You may 'live freely there', a playwright informed his London audience in 1605, 'without sergeants or courtiers or lawyers or intelligencers'. Land was free, rents rare, and opportunity unlimited. The body politic itself would be cleansed, or so at least Sir Edwin Sandys hoped in one of his more Utopian moments when he envisaged for Virginia 'a form of government as may be to the greatest benefit and comfort of the people, and whereby all injustice, grievances and oppression may be prevented'. As it happened, a large number of Englishmen were to taste of these benefits quite involuntarily. From the very beginning it was the practice to transport criminals and other offenders to the new lands. Straightforward felons formed a minority of the transportees: no more than about one hundred and eighty appear to have been sent to America before 1640. But there were other categories: poor children, orphans, vagabonds, women of all conditions, unemployed men whose arms would supplement the exiguous labour force, who were periodically sent to the colonies. Thereby, it was claimed with much truth, 'many men of excellent wits and of diverse singular gifts . . . that are not able to live in England, may be raised again'. Many of these poorer emigrants would have had to serve some time as menials, but eventually most white people attained their liberty and even won some moderate living for themselves. Not without reason did Captain John Smith in 1624 call America 'the poor man's best country in the world'.

The general picture presented here is, of course, optimistic. Much of the praise and promise was mere propaganda. Not all the colonies were as well off as seventeenth-century Massachusetts where, as C. M. Andrews observes, 'all classes of the population—the lower classes to an extent never experienced in old England—were clothed, housed and fed comfortably'. New arrivals sometimes expected too much from the glowing picture that had been presented to them. 'I have my selfe heard some say', reported a settler in 1634, 'that they heard it was a rich land, a brave country, but when they came there they could see nothing but a few canvis boothes and old houses, supposing at the first to have found walled towns, fortifications and corne fields, as if townes could have built themselves.' Many emigrants were of unsuitable temperament. The Virginia Company in 1616 complained that too many of them were 'lascivious sons, masters of bad servants, and wives of ill husbands', who would rather starve than work; and the directors had to appeal to England for 'good and sufficient men . . . of birth and quality'.

The importance of the American experience was unique. Liberation from the feudal structure of Europe, from its class conventions, its economic disabilities and its religious oppression, opened up a new horizon for all levels of society, and helped in turn to provoke change in Europe. 'I have lived in a country', the preacher Hugh Peter, recently back from America, told the Long Parliament in 1645, 'where in seven years I never saw beggar, nor heard an oath, nor looked upon a drunkard. Why should there be beggars in your Israel where there is so much work to do?'

THE SPANISH EMPIRE

The results of the Spanish conquest of America were if anything even more remarkable. No systematic colonisation was undertaken by the authorities, nor were any chartered companies formed for this purpose; instead, America became the hunting-ground of any Spaniard, of whatever class, who cared to make his fortune. The principal conquistadors were social nonentities: Cortés was the son of a 'poor and humble' captain of infantry, as we are told by Las Casas, who knew the father; Francisco Pizarro was a swineherd; Valdivia and Alvarado did not even know where they were born. Yet some who managed to survive achieved an apotheosis. Cortés became in 1529 a marquis of Spain, with the grant of an immense territory in Mexico comprising more than twenty large towns and villages and upwards of twenty-three thousand Indian vassals, all in complete feudal sovereignty. His elevation to this rank pinpoints one cardinal difference between English and Spanish America: here in the south the trappings of feudalism, of the *Reconquista*, the frontier against the barbarian, were transplanted from Spain. Even though the majority of Spanish emigrants to America were from humble professions, and invariably came out to seek for new opportunities, the societies which they settled into and created continued to reflect the social patterns of Spain.

At first this did not seem a likely development. The nature of the early settlements, the careers of the conquistadors themselves, showed that birth counted for nothing, and that advancement was open to all. An effort was made to exclude certain undesirable interests. The governor of Paraguay asked, for example, that no lawyers be allowed to come out to the colony, 'because in newly settled countries they encourage dissensions and litigation among the people'. After the conquest of Mexico, we are informed by Bernal Díaz, the Spaniards asked 'that His Majesty would be pleased not to suffer any scholars or men of letters to come into this country, to throw us into confusion with their learning, quibbling and books'. The backbone of the colony continued to be the small men who had transported themselves across the Atlantic: the shoemakers, blacksmiths, swordsmiths, cooks, plasterers and masons.

One factor barred the way to a democratic society: the ease of attaining wealth. Wealth can be a spur to social mobility, as indeed it was in America; but in the long run it made the white colonists into a leisured class exploiting the native population. The riches of the mainland were so tempting that the early settlers in the West Indian islands quickly abandoned their homes. 'Being men fond of adventure', observed the historian Fernández de Oviedo, 'those who go to the Indies for the most part are unmarried and therefore do not feel obliged to reside in any one place. Since new lands have been discovered and are being discovered every day, those men believe that they will swell their purses more quickly in new territory.' A highly mobile settler class like this needed some secure and fixed source of labour to exploit the land and feed the population: this was readily supplied by the Indians and subsequently by negroes. A large proportion of immigrants, particularly in the West Indies, consequently found that work was unnecessary and that their race alone gave them a right to wealth. 'In the Indies', reported a magistrate of Hispaniola in 1550, 'Spaniards do not work. All Spaniards who go there immediately become gentlemen.' The defender of the Indians, Fray Bartolomé de las Casas, was more savage in his assessment:

> As they now saw themselves as lords of the native rulers, served and feared by all their people, the Spaniards more and more forgot their origins, and their arrogance, presumption, luxury and contempt for these most humble people increased. When they went out, though they had neither mules nor horses they would not walk any distance but insisted on being borne on the shoulders of the unfortunate Indians . . . It was comical to see their presumption and vanity, and how they esteemed and exalted themselves.

Developing into a colonialist regime far harsher than Ireland, Spanish America certainly offered the underprivileged of the mother country a new perspective in life, but it did so only at the cost of reproducing once again the inegalitarian structure of

European society. To many Spaniards, and above all to the missionaries, this seemed a betrayal of Spain's mission in the world. Here, they had felt, was a virgin continent in which the noblest aspirations of man could have borne fruit. Here a new start could be made. To prove it, the bishop of Michoacán, Vasco de Quiroga, founded a Utopian community based expressly on the work by Thomas More. Like other experiments, notably those of Las Casas, this failed. New America, far from learning from the errors of the past, was to repeat the mistakes that old Europe had made. The attempt to break away from the stratified society of Habsburg Spain to an age of primitive equality and simplicity, collapsed well before the end of the sixteenth century.

The New World was only one, if the most exotic, of the ways in which a man could try to better his social status. The situation in Europe too was such that the condition of men's fortunes was rapidly changing.

THE COST OF LIVING

Social relations in the Old World were being subjected, precisely in the sixteenth century, to a new factor that affected all classes and helped to accelerate the rate of change: a rise in the cost of living. The complaints that have been culled by historians from contemporary accounts are legion. Here in Spain in 1513 is a writer (Alonso Herrera) claiming that 'a pound of mutton now costs as much as a whole sheep used to'; in Germany in 1538 another (Sebastian Franck) claiming that 'everything costs more, and one deals now in groats rather than pennies'; in England in 1549 another (Sir Thomas Smith) demonstrating that 'sixpence a day will not now go as far as fourpence would aforetime; also where forty shillings a year was good honest wages for a yeoman afore this time, and twenty pence a week's wages was sufficient, now double as much will scant bear their charges'; in France in 1568 another (Jean Bodin) to testify that 'the price of things fifty or sixty years ago was ten times less than at present'. Men of all ranks in society were witnesses to this inflation. The famous Italian engineer, Gianbattista Antonelli, on contract to Philip II, claimed in 1581 that in Spain 'the prices of goods have risen so much that seigneurs, gentlemen, commoners and the clergy cannot live on their incomes'.

Researches so far undertaken into price history show that nearly all the items that made up the ordinary stock of consumer goods rose steeply in cost over a period of about a century or so.

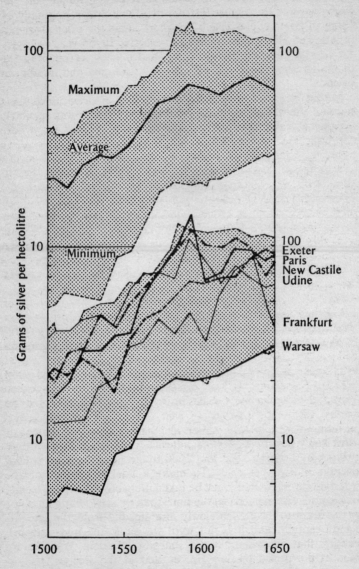

Figure 9 The inflation of wheat prices in Europe.

To gauge the reality of the price rise we cannot do better than to look at the cost of a basic commodity—wheat—on the European market. Figure 9 (from diagrams drawn originally by Fernand Braudel and Frank Spooner) shows the price of wheat, in grams of silver per hectolitre and assessed in ten-year averages, for various parts of Europe. The shaded area surrounding the diagrams shows the range between maximum and minimum prices.

Wheat has been chosen as an indicator of price movements because the data on it is plentiful and because it was regularly adopted as a market standard even though it was not everywhere the basic food of the people. The direction of the price curve taken by wheat was also taken by most other items in general consumption. If we wish to have a more reliable guide than this to the cost of living, we must add together the prices of several basic commodities, giving each a weighted value in the total, and so construct a sort of cost-of-living index. This has been done by E. H. Phelps Brown and Sheila V. Hopkins for a number of items consumed in the south of England between 1264 and 1954. The results for the period 1450-1700, shown in Figure 10, suggest that a rise in prices did occur on such a scale as to affect the life of the majority of the population.

A closer look at the extent of the rise shown here and in other sources may raise doubts about the correctness of using the term 'price revolution'. The Brown-Hopkins index, for example, indicates that the annual average rate of increase in England between 1532 and 1660 was 0.86 per cent, and even in the great inflationary period under the Tudors, from 1532 to 1580, did not exceed 1.5 per cent. To take a period in modern times, between 1935 and 1956 wholesale prices in Britain almost quadrupled, an annual rate of over seven per cent. Was the sixteenth-century increase so revolutionary after all? The pace of the rise was admittedly slow by modern standards. In Florence, for example, prices rose between 1552 and 1600 by no more than an annual average of two per cent. To make a fair assessment of the question several factors must be taken into account. The intensity of the price rise depends on the time-span we are looking at, since prices seem to have risen slowly and steadily from the late fifteenth century, and it is not until we get to the mid-sixteenth century that we encounter the sharpest inflation. Whether we look at the period of slow rise or that of the steepest rise, it remains true that it was the unprecedented nature of the phenomenon that most struck contemporaries and that has caused historians to apply the word 'revolution' to it. The impact of the rise was also distinctive. The sixteenth century, unlike our own age, was less able to adapt to a fall in the purchasing power of money and a rise in the price of a restricted choice of goods. If bread doubled in price, people starved; nowadays they can eat potatoes. Moreover, to calculate an annual increase over an extended period can be misleading, for this obscures the frequent and catastrophic short-term leaps in the price curve. Finally, nobody now seriously discusses the 'price revolution' in terms of rising prices only; the whole exercise is distorted unless we can bring into perspective other factors—wages, for example, and rents—that made the change in prices only too grim a reality in the life of large sections of the population.

CAUSES OF THE PRICE RISE

As in all periods of scarcity people naturally blamed the price rise on the usual villains, the merchants and speculators; and the authorities also came in for their share of criticism. The unnecessary export of food for profit, at a time when it was badly needed at home, was a common and regular complaint, and on occasion led to riot and sedition. The Castilian cortes of 1548 claimed that 'in the last few years the heavy purchases of wool, silk, iron, steel, other merchandise and provisions, by foreigners' had led to an immoderate increase in the price level. In 1551 it was the same complaint, with the claim that 'the principal cause of the rising prices of bread and other food is that (resident) aliens speculate in all kinds of provisions'. Monopoly interests in food and other commodities were blamed by Bodin in the 1560s for much of the high prices and scarcity in France. In England, too, the author of a 1549 tract, in an attempt to explain the high price of goods such as wool of which there appeared to be no scarcity, concluded that the 'principal cause is the engrossing of things into few men's hands'. These 'few men' who were universally held to blame, varied from country to country. In England they tended to be the landlords; there were also the hoarders of corn, men whom Archbishop Laud in a picturesque Biblical phrase was later to accuse of 'grynding the faces of the poor'. They were, on the continent, the wheat-merchants, the corrupt officials, the foreign usurers: the men who were murdered by the mob in Naples in 1585 and in Dauphiné in 1588.

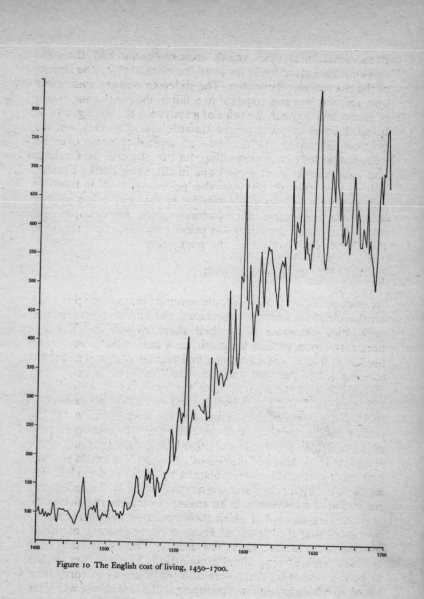

Figure 10 The English cost of living, 1450–1700.

In most cases the people were right to blame the men they did. Rents *were* being raised, food *was* being hoarded. But few would have understood that the problem could not be solved even by the speculators. The basic unit on which everyone was relying for financial stability, the coin of the realm, was itself being devalued. In England Henry VIII debased the coinage on several occasions in the early sixteenth century. Between 1543 and 1551 the amount of silver in English coins was reduced by over two-thirds, and wage-earners found the purchasing power of their debased money greatly reduced. The very poor, who subsisted mainly on very small change, found that much of it had now been made worthless; while traders raised prices so as to recoup their losses. Only in 1560 did Elizabeth eventually attempt to stabilise the coinage and strengthen it against foreign speculation. Surprisingly enough, England after 1560 was the only major European country to have a currency that did not get devalued. All other countries, from Russia and Poland to France and Spain, suffered some degree of monetary inflation as a result of a reduction in the amount of silver in the coinage. Spain began debasing coinage fairly late in the day. Minimal reductions in the silver content of coins occurred under Charles V and Philip II, but it was not until the reign of Philip III that silver began to disappear from the coinage entirely and the government resorted to extensive debasement. The complaints of Spaniards who suffered from the new debased coin gave some indication of how people in other European countries must have suffered when similar measures were taken: as in Poland, for instance, where the silver content of the *grosz* was reducd by two-thirds between 1578 and 1650.

A curious problem rises in any consideration of the few dates so far given. English monetary difficulties, like those of France, can be traced to the early sixteenth century at least; Spanish and Polish money, on the other hand, remained stable until the end of the century. Yet for all these countries a continuous rise in prices, whether or not associated with monetary inflation, was a common experience. It appears that the price rise was only partly to be blamed on the recoinages of the period. This fact struck Jean Bodin with peculiar force. In his *Discours . . . et Response aux Paradoxes de M. de Malestroict* (1568), an attack on a writer who denied that a price rise even existed, Bodin pointed out the fallacy of relating price levels only to the silver or gold content of coins. For Bodin 'the principal and almost the only' cause of the price rise was '(a reason that no one has yet suggested) the abundance of gold and silver' from America. Bodin's argument was to become the classic exposition of the origins of the price revolution, particularly after a vast array of data accumulated by Professor Earl J. Hamilton lent weighty support to it. The argument, very briefly, is that after the discovery of America the import of bullion flowed not only into Spain but also into Europe, where it supplemented the flow of coin and began to push up prices. Any increase in bullion before the discovery of the American mines was attributed to increased output by the silver mines of central Europe. In very crude terms, then, the volume of silver increased relative to that of goods, and the value of the latter increased correspondingly. This close interrelation between bullion and prices appeared to have been proved beyond doubt by the following graph, Figure 11, in which Hamilton depicted the relationship between bullion imports to Spain, and Spanish prices.

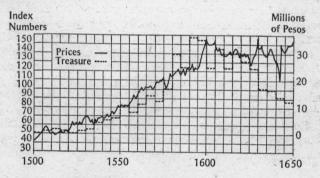

Figure 11 Bullion imports and price inflation in Spain.

It was not until about the mid-sixteenth century that European writers began to look on American silver as a possible cause of the rise in prices. Probably the first to connect the two phenomena was the Salamanca jurist Martín de Azpilcueta, who in 1556 argued that 'in Spain, in times when money was scarcer, saleable goods and labour were given for very much less than after the discovery of the Indies, which flooded the country with gold and silver. The reason for this is that money is worth more where and when it is scarce than where and when it is abundant.'

Francisco López de Gómara, historiographer of Charles V and biographer of Cortés, made a similar observation in 1558, in a work that remained unpublished until 1912. The author usually given the credit for the formulation and popularisation of the argument is Jean Bodin. Certainly in France Bodin's ideas were taken up and reproduced by contemporary students of the economic situation, and in Spain he was read and popularised by the eminent writer Sancho de Moncada. In England, meanwhile, the author of the *Discourse of the Common Weal* took for granted in 1581 the role played by 'the great store and plenty of treasure, which is walking in these partes of the world, far more in these our days than ever our forefathers have seen in times past. Who doth not understand of the infinite sums of gold and silver which are gathered from the Indies and other countries and so yearly transported into these coasts?'

Gerard Malynes, a prominent English merchant, argued in 1601 that 'the great store or abundance of money and bullion, which of late years is come from the West Indies into Christendom, hath made everything dearer'. By this date the explanation was clearly well accepted.

Modern historians, however, have been very wary of accepting the hypothesis as it stands. Just as price inflation appears to have had no necessary relationship to monetary debasement, so it can be shown that prices began to rise well before American silver made any appreciable impact on certain countries. England is the most obvious case, though several other countries could equally well be cited. Large quantities of bullion did not begin to operate, Spain until the 1540s, when the Bolivian mines began to operate, and certainly very little of this metal could have entered England before mid-century. Yet already by 1550 the price level there had doubled: where the Brown-Hopkins index for 1510 is one hundred and three, in 1550 it is two hundred and sixty-two. The situation of France is more difficult to assess since, as Bodin correctly pointed out, increased trade with Spain, seasonal emigration and the growth of Lyon and Paris as international business centres all helped to attract specie into the country. In Italy there can be little doubt about the timing. Significant amounts of bullion to finance the Spanish troops did not begin to arrive until the 1570s, reaching a flood in the 1580s, but already in the 1530s the price curve was moving sharply upward.

Difficulties arise even in the case of Spain. Hamilton's graph, reproduced above in Figure 11, would seem to prove his conclusion that 'beyond question the "abundant mines of America" were the principal cause of the Price Revolution in Spain'. The coincidence of the two trends in the graph can nevertheless be questioned. It is extremely difficult to get absolutely reliable figures for the import of bullion, and Hamilton, to whom all historians stand in debt for his painstaking and pioneering researches, is still open to some criticism. He not only fails to take any account of smuggled specie (often a substantial proportion of the whole) but also sometimes omits even officially registered consignments. The curve for prices, moreover, can be plotted on a different scale to show that prices rose proportionally higher in the early part of the century, before the large shipments of bullion. In any case, any graph that tried to show the relation between bullion and prices should offer us a curve not for imports alone but for the total volume of bullion within the country, since it was not imported money alone that modified prices so much as the total of coin used in transactions. It should also be pointed out that the bullion imported into Spain did not always stay there, a fact of which contemporaries were well aware. As early as 1558 the *arbitrista* Luis Ortiz presented the crown with a reasoned plea against the export of bullion in view of its scarcity within the realm. By 1600, when Martín González de Cellórigo wrote his *Memorial de la política necesaria*, the situation was expressed in a paradox: 'If Spain has no gold or silver coin, it is because she has some; and what makes her poor is her wealth: so that here are two contradictions which, though they cannot be formally reconciled, must necessarily in our Spain be both considered as true.' Hamilton was, of course, aware that the beginning of the rise in prices in Spain preceded the large-scale import of bullion, but he offered no proof of any sort for his suggestion that the output of the German silver mines may have been responsible. In short, considerable doubt can be thrown on the argument that bullion imports had a unique role to play in the early stages of the price rise.

For its validity the argument relies principally on the quantity theory of money, according to which a variation in the volume of money has a proportionate effect on prices. Expressed in an equation formulated by the economist Irving Fisher, the quantity theory may be expressed simply as $MV=PT$, where $M=$ money, $V=$ its velocity of circulation, $P=$ the general price level and $T=$ the total volume of transactions. When V and T are constant, M and P clearly determine each other directly; when, in other words, the same number of people are buying the same number of goods, the injection of an additional amount of money

69

will cause prices to rise proportionately. It is not our purpose here to discuss the Fisher equation, which has been subjected to a wide range of criticisms by economists. There is a tendency at present to regard it as unhelpful and sometimes misleading as a method of approach. Probably the main criticism of its use is that it over-emphasises the importance of M in determining P, and ignores the roles of V and T.

Evidence for quantity of money, velocity of circulation and volume of goods is difficult to come by. The German historian Wiebe, and others after him, drew up figures showing an increase in the European stock of bullion, but economic historians have been reluctant to rely on their findings. Very little is known of the output and exchange of commodities in this period. But we have already seen that a considerable increase in population did occur in the sixteenth century. This could mean more people as purchasers and hence a higher rate of turnover of cash (V). . It could also mean a change in the number of transactions (T).

There are at least three pieces of evidence which suggest a causal relationship between population and prices in the sixteenth century. We know that there was a regular and widespread rise in land values, a positive indication of land hunger on the part of expanding population. We know that there was in most areas a pronounced fall in real wages, which points to the swelling of the labour force, so that labour became cheaper. Both these factors will be discussed presently. Finally, and perhaps most significant, not all prices rose equally or at the same rate. In Spain, Hamilton demonstrates that 'throughout the first three-quarters of the sixteenth century agricultural prices rose considerably faster than the non-agricultural'. The reason he suggests for this is that agricultural production declined. This is only partially correct, for in some respects production seems to have increased. 'Even mountains disappeared', testified Florián de Ocampo in 1552, 'as everything in Castile was ploughed up for sowing'. Throughout Old Castile, one of the few regions so far studied, common lands were reclaimed into steadily advancing areas of tillage. It was not that produce from the land declined, but that it was still insufficient for the needs of an expanding population.

We know that, like Castile, the rest of sixteenth-century Europe experienced a great resurgence in agricultural production. If the population had been stable, this would have meant that agricultural produce would be cheaper than industrial

70

goods. However, the Brown-Hopkins calculations for prices in three selected countries show that, with the period 1451-75 represented by an index of one hundred, in 1601-20 the index stood as follows:

	Alsace	South England	France
Price index of foodstuffs	517	555	729
Price index of industrial goods	294	265	335

In each case, the food prices rose about twice as much as the other commodities. This was clearly a selective inflation in which the basic consumables most in demand by an increasing population rose in price. The picture holds true also for countries such as Belgium, Germany and Poland, for which detailed information is available. An explanation along these lines would go some way towards demonstrating why prices began to rise even before the arrival of bullion from America. From the same premises it could be argued that T, in the Fisher equation, decreased in so far as production could not keep up with the needs of a growing population. It would none the less be impossible to eliminate silver from the picture altogether, for it played a profound part in aggravating the malaise — and principally the monetary inflation — that much of Europe suffered in the wake of the price rise.

The rise in prices was not everywhere of the same dimensions. We need only look at Figure 9 to realise that Spain and France suffered the most severely, while regions far from the western trading area, such as Poland, continued to maintain much lower price levels even though the inflation may have been of the same order. If we measure price levels in several European cities in 1551-1600 as a proportion of Dutch prices (taken as one hundred per cent), the prices can be seen to be less inflated as one moves eastwards. French and Spanish levels in general exceed the Dutch level. At Frankfurt the level is ninety-three per cent, at Augsburg seventy-three per cent, at Vienna sixty-one per cent, at Danzig fifty-three per cent and at Warsaw forty-six per cent. Despite this imbalance between parts of the continent the rise was undoubtedly a European phenomenon, affecting all countries to a greater or lesser degree, and what is more our concern, affecting all social classes.

INCOMES AND THE PRICE REVOLUTION

If we were to consider the level of prices alone, the often moderate degree of inflation and the frequent periods of depression would give us cause to wonder whether anything revolutionary was happening. It may be argued with good reason that the use of the word 'revolution' in this context is misleading. Yet the testimony of contemporaries suggests that there were many serious consequences of the price rise. In a less flexible economy than ours is today, with large sections of the people, both workers and landlords, subsisting on traditionally fixed incomes, the impact of creeping inflation could be catastrophic. Basing himself on 'the common report of all ancient men living in these days', an English commentator of 1581 observed that 'in times past, and within the memory of man, he hath been accounted a rich and wealthy man and well able to keep house among his neighbours, which (i.e. who) was clearly worth thirty or forty pounds; but in these our days the man of that estimation is so far (in the common opinion) from a good housekeeper or man of wealth, that he is reputed the next neighbour to a beggar'. This account need not be accepted literally for us to understand the point being made.

We shall be considering here only the wages of the labouring population, and shall deal with other incomes in later sections. The bare statistics show that the income of the wage-labourer did manage to rise in this period for most of the professions for which we have data. In Spain the average money wage for a worker rose from an index of fifty in the ten-year period 1511-20 to one of one hundred and sixty-five in 1611-20. In Poland in the city of Lwow, wages which stood at an index of one hundred and five in 1521-30 had risen by 1621-30 to one of two hundred and forty-four. In southern England the daily wages of building-workers rose, for a labourer, from fourpence in 1548 to a shilling in 1642, and for a craftsman from sixpence in 1548 to one shilling and sixpence in 1642. Wages therefore doubled or trebled in the course of a century. In normal times this may have sufficed to keep up with rising prices. The circumstances of the period have, however, to be taken into consideration. The trebling of a wage does not necessarily mean a trebling of purchasing power. Prices may have (as they did) increased four or five times, and the coin in which wages were paid may have been debased and devalued. Rather than look at a man's money wages, his nominal wages, it would be more illuminating to look at his real wages, the purchasing power of his money. Wages in themselves are in any case no indication of a labourer's economic position, since seasonal unemployment was certainly high in many trades, and what a labourer earned in six months may well have had to suffice him for a further six months when he would be out of work.

One of the ways in which to assess a labourer's real wages during this period would be to assume that he was regularly employed, and to estimate his real wage in terms of how many consumables it would buy. This has been done for building workers by E. H. Phelps Brown and Sheila Hopkins. Their results for Valencia, Vienna and Augsburg are shown in Figure 12.

The information given in this diagram confirms what is known from other sources of the grave economic difficulties facing workers. It has been shown, for instance, that in the town of Speyer between 1520 and 1621 wages doubled and sometimes trebled, but over the same period the price of rye, a basic staple food, increased by fifteen times, that of wheat thirteen times, that of peas fourteen times, of meat sixfold, and of salt sixfold. Most of the wages we have touched on have been industrial ones, but it is not surprising to learn that agricultural wages also fell in real terms. In Poitou, a farmhand's wages in 1578 could purchase only fifty-two per cent of what they could have bought in 1470, and the income of a mower had likewise declined to fifty-eight per cent of its former value. In the south of France, in Languedoc, agricultural wages that had stood at an index of one hundred in 1500 fell to an index of fifty-four by 1600. All sections of the working class, both urban and rural, in all European countries, were severely hit. Historians who speak lightly of a Golden Age in these years, whether of Spain or of any other country, tend to forget that the triumphs of the rulers and of their culture were founded on the protracted miseries of the vast majority of the population.

It should be remembered, however, that a survey of wages alone does not give us the full story, since actual income could be either greater or less than the nominal wage. The accounts of the chapter-house of the church of Notre Dame in Antwerp in the sixteenth century show that even workers in regular employment were unemployed, and therefore unpaid, for about one sixth of the year. In such a case their actual income for the whole year would clearly stand at a lower level than the nominal wage rate. On the other hand, there were those for whom a money wage formed only a small part of income, since they were paid in kind

—usually one or two meals daily—and were consequently less dependent on ready cash. This group formed a large proportion of the working class in the towns, principally the unskilled labourers; and over large areas of Europe formed an absolute majority of the rural working population. Some of the more depressed of dependent peasantry were paid entirely in kind. Two conclusions follow from this. Firstly, to quote R. H. Tawney, 'the social problem in the sixteenth century was not a problem of wages (because so few persons depended entirely on wages for a living), but of rents and fines, prices and usury, matters which concern the small-holder or the small master craftsman as much

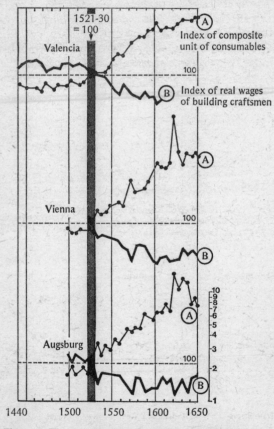

Figure 12 The cost of living in three European cities.

as the wage-earner'. Secondly, it is quite possible that many of those who subsisted in part or whole on payment in kind did not suffer from the price rise as much as Figure 12, which is based on wage payments, indicates. It is even possible to find that the wages of some workers rose higher than the level of prices: this is true of sixteenth-century Belgium, where, however, the special circumstance of mass emigration and economic crisis would have helped to keep skilled labour in good demand.

When all allowance is made for these modifying statements, it remains true that over most of Europe an alarming decline in living standards made the common labourer, both in town and country, a primary casualty of the price revolution. This is made plain by Figure 13, which illustrates the relationship between grain prices, industrial prices and wages, in six European countries in the sixteenth century. The sluggish movement of income levels arose from various causes, perhaps the most relevant being the growth in the size of the labour pool owing to

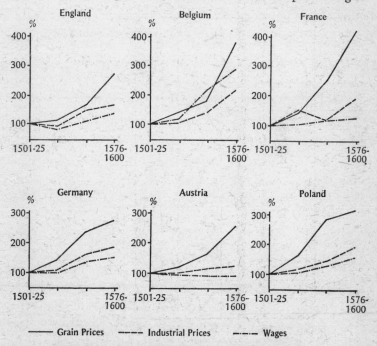

Figure 13 The decline in living standards in the sixteenth century.

increased population; but the result in political terms was every-where the same. The growing insubordination of the lower classes was one of the most striking aspects of this century of change and crisis. It is a relatively easy exercise to correlate the great civil out-bursts of the period with moments when some unlooked-for disaster, the bad winter of 1565-6 or the poor harvests after 1594, made life totally intolerable for those who had only by a miracle managed to tolerate it at all.

LAND AND THE PRICE REVOLUTION

The vital unit of wealth in Europe was not bullion but land, and it was the changes effected in both the price and utilisation of land that made the sixteenth-century inflation memorable to con-temporaries. Writing in 1549, Sir Thomas Smith observed in his *Discourse of the Common Weal* that there were those who profited and those who lost in the process. Those who profited were 'all such as have takings, or farms in their own maintenance, at the old rent; for where they pay after the old rate, they will sell after the new; that is, they pay for their land good cheap and sell all things growing thereof dear'. The losers, on the other hand, were 'all noble men and gentlemen and all other that live by a stinted (i.e. fixed) rent or stipend, or do not maner (i.e. work) the ground, or do occupy no buying or selling'. Because of the decline in their fixed rents, the nobles had to take steps to recoup their incomes, 'and therefore gentlemen do so much study the increase of their lands, enhancing of their rents, and so take farms and pastures into their own hands'.

These valuable comments on the English situation were no less true when applied to the rest of Europe. But though Smith's observations were generally valid, he tended to give too much emphasis to his argument that tenants profited while landlords suffered. He gave a picture of gentry who:

> seeing the charges of household so much as by no provision they make can by holpen, they give over their households, and get them chambers in London, or about the court; and there spend their time, some of them with a servant or two where he was wont to keep thirty or forty persons daily in his house and to do good in the country, in keeping good order and rule among his neighbours.

While it is true that a number of the ruling class became reduced in their means during these years, with results that we shall look at subsequently, there is no doubt that most of them

76

adjusted to the situation wherever possible and made a concerted effort to keep hold of their property. The consequence was a deliberate rise in the rents paid by tenants both in town and in country.

Rent increases were universally condemned by contemporaries as plain profiteering and cold-blooded usury. The English writer Robert Crowley in 1550 had no doubt that he was pointing his finger at the right culprits when he denounced:

> the great farmers, the graziers, the rich butchers, the men of law, the merchants, the gentlemen, the knights, the lords, and I cannot tell who; men that have no name because they are doers in all things that any gain hangeth upon. Men without conscience. Men utterly void of God's fear. Yea, men that live as though there were no God at all! Men that would have all in their own hands; men that would leave nothing for others; men that would be alone on the earth; men that be never satisfied. Cormorants, greedy gulls; yea, men that would eat up men, women and children, are the causes of sedition! They take our houses over our heads, they buy our grounds out of our hands, they raise our rents, they levy great (yea, unreasonable) fines, they enclose our commons! No custom, no law or statute can keep them from oppressing us in such sort, that we know not which way to turn us to live.

English statesmen, concerned for the well-being of the commonwealth, were no less quick to denounce the rent-raisers as the real cause of the economic troubles of the people. Yet for many landlords, as Smith (himself a landlord) realised, the raising of rents was all too necessary an operation. The price rise would have told heavily against them if they had not been able to increase their income in this way (where tenants' rents were fixed by written feudal agreements even this was often impossible), or otherwise by joining the market as producers in order to take advantage of the high agricultural prices.

There is abundant evidence of the rise in land values and rent. The trend was not everywhere the same, as we can see from the example of rural Languedoc, where in the sixteenth century land rents appear to have remained fairly stationary, and to have risen only in the early seventeenth century. But in other parts of Europe the development was unmistakable. Figures for the estate of Eiderstedt in Schleswig-Holstein show that a rent of 10.75 marks per hectare of arable in the period 1526-50 had risen by 1576-1600 to one of thirty-one marks; while over the same period the market price of the hectare rose from an index of one hundred to an index of six hundred and sixty-two. In Altenburg in Saxony an estate which sold for four thousand one hundred gulden in 1578 sold for eight thousand nine hundred and fifty in 1615. In Poitou land which sold for a price index of one hundred in 1531 was sold in 1601 at an index of five hundred and twenty. Bishop Latimer in England complained in the 1550s that his own father had a farm that had been leased to him originally at £3 a year whereas now the rent was over £16. 'In my time', observed William Harrison in the 1580s, '£4 of rent be improved to £40, £50 or £100'. These claims may have been exaggerated, but detailed research supports their burden. In East Anglia the rent of arable land rose sixfold between 1590 and 1650, a pointer not merely to the value of arable but also to its importance over pasture, whose rental in the same period rose no more than two or three times.

English landowners seem to have been extremely efficient in increasing their returns. On the Essex estate of the Petre family, land producing rent of £1,400 in 1572 was producing £2,450 in 1595 and over £4,200 in 1640. In the period 1619-51 the rents on the twelve Yorkshire manors belonging to the Saviles of Thornhill were raised by over four hundred per cent. On new additions to the estates of the Herbert family in Wiltshire, rents rose from an index one hundred in 1510-19 to one of eight hundred and twenty-nine in 1610-19, an eightfold increase. On new lands of the Seymour family in the same county, rents increased from an index one hundred in 1510-19 to nine hundred and fifty-one in 1600-9, more than nine times. The movement of rent on these newly acquired manors is illustrated in Figure 14.

It would be wrong to assume that rent increases invariably represented a clear profit, or that tenants always suffered. The gentry often had heavy expenses of administration and maintenance that may have only just been met by rent rises. Moreover, agricultural tenants could and did make profits, particularly when they were farmers of moderately good means. The rapid rise in the market price of cereals, meat and wool from their estates would readily compensate for having to pay more to a landlord. In the village of Wigston Magna, in Leicestershire, the whole of the late sixteenth century was a time of profit for the small farmers, because the steep rise in the price of foodstuffs they sold on the market more than compensated for any other expenses such as rents or taxes. This phenomenon of prices rising even higher than rents was commented upon by a character in the East Frisian Chronicle (1545) of Beninga: 'When you consider how butter, cheese and everything that grows on the land and that a labourer has to buy, cost a great deal and have more than doubled in price in the last twenty years, taxes and rents cannot be said to have risen to the same extent.'

In addition to profiting from the price rise, small farmers could be protected from rack-renting by the length of their tenancies. In Old Castile, for instance, as in Lwow (Poland), for much of the sixteenth century long-term contracts kept the peasant at least partly secure, and it was only in the seventeenth century that leases were revised and given out for very short periods. Explaining the pattern in Old Castile, Bennassar observes that 'length of tenancy and fixity of rent could not but encourage the peasant to improve his land, but the stipulation in at least ninety per cent of cases that the rent be paid in kind, did not allow him to profit to the full from the rise in prices'.

The attempt to revise fixed rents was made not only in the country but also in the towns. In England Crowley complained of the nobles and the landlords that 'some have purchased, and some taken by leases, whole alleys, whole rents, whole rows, yea whole streets and lanes, so that the rents be raised, some double, some triple, and some fourfold to that they were within these twelve years last past'.

It is difficult to find evidence to support Crowley, for though the cost of living in towns, and above all in London, may have been rising, other reasons than the simple greed of landlords were also in operation. The movement of population to the towns, universal at this time, must automatically have pushed rents up and opened opportunities for speculators. Urbanisation of the country gentry would have had the same effect. Whatever the cause, town rents did rise sharply. In Valladolid in the mid-sixteenth century, admittedly at a time when the court was still in the city, house rents appear to have risen within a decade by anything from fifty to eighty per cent. In Lwow, the rents of business premises increased from 1500 to 1550 by something between one hundred and fifty and eight hundred per cent. In Paris, rents increased tenfold between 1550 and 1670 (though some of this increase may have been offset by inflation).

It would hardly be an exaggeration to say that the 'land revolution' which followed the rise in prices was even more significant than the 'price revolution' itself. We need justify the statement only by outlining three main reasons. In the first place, the land protected the privileged. The holders of estates and

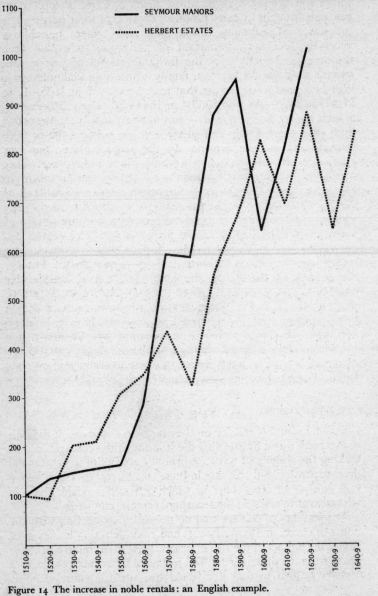

Figure 14 The increase in noble rentals: an English example.

80

manors in Germany, France, England, Italy, the noble lords whose soil produced corn, whose fields pastured sheep, whose peasants brought in dairy produce, these kept their heads above the waves of inflation, raised their rents where possible or necessary, but most important of all began to exploit their resources to benefit from the favourable level of prices. One success story was the Seymour family, whose manorial holdings in Wiltshire produced receipts that rose from £475 in 1575—6, to £1,429 in 1639—40, and £3,204 in 1649—50. The aristocracy — at least the greater part of it — was not only saved: it entrenched itself even more firmly and surely into the political life of both western and eastern Europe. In the second place, the sure guarantee offered by land in a world where most other values seemed to be collapsing inspired those who had been successful in their own fragile enterprises — finance, commerce — to think of their families and to buy an estate or two on which to spend their declining days. Land was both the conserver and the solvent of society; while preserving the old forces, it also gave greater opportunities for wealth and mobility to those who had made their fortunes in professions frowned on by the upper classes. Finally, the process of change on the land produced a considerable number of casualties. In England the independent small farmer, the yeoman, tended to disappear (not only downwards, it should be emphasised, but also upwards). Everywhere, both in England and on the continent, even in lands which like Sweden had a relatively free peasantry, changes in land values and soil exploitation led to the expropriation of a section of the peasant class and to the growth of unemployment both urban and rural.

GOVERNMENTS AND THE PRICE REVOLUTION

Inflation inevitably reacted on the machinery of state. It did this in two main ways: by affecting the stability of the coinage, and by making the waging of war (the primary activity of governments) more expensive. Subordinate to these considerations there were a vast number of other ways in which difficulties could arise, in administrative costs, in the securing of credit, and so on.

The stability of coinage had no necessary connection with the influx of silver, and governments had been debasing money even before the impact of the rise in prices, their main motive being to profit from the debasement. The inflow of silver, however, had a decisive impact in that it affected the intrinsic value of coins, whose silver content varied from country to country. Inflation of prices led naturally to a fall in the real value of money, and no one suffered from this more than the royal treasuries, whose revenues fell.

On the continent the struggle to stabilise the coinage in the sixteenth century is closely connected with the American silver sent abroad in great waves by Spain to finance its troops. Spain became the international pace-setter. Already in 1557 the collapse of its credit and the declaration of bankruptcy brought with it a universal declaration of bankruptcy in France, the Netherlands, Naples and Milan, making necessary the peace of Cateau-Cambrésis in 1559. To recover its fiscal stability and imperial position, Spain had to divert large resources of silver to Italy and the Netherlands. France, too, received a large volume of silver, not only indirectly through trade but also directly through the subsidies paid by Spain to the Catholic League in the 1580s. In all these countries silver began to exercise an inflationary role, aggravated quite naturally by the uncertainties of constant war. In Italy the silver began to be issued by the mints as coin: in Naples alone, between 1548 and 1587, ten and a half million ducats were put into circulation in this way. Yet by 1587 only seven hundred thousand of this remained in circulation. The rest had fallen into the hands of speculators and hoarders, ordinary people who were insuring themselves against bad money. In France the same phenomenon occurred. First there was an inflation of the silver coinage, then when attempts were made (as in 1602) to limit the face value of the coins, they began to disappear from circulation. Counterfeit or debased coin flowed in to take its place. Foreign speculators were active, as a report from Lyon in 1601 claimed: 'the German and Swiss traders in this city, under the shelter of their privileges, are amassing coin to carry out of the realm'.

Spain, the source of silver, was the greatest sufferer. Philip II had fought against the rise in prices without ever allowing himself to debase either the silver or the vellon coinage. Philip III, however, opened his reign by allowing (in 1599) the issue of vellon without any silver content. The government made a profit out of this, as it also did in 1602 when it ordered a reduction in size of the copper coins. The coining of more copper in subsequent years was supposed to cure the scarcity of money; instead it had two main adverse effects. It led to severe inflation, and it all but eliminated silver from circulation. The price level in Spain achieved heights paralleled almost nowhere else in Europe; and copper, rather than silver, came to represent over ninety-eight per cent of the coin being used in Spain in 1650.

England was the only country to maintain a relatively stable coinage in this period, thanks to the recoinage undertaken by Elizabeth in 1560-1, an exercise that took several years to complete, restored public confidence in the currency, and brought in a small profit to the crown. Elsewhere in Europe the intrinsic value of the coinage fell repeatedly, almost from year to year. Just as regularly, then, prices tended to rise, and the costs of the state tended to spiral upwards.

A lower real return from taxation, and higher costs of war, were the unhappy lot of all governments in the age of the price revolution. The plight of the early Stuarts in England is reflected in the plaint of Lord Treasurer Cranfield in 1623: 'you cannot easily conceive into what straits I am daily driven for supply of money for His Majesty's occasions, which the exchequer is not able to support, they are so infinite and of so many pressing natures'. In France the wars of the late sixteenth century crippled the monarchy, which repeatedly suspended payment of interest on the *rentes* and repudiated its debts. When Sully came to power his first act was not to pay the debts of the crown but to repudiate them and in effect declare a bankruptcy. In Spain, the worst hit of all, the government repudiated its debts regularly every twenty years: in 1557, 1575, 1596, 1607, 1627, 1647.

'War is extremely expensive to him,' wrote a Frenchman in 1597 about Philip II, 'and costs him more than it does any other prince.' The statement was a truism, in view of the fact that Spain — or rather, Castile — had to finance the largest empire in the world. It becomes more real to us, however, if we look at the expenses that forced the bankruptcy of 1575. A memorandum of April 1574 drawn up by Juan de Ovando put the crown's income for the coming year at a presumed 5,642,304 ducats, of which only one million was expected from America in the form of bullion. The crown's total debts at that date (as distinct from its current obligations) amounted to 73,908,271 ducats, of which four millions were owing in the Netherlands. The figures must not be accepted at face value, since other estimates made at the same time differed slightly, but the proporation of the debt appears all too credible.

The ironic feature of such a situation is that it was precisely in this period that European governments appeared to be interested in establishing 'absolutism'. To the political opponents of the Stuarts and of Richelieu, one essential aspect of 'absolutism' was the attempt to meet the financial stringency of the times by raising taxation through unorthodox methods. The years of political crisis in France after 1630, and the Eleven Years tyranny in England, were both connected above all with public finance. The revolutionary 1640s, when popular uprisings throughout Europe chose taxation as their primary grievance, showed that the problem remained unsolved. The long period of the price rise had come to an end by then, but the problems it had accumulated continued to plague governments. Where the irony lay was in the fact that no government could become 'absolutist' unless it had made itself financially independent; but financial independence was not so easily gained. An inflationary period was the worst possible time for a state to seek to make itself independent of the parliamentary process, when it was only by the consent of the governed that taxes could be increased to meet the rising costs of government.

TOWARDS THE 17th CENTURY CRISIS

As we move from the intensive period of the price rise into the seventeenth century, there is a levelling-off of the pace of inflation and a corresponding change in the momentum of the economy. The essential indicator was, once again, Spain. The great crisis of bankruptcy and plague at the end of the century in Castile brought the era of expansion to a sudden end. The change was matched in the political sphere by the passing of three monarchs: Philip II in 1598, Elizabeth in 1603, Henry IV in 1610. Spain now faced a future in which England and France, despite all the efforts of Philip, had consolidated themselves as potentially the two most powerful states in Europe. Internally, Castile entered on an era of declining population; the peninsula was in the grip of severe financial troubles; and America, so long a support of the royal treasury, began to withdraw its aid.

As America was the symbol of the price rise, so it now became a symbol of its regression. The peak period for import of treasure into Spain was the ten-year span 1591-1600, with nearly three billion grams of silver and nineteen million of gold. After 1600-10 there was a rapid decline of bullion imports over the first half of the century. The share going to the Spanish crown fell from nearly eleven million pesos in 1601-5 to only six hundred thousands in the five years 1656-60. The decline of imports does not mean that silver ceased to play its part in the running of the Spanish war-machine. Well into mid-century Olivares was dispatching shipments to Italy to meet the inexhaustible demands of the Thirty Years War.

The decline in silver is significant for it ushers in an age of copper. In Spain the trend was set by the issue of pure copper coinage in 1599, and the country became the outstanding victim of vellon inflation. As silver became scarce and disappeared, so governments had to resort to a debased or non-silver coinage. After 1602, France began to issue copper coins in the absence of enough silver. As the rich copper mines of Sweden began to pour out their produce, the danger of vellon inflation spread throughout Europe. In Moscow, Lwow and Danzig the currency rose in value by as much as three times around the year 1620. In Germany a pamphleteer of 1632 complained that 'for the last few years the minting of copper has caused great confusion in Germany and Spain'. The course of the war in central Europe did nothing to alleviate the problem. In Germany the currency crisis centring round 1620 became known as the *Kipper und Wipperzeit*, and unbalanced prices even more severely than the war itself.

> In our town men say it's Kipper,
> But neighbour Hans, he says it's Wipper,

began a song of the time current in Frankfurt (a Kipper was a coin-clipper). Clipping, speculation, profiteering by mints, were among the causes of the crisis. The imperial *thaler* rose to five times its face value in Alsace and Brandenburg, between 1619 and 1622. Commodity prices naturally followed suit. In Alsace, for example, the price of wine between November 1617 and November 1622 rose by over six hundred per cent. In Leipzig prices in 1621-2 rose to levels they were never to surpass throughout the worst years of the war. Contemporary with this came a continent-wide depression in agriculture. In France, England, Germany, Italy, grain prices tumbled. Shrinking markets and the collapse of credit made the burgomaster of Lubeck complain that in the years 1603-20 the rate of interest rose to 'unchristian heights never known since the world began'.

The temporary shift from silver was a pointer to an even more profound malaise. The fall in supplies of American bullion was matched equally, and in the same period around 1610-20, by the beginnings of a fall in the total volume of commerce between Spain and the Indies. In the strictest terms this meant a regression in the Atlantic trade, but Spain was also a European, a Mediterranean, power; so that the fall also reflected Spain's position in Europe. The commercial dislocation was one that tended to affect not only Spain but the whole of the European trading area, including the Baltic and the Mediterranean. England suffered a major trade crisis in these years (from 1616), caused partly by an incompetent attempt at reorganising the cloth export trade, partly by currency manipulations abroad and heavy competition from the Dutch. The crisis saw the parting of the ways between northern and southern Europe. In the north recovery was slow: of the eastern Baltic ports the only one to expand markedly was Riga, and others such as Danzig remained in relative decline until mid-century; while in England a series of crises in the first half of the century depressed trade periodically and led the Venetian ambassador in 1640 to write from London that 'the trade of this city and kingdom is stopping altogether'. It is reasonable, on this evidence, to see the crisis of 1620 as a prelude to the mid-century crisis. But at least in the north these difficult years led to readjustment in trade patterns, and did not involve any long-term decline in commercial strength. In the Mediterranean, on the other hand, the 1620s initiated a decline from which there was no real recovery. Here the decade 1610-20 ushered in a period of falling prices in the two principal trading areas, Spain and Italy. Though prices rose for a while after the 1620s, the trend was set: the south suffered a prolonged depression in the seventeenth century. There was a decisive shift in the balance of trade. Italy's export trade fell, Spain's shipping declined. In an age when foreign trade was a firm guide to economic strength, and a far firmer guide than industrial production, these facts were significant.

The invasion of the Mediterranean by foreign interests became an irreversible development. Already in the sixteenth century the problem of feeding the expanding population of the area had led to imports of grain from the north and the Baltic. After the great hunger of the 1590s northern grain implanted itself firmly in southern markets. It is possible that in the seventeenth century the Mediterranean, aided for example by Sicilian grain exports, managed to feed itself. But by then the foreign ships had found other articles in which to trade: tin and lead, timber and textiles.

The English were ahead of the others. In the port of Livorno there were six English vessels in 1590-1, three in 1591-2, but sixteen in 1592-3. In 1582 the English had already gained the right to trade freely in Malta. The next stop was the Levant, reconnoitred by the Levant Company, founded only the year before and numbering fifteen vessels by 1595. By 1620 their warships were in the Mediterranean.

They were followed soon by the Dutch, particularly after the conclusion of the Twelve Years Truce in 1609. In 1611 the States General named their first consul for the Levant, and the next year their first consulate was opened in Italy, at Livorno. The rate of Dutch expansion can be measured ironically by the number of their ships captured by Algerian corsairs: in 1617 it was thirty, in 1618 twenty-two; in 1620 as much as eighty-two. Then came the great depression, when even foreign ships had to withdraw from the Mediterranean. The Algerians in 1622 captured only one Dutch ship, in 1623 none. In 1623 the Dutch trade representative in Constantinople was writing home to say that he had received no directives for two years. But when the crisis was over the northern traders were back. The changing naval structure of the Mediterranean, where English and Dutch sailors could venture without fear of reprisal from the Catholic powers, indicated a major shift in international trade. Decay of commerce, decay of population (the plagues of 1599 in Castile, of 1630 in Italy), these were the signs of the passing of initiative in Europe to the countries of the north, to Sweden, the United Provinces and England.

For these three Protestant countries — the only ones in the early seventeenth century to have any pretension to naval power — it was to be a golden age, but for differing reasons. The Swedes celebrated these years as their greatest imperial age; for the Dutch it was a time of colonial expansion, cultural consolidation and commercial greatness; the English alone had to survive the rigours of Stuart rule for half a century, yet even for them the period brought the foundations of commercial and imperial power. France, alone of western countries, remained poised on the threshold without quite, like its Protestant neighbours, crossing over into the ebullience of empire.

But even if it is possible by the early 1600s to talk of southern decline and northern destiny, the essential unity of Europe remains as a check on our generalisations. The southern countries, for all their decay, took an unconscionably long time to collapse. Until the 1640s at least, Spain was with reason looked upon as the most powerful country in the world. And if we argue that Spain collapsed at mid-century, we must concede that it was followed soon after by Sweden and, in a less obvious way, by the United Provinces. The division, then, between a weak south and a resurgent north is not as easy to sustain as it may seem, even though by certain criteria — mainly economic — it is a valid and useful one.

The fact is that in the long run both northern and southern Europe shared in the same process of development. The political divergences must be recalled to the essential unity imposed by the economic situation. We are given a hint of this by the crisis of the 1620s, which was international in scope. The mid-seventeenth-century crisis was similarly international in character. One way to look at this would be to emphasise the price trend, the downswing in the 1620s, and then from about mid-century the secular depression: in Milan from 1637, in Languedoc from 1654, in Beauvais from 1662, in Danzig from 1663. This movement, radiating out initially from the Mediterranean area (which is why Spain and Italy are usually described as being the first to decline), was one in which all Europe shared and which severely modified its economic and social structure. Since such an interpretation of history in terms of price data may appear to be too mechanistic, however, it is essentially the social, the human, aspects of the crisis of the seventeenth century that will be discussed in the chapters that follow. The outstanding feature of the crisis is the unity it seems to impose on all European countries, regardless of their development relative to each other. It is by studying the crisis as a unity that we can isolate those factors that contributed to change in European society.

3 THE GROWTH OF CAPITALISM

It is Faith that brings salvation. Faith in money-value as the immanent spirit of commodities, faith in the mode of production and its predestined order, faith in the individual agents of production as mere personifications of self-expanding capital.

KARL MARX, Capital, vol. III

We do not see usuries forbidden to us, except in so far as they are repugnant both to justice and charity.

Letter of John Calvin (1545)

The sixteenth and seventeenth centuries in Europe witnessed a transition from the primary accumulation of capital to the full practice of commercial capitalism. The growth of mercantile (rather than industrial) capital is so prominent a feature of the age that many historians have no hesitation in dubbing it the 'age of mercantilism'. Both the terms 'capitalism' and 'mercantilism' that come to prominence in this context are difficult ones to define. Ironically, neither has direct relevance to the period we are discussing, since the origins of capitalism can be sought far earlier than the sixteenth century and the heyday of mercantilism came mainly after 1660. It is impossible, all the same, to look at the political economy of Europe without attempting to use these and similar terms of uncertain definition.

RELIGION AND CAPITALISM: THE END OF A CONTROVERSY

In his study on *The Protestant Ethic and the Spirit of Capitalism*, first published in 1904, the German sociologist Max Weber argued that the Protestant churches, and particularly the Calvinist faith, had contributed to the creation of an outlook that encouraged financial thrift and business enterprise. This outlook, he argued, did not itself create capitalism.

We have no intention whatever (he claimed) of maintaining such a foolish and doctrinaire thesis as that the spirit of capitalism could only have arisen as the result of certain effects of the Reformation, or even that capitalism as an economic system is a creation of the Reformation. In itself, the fact that certain important forms of capitalistic business organization are known to be considerably older than the Reformation is a sufficient refutation of such a claim. On the contrary, we only wish to ascertain whether and to what extent religious forces have taken part in the qualitative formation and the quantitative expansion of that spirit over the world.

Weber argued that the new Reformation ethic had encouraged the further development of capitalism, because those who believed in it felt that capital accumulation was sanctioned by the divine purpose. Old mediaeval scruples about usury and interest therefore vanished before a teaching that could justify the making of wealth by the highest moral criteria. Capitalism had found its ideologues: henceforward the Calvinist middle classes became the great promoters of capitalist advance, and the trading circles of England and Holland became their standard-bearers.

The very frail supports for Weber's structure were being easily demolished by critics when in 1926 R. H. Tawney produced his brilliant study on *Religion and the Rise of Capitalism*, a work which disagreed with many of Weber's premises but which, through a survey of the controversy over usury and other matters, tended in the last analysis to agree with his position. 'The "capitalist spirit" ', Tawney argued, 'is as old as history, and was not the offspring of Puritanism. But it found in certain aspects of later Puritanism a tonic which braced its energies and fortified its already vigorous temper.' In spite of the careful phrasing of this passage, which suggests a very guarded attitude towards Weber, Tawney, like other historians from a Protestant background, may to some extent be said to have shared Weber's attitude.

Discussion of the views of Weber and Tawney has since become so common and obligatory an exercise for students of history that it seems appropriate to emphasise that the controversy has long been a sterile one, profitless both to students and to professional historians. Valuable and stimulating as the contributions of these two great writers have been, it is fair to point out that no one now believes that the Protestant religion *qua* religion played any unique part in the development of European capitalism.

Although it is the historical evidence for the Weber thesis that is really at issue, it seems clear that Weber's methodological approach should be fundamentally questioned. Weber's philosophical idealism made him and his followers posit a meta-physical 'spirit' which modified the whole trend towards capitalism. While agreeing that such a 'spirit' is essential to capitalist growth, later historians have rejected the assumption that it is a prerequisite for such growth. It was, in other words, capitalism that promoted the capitalist spirit, and not the reverse. The views of Marx in this respect provide a valuable corrective to those of Weber. Capitalism for Weber tended to be an attitude of mind: to Marx, however, it was a method of production, rooted not in mental perspectives so much as in the actual events of history. Capitalism for Marx was promoted through the exploitation and expropriation of working-people, which contributed to the accumulation of capital within the hands of a new forward-looking class.

The misleading nature of the arguments put forward by Weber, who was not a historian but a sociologist, are well described in the following passage from Tawney, which we shall quote at length.

If capitalism means (writes Tawney) the direction of industry by the owners of capital for their own pecuniary gain, and the social relations which establish themselves between them and the wage-earning proletariat whom they control, then capitalism had existed on a grand scale both in mediaeval Italy and in mediaeval Flanders. If by the capitalist spirit is meant the temper which is prepared to sacrifice all moral scruples to the pursuit of profit, it had been only too familiar to the saints and sages of the Middle Ages. It was the economic imperialism of Catholic Portugal and Spain, not the less imposing, if more solid, achievements of the Protestant powers, which impressed contemporaries down to the Armada. It was predominantly Catholic cities which were the commercial capitals of Europe, and Catholic bankers who were its leading financiers. Nor is the suggestion that Protestant opinion looked with indulgence on the temper which attacked restraints on economic enterprise better founded. If it is true that the Reformation released forces which were to act as a solvent of the traditional attitude of religious thought to social and economic issues, it did so without design, and against the intention of most reformers . . . . To think of the abdication of religion from its theoretical primacy over economic activity and social institutions as synchronizing with the revolt from Rome is to antedate a movement which was not finally accomplished for another century and a half, and which owed as much to changes in economic and political organization as it did to developments in the sphere of religious thought.

The Anglo-Saxon example was Weber's chief method of illustrating his thesis, and Tawney himself relied on the Puritan writers, specifically Richard Baxter, to show how great a contribution to capitalism was made by their ethic. Yet the English example is not necessarily the most suitable to adopt, if only because Englishmen had fallen victim to their own propaganda and actually begun to believe in some well-repeated attitudes. We have, for example, a pamphleteer in 1671 claiming that 'there is a kind of natural unaptness in the Popish religion to business, whereas on the contrary among the Reformed the greater their zeal the greater their inclination to trade and industry'. A large body of English Protestant literature equated popery with idleness, for no other reason apparently than that Catholic clergy did not work (while, presumably, Protestant clergy did) and that Catholic countries had too many feast-days that kept people idle (while presumably Protestant countries had few idle hands and continuous full employment). In reality there was not and could not have been any basic difference between countries on the grounds of their religion alone, as the above quotation from Tawney is at pains to argue. Catholic economists and statesmen were no less aware than their Protestant counterparts that feast-days must be kept to a minimum and that vagrancy, including clerical vagrancy, must be checked. Idleness and unemployment were as rife in England as in Spain, if we may believe the economist Thomas Mun who in the 1620s denounced his compatriots for 'mis-spending of our time in idleness and pleasure'. Did the Puritan ethic ever cure these bad habits and so contribute to thrift? The question will never be adequately answered, since historians differ in the extent to which they think the Calvinist spirit was influential in England. Using the most rigid criteria, it may even be argued that the Puritans, always a minority group, were only ever predominant in England in the mid-seventeenth century. After this, it can be argued, the English reverted to their old ways, and by 1663 a French traveller could claim that the English were 'naturally lazy and spend half their time taking tobacco'.

If we choose a more thoroughly Calvinist country, the United Provinces (where, however, over half the population were still Catholic by the seventeenth century), we find that the business ethic was not primarily associated with Calvinism. What is at dispute here is not Calvin's own views, important as these are, so much as the practical contribution which he and his followers may have made to the ready acceptance of usury as a key factor in capitalist development. It is generally agreed that Calvin's thought on usury was in all essentials traditional, but that he introduced certain nuances that his followers were later to develop into a more liberal theory. For a century or more there was little sign of Calvin having introduced any radical changes from the standard Catholic position. The result was that in the most formative period of the growth of Dutch power, there was no obvious identity between the official religion and the development of capitalist methods. The theologians remained firmly opposed to any practice of usury that stepped outside the traditional (that is, the mediaeval) limits. Decisions reached at the general synod of Emden in 1571, the provincial synod of Dort in 1574 and the national synod at Middelburg in 1581, show strong opposition to usury. The second of these synods actually ruled against allowing bankers to approach the communion table. As late as 1646 we have a reasoned statement by the leading theologians of Dutch Calvinism in which they denounced high interest rates, and interest on loans to the poor; at the same time they accepted that usurers should be excluded from communion.

There was also, it is true, another side to the Dutch Church. It was in 1638 that Claude Saumaise published his *De Usuris* (On Usury) in which for the first time a Calvinist teacher went further than Calvin in liberalising the attitude to profits. The year after this came his *De modo usurarum liber* (On the nature of Usury). There was still strong opposition to his views from the clergy, and it was not until 1658 that a local synod, at Leiden, openly disapproved of 'the prejudice against usury'. But it required the hand of the secular authority, that of the State of Holland in 1658, actually to rule that no banker should be excluded from communion simply because he practised usury. We have a situation, then, where the capitalist ethic was certainly not predominant among Calvinist thinkers during the most formative period of Calvinism, the late sixteenth century; and where the pastors of the Calvinist churches themselves appeared to be unaware that their religion winked at usury. The very tardy acceptance of usury may also be demonstrated by reference to Calvin's own Geneva, but perhaps the most striking example is that other most Calvinist country, Scotland (or at least lowland Scotland), which gives even less encouragement to any thesis attempting to link capitalist enterprise with the faith of John Calvin and John Knox.

The great advantage of the argument from religion is that any religion can, with some effort, be identified with the rise of a capitalist spirit. Werner Sombart has therefore with ample justification argued that it was Catholicism, not Protestantism, that played the role outlined by Weber. The papal financial system, and thinking of theologians such as St Antonine of Florence and Cardinal Cajetan, the practice of capitalism in Italy and in Catholic Antwerp, all these can be fitted into a very plausible thesis. H. M. Robertson likewise, in an effort to create a *reductio ad absurdum,* argues from the tolerant attitude of German Jesuits towards the taking of interest at five per cent, that the Society was one of the forerunners of the capitalist spirit.

The fact is, as Henri Hauser pointed out long ago, that the debate over usury is not necessarily the central issue. Hauser observed correctly that there were two main questions at stake: who were the first thinkers to allow usury, and why were some Protestant nations more progressive than Catholic; and that Weber confused the two issues, identified some of the thinkers of the first question with the Protestant nations of the second, and came out with the formula that Puritanism=Capitalism. In this way several unrelated questions of undoubted historical interest were confused together for the purpose of a stimulating but ultimately false thesis.

Supporters of the Weber thesis argued from two mistaken positions. They adopted the wrong causation, for, as H. M. Robertson puts it, 'it was the development of industry and commerce that promoted habits of diligence; not Calvinistically inspired habits of diligence that promoted industry and commerce'. They also adopted the wrong historical sequence, by looking first at the successful enterprises of the English and Dutch, and then arguing back to the success of the religion involved. Weber's method is open to criticism here, since he adopted the ideology of an eighteenth-century American, Benjamin Franklin, as the prototype of the ideology of his sixteenth-century Europeans.

A look at the sixteenth century displays the complete impartiality of God as to which faith he was favouring economically. Even by the late seventeenth century the Catholic countries were not noticeably more backward than the Protestant. When the various factors involved in commercial expansion, agricultural growth and industrial progress are examined, when the position of working men and the availability of capital are considered, there is no doubt that religion is seen to be one of the factors of least consequence in any study of the origins of capital enterprise.

REFUGEES AND CAPITALISM

> There is no one who does not know (announced Jacques Savary in his *Dictionnaire Universel de Commerce* (1723)) that the city of Amsterdam is one of the cities with the greatest trade that there is in the world, whether by the amount of money remitted by her merchants and bankers to all foreign countries, or by the almost infinite number of commodities with which her warehouses are filled, and which come in and go out unceasingly in the commerce which she carries on even to the ends of the earth.

Amsterdam was a Protestant city, but only formally so; in practice it was a home for every religious persuasion, and its tolerant policy in matters of faith made the phrase 'an Amsterdam of religions' proverbial. If foreigners came there, more often than not it was because the liberal religious policy allowed them to exercise their business activities in peace. And not only in Amsterdam but throughout Europe, it was the refugees, bereft of home and fortune, seeking only the toleration that would allow them to prosper, who promoted the spread of capitalism. In England, in Holland, in Germany, in Switzerland, it was the foreigner and stranger who came to settle and to develop the business which religious strife had forced him to abandon in his own land.

It is easier to describe this phenomenon than to explain it. Historians like Brentano have argued that the stranger from a developed community is a unique vehicle for economic enterprise, and is most fitted to manage the affairs of his hosts in a profitable way, not being bound by their ethical standards. It was common experience in mediaeval England, for example, to find Italians and Flemings in control of sections of the finances; and in Spain even into the sixteenth century the Genoese dominated financial business. Amintore Fanfani has argued that the international trader and merchant 'did most to favour the rise of the capitalist spirit', simply because his international activities freed him from the moral constraints of any one society. This classic role of the stranger took on new significance in an age when whole communities were displaced on account of religion.

The peak period of emigration for religious reasons was in the second half of the sixteenth century. Since this was the age of resurgent Catholicism, most of the émigrés happened to be Protestant. Their religion was in itself of no great significance, and it is difficult to categorise them theologically since they tended to come from, as well as to merge into, widely varying religious traditions. What is important is the undoubted effect they had on the financial and economic life of Europe. Where the émigrés sprang from an economically progressive background they tended to take their skills with them, and so contributed to the extension of technical enterprise. The most notable contributions were made by refugees from what had been the two most advanced regions in Europe both industrially and commercially: Italy and the southern Netherlands.

The Italian émigrés had directed their footsteps to Switzerland since the early days of the Reformation and it was there, in the German-speaking areas above all, that their influence was greatest. They came principally from Vicenza, Cremona, Locarno and Lucca, and their chief contribution to the world outside lay in the production of textiles. Zurich's economic success came to be founded on the work of the Locarno entrepreneur Evangelista Zanino, who established the first large-scale textile industry (mainly velvets) in German Switzerland. Zanino dominated the city's industrial life for most of the late sixteenth century. He spent most of his time away from Switzerland on business missions while his brothers looked after the factories in Zurich. He died in 1603. The Pellizzari, who first came from Vicenza in 1553, flourished in both Basel and Geneva, and prepared the way for other immigrants. Their work in Geneva was soon overshadowed by other people such as the Lucca capitalist Paolo Arnolfini, who went there in 1570.

The most important of the Lucca refugees was Francesco Turrettini (1547-1628), who first came to Geneva in 1575. Travel and business-training in Antwerp, Frankfurt and Zurich occupied him for the next few years and it was not until 1593 that he returned to Geneva to found the Grande Boutique, the biggest Genevan silk company of its time. His co-founders, refugee entrepreneurs like Cesare Balbani and Pompeo Diodati, are evidence of the great influence exercised by Italian capitalists. The capital of the Grande Boutique grew in twenty years from eighteen thousand to one hundred and twenty thousand crowns. Turrettini was beyond all doubt the most important foreign capitalist to come to Switzerland. His business expanded into the early years of the seventeenth century but he, like other entrepreneurs, was hit by the 1620 economic crisis. The Grande Boutique was wound up in 1627 and replaced by another firm, in which members of his family continued to have a large interest. The year after this, in March 1628, Turrettini died, leaving a fortune of over two hundred thousand crowns, making him the wealthiest foreign entrepreneur in the country. His career was to be paralleled among many other European émigrés.

The Italians in Switzerland were responsible for the introduction of new production methods and new fabrics (they brought in mulberry culture). More than this, it was they who initiated large-scale enterprise in the area, and freed Switzerland to some extent from economic dependence on its neighbours. Although capitalist methods had already existed in the country, the Italians made further advances by breaking through the guild system, establishing a new industrial organisation and forming trading companies.

The Italian influence elsewhere in Europe was limited because few refugees went farther than Switzerland. In England, probably the next most popular place of refuge, the Italians were the smallest of all the foreign communities. They were active in southern Germany, but more as itinerant merchants than as domiciled entrepreneurs. In Leipzig, for example, only one important Italian merchant seems to have taken up citizenship in the whole of the period 1551–1650. In England the most prominent Italians tended to be financiers rather than entrepreneurs. Horatio Palavicino, a Genoese by origin but nevertheless fully anglicised, emerged in the 1570s in London and Antwerp as one of the wealthiest financiers of England, with family links in the Low Countries, Spain and Italy. He engineered huge loans on Elizabeth's behalf in 1578 and thereafter, was knighted in 1587 after important financial services to England on the continent, and died in 1600 worth about £100,000.

These few details underline a fact which hardly needs emphasis: that it was the Italians above all who were the ambassadors of financial capital, a function they had retained ever since the Middle Ages and the Renaissance. Their names were legion: the Florentine Lodovico Diaceto, who made and lost his fortune in the French Wars of Religion; the Lucca firm of the Bonvisi, who flourished throughout the sixteenth century, drawing their fortune mainly from Antwerp and Lyon, until they collapsed at the latter town in 1629; Zametti, also of Lucca, who became the chief banker of Henry IV of France, and whose son ended as a bishop of France. They served all governments and all countries.

The industrial expertise of the Italians was limited for the most part to Switzerland: the Netherlanders, on the other hand, made themselves active throughout Europe. Their dispersion arose principally from the decay of trade at Antwerp. Some left merely in order to recoup their fortunes (with the result that many émigrés were Catholic), and we can find them abroad even before the Dutch revolt affected the city; but the more substantial part went as a direct result of the religious situation and the havoc wreaked on economic life by the war. By the end of the sixteenth century all the major west German cities had a strong representation of Flemish and Walloon capitalists. Of the foreign firms in Cologne at this time, there were about fifteen to twenty-five Portuguese, about forty Italian and about sixty Nether-landish.

Wherever they went in Germany, both merchants and artisans had grave difficulties in getting accepted by their host com-munities. Frankfurt is a case in point. Together with Hamburg it was the largest centre for Netherlands émigrés. Discrimination occurred for that very reason. The merchants were hit by two laws, one in 1583 which forbade the exiles to buy houses without permission from the city council, and one in 1586 which decreed that no foreigner could become a citizen unless he married into the family of a citizen. The artisans for their part were hit by severe guild restrictions, which regulated the terms under which they could work or set up business. Not surprisingly, for many Netherlanders Frankfurt became only a brief stopping-place. Their experience shows that the economic talents of the exiles were not readily welcomed everywhere.

Despite this, there is ample evidence of the important contri-bution made by the exiles to the life of Frankfurt. The Belgians (we may call them such since they were almost exclusively from the southern Netherlands) came in large numbers, the peak years being 1560 and 1561 when an annual two thousand or more refugees arrived. Despite opposition, a large number succeeded in gaining citizenship, and in the years 1554-61 as many as 38.4 per cent of all new citizens were Belgians.

The majority of these new citizens came from the industrial, French-speaking areas of the Netherlands. Of those gaining citizenship between 1554 and 1561 nearly eighty per cent were Walloons. In Frankfurt they soon played a preponderant role in those callings to which they had been trained. Undoubtedly the best represented trade was the textile industry: nearly forty-seven per cent of the Belgians who were citizens of Frankfurt in 1561 were in one or other of the branches of this industry. The production of silk was introduced by the newcomers, and they became the biggest dealers in nearly all the principal commodities. The biggest traders in drugs were Johann Heuss and Jacob Bernoully from Antwerp; in sugar the biggest traders were the de Hamel family from Tournai, while Anton and Daniel Meerman from Antwerp were also prominent; the biggest jeweller in Frankfurt was Daniel de Briers from Antwerp, while Antwerpers like Mertens, Hensberg, Moors and Uffeln were the wealthiest gold- and silver-smiths.

Wherever they went in Germany the exiles made their mark. They founded Frankenthal in 1562, specifically as an industrial centre. Neuhanau was founded by them in 1597, Mannheim in 1607. The most conspicuous contribution was made less at the artisan level (which mainly involved the textile industry) than in the world of mercantile capital, where we find Antwerp financiers everywhere: men like Louis de Behaut in Hamburg; Godfried Houtappels, Simon de Decker and Jean Resteau in Cologne; the Heldewiers in Frankfurt. The key role of Antwerp merchants in German trade, a role which was out of all proportion to their numbers, can be seen by looking at Figure 15, which shows the areas of origin of foreign merchants and traders who took citizenship in Leipzig in the period 1551-1650.

In this period only ten Netherlands merchants (as distinct from other trades) obtained citzenship of the city, in contrast to a great number from elsewhere. Six of the ten came in the years 1555-90: these were the wealthy merchants Dominicus Breun, Marcus Mertens, Sebastian van der Velde, and Hans Cuvelier, all from Antwerp, Heinrich Cramer von Claussbruch from Arras, and Heinrich von Ryssel from Maastricht. Their numbers give little hint of their importance, for they were in reality among the most prominent and wealthy traders of Leipzig. It was to this little group that Saxony owed the beginnings of capitalist and industrial expansion in the sixteenth century. The Elector Augustus adopted a deliberate policy of attracting the Netherlanders. He introduced textile-workers to found the factory at Torgau; in 1566 brick-workers were brought in. Concessions such as freedom from taxes were given. This was the case with Cramer, who in 1579 was encouraged to set up a textile-factory on his estate at

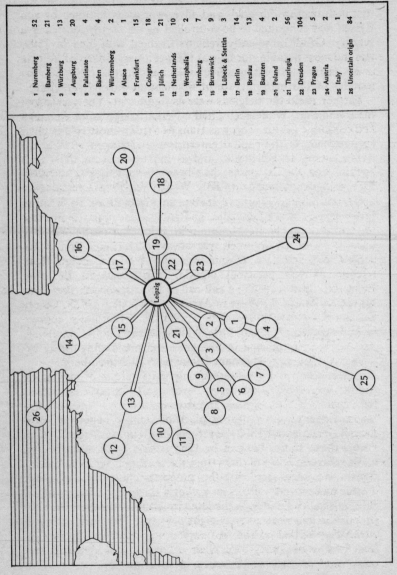

1	Nuremberg	52
2	Bamberg	21
3	Würzburg	13
4	Augsburg	20
5	Palatinate	4
6	Baden	4
7	Württemberg	2
8	Alsace	1
9	Frankfurt	15
10	Cologne	18
11	Jülich	21
12	Netherlands	10
13	Westphalia	2
14	Hamburg	7
15	Brunswick	9
16	Lübeck & Stettin	3
17	Berlin	14
18	Breslau	13
19	Bautzen	4
20	Poland	2
21	Thuringia	56
22	Dresden	104
23	Prague	5
24	Austria	2
25	Italy	1
26	Uncertain origin	84

Figure 15 Foreign merchants in the trade of Leipzig, 1551–1650.

Menselwitz, near Leipzig, to be staffed with Belgian workers, and to be free from the controls laid down by the guilds. In 1588 the first manufacture for gold- and silver-work was founded by von Ryssel, and continued to be controlled by his family for nearly a century. Of all these entrepreneurs Cramer, who died in 1599, was the most notable, for he was the wealthiest citizen of Leipzig in his time, the most powerful merchant in the city, and the founder of the manufacture of woollens in Saxony-Altenburg.

Farther afield the Belgians were as significant. The greatest of the *condottieri*, Wallenstein, had a Netherlander as his financial and economic genius. This was Hans de Witte, whose role as chief entrepreneur in the capital enterprises undertaken on Wallenstein's estates in Friedland, and as moneylender to the Czech nobility and the Emperor, has been thoroughly documented. Born in Antwerp in about 1583, Witte (who always remained a Calvinist) came to Prague in 1600 or so. He built up his fortunes in association with other exiles, and grasped his opportunity after the battle of the White Mountain in 1620. The participation of fellow-Belgians in his work was always important. One of his earliest colleagues in Prague was the Walloon émigré Jean Matieu. Witte's principal banking correspondents in other European cities read like a roll-call of the dispersion: there was his cousin Arnold de Witte in Antwerp, the Italian Giulio Cesare Pestalozzi in Augsburg, the prominent Netherlands refugee Daniel de Briers in Frankfurt, Walter de Hertoge in Hamburg, Anton Frey-Aldenhoven in Cologne, and the distinguished ex-Antwerp merchant Abraham Blommaert in Nuremberg.

These examples have stressed only the interests of mercantile capital originating in Antwerp. Beyond this, we must emphasise the export of technology and industry from the southern Netherlands. England, as a nearby place of refuge, benefited enormously. From about 1550 the refugee communities began to take visible shape there. London by 1568 is said to have harboured 6,704 refugees, 5,225 of them from the southern Netherlands (the figures are unreliable, but the proportion seems reasonable). Textile traders and workers formed over thirty-five per cent of the refugee total in London in the late sixteenth century; by 1635 the proportion had risen to sixty-eight per cent. The main centre at which they settled outside the capital was Norwich, a city that benefited so obviously from their activity that a contemporary could sum up their contribution in these terms:

In primis, they brought a great commodity thither, viz. the making of bays (etc.) . . . item — by their means our city is well inhabited, and decayed houses reedified and repaired . . . item — they dig and delve a number of acres of ground and do sow flax, and do make it out in linen cloth, which sets many on work . . . item — they dig and delve a great quantity of ground for roots which is a great succour and sustenance for the poor . . . item — they live wholly of themselves without charge, and do beg of no man, and do sustain all their own poor people. . . .

The several contributions made by immigrants, the introduction of glass-engraving, new potteries, lace-making and the like, are well known. In general it should be remembered how easily and commonly the use of the word 'Dutch' by English contemporaries hid the fact that Antwerpers and Belgians were meant: the 'Dutch' multiple loom, for instance, which was introduced in the 1560s and revolutionised weaving; the 'Dutch' merchants, like John Carré (of Antwerp) who brought in glass-workers to England; and the eighteen 'Dutch' financiers (nearly all came from the southern Netherlands) who were arrested on currency charges in 1618-19 and who initiated the great part played in London finance by 'Dutch' bankers; and even the 'Dutch' churches set up by Flemish immigrants. A treatise written in 1577 summed up the position as follows:

By reason of the troubles grown in other countries, the making of bays . . . and many other things made of wool is mightily increased in England. . . . For this cause we ought to favour the strangers from whom we learned so great benefits . . ., because we (the English) are not so good devisers as followers of others.

The 'strangers', it should be noted, were not always refugees. A survey in 1573, for example, reveals that just over half the foreigners entering London that year came for economic rather than religious reasons. By the same token a few Catholics could be found among the general majority of Protestant immigrants.

Finally, and most important of all, the contribution of the Antwerp exiles to the growth of Amsterdam and the economy of the Dutch Republic was transcendent. Numerically the refugees from the southern Netherlands were very significant indeed, but it was in their quality and function that their principal importance lay. Amsterdam became inevitably their chief goal. Over thirty per cent of those obtaining citizenship in Amsterdam in the years 1575-1606 were from the south, and of the southern immigrants to the city in this period over fifty per cent came from Antwerp alone. The immigrants included names that were soon to rank among the most prominent in the north: Johan de Brauw and François Fagel from Flanders, Frans van Aerssen from Brussels, Daniel Heinsius from Ghent, Louis Elsevier from Antwerp, Gomarus from Bruges, Justus Lipsius from Overijssche. But it was the financiers and the magnates of commerce and industry whose presence really helped to transform the potential of the United Provinces: men such as Louis de Geer from Liège, Isaac Lemaire from Tournai, Balthasar de Moucheron from Louvain, Willem Usselinex from Antwerp, and scores of others from Liège (like Trip and De Besche), Antwerp (like Heldewier, Della Faille, Dirk von Os and Balthasar Coymans) and elsewhere in the south.

Their contribution lay, first and most obviously, in the sphere of merchant capital. Of the three hundred and twenty biggest account-holders in the Amsterdam Exchange Bank in 1610, over half came from the south. By 1631 it was estimated that one-third of the wealthiest Amsterdammers were southern by origin. A comparable picture might be drawn of Rotterdam, where one of the wealthiest and most influential merchant citizens was Johan van de Veken, a Catholic from Malines. Southerners took the lead in all the great enterprises of Dutch commercial and imperial expansion. It was, for instance, Olivier Brunel from Brussels who laid the basis for Dutch trade to the White Sea; Balthasar Moucheron who became the first and most eminent projector of the expeditions to the North Pole and Novaya Zemlya; Lemaire and von Os who were the two biggest stockholders in the East India Company, that cornerstone of Dutch prosperity; Usselincx who founded the West India Company, which nearly won Brazil for the Dutch.

Perhaps even more notable was the influence on Dutch industrial prosperity. Antwerp and the south became the power-house for the rapid expansion of those manufactures that were needed for commercial success. The textile industry was the main beneficiary as émigrés came from Hainault and Flanders to Haarlem, Leiden and Middelburg. They fled not sofely for religious reasons but because war and the stoppage of trade in the south had hit at industries and at their own livelihood. Whole communities and industries transported themselves northwards. Almost overnight, great industrial centres of the south became depopulated. Haarlem won its bleaching industry from the southern provinces, Leiden its prolific textile industry. New handicrafts, such as the working of gold and silver, were introduced: of the thirty-eight goldsmiths who became citizens of Amsterdam in 1585, twenty-eight came from the south. If we take the principal trades represented in accessions to citizenship in Amsterdam over the period 1575-1606, we find that twenty-two per cent of the clothiers came from Belgium, thirty-seven per cent of the textile manufacturers, and nearly thirty-five per cent of the merchants. These figures give us some indication of the great loss suffered by Belgium as a result of the war in the Netherlands, and of the great gain made by the United Provinces.

The work of Antwerp did not stop there. From their new homes in the northern provinces the Belgians extended their influence throughout western Europe. In France the 'Dutch' established themselves prominently at Paris as well as in the citadel of French Protestantism, La Rochelle. The French historian Mathorez has no hesitation in claiming that 'the seventeenth century (i.e. 1598-1685) was the great period of Dutch penetration into France'. How Dutch were these Dutchmen? The most prominent of them, used repeatedly by Richelieu as a financial agent, was Jan Hoeufft, no Dutchman but a southerner, a Brabanter who had fled his home and become naturalised in France in 1601. His brother Mattheus settled in Amsterdam as a financier, and helped France thereby to draw on credit in the Dutch capital. The task of draining marshes in France was entrusted in 1599 to another Brabanter, Humphrey Bradley, without whose large capital investment the task could never have commenced. No other 'Dutch' financiers of the early seventeenth century equalled these two Belgians in the size of their outlay. There were others, like the Meerman family who founded prosperous sugar-refineries in Bordeaux, and the flourishing Crucius family of La Rochelle. Mathorez assumes them to be Dutch, which would not conflict with the known influence of 'Dutch' control over the external trade of these two large French ports. The facts are otherwise. The Crucius family came from Hainault, in Belgium, and the Meerman family were originally merchants of Antwerp. Both had extensive interests not only in France but also in Germany, where they had a firm base in Frankfurt. It is interesting to note that one of the immigrants to France in these troubled times was an artist, almost certainly from Belgium, called Noël Bernard, whose grandson Samuel refused to follow the vocations of his father and grandfather, and instead turned to capital enterprise, which made him eventually the greatest and wealthiest of all the financiers of Louis XIV. Samuel Bernard's success symbolises the great importance of Belgian finance in the history of France.

Not France alone, but all Europe, was open to the Belgian entrepreneurs. As an example we may take the Marcelis family. Gabriel Marcelis fled from Antwerp during the wars, settled down in Hamburg, and built up business connections in Amsterdam and Copenhagen. His three sons Gabriel, Celio and Pieter each became based on Amsterdam, from where they extended their interests to northern Europe with a particular commitment to the munitions industry. The younger Gabriel became in the 1640s a leading financier to the Danish government and in 1645 helped to raise a fleet for Denmark against the Swedes. Celio served as entrepreneur and arms contractor to the Danish government, while Pieter had interests in the ironworks of Muscovy. Across the sea in Sweden, even their extensive activities were outdone by those of another southern Netherlander: Louis de Geer of Liège.

De Geer (1587-1652) was one of the outstanding capitalists of the century. Though born in Liège he was brought up in the United Provinces after 1596 and moved to Amsterdam in 1615. De Geer began his career as a military financier: he made loans to Sweden, England and France, and helped pay the armies of Gustav Adolf and Mansfeld in Germany. In the 1620s he moved to Sweden where he continued to finance Gustav Adolf, and at the same time began to develop the Swedish mining industry, for which he imported Walloon workers. Finance, mining and munitions were the three mainstays of de Geer's vast empire. In 1645, when Sweden went to war with Denmark it was he who went to Holland to collect and equip a fleet under the Swedish flag. Sailing to the Baltic, the fleet after an initial reverse defeated the Danish fleet, which had itself been partly equipped by Marcelis' Dutch resources.

The pattern of the dispersion from Italy and the Netherlands is straightforward. These were economically advanced areas which, in the autumn of their life, scattered their seed over the world and brought out in due season new growth, new industry, new capital development. Emigrés from less developed areas, however, also had a significant part to play in the growth of capitalism. The Huguenots came from no notably advanced region, and made little contribution to technological innovation, yet their presence was everywhere welcomed as a spur to progress. The first great emigration from France occurred in the late sixteenth century. The overwhelming majority of these refugees, about ninety per cent, were town dwellers, and the industrial professions were predominant among them. We know the professions of just over half of the newcomers listed in the *Livre des Habitants* of Geneva. Of this half, sixty-eight per cent in the period 1549-60 were manual workers, the great majority in textiles. In 1572-4, over one-fifth of the known trades consisted of textile-workers. In 1585-7 nearly one-third of known trades consisted of textile-workers, and artisans as a whole formed fifty-six per cent of the total. These figures suggest that a large and active labour force was being introduced into Geneva. The result was an undoubted stimulus to the city's industry, from which Turrettini and other capitalists benefited. There were three trades in particular that the refugees helped to promote. Watchmaking was introduced into Geneva at this period by Huguenot craftsmen, and continued to be dominated by workers of that nation. Textiles could not fail to be affected by the mass immigration of artisans. Finally, the Genevan book industry received an exceptional stimulus from the hundreds of printers and booksellers who had fled from France. Other parts of Switzerland also benefited, perhaps more modestly, from the French. The lace industry, for example, was brought to Basel in 1573 by Antoine Lescailles, a refugee from Lorraine. Contributions like these came from a religious minority that had turned to economic enterprise because it had been denied the possibility of social and political power.

A similar explanation may be offered for the undoubted stimulus given by Jews to capitalism. The Jew as an outcast from Christendom had for long been associated with usury, a practice which seems to have been permitted to them as strangers though it was in principle forbidden to Christians. As strangers, the Jews were not bound by the rules of society: they prospered, but were consequently hated. Utilised everywhere as essential to financial enterprise, the Jews were also repeatedly expelled from most parts of Europe in the fifteenth and sixteenth centuries, the biggest of these exercises being their expulsion from the Spanish dominions in 1492. By the sixteenth century they had become constant refugees like so many of the Christian sectaries. In some trading cities, the Jews were welcomed freely. By 1600 the most prosperous commercial centres of western Europe, Amsterdam, Hamburg and Frankfurt, were also the cities with the largest Jewish communities. Inevitably contemporaries no less than economists like the nineteenth-century German historian Werner Sombart were quick to point out that there must be some link between the Jewish genius and material progress.

Untenable as such a view may be, the history of western European Jewish enterprise in this period certainly supplies material for debate. In some parts of Europe, as in Rome (where in 1592 there was a population of about three thousand five hundred Jews), the Jews were still largely restricted to their mediaeval role as lenders of money. In the expanding cities of the north, however, they were prominent in the field of capital enterprise. In Antwerp they had established themselves, thanks to their links in Spain and Portugal, as one of the most useful business communities. Though repeated enactments in the early sixteenth century had attempted to expel them, they continued to function, not of course as 'Jews' (after 1492 that was impossible in a Spanish-controlled country) but as converted Jews, *conversos,* or Marranos as they were known in the north. When the great emigration from Antwerp occurred, they too departed. The firm of Felipe Dinis, for example, established at Hamburg, had moved from Antwerp in the 1560s. Perhaps the best known of the Marrano exiles at this period was Marcus Pērez (1527-72), of Spanish origin, who was to become one of the earliest financiers of William the Silent. He fled from Antwerp in 1566 and moved to Basel, where he tried somewhat unsuccessfully to introduce new industrial schemes. Some testimony to the value of the Marranos is given by a committee set up in 1653 to consider whether they should be allowed back into Antwerp; the conclusion was that 'by the trade which they will expand far beyond its present limits, the benefit derived will be for the good of the whole land'.

The re-emigration of Jews to Germany, the United Provinces and elsewhere solved few of the community's problems. Even in cities where they were 'freely' accepted, there were serious restrictions. Both Hamburg and Frankfurt, for instance, had ghettoes to which Jews were confined. They were, moreover, subject to extensive civil disabilities, and it was unusual for a Jew to be granted citizenship. Even in Amsterdam's large community, the records indicate that from 1575 to 1606 only seven Portuguese Jews received this privilege. In Hamburg, special terms had to be agreed upon in 1612 to allow Jews to reside and to trade. Once these hurdles were overcome, Jews prospered. In Frankfurt they became a thriving part of the city's commercial life until the Fettmilch uprising in 1612, when the Jewish quarter was sacked.

In Hamburg and in Amsterdam the wealthiest members of the community were Portuguese Jews, merchants who still maintained their links with the peninsula, and who consequently gave the northern Europeans a convenient inroad into the Spanish and particularly the Portuguese empire overseas. In Hamburg the Marranos handled a large part of the trade from Iberia. Of the sixteen firms importing spices, eleven were Portuguese. In all, of the forty-one merchants importing from Portugal in 1612, eighteen were Jewish, the biggest of them all being the wealthy merchant Ruy Fernández Cardoso. In Amsterdam the Jews played a far less prominent part than is usually attributed to them. As late as 1630 there appear to have been only about a thousand Jews in the city, none of them outstandingly wealthy. Many had come from Antwerp, others had come directly from Portugal. The Jewish traders made a contribution to silk manufactures, to the import of sugar (from Brazil) and sugar-refining, and were also prominent in the jewellery and diamond business. They were particularly active in printing, since Amsterdam was the only centre in Europe to be able to print Jewish books freely. Perhaps their most outstanding achievement in the seventeenth century was to allow Dutch interests to infiltrate, and for some time even to possess, the Portuguese lands in northern Brazil.

Elsewhere in Europe the Jews had a modest role to play. In England there was a small community long before Cromwell conceded them the right to enter the country legally. The early sixteenth-century community in London centred round agents of the Antwerp firm of Mendes. By 1550 the London Jews numbered about one hundred. In 1625 a pamphleteer could claim that 'a store of Jews we have in England; a few in Court; many in the city; more in the country'. Under Cromwell and after his time, the Jews in England were distinguished by their connections in the world of finance. Whatever their contribution may have been, they were certainly not a unique factor in the formation of capitalism. It is true that they had valuable international links, particularly between members of their own race, thereby promoting the essentially international nature of capitalist development. But in this they did no more than the other refugees of the period.

What was the function of the other foreign financiers, the small groups, particularly of Italians, who flourished at European courts? These men have little or no part to play in our picture. The Florentine and Genoese bankers of the Holy See in the late sixteenth century, the financiers of the Spanish crown — Grimaldi, Centurioni, Spinola, Pallavicino — made little contribution to capital or industrial growth. They helped to promote credit, as their predecessors had done before them. Beyond that they were creatures from a past age, members by now of a *rentier* class, drifting round the halls of the southern princes in the vain hope of recovering their unpaid debts, until one by one in the course of the century they were snuffed out by bankruptcy.

Persecution of racial and religious minorities had an effect out of all proportion to the number of refugees involved. From the industrial centres of northern Italy, the rich metropolis of Antwerp, the ghettoes of Spain and Portugal, the artisan homesteads of France, a stream of self-made men, tried by long adversity and deprived finally of their homes, went out to live among strangers and to develop among them their very considerable talents. In this movement of people we can see almost visibly represented[1] the passing of capitalist leadership from Catholic to Protestant Europe. The fact that many of the émigré enterepreneurs were Calvinists, like Turrettini, Marcus Pérez, Witte and de Geer, was an accident governed either by the milieu they had come from or that in which they sought refuge. By the seventeenth century their importance to capitalism was being cited even in Catholic countries as proof that religious toleration was a necessary prerequisite of economic expansion.

MONEY AND CAPITALISM

Money played a relatively small part in the lives of the people of Europe. Barter and exchange still had inordinate importance in some regions, and in entire areas (such as in Sweden) metallic money was not used as a medium of exchange. The principal reason for this was that agricultural communities continued to be domestically self-sufficient. It was only when the town economy became bound up with the rural areas, and when external trade had become necessary, that the need for money as a unit of exchange became felt. Even then there were two important factors that modified the functions of precious metals in the economy. In the first place, the common people rarely saw or held in their hands a coin made of gold or silver; for the most part they traded in small change, in units of copper or other baser metals of which small coins tended to be made. The circulation of gold and silver was severely restricted, and tended to be concentrated in the hands of a small number of traders. In the second place, credit may well have played a larger part than cash transactions in the ordinary activities of agricultural producers. On either count, we have the *form* of a money or cash economy, but are still quite far from the reality.

This general picture can be filled out in detail, at least for certain parts of Europe. In the primitive economies of the Baltic littoral, in the Balkans, in large areas of western Europe, a money economy was still in the process of formation. It was not until its copper mines began to pour out their wealth that Sweden even began to be supplied with enough metal to form a coinage. Meanwhile the peasantry paid their dues in the shape of labour services, and received their wages in kind rather than cash. The proportion of income received in cash either by peasants or by landlords was very small in most agrarian areas in Europe. The bishopric of Olomouc in Bohemia in 1636, for example, drew its income almost exclusively from three sources: agricultural output, labour services, and taxes in kind (only occasionally in cash). In the Beauvaisis in France in the seventeenth century, harvesters and vineyard workers were given their meals and a small monetary payment: no question here of gold or silver coin. Textile-workers in rural areas sometimes had to be content merely with a piece of the cloth they had woven. Peasant debts in Beauvais were repaid either in kind or in labour. Elsewhere in rural sixteenth-century France even the upper-classes were not over-conversant with cash. Cases that we know of traders in Poitou, in Lyon and in Toulouse, show that it was exceptional to turn fortunes into cash. What mattered was land, or the accumulation of credit, and it was there that energies appear to have been directed. It is in Beauvaisis too that we can see the operation of agricultural credit. Indebted peasants would sign sworn recognisances of debts on slips of paper, and the slips would serve to represent capital, to be sold or transferred according to demand.

Coexisting with this still primitive world was an increasingly sophisticated apparatus of financial capitalism. The commutation of feudal dues to cash, the expansion of industry, trade and markets, the collapse of the ban on usury, meant that money was assuming a more important part in the affairs of the community. The volume of money in Europe also increased appreciably in this period. In one sense it increased as a result of growing population, greater demand and greater velocity of circulation. But it also increased in absolute terms, and here one can appeal to the unquestionable evidence of bullion imports into Europe from America, imported not only through the official channels so carefully listed by Earl J. Hamilton, but also through unofficial means, through smuggling and privateering. One can appeal moreover to the several coinages, re-coinages and debasements of the period, all of which were aimed at getting more cash into circulation. The distribution of this money was, as we have seen, confined largely to the urban and the upper, trading classes, and was excluded in general from the lives of the common people and the countryside. In this century of inflation, however, money was rapidly becoming a significant reality for the latter as well.

The most interesting development in the money economy of the sixteenth century was the manipulation of capital by means of credit. Credit as such was not new, nor did it obtain its greatest triumphs until well after this period, but it was now that the activities of financiers brought a new perspective into the utilisation of capital. In Marx's words, 'the two characteristics immanent in the credit system are, on the one hand to develop the incentive of capitalist production . . . on the other hand, to constitute the form of transition to a new mode of production'. Marx was referring to the modern credit system, but his remarks have equal value in the context of our period, where credit provided an essential instrument for the move to capitalism. It did this firstly by making capital more mobile and facilitating investment, secondly by enabling the chief manipulators of credit, the bourgeoisie, to accumulate property in their hands at the expense both of the rural and the noble classes.

The machinery of credit varied immensely from country to country. At the lowest level it rested on the activities of moneylenders. In sixteenth-century England, as Tawney has observed, 'the vast majority of lenders were, in the rural districts, farmers, yeomen or gentlemen, and in the towns, merchants, shopkeepers, mercers, tailors, drapers, haberdashers, grocers and similar tradesmen'. The concentration of moneylending activities in the hands of a small specialist group was not yet developed. The handling of money remained principally in the hands of those who, like goldsmiths or textile merchants, were primarily connected with individual trades. In time, however, it was these very goldsmiths and merchants who abandoned their actual trades as the volume of purely monetary transactions grew. A profession that became very important in the world of finance by the late sixteenth century was that of the notaries, clerks whose original task had been the management of business and legal affairs but who, by their indispensability at a time of increasing turnover in landed property and expansion of trade, drew a great deal of financial business to themselves and became leading money-brokers. The several trades engaged in this sort of finance tended to deal with actual coin, and of those interested in coin none was more prominent than the goldsmiths, who are usually credited in English history with being the predecessors of modern banking. In the sixteenth century, however, all money-brokers, not merely the goldsmiths, took part in coin transactions. The brokers not only made loans, they also accepted deposits of cash. By 1660, a contemporary could report that 'the goldsmiths in Lombard street . . . are just in the nature of bankers at Amsterdam . . . , keeping at this day many great merchants of London cashes'. This system of deposit with private brokers had been practised through much of western Europe well before 1550, and gave rise to two important developments. The taking of deposits clearly meant that brokers had now become private bankers. Moreover, where bankers did not charge for the deposit service, they tended to lend the money out in the modern way. A depositor who called for his capital might get it in cash or, as often happened, in credit. He might even be granted an overdraft in order to increase his confidence in the deposit banker. The extension of deposit and of credit services was an essential feature of the private banks which flourished more in their traditional home, the Mediterranean lands, than in northern Europe.

The very nature of private banks bred insecurity. Their capital was small, and deposits were often put into very risky ventures. The practice of credit was shaky, since it needed only a few persistent rumours to cause a run on the bank and hence its collapse. For a banker who dealt in international exchange a crisis anywhere, in Antwerp, in Spain, could bring several private firms collapsing in ruin. This was what happened in continental Europe when the Spanish monarchy renounced its debts in 1557 and in subsequent years. The uncertainty of credit hit not only the big financiers but also all the smaller men in France, Germany, the Netherlands and Italy, who could not protect themselves. In Venice alone the statesman Contarini claimed in 1584 that of one hundred and three private banks that had once existed in the city, ninety-six had come to an unhappy end. In France the wars of religion precipitated disaster. In 1575 there were still forty-one banks at Lyon, in 1580 there were a score, in 1592 only four. The years 1587-9 seem to have been particularly fatal, for in Spain and Italy alone there were then twenty bankruptcies among the large bankers.

Financial uncertainty in the face of these collapses was one of the main pressures behind the growing demand for public banks. Early sixteenth-century firms had been called 'public', but this meant only that they were licensed by public authority. In the late sixteenth century several old banking foundations put themselves on a more truly public footing. In 1586 the Casa di San Giorgio of Genoa opened public deposit facilities; other banks did the same in 1587 in Venice and Messina, in 1597 at Milan, in 1605 at Rome. In the territories of the crown of Aragon, public bank facilities had existed since the early fifteenth century, notably in Barcelona and Valencia: these institutions were now given new life. The essential feature of a public bank was that it was open to both private and governmental clients, but the bulk of the capital supporting it was in fact 'public' or municipal. In Valencia for example the *Taula* or bank was both treasurer and administrator of the city's finances. Since financial security rather than enterprise was the watchword of these public banks, credit was seldom allowed. Despite this, the evolution was a promising one, and led in 1609 to the foundation of a public exchange bank in Amsterdam.

The weakness of private banks and the lack of credit offered by public banks meant that speculative finance had to look elsewhere for a profit. This was where the merchant-bankers (already well-established in mediaeval times) came in. Although referred to almost universally at the time as 'bankers', they were properly speaking *financiers*, since their commerce was with money, merchandise and credit, and they seldom operated along deposit and banking lines. They began as small capitalists, dealers in merchandise, and branched out into the international exchange of money that was necessary to promote trade. Since cash could not be transferred internationally, credit was, and the principal instrument used for this was the bill of exchange.

The bill of exchange was the most important of the means of credit with which we are concerned. Originating and widely used in an earlier epoch it had by the mid-sixteenth century become firmly accepted in the financial world. As the Antwerp financier

Jan Impyn observed in 1543, 'One can no more trade without bills of exchange than sail without water.' The bills of the sixteenth century, however, often had little connection with trade. In Tawney's words, the bill 'had been used in the Middle Ages mainly as an instrument for paying international debts and had been drawn against tangible goods. What puzzled and enraged moralists and statesmen in the sixteenth century was that its use was being extended from paying for imports to the making of advances and the raising of loans, without goods passing at all.' A bill advanced in Antwerp, for example, to be paid at Lyon within three months, would be simply a financial transaction, a loan. In two important respects, however, this would be more significant than an ordinary loan. The period of time involved meant that credit was being extended. Moreover, though the payment in Lyon was of exactly the sum loaned, the costs of the transaction as well as the difference in exchange rates would be added to the bill, and these costs would accumulate until the bill was redeemed. This plainly created a capital market, in which both credit and usury (the 'costs') were being practised, but under disguise. Financiers could in this way lend and borrow money anywhere in Europe, and profit from it in the bargain. 'In other words', to quote Tawney again, 'the exchanges kept capital fluid throughout the whole world of commerce, put the reserves, not merely of the national but of the European market at the disposal of any firm of good standing, and supplied a convenient channel of investment to merchants and bankers who desired to earn a high rate of interest on short loans.'

The great fillip to the money market, and the principal reason for the emergence in the sixteenth century of great firms such as Fugger, Grimaldi and Herwarth, was the insatiable demand for cash made by the national monarchies of western Europe. The intervention of the state in finance encouraged financiers to group together in combines in order to meet its demands: the trend in finance, no less than in commerce and industry, was towards concentration and monopoly. Great firms like the Fuggers and Welsers were, as Ehrenberg has shown, not family enterprises so much as combinations of capitalists who put their money into the firm in return for a fixed rate of interest.

The pooling of capital brought in record returns. The Genoese financier Niccolò Grimaldi, who began his career in 1515 with eighty thousand ducats, had by 1575 increased his capital sum to over five millions; the Fuggers, whose assets in 1511 came to

196,761 florins, had 2,021,202 in 1527, an annual profit of over fifty-four per cent. To be a creditor of the state was clearly an advantage, particularly when this favoured position allowed one some control over government income and over commercial policy. Moreover the financiers as individuals could and did rise in the social ladder: the Fuggers, for instance, became princes of the Empire. But the disadvantages of involvement with the state were to become all too apparent after the international crash of 1557. The bankruptcies of the Spanish crown in particular were fatal for financiers. In 1557 Philip II defaulted on current debts amounting to seven million ducats, in 1575 the sum involved was in the region of fifteen million. On each occasion the sum was not wiped out but consolidated: the financiers were to be paid annuities at a fixed rate until the debt was wiped out. Both municipalities and governments throughout Europe (with the outstanding exception of England) used this method to deal with debts they could not meet. The process helped to destroy the great finance houses, but it also created a new phenomenon: a national debt.

In the sixteenth century most governments tended to be behind in the payment of debts. They invariably spent their income one, two or more years in advance. Although this was common practice, it was never looked on with favour, and ministers like Sully were concerned above all with retrenchment, with balancing the books. By the seventeenth century the economically most progressive countries had come to realise that a large debt was not necessarily a liability. We find a Venetian ambassador to the United Provinces reporting in 1620 that 'the province of Holland alone has a debt of forty million florins, for which it pays six and a quarter per cent interest. It could easily get rid of its debts by raising taxes, but the creditors of the state will not have it so. I have heard it said that the merchants have so much capital available that the state can obtain from them all that it requires.' The debt in this case was looked upon as a sound investment by the creditors of the state. Writing in 1673 Sir William Temple observed that increases to the debt in Holland were so popular that 'whoever is admitted to bring in his money takes it for a great deal of honour; and when they pay off any part of the principal, those it belongs to receive it with tears, not knowing how to dispose of it to interest with such safety and ease'.

The growth of a public debt had two important consequences. It brought into existence in the sixteenth century a large *rentier* class, drawn principally from the bourgeoisie. It also reinforced

115

the financial and political stability of the government, by post-poning any settlement of fiscal arrears and by tying creditors more closely to the regime. In Spain, which thanks to its expensive imperial programme had become committed to deficit finance, the public annuities or *juros* became the mainstay of the social order. As the years went on, the public debt accumulated, with the possibility of full repayment receding further than ever into the future.

While the growth of a public debt is an example of the extension of credit, the ultimate effect of credit facilities of this sort was non-productive and anti-capitalistic. Money became immobile, was tied up in institutions, and served only to support a *rentier* class. When the volume of financial business required it, the establishment of a public bank of the new type was seen to be far more advantageous. The result was the foundation in 1609 of the Exchange Bank of Amsterdam, with exchange and deposit facilities and, from 1614, lending facilities. The Amsterdam Bank, which was to be cited thereafter as a model for all other nations, became prized by its investors for its security, but its principal function was the promotion of commerce, industry and the money market. It had seven hundred and eight depositors in 1611, and two thousand, six hundred and ninety-eight in 1701. Deposits rose from 925,562 florins in 1611 to 16,284,849 in 1700. The greatest capitalists of Amsterdam, those in particular with international interests, were among this number. The great machine to which the Bank was geared was that of commercial capitalism, and in order to serve this world of commerce a vast volume of credit was made available. Bullion holdings in both gold and silver certainly existed to support any credit, but the amount of monetary transactions, their international scope, and the speed with which they were carried out, enabled a fund of credit to be built up which made dependence on hard cash less essential than in other trading centres of Europe.

TRADE AND CAPITALISM

The formation of capital depended principally on commerce. The great increase in financial activity and banking enterprise was simply a reflection of expanding trade. Amsterdam's wealth was founded not on the speculative world of the exchanges but on the real world of trade and the profits it created. All economic activity in Europe was directed to commercial ends, and outside Europe it was once again trade that preoccupied Europeans. Far from this preoccupation being merely an economic one, it tended to become so important as to interest and even to obsess the state, for whom trade finally became synonymous with power.

The new forms of trading that developed in the sixteenth and seventeenth centuries had a formidable number of obstacles to surmount. Markets were still necessarily small and restricted. Transport, whether by land or sea, was slow, and perishable goods therefore had their market restricted by the time factor. With poor roads and especially in time of war, land transport was risky. Sea or river transport was the most reliable for bulk goods, but natural disaster and piracy made this method equally vulnerable. 'It's not usually good business to transport wheat by sea', complained the merchant Simon Ruiz of Medina del Campo, in 1591. 'I have seen those who have lost a great deal that way.' Time was no less vital a concern than mere loss: when wheat from the Baltic reached its destinations in the Mediterranean in the 1590s, it was already a year old. Grain could and did spoil in shorter periods than this. The difficulty of taking goods any great distance by land was caused not only by stubborn terrain and poor roads, but also by the lack of effective motive power, horses or mules being the principal draught animals. Even when roads were improved (as much for military as for commercial purposes) and canals built, markets were not appreciably enlarged. There were, in short, no technological innovations to overcome the old barriers of space and time.

The human barriers were no less noteworthy. Politically and fiscally, *ancien régime* Europe was an enormous mass of small independent jurisdictions which interfered constantly with the free passage of trade. A road or a river which passed over the territory of several noble seigneurs was likely to have a separate toll post at each territory. Travelling from his home town to Cologne in the late sixteenth century, the Basel merchant Andreas Ryff counted no less than thirty-one customs barriers which' goods would have had to negotiate in this way. The River Elbe at the same period had thirty-five customs posts, while the Danube in Lower Austria alone had seventy-seven. In 1567 the River Loire and its tributaries had two hundred tolls, collected in one hundred and twenty different spots. On the Rhone in the seventeenth century, the short stretch from the Savoy frontier to Arles alone had forty tolls. The cumulative effect of all this on costs and distribution is obvious.

The result of these hindrances to internal trade was that the great leap in the volume of transactions came in coastal and international traffic; in, that is, external sea transport. It was shipping that counted, and it was the English and Dutch above all who were the pace-setters. The profits to be gained from sea trade were comfortable, even in European waters. Transport costs by ship were lower. Sending hops from the Netherlands to England, for example, incurred only a five per cent capital expense in the late sixteenth century; shipping flax from Reval to Lübeck at the same period cost only six per cent. Over longer journeys the expenses were higher, but few traders undertook these unless the returns were commensurate. The sending of ships from Antwerp to Seville earned the Antwerp firm of Della Faille regular profits of one hundred per cent, ample reward for the initial outlay. In colonial ventures to America and Asia, of course, the returns were so enormous as to seem staggering to modern eyes. Early expeditions to India brought back goods worth as much as sixty times the original costs. By the seventeenth century profits of one hundred per cent were being marked up regularly by the English East India Company (in 1617 it made a profit of five hundred per cent), and Sir Walter Ralegh actually referred to a hundred per cent profit from one colonial enterprise as 'a small return'.

The key role of shipping in the development of markets has encouraged some historians to consider it as in some way comparable to an index of a country's economic growth. From this point of view, the volume of external trade, shown in figures for shipping, would be a direct reflection of productivity. Clearly this assumption can be seriously questioned. But there is also little doubt that the nations with the most flourishing sea trade were, to use a superfluous and tautological phrase, economically the most active. The passing of economic supremacy from the Mediterranean to the north, for example, can be seen clearly in the shipping routes. In the early sixteenth century the power of Venice and Spain in the inland sea was still paramount, and even in 1571 at Lepanto they alone were capable of resisting the vanguard of Islam. By the end of the sixteenth century, as we have already seen, the English and Dutch were beginning to supersede them on the trade routes. The volume of Venetian and other Italian merchant shipping declined. The merchant tonnage of England increased meanwhile from an estimated total of sixty-seven thousand tons in 1582 to one hundred and fifteen thousand in 1629 and three hundred and forty thousand in 1686. By the mid-seventeenth century the bulk of trade in the Mediterranean and to the Levant was falling more and more into English hands.

The English tonnage figures reflect the revolutionary increase in both land and sea trade in the sixteenth century. Venice and Spain, the two most notable Mediterranean powers, shared in this expansion until the late sixteenth century, although for Spain, as we shall see, the effort was directed principally outwards over the Atlantic. A novel factor was the rise of Dutch sea power, which soon outpaced all competitors. One index to this rise is the growth in the trade of Amsterdam. In 1589, shortly after the closing of the River Scheldt, the port charges collected at Amsterdam amounted to about two hundred and fifty thousand guilders. In 1620 the charges came to three hundred and ten per cent of this figure. By 1638, they were four hundred and twenty-three per cent, and by the end of the century eight hundred and five per cent, of the takings in 1589. Vitally important as the opening up of the Orient was to be to Dutch success, their commitment was always primarily to the Baltic, which in our period replaced the Mediterranean as the focus of international interest. As late as 1666 it was estimated that three-quarters of the capital active on the Amsterdam exchange was engaged in the Baltic trade. 'The source and root of the most notable commerce and navigation of these lands', De Witt described the Baltic grain trade in 1671. It was a trade which in the period 1562-1657 attracted into the Baltic some 113,212 Dutch ships, a figure which represents only those officially registered in the Sound tolls and which may account for no more than three-quarters of the real total.

What had made the great expansion of commercial activity possible? On the whole we can point to four main internal causes: the ease of credit, the growth of insurance, technical improvements in shipbuilding, and the creation of joint-stock companies. The necessity for credit was widespread, particularly since without it there was little possibility of the one great stimulant—the willingness to take commercial risks—developing. Small merchants could in this way commit themselves to enterprises on which the returns were wholly speculative, and long-distance trade could replace the certainties of local trade. There was also the consideration that the turnover from any large capital commitment was slow in materialising, as for instance with the Seville shipments of the Antwerp firm of Della Faille, whose operations lasted between nine and thirteen months. An extension of credit while capital was tied up in one enterprise would allow the next to be put into operation. The use of the bill of exchange in matters like this speeded up the mobility of capital and simplified the task of the merchant. The development of insurance, especially marine insurance, was of comparable importance, since it underwrote very firmly that most important feature of the capitalist, the willingness to take risks.

Improvements in shipbuilding were a logical consequence rather than a cause of expanding trade. The initial problem was simply that of building a vessel with a large enough freightage to make long-distance trade profitable. The problem was complicated by the fact that merchant vessels would have to vary according to the sea in which they sailed, and allowance might have to be made for armament. The most successful of all merchant ships that evolved in this period under the Dutch, who were always the pace-setters in shipbuilding techniques, was the *fluyt*. Designed especially for the Baltic trade, with few or no guns, this vessel was unsuitable for use in the Atlantic or the Mediterranean, and had a restricted sphere of operations. It became symbolic none the less of the supremacy in European waters of the capitalists of the United Provinces.

None of the factors we have touched on involved any radical innovation in technique. The same cannot be said of the joint-stock company, which marked a significant departure from previous practice. Trading companies, or regulated companies, had consisted of a number of merchants trading together with joint capital for the duration of an operation. At the end of each operation the proceeds were shared and the enterprise wound up, after which the merchants were theoretically free to depart with their capital. The joint-stock company, properly so called, consisted not so much in the cooperation of merchants as in the permanent funding of capital, which existed continuously and was not split up after each operation. The restricted world of personal participation and private partnerships in trade was superseded by a framework in which merchants did not need to participate at all: they purchased stock in the company, which traded on their behalf. By drawing on investments from different sources, not merely from merchants, a company's directors could build up a considerable stock of ready capital which enabled them to pursue long-term projects. At the same time merchants could take part by proxy in several enterprises at once, without prejudice to those that might require personal attention. For the first time, then, the joint-stock company created the possibility of large-scale, long-term commercial enterprises of a monopolistic nature, the tendency to monopoly lying in the fact that there could be little competition with the resources controlled by the company. (Regulated companies, it is true, also tended to become monopolies, but in theory there could be limited competition among members of the company.)

The first big firm in England to adopt a joint-stock (of lesser firms, the Muscovy Company had been first with a joint-stock in 1553) was the East India Company, which began in 1600 as a regulated company and changed in 1612 to a common fund; it was not until 1657 that this fund was treated as permanent. Other organisations, both in England and abroad, followed suit, so that by the mid-seventeenth century the joint-stock company was a common phenomenon. By 1703 the capital of English joint-stock companies had reached eight million pounds. More important than the sum involved was the significance of companies for the development of capitalism. With them, it has been observed, 'capital was king'. The strengthening of monopoly, the advantage acquired by the big entrepreneurs, led to a concentration of economic power in the hands of a few big capitalists. This concentration of mercantile capital promoted the wealth and position of the trading classes and stimulated industry, for, as Professor van der Wee observes, it was the expansion of commercial capitalism that 'gave reorganised industrial production the final stimulus for irresistible growth'.

The state could not fail to be interested in the advantages of commerce. The English writer Roger Coke claimed in 1671 that 'the end of trade is threefold, viz. Strength, Wealth, and Employment for all sorts of People'. On all these counts the government would have reason to interfere in, though not necessarily to control, trade policy. The passing of the English Navigation Act of 1651 is usually taken to be the culmination of such a trend of intervention, and in France the policies of Colbert are similarly accepted as an example of what is known as mercantilism. The spheres in which the state was concerned can easily be listed: shipping (particularly for defence), the colonies, bullion imports, industrial exports and so on. The promotion of trade was, by the mid-seventeenth century, seen to be a primary concern of the state, not only because it assured profit, but also because it ensured power. As Sir Josiah Child put it, it was 'absolutely necessary that Profit and Power ought jointly to be considered'.

With the intervention of the state, commercial capitalism found a powerful ally. Their interests were not always the same, and the adoption by the state of a policy of war, for instance, was often bitterly resented by merchants who knew that it would disrupt trade and lose markets. But for the most part in the two principal trading nations, England and Holland, the interests of the merchant community tended to prevail, and as a result monopoly companies thrived.

INDUSTRIAL ORGANISATION

The concept of 'industry' plays an inordinate part in surveys of the economic life of what was still a completely pre-industrial age. So few people were involved in industries, and so small a proportion of capital was invested in it, that we may rightly look with suspicion on historians who measure progress in this period by the output of coal or textiles. Indeed, a respectable argument of long standing, put forward over twenty years ago by Professor John U. Nef, claimed to find the seeds of an industrial revolution in this period. Persuasive as Nef's argument may have been at one time, it cannot be accepted today without qualification. Production rose by leaps and bounds in some industries and in some areas at this epoch, but they were purely quantitative increases that lacked the qualitative technological and social advances that alone made the Industrial Revolution possible.

Was there then no industrial progress in the sixteenth and seventeenth centuries? If this chapter has indicated anything so far, it is surely that progress did occur. The dispersal of techniques by refugee workers helped to found new industries; the activity of entrepreneurs and capitalists helped to create money for investment in industry; and, most obvious of all, commerce would not have expanded had there not been a greater volume of goods in which to trade. This picture of economic health cannot be accepted at face value, however. The sum total of the increased output in industry still accounted for only a fraction of the total of goods or of capital active on the market. Moreover, industry still laboured under fairly primitive conditions of guild control, utilisation of labour and so on. We shall look briefly here at some of the features of industry in the sixteenth and seventeenth centuries.

There was no large-scale industrial enterprise of which we have knowledge in the period. The most important industry in Europe was textiles, but as in earlier epochs textiles everywhere tended to be worked through the putting-out system, in which domestic looms were operated individually, and sometimes even widely scattered, though they may have come under the direction of a central agent or capitalist. It was, in short, rare to have a great number of working looms concentrated under one roof, as in the modern factory. There were one or two outstanding exceptions to this rule, such as the large Gobelins mills managed by the Van Robais in France, which kept as many as one thousand seven hundred workers together in one enterprise, divided into departments. Even larger numbers might be found in the ship-building industry: it has been estimated that the Venetian Arsenal in 1560 employed some 2,346 artisans. Mining was one other industry that could be said to have employed labour intensively, but here again it is difficult to find many large-scale enterprises, even in the coal industry. Big collieries tended to have about one hundred workers in them: the biggest Liège coal mine in the early sixteenth century had one hundred and twenty, Kincardine colliery in Scotland in 1679 had seventy-one; the Grand Lease colliery near Newcastle in the early seventeenth century was exceptional in having somewhere near five hundred persons at work both below and above the surface. A unique position among mining concerns was held by the alum mines at Tolfa (near Rome). In 1557 it employed seven hundred and eleven labourers, making it the largest mining complex and one of the biggest industrial enterprises of its time. Contemporaries were impressed by even moderate size, as when Guicciardini in the mid-sixteenth century applied the term 'forges of Vulcan' to an ironworks which in reality produced no more than eight hundred and forty-two tons in the year. Enterprises seemed large because there was so little to compare them with. The concentration and division of labour was still in its infancy.

It was not the size but the number of enterprises that contributed to the multiplication of capital. Entrepreneurs could be found with investments in several varied industries, and it was their activity on which growth ultimately depended. They, in turn, would invest only if they could see some way of breaking through the existing restrictions on production. The several interesting technical innovations of this time (such as the multiple or 'Dutch' loom) met with bitter opposition from guilds as well as workpeople, so that it was a primary concern of the capitalist to by-pass the guilds.

This was not so easy to do. By mediaeval precedent the guilds, which represented individual crafts or groups of crafts, regulated conditions of employment, training and production. The guild rules laid down at Liège for the cloth industry were typical. In 1589 the corporations allowed only single-frame looms 'so that the poor as well as the rich can live, and not be oppressed by the rich'; production was limited to 'only two pieces of cloth a week', and no more than twelve pounds of wool could be bought at any one time. In 1618 they determined that the length of an apprentice's training should be eight years. These few rules, taken together, would if obeyed have meant a severe restriction in the number of skilled workers, the volume of production, the speed of production and the variety of technique. The rules were totally anti-capitalist, and would have restricted textile production to being a cottage industry. Admirable as the aims of the guilds may have been in trying to protect their small producers, they were an open hindrance to a developing industry.

Several factors combined to out-manoeuvre the corporations. Immigration of foreign workers was a powerful solvent, as we can see from the protest drawn up by English guilds in 1616 against alien immigrants on the grounds that they 'keepe their misteries to themselves, which hath made them bould of late to devise engines for workinge of tape, lace, ribbin and such, wherein one man doth more amongst them than seven Englishemen can doe'. No longer would the native guilds have a monopoly of technical knowledge. The rules of the guilds, moreover, applied only to the old sections of the economy and to established trades. They found it difficult to extend their restrictions to cover new industries and new methods of work. In addition, though the state sympathised strongly with the guilds and made every effort to reinforce their control, it allowed so many individual exceptions that the system was slowly undermined. New, independent and wealthy capitalists, for instance, were given extensive concessions by the crown for fiscal or other reasons. Finally, the various factors operative in an age such as this, where change was universal and where old rules ceased to apply to new situations, made the demise of the old guild organisation inevitable.

With concessions from European monarchs clutched in either hand, the capitalists of these years pressed on bravely in their search for Mammon. It was in these years that for the first time an unwary public began to be aware that the 'freedom' given to the entrepreneur all too often meant 'monopoly'. Already in Liège in 1562 the small but thriving iron industry was controlled by a ring of twenty-five merchants. In Dordrecht by 1600 a group of twenty merchants ran three-quarters of the iron trade. By 1603 the wealthy Catholic capitalist Jean Curtius had a monopoly of Liège's booming arms industry. In Louis de Geer the trend reached its climax. In the sense in which we are using it here, 'monopoly' means a concentration of capital, not simply the control of an industry by one or more individuals, and it was in this sense that monopoly became significant by the seventeenth century, for it focused the energies of several entrepreneurs on to one industry and thereby allowed the industry sufficient capital investment to expand rapidly.

How did the working population react to the obvious change in their terms of employment posed by the new developments? Their initial reaction seems to have been that the guild system was antiquated, did not represent their interests and was unable to meet the challenge of capitalist methods. It is true that methods of exploitation being evolved by employers exceeded the worst fears of the helpless guilds. The cotton industry of Lancashire, first introduced by Belgian immigrants, controlled a rapidly expanding putting-out system which employed large numbers of poor people, so much so that by the late seventeenth century (1696) it was reported that 'the number of poor that are employed in the manufactures of Manchester by a modest computation are above fourtie thousand'. With the payment of low wages, this was the beginning of sweated labour. In Holland by the late sixteenth century, low wages and the exploitation of women and children were already established. In 1597 a decree condemned certain employers who had reduced young children to actual 'slavery'. The judges sometimes stepped in to condemn child labour, as in 1636 in Delft; but then came the textile boom in Leiden in the years 1638-48, when that city's employers imported four thousand orphan children from Liège to help work the looms. Conditions grew so bad that in 1646 an edict had to be passed to prohibit the children working for more than fourteen hours a day. These examples represent sophisticated practice, but even by the late sixteenth century working conditions could and did lead to agitation. The employers, declared the printers who appealed to the Parlement of Paris in 1577, were exploiters who became rich 'at the price of the sweat and hard labour of the worker'.

In the new situation of the sixteenth century several different

125

antagonisms arose within the general body of employers and employed. The small master fought for his independence from the guild no less than the big capitalist did. Here we shall concern ourselves only with a few cases of the strife between employers and workingmen. Those strikes of which we have details tended to originate among the more privileged trades, above all the printers. In Paris and in Lyon in 1567 and 1571 there were riots involving printers who, in addition to their old complaints about working hours, demanded the setting up of new unions to represent themselves, and the establishment of arbitration machinery. The big strike of 1571-2 in both cities was followed by government attempts to regulate the wage structure. Dissatisfaction led in 1577 to an actual demonstration through the streets of Paris on 22 January, with placards denouncing the comforts of the rich. Nevertheless the government refused to allow new unions to be set up, and took steps in 1579 against a strike of Paris bakers, as well as in 1583 against the tailors of Paris.

The printers were equally active in the Netherlands, and the most famous of the strikes in the sixteenth century involved them. One such strike, born of the economic dislocation of the late 1560s, illustrates how difficult it was for the disaffected to win. In 1572 the famous publisher Christophe Plantin complained of 'malice and conspiracy among all our workers', who had gone on strike for better conditions. Rather than give way, Plantin operated a lock-out, and told his workers that he would shut down the press. Fearing for their jobs the men came back after a few weeks and, as Plantin observed later in triumph, 'all of them now show themselves as willing to be of good service to me, as previously they showed themselves to be rebellious and discontented'. When workers such as these were prohibited from forming their own unions, they tended in the face of repression to form underground trades societies of a secret nature. As known in France, these societies involved oaths, initiation ceremonies and other quasi-religious paraphernalia. They flourished among French workers in the late sixteenth and early seventeenth centuries, though penalties of death were threatened (1618), and laws were passed against them on various occasions. Despite the cabbalistic ceremonies, they were real cooperative unions: they aided out-of-work members from the trades which were represented. Rival societies adopted exotic names such as Children of Solomon or Wolves or Children of Master Jacques, and sometimes attacked each other. But it was the threat implicit in their secrecy, in the fact that they helped to organise strikes, and were capable of uniting the working classes, that made them anathema to the state, and a vigorous campaign was carried out against them not only by the government but also by the Church. The faculty of the theology at Paris, for example, took it upon itself in 1655 to prohibit the workers' societies, or *compagnonnages* as they were called.

We know little about strikes in the industrial centres at this time. Leiden was one city which had regular strikes, in 1637, 1643 and 1648, with a particularly dangerous outbreak in 1638. At Amiens in the seventeenth century there were regular industrial disputes among the textile workers; particularly in the years 1620-35. In 1621 the workers protested against the employment of cheap foreign labour. By 1623 a union had been formed and 'they all simultantously quit their work, and those who did not wish to do so freely were forced to do so by the chief strikers, who numbered about twenty or thirty and were known as "big brothers"'. Strikes must have been very regular, to judge by the ease with which they could be called. It is another matter to assess the significance of such events, particularly in a period when the worker had not yet been alienated from his environment. What is clear is that their importance should not be exaggerated, since they were seldom outright confrontations, and were often provoked by other than industrial causes, such as bread shortages. At the same time it would be unwise to question the growth of some sort of proletariat (this will be discussed in Chapter 11), and of an increasingly militant mood on the part of the better organised workers. In Lyon, for example, which might well pass for one of Europe's first industrial cities, the labouring population was probably somewhere near two-thirds of the entire urban total. Some of the new unions were apparently quite large, and Rouen is said to have had several thousands of *compagnons* in the early seventeenth century. Finally, if proof of the militancy of the workers is required we need only look at the prominent part that some trades played in the riots and rebellions of this period.

ECONOMIC GROWTH AND CAPITALISM

Unfortunately, any serious discussion of capitalism must discuss capital, and there is almost no data in this period on capital formation and growth. Some historians have therefore not concerned themselves with the question, on the grounds that it was still a pre-capitalist epoch; or else they have discussed capitalism solely in the context of finance, as though money by itself were capital. In view of the changes in the structure of the European economy, however, it is clear that one issue of great importance is that of the primary accumulation of capital. This will be looked at very briefly here, if only because we hope to substantiate general statements here with evidence in subsequent chapters. Our concern is less with the economics of primary accumulation, which after all was a historical process that had long functioned, than with three factors of more immediate relevance: the impact of overseas expansion on European internal growth, the practice of savings and the contribution of agricultural accumulation.

The economic effects of the opening of trade routes to Asia and to America were so profound and wide-ranging that it is impossible to define all their aspects adequately, nor have historians attempted to do so. Within the period we are covering attention has usually been paid first of all to the import of foreign treasure into Europe. The introduction of massive quantities of precious metal into European markets, quantities that have never been accurately measured and for which only global estimates are available, could not fail to revolutionise the pace of commercial activity. Some idea of the importance attached to American silver may be obtained simply by reading the correspondence of the Antwerp merchants and their colleagues in other European countries, notably Spain. The bullion was wealth, but also created wealth through the transactions it helped to promote and through the coinage which governments minted from it. The result was a constant search for more bullion. On the trade routes of the Spanish empire in Europe it was obtainable without much difficulty. Countries not athwart those routes had more trouble, and the English solved this problem by a vigorous resort to privateering and war. Large profits were made in London from piracy directed against Spain and Spanish America, and the returns were invested in normal commercial concerns. As the Venetian ambassador commented in 1617, 'Nothing is thought to have enriched the English more or done so much to allow many individuals to amass the wealth they are known to possess, as the wars with the Spaniards in the time of Queen Elizabeth.'

Imports of treasure were perhaps the most significant result of the discoveries. Economic thought in Europe was profoundly affected by it, and the result was a long-lasting emphasis on the need to accumulate as much bullion as possible, for in bullion lay wealth. This supposition was of course true. The whole European economy was stimulated by the injection of precious metals, which did not remain in their principal resting places (such as the Iberian peninsula) but were transmitted outward to northern Europe and eastward through Italy to the Levant (in 1595 Venice alone sent 29,400 pounds weight of silver to Syria to pay for trade). But though bullion might raise price levels and so enhance industrial growth, it was not necessarily a spur to capitalism.

Growth depended directly on production, trade and markets. The great disadvantage of the new discoveries was that they offered no markets to the European producer. English industrialists who in the eighteenth and nineteenth centuries could force their textiles by armed might on the peasants of India and China were in the seventeenth century unable to sell their woollens to Asians who had no need of them. The Spanish authorities evolved a special monopoly system to deal with this situation. Only Spanish manufactured goods could be taken to America, and to ensure a market for them the American settlers were forbidden to develop certain industries. At one time or another production of several essential items was forbidden in America: wine, olive oil, textiles, were among the most important. In theory Spain should therefore have been in a position to supply these needs. The settlers, however, soon built up a native industry of these goods in areas where their production was possible. Where they could not be produced, reliance was placed on Spanish supplies, which were notoriously inadequate. In 1555 the clergy of Hispaniola were complaining that 'provisions arrive from Spain at intervals of years, and we are without bread, wine, soap, oil, cloth, linens. When they arrive, the prices are exorbitant.' By 1566 the bishop of Cuba could report that 'the sacrifice of the Mass has not been offered many a time for lack of wine. Today, when extreme poverty exists here, the fleet arrives and a yard of canvas costs a *castellan*, a sheet of paper a *real*; everything from Spain, even what the soil produces, is very expensive'. Foreign ships — English, Dutch and French — soon broke into the monopoly and began supplying America with their own manufactures. Deprived of its markets abroad, Spain also failed to profit from the advantage that American produce might have given. The American spices never became popular, chocolate did not become a fashionable drink until the seventeenth century and tobacco likewise caught on only in the seventeenth century. Bullion, the most valuable American commodity, had ultimately disastrous effects on the Spanish economy. In short Spain's overseas possessions did not stimulate domestic industry enough to push the country further on the way to capitalist growth.

Substantially the same problem of the lack of markets faced the English and Dutch, who solved their difficulties in a brilliant way. The Dutch in the early seventeenth century made themselves masters of the bulk of the carrying trade in the former Portuguese possessions in the East Indies. In this way they also established a virtual monopoly of the trade to Europe in spices and later in coffee. The problem of how to sell European produce to Asia became a secondary one in this case, since the bullion to pay for spices was in fact obtained in Asia from the profits of the carrying trade. The English East India Company, on the other hand, was not afraid to take bullion out of Europe to pay for its purchases. In the first ten years of its existence the total exports of the Company came to £170,673, of which as much as £119,202 was bullion. Those who felt that the whole purpose of empire was to bring bullion to Europe were not surprisingly rather concerned. It was for them that Thomas Mun explained in his *England's Treasure by Forraign Trade* (1664):

> If we send one hundred pounds into the East Indies to buy pepper there and bring it hither, and from hence send it to Italy or Turkey it must yield seven hundred thousand pounds at least in those places in regard of the excessive charges which the merchant disburseth in those long voyages, in shipping, wages, victuals, insurance, interest, customs, imposts and the like, all which notwithstanding the king and the kingdom gets.

The trading companies of the English and Dutch, and the commodities they brought back to Europe, were the basis of the highly successful commercial capitalism of these two Protestant powers. Spain, with easy access to bullion, neglected its merchant navy; the maritime powers found treasure through trade and re-exports. In this way the foreign discoveries made their contribution to wealth in Europe.

Did Europeans seize the advantage? The investment habits of each nation depended very much on its economic position and its social norms. In a world where the most productive enterprise was trade, we must necessarily consider the attitude of moneyed people towards trade. We immediately come up against the

130

realisation that not only did entire sections of the propertied classes disapprove of trade (as, for instance, the nobility in western Europe), but many who made their fortunes in trade were not interested in reinvesting in the process by which they had benefited. Capital that had been created, savings that had been made, were therefore diverted to items of greater social estimation, such as public office or land. In short, it was difficult for capitalism to thrive if the social system and the relationship between classes prevented it. A particularly ironic example is that of Atlantic slavery, which exhibited all the features of a good capitalist enterprise, but which in its results reinforced the feudal structure of labour wherever it was introduced. Despite these drawbacks, it seems undeniable that with the collapse of traditional ethics on usury, habits of saving and investment were advancing.

The way in which capital went to work through savings can be illustrated from Holland. Profits there could not be put so easily into land, since there was little available; nor did the purchase of public office occupy so large a part in social priorities as elsewhere. Savings therefore went into *rentes* (into, that is, municipal loans), into shipping, fishing and drainage enterprises. The important part played by the concept of savings among the Dutch was emphasised by Sir William Temple in the seventeenth century when he observed of Hollanders that 'their common Riches lye in every Man's having more than he spends; or, to say it properly, in every Man's spending less than he has coming in, be that what it will'. The willingness of small investors to use their savings to good purpose must have contributed substantially to the ready availability of money, a direct cause of the low interest rates in Holland. It was upon these low interest rates (in the early seventeenth century a merchant in good standing could obtain credit at from three to four-and-a-half per cent interest) that the successes of Dutch commercial capitalism rested.

Because of the minor importance of capitalist industry at a time when the economy was overwhelmingly agricultural, primary importance must be given to the agrarian rather than the industrial or even commercial accumulation of capital. Commercial accumulation was of immense importance in England and Holland, but nearly everywhere else in Europe this sector was a minor source of capital. It was land that counted. This attention may seem misplaced, since we tend to accept the picture that agricultural profits and qualitative change in methods of land exploitation only occurred in the eighteenth century, so that only in the eighteenth century was surplus capital accumulated from the land and then invested in the industrial revolution. Such a picture is in some respects unfair to the achievements of the previous century.

In England, as we shall see later, there appears to have been a major improvement in agricultural methods. New crops and grasses were introduced; the production of fodder, corn, meat and dairy goods was increased; enclosures, prohibited by royal policy before 1640, went on apace after that date. It is true that the fruits of this improvement were not greatly significant until the eighteenth century, but even in the earlier epoch a basis was being laid for the reallocation (through enclosures) of labour from the land to the clothing industry, and for higher production of food which would help to free England from dependence on imports. Eastern Europe gives by far the clearest case of the use of capitalist methods in agriculture, so much so that the system of great estates worked by serf labour has frequently been called 'feudal capitalism'. This term also warns us not to overestimate the significance of the system. It is true that production for external markets and the creation of a surplus were among the essential features of the serf estates, but the important point is that this surplus capital was not invested in economic enterprise. The great lords who owned the estates converted their profits instead into private luxuries.

CAPITALISM, WAR AND PROGRESS

In a study written a generation ago, Professor John Nef argued that war was unhelpful to capitalist enterprise and that the wars of the period 1562 to 1648 'moved most of continental Europe less in the direction of nineteenth-century capitalism than away from it'. Wars, he argued, were destructive and wasteful of human effort, and the eventual emergence of England to industrial leadership could be attributed in no small measure to its refusal to get involved in continental wars. In view of the great number of wars in this period, it is worth considering whether they were after all so unhelpful to capitalist growth.

One difficulty lies in talking about wars in general, for it is certain that wars could differ radically from each other. Firstly, a war could have both advantageous and deleterious effects. The first Anglo-Dutch war, which followed the Navigation Act of 1651, was described in the following words by one of its supporters, Sir Arthur Haselrig: 'At the end of (the Rump parliament), scarce a sight to be seen that we had had a war. Trade flourished; the City of London grew rich; we were the most potent by sea that ever was known in England.' While it was true that the Dutch suffered from the war of 1652-4 (Holland was described as 'dead, corn dear, fishing prevented and the people very unquiet'), the war also had some bad effects on England, notably financial loss and the interruption of commerce. Secondly, it is important to determine whether we are talking about internal or external wars, for contemporaries saw each in a totally different light. The mercantilist thinkers of the seventeenth century often advocated war as a matter of state policy, but they seldom conceived of it as being beneficial to the economy as a whole. Colbert considered that war might be profitable in the acquisitive sense: it could increase the national stocks of gold and silver. But neither he nor anyone else thought that war could have any benefits beyond bullionist, territorial and commercial expansion. For such thinkers war was often beneficial, but only if carried out on someone else's territory. Wars fought at home could only be harmful, since they damaged one's own property. A third distinction needs to be made, in the nature of war itself. It is commonplace to attribute German's decline in the seventeenth century to 'war', whereas this was only one of the many factors affecting German development. In this German example, war is credited with too much evil. But other examples show that war often omits to receive due credit. In discussing the expansion of European trade, Nef argues that 'not war but commerce set the pace', an argument difficult to justify when so often it was trade that followed the flag. These three simple points require a little expanding in order to help us see how the practice of war came to be an integral feature of early modern capitalism.

The cruelty and destructiveness of war can never be in doubt. But in this as in all periods there were those who profited, and whose profits were the foundation of capitalist successes. To that extent it is permissible to talk of the 'benefits' of war. If we take the case of England, it is strange to be told that England was continually at peace when in fact it was regularly at war, officially or unofficially. The privateers under Queen Elizabeth brought considerable amounts of bullion home from their expeditions. Though the Anglo-Spanish war which ended in 1604 was followed within a decade by a slump in the cloth trade, the wealth of merchants in Jacobean London still testified to the profits available from privateering, and the failure of the smaller trading firms led to the concentration of monopoly capital in the hands of the chief commercial companies. Despite shipping losses, the war witnessed a boom in shipbuilding, and a corresponding increase in England's merchant marine. The same to some extent is true of the first Anglo-Dutch war (1652-4), which increased English tonnage simply through the number of Dutch prizes taken. An even more convincing picture of war as a stimulus to shipbuilding can be made out for the Dutch Republic. On the industrial level, we need only indicate the armaments industry, in all countries but notably in both the northern and the southern Netherlands. It was armaments that made magnates of men like Crucius, de Geer and Marcelis, and through them in turn that trade was vitalised. In Sweden the needs of war stimulated the metallurgical industry, both in copper and iron. As early as 1629 Sweden had become self-sufficient in war production and did not need to import war material. The growth of the iron industry, and the development of capitalist forms of organisation under businessmen such as de Geer, were among the most important direct results of a policy which boosted industrial investment for the purpose of war.

For the historian Werner Sombart, war helped capitalism in three main ways: in the development of heavy industry for military purposes, the growth of industrial investment, and the financial methods that led to a development of the capital market. The first two factors can be illustrated in detail from the case of Sweden, and if for 'industry' we read 'commerce' the second factor is obviously central to the development of England and the Dutch. The third factor, though operative before 1660, developed more rapidly after that date. War led to the need to finance expeditions far abroad, and in a bullion-conscious age the export of specie was the worst possible solution. This was one of the principal reasons for the rapid development and use of bills of exchange among countries at war, through the agency of an international clearing house, as Amsterdam had now become.

The few references to war that we have given emphasise the importance of distinguishing between internal and external wars, for England, though never invaded, certainly drew capital benefits; and so also did Holland and Sweden. A war waged on someone else's territory could have no obvious ill effects on one's own country. The Swedes perfected this approach. Maintaining themselves in Germany through French and Dutch subsidies, the contributions of other allies, and living off the country, they made the maximum *bellum se ipsum alet* a reality. In December 1634 Oxenstierna claimed, though with some exaggeration, that 'we have now, by the space of four years, sent as good as no money out of the kingdom to the German war'. Interestingly enough, by the end of the seventeenth-century some mercantilist thinkers moved round to the belief that *internal* wars were economically preferable. The English writer Davenant emphasised that it was more profitable to have a war inside than outside the country, because if carried on abroad it drew money out of the country. Basing themselves on the experience of their own country, Spanish writers were soon to come round to the same belief.

The relationship of war to commerce, finally, is one that hardly needs elaboration. Naval wars were not merely a question of short-term profits. They were the perfect instrument of aggressive mercantilism. Though Cromwell depressed shipping by a foolishly calculated war policy against Spanish territories, his contemporaries boosted shipping by a careful combination of trade and war. Just as under Elizabeth several big members of the Barbary and Levant companies resorted to privateering to protect and extend trade, so the English campaigns in the Mediterranean at the beginning of the eighteenth century destroyed French naval power, consolidated trading positions in Italy and the Levant, and built up a system of naval bases to ensure the smooth passage of English commerce. In the Baltic, as in the Mediterranean, trade followed the flag. Peace was irrelevant in a society where trade was the carrying on of war by other means.

II

SOCIETY

4 NOBLES AND GENTLEMEN

In so far as we are born of good lineage, we are the best.

The nobleman STEFANO GUAZZO,
La civil conversatione (1584)

The causes whereby the great seigneurs, gentlemen and principal people of this realm are wasted and destroyed are the many usurious purchases and debts which they contract.

The cortes of Castile (1563)

By the late sixteenth century so startling a change had occurred in the commanding position once held in society by the European nobility that contemporaries were quick to remark it in their memoirs. They tended to emphasise above all the economic decline of certain sections of the aristocracy and their replacement in both economic and political life by newcomers from a lower social stratum. To some extent it is not difficult to describe and to explain these developments. We would be misleading ourselves, however, if we were to dwell only on the theme of decline, for events were in many ways more complex than this, and it is impossible to make any convenient generalisations that apply to several European countries simultaneously. The peculiar importance of the aristocracy and the gentry (who will for most purposes be treated together with the aristocracy here) lay at this time in their almost complete monopoly of political power and social position. It was consequently a serious matter when the monopoly began to be broken, when new forces intruded into the sacred sphere of government, and when the concept of nobility itself began to change.

A NEW NOBLE ETHIC

The words 'aristocrat', 'noble' and 'gentleman' will be used interchangeably here, for the simple reason that most contemporaries used them in that way. All countries tended to divide the noble class into two grades at least, the greater and the lesser. When the Englishman Sir William Segar wrote his *Honour military and civil* in 1602 he used the word 'gentleman' to describe the uppermost social category and then proceeded to subdivide as follows: 'Of Gentlemen, the first and principal is the King, Prince, Dukes, Marquesses, Earls, Viscounts and Barons. These are the Nobility, and be called Lords or Noblemen. Next to these be Knights, Esquires and simple Gentlemen, which last number may be called Nobilitas minor.' Segar was distinguishing between the titled nobility and others, but in many other countries a clear distinction was made within the titled class itself, as in Spain where grandees were a grade above the ordinary *títulos*. Single words such as *noblesse* or *nobleza* therefore tended on the continent to cover a widely differentiated class, and in eastern Europe the *szlachta,* for instance, referred not merely to gentry or nobles but to the whole aristocratic estate of Poland. Under one term, then, a whole spectrum of ranks could be covered.

Words could also be used to denote values, and here an important distinction occurred, for 'nobility' used in this way tended to refer to the outward rank of a person, and 'gentility' to the interior virtue which should accompany it. 'Nobility', for example, could be bought and sold, but 'gentility' could only be inculcated. The king could make a nobleman, it was commonly and widely said, but not a gentleman. The distinction was no mere academic one, but a real political one, for it raised the question: by what right do the nobles govern? Do they govern by hereditary right and entrenched privilege, regardless of whether they are really the best class of society, the possessors of virtue? Or do they rule because they are in fact the best, a true aristocracy of quality? By the end of the sixteenth century there were still many who held that lineage conferred power, because a nobleman was by definition a gentleman. As the Monferrat noble Stefano Guazzo wrote in 1584: 'in so far as we are born of good lineage, we are the best'. Alessandro Sardo in his *Discorsi* (1587) maintained that nobility was conferred not by virtue but by birth and lineage, and could not be destroyed even by evil acts. As against this traditionalist position, the post-Renaissance thinkers began to adopt a new approach, one which was often dictated by the need to find a place in the political establishment for a class of successful merchants and civil servants impatient of a too rigid social structure.

The new mood was indicated by several writers, among them Guillaume de la Perrière, who claimed in his *Le miroir politique*

(1567) that 'the stock and lineage maketh not a man noble or ignoble, but use, education, instruction and bringing up maketh him so'. The Renaissance emphasis was on virtue, education and service to the state, and of these three qualities there can be little doubt that service was what in the end came to be the chief rationale of the new ethic. Among the most significant treatises concerned with this was Girolamo Muzio's *Il Gentilhuomo* (Venice 1575). Although he begins by saying that 'nobility is a splendour which proceeds from virtue', Muzio finds that the noble class has long since lost its honour, and turns his attention from a degraded traditional nobility to a new civic nobility created by the state because of its virtue (i.e. its services). The government must still be aristocratic, though it must be entrusted not to the old militaristic nobles but to an aristocracy that had distinguished itself in letters and laws.

Although we may suspect that many tracts like this were written from a definitely anti-noble and pro-bourgeois point of view, the fact remains that most writers were genuinely concerned to rejuvenate the nobility, if only to preserve the social order from disruption. The response to the propaganda was encouraging, though there is no statistical evidence to show how great a cultural change was effected in the European aristocracy. While the noble class had the greatest opportunities for education, it did not always exploit the advantage to the full. Nor did nobles make adequate use of the other opportunities that might have perpetuated the rule of their caste. The result was that under the pressure of economic and political changes a grave crisis occurred in the ranks of the aristocracy.

HABITS OF VIOLENCE

Was the European nobility as antiquated and outdated in its functions as historians have asserted, and as even some contemporaries claimed? The question can be answered most simply by looking at the allegedly quarrelsome habits of the aristocracy. The military significance of the nobles lay in their own private armed retinues as well as in the troops which they called out in service of the king. Both attributes were wholly feudal, though the second was in form at least meant to be a service to the centralised state. On both counts, the nobility controlled most of the fighting forces within the realm. It is not surprising if in these circumstances most of the violent acts recorded by contemporaries emanated from the aristocracy. Any criticism of the nobles, then, must be tempered by the knowledge that they had a near monopoly of methods of violence, and in many parts of Europe they alone were permitted to sport arms.

The nobles were acting within a power structure with which they were familiar, one in which they had grown up and which they expected to see perpetuated. This situation would continue to hold good in parts of central and eastern Europe where territorial authority was still very fragmented and the power of the crown weak. Indeed in the Russia of Ivan the Terrible even more power for violence was put into the hands of the so-called 'service nobility' so as to enable them to extend the authority of the crown through terror. But in the nation states of western Europe private violence was becoming more and more of an anachronism because it openly contravened public order, the order, that is, maintained by the crown. Royal action against the military power of strong vassals was necessarily very cautious. For one thing, the royal or national army was still in the mid-sixteenth century, and in some countries still even in the mid-seventeenth century, a feudal one. Under Henry VIII in 1523, one-third of the total English army was directly contributed by the titular aristocracy. In France the king still had to resort to the feudal musters known as the *ban et arrière-ban,* which admittedly produced few results but, as the Frondes showed, the forces mustered by the nobles could still outnumber those that the crown might put together on its own authority.

Throughout the period we are looking at, the nobles retained the military initiative. Not until the approach of the mid-seventeenth century was a serious move made (by Prince Maurice in Holland, by Gustav Adolf in Sweden) to form a national army free of feudal allegiances, and only with Cromwell's New Model Army was a thoroughly democratic national force created. In other respects the nobles set the pace. The civil wars in France were pre-eminently decided by combinations among aristocratic factions, and the balance of power between noble interests had some part to play in the Netherlands, Poland and elsewhere. In such conditions it was not unusual to find examples of excessive violence. The French case is particularly striking. We have the complaints of the representatives of the town of Epernay in 1560 that 'the nobility today is so unbridled and unlicensed that it devotes itself solely to the sword and to killings'. François de la Noue, himself a veteran of many wars, condemned in 1585 those gentry who considered that 'the marks of nobility were to make oneself feared, to beat and to hang at will'. It was not only the French wars, but other disturbances as well, that illustrated the power of the nobles to threaten the state: in England the rebellions against Elizabeth by the northern earls in 1569 and by Essex in 1601, in France the rebellions against Louis XIII by the Protestants, and by the Montmorency faction in 1632.

The indignation of contemporaries was aroused less by political rebellion than by arbitrary personal violence, in which the nobles had a distinctive record. During the civil wars in France there were several commentators who claimed to see the campaigns as a plot by nobles of either faith to exploit the people. 'It appears that the nobles and the enemy have sworn to bring about the total ruin of the people', protested a Catholic writer in 1573. Was there not ample evidence, claimed a writer in Dauphiné, that the nobles seldom attacked each other's property, even if they were on opposite sides, and only sacked the houses of commoners? Frenchmen were like the lamb led to the slaughter. The Huguenot and Catholic nobility, it was reported from Languedoc, 'openly help each other; the one group holds the lamb while the other cuts its throat'. Nobles who turned to banditry, especially in times of war, were all too common. The French civil wars were notorious for the appearance of noble brigands, chief among them the Leaguer La Fontenelle, who operated in Brittany until 1602. Claude Haton in 1578 reported the activities in Champagne of a group of seigneurs 'perpetrating unmentionable and incredible beatings, robberies, rapes, thefts, murders, arson and every kind of crime, without any respect of persons, of whatever rank'. Under Louis XIII many of the lords continued these habits of violence, as they could well afford to, for they had their own private armies and clientele. The Duc de la Rochefoucauld raised fifteen hundred gentlemen within four days for the siege of La Rochelle, and said proudly to the king, 'Sire, there is not one who is not related to me'. With this extent of local influence, some seigneurs degenerated into tyranny. One such was Gabriel Foucault, Vicomte de Daugnon, governor of La Marche, described by the commentator Tallemant des Réaux as 'a great robber, a great borrower who never returned, and a great distributor of blows with a club'. It was he who rewarded his retainers by granting them other people's daughters whom he had carried off. Noble brigands were commonplace in southern Europe, and many of the bands operating in Castile in the time of

143

Philip IV were led by gentry. The most famous of sixteenth-century Catalan bandits, Rocaguinarda, was noble. It was in Italy, however, that the great feudal lords resorted openly to violence. The year 1578 saw the emergence of Alfonso Piccolomini, Duke of Montemarciano, who for thirteen years thereafter operated as the biggest seigneur-brigand in Italy. It was against the feudal anarchy represented by men like this that Pope Sixtus V struggled with some success. When the Grand Duke Ramberto Malatesta began to operate as a bandit within the papal states, Sixtus promptly had him arrested and executed in 1587.

By the mid-seventeenth century, a great deal of this brigandage and anarchy had been eliminated, for it was too open a threat to the state for the state to turn a blind eye. It was somewhat different with the limited violence associated with feuds, duels and simple crime. These tended to continue regardless of state policy. Edicts against duels, for example, were always failures. If a nobleman felt he had to defend his honour he would defend it, and the constant repetition of edicts against duelling illustrates the failure to stop the practice. In the Duchy of Lorraine formal and solemn prohibitions of duelling can be found in 1586, 1591, 1603, 1609, 1614, 1617, 1626 and so on almost indefinitely. French governments were equally concerned about the practice, and Sully was bitterly opposed to it. Richelieu's well-known hostility was neither novel nor effective. He ordered the execution of Montmorency-Bouteville merely because his victim had provoked him; moreover, as he said in 1632, 'the king needs to make examples'. But duelling went on long after Richelieu. In any case, the cardinal was not inspired by any anti-noble sentiment when issuing his edict against duelling. On the contrary, the measure was intended to stop a highly valued ruling class from self-destruction, 'nothing being dearer to me', as Louis XIII observed, 'than to do all I can to preserve my nobles'. The evidence of the marshal Duke of Gramont is telling: according to him, duelling alone cost the lives of nine hundred gentlemen during the Regency of Anne of Austria.

Easy as it is to accumulate evidence of such activities, the fact remains that by the seventeenth century aristocratic violence was becoming the exception rather than the rule. The deliberate policy of law enforcement adopted by the western monarchies, the gradual impoverishment of many noble families and subsequent economies in retinue, a growing preference for litigation rather than brigandage, were among the main reasons for this. For England, Professor Stone has demonstrated convincingly that the armaments as well as the retainers kept by leading aristocrats had dwindled sharply by the early seventeenth century. The firm hand of government was beginning to intervene. We find an English judge in 1592 warning the Earl of Shrewsbury that 'when in the country you dwell in you will needs enter in a war with the inferiors therein, we think it both justice, equity and wisdom to take care that the weaker part be not put down by the mightier'. In Spain in 1597 it was said of Philip II by a contemporary, the writer Castillo de Bobadilla, that he had humiliated the nobles, and 'did not pardon them with his usual clemency, nor did he respect their estates, and there is no judge now who cannot act against them and take their silver and horses'. In these statements it is possible to see the definite emergence of a rule of law which, though still incapable of curbing the independence of the nobility, went some way towards making them accept the norms of conduct laid down by the state.

THE NOBILITY IN BUSINESS

The pacification of the nobility, the undermining of the belief that the nobleman was essentially a warrior, gave place to a new ethic. In much the same way, other long-cherished prejudices of the noble class were changing rapidly. Perhaps the best known of these attitudes was the belief that nobles should not work for their living, that gentlemen should not soil their hands with labour. For various reasons, this conviction had great force in southern Europe, and less in the north. It is well known that in sixteenth-century Spain no *hidalgo* could compromise his honour by trade. To work for gain or profit was demeaning. As the Ferrarese noble Sardo observed, 'inherited wealth is more honest than earned wealth, in view of the vile gain needed to obtain the latter'. These may have been admirable sentiments on the lips of one who stood to inherit wealth. But in a world where very many sought to redress fallen fortunes, there would always be those who could not accept the prejudice against trade. In England there had never been any real objection, either socially or in principle, to noble participation in business. To examine the change in outlook, then, it is to the Latin countries that we must first turn.

Among the writers in the late sixteenth century who argued in favour of trade was the French jurist André Tiraqueu, whose

Commentarii de nobilitate (Commentary on nobility) (Basel 1561) claimed that commerce did not derogate from nobility when it was the only possible way of making ends meet. In Italy the jurist Benvenuto Stracca, representing it is true a more conservative view than had formerly prevailed in Venice, made it clear in his *Tractatus de mercatura* (Treatise on trade) (Venice 1575) that a noble could take part in large-scale trading but not in petty commerce, nor must he participate in person but only as a director. These distinctions were standard ones that came to be widely accepted. Despite such writings, the preponderant attitude was the traditionalist one. As the sixteenth-century French jurist Loyseau affirmed in his *Traité des Ordres,* 'it is gain, whether vile or sordid, that derogates from nobility, whose proper role is to live off rents'. Derogation, *dérogeance,* was a technical term with a very serious meaning, namely the possible loss of noble status. Like other jurists, Loyseau admitted that to take part in commerce did not result in a loss, but merely a suspension, of noble status: 'all that is necessary for rehabilitation are letters signed by the king'. Certainly in France it was the king and government that did most to break down the old attitude to commerce. At the turn of the century, for instance, when the Parlement of Lyon demanded that merchants who became nobles should live *'noblement'* (that is, should no longer trade), the royal council declared in June 1607 that 'the King wishes them to enjoy fully and freely the privileges of nobility, as though they were nobles of ancient lineage, and they may continue to do business and trade, both in money and banking as in any other large-scale trading'.

This official verdict merely followed several others of a similar nature, and confirmed the interest of the government in seeing the nobles put their money where it most benefited the state. It is with Richelieu that we get the most precise statements of policy. In the Code Michau of 1629, for which both he and Marillac were responsible, a clause declared that 'all nobles who directly or indirectly take shares in ships and their merchandise, shall not lose their noble status'. By the time of Colbert no real infamy attached to nobles who traded. Indeed by the end of the seventeenth century even Spain appears to have abandoned the traditional attitude, for the code of laws shows a declaration, adopted in both Aragon and Castile (in 1626 and 1682 respectively), that the manufacture and trade of textiles was no bar to nobility; and in Segovia, centre of the cloth industry of Castile, most of the owners of factories were nobles.

146

Elsewhere in Europe there was so little objection to aristocratic entrepreneurship that we find everywhere nobles involved in industrial and commercial activity. It is sometimes said that, in western Europe at least, the nobles seldom traded and were more concerned with industry. In England Dudley Digges in 1604 claimed that 'to play the merchant was only for gentlemen of Florence, Venice or the like'; in other words, only decadent foreigners dabbled in trade. It is hardly wise to trust the evidence of Digges. If nobles preferred industry to trade, there were very good reasons for it: they tended to be landed, and the land produced ore, coal, metals, wood and many similar items which it was only logical for the landowner himself to invest in. Trade, particularly overseas trade, was hardly a priority for a man with a rich industry in his own back garden. This did not mean that a noble industrialist was prejudiced against commerce, for very many industrialists also took an interest in exchanging and exporting.

The attempt to alter established attitudes is shown by the existence at this period in both Lorraine and France of the terms *gentilshommes-verriers* and *gentilshommes-mineurs,* which referred to those who enjoyed noble privileges as a result of their participation in the industries concerned, glass manufacture and mining. Some nobles participated in glassmaking. Others in the leading cities—Lyon and Bordeaux for instance—were permitted to engage in trade by royal charter. In England there was little need to break down the barriers. There the nobles distinguished themselves by the exploitation of mines on their estates and by their promotion of mercantile enterprises. 'In the Elizabethan period', we are told, 'the most active entrepreneur in the country was not some busy merchant or thrusting member of the new gentry, but a peer of ancient stock, George Talbot, ninth earl of Shrewsbury.' He was a large-scale farmer, a shipowner, an iron-master, and the master of a steel-works, coalmines and glassworks; in addition he had interests in trading companies. The most prominent aristocratic names in the realm, among them Norfolk, Devonshire and Arundel, were associated with industrial enterprises. The scale of their commitment was not very large. Not all the nobles were direct enterpreneurs: a few merely lent their names. No aristocrat relied on industry alone for his income. The biggest profits were still in land, and it was to urban development and to fen drainage that nobles tended to turn after about 1600. When all allowances are made, however, noble participation in business was still highly significant. 'The peerage fulfilled a role', Professor Stone reminds us, 'that no other class, neither the gentry nor the merchants, was able or willing to rival.' Though their contribution to economic growth was quantitatively small, it was financially adventurous. It was the peers who risked their money in industrial and trading endeavours to an extent that certainly brought ruin to many, but also helped to pave the way for the later injection of capital by other classes.

In other countries besides England the pattern was not very different. To take seventeenth-century Scotland, there the Earl of Wemyss told Cromwell in 1658 that the estate of many Scottish 'noblemen, gentlemen and others doth consist very much in coalworks', so giving them a special position as capitalists. Significantly, the noble entrepreneurs of Scotland relied on a depressed labour force in their coalworks. This combination of feudalism and capitalism was common on the continent, where the wealthy noble merchants and industrialists of Holstein, Prussia, Bohemia, Poland and Russia benefited from the availability of cheap labour that followed changes in the agrarian economy. Heinrich Rantzau, the first and greatest of the sixteenth-century Holstein aristocratic entrepreneurs, made huge profits from demesne farming and ploughed much of this back into industries on his estates. He established thirty-nine mills for the production of lumber, flour and oil, and for the manufacture of articles from copper, brass and iron. Both landed and industrial produce was traded abroad, so that the richest merchants in Kiel, for example, were nobles. After the crisis years of the early seventeenth century the Holstein nobility tended to withdraw from business and turn to their estates. We even find one aristocrat, Duke Johann Adolph of Holstein-Gottorf, claiming in 1615 that 'trade is not proper for noblemen'.

In central and eastern Europe the nobles did not give up so easily. It is precisely in the early seventeenth century that we find the biggest capitalist concern in central Europe being brought into existence in the duchy of Friedland by Wallenstein. There were, it is true, special features connected with Friedland: it was both financed by, and geared to, war; and its industries, among them munitions, were not primarily concerned with peaceful trade. But Friedland illustrates clearly the common situation, which is worth emphasising, that only the nobles had the means of raising capital and putting it to work. In areas where the bourgeoisie was weak, or in the process of decline, it was the nobility who took control of both trade and industry. The important fact that does emerge if we take the whole of Europe into consideration, rather than confining ourselves to a narrow western European viewpoint, is that the greater part of the nobility of the continent were active in business, not excluding trade.

In Sweden the nobles were prominent as entrepreneurs from the sixteenth century. They tended to work the mines on their own estates — principally in iron ore — and from mining they moved to trade. Trading profits allowed them to accumulate capital which they invested in forges and manufactories, and also lent out at interest. Their investment in trade was assured by a guaranteed privilege that they could export the produce of their own estates free of duty. Many of the wealthiest nobles consequently purchased ships. The nobility of the German lands varied in their application. In Brandenburg, as we shall see presently, they tended to monopolise both industry and trade. The heart of Germany owes its industrial beginnings to them, for it was the encouragement of the princes that allowed the refugee entrepreneurs to take root. In Lower Saxony Duke Anton I von Oldenburg encouraged his nobles to take a personal interest in market procedures, from which came a class of noble capitalists. One of these was Stats von Münchhausen, who based his enterprise on land, but then invested his agricultural profits in ironmongery and timber. His fortune grew to be immense: by 1618 he was said to possess over ten tons of gold and over one million *thaler*. Some of this money went into building himself the castle of Bevern on the River Weser. On the Baltic coast, in Pomerania, the family of Loytze, from the city of Stettin, made themselves into the 'Fuggers of the north' through reinvesting the profits they made from land. When their firm collapsed in 1572 a large number of the nobility fell into difficulties and the Chancellor of Pomerania committed suicide because of his losses.

Hungary may be taken as a brief example of the situation in the eastern countries. Since the economy was in no sense industrialised, Hungarian foreign trade consisted in the export of agricultural goods and the import of industrial goods. The nobles were lords of the soil and by extension dominated the trade in its produce. Hungarian seigneurs were consequently both farmers and merchants. In his autobiography the seventeenth-century Transylvanian nobleman Bethlen Miklos tells us that he took part in the trade of wheat and of wine. Moreover, 'I have traded in salt without losing anything; on the contrary it is by these three items (wheat, wine and salt) that I have gained nearly all my goods, for the revenue from my lands alone would never have met all the expenses I had to make'. Bethlen also traded in cattle, sheep, honey and wax.

In Russia, conditions differed so radically from those in western Europe that a shocked Austrian ambassador reported in 1661 that 'all the people of quality and even the ambassadors sent to foreign princes, trade publicly. They buy, they sell, and they exchange without a qualm, thereby making their elevated rank, venerable that it is, subservient to their avarice.' He could have added that the tsar himself was the biggest of Russian businessmen, with profitable interests in both trade and industry. Industrial enterprise of every sort existed on the estates of tsars, monasteries and boyars. Among the biggest noble merchants of the sixteenth century were the Stroganov family, whose members had international trade connections. To serve the producing and trading interests of the elite, a servile labour force was brought into existence: industrial serfdom was a reality, and workers in this depressed category were known as 'state serfs'.

These few considerations make it clear that over much of Europe the nobleman was far from being the indolent parasite he has often been represented to be. On the contrary, he was often the creator rather than the consumer of wealth. Whatever the country, in either east or west, aristocrats concerned themselves with industry and trade if the economic conditions were suitable and if there was no other entrepreneurial class at hand. Viewed in these general terms, it is possible to see why the French nobles tended not to trade while the Russians did. This still leaves out the very important factor that in some western countries there did exist a strong social prejudice against profit-making through commerce, and that in the seventeenth century this prejudice was strong enough to affect the entrepreneurial activities of, for instance, the Italian mercantile nobility, members of families that had originated from bourgeois merchants.

The nobility in business, it should be emphasised, were not necessarily fulfilling a progressive function. In central and eastern Europe the entry of aristocrats into business checked the growth of an independent merchant class, and in some cities destroyed an existing trading sector. The manipulation of capital by the feudal classes hindered the development of a strong bourgeoisie, and the rise of landed noble traders led to the decay of urban centres. All this was ultimately to have unfavourable consequences for the economic life of the areas concerned. 'Feudal capitalism' sounds like a contradiction in terms, but it was also a contradiction in reality. It was really only in those countries where an energetic middle class took over economic development that the contribution of the nobility can be seen as a beneficial, creative and adventurous step forward.

ARISTOCRATIC WEALTH AND WASTE

If there was one essential mark of nobility that superseded all others, it was wealth: the aristocracy were the rich. Those who were well-established in the noble class would have preferred to equate their status with blood, but the common practice of nations was against them. As a Spanish writer of this time, Arce Otalora, observed: 'it is the law and custom in all Italy, Germany and France, that those who do not live nobly do not enjoy the privilege of nobility'. In Spain too, he could have added, the ancient laws of Castile declared that 'if any nobleman falls into poverty and cannot maintain his noble status, he shall become a commoner, and all his children with him'. The equation of wealth and nobility created several problems, of which the most disturbing for the hereditary aristocracy was the ability of newly-enriched men to rise into their ranks. The nobles consequently clung desperately to the principle of a blood elite that did not cease to be an elite merely because it had become impoverished. The returns made for the feudal levy (*arrière-ban*) in France under Louis XIII illustrate how widespread the impoverishment was: they show clearly that the provincial nobility was structured like a pyramid, where the peak was made up of the few wealthy and the base was occupied by a vast number of penniless gentlemen. For these many, the term 'noble but poor' came to be a common description used by administrative officials, who were well aware of the contradiction in terms. The account-books of the French treasury in 1614 have entries in which sums of ten or more *livres* were given out as charity to 'poor gentlemen' in order 'to help them to live'. In Spain where the proportion of self-styled gentry (*hidalgos*) was far higher than in France, the phenomenon of an impoverished nobility was so commonplace that it became a standard, indeed a predominant, theme of the literature and art of the period. Yet in spite of these poor nobles, wealth remained

151

the hallmark of the peers of Europe. In what did it consist?

Apart from some commitments to capitalist activity in trade and production, the noble class everywhere relied on the land for its income, though its concern with it varied very widely. In western Europe as a whole the nobles were drifting away from their estates and becoming absentee landlords rather than agricultural producers; in the east, they were becoming more involved than ever in the exploitation of land. The nature of noble property thus differed between these two areas. A flourishing money economy in the west meant that everything could be made to yield cash immediately: estates were rented out, houses let, and offices of state bought and sold.

In England the movement away from direct exploitation of the soil was notable. Before 1600 the receipts of the Earl of Rutland from demesne farming came to about one-fifth of his income; after 1613, when leasing of land had begun, they fell to about one-twentieth. By the mid-seventeenth century most English great nobles had become absentee landlords. As land became capitalised, so it ceased to occupy the principal part in revenue that it had once had. Many of the most privileged nobles turned to the profits from other sources, from rents, pensions and public office.

The balance between landed and other income can be illustrated by a few rough examples, taken from senior nobles and officers of state, who admittedly were in a better position than most to secure income from sources other than feudal rights. The Marshal d'Ancre, the French royal favourite, in 1617 had a fortune of over seven million francs, of which only one million came from land, the rest deriving from offices and other sources of government revenue. Of the hereditary aristocracy, the Duc d'Epernon in about 1640 had an annual revenue of three hundred and forty-three thousand *livres,* of which only half came from his twenty-three estates. In Spain in 1622 the Duke of Lerma drew up a statement of his own income for the king: of his total assets of one hundred and twenty thousand ducats, nearly two-thirds came from the fruits of office, and only one-third from land. The Duke of Béjar in 1630 drew only thirty-five per cent of his income from demesne; of the rest, the highest proportion, forty-five per cent, came from fiscal rights.

These nobles were wealthy, and they were the few. The majority, as Richelieu observed in 1614, 'as poor in money as they are rich in honour, cannot obtain posts in the royal household or judicial offices, since one can only attain such honours through means which they do not possess'. The distributor of favours was the court, which was a phenomenon limited perhaps to only five centres in Europe: London, Paris, Vienna, Madrid and, for good measure, Rome. Other countries had their centres of government and their focus of social life. But only in these five was the court a combination of both city and monarch's residence (Madrid was in fact called simply *la Corte*), of both political and social life, and above all the heart of a growing bureaucracy which allowed open trafficking in official posts.

Rome would appear at first glance to be an exception among these five. But it was, in fact, the archetypal court. Staffed by wealthy aristocrats such as the Colonna and Orsini, scene of the most extravagant displays of luxury, Rome was the dispenser of patronage to the largest bureaucracy in the world, that of the Church. In France the court had become the focus of aristocratic attention long before the reign of Louis XIV. Royal patronage was responsible not merely for the rise of *parvenus* like d'Ancre, but also for the support of the noble class, the lesser of whom received gratuities while the greater received enormous pensions. From 1611 to 1617 a total of fourteen million *livres* was paid out in pensions to nine nobles, among them Condé, who received three million, five hundred thousand *livres*. A lucrative source of income to king and courtier alike was the sale of offices: thus Sully sold the captaincy of the Bastille for three hundred thousand *livres*, and the Marquis de Rambouillet sold the post of master of the royal wardrobe for the same sum. The English nobles had similar ways of exploiting the court. They received lands in gifts or on lease, whether from the dissolved monasteries or from Ireland or some other source. They obtained cash gifts (James I in the peak year 1611 gave away £43,600 to Scots favourites) or annuities; and benefiting from influence they secured trade privileges, tax-farms and monopolies to such an extent that the merchant class began to direct its resentment over arbitrary economic policies against the crown. Madrid, the most bureaucratic of all European cities, and one where the aristocracy was most in power, more than equalled all other courts in the advantages it offered to seekers after favour. The nobles sought not so much cash (though this was given) as other *mercedes* or favours: lucrative offices in Spain or the Indies, annuities (*juros*), land and similar privileges. Houses which had fallen on evil times expected the crown to rescue them as a matter of right, so much so that the Duke of Sessa died in 1606 'out of melancholy at being ruined and because the king did not give him a *merced* to pay his debts'. In fact, Philip III actually met one quarter of the dead duke's debts, and settled an income on his widow and son.

Fortified then by ancestral lands and by the favours of the great monarchies, the noble class was far from being as impoverished as some of its individual members undoubtedly were. The aristocracy of Church and State went through difficult times, but was never in any danger of losing the pre-eminence that wealth and tradition bestowed on it.

What danger there was tended to come from the need to 'live nobly'. Even by contemporary standards a great deal of money was spent wastefully. What has been called 'conspicuous consumption' was often no more than the attempt to keep up appearances. As the Spanish Duke of Béjar confessed in 1626: 'Everyone judges me to be rich, and I do not wish outsiders to know differently because it would not be to my credit for them to understand that I am poor.' All too frequently, however, the policy of keeping up appearances was financially suicidal. The system of keeping a large household of retainers and servants provides one example. In England in 1571 the Earl of Pembroke had two hundred and ten men wearing his livery, and in 1612 we find the Earl of Rutland with a following of about two hundred. Retaining encouraged violence between rival households, kept up the trappings of an outworn feudalism, made idleness fashionable and impoverished the nobility. Governments consequently legislated against it. One contemporary interpretation of the English Statute of Retainers of 1504 is given by Bacon, who reported that 'the kings of this realm, finding long since that kind of commandment in noblemen unsafe unto their crown and inconvenient unto their people, thought meet to restrain the same provision of laws; whereupon grew the Statute of Retainers; so as men now depend upon the prince and the laws and upon no other'. This view, a governmental one, reflected the concern for public order. But some disorder continued and so too did the large households. Among the Spanish laws, for instance, we find one of 1623 that limited personal households to only eighteen persons; yet a half-century later the chief minister, the count of Oropesa, had one of seventy-four. In Rome, well into the late sixteenth century the princes of the Church kept up truly princely households that ran into hundreds, including numerous slaves. It was of this Rome that a Venetian ambassador spoke in 1595 when he reported that 'in our days luxury and comfort have been introduced into all countries and all courts, even among the most distant and barbarous nations; likewise at Rome, where it seems that the field lies open to these influences even more than elsewhere'. In the early seventeenth century, as though to confirm these words, the French ambassador in Poland observed that 'the Poles live in incredible luxury and pomp. Many of the nobles are followed by five and six hundred retainers.' As a rule this immoderate ostentation of followers was too expensive for nobles to maintain for a long time, and a choice between economy and bankruptcy soon presented itself.

In several other obvious ways too, conspicuous expenditure could be ruinous. Luxurious clothes, which figure prominently in La Noue's denunciations of the French nobility, eating, gambling, hunting and similar pastimes were indulged in on a scale that made commoners gasp. The banquets held in Rome by the cardinals and the Pope were legendary. Secular princes were no less given to over-eating, especially at diplomatic functions. It was no doubt the urge to impress that made the Englishman Lord Hay give a feast in 1621 to the French ambassador, in the preparation of which one hundred cooks were employed eight days to cook one thousand six hundred dishes. In a previous chapter we have noted the extravagant wedding feast of the Bohemian noble William of Rožmberk in 1587. His brother Peter was likewise said to feed daily one hundred and ninety-two persons at fourteen tables. Many nobles dreaded such feasts. When in 1643 the Admiral of Castile gave a great dinner to the ambassadors of the Grisons, 'the other seigneurs', reported a Jesuit contemporary, 'who had also been asked to entertain, were fearful of the event because they could not do more than he. The times were not propitious for such excessive expenditure; but if they spent less it would be observed. They did not know what decision to make, and said that the times were hard.' Yet they put a brave face on it, and continued their lavish displays. Few items contributed more to status, or annoyed governments more, than the purchase and embellishment of coaches. In every European court a minor fortune was poured out on the attempt to possess a more elegant coach than one's peers. This was one of the more important items to feature in the sumptuary laws of the time. Governments objected for two principal reasons: firstly, because by displaying coaches which were more luxurious than those owned by their social superiors the nobles contravened the rules of precedence and aroused social tension; secondly, because the use of ornaments such as gold and silver was in violation of public policy regarding precious metals.

Such extravagances had their victims, as we can see in the many known cases of nobles who literally wasted their substance away, one such being the Earl of Oxford who between 1575 and 1586 went through his landed income of over £2,000 a year, as well as over £70,000 which he realised from the sale of his entire property. In France one of the generals of the galleys under Louis XIII, Pont-Courbay, with a handsome revenue of sixty thousand *livres* a year, and a household of forty-four servants to maintain, managed to run up debts of four hundred thousand *livres* within the short space of two years. The Prince of Conti, a French prince of the blood, had landed assets in 1655 of about five million *livres*, with income therefrom of two hundred thousand *livres* a year. But his expenditure that year amounted to the incredible sum of over one million. His annual pension from the king, half a million *livres*, helped to cover half the debt. To meet the rest, Conti sold his governorship of the province of Berry.

Outstanding among the items of expenditure, particularly since many of the results may still be seen today, was the building of residences. The late sixteenth and early seventeenth centuries were the great era of rebuilding in Europe. One motive seems to have been preponderant: the ambition of the rich to build homes worthy of their own wealth and status; homes, moreover, that would surpass those of all their rivals. Coming home from their wars in Italy and in Flanders, the aristocracy settled down to impress their neighbours and their sovereign with their splendid way of life. 'What has been created in the past is small in comparison with our own time', observed La Noue in 1585, 'since we see the quality of buildings and the number of those who build them far exceed any yet known, particularly among the nobility, who devote themselves to it more for glory than out of necessity.' In England the great rural reconstruction of this epoch, shown by the number of farmhouses and countryhouses that were rebuilt between about 1570 and 1640 in at least four different counties, was paralleled by the work of the nobility who built themselves mansions both in the country and in London. This was the age when Burghley House, Chatsworth, Hardwick, Hatfield and Longleat made their appearance in the world. All ranks of the aristocracy joined in the struggle to build bigger and better houses. 'There was never the like number of fair and stately houses as have been built and set up from the ground since (Queen Elizabeth's) reign', wrote Bacon in 1592. 'No kingdom in the world spent so much in building as we did in (King James') time', reflected another contemporary. The process may certainly have seemed unique to an Englishman, in view of the enormous sums expended on building. The visitor to London had but to look at Somerset House or the Banqueting House at Whitehall, to see how the fever had spread to the city. But it was a fever that had its parallels elsewhere in Europe, for the nobility, when not building on their estates, were moving into the cities, and with them came a new impetus to the urban building programme.

When nobles had their estates in the mountains or at frontiers, they built castles, not the defensive ones of a past age but new, luxurious architectural monuments. The aristocracy of central and northern Europe seem to have followed this practice, particularly when their profits from agriculture allowed them to do so. It was in this period that Duke Ernst von Schaumburg built Bückeburg castle and a church with it, both richly decorated. Münchhausen, we have already seen, put some of his profits into a castle. The gentry of Pomerania, Mecklenburg and East Prussia chose this time to build themselves large and luxurious manor houses, furnished with tapestries, crystal and all the ornamentation they could import from elsewhere. From these princely and isolated houses they governed their vast estates.

This isolation in the countryside was usually typical of the noble class, even in the mid-sixteenth century. They felt more at home in the country, 'as if', mocked a French writer in 1600, 'there was a contradiction between being a gentleman and bearing arms, and living in a town'. But there was a certain self-sufficiency about the country life that gave it a flavour all its own, as we can see in the diary of one French country seigneur, Gouberville. This entry, under 6 February 1555, for instance: '*Ce jour là il ne cessa de plouvoyr. Mes gens furent aux champs, mais la pluie les rachassa. Au soir, toute la vesprée nous leusmes en Amadis des Gaules comme il vainquit Dardan.*' It was Noël du Fail who observed at this time that 'our French towns certainly have some attraction, but are suitable only for lawyers, merchants and artisans. You can say with assurance when you see a gentleman in the town that he is there either as a visitor or a guest, either to pay or to be paid, to borrow money at enormous interest or to spend it profligately.' 'The nobles', reported the Venetian envoy Soranzo in 1558 during his stay in France, 'live not in the cities but in the villages and in their châteaux.' For him to make such an observation, is a clear reminder that in Italy, as in Spain and in parts of Germany, nobles were by contrast town-dwellers. But over the greater part of Europe the class distinction between town and country was a fairly well-defined one.

In western Europe the drift from the land, and the growing attraction of the capital city, altered this picture to some extent. The aristocracy brought capital to the city and invested it in splendid new edifices. This development coincided with the Counter Reformation, which inspired much of the architectural boom that took place. Inevitably the pattern was set by the Rome of the Counter Reformation, where the popes, particularly Pius IV and Sixtus V, set out deliberately to recreate the Eternal City as the most beautiful urban centre in Europe. In this renovated city the princes and cardinals built their palaces and villas, splendid residences named after their builders, like the villa d'Este at Tivoli or the Farnese villa at Caprarola. Most of the building at Rome took place in the second half of the sixteenth century, coinciding with the end of the Italian wars. It was after these wars, too, La Noue infoms us, that French gentlemen returning home yearned to build houses as they built them in Italy. Châteaux and decorative gardens began to spring up all over France. The cost to the peasantry was severe, for villages were destroyed as the sumptuous new dwellings and their vast parks began to invade the countryside. 'Oh, golden age!' exclaimed a French writer of 1622 with bitter irony: 'now we see our countryside enriched with superb buildings, the sight of which wipes out antiquity; and not only are there houses of the bourgeoisie but also superb châteaux of judges, nobles and financiers which in less than a year have destroyed a thousand peasant homes in order to build one noble one.'

In Paris the rebuilding was given a great impetus by Henry IV, who altered the royal palaces and laid out spacious new squares such as the Place Dauphine. The nobles contributed to the proliferation of *hôtels*, large aristocratic town mansions, for which Richelieu himself set the style with his own Palais-Cardinal, just as Sully before him had built the Hôtel Sully.

> L'univers entier ne peut rien voir d'égal
> Aux superbes dehors du Palais-Cardinal

wrote Corneille. So imposing were the noble houses that when the

Duc de Nevers had an *hôtel* built for himself the king murmured that he found it 'a bit too magnificent to be facing the Louvre'. What little we know of other areas of western Europe suggests the same important contribution by the nobility to the urban development programme. Thus Valladolid at the beginning of the seventeenth century, at a date when it had long ceased to be the capital of Spain, was said to have contained about four hundred seigneurial houses and palaces.

Few nobles could commit themselves to luxury expenditure and yet hope to see the family fortune survive for another generation. The very wealthiest could and did survive. But even for them there were pitfalls that had to be avoided, in a world where economic crisis threatened all social classes.

CHANGING FORTUNES AND NEW MEN

One point on which most contemporary witnesses seem to have agreed was that there had been a sharp fall in the fortunes of the aristocracy. 'The lords in former times were far stronger, more warlike, better followed, living in their countries, than now they are', observed Sir Walter Ralegh in the early seventeenth century. 'There have been in ages past', claimed Bacon in 1592, 'noblemen both of greater possessions and of greater commandment and sway than any are at this day.' The reasons for this decay varied from one part of Europe to the other. In the United Provinces the aristocracy had lost many estates during the war of independence. In France it was the civil wars that helped to ruin large sections of nobility. 'How many French gentlemen', wrote La Noue, 'are shorn of the riches that their houses were once adorned with under Louis XII and Francis I! One sees them now going in want of several necessities, the exceptions being those few houses that have been built recently and others which by good management have been upkept and enriched.' Four-fifths of the aristocracy were impoverished, he claimed with obvious exaggeration, and 'all the nobility can do now is to make ends meet by staying at home'. In Spain too the complaints were legion. The city of Seville, remonstrating in 1627 against the steep inflation, argued that 'it is the nobility in particular that are affected, since they have to keep themselves on incomes that will not buy today what could be bought previously with one-fourth of the same'. 'The greater part of the grandees of Spain', observed a French visitor under Philip IV, 'are ruined even though they possess large revenues.' In Russia the greater nobility suffered severely in the *oprichnina* period (1564-72) which destroyed much of their military and landed power. In Naples by the end of the sixteenth century, of one hundred and forty-eight noble families as many as fifty were too poor to maintain their rank and position.

This apparently unquestionable decline of the feudal classes was neither as universal nor as straightforward as it may appear to be. In no European country, not even bourgeois Holland, did the nobility decline absolutely. Many grandees and great houses perished through wars and economic difficulties, but their places were soon taken by others. Many lesser nobles decayed, but were immediately reinforced from below by those who had risen up the social ladder. It is true that in western Europe much wealth was passing into the hands of the middle class, but this occurred only in a few countries; elsewhere the noble grip was never relaxed, and in eastern Europe the noble class actually rose to predominance over the ruins of the bourgeoisie. Even where the aristocracy had clearly declined in wealth, it did not immediately cease to exercise its leading role in government and in society.

How and why did some nobles decline? Conspicuous consumption in all its forms was clearly a major cause. What made such consumption ruinous in this period more than any other was the combination of high expenditure with diminishing revenues and rising costs in a century of price inflation. The increase in the cost of food, building, clothes and luxuries was remarkable enough. It became catastrophic when there was no proportionate increase in the basic source of noble revenue, the land. Though the land may not have always formed the major source of income, it was certainly the most important, for noble houses almost without exception depended on it for supplies and rents. Only a small minority of nobles in public office benefited from lucrative salaries and pensions and did not require great estates to fall back on.

The decline of the Venetian nobility has few parallels elsewhere in Europe. Mercantile in its origins, this ruling class found its fortunes tied up with Venetian commerce, and when that decayed they found it difficult to adjust to other forms of entrepreneurial activity such as the textile industry. In addition by the late sixteenth century the Venetian nobility had become exclusive and caste-ridden, and frowned on the entry of any newcomers into its ranks. By the early seventeenth century they were in a state of irretrievable collapse. Their numbers declined from a total of two thousand and ninety in the year 1609 to one thousand six hundred and sixty in the year 1631. The English ambassador in 1612 summed up their development: 'They here change theyr manners, they have growne factious, vindicative, loose and unthriftie. Theyr former course of life was merchandising; which is now quite left and they looke to landward, buieng house and lands, furnishing themselfs with coch and horses, and giving themselfs the good time with more shew and gallantrie than was wont.'

Despite their growing economic difficulties, the aristocracy of western Europe appear not to have attempted to better themselves through agriculture. There was every reason why they should have turned to the land. In an age of rising population and inflation of agricultural prices, there was a clear demand for more food, and the period should have seen an expansion of estate farming. Such an expansion did occur in the late sixteenth century and the early years of the seventeenth, but on aristocratic lands it did not occur on a scale that might have benefited their class. There were, it is true, numerous and important exceptions. In Piedmont the nobles seem for the most part to have invested in the soil, since other investments offered limited scope. In the early seventeenth century their return from the land came to over five per cent of invested capital, a good annual gain from their outlay. Then there were outstanding cases like the French Marquis de Gamaches who in the mid-seventeenth century made enough profits from his soil and his investments to be able to give his daughter a dowry of one hundred and eight thousand *livres*. Writing of England in 1600, Thomas Wilson testified that 'the gentlemen which were wont to addict themselves to the wars are now for the most part grown to become good husbands and know as well how to improve their lands to the uttermost as the farmer or countryman, so that they take their farms into their hands as the leases expire and either till themselves or else let them out to those who will give most'. An example is provided by the estates of the Percy family, which were fairly well administered and produced a net annual income that rose from £3,602 in 1582 to £12,978 in 1636. But, to adjust Wilson's picture, it must be understood that it was animal husbandry rather than arable farming to which the nobles attended. Aristocrats like the Duke of Norfolk and the Earl of Shrewsbury were among the biggest sheepowners in England. Not many nobles made efforts to till their own demesne, if we may accept the evidence of those many who, like the Earl of Rutland, preferred to lease their ground profitably rather than farm it themselves. To make up for the smaller domestic food supply, Rutland claimed much of his rents in kind, to such an extent that in 1611 he got all his oats and most of his wheat in the form of rent, and only his rye and barley from demesne; most of his cattle meat, on the other hand, came from domestic pasture.

In France it would be fair to assume that Henry IV's known enthusiasm for Olivier de Serres' *Théatre de l'Agriculture* (1600) was reflected in the attitudes of the provincial nobility, but the assumption is mistaken. Everywhere after the civil wars the higher nobility appear to have been unable to settle down to administer their estates. Gentlemen who had no capital beyond their lands, yet who needed some if they were to 'live nobly', found themselves obliged to run up debts. They alienated lands, or raised rents, in an effort to make ends meet; but seldom did they commit themselves to actual farming of the soil. The result was that here, as in Spain, the biggest landowning class absented itself from the land. In other countries where the economic and political position differed somewhat, nobles remained on the land. In Denmark, for example, where as late as 1625 only five per cent of all nobles held public office, eighty-five per cent still lived primarily off the revenue from land. But for them too the crisis was similar. By 1604 the royal council informed King Christian IV that 'an important section of the nobility already has enormous monetary debts'.

Nobles who were unable to exploit the land directly leased it out. The inflation of the sixteenth century made leases and rents a particularly vital issue. There were two main problems: the exploitation of existing rents, and the further leasing out or sale of demesne. As we have seen in the previous chapter, rents were increased by noble landlords in an attempt to keep pace with the price rise. On the Welsh estates of the Somerset family, rents doubled between 1549 and 1583. The sharpest rises appear to have come ofter this period, if we assume to be representative a sample taken by Professor Stone from the estates of seventeen families in different parts of England and Wales, which shows that rents doubled between about 1590 and 1640. Comparing this information with Figure 14 (p. 80), it seems that rents often kept pace with agricultural prices in the early seventeenth century, so that landlords who leased their properties could obtain a good profit. Unfortunately it is difficult to extend this generalisation to the whole of Europe, since conditions varied so widely.

What is certain is that the movement of rent is not by itself a reliable guide to the economic viability of the great estates, for while some rents could be and were raised, others that had been settled by feudal custom and by written agreement could not be raised so easily. A landlord who was burdened with too many customary tenants of this sort, tenants moreover who enjoyed very long leases, would find that the income he received was out of all proportion to the real value of the land. It was calculated in 1624, for instance, that the copyholder[1] tenants of the Earl of Southampton were paying him a total rent of £272, while the actual value of their tenancies was £2,372. A powerful lord could use threats to persuade tenants to exchange their copyholds for ordinary leases. But equally powerful forces could block such moves: the unquestionable legal right of tenants to hold to their customary rent, the danger of rebellion, the social pressures that demanded good relations between landlord and tenant. The method of exploiting existing rents was no less significant than the rise or fall in real value of the rents themselves. There seems to be little doubt in this respect that the English nobility, like their contemporaries in central and eastern Europe, were more assiduous landlords than those of France and Spain. Confusion still existed in estate accounts and other branches of management in England, but many noble houses found able stewards who put some order into manorial administration. In France and Spain, on the other hand, where the higher aristocracy were habitually absent from the land, stewards were notoriously incapable of running the estates or, perhaps more important, of producing enough revenue from the estate to pay for conspicuous expenditure at court.

The leasing out of demesne on new leases was always the most profitable alternative to revising customary dues. The trend was an old one, and meant that land directly exploited by the lord was in fact far less than the nominal extent of his estates. In general the nobility of western Europe were thus a *rentier* rather than a producing class. Being divorced from the soil they had little comprehension of the problems associated with it: the troubles of tenants, poor returns from rents and farming. Worst of all, as *rentiers* they treated their possessions as a source of supply, and seldom if ever did they actually put capital back into

1 Copyhold meant that a tenant held land by right of an entry in the manorial roll; the rent was specified in the roll entry.

163

the land. At most, leasing put off the evil day of reckoning. When that day came, the land would have to be sold (except, that is, where the laws of entail prohibited alienation).

The process was common enough at the time. What is important, however, is to establish whether so many gentlemen declined economically that it had a qualitative effect on the numbers and composition of the nobility. There may be no adequate answers to this problem. In England families such as the Cliffords and Stanleys among the nobility, in Spain the great houses of Enríquez and Osuna, were among the more prominent casualties; but names like these could be multiplied without any clear evidence that they represented a significant proportion of their class. In France and the Netherlands there was obvious shrinkage in numbers, but this was a natural consequence of the civil wars of the late sixteenth century. In the United Provinces the remnant of the nobility had shrunk to a small group who, according to Sir William Temple in 1673, protected their diminished numbers by refusing to marry below their rank. At the same time, they affected an exclusiveness which showed itself in the adoption of French dress, manners and speech. Such exclusiveness, as we know from the example of the Venetian nobles, led inevitably to shrinkage and decline.

Elsewhere the decline, if decline there was, consisted in a diminution of wealth. The French writer Jacques Hurault, in his *Discours* (1591) claimed that 'the Third Estate is the most numerous of the three, and would be the richest if taxed less. The nobility is the least in number, and the least wealthy of the three, but the prince only taxes it with military service.' The statement is misleading, since no members of the middle class could have compared in wealth with the great seigneurs, nor in fact were the nobles always free from obligations to the crown. By the 'nobility', moreover, we must understand a status rather than a title, since the term clearly covers all those rural gentry and younger sons who swelled the lower ranks of the aristocracy. Looked at in this way, it is easy to conceive of the nobility as being poor. In Denmark, of the five hundred or so noble landowners existing in 1625, about one-third held over three-fourths of all the landed property. With such a concentration of landed wealth, common to all aristocracies, it was inevitable that very many members of the class were poor. In 1591 the Danish historian Vedel deplored seeing gentlemen begging in the streets of Kiel. We have already observed Richelieu describing the French nobles of 1614 as 'poor in money but rich in honour'. So hard pressed were many of them that Louis XIII reminded his judges in a decree of 1639 'not to imprison them for debt, nor to sell their goods'.

The section of nobility that historians have usually represented as being worst off were the country gentry, and the evidence seems to support their picture. In Beauvais in the late seventeenth century, for instance, a good third of the noble families could be classified as poor, and it seems certain that several of them were even in receipt of surreptitious poor relief. The rise and rapid fall of one French family can be traced in the case of Nicolas de Brichanteau, seigneur of Beauvais-Nangis, captain of a troop of fifty men, who died in 1563. His son Antoine rose to prominence in the army, won royal favour and ended up as admiral of France and colonel of the guard. Excessive expenditure in this exalted position began his ruin. His son Nicolas tried to make his way at court but the family's debts caught up with him. In 1610 the estate of Nangis was covered with debts, accumulated at court, of up to four times its value. Nicolas was thereupon forced to retire to his estates in poverty.

The decay of sections of the Spanish aristocracy was a notable phenomenon. In the absence of civil wars of centralising absolutism, the problems of the Spanish nobles must be explained in purely financial terms. 'The grandees, *títulos* and individual gentlemen who own lands and other rents today', wrote a contemporary in 1660, 'are completely deprived of any revenue because of the decline of the population and of the number of farm labourers, and because prices have risen so disproportionately on account of the taxes that labourers command more than three times the wages that they used to.' Absentee landlordism seems to have played a major part in the growing gap between expenditure at court and income from estates. 'Many of the Castilian *títulos*', reported a Jesuit in 1640, 'have excused themselves from court because of the great want in their finances, and His Majesty has ordered them to go to their estates and not to leave without his express command, since he wishes them to save up so as to serve him in some other occasion.' The suggested remedy is as revealing as the plight, since both king and nobles appear to have considered estates not as territory to be developed but as wealth to be exploited. A great part of this wealth went on ostentation as befitted one's rank, with the result that in Spain too there grew up a large corpus of sumptuary laws.

Attempting on one hand to meet all the demands made on them for life at court and for duties connected with the royal service, and on the other hand attempting to keep pace with the catastrophic inflation, the Spanish nobility went cap in hand to the moneylenders. The names of the greatest lords of Castile — the dukes of Alburquerque and Osuna, the counts of Benavente and Lemos, the marquises of Santa Cruz and Aguilar — figure among the list of debtors to the bourgeoisie of Valladolid. The reasons for which they borrowed are interesting. Alburquerque borrowed in 1597 to pay the costs of a court case, Aguilar borrowed in the same year to pay a tax to the king, Benavente borrowed in 1581 (the large sum of forty-five thousand ducats) to pay his daughter's dowry. It was in part the financial straits of a century of growing disaster that made the nobility of Castile refuse in 1639 to contribute towards the costs of Olivares' campaign against France. When they likewise refused to serve in person in the war, Philip IV in January 1640 denounced their lack of cooperation and pointed out (what was of course untrue) 'how much the opposite holds true in France'.

The feudal nobility of Naples also suffered like their peers elsewhere. Their sales of land were an appropriate comment on their debts. The Prince of Bisignano, who possessed sixty-five estates in Calabria and other regions, was so overwhelmed by debts that by 1636 all his holdings were sold up. Of twenty-five estates held by the princes of Molfetta in 1551, fifteen were sold by the early seventeenth century. The family of the marquises of Acaya alienated six of the ten fiefs they held in the terra d'Otranto. Even jurisdictions over towns were the object of private transactions. Between 1610 and 1640 alone, in eight of the twelve provinces of the kingdom of Naples at least two hundred and fifteen communities were alienated, by families with names as distinguished as Carrafa, Pignatelli and Orsini.

The changing fortunes of the higher and lower nobility are in themselves, as we shall see, not adequate proof of a decline of their class. The phenomenon of vast debts was common in England, for instance, but most debtors seem to have overcome this either through royal favour or through good fortune. Some attempted to meet their debts by selling lands. The fourth Earl of Huntingdon, who had debts in 1596 of about £18,000, sold up about £20,000 worth of his lands in the years 1591-1600. One of the bigger debtors in England was the ill-fated Earl of Essex, who had debts in 1601 of about £25,000, and had sold lands worth over £40,000 in the previous decade. The Earl of Arundel was one whose debts exceeded £100,000. Ruin was not, however, always the wages of debt. When property was mortgaged and lands sold in an attempt to build up credit some sort of delay had been introduced into the otherwise inevitable ruin of a house.

These observations indicate beyond doubt that many noble families, some of them the greatest in the land, decayed and fell on hard times through financial troubles. 'How many noble families have there been whose memory is utterly abolished!' wrote an Englishman in 1603. 'How many flourishing houses have we seen which oblivion hath now obfuscated!' If so many aristocrats passed from the scene, what happened to their wealth? In so far as the principal item of wealth passing out of noble hands was land, it was generally the bourgeoisie who benefited. In Naples the space left vacant by the old aristocracy was filled by Genoese, Tuscan and Venetian merchants, and by Neapolitan bourgeois and office holders. In Spain the creditors of the nobility were bourgeois and government officials. A Norman noble expressed his hatred of the urban bourgeoisie in 1656 by claiming that:

> Three things have ruined the nobility: facility in finding money, luxury, and war. In peace they are consumed by luxury; in war, since they have no money in reserve, the most comfortable gentleman can go only by mortgaging his field and his mill. So true is this that it can be proved that since 1492, when money became more common, men from the towns have acquired more than six million gold *livres* of revenues from noble lands owned by gentlemen rendering service in war according to the nature and quality of their fiefs . . . Men from the towns lend money (and as a result) all the proprietors are chased from the countryside.

But in some parts of Europe it was another group that seems to have profited, a group which had its lower ranks in the bourgeoisie and its upper ranks in the nobility. For convenience this group will be referred to as the gentry. The rise of the gentry at the expense of the old aristocracy is a thesis much debated among Anglo-Saxon historians. Some of the insularity of the debate can be removed if we consider the rise as a European and not merely an English phenomenon. It will also remove ambiguities if we make it plain that for the most part the gentry is being treated here as part of the noble class, so that what we are discussing is not the transference of property and wealth from one class to another so much as the transfer of property and hence the

167

shifting of equilibrium within the same class.

The English gentry were not for the most part men of a bourgeois cast of mind. 'I scorn base getting and unworthy penurious saving', wrote one of them, Sir John Oglander, in 1647, thereby disavowing two of the main hallmarks of the bourgeois. As Professor Trevor-Roper has pointed out, 'it was an aristocratic age, and the gentry accepted — in general — the standards of value and conduct of the aristocracy'. Their fortunes followed much the same lines as those of the higher aristocracy. Some of them fell on hard times, were unable to meet their debts, sold their property; others prospered from the mistakes of others, invested in land or business at a time when the returns were promising, and founded great fortunes. In the late sixteenth and early seventeenth centuries the English gentry as a whole increased in numbers and in wealth, due principally to the great turnover of land in the property market. How this worked may be illustrated by the sales of land made by Lord Henry Berkeley between 1561 and 1613. Of a total sales value of about £42,000, over £39,000 in land was sold to thirteen members of the higher gentry, the balance being purchased by twenty-five other persons of unspecified rank. Building their fortunes in this way, by purchase of property, many new families made their way up the social ladder. In Wiltshire between 1565 and 1602 no less than one hundred and nine new gentry names had been added to the original total of two hundred and three. This swelling in their numbers and wealth gave the gentry a new significance in the eyes of contemporaries. The political theorist James Harrington went so far as to claim in his *Oceana* (1656) that the gentry had become the richest estate in the realm. To use his own words, 'in our days, the clergy being destroyed, the lands in possession of the people overbalance those held by the nobility, at least nine in ten'. Another contemporary claimed in 1600 that the richer gentry had the incomes of an earl, and it was said in 1628 that the House of Commons could buy the House of Lords three times over. Like many contemporary claims, these statements have little proof to support them. It is true that the number of gentry increased, and most likely, as a group they held more wealth in their hands by 1660 than a century previously. But it still remains to be demonstrated conclusively that economic power had passed from the aristocracy to the gentry, and that the civil war of 1642 was a struggle over the transference of the political power that corresponded to this wealth.

The emergence of the gentry cannot in any case be measured merely in terms of wealth, for there were still few of them who could compete with the great aristocratic landlords, and even the sales of royalist lands during the republican period did not create a new much-landed gentry class. If their significance is to be gauged, it must be in terms of a steady accumulation of power in the countryside (rather than at court, where few gentry prospered), based largely on land, it is true, but precipitated by the events of the 1640s and by the devolution of authority, in those years of crisis and beyond 1688, upon the one class which had maintained its hold on the people of England.

Elsewhere in Europe the gentry made far more obvious inroads into the position of the old magnates. This was the case particularly in Russia and Poland. The rise of the Russian gentry is associated above all with the struggle of the boyars and magnates against the absolutism of Ivan IV (the Terrible). Ivan's attempt in the years 1564 to 1572 to crush the aristocratic opposition ruthlessly by confiscating their lands and destroying their persons, was from the political point of view a complete success. Ivan's two principal demands were for a reliable military force and for adequate revenue for the crown. He obtained both these by introducing the basic features of the 'service state', in which, as one historian phrases it, 'whatever privileges or freedoms a subject might enjoy were his only because the state allowed them to him as a perquisite of the function he performed in its service'. In 1556, for instance, the tsar decreed that each landlord was to supply a fully equipped horse-soldier for a certain number of units of land; alternatively, this service could be commuted into a money payment. This was clearly to introduce feudal principles that were falling into disuse in western Europe. Ivan, however, went further. He arbitrarily divided his kingdom up into a vast demesne territory controlled by a court called an *oprichnina*, comprising half of Muscovy and particularly the area around Moscow; and a territory in which boyar landownership was conceded, the *zemshchina*. Within the *oprichnina* area boyar power was abolished, estates destroyed and opponents executed. To enable this revolution to succeed, Ivan gathered to him the gentry class, the *dvoryanstvo*, who were liberally rewarded out of the lands confiscated from the boyars. Writing to the tsar in 1573 of the excesses committed by the *oprichniki*, the executors of Ivan's policies in the *oprichnina*, the opposition boyar prince Kurbsky denounced 'the laying waste of your land, both by you yourself and by your children of darkness (the *oprichniki*)'. 'Who will decorate the graves and gild the tombs of those countless martyrs killed by you and your children of darkness?' Even the Fugger newsletters reported in 1572 from Moscow that 'the Muscovite himself ravages and despoils his own land and nation'. Kurbsky's rhetoric mirrored the very great immediate evils brought about by the *oprichnina;* political and social discontent was widespread, agriculture was ruined, depopulation was commonplace (between 1566 and 1574, for instance, the town of Murom lost four hundred and seventy-six of its five hundred and eighty-seven homesteads), and the military defences of Muscovy were shattered.

On the ruins of this old order, the gentry rose into prominence as the new noble class. The process which received so great an impetus from Ivan the Terrible was continued into the early seventeenth century under the Romanovs. In 1566 Ivan had summoned an assembly called the Zemsky Sobor, consisting mainly of gentry in the service of the crown, to serve as a counterbalance to the boyar assembly. The gentry were also granted estates, but on new terms of tenure; for whereas the old magnates had held their lands freely, as *votchina,* the new landowners held it on terms of service, as *pomestye.* The gentry landowners were known correspondingly as *pomeshchiki,* and it was through them that the Russian state was governed under the Romanovs.

As the Russian gentry established their predominance through the land, so too the Polish gentry, the *szlachta,* became the noble class of Poland by extending their control over the soil and over agricultural production. In the early fifteenth century the noble estate was composed on the one hand of the great magnates with vast demesnes — families such as the Ostorogs, the Leszcynskis and the Radziwills — and on the other of the numerous company of knights and gentry. The latter increased their political power primarily by acting as a body to secure constitutional guarantees of their rights and status, and by establishing their authority at a local level through county committees or *sejms.* By the late fifteenth century the local *sejms* had given rise to a national Sejm or parliament composed of three orders: the king, a senate (consisting of bishops and senior nobles in the administration), and a chamber of deputies (consisting almost entirely of *szlachta*). The constitution of this parliament was officially confirmed by the king in 1505, when he promised not to act on any important issue without its consent. Numerically superior in the Sejm, the gentry

170

inevitably came to dominate its councils and used it to promulgate legislation that served their own interests. By the late sixteenth century, despite the continuing influence of the great magnates, it was the *szlachta* who represented the nobility of Poland.

Like the gentry elsewhere, the *szlachta* were not an economically homogeneous group. Throughout the Polish territories (essentially, Poland and the Grand Duchy of Lithuania) the noble class made up somewhat less than ten per cent of the population. But over half of this number were very minor gentry indeed, enjoying noble rights and status, but possessing little more land than an ordinary peasant. Despite this, it was the land that was the basis of *szlachta* power, and to defend their interests they took care to limit the powers both of the clergy and of the townships. Clerical posts were infiltrated by gentry, and the Church was deprived in 1562 of its disciplinary powers over heresy. In 1565 the Sejm restricted the activities of the merchant class. In this way the so-called 'republic of nobles' came into being, where all gentry, of high and low degree, shared equally in the government of Poland.

In other lands of central and eastern Europe it is also possible to talk of a rise of the gentry, associated with a change in the exploitation of the soil. Perhaps the most outstanding example is East Prussia, where the new nobles, the Junkers, made their appearance in the fifteenth century from the knights, soldiers and adventurers of the German frontier. The process of recruitment of this new landed estate, which must be looked upon essentially as a squirearchy or gentry, since it possessed little of the elitist ethic of the nobility of western Europe, continued throughout the sixteenth and early seventeenth centuries. The contrast between the landed nobility of the east and the leisured classes of the west was a profound one, and justifies us looking at the eastern aristocracy in more detail later.

THE POLITICAL CRISIS OF THE ARISTOCRACY

The fluctuation in wealth of sections of the noble class was only one component of the crisis they were undergoing. Even where large numbers of the old peerage had declined in fortune, there was no sign that the class as a whole had decayed. This indeed was one of the paradoxes of the time, for lords and ladies continued to live in splendour while the fundamental presuppositions of their function were being questioned. As the Venetian ambassador remarked in 1622 of the English aristocracy, who can stand here as an example of others: 'the magnates are mostly hated for their vain ostentation, better suited to their ancient power than their present condition'. The implication is plain, that it was power no less than wealth that had passed out of the hands of the nobility.

The principal reason for this was the increase in the strength of the crown. Nowhere in western Europe was the increase quite as spectacular as that of Russian despotism, but the trend in favour of an administratively centralised state was irresistible. The aristocracy everywhere was affected in three main ways: by the reduction of military power, by exclusion from high government office and by a general restriction of privileges. The last of these points refers simply to such matters as duelling, the sumptuary laws, liability to prosecution by the royal courts, and other similar innovations which curtailed the independence of nobles.

It would be an error to assume that rulers and governments favouring absolute monarchy were hostile to the interests of the aristocracy. On the contrary, they were passionately devoted to the noble class as the natural and traditional rulers of the people, and the only foundation of the state. The well-quoted lines of Shakespeare

> Take but degree away, untune that string,
> And, hark, what discord follows

rang too true in the ears of the authorities for them to conceive in any way of removing rank and degree, of undermining the position of the hereditary lords of the land. If the absolute rulers attacked their nobles it was not in order to destroy them; and if they did happen to destroy them they were quick to raise up new blood to replace them. They did not object to the personnel or wealth of the aristocracy, but to their incapacity as a governing class, 'their contempt of the various branches of knowledge and the little trouble they take to fit themselves for various posts', as Henry IV's prime minister, the Duke of Sully, put it. It was never the purpose of absolute monarchy to supersede the nobles in posts of influence, or to resort to bourgeois ministers; the whole mentality of absolutism was too anti-democratic, too essentially aristocratic for that. As the state grew in power, therefore, it found itself in an increasingly illogical position; for on the one hand it relied upon and fostered the hereditary ruling class, and on the other it was obliged to look outside the ranks of that class for the necessary cooperation in setting up a strong administration. This created an internal contradiction within absolutism, one that would be resolved by radical, even violent, methods in the course of the seventeenth century.

The first and greatest danger facing the monarchies was the armed might of the nobles. Ivan the Terrible solved his problem in a particularly brutal fashion. In western Europe, where the feudal principle had been strongest, the reduction of military powers was to be a long and difficult process. In Spain the Catholic monarchs had so far succeeded in their pacification that the armies raised by the *Comuneros* in 1520 (under Charles V) were the last to be sent against the crown within Spain until the end of the *ancien régime*. The martial spirit of Spain was spent instead on foreign fields, in Europe or America. The rapid degeneration of Spanish valour in the course of the sixteenth century is shown most markedly by the inability to win back Portugal, and by the failure of Spanish grandees to respond to the needs of their country. Outside Spain, much aristocratic revolt was governed by religion: thus the rebellion of the northern earls in England in 1569 and the Huguenot revolt in France in the 1620s, although modified greatly by regional sympathies, took their origin in religion. The last attempt at a non-religious rising in England before the civil war was that of the Earl of Essex in 1601. In France the feudal principle took much longer to subdue, its last great appearance being in the aristocratic Fronde of 1649-53.

Only in the case of England has any attempt been made to examine the decline in the military strength of the nobles. There, as Sir Walter Ralegh observed at the beginning of the seventeenth century, 'the force by which our kings in former times were troubled is vanished away'. It had vanished because of the crown's own efforts in statutes and by direct action to restrict the amount of retainers kept by the peers; but also because the nobles themselves were no longer able to afford private armies, and because — as in Spain — the nobles were ceasing to have any personal experience of war (while three-quarters of the titled peerage of England had been in service before mid-century, by 1576 only one in four had had military experience). In France, where feudal habits persisted longer than in England, private armies were fairly commonplace even in the 1650s; and thanks to a century of almost continuous war both within and without the country the opportunity for service was never lacking. With 1653, however, and the defeat of Condé, the last feudal revolt of the *ancien régime* came to an end.

The armed rebellions of the nobility arose in part from their exclusion from government, and cannot be looked at in isolation from that factor. In mediaeval times it had been the right of the magnates to give advice to the king, usually through the council. It had also been their duty to occupy the chief defensive and administrative posts in the provinces. In the late fifteenth century, and still more after the Reformation era, rulers withdrew their confidence from unreliable or dissentient nobles, and remodelled their administration with the help of lesser men whom they could trust and who did not rely on any great lord for preferment. It has been habitual to refer to many of these men as commoners, and some of them were indeed of undistinguished origin. But in less than a lifetime they had without exception established themselves as gentlemen of influence and position. By the late sixteenth century there were no real 'commoners' in the offices of the great monarchies. Secretaries of state like Walsingham and Antonio Pérez were gentry of the first order. This was to be the pattern also for the seventeenth century, where no senior administrators of humble origin remained humble. Historians who see in the employment of a non-noble secretary something as significant as an alliance between absolute monarchy and the middle classes, are clearly indulging their fancies. It is true that the hereditary magnates felt offended at the employment of such people, but that was the logic of the whole situation: to govern independently of noble factions the ruler had to look outside their ranks.

The absence of revolt in Spain is explained by the complete hold which the nobles maintained over all aspects of administration, making this an example of a state where 'absolutism' operated with the aid of the aristocracy. The councils of state were staffed by noblemen, noble families dominated the countryside and the municipalities. Olivares was the first great minister to be wary of noble power. He informed Philip IV on one occasion that 'I regard it as inexpedient to give them great offices in justice and finance'; and it was under his regime that relations between crown and nobles were the most strained. 'If the basis of nobility is not to pay taxes,' complained one noble, 'in this era, because of the immense flood of requests for donations, the lustre of the privilege has been extinguished.' There was some justice in the complaint, since even if the nobles were exempt from taxation they often paid handsomely through the free gifts the government demanded at every emergency. But the fact remains that Olivares failed in all his major enterprises, and the sway of the aristocracy was undiminished. A census of New Castile made for Philip II in 1597 showed that the lords controlled nearly forty per cent of the towns and thirty-four per cent of the population at that date. In Old Castile by the eighteenth century forty-seven per cent of the population was living under seigneurial jurisdiction, in the province of Salamanca as much as sixty per cent. Great nobles such as the Constable of Castile and the Duke of Infantado were seigneurs in over 500 towns each. The most important cities of the realm, among them Seville and Toledo, were controlled entirely by aristocratic oligarchies. If some nobles declined, then, the power of their class did not.

The Tudor monarchy in England (1485-1603) introduced administrative changes that completely altered the balance of power in the realm. The extensive authority assumed by the royal council in London and in the provinces (in the north and in Wales, for instance), was wielded by nobles and prelates who had adopted the cause of the crown. But the men on whom the real task of administration fell more and more were the gentry, the class from whom sheriffs and justices of the peace tended to be chosen. The gentry were, in addition, the group that formed the bulk of the membership of the House of Commons, whose constitutional importance grew enormously in the late sixteenth century. Cut off for the most part from participation in local and central government, a task for which they never had much taste anyway, the aristocracy depended for advancement on the great offices of state that lay within the gift of the king — lord-lieutenantcies of counties, posts and sinecures in the royal household and in the military and diplomatic services. The traditional loyalty and deference to peers in their country seats still continued to a very great extent, but even this link was dissolving as feudal tenures disappeared and tenants became less dependent on their lords. Inevitably, then, the peers gravitated towards the court, and it remained for the crown to decide among which groups favours should be divided. Official policy welcomed the opportunity to have nobles serve usefully under the crown. 'Gratify your nobility', Burghley advised Elizabeth in 1579, 'and the principal persons of your realm, to bind them fast to you'.

The difficulty was that there were too few available offices and too many aspirants. In the struggle for places, the aristocracy found themselves hard pressed by the rising gentry. It was said, for instance, that there were three to four hundred candidates for the top twenty posts in the new household of young Prince Charles in 1638. With competition of this magnitude at all levels of the court administration, the number of those disappointed is likely to have been very large. Office, whether in England or on the continent, offered position (often inheritable), influence and income. To those nobility and gentry who had mortgaged their future through extravagance, deprivation of office meant disaster.

The efforts of the French monarchy to tame its nobles are associated principally with the policy of Richelieu, but there can be no doubt that the efforts of Catherine de Medici as well as of Henry IV and of d'Ancre were directed to the same end, which was an obvious one in view of the constant militancy of the magnates, particularly the Protestant ones. Effective measures against them began only with Richelieu, who perforce adopted a policy of selective victimisation, since he could not nor wished to act against them as a class. Court plots against the cardinal, which had repercussions in the provinces, were repressed and their leaders executed: the Count of Chalais in 1626, the Duke of Montmorency in 1632, the Marquis of Cinq-Mars in 1642. The great military commands were likewise taken away from the grandees and suppressed: the office of admiral of France was abolished in 1627, together with that of constable of France. Governorships of strategically sensitive provinces were taken away from great nobles like Vendôme (Brittany), Guise (Provence) and Soissons (Champagne), and given to those who were more reliable, or else to lieutenants-general subordinate to the crown.

Measures like these were to some extent effective, but touched only the very great. How the mass of the nobles reacted to the general direction of policy may be seen more closely through, for example, the *cahiers* drawn up by the country gentry and nobility of Angoumois for an Estates General projected for 1649 by the French government but never summoned. Some of the key complaints in these *cahiers* concern the inability of the aristocracy to maintain their rightful authority in, for instance, seigneurial jurisdictions, on which royal judges had been encroaching. Their administrative control in the provinces had, moreover, been threatened by the intendants, wherefore the crown was 'very humbly requested not to reestablish them'. Gravest of all, they felt, was

> the notable prejudice suffered by the nobility from the sale of offices, both in the royal household and in the army as well as in judicial posts, into which entry is almost impossible because of the excessive price, so that it grieves them to be deprived of posts they formerly possessed, and to see them at present fall into the hands of people of no birth, merit or capacity.

Though an Estates General did not meet, in 1651 the nobles held an assembly of their own, in which the crown was bitterly criticised not only for the destruction of the noble right to a monopoly of offices of state, but also for the burden of taxation falling on them. 'The nobles', they claimed, 'are subjected to all kinds of *tailles* and taxes, and their lands diminish in value as often as *tailles* are paid.' On these and several other grounds, they felt they had genuine grievances against the state.

While there was some justice in complaints like these, it should be emphasised that only a proportion of the nobles may have suffered unduly. Many nobles continued to occupy important posts in the administration, benefited financially from public office and court favour, and gave a decidedly aristocratic flavour to government. If nobles became impoverished, the government was not always to blame; nor could the court adequately reward the hundreds of office-seekers from their ranks.

The problem of the alienation of the nobility from government was, as we have already observed, an inherent contradiction of absolutism, and the heart of the political crisis of the aristocracy. While wishing to gratify the nobles, the crown was unwilling to grant them real power. One of the ways adopted to circumvent this problem was to grant personal honours in great numbers, either free or for cash. The result was an enormous inflation in the size of the aristocracy which, at the very moment of its greatest difficulties, found itself multiplied by the intake of hundreds of newcomers.

The Spanish monarchy was the ideal setting for this sort of growth. The titled aristocracy multiplied in numbers in the early seventeenth century. Where there had been only one hundred and twenty-four titled nobles in 1597 by 1631 there were two hundred and forty-one, and under Philip IV alone nearly one hundred new titles were created. The growth in distribution of honours can also be illustrated strikingly by looking at the sharp increase in membership of the orders of chivalry. The motives behind royal policy were explained concisely by Philip IV in 1625: 'Without reward and punishment no monarchy can be preserved. Now rewards may be either financial or honorific. We have no money, so we have thought it right and necessary to remedy the fault by increasing the number of honours'. The increase was startling. In the twenty-five years from 1551 to 1575 no more than 354 new members of the Order of Santiago had been created; from 1621 to 1645, the total shot up to 2,288. In Spanish-ruled Naples an equally notable increase occurred. There the number of titled barons increased by over three hundred per cent between 1590 (when the total number was one hundred and eighteen) and 1669.

In England James I accelerated the process, many of the honours he created being given away and not sold. Before his accession in March 1603 England had about five hundred knights. In the first four months of his reign he dubbed no fewer than nine hundred and six new knights, and by December 1604 the total of new knights alone had risen to one thousand one hundred and sixty-one. The increases in the ranks of the titled aristocracy were by their nature even more startling. In the thirteen years 1615-28 James and his son Charles I increased the numbers of the English peerage from eighty-one to one hundred and twenty-six, the rise being greatest among the earls, who rose from twenty-seven to sixty-five. These increases, of fifty-six and one hundred and forty-one per cent respectively, have been called 'one of the most radical transformations of the English titular aristocracy that has ever occurred'. This suggests a unique phenomenon, however, and it should be remembered that some other European countries suffered an even more remarkable increase. In Sweden Queen Christina within the space of ten years doubled the number of noble families and sextupled the number of counts and barons. In Spain Charles II, who came to the throne in 1665, created in the thirty-five years of his reign as many new honours for the aristocracy as all his Habsburg predecessors had done in the two preceding centuries.

The inflation of honours did not necessarily placate or gratify the already discontented peerage. Hereditary nobles became even more resentful of newcomers. 'It may be doubted,' wrote an Englishman of the next generation, Sir Edward Walker, 'whether the dispensing of honours with so liberal a hand was not one of the beginnings of general discontents, expecially among persons

178

of great extraction.' The fact is that most of the new creations conferred status but not power. Commoners were ennobled but neither the new nor the old nobility was given office or income, and both crown and aristocracy suffered in prestige.

The remarkable resilience of the noble class in the face of economic decline and political and military decay is to some extent illusory. Left to themselves the nobility may well have been overcome by the crisis. But their most powerful ally, precisely the one responsible for many of their difficulties, was the crown. And though the crown was always devoted to the social and political preponderance of the class, in one particular respect it guaranteed the continuing existence of that class: through the entail. This was one factor above all others that seems to have saved the aristocracy. The case of Denmark is illustrative. By 1660 the total debts of the Danish nobility are estimated to have amounted to one-third of the value of all noble land. In many other countries this would have led to wholesale alienation of the land. But the system of privileges which the crown had granted to the nobles in the mid-sixteenth century meant that noble land seldom moved outside the class, and if it was sold it merely went to another nobleman. Though the Danish case does not refer to the entail as such, it illustrates a system of privileges which was very similar. It was in Spain that the entail or *mayorazgo* achieved what may be termed its greatest success. Heads of great houses and all their dependents periodically pleaded poverty, a comprehensible situation when the laws of the entail would not allow them to alienate family property; but it was thanks to this that the houses lived on even though some members died in near penury. Spanish noble entails were hedged around with many privileges, not the least of which was that debts could be contracted on the entail even though the property itself could never be alienated.

Entail and primogeniture were the two principal ways of preserving the integrity of noble property. Primogeniture had been practised in England since the Middle Ages; entails became common there only in the seventeenth century. In Spain entails had been common in the fifteenth century and they were specifically allowed by the Laws of Toro in 1505. In France and Germany entails were common by the seventeenth century, in Italy they were widely practised in the sixteenth. One drawback of the entail was that by disallowing the alienation of estates it depressed the land market at a time when land was in regular demand. For this reason primogeniture might sometimes be preferable. The rulers of Piedmont, for example, attempted (in 1598) to limit the period of entail, and in 1648 Charles Emmanuel II issued an edict encouraging the practice of primogeniture, 'since it so concerns us to maintain and develop the splendour of the nobility'.

Thanks to the paternal care of their kings the European aristocracy surmounted many of their problems. Their estates were protected by law, their pockets were often flattered by pensions, they were exempted from most taxation, their persons were often granted immunity from criminal proceedings. But it was in the difficult years of the mid-century that the contradictions in their position became once more apparent, and led to a turning-point which may properly be called their moment of gravest crisis.

5 THE
EUROPEAN BOURGEOISIE

Another kind of person has risen among us, born to bring about the
ruin of others . . . The *rentiers,* ignorant and unlettered individuals
who amass great wealth without trouble, without labour and without
risk: great do-nothings who commerce only with notaries in order to
receive back-payments. It is they who have chased the two pillars of
the state, the gentry and the peasantry, from their ancient holdings.

Memoir by a Norman noble (*ca* 1656)

The number of office-holders that we have shames the state and
brings its administration into contempt.

NOEL DU FAIL (1576)

For the French jurist Charles Loyseau, author of the *Traité des
Ordres* (1613), a *bourgeois* was simply the inhabitant of a town or
bourg. When discussing the middle classes, he preferred to talk
of them as the Third Estate, a group that included such worthies
as men of letters, financial officials, lawyers and merchants. But
even by the early seventeenth century it was already becoming
common among some French writers to use the word more in a
class than in a residential sense, and to be termed 'bourgeois de
Paris', for instance, meant something very substantial in terms of
social values by the mid-century. This later use of the word
became common in the English language, where a burgher or
burgess was a citizen, even an official, rather than simply a
resident. Yet despite the different functions of the words
bourgeois and *bourgeoisie, bürger* and *bürgertum,* one undeniably common factor stood out: for all practical purposes the
middle class of people were townspeople, and the towns were the
principal environment of the bourgeoisie.

It was from the social and economic life of the towns that the
bourgeoisie drew their fortunes. Like the nobility, they were not a
homogeneous class. At the lowest level they consisted of petty
traders, minor officials, prosperous craftsmen and others who
tended to have independent means and were not in the employ of

another. At a higher level they were made up of bureaucrats, lawyers and others in the public service. At this level, too, the bourgeoisie were the capitalist class, makers of fortunes in wholesale trade, long-distance commerce, and moneylending. From this it is clear that the bourgeoisie were conceived to be sandwiched between two other classes, those at the bottom who had to toil for their living, and those who lived off unearned income at the top. These three categories cannot be taken literally, however, since there were an infinite number of levels leading from one category to the next.

Since the bourgeoisie had a clear function to carry out in the life of the towns, it is obvious that they must have existed wherever urban growth could be found. In this sense, there had always been a middle class. The difficulty is that when some historians refer to the 'bourgeoisie' they tend to refer in particular to its historic function as the entrepreneurial class, and of course an entrepreneurial bourgeoisie did not exist everywhere and was often of very recent standing. For simplicity of expression, however, the word 'bourgeoisie' will be used here rather than the equally valid term 'middle classes'.

Though we have defined the bourgeoisie as townspeople, they were not a stagnant urban class, and were constantly being recruited from the ranks below them. Some rose from the small shop, some from the plough. A surprisingly large number of small farmers set their hearts on giving their children a better start in life than they had had. This was the pattern in upper Poitou in the sixteenth century, where rich peasants put their sons through university, managed to buy a minor office for them, and so began their rise into the bourgeoisie. This might take generations. In Burgundy we have the example of the Ramillon family which in 1515 was still practising agriculture in the town of Charlay. By the seventeenth century some members of the family had moved to Varzy: there they took up small-trading, as a butcher or a baker. By 1671 Etienne Ramillon had become a merchant draper. In 1712 a grandson of his became an *avocat* to the parlement.

The movement from the small shop was likewise slow but certain. Loyseau observed confidently in his *Traité* that 'the merchants are the lowest of the people enjoying an honourable status, and are described as *honorables hommes* or *honnêtes personnes* and *bourgeois des villes,* titles not given to farmers or artisans and even less to labourers, who are all regarded as common people'. But a generation later in Paris notarial documents could be found describing even artisans by all these epithets. Since the descriptions were wholly unofficial, they were adopted with impunity by those who felt they had a right to them. In a society that was incredibly jealous of title and precedence, the successful arrogation of an honorific title was a sure sign of having achieved bourgeois status. 'Before this century', wrote a French observer in 1650, 'it was unknown for wives of secretaries, lawyers, notaries and traders to call themselves *Madame*'. The new development was a sign of mobility among sections of the lower middle class anxious to find their place in the sun.

THE ECONOMIC LIFE OF THE BOURGEOISIE

The fortunes they accumulated gave the bourgeoisie a power in terms of money that their numbers alone did not warrant. The numerical strength of the middle class at any one moment is difficult to define, if only because of the divisions within the group and because of the impossibility of finding a 'class' with clearly defined attributes. Where figures are available, they tend to describe a town oligarchy rather than an economic class, an oligarchy however that included the top merchants, office holders and clergy, so that at least the hard core of the bourgeoisie can be counted. In Venice in the late sixteenth century, for example, the *cittadini* were six per cent of the city's population. In Norwich in the early sixteenth century the upper middle class numbered about six per cent of the population and owned about sixty per cent of the lands and goods for which taxes were paid to the city. A further fourteen per cent could be included as coming within the definition of 'middle class', but these were somewhat poorer. If we adopt the holding of property as a sign of status, and make deductions from urban tax assessments, the propertied middle class emerge as a fairly small group. In sixteenth-century Coventry, forty-five per cent of the property seems to have been owned by only two per cent of the people. These few rich were indubitably middle class. It was the Coventry grocer Richard Marler, for instance, who paid about one-ninth of the town's subsidy contributions. In late seventeenth-century Beauvais there were three hundred or so, out of a total of three thousand two hundred and fifty tax-paying families, that could be considered as the upper bourgeoisie, and even within this group there was a small elite of about one hundred families. It is only for this sort of elite that adequate data is available, usually in the form of figures for those holding burgher or citizen rights and described as enjoying patrician privileges.

Most of the bourgeoisie achieved their status through one of two principal channels: trade or office. Through these means came the capital which led eventually to the purchase of land. By itself the term 'trade' is taken here to cover not only commerce but also industry and finance, each of which was a powerful stimulus to the concentration of fortunes in the hands of a small and privileged group of entrepreneurs. The seaports, industrial centres and market-towns of Europe were the obvious homes of the rising bourgeoisie, and it is consequently in towns like Amsterdam, Liège and Medina del Campo that we can best find the representatives of the new wealth.

We have already glanced at the part of Antwerp and Amsterdam in the expansion of capitalism. The growth of Amsterdam in the early seventeenth century was particularly remarkable, and we have had Sir William Temple's testimony that much of this derived from the bourgeois ethic of the Hollanders: 'their common Riches lye in every Man's having more than he spends; or, to say it properly, in every Man's spending less than he has coming in, be that what it will'. As a result of the international trading and financial concerns of Dutch merchants, and of the new opportunities opened up by the overseas empire, the commercial classes of Amsterdam became more exclusive in structure as they became more wealthy. Part of this exclusiveness came through marriage, since business fortunes tended to be consolidated by intermarriage between the great houses, and companies consequently became almost purely family concerns. But the exclusiveness also came through the monopoly which the merchant-burghers exercised over the social and political life of the city of Amsterdam. The priorities of the bourgeoisie began to alter. In 1615 a burgomaster of Amsterdam reported that the administrative elite, the regents, were either active or recently retired merchants. By 1652 the traders were complaining that the regents no longer got their money from an active commitment to trade, 'but derived their income from houses, lands and money at interest'. This was clearly an exaggeration, since the regents often still had close links, through marriage or investment, with commerce. But the trend was unmistakable. Trade had in many instances ceased to be the principal pursuit of the too-successful bourgeois.

In the principality of Liège, the majority of the bourgeoisie in the years 1577-8 drew their incomes from trade and finance. As was the rule everywhere in Europe at this time, industry was the smallest of enterprises. It was foreigners who came in to help develop what became one of the most important armament centres in Europe. From 1565 to 1607, four out of every five new admissions to the bourgeoisie of Liège were foreign. By 1595 it was a foreigner named Jean Curtius (from Den Bosch) who had the biggest single income in Liège, and it came from munitions. Together with Jacques le Roy of Antwerp, Curtius had a monopoly of arms manufactures in the principality. During his most active period of capital accumulation, in 1595-1603, Curtius invested in precisely the same interests that attracted the merchants of Amsterdam: land and rents. This was a tendency shared by the bourgeoisie of Liège, for nearly half the total amount of money invested in state loans (*rentes*) in 1595 came from members of this class.

It was only after one had made money from trade that one could become a financier. Simon Ruiz of Medina del Campo was the most distinguished of the very small group of Spaniards who, in the late sixteenth century, extended their operations from the textile trade to the lending of money. By 1576 he was lending money to Philip II and had begun to participate in the complex network of international exchanges through which the king managed to pay his troops in Antwerp and elsewhere. Thanks to the profit he made from these financial activities, Ruiz accumulated a considerable fortune. But the money was not kept in typically bourgeois channels. On the contrary, the next generation of his family dissipated the wealth and preferred to abandon the insecurities of the money-market for the more desirable honours of noble status.

Bourgeois who had made their money in trade formed only the first generation of wealth, and had their feet on only the first rung of the social ladder. Where they went from there depended on the society and country in which they lived. It was here that the differences between nations such as Holland and Italy or France became apparent. In a well-known passage, Jacques Savary summed up his view of the differences between the French and the Dutch:

From the moment that a merchant in France has acquired great wealth in trade, his children, far from following him in this profession, on the contrary enter public office . . . whereas in Holland the children of merchants ordinarily follow the profession

185

and the trade of their fathers, ally themselves with other merchant families, and give such considerable sums to their children when they marry that one of these will have greater wealth when he begins trading on his own, than the richest merchant of France will have when he stops trading to establish his family in other professions. Therefore since money is not withdrawn from trade but continues in it constantly from father to son, and from family to family as a result of the alliances which merchants make with one another, individual Dutch merchants can more easily undertake the Northern and Muscovy trades than individual French merchants can undertake them.

The contrast drawn by Savary was in one way a false one, since some of the Dutch bourgeoisie were no less attracted by office than those of France, and the drift into rentals and public office was quite considerable in Holland. But because of the different social structure in the two countries, the process took place far more rapidly and with more serious consequences in France.

The devotion of the French bourgeoisie to trade and industry was certainly half-hearted. Already in 1560 we have a complaint from the Chancellor L'Hospital that 'trade has decayed greatly because of the issue of *rentes* by the Hôtel-de-Ville', that is, by the city of Paris. No sooner had merchants made their fortunes than they chose to invest the proceeds in these municipal loans, which guaranteed a steady income for the foreseeable future. In this way traders withdrew their money from commerce and dropped out of business. Figures available for the bourgoisie in Amiens show that out of the names of twenty-seven principal merchants in the textile industry there in 1589-90, only six names remained thirty-five years later; while of thirty-eight surnames to be found in 1625, only seven remained by 1711. If these figures are correct, they show an appreciable movement of families out of business once their fortunes had been made. The process of moving out of commerce consisted simply in transferring assets to property that would give a steady but not necessarily high rate of interest. Security was being preferred to risk and the security involved was that of one's family and children. Wealth for its own sake, the capitalist ethic, was abandoned in favour of wealth that brought ease and social position. The fortune left by the Beauvais merchant Lucien Motte in 1650 shows the first beginnings of a movement out of trade into other interests: only four per cent of his money was invested in land, but as much as twenty-seven per cent represented *rentes* and assets external to commerce. The trend, as we have seen, was well known, and the government could not fail to regret what ill effect it must have had on the economy. 'What has hurt trade', stated a report to Richelieu in 1626, 'is that all the merchants, when they become rich, do not remain in commerce but spend their goods on offices for their children'. A Lyon merchant of about the same time, directing his protest against noble status rather than against office-holdings claimed that

> trade creates wealth; and nearly all the best families of Paris, Lyon, Rouen, Orléans and Bordeaux originate not only from lawyers, notaries and attorneys, but also from merchants. . . . The exchange in London, the fair at Lyon, the exchanges at Antwerp and Rouen, also yield yet more families. The merchant acquires, the office-holder keeps, the nobleman dissipates. . . . Our city has decayed only since it got involved with *rentes* and nobility.

The French bourgeois' ascent up the social ladder began with the purchase of office. Not only merchants, but other sections of the middle class commenced their climb in this way. Beyond office, there lay the purchase of land, and it was the movement to the land, hinted at so minimally in Lucien Motte's fortune, that was the most outstanding characteristic of bourgeois fortunes in this period. If we take the example of Toussaint Foy, tax officer for one region of Beauvais, we find that his fortune at his demise in 1660 was made up in the following way:

Lands	55.8 per cent
Cash and goods	14.1 per cent
Office	5.8 per cent
Rentes and credit	13.5 per cent
Houses	10.8 per cent

These figures for a bourgeois fortune at the end of our period allow us to turn our attention to the three most important feaures of the economic life of the bourgeoisie: their income from *rentes*, land and office.

A RENTIER AND A LANDED CLASS

Rentes, or annuities, played a fundamental part not only in diverting bourgeois money from trade, but also in easing the way to their conquest of the land. Unknown in England, where the monarchy found other ways to raise money, the *rentes* on the continent consisted of public loans to a needy government, and could be found in Italy in the Middle Ages. Most other states began to issue *rentes* in the fifteenth and sixteenth centuries. In France the *rentes,* though technically a loan to the crown, were issued by the Hôtel-de-Ville at Paris, which gave an annual interest on loans. In Spain there were two principal kinds of loan: the *juros,* issued by the state, and the *censos,* issued either by municipalities or by private individuals. In the same way, municipalities in Italy, Germany and the Low Countries issued loans on which annual interest was payable. In Italy the *monti,* as the consolidated public debts were called, had long played a key role in the financing of municipal policies.

Annuities, of whatever kind, were a tempting form of investment, particularly when the state offered high interest rates in an effort to attract investors. In an age when banking was relatively unknown, the authorities became bankers, borrowing from citizens and paying them their interest out of taxation. The system was all too successful. In late fifteenth-century Florence it led to the emergence of a *rentier* mentality among the wealthier bourgeoisie, and to the concentration of financial wealth in the hands of the upper rank of citizens since it was these who controlled the machinery of state. It is possible that this process actually prevented capital accumulation among those classes who were most interested in increasing production. In this way investment in the *monti* diverted capital from entrepreneurial activities. A comparable situation prevailed in other parts of Italy at a later period. In the Como region near the Duchy of Milan, a vigorous and wealthy middle class existed. In addition to their other interests, the citizens of Como devoted themselves to moneylending. Their clients were both peasant communities and the government, and from these the bourgeoisie drew their annuities, their *censi.* In 1663 the rural community of Gravedona, one among others, complained that it was crippled by debts because of the *censi* it had to pay to former councillors and officials of the city.

By itself, investment in *rentes* was not open to criticism. What was important was the priority given to it. The Amsterdam bourgeoisie was as large a *rentier* class as any in western Europe (Louis Trip, for instance, at his death in 1684 left something like one hundred and fifty-seven thousand florins in *rentes* alone), but Dutch investment in this sort of commodity took place only after the capital demands of commerce and industry had been met, so that *rentes* tended to eat up only a proportion of working capital. In Germany, France and Spain, on the other hand, the devotion to *rentes* amounted to a passion.

State loans were a popular investment and, as we have seen with the English national debt, could attract a very large amount of capital without obliging the midddle class there to rely solely on the debt for its income. For many English bourgeois investors, the debt would have been their alternative to the purchase of land, and an insurance against the future. For many investors in Spain, however, the *juros* represented quite simply their principal source of income. The nobles invested no less than the bourgeoisie, and examples of nobles who in 1680 depended on the *juros* alone for their cash income are revealing: the Viscount of Ambite 'whose whole income consisted in them', the Viscount de la Frontera 'who had no other income to live on', the Count of Toreno 'whose main source of income is these *juros*'. Innumerable bourgeois families, and particularly widows, drew on *juros* as though they were a pension scheme. It needs little effort to show that those who lived off the interest from state annuities were in effect living off the state, without making any productive contribution to it. Perhaps the most striking example of this, though not necessarily the only one of its kind, was the city of Valladolid, where two hundred and thirty-two citizens in the late sixteenth century drew more money from the government by way of *juros* than was actually paid by the whole city in taxes, so that the state was in practice subsidising the city.

In addition to using the state as a source of revenue, the bourgeoisie were also in a position to offer credit elsewhere. The *rentes* which they owned in this case were loans made to individuals, who in return for an immediate advance of cash undertook to pay their creditor an annuity in cash or in kind until the extinction of the debt. The transaction was not always so straightforward, and difficulties were sometimes put in the way of speedy redemption of the loan. *Rentes* of this sort, *censos, censi,* made the bourgeoisie creditors to two classes of people in particular, the peasantry and the nobility.

The peasantry and the village communities of Europe tended to depend exclusively on the moneylenders of the towns for the capital they needed in order to improve their landholdings. The cash available to the peasant was never very considerable; in times of deflation or disaster, when credit was most needed for improvement and survival, the situation became critical. The peasantry inevitably became the largest class of borrowers. The accounts of the Valladolid notary Antonio de Cigales show, for example, that in the years 1576-7 over fifty-one per cent of his debtors were peasants. The sums were invariably small, but certainly helped the peasant to make ends meet and to develop his holdings when necessary.

In nearly all regions of Europe, with the obvious exception of the east, the bourgeoisie played a significant part in helping rural reconstruction. This help was needed most of all after the great wars that ravaged peasant territories, in France after the civil wars and the Frondes, in Germany after the Thirty Years War. The credit which came to the rescue of rural communities on these occasions was usually bourgeois money, supplied by the merchants, retailers and officials in the towns. In this way capital was invested in agriculture, hopefully to the benefit of the peasant and the community as a whole.

It was when the question of payment of annuities and redemption of the loan arose that difficulties occurred. A peasant who did not manage to repay the loan when a good harvest came, often lost the chance forever. A bad year could bring with it the beginnings of an inability to pay; this in turn could and did lead to permanent indebtedness and final bankruptcy. The *rentier* could step in and confiscate the land-holding that had been the guarantee of the loan. In the long periods of agrarian depression which recurred in the rural economy, thousands of peasant holdings passed out of the hands of their owners into those of the urban bourgeoisie. Castile in the seventeenth century was amply populated with towns and villages labouring under the burden of *censos*: the village of Escurial (Cáceres province), for instance, with a population in 1679 of about 1,375, a capital of 9,712 ducats in property and cattle, and a total debt principal of 24,616 ducats of *censos*; or that of Aldeanueva de Figueroa, which in the years 1664 to 1686 alone alienated over one-third of its land to the bourgeoisie of Salamanca.

The transference of land from the peasantry is relatively easy to understand, but there were other sections of society that also became indebted to the *rentiers*. In the number of Antonio de Cigales' debtors for 1576-7, about ten per cent were artisans and thirteen per cent were holders of offices, while nearly three per cent were nobles. All of these did not necessarily lose their property, but the cross-section of society that did tend to lose land was surprisingly wide. An example from the early sixteenth century illustrates this. In one of the parishes in the Rouen area in 1521, of a total of two hundred and eighty-eight people selling their plots of lands, one hundred and eighty-three were peasant farmers, fifty-two were artisans, twenty were labourers, nineteen were bourgeois and fourteen were priests. The purchasers were almost without exception bourgeois.

The *rentes* therefore became an instrument for the deterioration and expropriation of an independent peasantry, and promoted the conquest of the soil by the urban classes. The transfer of land from peasant to bourgeois was not of course caused exclusively or directly by *rentes*. The economic circumstances of the early sixteenth century had already given a firm impetus to the process. But peasant indebtedness to *rentiers* certainly played a very large part in it. By the mid-sixteenth century over half the land around Montpellier was said to belong to the city's inhabitants. The extension of bourgeois hold on the land was unmistakable. Where tax officials held only six hectares of Montpellier territory in 1547, by 1680 they held two hundred and twenty.

The nobility also were prey to the activities of the town moneylenders. Outpaced by rising costs, inadequate exploitation of their estates, and by conspicuous consumption, they had to raise loans from the class that had most capital to spare. We have already seen the chief nobility of Castile indebted, sometimes for enormous sums, to the bourgeoisie of Valladolid. In this city the creditors were not only individuals: they were very often, as elsewhere in Spain, corporate bodies such as religious communities. The scale of indebtedness of the Castilian nobility was so alarming (thus the count of Benavente in the early seventeenth century paid out forty-five per cent of his annual income for *censos*) that towards the end of his reign Philip II stepped in to save his ruling class. By royal decrees, individual noble debtors were allowed to seek reductions in the rate of interest they paid; if this were refused by creditors, the nobles were allowed to redeem their *censos* — by creating new debts elsewhere in order to repay the old debts. So great was the demand for income from *censos* that reductions were readily conceded by the bourgeoisie.

Thanks to the debts contracted by the nobility, the urban classes proceeded to take over the ownership of the soil from nobles no less than from peasants. An extraordinary premium was set on land, as the fortune of Toussaint Foy, referred to above, shows. Land gave security and respectability and, above all, a pretension to noble status. The lands which seemed most attractive to a bourgeois with social aspirations were those that carried feudal and seigneurial rights with them, and many bourgeois were able quite legitimately to style themselves consequently as seigneur of such and such a fief. By itself, of course, the proprietorship of a *seigneurie* did not mean that one had become a noble; but the lordship of one or more sizeable estates was an irrefutable argument when presenting one's claims for a noble title.

The advancement of the bourgeoisie of the city of Dijon is a case in point. With a population in the early seventeenth century of about four thousand three hundred households (about twenty thousand people), the numbers of those who could be classified as bourgeois came to between six and eight thousand people. Though the core of this class was composed of lawyers, officials, members of the parlement and their like, there was also an admixture of gentry who had moved in from the countryside, attracted by the income from office. In their turn the bourgeoisie moved their interests (but not their persons) into the countryside. The wealthy trading interests of the Dijon patriciate bought land in order to give themselves that mark of distinction, that *qualité*, which bestowed status. By the mid-seventeenth century the city of Dijon had obtained a firm and irreversible grip on the land and estates surrounding it.

The same process occurred in seventeenth-century Amiens. There the bourgeoisie purchased land according to cash and rank: smaller merchants bought small lots, the *noblesse de robe* bought estates. The upper bourgeoisie drew nearly sixty per cent of its income from land and rents, a clear indication of the social values they cultivated. A survey drawn up in 1634 of all the landed fiefs in the possession of the bourgeoisie of Amiens revealed that a total of three hundred and fifty-one citizens, all commoners, held property that ranged from small parcels to large seigneurial estates. Of these large estates, twenty-eight retained feudal jurisdiction; eighteen of them belonged to the *noblesse de robe*, five to bourgeois citizens, and four to lawyers.

In Alsace the appropriation of land by the townspeople was at its height in the late sixteenth and early seventeenth centuries. Peasant communities suffered the worst, as usual. The territorial holdings of the town of Hagenau multiplied as a result of rural indebtedness. The city of Strassburg was second to none in its acquisitions. From the year 1587 comes a complaint that 'more and more from day to day grows the unheard-of pace at which houses and holdings pass into the hands of the Strassburgers'. But it was noble property that the bourgeoisie prized most, for its status and also for the belief that noble lands could claim exemption from taxation, regardless of their proprietor; a belief, it should be emphasised, that the laws tended to support. As the bourgeoisie accumulated both peasant and noble property, they began to alter the face of ownership in the countryside, and to become themselves the new seigneurs, often with extensive holdings. One bourgeois landholder of this type was Pierre Cécile, a *conseiller* of the Parlement at Dôle (Franche Comté). By the time of his death, in 1587, he was the owner of two hundred and fifty plots of land and meadow, three town houses, three small country houses, and fourteen vineyards scattered through the territory of over twenty-five different towns and villages.

The indebtedness of the rural nobility may be studied in the accounts of a leading judge of the Beauvais region. Of those who held *rentes* from Maître Tristan in 1647, nearly three-quarters were noblemen, all with distinguished names, including that of the family Rouvroy de Saint-Simon. Nearly all the lands, houses and *seigneuries* that fell into Maître Tristan's hands as a result of his activities as a *rentier* came from noble debtors. From the illustrious Gouffier family, descendants of two Admirals of France, a family moreover that was now overwhelmed by debts and had sold all its possessions in Picardy to bourgeois, Tristan bought the estates and fiefs of Juvignies and Verderel, which remained in his family for over a century. By the end of the seventeenth century, the Tristans had climbed to wealth over the decayed fortunes of impoverished noblemen, and in the early eighteenth century they obtained noble status through the purchase of an office at court. Their example, one among many even in the confines of Beauvaisis, illustrates the extraordinary extent to which *rentes* served to transfer land and property from the aristocracy to the rising middle classes, and helped eventually to create a new nobility in France.

The acquisition of land by the bourgeoisie has often been looked upon without qualification as a retrogressive, anti-capitalist development, above all since it took money out of commerce. Observations like those of Savary, quoted above, have reinforced this impression in the minds of students. It is very important therefore to look at the other side of the picture. There can be no doubt that the land tended to benefit wherever the new bourgeois seigneurs took their duties seriously and brought their habits of thrift to work on the agricultural economy. They introduced changes in routine and methods of exploitation. In the estates which the merchant classes acquired around Toulouse in the mid-sixteenth century, for instance, a rationalisation of labour was introduced. The number of tenants was reduced to an economic minimum, rents were asked for in kind rather than in cash, and share-cropping (métayage) was introduced to replace less profitable kinds of tenancy. The fact is that in many regions only the bourgeoisie had the capital necessary to revive agriculture, so long neglected by aristocrats who had seen their estates as property to be exploited, or by peasant-farmers who had been struggling against debts. Many bourgeois seigneurs took a profound interest in their lands and in Varzy, for instance, estate administration occupied a great deal of the time of the new owners. The bourgeoisie were not, in short, lazy. The help given by their capital investment was crucial above all after times of war, as we have already noted. After the grim 1630s in Alsace, it was the urban bourgeoisie of Strassburg and other towns who helped to restore village communities destroyed by war. In mid-seventeenth century Dijonnais, it was thanks to the bourgeois seigneurs that the villages were repopulated, the fields restored, the vineyards replanted and extended, and the cattle brought back. In many areas of Germany after the Thirty Years War it was the merchants of the cities who advanced the capital without which the rural areas could not have recovered. In purely economic terms, the advent of bourgeois landownership was nothing if not beneficial.

But in social terms, and in historical perspective, the metamorphis of the bourgeoisie into a *rentier* and a landowning class was a backward step, for the middle classes thereby adopted the pretensions, values and way of life of the nobility. Did they then succeed in gaining noble status as well?

THE ECONOMIC AND SOCIAL FUNCTION OF OFFICE

Professor Mousnier has described the progress of the bourgeoisie towards nobility in these terms: 'office began nobility, the fief added to it, the sword completed it'. Public position, in other words, was followed by the purchase of land, and ultimately by training one or more sons for the army: the full scale of noble values was thus achieved. The ascent did not necessarily always take this form. In his classic work on Dijon, Gaston Roupnel argued that more often than not the purchase of land preceded the purchase of office. Whatever the order we adopt, it remains true that the tenure of public office was one of the most powerful influences in the development of the European bourgeoisie. Already by the mid-sixteenth century it was a longstanding practice for both nobles and bourgeois to invest in office.

Public office brought status, and also an income. Being 'public', offices were open to all who cared to obtain them. It would appear, then, that office was an ideal vehicle for social mobility, and it is this which has made historians view it as an important factor contributing to social change. However, in some states office was not as exciting a proposition as this. The eastern European states had a minimal bureaucracy, in which office counted for little, and the royal household was the main dispenser of favours. In England too it was the royal household that counted, and favour or influence rather than money that won office; posts in Parliament or in county administration, all unpaid, were the reward of status and did not confer status, so they were not obvious channels of social mobility. In republics such as Venice or the United Provinces, the senior posts were controlled permanently by an oligarchy into which it was almost impossible to rise other than by marriage or favour. Sir William Temple observed of the Dutch merchants, for instance, that 'when they attain great wealth, (they) chuse to breed up their Sons in the way, and marry their daughters into the families of those others most generally credited in their towns, and thereby introduce their families into the way of government and honour, which consists not here in titles but in public employments'. In none of these states, therefore, did the sale of office, or venality of offices, ever gain a great hold, though it was often common, as in Venice, for minor offices to be bought and sold.

Office by itself did not encourage mobility; that occurred almost exclusively through venality of offices. And venality of office, far from being a common European phenomenon, was highly significant in France alone. It occurred in other countries, but more as an occasional method of granting favours or of raising money (the Spanish sales fall into these categories), then as a regular feature of the administration. Inevitably, then, a discussion of venality limits us to a consideration of the French bourgeoisie.

The initial purpose of the French crown in selling offices was to raise money, but by the mid-sixteenth century this had created a problem of major dimensions. In 1546 the Venetian ambassador reported that 'there is an infinite number of offices, and they increase every day'. Loyseau estimated that in the second half of the sixteenth century about fifty thousand new offices had been created, a figure which does not seem improbable when one looks at some of the figures for the growth of bureaucracy. The profession best represented in this spectacular growth was the law, this 'amazing flood of lawyers', as Noël du Fail put it. It was they who thronged the administrative bodies of the state at virtually every level—but only on paper. In practice the great majority of the new officials were absentees, men who had acquired the office for the social position it conferred and for the salary that went with it. The threat to the state, then, was not over-bureaucratisation, but absenteee officials, officials who had been appointed not because they were qualified but because they had paid for the post. So great was the demand for office that a considerable inflation in prices occurred. A judgeship in the Parlement of Paris, for instance, was officially valued in 1605 at eighteen thousand *livres;* under Louis XIII the price reached seventy thousand, and by 1660 the post was valued at one hundred and forty thousand.

Though venality was important in itself, it was the possibility of making an office inheritable that really institutionalised it. When the *Paulette* was introduced in 1604 it produced an immediate rise in the price of offices that could now be made hereditary legally. Offices continued to be accumulated as property to be passed on from father to son, but with greater security than before. It should nevertheless be remembered that long before the *Paulette* ways were found of keeping an office in the family, and the 1604 law merely formalised a common practice. The extent to which the bourgeoisie relied upon venality for their income can be shown in a few examples. In 1589 the fortune of Nicolas Caillot, *conseiller* of the Parlement of Rouen and son of a goldsmith, consisted twenty-two per cent in *rentes,* thirty-three per cent in rentals and forty-five per cent in the fruits of office; in terms of annual income, office was the most important item, producing fifty-six per cent of his revenue. In 1600 the revenues of Jean Godart, *sieur* de Bellebœuf and a senior financial official in Normandy, were drawn twenty-nine per cent from land, thirty-nine per cent from *rentes* and thirty-two per cent from offices.

The Norman official Jacques d'Amfreville, who died in 1629, left a fortune of which offices made up about thirty per cent and land forty-nine per cent.

Though these examples show office as a significant component, in fact many other examples could show a different picture; and office in any case was seldom considered as valuable as land. Loyseau's testimony is valuable: the bourgeoisie, he said, put

> inheritances (i.e. fiefs and lands) in the first place, as being the most solid and secure property, of which the family fortune should chiefly consist; offices next, for in addition to the profit, they gave rank, authority and employment to the head of the family and helped him to maintain the other property; and left *rentes* to the last since they merely brought extra revenue.

So great was the number of office holders in France that they were almost regarded as an Estate of the realm in themselves, 'the fourth Estate'. Through venality many humble families grew to produce the most eminent officials of the realm, and administrators such as Jeannin, Talon, Molé, Séguier, de Thou and others rose in this way. They formed a new nobility, the *noblesse de robe*, which could be differentiated into three distinct levels: the *petite robe*, consisting of lesser officials such as notaries and lawyers, the *moyenne robe*, predominantly in the provinces, which consisted of most members of the parlements and other judicial bodies, and the *grande robe*, consisting of the great officers of state who were commoners. So profound was their influence even at the centre of government that in 1624, of the thirty members of the Council of State, twenty-four were of the robe.

Through venality the bourgeoisie rose to govern France, but not without the bitter opposition of the upper classes. We have already seen the nobles protesting about the sale of office, which they regarded as their domain. Every Estates General in this period, up to the last one in 1614, protested at the 'frightful number of superfluous offices' (the clergy in the 1576 Estates). But so long as the state needed to sell offices, there was no alternative to venality.

The problem of office was not one to be blamed entirely on the state, nor even entirely on the bourgeoisie. The fact is that, quite apart from the social advancement offered by office, the system of higher education in most European countries was geared to the production every year of thousands of graduates in one principal subject—law. The logic of this development is something that still requires adequate discussion. In England, Germany, Spain, Italy, and not merely in France, an 'amazing flood of lawyers' poured out into public life, with widely varying results in each country. If they could not be absorbed into the administrative structure, as France absorbed them, what could be done with them?

RANK AND MOBILITY IN THE BOURGEOISIE

The rise of the middle classes was an unquestionable phenomenon of sixteenth-century Europe. Those who had made their way in trade, office and land were now concerned to consolidate the gains, in social status as well as in political influence, made by their class. Together with the increase in importance of the urban bourgeoisie went the growing importance of towns in the national economy. It was the moneyed urban bourgeoisie that began to set the pace, not only in England and Holland but also in other countries where working capital was obtainable only from this group. Their aspirations were widely resented as being subversive of the natural order of ranks. 'Who ever saw so many discontented persons', complained an English observer in 1578, 'so many irked with their own degrees, so few contented with their own calling, and such numbers desirous and greedy of change and novelties?' Even by that date, the process of bourgeois advancement was well under way in countries like France and a new 'nobility' had come into existence in the form of the *noblesse de robe*. The late sixteenth and early seventeenth centuries were a period of rapid social mobility during which serious inroads were made into the privileged position held by the old and partly impoverished aristocracy. The change cannot be better illustrated than by looking at Denmark. There in 1560 the merchant classes still described themselves in a petition as 'lowly branches shadowing under Your Majesty and the nobility of Denmark'. In 1658, however, the bourgeoisie of Copenhagen were openly calling for 'admission to offices and privileges on the same terms as the nobles'.

The evidence, clearly observed by many contemporaries, of new *parvenu* blood in the ranks of the gentry, was enough to arouse condemnation. In October 1560 at a meeting of the provincial estates at Angers a lawyer named Grimaudet poured his scorn on 'the infinity of false noblemen, whose fathers and ancestors wielded arms and performed acts of chivalry in grain-shops, wineshops, draperies, mills and farmsteads; and yet when they speak of their lineage they are descended from the crown, their roots spring from Charlemagne, Pompey and Caesar'. In 1581 the author of the *Miroir des Français,* Nicolas de Montaud, denounced 'certain gentlemen who have taken the title of nobility as soon as they emerge from their apprenticeships as shoemakers, weavers and cobblers'. In fact few successful bourgeois fitted into these categories, nor did they need to make fantastic claims about their descent, since their rise was too remarkable to disguise in this way. In any case, the political philosophy of the bourgeois was not always that of the old lineage-obsessed nobility.

The bourgeoisie could work their way up in society in as little as one generation, as with the sixteenth-century Lyon grocer Jean Camus, whose investments and purchases of land left him at the end of his life in possession of eight noble estates, some of which included villages and small towns. But the upper levels of French society were still extremely caste ridden, and, as we have seen, land and office as well as sword were the prerequisites of success. In Amiens the rise into the nobility took no more than one or two generations. Among the city's *noblesse de robe* in the mid-seventeenth century, office counted for between thirty and forty per cent of income, but the major part of the remainder came from land and *rentes.* Office was not an infallible path to status, if we can judge from Normandy where, between 1589 and 1643, of five hundred and forty-four patents of nobility that were granted only one hundred and seventeen (or 21·5 per cent) were issued to office-holders. Office and land by themselves were seldom enough, and to earn the right to enter the established caste a successful bourgeois had to prove that he could 'live nobly', maintain a certain style of life, and practise the profession most typical of the caste—war. In Amiens we can find different branches of one family involved simultaneously in one or other of the functions that went to make up the noble style of life.

In England there was an unprecedented improvement in the position of the middle classes, so much so that for some contemporaries such as Lord Clarendon it was the thrusting bourgeoisie who were the anti-royalist party during the civil war in England. There is no need to take the war as a point of reference in order to demonstrate Clarendon's argument. In both land and trade important changes in the distribution of wealth had occurred. To some extent any discussion about a rise of the bourgeoisie is confused by the long-standing debate over the gentry, since sections of the gentry were also improving their position, and in both wealth and status there was often little or nothing to differentiate the successful member of the middle classes from the successful gentleman.

The nobility of England, though an elite, was not a caste, and it required little effort to become part of its lower ranks. 'Who can live idly and without manual labour, and will bear the port, charge and countenance of a gentleman', claimed Sir Thomas Smith at the time, 'he shall be called master, for that is the title men give to esquires and other gentlemen, and shall be taken for a gentleman.' By this definition, one could become a gentleman simply by living as one, and without necessarily having any landed property. This was one of several ways in which the landed and mercantile classes became confused, making it difficult to distinguish origins. The confusion was increased by the tendency of gentry sons to engage themselves as apprentices to trade: we are told, for instance, that by the 1630s nearly a fifth of the London Stationers' Company apprentices came from gentry stock. When, therefore, it appears in 1635 there were nearly twelve hundred persons resident in London who described themselves as gentlemen and who also, for the most part, engaged in trade, it is difficult to determine what proportion of these people had actually risen through the ranks to win their status. This group of leisured urban members of the professional and trading class, unsupported by landed wealth, has been called the 'pseudo-gentry'.

But the middle classes in town and country also supplemented the ranks of the gentry proper. There were two main streams that contributed to this, the successful yeomen of the country and the rising town merchants who purchased land. With the yeoman it was certainly the mobility of land that facilitated social mobility. Independent landholders (though not necessarily freeholders), they benefited from the increased value of the soil, and as a class their average wealth probably doubled in the period 1600 to 1640. Living in the same environment as the country gentry, often more prosperous than many gentry, they rose almost imperceptibly into the higher status group. 'From thence in time', observed a contemporary in 1618, 'are derived many noble and worthy families.' Of the fifty-seven Yorkshire families granted arms between 1603 and 1642, over half were wealthy yeomen. Of a total of three hundred and thirty-five gentry in the county of Nor-

200

thamptonshire in the mid-seventeenth century, the great majority were newcomers not only to the county but also to the squirearchy, and at least three-quarters of them had only very recently arrived in their new status. A substantial proportion of them must have come from yeomen stock, and several would have been lawyers or traders in Northampton. The rate of mobility, however, was not always as high as this.

Land was important for urban mobility. By the early seventeenth century, we are reminded by Tawney, it was difficult to find a prominent London capitalist who was not also a substantial landowner. The contemporary Stow remarked that 'merchants and rich men (being satisfied with gain) do for the most part marry their children into the country, and convey themselves, after Cicero's counsel, *veluti ex portu in agros et possessiones*'. Like many other contemporary comments, this needs to be approached with care. For though land was clearly a spur to mobility, it was often (unlike France) no more than the last stage in the progress to status, nor did families who obtained land cease to trade. A study of the wealth of seventy-eight gentry families in Elizabethan Sussex shows that among the twenty-five wealthiest families only four were supported chiefly by land, while the majority had heads who were still — what they had been before emerging as 'gentry' — ironmasters, managers of forges and furnaces, merchants and lawyers. Similarly, if we look at the greater merchants of the city of London in the early seventeenth century, we find them living in the style of the gentry, with country estates and stewards to manage them, parks and gamekeepers to patrol them, and country houses which regularly dispensed hospitality. But three-quarters of the greater merchants, despite this formal commitment to the country, never moved their roots from London, and maintained both their business and their friends in the city throughout their career.

There was clearly also a downward movement in the social ladder at the same time, but contemporaries were not alarmed by the failures so much as by the successes. Noblemen were chagrined to see newcomers whose only title was their wealth, rise to prominence in public life. Merchants were likewise concerned that so many of their colleagues should desert their profession and adopt the unproductive habits of the aristocracy. Thomas Mun lamented that 'the memory of our richest merchants is suddenly extinguished; the son, being left rich, scorns the profession of his father, conceiving more honour to be a gentleman, to consume his estate in dark ignorance and excess, than to follow the steps of his father as an industrious merchant to maintain and advance his fortunes'. Success in society appears, however, to have had little effect on business enterprise in England, and Mun's lament refers more to the shifting fortunes of individual families than to any extensive diversion of capital from trade.

Many merchants must nevertheless have hesitated between the choice of profession or status, and in France the choice may well have been an agonising one. Claude Darc, merchant of Amance (Franche Comté), who died in 1597, solved his difficulties in a particularly appealing way. His daughters were married off to legal officials, so that their status was guaranteed. Of his two sons he chose the elder, Guillaume, to remain in the business; but he trained the younger, Simon, to become a doctor of laws. In this way one branch of the family would continue to accumulate wealth while the other sought position. In his will he spoke of Simon 'and all the expense he has caused me, both for the pursuit of his studies and for his upkeep these twenty-five years past, and at Paris, Freiburg, Cologne, Rome, Naples, Dôle and elsewhere that he has been up to now, for the eight years that it takes to become a doctor; all this has cost (God help me!) more than twelve thousand francs'. He also spoke of Guillaume, who had 'exposed the best years of his youth, and risked his person many times, to the peril and danger of the long journeys he made to distant and strange countries, and in those twenty years he has, by his work and labours, added to and increased the family fortune by much more than the said doctor has spent'. Two widely differing paths, but to each the father gave his wholehearted support.

In the United Provinces the achievement of national independence left the bourgeoisie firmly in control. The change in Amsterdam may be dated from the year 1578 when a coup or *Alteratie* led to the overthrow of the old regime, with its officials and clergy, and the staffing of the ruling council of the city with new bourgeoisie Calvinist members. In historical terms, the bourgeois continued to dominate the United Provinces because their trading interests had made them support the struggle against Spain. In geographical terms, it was the west and northwestern half of the country that had profited from the war of independence. 'Whereas it is generally the nature of war to ruin land and people', observed a burgomaster of Amsterdam, C. P.

Hooft, 'these countries on the contrary have been noticeably improved thereby.' Protected by their rivers and with the open sea before them, the bourgeoisie of Holland and Zealand had since the 1570s enjoyed virtual immunity from the war, so that while Spain was expending its strength against them in the south, they built up in the northwest a flourishing base on which the Dutch economy was to rest.

The eastern half of the country was, on the other hand, under developed, primarily agricultural and dominated by the noble class. It was the nobles of Guelderland and Overijssel in particular who were the main support of the House of Orange in its differences with the bourgeoisie of the west. Their relative weakness in the country as a whole gave control of administration to the bourgeois elite of the cities, the regent class. In the regent class of Holland we have a clear example of the way in which a highly successful section of the bourgeoisie developed. Senior administrative officers of the towns, the regents were drawn originally either from active merchants or from those who had recently retired from business. Their tenure of office inevitably became a comfortable monopoly, and tended to make them withdraw from active trade. The old clash between commerce and office-holding worked to the detriment of the former. By 1652 the Amsterdam merchants were complaining, rather like Thomas Mun, that the regents had ceased to support trade and were drawing their income 'from houses, lands, and money at interest'. The merchants of the late sixteenth century had become a *rentier* class in the seventeenth. The de Witts are an obvious example of the drift from trade. Cornelis de Witt, born in 1545, was burgomaster of Dordrecht and a successful trader in timber. The most prominent of his sons, Jacob, continued his father's business, but his growing involvement in public affairs (notably his opposition to William II of Orange in 1650) obliged him to dispose of the family business between 1632 and 1651. Jacob's son Johan, a distinguished member of the regent class, concentrated entirely on the duties of political office.

The Dutch bourgeoisie lived unpretentiously. Sir William Temple testified that 'of the two chief officers in my time, Vice-Admiral de Ruyter and the Pensioner de Witt . . . I never saw the first in clothes better than the commonest sea-captain . . . and in his own house neither was the size, building, furniture or entertainment at all exceeding the use of every common merchant and tradesman.' As for de Witt, 'he was seen usually in the streets on foot and alone, like the commonest burgher of the town'. 'Nor was this manner of life', adds Temple, 'used only by these particular men, but was the general fashion or mode among all the magistrates of the State.' This apparent austerity was only the prelude to the adoption of a neo-aristocratic way of life. Social mobility in the usual sense was an irrelevancy, since in practice the regent class by the seventeenth century ranked above the old nobility. In this position, the upper bourgeoisie adopted distinctly conservative habits. 'Their youths', reported Temple, 'after the course of their studies at home, travel for some years, as the sons of our gentry use to do.' When they went to university, they usually read civil law. Johan de Witt was one who read law at Leiden, and did the grand tour with his brother in 1645-7.

A patrician class arose in Holland, and its rise was accompanied by the abandonment of frugality. 'The old severe and frugal way of living is now almost quite out of date in Holland', Temple was to complain, having in mind the bourgeoisie of Amsterdam and the Hague. The trend towards luxury was illustrated by a pamphleteer of 1662 who called for the passing of sumptuary laws on the grounds that people were beginning to dress and live above their station. The intention was obviously to distinguish between the oligarchic elite of regents, magistrates and wealthy merchants, and the mass of the bourgeoisie.

Sumptuary laws were the standard method of attempting to preserve rank and check mobility, but the Dutch were relatively free of them. Elsewhere in Europe the pretensions of the middle classes were subject to both legislation and comment. 'I doubt not but it is lawfull for the nobilitie, the gentrie and magisterie, to weare rich attire', said Philip Stubbs in his *Anatomie of Abuses* (1583). 'As for private subjectes, it is not at any hand lawful that they should wear silkes, velvets, satens, damaskes, gold, silver and what they list.' The abundant sumptuary legislation in Europe at this period is proof that the authorities shared Stubb's views, though their motives, as we have already noted, were not exclusively concerned with the maintenance of degree. In any case, legislation was invariably a failure. The French crown was obliged to issue no less than thirteen sumptuary edicts between 1540 and 1615, but with little success. After 1604, when it repealed all existing sumptuary laws, the English government did not bother to dictate the rules of apparel to its subjects. As Bodin observed of France: 'Fine edicts have been passed, but to no purpose. For since people at court wear what is forbidden, everyone wears it, so that the officials are intimidated by the former and corrupted by the latter. Besides, in matters of dress he is always considered a fool and bore who does not dress according to the current fashion.'

The failure of the sumptuary laws was yet another demonstration of the worldly success of the middle classes.

THE RISE AND FALL OF THE BOURGEOISIE

England and the Dutch Republic could be described as model bourgeois states, since in them the spirit of enterprise, and the devotion to trade that marked the bourgeois were predominant. This is not of course an adequate explanation of the remarkable expansion of commercial capitalism in these countries above all others in Europe, but it is unquestionable that their business and trading classes played a fundamental role in their success story. Commerce flourished and towns expanded when the middle classes helped to direct economic and political policy. When on the other hand they had little direction of policy, and when their own interests diverted them from entrepreneurial activities, there were serious repercussions on economic life. This was the case in much of central and southern Europe.

In Spain the urban bourgeoisie played an important role in the seaports, in Barcelona, Valencia, Seville and the Basque country; but their function in the inland towns grew less important in the course of the sixteenth century. As in other countries, the simplest way for the state to control its bourgeoisie was to restrict the privileges of the towns. A start was made by Charles V after the revolt of the *Comuneros* in 1521. Under Philip II the main Castilian towns — eighteen of them — were entitled to send representatives to the Castilian cortes. Under him and his successors this privilege was gradually watered down, giving the urban classes little or no say in the formulation of policy. The deliberations of the cortes in the early seventeenth century show that it had become no more than an empty vehicle of grievances, with no power to win redress. Commercial decay was even more striking than political decline. Under Charles V and Philip II the fairs at Medina del Campo made Old Castile an integral part of the western European market, and successful merchants like Simon Ruiz represented the most enterprising section of the Castilian bourgeoisie. By the seventeenth century, however, Medina and the fairs and the native merchant class had all but vanished. The capital that had once been harvested from trade, the surplus that had gone into ambitious buildings like Simon Ruiz's hospital at Medina, were now replaced by the activities of foreign finance.

The weakness of the Castilian middle classes is all the more striking since they stood to profit from the unparalleled wealth offered by America. An explanation might be given along the lines that Spain had been robbed of its enterprising Jewish bourgeoisie in 1492, but for the fact that there was also a large and active group of non-Jewish traders in every major Spanish city, no less capable than the Jews. The explanation moreover ignores the fact that the Jews were still, as *conversos,* operating actively in the world of commerce, and that their numbers were periodically augmented by the immigration of Portuguese *conversos.* Apart from the political debility to which we have already referred, the one outstanding feature in the history of the Castilian bourgeoisie is its transformation into a *rentier* class.

We have already seen the bourgeoisie of Valladolid taking an active part in the procuring of *censos* from both the aristocracy and the peasantry; in addition they had a large interest in the *juros* issued by the government. At least in agriculture the *censos* had an initially beneficial effect, but in the long run they brought indebtedness and ruin to the rural classes. The effects on the *rentier* class were no better. To the constant untiring pursuit of *censos,* all sections of the bourgeoisie — lawyers, office-holders, clergy, merchants — diverted their capital. Money was diverted from productive enterprises because they were too risky and put into *censos* and *juros* because they brought a steady return. These investments consequently became a highly prized article of property. What other way was there of obtaining an income without working for it? Contemplating with dismay the effects of the *rentier* mentality, the Valladolid bourgeois Martín González de Cellórigo in 1600 condemned *censos* as a

> plague which has reduced these realms to utter poverty, since most or a majority of people have taken to living off them, and off the interest from money . . . Obsessed by rents, they have deserted the virtuous occupations of breeding and agriculture, and all that sustains men naturally. . . . It may well be said that the riches which should have brought wealth have brought poverty, since they have been so misused that the trader no longer trades, the farmer no longer farms, and many are unemployed and destitute.

In a passage that illustrates a phenomenon common to countries other than Spain, Cellórigo goes on to say:

> *Censos* are the plague and ruin of Spain. For the sweetness of the sure profit from *censos* the merchant leaves his trading, the artisan his employment, the peasant-farmer his farming, the shepherd his flock; and the noble sells his lands so as to exchange the one hundred they bring him for the five hundred the *juro* brings. . . . Through *censos* flourishing houses have perished, and common people have risen from their employment, trade and farming, into indolence; so that the kingdom has become a nation of idleness and vice.

The cortes of Castile were no less concerned about this problem when in the late sixteenth century they claimed that 'many have devoted themselves to *censos,* and thinking this to be a good way of living have abandoned their flocks and land and other trades from which the kingdom used to profit, and spend their fortunes on *censos*'.

For Cellorigo the transference of property brought about by *censos* had resulted in a form of social mobility that brought nothing but disaster to Spain. The middle classes in particular had abdicated their function in society:

> The greater part of the middling sort have joined the ranks of the rich, through the *censos* settlements and entails they have taken from them; and so they have attained a particular status, that of a self-made group; and since they belong neither to the rich nor to the poor nor to the middle, they have thrown the state into the confusion we now see it in. Many who were quite well off among them have joined the ranks of the rich; and others who were better off in trade, in their business, in their employment and in the middle class to which their fathers belonged, have joined the gentry. Many of the middle condition have also fallen into the ranks of the poor, since they so desired to leap into the ranks of the rich, and thence into that of the gentry, and so to live in idleness, that they toppled into the lowest class. . . . As a result many evil consequences affect the middling sort. For in addition to the decline in their numbers, and to being resented by both poor and rich, they are the ones who usually defend the rich, maintain the poor, preserve religious, enrich the clergy; it is they who sustain armies, serve the Prince, and pay the taxes. Yet now the middle class is so destitute, crushed, weak and enervated that, bearing as it does the whole weight of the state upon itself, it could not fall into a worse condition than it is in at present.

The decay of the Castilian middle classes cannot be separated from the general context of the economic development of Spain. There was no peculiar national characteristic which drove Castilians, among them a considerable proportion of *conversos,* to abandon industry and turn to *rentes*. The economic climate was against them. Spain suffered the most severely from the price rise, and the severe fluctuation of prices, aggravated by a disastrous inflation and debasement of the coinage, bred an atmosphere clearly unsuited to investment, since few moneyed men were willing to risk themselves for profits that could be and regularly were wiped out by monetary inflation. In so far as the inflation was caused by too rapid an injection of wealth from America, it was bullion, claimed Cellórigo, that had impoverished Spain, 'not of itself, for that would be to deny its essence, but because of those who enjoy it, since they do not know how to use it'.

The vigour of the bourgeoisie, then, must be judged not only by their own priorities but also by the state of the economy. In the case of Italy there can be little doubt that economic decline was an important factor. The slowing down of the Venetian textile industry in the late sixteenth century, and its decline after the opening of the seventeenth century, for instance, could not fail to lead to a redistribution of investment. Increasing difficulties in the Levant trade, and growing commercial rivalry from other Italian cities and from northern countries, made the comparative security of land and rentals more desirable. Nobles, citizens and people of Venice purchased property and estates on the mainland, the Terraferma, particularly at the end of the sixteenth and the beginning of the seventeenth century. At the same time, in Venice, as in other cities, opportunities to live as a *rentier* were readily available. The decline of commerce, therefore, no less than success in business, encouraged the merchant classes to leave their traditional occupations in favour of security and status. Gradually the mercantile oligarchy became a patriciate, as in the city of Lucca; and in the city of Como, while maintaining hold on its business interests, it extended itself into the collecting of interest from loans it had made to the government or to rural communities. The drift was towards a more leisured life.

Developments in the duchy of Milan give a clear illustration of how the successful bourgeoisie, once they had made their fortune, drifted to the land. Historians used to blame the economic decline of the duchy on its long period of domination by Spain, but substantial responsibility must be assumed by the merchant class. Many of the great merchants and industrialists of the fifteenth century had, by the seventeenth, joined the ruling feudal classes. The Missaglia family, prominent armament manufacturers of the fifteenth century, obtained a noble title at the end of their period of greatest success, and withdrew their capital from the business. Sixteenth-century merchants like the Cusani diverted their money from trade to the purchase of land. Bourgeois who had spent their career in the public service (families like the Borromeos, patricians like the Moroni), members of the professions, and office-holders, all committed their fortunes to the land, from which they derived a noble title and feudal rents. When privilege and status were so readily obtainable, why pursue vile gain?

While the decay of the Mediterranean bourgeoisie was closely connected with general economic factors, the fate of the central and east European trading classes was in addition modified by political forces. In a part of the continent with a lower density of population than western Europe, the towns were smaller and weaker, and so more likely to be dominated by the rural areas. The long struggle between the traders of the towns and the producers in the countryside, a struggle which in Russia lay behind the great urban revolts of 1648, was resolved throughout most of central and eastern Europe in the course of the sixteenth century in favour of the producers.

The distinction between town and country that we have just applied to Russia is not, of course, wholly accurate. In a relatively primitive economy no such division can be made. This becomes clear when we consider the Russian 'bourgeoisie', who can usually be regarded as the trading classes of the towns, the *posadskie lyudi*; but also consisted of the rural traders, inhabitants of the villages known as *slobody*. The wealthier traders too had their interests in both town and country. It was perhaps this lack of differentiation, in addition to the feudal structure of Russian society, that repressed the growth of an autonomous urban bourgeoisie. There was no field that the traders and merchants could specifically call their own. We have already seen that the nobility and monasteries dominated large-scale trade and industry. The chief minister Morozov, who fell from power in 1648, traded in grain, mined and produced potash, possessed distilleries and mills, exploited iron mines and ran a metallurgical industry. He was at once a great landowner, a merchant, an industrialist, entrepreneur and usurer. When princes of both State and Church promoted capitalism to this extent, what function could the nascent bourgeoisie possibly have?

What gave the conflict between traders and producers

elsewhere in Europe its peculiar importance was that the latter, owners of the soil and of the peasantry, were the noble class. Strengthened in their possession of land by the seizure of Church property after the Reformation, the nobility gradually came to exercise within the state a political preponderance that no ruler could dispute. At the political level this had a serious effect upon the bourgeoisie, since the rulers repeatedly took the side of the nobles in constitutional disputes with the towns, so that the voice of the towns in the Estates of each realm was progressively weakened. But it was the economic factor that was decisive. The fate of urban privileges in Brandenburg provides an example. As elsewhere in central Europe, brewing was a leading industry of the towns. The nobility enjoyed some exemption from taxes on this commodity, and consequently were able to produce cheaper beer than the urban breweries, in open violation of the law which equalised beer prices. They soon took over much of the rural market and brought depression to the towns: in 1595 the authorities counted eight hundred and ninety-one ruined breweries in the towns of Brandenburg, while new ones continued to spring up in the countryside. Commerce, long an activity of the town bourgeoisie, suffered similarly. When the nobles began to develop production of corn from their estates, they also began to find ways of transporting it themselves in order to avoid the middlemen in the towns. Despite some attempt to restrict this, by the mid-sixteenth century the nobility were exporting their corn freely. By the early seventeenth century the Brandenburg gentry were claiming that they were entitled to export freely by both land and water, and that they were exempt from tolls and duties. The authorities were unable to intervene.

The result was the decline of the towns and their trading population. At times the towns even had to suffer famine because of the way in which the producers held back supplies in order to speculate in prices. It was not corn and beer only, but all the other produce of the land, in which the gentry began to deal on the basis of the unequal privileges they were accorded. The towns lost their privileged trading and industrial position, and the noble class rose at the expense of the bourgeoisie. The picture was the same throughout the northeast. In Prussia and in Pomerania too, exemption from taxes gave the gentry a clear field in the sphere of corn and beer. After a century of complaints the great port of Königsberg in 1634 claimed that nothing had been done to remedy the situation. The economic and commercial decay of the towns, and the weakening of the bourgeoisie, continued in the course of the seventeenth century, and the trend was consolidated in the 1650s and 1660s by the various measures of state control adopted by the rulers of Brandenburg-Prussia.

In the east the case of Hungary presents a similar picture. Suffering from the burden of the long wars against the Turks, Hungary underwent both a political crisis and a crisis of production. Anxious to rescue their fortunes, the nobles, the agrarian producers, laid claims to control over distribution as well as over production. Some concessions were made when in 1563 the kingdom passed a law permitting nobles who were refugees from the Turks to buy houses in the towns and to import wine from the countryside free, provided this was for their own use only. Once granted to a section of the nobility, these privileges opened the way to the nobles as a whole to establish themselves in the towns and, what is more, through marriage with the urban patriciate to take part in the government of the towns. It was in vain in 1574 that the cities presented a demand that landlords should not be allowed to trade in agricultural produce. The diet ruled that provided the customs duty was paid they could trade both internally and externally in all goods. Inevitably the towns and the bourgeoisie collapsed before the economic domination of the gentry.

The central German bourgeoisie had complex characteristics that have never been adequately studied. It is perhaps true to say, however, that here as in western Europe social success compromised the business ethic of the middle classes. This applies not only to traders and financiers who rose in the world, but also in particular to the vast number of office-seekers in the German states. Perhaps the most famous of the merchant-bankers of the early sixteenth century, the Fuggers, were typical of the traditionalist outlook that restricted the successful bourgeois. The family entered the ranks of the nobility of the Empire; moreover they purchased land extensively, and conducted the business of their estates in the finest feudal manner. The decay of considerable sections of the trading classes may also be deduced from the decline in Germany's economic fortunes with the disappearance of Hanse supremacy in the northern towns, and the depression that set into the trading centres of southern Germany with the decline of Italian trade and of Antwerp. But this was merely a shifting of economic forces, not an absolute decline, and the merchant classes of Hamburg and Leipzig, to name two centres, were flourishing both before and after the Thirty Years War.

It was the tenure of office that characterised the bourgeoisie in most central German cities. An imperial decree of 1530 described the urban middle classes as falling into roughly three categories: the common citizens (including retail shopkeepers and journeymen), then above them the merchants and master craftsmen, and finally the patrician class of office-holders. In smaller towns the last two groups tended to merge, in line with the fact that even self-made men allowed themselves to be attracted by office and by 'living off investments and rents' (to quote the 1530 decree). Merchant families did supply recruits to the class of officials. But by far the vast majority of recruits came from the body of university graduates (who here as everywhere else in western Europe tended to study law in order to enter the administration), drawn from patrician families and therefore assured of a place in the elite after graduating. In Württemberg in the mid-sixteenth century this group occupied nearly three-quarters of the places in public administration. Here was a flourishing middle class, a rising bourgeoisie, yet one which had clearly divorced itself from any part in the production of wealth, and had committed itself to the ideals of office and *rentes,* ideals which in a monarchical regime were a prelude to the attainment of noble status.

Attracted by ideals which involved living off unearned income, the upper bourgeoisie of a large part of Europe had virtually resigned from their class; elsewhere, unfavourable economic circumstances weakened the position of both towns and bourgeoisie. How significant was this for the general development of European history?

THE BOURGEOISIE AND THE EUROPEAN CRISIS

Though little agreement is possible about the existence of a so-called bourgeois spirit or ethic, there can be little doubt that in historical perspective the sections of the urban population we normally call bourgeois — ranging from small independent artisans to the upper ranks of the patriciate — were the most vigorous section of the population. They were often conservative, above all when attempting to preserve the guild system; but economic enterprise, commercial adventure and the accumulation of capital were associated primarily with them. Inevitably their elimination or withdrawal from the political and economic life of a country tended to create a serious crisis.

The bourgeoisie played a fundamental role in the evolution of the European crisis. The decay of the great trade routes of the Renaissance — the links between the Mediterranean and southern Germany and Belgium — is associated with the end of one phase in the history of the European bourgeoisie. When that phase had passed, when Venice was in decline, the Spanish empire in decay, and Antwerp desolate, the future shifted to the bourgeoisie of northwest Europe. The shift in the balance of economic forces towards the northwest cannot be explained in terms of class; but any explanation that leaves out of account the role — which was obvious to contemporaries — of the middling sort of people, does violence to the facts. Spanish thinkers from Cellórigo down through the Count-Duke of Olivares were only too well aware of the link between decline and an ineffective bourgeoisie. 'Our republic', Cellórigo exaggerated, 'has reached the two extremes of rich and poor, with no middle condition to bridge them.' In one of his more extravagant plans, Olivares even thought of bringing the Jews back, to inject new life and capital into Spanish society.

The bourgeoisie, in short, were essential to economic expansion. The simplest case-history to illustrate this point is Sweden, which in the early seventeenth century seemed to all Europe to be the third great Protestant giant. Though Sweden developed rapidly in the course of the century, however, its economic vigour was incomparably smaller than its military strength, not least because of the virtual absence of an effective middle class of capitalists and lawyers. The contrast with the maritime powers was striking. For despite what we know of the conservative structure of English and Dutch society, there was an obvious sense in which the two states might appear, to their European competitors at least, to have been bourgeois in spirit. Whatever the priorities of life at home, abroad the commercial success of the Protestant powers was based on a steady investment of capital by gentry and mercantile bourgeoisie. A recent study of over five thousand native investors in England's overseas trading companies in the period 1575-1630 arrives at the following figures: 73.5 per cent of the investors were bourgeois merchants, 2.4 per cent were merchants who had been knighted, 9.9 per cent were knights, 9.3 per cent were gentry, 3.5 per cent were peers and 1.4 per cent were yeomen and men in professions. The gentry were prominent in the companies, some of which were largely or wholly composed of noble and gentry members, such as the Virginia Company (44.7 per cent membership) and the Africa Company (78.9 per cent membership). Moreover the gentry in these fifty-six years invested something like £1,500,000 in the companies. But it was the bourgeois merchants who were beyond all doubt the foundation of England's commercial greatness. At no time after the early seventeenth century did any other country (save only Holland) succeed in mobilising the resources of its middle classes so successfully. The hopeful pleas of the Code Michau in France were indicative of the failure of the French state to achieve anything comparable to what the English or the Dutch had done.

The shift in power, signalled by the commercial preponderance of the Anglo-Dutch bourgeoisie, was only one aspect of the crisis. Internally, serious fissures were set up in the lives of some states by the decay of their bourgeoisie. The situation may perhaps be seen at its most serious in central and eastern Europe, where the political and economic decline of the towns, added to the rapid development of a gentry-dominated system of agriculture based on serfdom, led to a prolonged struggle between town and country. The bitterest epoch of the struggle was in the mid-seventeenth century, leading in Brandenburg (by the *Recess* of 1653) and in Russia (by the *Ulozhenie* of 1649) to the victory of the feudal classes. In the east, therefore, the countryside won its battle against the towns; whereas in the west the opposite was true. The critical situation of these years was of course paralleled in other parts of Europe: a key feature of the revolt of Naples in 1647, for instance, as of the Frondes in 1649, was the attempt of an aristocracy fortified by bourgeois blood to take over the machinery of state. It is true to say that on the whole those countries which lacked a strong bourgeoisie were the very ones to succumb in the moment of crisis and to accept a system of absolute rule, operated not necessarily by a single ruler but by the entire aristocratic class.

The countries, on the other hand, which showed the most vigorous opposition to absolutist trends in government, and which evolved a body of theory to support their stand, were those — notably England and Holland — where the gentry and bourgeoisie made spectacular attempts to preserve their material gains from attack. It is clear, then, that though the whole of Europe suffered from a period of intense crisis in the middle seventeenth century, the causes and circumstances of the

214

crisis, at least in social terms, differed from one end of the continent to the other. Though the bourgeoisie were at the centre of events, their significance varied greatly according to situation.

BETRAYAL BY THE BOURGEOISIE?

It was once the fashion for Anglo-Saxon historians to present the sixteenth and seventeenth centuries as a great age of triumphs for the bourgeoisie, who were supposed to have been uniquely industrious and largely Puritan, and who were alleged to have prepared England for its destiny as a world power. Behind this strange mixture of Weber and Marx, we can discern nothing more alarming than the Whig history of a past generation, with its firmly nationalist and strongly Protestant overtones. The attempt to present the bourgeoisie as the revolutionary and progressive class in seventeenth-century England (a myth still upheld by pseudo-Marxist historiography), has long since ceased to be convincing in view of the detailed studies that have been made of the English civil war. This is not to call in question their leading role as capitalists and traders; but beyond this economic function the middle classes were not notably progressive or socially radical.

In Europe as a whole the bourgeoisie suffered from two grave weaknesses: they were an incoherent class; and they were rigidly conservative. It may be questioned whether they were so incoherent. They were, after all, a vigorous rising group, creators and promoters of wealth, jealous of their political privileges and sometimes also of their religion. Studying a part of Europe not commonly remembered for its middle class, Franche Comté, Lucien Febvre has demonstrated none the less that the bourgeoisie there were probably the most active social group in the country. As traders, they devoted themselves regularly to work, and travelled widely throughout Europe in order to promote their commerce. As landowners, they developed the soil, and used their estates for extensive social activities such as riding and hunting. Male members of the family knew how to fight and had been to war. They were also the most cultured class in the country, to judge by the domestic libraries they possessed; moreover, their sons were educated in several foreign countries. The picture could be repeated for England and other states, but is not sufficient evidence. For by 'coherence' here we mean a sense of identity, and this the bourgeoisie seem to have notably lacked. Of all social strata, they were those least entitled to be described as a 'class'. The common people, as we shall see, were often very aware of their identity, and the nobles spent much time discussing theirs; but the middling sort remained undifferentiated in their own minds. In ethical terms the bourgeoisie had not yet found itself. One looks in vain among the private records of merchants and capitalists for memoirs which might give us some idea of their outlook, hopes and ideals. Instead we have to rely on the accounts of public commentators like Jacques Savary, or theologians like Richard Baxter. A diligent historian can piece together fragments like these and claim to have established what the bourgeois mentality was. Yet this is something quite different from what the bourgeois himself might have written.

For him, as for Loyseau, his principal identity referred not to a class but merely to his station in life, a station which was liable to improve constantly. Unlike the nobles, who knew and recognised the members of their own grouping, regardless of civic boundaries, the bourgeois (apart from his civic loyalties) felt that he belonged ultimately only to the rank towards which he aspired. Hence, as we have seen, social mobility involved the acceptance by the bourgeoisie of the ideals of a class which was technically alien to theirs. In this sense, their 'incoherence' led the more successful members into the acceptance of what we might call conservatism. The extent of this conservatism of course varied from country to country. In some the successful bourgeois turned his back on trade and capital earnings. It is this trend that Professor Braudel has categorised as a great 'betrayal by the bourgeoisie'. But in countries where the gentry also traded, as in England, there was no need to jettison commerce as the price of social success. In republics, it was easiest of all for the bourgeoisie to adapt to their new status: oligarchies were formed and, in time, aristocracies. In the Italian state of Lucca the commercial ruling oligarchy which had formerly described itself as *patres, patricii senatoresque*, altered its description by the end of the sixteenth century to *nobilitas*; while the group formerly dignified as *plebs et populus* was downgraded to the rank of *ignobilitas*. The function and status of the new nobility of Lucca were discussed for the first time by the writer Pompeo Rocchi in his *Il gentilhuomo* (1568). The Dutch oligarchy of the seventeenth century never reverted quite as radically, but the structure of its society was described in no uncertain terms in the early eighteenth century by an Englishman who declared that 'their government is aristocratical: so that the so much boasted liberty of the Dutch is not to be understood in the general and absolute sense, but *cum grano salis*'.

It was with the French bourgeoisie that the reaction was most marked. Their apologists adopted the view that, to quote a seventeenth-century president of the Parlement of Paris, 'there is only one kind of nobility, and it is acquired through service either in the army or in the judiciary, but the rights and prerogatives are the same'. The notion of service likewise formed the basis of the theories that the Huguenot writer Louis Turquet de Mayerne put down in his *De la monarchie aristodémocratique* (written 1591, published 1611). Mayerne totally rejected the old concepts of nobility. Of nobility by birth he claimed that 'birth is neither the origin nor basis of nobility'. Wealth, on the other hand, was a necessary prerequisite, since 'a poor nobility is useless to the state'. To justify social mobility, he asserted that 'the common people are the seed-ground of the nobility'. Finally, the definition: 'true nobility has its basis only in good acts; in the work, I mean, of men who deserve well of the state'. And, in effect, 'proper fulfilment of one's public office ennobles a man'. What this meant was simply that Mayerne was trying to create a bourgeois concept of *noblesse*, to enable the bourgoisie to replace the old ruling class. Only the merchant, he argued, deserved nobility, for he proved it by his worldly success; moreover, he benefited the realm through trade, which enriched the country and also gave him a knowledge of public affairs that no other profession did. Arms and war, then, were an ignoble profession; what was noble was trade, finance and agriculture. It was precisely in revolutionary sentiments like these that the conservative aspirations of the bourgeoisie were, paradoxically, most clearly expressed; for if Mayerne wished to overthrow one nobility it was only to replace it by another.

Despite the conservative orientation of the middle classes, the 'betrayal', such as it was, was limited mainly to the three principal Latin countries. The Germanic northern countries had their own forms of social reaction, which on the whole did not include the abdication of the bourgeoisie from the professions that had put them where they were.

6 THE PEASANT ECONOMY

Du sehr verachter Bauernstand
Bist doch der beste in dem Land
Kein Mann dich gnugsam preisen kann
Wann er dich nur recht siehet an.

Wie stünd es jetzund um die Welt
Hätt Adam nicht gebaut das Feld?
Mid Hacken nährt sich anfangs der
Von dem die Fürsten kommen her.[1]

GRIMMELSHAUSEN, *Simplicissimus* (1668)

Whosoever doth not maintain the plough destroys this Kingdom.

SIR ROBERT CECIL (1601)

By far the most important sector of the economy before the era of industrial capitalism was the land; by far the largest and most essential sector of the population was the peasantry. Agriculture was consequently the mainstay of economy, society and state. The peasant classes were, correspondingly, the mainstay of all three. In a well-known German print of the sixteenth century, the tree of society is illustrated with peasants as the roots and — after the ascent branch by branch through the lower and upper classes, king and pope — perhaps even more significantly, as the crown of the tree. It was, in short, more commonly accepted than we may realise that the agricultural labourers were the very basis of the state. The quotation given above from Robert Cecil, Elizabeth's secretary of state, emphasises the concern felt by the authorities for this sector. Unlike the industrial workers, peasants were seldom a despised class. This seems odd when we realise in what miserable conditions the majority of the rural classes toiled in the early modern period. Yet traditional respect for the soil and its fruits, a respect hallowed by the seasonal rites of the Church, continued to adhere to the class that worked the land.

1 You, much despised peasantry, are yet the finest in the land; no man can esteem you too highly, when once he sees your worth. How would it be now in the world had Adam not tilled the soil? It was originally the hoe that sustained him, the man from whom princes arose.

By the seventeenth century artists began to represent peasants as drunken, boorish louts, a sign no doubt of a growing lack of comprehension among the expanding urban population. But the respect attached to the status of peasant still retained a powerful influence over both social attitudes and political policy. It would be mistaken to interpret this respect in economic terms only, though concern for the chief producing class was naturally widespread. There were two main ethical reasons why Europeans defended the peasant in this period: first, because he embodied the traditional values of society; second, because his position was being undermined by forces disruptive of the old order.

The view that the peasant was the fount of society is clearly expressed in the mid-seventeenth-century quotation given at the head of this chapter. Adam was the first peasant: all men and all nobles were therefore descended from peasants. Far from being a revolutionary assertion, this claim was commonplace. It can be found in the literature of most countries in Europe. In the peasant was to be found those virtues of labour, patience, subordination, duty and piety that every Christian priest praised from his pulpit. The peasant was not sullied by the sins of the townsmen, by the search for profit. He represented a self-contained unit, who lived off no other man, and who trusted in God.

Such at least was the myth, and it was by no means a harmless one, for it determined the prejudices of many centuries of mless one, for it determined the prejudices of many centuries of Christian civilisation. In economic life the acceptance of subsistence agriculture as natural and good and of trade, particularly in trade for profit, as bad, had a persistently regressive effect. Social groups which did not engage in agriculture to any appreciable extent were ostracised as economic parasites who would not soil their hands with true work: hence the popular basis of anti-Semitism, since Jews tended to be an urban minority, and were devoted to the unnatural vice of usury.

In an age when land values were changing rapidly and the function of rural labourers was being disturbed, those who were concerned for social justice were alarmed most of all by the depressed state of the peasant classes. In England in particular the sixteenth century witnessed an effort by numerous writers to preserve the position of the independent labourer in rural society. In the process, the virtues of the English yeomanry were highly idealised, as though the fate of the kingdom virtually depended on their freedom. On the whole, the English managed to keep a class of free tillers of the soil. On the continent, the trend was quite different.

THE AGRARIAN ECONOMY

The sixteenth century seems to have lived under the shadow of controversies over depopulation: in England the deserted villages, in central Europe the *Wüstungen*, were still evidence of disappearing towns. And despite the very clear rise in population figures during the period, few towns returned to life. Cities grew, existing towns expanded, but the fields expanded too, and in the partnership between town and country it was the latter that was the superior partner. The major part of the working population was occupied on the land; essential food supplies came from the land alone. For all the quick profits brought by commerce and retailing, it was on the soil that the livelihood of most people depended. Hence the great ease with which disruption could be caused by bad weather, by poor harvests, by the passage of troops; hence too the concern of economists whenever the area of tillage was threatened by pasture-farming. In general the years up to the mid-seventeenth century were flourishing ones for agriculture, and little threat to the supremacy of the soil existed.

The dominant trend of the century 1550-1650 was the extension of arable. It expressed itself in three ways: in the conversion of common and pasture land to arable, in the reclamation of land from the sea, and in the advance of the plough into what had formerly been forest land. The last of these was perhaps the least significant. Though woodland was continually eroded in this period the causes tended to include sales of trees by impecunious forest owners (including the crown), levelling of woods to build and to lay out parks (a common habit of nobles throughout Europe), and thefts of wood by peasants. In England in the early seventeenth century a report claimed very plausibly that 'the principal and especial cause of spoil in forests and parks is the poorest sort of people inhabiting and bordering near the same'. Thanks to the high price of firewood and timber, forest owners themselves were reluctant to alienate their woods or convert to arable. But the fact remains that forests were eroded and destroyed, so that the state had to step in to protect them. In both France and Spain there was continuous legislation to protect forests, and in France the crown even made its legislation apply to all feudal and private woods, on the grounds that these were within the scope of its sovereignty. Trees were a major public concern because they supplied fuel, were used in shipbuilding, and were essential for the prevention of soil erosion. Charles I of England, however, seems to have appreciated forests less for these reasons than because they were a useful source of income in sales of trees (the French crown also broke its own laws in this way), and were perfect for hunting in. The very volume of legislation protecting trees was a guide to the assaults on forests. Inevitably, where wood was destroyed arable crept in: 'the countryside is being deforested', as the estates of Languedoc complained with some exaggeration in 1546. In England by the early seventeenth century the argument that arable land would be more profitable to the nation than forest, began to gather force; it found its parliamentary expression in the October 1653 Act for the Disafforestation, Sale and Improvement of Royal Forests. Despite this act, no major changes occurred, and the plough was not a major destroyer of forests.

The conversion of pasture to arable was obviously not a universal rule, for pasture was necessary for livestock, which meant meat and wool, two exceptionally important items. Though arable tended to predominate, it is not easy to measure the change in terms of acreage. Perhaps the simplest and most ready guide to the trend was the relative value of land, as in East Anglia where, as we have already seen, the rent of arable rose sixfold between 1590 and 1650 while that of pasture rose by only two or three times. It is in the reclamation of land from the sea that the demand for arable emerges most clearly. Reclamation became a major industry in which the Walloons and Dutch proved to be the most experienced engineers. Large areas were reclaimed for the United Provinces from the sea: between 1565 and 1590, eight thousand and forty-six hectares were won back, and from 1590 to 1615 a total of thirty-six thousand two hundred and thirteen hectares, the largest area to have been reclaimed for two centuries. Other areas of Europe were no less active in the task. In Schleswig-Holstein by the year 1650 about twenty-five thousand hectares of marshland on the coast had been reclaimed. Henry IV of France invited a distinguished team of Netherlanders under Humphrey Bradley to supervise drainage of marshes in France, and it was Netherlanders, profiting from their long experience, who played a leading part in most reclamation schemes elsewhere on the continent, in Italy and in Germany. For the reclamation of land near Ferrara in 1598, for example, Dutch engineers were employed. In England the long-mooted drainage of the Fens was periodically postponed for lack of capital, and it was not until adequate money could be collected by Charles I that the scheme was eventually put into effect. The engineer employed for the task was Cornelius Vermuyden, who promised to reclaim 'a continent of about 400,000 acres, which being made winter ground would be an unexpected benefit to the Commonwealth of £600,000 per annum and upwards'. Something close to this figure was in fact won back permanently from the sea, and produced some of the richest arable land in England.

The principal reason for the great extension of land and arable was a greater demand for food. There was of course a considerable variation at different periods between the demand for meat and the demand for agricultural produce. The essential point is that the demand was created by the rapidly expanding population of the late sixteenth century, and was reflected in high prices for food. It was high cereal prices above all that encouraged farmers to make their profits by putting their land under the plough. For a time food crops made unopposed headway: pasture land was converted to arable when animal husbandry proved to be less profitable, and in one area at least, in Maine (north-west France), even vineyards were converted to cornfields. In eastern Europe, population increase played no significant part in the shift to arable. There the more immediate reason was the favourable price situation of the western European market, and it was to supply this market that cereal production was developed. Between west and east, then, there were somewhat different reasons for the same economic development.

The emphasis on agriculture was accompanied by a spate of books on the subject, notably in the century after 1550. The best-known English writer was Sir Anthony Fitzherbert. In France the late sixteenth-century works of Belon, Choyselat and Estienne were followed in 1600 by the most famous of the French books, Olivier de Serres' *Théatre d'Agriculture*, which went through numerous editions within a generation. In Germany the most notable treatise was Conrad Heresbach's 1570 dialogue *De re rustica* (On agriculture), which was followed in the early seventeenth century by Jacob Coler's *Oeconomia ruralis* (Rural economy), a combination of two works he had written and first published in the 1590s. In Poland the most popular work, *Notaty gospodarskie* (Notes on the rural economy), was published in 1588 by a nobleman, Anselm Gostomski, and held the field for a full century. Many of the books on agriculture were merely technical manuals, but the best were influenced by an urgent social philosophy. It was the express intention of Olivier de Serres, for instance, to recall the ever-growing numbers of absentee noble landlords in France to the delights as well as the profits of estate farming.

Despite the boom conditions that prevailed for agriculture in the century up to about 1650, it seems true to say that no real technical advance in production was achieved. This is all the more surprising since in nearly every other sphere revolutionary changes were occurring. Yet on the land the field-systems, rotation methods, tools and crops and fodder utilisation, changed very little. If progress is to be measured by output, the evidence seems to be that the yield ratios of seed (that is, the ratio between seed sown and seed harvested) did not increase remarkably in western Europe over the average, which varied between 6 and 8:9 for wheat. Instead, the ratios decreased as the agricultural depression of the mid-seventeenth century set in. This surprising stability in cereal production contrasts sharply with two outstanding features of the period: the great extension of cultivated land, which at least in drainage enterprises involved an unprecedented injection of capital and machinery; and the fundamental change in social relationships, which in western Europe can be identified roughly with the decline of feudalism, and in eastern Europe with the onset of a new feudalism.

This contradictory picture of agricultural development has led one historian to question its validity for England. Dr Eric Kerridge has argued that it was precisely the sixteenth and seventeenth centuries that witnessed the so-called 'agricultural revolution' in England, and that 'all its main achievements fell before 1720, most of them before 1673, and many of them much earlier still'. On this estimate, the period 1560-1673 witnessed important changes, including the floating of water-meadows, the substitution of up-and-down husbandry (alternative grass and tillage) for permanent tillage or grass, the introduction of new fallow crops and grasses (turnips, clover, etc.), marsh drainage, manuring and stock-breeding. The effects of these changes may not have been immediately felt, and in any case the depression of the late seventeenth and early eighteenth century would have restricted expansion. Dr Kerridge claims nevertheless that crop yields were raised over a wide area, and that 'foodstuff production must at least have doubled between 1540 and 1700'. It was thanks to the changes effected in this period that Sir William Petty could claim in 1676 that

> it is manifest that by reason of the dreyning of fens, watering of dry grounds, improving of forests and commons, making of heathy and barren grounds to bear saint-foyne and clovergrass, meliorating and multiplying several sorts of fruits and garden-stuff, making some rivers navigable etc — I say it is manifest, that the land in its present condition is able to bear more provision and commodities than it was forty years ago.

WHO OWNED THE LAND?

We are so used to thinking of the peasantry as a depressed population, and of the nobility as the landowning class, that it is salutary to be reminded that in western Europe the peasants owned by far the greatest proportion of land. The very general figures that are available refer mainly to the eighteenth century, but can be applied fairly safely to the seventeenth when, if anything, more land would have been in the hands of the rural classes. In France it has been estimated that about half the land was held by peasants, varying from a proportion of twenty per cent in Brittany and Normandy to over fifty per cent in Dauphiné. In west Germany, in Brunswick, the nobles held only eight per cent, the peasants 67.5 per cent of all agricultural land. The elementary logic of economy meant that those who exploited the soil tended, in those parts of Europe not dominated by *latifundia*, to be the proprietors.

This picture of a landowning peasantry is of course an entirely fallacious one. Firstly, and most obviously, the peasantry as the largest class were too numerous for the land available to them, and their holdings were invariably inadequate. Fifty per cent of French land, for instance, had to suffice for the ninety per cent of the population that worked in the country. The average peasant holding was therefore only in exceptional circumstances capable of supporting a rural family comfortably. A clear example is supplied by the town of Roquevaire in Lower Provence, of which we have details for the year 1663. The landed property there was apportioned as follows: the clergy owned one per cent, the bourgeoisie nineteen per cent, the nobles twenty-three per cent, and the peasants held fifty-seven per cent. On the face of it this gave the peasantry the lion's share of the soil. But the landholding community at Roquevaire was made up of nine nobles, twelve bourgeois and over one hundred and fifty peasant proprietors, so that roughly speaking each noble family held nine times and each bourgeois family three times as much as the average peasant landed family. Secondly, peasant tenure of the soil cannot be dissociated from the obligations that might bind either soil or peasant or both. The free peasantry were a minority class and tended to be confined to the north of Europe and to the Baltic lands. Elsewhere few were freeholders. They might be personally free, as in most of western Europe, but their land was for the most part not held in full propriety, and had to fulfil various obligations to a lord. In effect this meant a tenancy, not ownership. Where the feudal system was operative, in various parts of France, eastern Spain, Italy and central and eastern Europe, they had to perform services both in kind and in labour for their lord, a duty which restricted their own personal freedom. All peasants, whether free or not, were in any case finding that the basis of their independence and prosperity was being steadily eroded by developments (such as taxation) which were beyond their control. Finally, it is necessary to remember that there were a huge number of the rural population that held no land at all.

The wide differences in the state of the rural classes in Europe make it important for us to look at them more in terms of areas than we have had to do for other sections of society.

THE ENGLISH PEASANTRY

Thanks to the administrative and legal structure of feudalism in England, where the forms of Roman law never took root, the English peasant farmer was almost totally free by the sixteenth century. The landed peasants in some areas continued to pay traditional dues to manorial lords, but the proportion was not numerically or socially significant. Those who did not farm their own land made up a rural labouring sector which formed as much as a third of the total country population. As in any period of change, the peasant farmers developed both upwards and downwards: in the former case, they improved their lot and moved into the yeomanry or gentry; in the latter, they augmented what was, in an age of expanding population, a growing rural proletariat. Generalisations like these become more comprehensible if we look at one detailed example.

The village of Wigston Magna, in Leicestershire, doubled its numbers from about seventy to one hundred and forty households in the course of the century 1525 – 1625, thereby becoming one of the most thriving villages in the English Midlands. A breakdown of the occupations of the villagers in the late seventeenth century shows that thirty-six per cent depended on agriculture for a living, thirty per cent on crafts and trades connected with the land, and seventeen per cent on framework-knitting. In addition sixteen per cent were simply described as 'poor'. The peasant farmers benefited from the rise in food prices during the century of inflation, and accumulated a comfortable surplus, which in the years up to the early seventeenth century was largely untouched by taxation. The forms of feudal organisation vanished here in 1606 when the last manor was sold by its lord, and the villagers refused to continue to pay the feudal dues to the new occupants. The end of manorial control also meant the end of tenure by copyhold, for the rolls which proved tenure used to be kept by the lord. All tenure now became freehold. As the village developed, its economic life became more diversified. The peasant farmers grew wealthier, because of the demand for their food produce; but the smaller peasants were unable to compete with the larger producers, and as population increased the land-holdings of the smaller peasantry became even more inadequate. Beside the prosperous farmer there now appeared the beginnings of the rural proletariat. The village world of subsistence economy was also being invaded more and more, in proportion to the growth of commerce for the market, by money. Cash transactions became more common, and a ready example can be found in the giving of marriage settlements in cash rather than in kind.

The growth of rural poverty was a notable feature of the period. In the Midlands the cost of living for a farm labourer rose sixfold between 1500 and 1640, while his real wages over the same period fell by about fifty per cent. Not surprisingly, economic distress among the rural population was widespread, and contributed primarily to the growing numbers of vagrants, who were often no more than landless labourers seeking employment. The situation did of course vary widely in other parts of England, and there were even a few patriarchal figures such as Sir George Sondes of Lees Court in Kent who for thirty years spent, in his own words, 'at least a thousand pounds a year' in giving economic help to his farm labourers.

Significantly, however, even the average tenant farmer was not exactly rich. A hypothetical example drawn up by one historian illustrates this. The average small farmer in the early seventeenth century might have a farm of thirty acres, using a three-field system. The two principal costs would have been the payment of rent to a landlord, and the requirements of seed: together these might take up two-thirds of the outgoings of the farm. As much as one-quarter of the crop yield would be retained for purposes of seed to be sown the following year. There would be a few sheep, and oxen for the plough. In a normal year a farm like this might give a net profit of about £15, which would be a less than comfortable margin with which to work.

An independent and free community like Wigston Magna, then, might be representative in that it illustrates the end of feudal control, and the increase of both wealth and poverty; but it is not a clear example of what was perhaps the dominant trend of the late sixteenth and early seventeenth centuries, the redistribution of landed income in favour of the landed class. Small farmers and farm labourers had an increasingly difficult time; the former, because it was a constant struggle to make output exceed the level of rents, the latter, because wages fell rather than rose. A small landowner might profit, but he had to compete with the greater marketing power of the larger producers. In social terms, it was not a comfortable period for the mass of the rural population. In purely economic terms, however, it was a period of rapid progress in production, in the development of the market, and in capital formation.

THE WEST EUROPEAN PEASANTRY

We are concerned here not so much with describing the peasantry, a task beyond our scope, as with defining certain aspects of the changing structure of the peasant economy. We have already observed that, formally speaking, the peasantry held the greater part of the soil in western Europe. In seventeenth-century Sweden, for instance, the peasantry held half the land, the crown about one-third, and the nobility about one-fifth. However, such figures are largely meaningless as far as the peasants are concerned, since they fail to tell us exactly how much land the average peasant held. On the whole, the west European peasant was free, in the sense that he was not personally dependent in the way that the serfs of mediaeval and of eastern Europe were. But this freedom was at all times hedged about with important qualifications which often made it merely nominal.

Perhaps the most important qualification was the amount of land held. The average peasant holding was barely enough to support a man and his family; moreover, it tended to be a tenancy rather than a freehold. Even where land was held free, as in Castile, it was seldom enough to assure a regular and reliable income. The smallness of holdings was a phenomenon that was aggravated by the population rise of the late sixteenth century, which caused an even greater division of the soil into allotments. Within the peasant class, there was a readily recognisable structure of landholding: at the top were a small handful of well-landed independent farmers and at the bottom a large number of peasants with very much smaller rented holdings. Goubert suggests that in the French district of Beauvaisis in the seventeenth century a typical village community of about one hundred families would have one or two very rich *laboureurs* (peasant farmers), five or six middling *laboureurs*, and about twenty middling peasants (whom he groups together as *haricotiers).* Even below these, however, were the much larger class of farm-workers and day-labourers of various sorts who in most countries (certainly in France and in England) made up the majority of the rural population. For his Beauvais community, Goubert suggests a figure of up to fifty families of these *manouvriers.* In the Dijonnais in Burgundy these workers were the vast majority of the male adults in the countryside, and totally outnumbered the peasant farmers. The farm-labourers were usually fixed in their residence, while day-labourers had so little means of their own that they were more often on the move, particularly into the towns. What this picture suggests is that it is mistaken to look on the landholding peasant as the largest sector of the rural population: he was the most typical, certainly, and the most important, but not always the most numerous.

A second qualifying factor that affected the status of the peasant was the proprietor under whom he worked. The Swedish peasants, for example, would be divided into three categories: crown peasants, nobles' peasants, and tax-paying peasants. The last category of peasant was so called because he was a freeholder, and his only obligation was the payment of taxes to the state. He was perhaps more fortunate than crown peasants, who paid rent, rendered labour services for a set number of days in the year, and had to pay renewal fees when their leases expired; or than the peasants of the nobility, who shared similar conditions to crown peasants, but were more at the mercy of their landlords. In Sweden the peasants in private hands were exempt from ordinary taxation: this was not the case in most other countries.

In New Castile, to take one Spanish region for which we have some information, the landholding peasant was very much in a minority. Over half the rural population here consisted of agricultural labourers, and the general average was more in the region of seventy per cent. The 'peasant' in New Castile was more often than not an agricultural worker. In many villages there were no peasants at all: all were labourers dependent on employment, frequently starving when there was no way of securing a living. The peasants then were no more than a quarter or a third of the rural population, but even of this number only a minority held their own land. As in many other parts of Europe the soil consisted principally of common fields and of land owned by nobles, clergy and townsmen: the peasant's private plot was exceptional.

The various obligations of peasants can be illustrated by reference to a few examples. In the west German lands labour services formed part of the system of estate economy known as *Grundherrschaft*. In Brunswick the labour dues were formalised by a law of 1597. According to this the peasantry in that state owed weekly services: an *Ackermann* (peasant farmer) was to give two days statute-labour with his plough-team, a *Halbspänner* (or holder of half a hide of land) was to give one day. When it came to purely manual labour, the peasants owed services varying from two days to half a day a week. By any standards these were fairly heavy demands, yet they occurred in a system which is usually described as a free one in contrast to the serfdom of the east. Labour services with a plough, for example, were onerous, since the team was required to supply two persons and four horses, with a cart. The enormous utility of these services to the landlords is shown by the fact that in the demesne of Gandersheim in the fifty years 1610-60 no work-horses at all were kept, since all the ploughing was done by labour teams. In the year 1639, the demesne obtained 248 ploughing days from labour teams, more than enough for its needs. Nowhere in western Europe outside the German lands and Denmark were labour services so frequent.

The peasant rendered in cash if not in kind. In France and Spain it was the tax system that gave most cause for offence, and it is arguable that taxes were ultimately more ruinous to the peasant economy than labour services.

If, when he sowed his ground (observed a distinguished French lawyer, La Barre, in 1622) the peasant really realised for whom he

229

was doing it, he would not sow. For he is the one to profit least from his labour. The first handful of grain he casts on the soil is for God, so he throws it freely. The second goes to the birds; the third for ground-rents; the fourth for tithes; the fifth for *tailles*, taxes and impositions. And all that goes even before he has anything for himself.

Census returns of 1575-80 for the peasantry of New Castile confirm the plight of the peasant producer, who was obliged on the average to consign well over half his harvest to the payment of taxes and dues of various kinds. The lightest of his burdens tended to be the traditional dues payable to the seigneur. Tithes, which were usually assessed at a strict tenth, came to ten times the value of seigneurial dues. One contemporary commentator, Lope de Deza, asserted in 1618 that the tithes in Toledo province equalled all other taxes in value, but (such was the nature of loyalty to the Church that all writers shared) rather than recommend an end to tithes he suggested that all the other taxes be suppressed. After tithes the peasant had to pay his taxes to the crown; these came to about the same value as the tithes. Finally, and most important of all, came the land rents. In New Castile these took up between one-third and one-half of a peasant's harvest. Quite often the rent would amount to three or four times the value of the tithes. Adding up the rent and the taxes, little could have remained to the producer, as we gather from one village near Toledo which complained in 1580 that 'after paying the rent, nothing was left them'. Nor was this an end to the sorrows of the peasantry for, as we have already seen, those who fell into difficulties borrowed money and found themselves bound by *censos*. Rural indebtedness was all too common. 'In short', complained the cortes of Castile in 1598 when presenting a petition against *censos*, 'everything tends towards the destruction of the poor peasantry and the increase in property, authority and power of the rich.'

A more particular view of the presumed weight of the tax structure in France may be gained from the peasants of Beauvaisis in the mid-seventeenth century. The average peasant *(haricotier)* worked about five hectares of land. The payment of taxes to the crown would take up about one-fifth of his output (the *taille* accounted for most of this), leaving him with eighty per cent of his harvest. The tithe and church taxes would take up another eight per cent of his revenue, and other taxes would account for four per cent more, so that eventually the peasant would be left with sixty-eight per cent of the harvest. Another twenty per cent, however, would have to be set aside for running costs and for the reservation of seed to be sown the following year. This left forty-eight per cent, and still the outgoings were not at an end, for the rent to the proprietor of the land remained to be paid. This varied widely, depending on the system of tenure. What the peasant received eventually might be only a small fraction of his original harvest. This, of course, was in a normal year; and takes no account of the possibility that the peasant might have debts to be repaid out of his income. If the year had been a bad one, as all too frequently it was, or if his debts were many, which was generally true, the peasant faced disaster.

The rise in the burden of taxation on the peasantry was a general western European phenomenon, and it occurred at approximately the same time, from the 1630s onwards. In France it was caused by Richelieu's fiscal policy, in Spain by the policy of Olivares, in Sweden by the demands of the overseas war effort. The final result was to even out the differences in the economic level of the peasantry, and to reduce them to a common misery. The smaller French peasantry were unable to benefit from the favourable price situation of the period, not only because as a rule they did not have a marketable surplus, but also because taxes increased at a far higher rate than prices.

Over and above the immediate ills of taxes and bad harvests, the long-term situation of the farm labourers, whom we have already described as the largest rural class, deteriorated. As in England and in eastern Europe, their earning power declined. In Languedoc between 1500 and 1600 the money wages of agricultural labourers fell from an index of one hundred to fifty-four. As economic difficulties faced both labourers and smallholding peasants, a depression of the rural masses set in. This was to exercise a profound influence on the revolutionary political mood of the mid-seventeenth century.

Two main consequences followed from the difficulties facing the peasantry. As they fell into debt, surrendered their tenancies, and drifted from the soil in despair, their holdings were taken over by others. From this arose the two phenomena of the concentration of estates and the appropriation of rural holdings by the urban classes. We have already observed how the bourgeoisie played an important part in the latter phenomenon. In Beauvaisis by the end of the seventeenth century the bourgeois of the city of Beauvais held about 13·5 per cent of land, as against twenty to

231

twenty-five per cent held by the nobility. In the province of Como in Italy the expropriation of the peasantry reached its height in the crisis years 1620-50, and most of the land that changed ownership fell into the hands of the bourgeoisie or of the Church. The same process occurred in Spain and in Germany. In Brunswick, already as early as 1546 about thirty-four per cent of the farmland in the district of Wolfenbüttel was being developed by tenants of the bourgeoisie.

The concentration of estates was a long-term process. Among several examples of this important development, which set the tone for relationships on the land in the eighteenth century, we may cite the village of Manguio in Languedoc, which in 1595 had only one estate exceeding one hundred hectares, but in 1653 had three and by 1770 eight.

SEIGNEUR AND SOIL IN EASTERN EUROPE

The sixteenth century saw the emergence of the gentry in eastern Europe to a position of economic power and political influence. The Junkers of East Prussia, the *szlachta* of Poland, the *pomeshchiki* of Muscovy, now took their place beside the old noble class. Their social function and style of life approximated closely to that of the traditional aristocracy and because of this it is possible for us to use the one term 'nobility' to refer loosely to the upper stratum of society in most east European countries. The basis of power of this stratum was possession of the land, and it is in terms of land that we must discuss the changing roles of seigneur and peasant in the east.

Why should eastern Europe (east, that is, of the Elbe) be discussed separately from the west? Though generalisations tend to be misleading, the following points indicate the special conditions prevailing in the east. The eastern countries were far less densely populated than the west: the density of population in Poland, for example, varied from fourteen per square kilometre in Greater Poland to three per square kilometre in the Ukraine. The result was that there was a proportionally smaller labour force to serve a large area of cultivated soil. The eastern lands were less economically advanced than the west. The machinery of a centralised state had not come into existence anywhere in the east, so that the nobility were a far more autonomous class than in western Europe. Without a strong state, and without any tradition of service to such a state, the eastern nobility concentrated their efforts on farming their lands and on acquiring wealth and influence on a territorial basis.

The predominance of the noble class is a striking feature of the history of eastern Europe. This arose principally from the relative weakness of the towns and bourgeoisie, a subject we have looked at in the previous chapter. The paucity of large towns (of the seven hundred towns in Poland at the beginning of the seventeenth century only eight had a population exceeding ten thousand), the corresponding lack of a vigorous bourgeoisie, and the constitutional weakness of the Third Estate, gave the country nobility an inestimable advantage. The result was the rapid aristocratisation of eastern governments and the decay of the bourgeois trading interest. The constitutional triumph of the gentry and nobles was simply a reflection of their now well-assured domination of the soil.

Noble tenure of the soil did not by itself give the impetus to an expansion of production and further exploitation of the peasantry. That impetus came from the general economic situation in Europe. The eastern ports had since the fifteenth century been suppliers of grain to western Europe. The produce of eastern estates, therefore, and the trade activity of ports like Königsberg and Gdansk (Danzig), were closely tied to the market demands of western Europe. With the important exception of Russia, most eastern countries were to some extent part of the European market. This was true even of landlocked territories such as Hungary, since thanks to its political status as a Habsburg sphere of influence western Hungary exported agricultural goods through Vienna and south Germany. The close commercial link between east and west, despite their dissimilar economic development, is reflected in the prices of grain and food. Though the *level* of prices remained lower in the east (over the fifty years 1551-1600 prices at Danzig were only fifty-three per cent of those at Amsterdam, and those at Warsaw only forty-six per cent), the order of inflation was comparable to that in the west. In Poland, for example, the rise in grain prices reached its peak in the late sixteenth century, the difference between the second and the third quarter of the century being of the order of seventy-five per cent. The parallel with western trends is most obvious in the price data for Danzig, a port whose activity would naturally reflect the western market. The increasing demands of the western, and even the Mediterranean, market had the effect of causing prices to spiral steeply. The consequent rise in food prices within

Poland, aggravated by the growth of exports, is shown in Figure 16.

It was this rise in cereal and food prices, caused principally by foreign demand, that supplied the incentive required by the landowners of the east. In addition, the different price levels between east and west guaranteed a profit for all, both exporters in the east and importers in the west, concerned in the grain traffic. The rise in prices brought to a head the various social and political developments involving the eastern nobility. While demesne farming declined in western Europe and the nobles attempted to secure incomes from other sources than agricultural production, in much of central and eastern Europe the nobles went back to the land as a source of wealth. The benefits to be obtained from farming are shown by the returns for an estate of the Rantzau family in Holstein in 1600. Of an annual income of five thousand marks, only two hundred and fifty came from peasant rents. The rest came from livestock, grain and dairy produce.

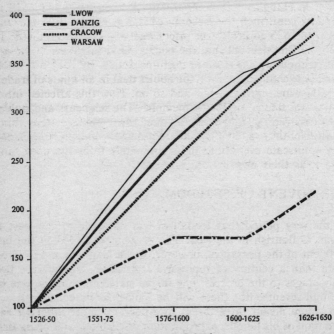

Figure 16 The inflation of food prices in Poland.

Peasant and waste-lands were absorbed into demesne, and the production of grain for a lucrative market became a primary occupation. In countries without access to the sea, grain did not necessarily dominate the economy of the great estates. On the contrary, in Bohemia the principal item of production for both the internal and the external market was beer; and in Hungary wine was by far the most important source of income and capital. Both ecclesiastical and secular lords shared in this expansion of production, which increased their capital earnings and allowed them to operate a virtual monopoly over economic activity. The price rise, fatal to seigneurs in the west, consolidated their power in the east.

Noble entrepreneurship took a great step forward. 'The nobles in past years', commented a Pomeranian official in the late sixteenth century, 'have not been very industrious and keen to make their living. But now in recent years they have become better at it, and since the country existed the nobility has never been so rich and powerful as nowadays.' The progress of the gentry in Hungary was comparable. A royal decree of 1618 in Hungary confirmed the freedom of the gentry from excise and taxes. In 1625 controls over prices and wages were removed. In 1630 the Diet decreed that the nobles could take part in foreign trade without paying taxes or customs duties. By 1655 a memoir of the time could claim that 'the nobles deal in all kinds of trade', in corn, wine, cattle, honey and so on. How this affected other classes was described by the memoir: 'The seigneurs and nobles take over trading; they seize for themselves whatever they think profitable; they exclude the common people and the merchants; they confiscate everything indiscriminately from the poor, and hold it as their own private property.'

THE ADVENT OF SERFDOM

At the very period that feudalism was decaying in the west it began to flourish in the east. The process which led to the enserfment of the peasantry, however, was a long one and covered more than a century of repressive legislation. There were two main stages to the process, one in the sixteenth century, one in the mid-seventeenth; these will be looked at independently.

Serfdom meant three things to a peasant: more intensive exploitation of his labour, expropriation of his land, and being tied to the soil (or to a lord). In order of time, the exploitation came first. The growth of demesne farming meant a greater demand for labour, but the peasants were not available in adequate numbers nor were they all obliged to perform regular labour services. It became the task of the landlords to secure an adequate volume of labour, and this they attempted to do by increasing the burdens on dependent peasants. Many of these fled when the new burdens were imposed, and this only aggravated the labour problem. The power of the state was therefore called in to help solve the difficulty. The legislation that was passed by various governments from the early sixteenth century onwards had one aim in mind: to bind the peasant as closely as possible to the soil and deprive him of freedom of movement. A secondary task of the laws was to increase the burdens, particularly the labour obligations, of the peasants. No better proof can be found of the fact that the machinery of state was serving the interests of the feudal class.

In Prussia, ordinances of 1526, 1540, 1577, 1612, and 1633 progressively limited the right of a peasant to move from his land, or to inherit property. Labour burdens were increased and lords were given the right to exploit the labour of a peasant's children. In Brandenburg, laws of 1518, 1536, and subsequent years likewise tied peasants to the soil, and the question of labour was settled in the early seventeenth century when the High Court ruled that all peasants were liable to unlimited services unless they could prove the contrary. In the Habsburg lands the trend was the same, but the particular problem of these frontier provinces — proximity to the Turks — caused shifts in policy. The general picture can be illustrated by the case of Hungary. Laws of 1514 and 1548 fixed official limits for the labour service (*robot*), but in practice peasants were exploited well above the authorised level of fifty-two days a year. This situation led to the flight of peasants, which in its turn provoked legislation tying the worker to the soil, as measures of 1556 and 1608 stipulated.

The importance of labour services cannot be underrated. Unlike the west, where hired labour was common, many central European estates had to survive largely off feudal services. As in the west, peasant obligations also consisted of tribute in cash and in kind. Since labour rather than tribute was required on the great estates, it became the universal rule in eastern Europe to commute services in cash and in kind into labour services. This can be seen, for example, in Brandenburg, where in 1608 the Von Arnim family, in the Uckermark, was granted a general permit to

236

use the services of its subjects instead of their rents. Extension of labour services became general in this region. By the end of the sixteenth century most of the villages owned by the cathedral chapter of Havelberg had to render about ninety days' labour in the year. Peasants belonging to the Margrave in the vicinity of Wittstock in 1601 had to serve as much as three days in the week normally, and had to give unlimited service during harvest-time. This process was accompanied by attempts to tie the peasant to the soil. At the end of the fifteenth century a law had declared that any peasant leaving a domain must find a replacement before he could leave. In the sixteenth century this law was made a general rule. In 1536 no peasant was allowed to be admitted to any town or domain unless he could produce a letter from his lord showing he had left with his consent.

The expropriation of the peasantry followed inevitably from any intensification of tax or labour dues. The number of free peasants had never been high. In Bavaria, even by the liberating eighteenth century they numbered only four per cent of the peasant population. A community of free and independent peasantry like the *Cölmer* of Prussia was exceptional. In Bohemia by 1654 no more than about five hundred peasants out of a total of sixty-four thousand were personally free. The vast majority was economically underprivileged and heavily dependent. In a time of crisis they fell easily into debt and so into the hands of the principal moneylender — the landlord himself. Indebtedness of an impoverished peasantry became one of the essential factors in the evolution of serfdom. There were several categories of peasant, ranging from the relatively free to the wholly servile, but all were reduced by poverty to a common level of existence. The peasants of Pomerania, whom we may take as an illustration, are described thus for us by a contemporary writing in the 1540s:

The peasants' position is by no means equal. Some possess the heritage of their farms, give moderate dues and have to render limited services. These are well off and rich; and if one of them wants to leave the farm with his children, he sells it with his lord's consent, gives him a tithe of the purchase price, and departs freely with his children and chattels wherever he wants to go. But with the others it is different; for they do not possess the heritage of their holdings and have to serve their master whenever he wants them. Often they cannot do their own work because of the services and thus they become impoverished and abscond . . . They are in practice villeins, for the lord gets rid of them when he pleases.

237

In fact, by the end of the sixteenth century there was little to separate these two categories, since the free peasants became increasingly restricted to the land, were heavily taxed, and burdened with new labour services. In Brandenburg the same deterioration can be seen. In 1552 a local writer said in his description of the New Mark: *'Rustici omnes in liberate educati sunt: tota enim Marchia neminem habet servili conditione natum.'* Fifty years later the jurist Scheplitz commented on the same passage: *'vix dici potest'*. In 1632, for the first time, some peasants of the Ucker and the New Mark were classified simply as *leibeigen*, serfs.

It was in Russia that the reduction in status was most marked. Before the final legislation of serfdom there had been varying grades of peasants, from slaves and villeins, who were found usually on noble demesnes, to completely free peasants and independent landholders. Between these extremes there were the normal categories of tenants, with different degrees of obligations. The second half of the sixteenth century witnessed a severe dislocation of the Russian state, caused principally by wars and by the *oprichnina*. In the depression and depopulation that followed these events, the landlords found it very difficult to secure an adequate labour force. Thousands of peasants had emigrated beyond Muscovy, and the attempt by the landlords (the *pomeshchiki*) to exploit those who remained served only to aggravate the flight from the land. As feudatories of the crown, the *pomeshchiki* appealed to it for help. In the spate of legislation that emerged between the late sixteenth century and the mid-seventeenth century, all categories of peasants suffered, both dependent and free. As usual, the laws concentrated on restricting the peasants' ability to move. The first of these laws was in 1580. Its effectiveness can be seen in the monastery of Volokolamsk where in 1579-80 as many as seventy-six peasants fled and twenty were attracted in; in 1581 not a single peasant moved. But it was difficult to obtain satisfactory observance of the law everywhere, as shown by the need for decrees in subsequent years. Of these, the most important were passed in 1597 and 1607. It is important to observe that these laws, unlike similar ones elsewhere, bound the peasants not to the soil but to their lord: the dependence was wholly personal. While this was going on, the liability of the peasants to taxes and to labour services (*barshchina*) was being increased. Labour services were a major obligation not only in central Russia, for as landlords elsewhere found it more profitable than ordinary dues in kind, they began to extend it to their peasants. The mounting difficulties faced by free peasants obliged very many to borrow and hence to fall into debt. A combination of several factors had by the early seventeenth century reduced the Russian peasants to the common status of serfs. Finally, in 1649, this was constitutionally legalised.

In the course of these developments, many of the peasants of eastern Europe lost their land. Oppressed by debt, victims of necessity or of sheer superior force, they surrendered or sold their holdings to the nobles. For the nobles appropriation of land was nothing new. The spoils obtained from the Church during the Reformation gave them the basis for new extensions to their territory. In 1540 in Brandenburg the Margrave granted the nobles of the Old Mark, and later those of the whole country, the right to buy out their peasants and to replace peasant holdings by demesne. With the active support of the rulers, who themselves bought land, the nobles replaced smallholdings by large estates. Between about 1575 and 1624, according to a survey of the latter year, 441 peasants out of a total of 7,988 were bought out in the Middle Mark. The result was an increase of demesne lands in this area by over fifty per cent and a decrease in peasant lands by about eight per cent. In northeast Estonia, where the landlords likewise took over peasant lands, the number of estates increased from about forty-five in the early seventeenth century to one hundred and thirty-five in 1696.

The new estates were of considerable size, and big estates remained a feature of the trans-Elbe economy. In Mecklenburg, Pomerania and the central area of East Prussia, over half the estates extended to more than one hundred hectares each of agricultural land. In Prussia and Brandenburg, between thirty and fifty per cent were of this size. West of the Elbe, estates were usually much smaller than this. Several peasant properties were usually amalgamated to form a manor. In Saxony the manor of Tauscha was created in the mid-sixteenth century out of seven farms totalling twelve *Hufen* (hides). The manor of Wünschendorf, near Pirna, was erected in 1610 out of five farms totalling four-and-a-half *Hufen*. The process of alienation of peasant property is shown in the following table, which gives details for holdings in the Russian district of Varzuga, by the White Sea. The unit of land is the *luk*, which varied in size but tended to consist of about three hectares of agricultural and woodland.

Owners of lands (in luki)	1563	1575	1586	1614	1622
Peasants	830⅓	726⅓	429	266½	—
Monasteries	36	128	549	549	549
Patriarchate	—	—	—	—	266½
Other	—	12	21½	21½	21½
	866⅓	866⅓	865½	837	837

While the rise of the manorial estates was at the expense of the peasants, however, the degree of expropriation must be set in proportion. Serfdom had come to stay, but it would be untrue to imagine that all the peasants of central and eastern Europe were enslaved and deprived totally of their property. Figures that are available suggest that the pace of expropriation was slow. Even by 1624 in the Middle Mark of Brandenburg the peasants still technically held four *Hufen* to every one held in demesne. Of all the land in Prussia, according to an estimate of the early seventeenth century, the free *Cölmer* held fifteen per cent, the nobles thirty-six per cent, and the peasants forty-nine per cent. Yet these were among the regions which apparently suffered most from the coming of serfdom. In some areas the peasant losses were even smaller. In Saxony, which admittedly suffered less from the rise of noble estates, it has been estimated that the overall loss of peasant land up to the eighteenth century did not exceed five per cent of peasant holdings. The peasantry, in short, suffered more through the deterioration of their personal status and economic independence than through the outright loss of their land.

What opposition, if any, was there to these developments? The towns and their burghers clearly resented the economic power which the introduction of serfdom granted the nobility. In certain areas of Germany and western Europe the bourgeoisie themselves shared in the expropriation of the peasantry; but in the east this was almost unknown, and indeed there the nobles actually began to expropriate the burghers as well. The towns were therefore fighting for their lives when they attempted to resist the encroachments of the landed classes. This explains the bitter struggle between the Baltic ports and the noble estate. Among the cities to resist most strongly was Reval, which carried on a long but ultimately hopeless fight against the nobility of Estonia. The burghers objected in particular to the fact that the nobles traded directly with the Dutch, and in 1594 obtained an order prohibiting this, but the order was repealed later in the same year. In the same way the city of Riga was engaged in a struggle with the nobles of Livonia. Königsberg committed itself even more directly than this, to protest against the legislation of serfdom in Prussia. The city refused to observe the terms of edicts which restricted the privileges of peasants, and maintained firmly that all peasants fleeing to it were beyond the jurisdiction of their masters. In 1634 the city authorities in a joint statement claimed that all peasants in Prussia were free and not serfs, and that they and their children were entitled to freedom of movement. After denouncing exploitation by the Junkers, Königsberg went on to reject totally the practice of serfdom. Many burghers from other towns also had the courage to denounce serfdom. Among them was the Stralsund alderman Balthasar Prutze, a member of one of the town's leading families, whose father and grandfather before him had been burgomasters. A report by Prutze in 1614 described the state of the peasantry of Pomerania as follows:

> Everywhere that this barbaric and as it were Egyptian servitude appears, we see poor people and in consequence no rich gentry but, rather, impoverished lands; while on the contrary where the peasants till their own fields the people are rich and capable of paying their taxes . . . In our territory serfdom did not exist fifty or a hundred years ago, nor was it known even before that, but latterly it has been brought in on a large scale and unnoticed, through the help of the authorities. . . . To sanction this, steps were taken for some of the jurists to draw up regulations whereby: a peasant cannot sue his landlords without special permission, or make any claim, much less a criminal suit, against him; cannot will away his property; cannot marry without the lord's permission; cannot send his children to the towns to learn a trade without permission, nor give them a marriage portion nor marry them off, nor leave an inheritance. . . . But he must follow the lord as a vassal, give him aid and support against his enemies, contribute to the marriage portion of his daughter, accept him as judge even in cases that concern him . . . plough, harrow, sow, harvest and thresh in the lord's fields with all his capacity, even to the neglect of his own; perform other services, carry timber and tend, without payment; feed and lodge himself; put up with beating; lend his horse and hands; and perform other services required by the lord, or in default of services give money, or for money give corn. . . .

In some countries the authorities were unsympathetic to serfdom. This clearly was not the case in Russia, where the tsar, one great landowner among other landowners, was interested in supporting the *pomeshchiki*. Nor was it the case in those areas where the nobles dominated both political and economic life. But in parts of central Europe the rulers were strong enough to act differently. In Saxony the rulers pursued a consistent policy of 'protecting' the peasants, since the passing of land out of the hands of the peasantry not only strengthened the nobility but also exempted the land from taxation. Feeling that if anyone was to be enriched it should be themselves, the Saxon rulers bought up land from both peasants and nobles: the Elector Maurice had up to 1564 spent seven hundred and five thousand florins on land purchases, and the Elector John George I bought up no fewer than four towns and one hundred and eight villages between 1590 and 1626. Meanwhile successive laws — in 1563, 1609, 1623 and 1669 in particular — restricted the burdens of Saxon peasants and the alienation of their land. In Bavaria also there was only a limited move towards serfdom, since the principal landowners were the state and the Church, and neither had any interest in changing the methods of exploitation already in existence. The Duke of Bavaria was lord over at least twenty per cent of the country's peasants and moreover exercised jurisdiction over some fifty per cent, while the Church was lord over about half the peasantry of the country. From these examples it is clear that the advancement of serfdom depended for its success very much on the preponderance of one social class, the landed nobility.

It is difficult to generalise about what part the Church played in this picture. Certainly the farther east we go the more obvious it becomes that the Church was among the biggest landowners, and that in the eastern countries it contributed as much as any other landlord to the growth of serfdom. The territory held by the Russian monasteries in the 1580s was very considerable: in the Moscow district they held thirty-six per cent of all arable land, in the Pskov district fifty-two per cent. Some of this was land they had been donated during the *oprichnina*, when the nobles, fearing confiscation, handed their estates over to the Church in return for a life tenancy. In 1570-1 alone, ninety-nine such estates were given to monasteries in Muscovy. Vast areas of land with enormous economic potential were thus in the hands of the Church. In Poland the archbishopric of Gniezno, of which a detailed study has been made, possessed (by the eighteenth century) scattered holdings that included no less than four hundred and twenty-six villages and thirteen towns. In Poland and Russia production on ecclesiastical estates was directed towards an external market, so that the Church had a vested interest in the measures taken to control mobility of labour. The reason the large holdings of the Church in Bavaria, Austria and other regions did not tend to contribute to serfdom was partly because of the political power of the state, partly because the labour problem was not so acute, and partly because the holdings were not principally directed to production for external markets.

By the beginning of the seventeenth century a combination of economic and political factors had reduced the peasantry of much of central and eastern Europe to a state approaching servitude. Friedrich Engels once described this state as a 'second serfdom' (*zweite Leibeigenschaft*) since it differed both in time and nature from the early period of European serfdom. There were two distinctive features that created the new serfdom and were essential to its growth: the consolidation of landed power in the hands of the noble class, and the dedication of the manorial economy to the produce of grain for a (usually external) market. On these terms, did serfdom justify itself economically?

It would appear that the serf economy was relatively profitable for the first century of its existence, up to the crisis of the mid-seventeenth century (we are not here concerned with the profits from serfdom in the eighteenth century and thereafter). The surplus value reaped by the landlords from the labour of the depressed peasantry, and the imbalance in grain prices between eastern and western Europe, assured steady profits and an expansion of the export trade. The exports of grain from the ports of the eastern Baltic increased in volume steadily from the sixteenth to the seventeenth century. For the whole of this period the principal grain to be exported was rye, whose volume was often ten times as great as that of the wheat exported. Poland's exports of rye grew from about twenty thousand tons a year in the early sixteenth century to about one hundred and seventy thousand tons in 1618. The biggest import area was Amsterdam, which in 1600, for example, took over eighty per cent of Danzig's rye exports. Of this, Amsterdam itself used only twenty-five per cent, so that substantial profits were made in the west through re-exports.

To examine estate production it is necessary to choose areas not visibly affected by the wars of the seventeenth century. Details for some eastern Baltic demesnes that were outside the main track of armies, confirm the increase in output over the century 1550-1650. The takings on one East Prussian estate are analysed in Figure 17.

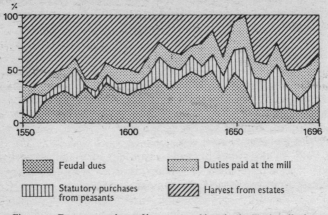

Figure 17 Demesnes under serfdom: corn takings in the Tapiau district, 1550–1696, in five-year periods.

Though all these data point the same way they are to some extent misleading, for neither an increase in exports nor the growth of production is a reliable guide to the efficiency with which the land was exploited under serfdom. In fact, it seems almost beyond doubt that, from the very first, serfdom was one of the most inefficient forms of agricultural labour to be used on the continent of Europe. The higher overall output of grain, for example, seems to have resulted not from the superior efficiency of serf labour over free labour, but quite simply from the expansion of acreage put under the plough, a process made possible by the two distinctive features we have noted above (noble control of the soil, and production for the market). If farms increased their output, it was because they grew larger. This was certainly the case in the great estates of Estonia in the seventeenth century. Similarly in East Prussia a study of ten selected farms shows that between 1600 and 1640 they increased their acreage by 157.6 per cent. In addition it must be borne in mind that very few estates were run solely on serf labour, and that there were elements of tax, tithe and wage labour which allow us to study the productivity of different sections of one estate. In the district of Tapiau in East Prussia, for instance, over the period 1550-1696 only forty-five per cent of grain came from the demesne itself; the major part came from dependent peasants who paid rent in kind

244

(twenty-six per cent of grain revenue), in taxes for the use of the lord's mill (fourteen per cent), and in other dues. It is possible to argue that on an estate like this it was the proportion of grain *not* produced by serf labour that increased, while the use of serfs (exclusively on demesne) led to no notable increase in production unless the acreage of the demesne was extended.

Some evidence of this sort can be found in the seigneurial estates in seventeenth-century Hungary, where the yield-ratios for grain generally varied from 2.5 to 3.5. This can be contrasted with the output of peasant producers, who managed to double these figures. Figures for the production of wheat suggest that while the demesnes had a yield-ratio of six the peasants had one of twelve. In viticulture the same situation prevailed. When wage labour was used instead of labour services, productivity in the seventeenth century trebled. The conclusion to be drawn from this was obviously that peasants were less efficient when rendering labour services to another than when working for themselves. As a result there was a tendency, in viticulture at least, to move away from labour services, and we find that on the estates of the Rákóczi family in the seventeenth century about ninety per cent of the vines were cultivated by hired labour. There were practical limits to this trend, and serfdom continued to be the basic feature of labour relations.

Taking eastern Europe as a whole, serfdom seems to have dampened output in the early modern period (this need not have affected profits unduly, because of the high prices still obtainable in the west). Figures for Polish estates indicate that the yield ratio for wheat in 1550-99 was 4.7, and that this fell to 4.6 in 1600-49 and to 2.5 in 1650-99. The ratios for rye in the same periods were 4.0, 3.5 and 3.1. The figures suggest a decline as serfdom intensified. Even at their highest level of output the demesnes of eastern Europe never managed to produce as much as those in the west. A comparison of the estates of East Prussia with those of Brunswick (in west Germany) shows that while the former over the period 1550-1695 averaged a yield of about seven hundred and sixty kilograms a hectare, the latter over the years 1540-1676 averaged eight hundred and ten. In the late sixteenth and early seventeenth centuries as a whole, the eastern countries had yield ratios for wheat that varied between 3 and 5.9, while in England, the Netherlands and France the ratios were almost double, varying from 6 to 8.9.

THE SEVENTEENTH-CENTURY CRISIS AND THE ESTABLISHMENT OF SERFDOM

Three main factors led to a further intensification of serfdom in the east: an international economic depression centring on the mid-seventeenth century, the havoc caused by war and particularly by the Thirty Years War, and internal contradictions in the structure of serfdom.

The agricultural depression that commenced towards the middle of the seventeenth century had an effect on the whole European economy. Among its principal symptoms were falling cereal prices, the conversion of arable to pasture, and a decline in the reclamation of land from the sea. With west European supplies of grain more than adequate for current consumption, there was a fall in demand for Baltic grain. In Danzig the prices of cereals fell sharply, while that of meat rose. In the estates of the archbishopric of Gniezno, the acreage under cultivation began to decline. After about mid-century, there was a general decline both in acreage and in production, caused in part at least by the shrinking of the market. To make up for declining income, the landlords increased their pressure on the peasantry. In Prussia the dues demanded of the peasants were raised repeatedly, and labour obligations were made so onerous that in 1664 the peasants of one area complained that 'they could no longer endure such heavy statutory labour services'.

It was the wars that caused the greatest ruin, most directly. The eastern lands were subject to lengthy and destructive military campaigns. In the late sixteenth century Russian pressure was directed westwards in wars that devastated Livonia from 1558 to 1582. In the seventeenth century it was the Swedes who were the aggressors. Almost continuously throughout the early 1600s they intervened in the Baltic lands against Russia and Poland. Though the eastern lands were not formally in the Thirty Years War they suffered no less. Poland suffered particularly badly from the Swedish invasions of 1626-9 and 1655-60. The population losses suffered by Greater Poland in these years have been estimated at forty-two per cent, those suffered by Little Poland at twenty-seven per cent. Probably the worst affected region was Masovia, which lost about sixty-four per cent of its population, suffered the destruction of ten per cent of its villages, and had eighty-five per cent of its cultivated land put out of use.

The greatest scourge was undoubtedly the Thirty Years War. We have already glanced at its effect on population. The decline in population owing to death or emigration had serious repercussions on the agrarian economy. If few small towns or settlements disappeared permanently, and few village sites were replaced by forest land, the exceptions, temporary or permanent, were enough to cause a crisis on the land. The crisis was twofold, involving both labour and capital. Wartime disruption had forced many independent peasants to leave the countryside for the cities; while dependent peasants, long smarting under labour obligations, drifted willingly from the land. When seed-time and harvest came round the landowners found their work force greatly reduced, and were obliged to pay their regular as well as their hired labourers a favourable wage. Inevitably the peasants found that there was a premium on their labour, a factor which made seigneurs even more anxious to tie down the labour force. In several respects the position of the peasantry deteriorated. Where their landholdings were large enough for sustenance but small enough to be restored without any great capital resources, they could continue to live on the land. Where, however, the plot had been sold during the war to a thrifty landlord, or where it had been so ruined or neglected as to need some capital for investment, there was no way of getting back to the land without money. In the current manpower crisis labour became far more valuable than land, and many peasants found it more immediately profitable to become day-labourers than to till the soil.

In these circumstances it was possible to buy up deserted land at bargain prices. Nobles and landlords with the necessary capital accumulated property formerly belonging to independent villages and free peasants. The restoration of agriculture was consequently carried out in accordance with the wishes of the landlord class. Only as many peasant dwellings were restored, for example, as was consonant with the needs of the new owners of the soil. Manors replaced villages. In one case near Stralsund, fourteen peasant holdings were replaced by one large estate. The process was multiplied elsewhere in Pomerania and throughout the German lands. The peasant communities were unable to resist the process, since many of them were heavily in debt and saw little alternative to selling out. When the village of Boersch in Alsace tried to borrow money to maintain its position, it managed to obtain a loan in Strassburg but only at the rate of twenty-eight per cent interest. Both individually and communally, the peasantry were ushered into a period of economic ruin. The noble peasantry eulogised by Grimmelshausen (in the quotation at the head of this chapter) were a class superseded by the princes they claimed to have sired. The worst areas for estate consolidation appear to have been Mecklenburg and Pomerania: in the district of Stargard in Mecklenburg, where the war virtually annihilated the peasantry, three-fourths of peasant holdings fell into noble hands.

Finally, contradictions and weaknesses in the practice of serfdom up to the seventeenth century called for an intensification of the system. The fact that peasant flights increased in proportion to feudal obligations, for instance, was clearly self-defeating. The flight of peasants from Brandenburg to Poland resulted in a settlement at the River Netze by the New Mark: there by 1620 more than forty villages had been founded by refugee peasants. A maximum effort was therefore made in the mid-seventeenth century to obtain complete immobility of labour.

As a result of the great need for such immobility, serfdom in all its legislative fullness was introduced. Earlier attitudes to legislation had been casual and unhurried. When in 1616 regulations for the peasants of Pomerania-Stettin were drawn up, these were described as '*homines proprii et coloni gelbae adscripti*', a major change in their status no doubt but one that was not formalised in an official code. In subsequent years the authorities made every attempt to give formal legal validity to serfdom. In Estonia a law of 1632 began combating peasant flights, and by mid-century stability of the labour force had been obtained. A system of contractual serfdom, based on that practised by the Swedish estates of the De La Gardie family on the island of Osel, was introduced. In Russia a major social and political crisis preceded the passing of the Code of Laws, the *Ulozhenie*, of 1649. As a result of the crisis, in which the victory of the landed nobility was confirmed, the Russian peasantry were fully enserfed. All peasants and their families were declared bound to their masters, with no right of departure, and no right to asylum in the cities. No distinction was made between peasants and villeins: both had to serve on the same terms and with the same obligations and lack of freedom. Like the *Ulozhenie*, the *Recess* (or Code) granted by the Elector of Brandenburg in 1653 was influenced by the nobility. For the first time, this edict assumed that the peasants were serfs, and laid the onus on the peasant to prove that he was not one. In the Swedish-occupied territories, such as Pomerania-Wolgast, energetic opposition to serfdom was shown by the Swedish authorities. But the situation proved uncontrollable, and in 1645 and 1670 laws issued by them gave additional legislative confirmation to the existence of serfdom in Pomerania.

It was not only in the east that the peasantry suffered. In western Europe too, and particularly where the Thirty Years War had had some impact, the years of depression brought a worsening in the status of the rural classes.

The Dijonnais, in Burgundy, to choose a French example, was severely devastated by both friendly and enemy troops during the war. 'For ten leagues around Dijon, everything has been destroyed both by the Swedes and by the enemy', wrote Condé to Richelieu in 1636. The village communities in the area were financially ruined as a result of the campaigns. To pay off the debts, rights were sold to creditors and both common and forest lands were alienated. One village, Noiron-les-Cîteaux, was a free community which in 1557 had a rich domain and paid only a small taille. By 1666 the domain had vanished in alienations, and to the taille had been added a heavier taille, payments in kind, corvées and a tithe. Generally such villages fell into the hands of the bourgeoisie of Dijon, who were responsible for initiating what may accurately be called a feudal reaction, since the properties now became no less than fiefs, their only gain being that agriculture was soon restored to its former flourishing condition as a result of the investment of capital by the new bourgeois seigneurs.

Did the establishment of serfdom take eastern Europe back into the Middle Ages? This is a difficult question over which some historians differ. On the face of it, it looks as if the imposition of the forms of feudalism — demesne economy, labour services, the *pomestie* — was a step backwards. There are serious reasons for questioning the viability of an economy and society based on serf labour. Pure serfdom, in the sense of a man being bound absolutely to a master or to the soil, seems to have been, as we have argued, less efficient than a system of wage labour or other less servile form of exploitation. Yet serfdom based on total dependence was in many regions the only way of securing a guaranteed labour force. Part of the problem is to explain how the nobility managed to prosper on this outmoded type of labour, and what changes, if any, occurred in the economy as a result. The profits came of course from the production of goods, primarily grain, for an external market. In Russia the market was not abroad but internal and eastwards. It is this *production for a market* that is a clear contradiction of any idea that the 'second serfdom' was mediaeval, for the old-type manorial economy had not been geared to a market and to profits. The 'second serfdom', then, was a new economic system in its own right, created by the particular conditions of its epoch, and had little in common with the Middle Ages, despite the striking institutional resemblances.

From this, however, it has been argued that the system was actually progressive, and opened the way to the development of capitalism. The paradoxical term 'feudal capitalism' has been used, in which the word 'feudal' applies to the use of labour services and 'capitalism' to the gearing of production to an export market. The concept is an appealing one, if only because of the paradox it contains. To substantiate it, we must see whether two essential features of the transition to capitalism — the existence of a money economy and of technological change in the means of production — are present in the 'second serfdom'. It is here that difficulties arise. A money economy was obviously growing, on the basis of trade and the profits from it that accumulated in the hands of the nobles; moreover, the development of great estates, producing for an external market, necessarily entailed some changes in methods of land exploitation. But it is very difficult to admit that a system in which little money changed hands, in which most workers were not paid wages, and in which the really significant accumulation was of lands rather than of capital, was a 'money economy'. It has indeed been maintained that, for Poland at least, the whole serf economy of the sixteenth to the eighteenth centuries lacked any significant capital accumulation. The issue has not been explored historically, but what non-statistical evidence there is tends to suggest that the great landlords, for all their devotion to estate management, were uncapitalistic in their outlook. The luxurious way of life of the gentry of Pomerania and East Prussia, the manors they built with delicate and rich furnishings imported from the west, are clear indications of where surplus capital was being invested. Moreover the later generation of landlords was not always as enterprising as the earlier. In Hungary we have the case of a prominent noble, Gy. Hédérváry, who in 1542 could express himself in these words: 'My one aim is to buy a ship, and to transport thousands of bushels of barley and wheat. I shall carry barley, flour and other provisions.' But a century later, in 1642, one of his descendants, I. Hédervary, had developed different habits. Writing to a cousin, he explained that 'he should not hold my marriage and my ex-

1 This print from a contemporary broadside illustrates the Great Plague of London in 1665. Cities, with their denser population, were particularly vulnerable. Naples, perhaps the largest European city, lost nearly half its inhabitants in the plague of 1656

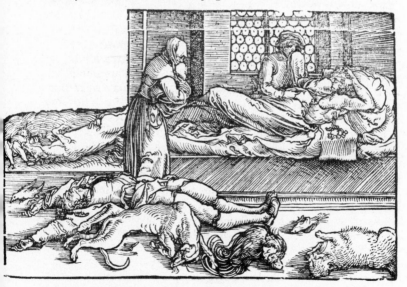

2 The stench of death, portrayed in a sixteenth-century German print showing the impact of an epidemic on both men and beasts

3 Pieter Breughel's horrifying painting of *The Triumph of Death* goes beyond medieval moralising, and emphasises in grim detail the violence of the late sixteenth century

Ce chariot dargent que la monoye tire,
Est bien couronne des plus gros de ce temps,
Mais il est mal suiuy de pauures payzans;
Que disette retient enchaineen son Empire.

Ils tachent bien pourtant dy pouuoir paruenir,
Et quelques vns dentre eux s'aduance sur la chaine,
Mais leurs effortz sont vains, pauureté les entraine,
Et leur fait eschapper ce quils pensoient tenir.

L'argent les aueugle.

Riche comme en Iuif.
Quand il
seroit aussi scauant qu'un
St Paul sil n'a de l'argent c'est
un sot.
Pauure fortune.

4 (*top*) Envy of the economic success of the Jews
became a fundamental cause of anti-Semitism. It led
in Frankfurt in 1614, during the disturbances known
as the Fettmilch uprising, to the sacking of the
prosperous Jewish ghetto

5 (*above*) Lagniet's 1657 illustration shows money as a
universal motive force, with Jewish financiers leading
its pursuit. Peasants also follow in its wake, but are so
chained down by poverty and misery that they are
unable to achieve wealth

6 (*left*) This elaborate Belgian painting of 1544, showing the various activities involved in mining and extraction, is a good illustration of the fact that industrial activity was very often the preserve of the landed noble (the chateau stands to the right of the picture)

7 (*below left*) Interior (1576) of the workshop of Etienne Delaulne, a celebrated goldsmith of Paris. The engraving was done by Delaulne himself

8 (*below right*) An armament workshop and foundry, in a sixteenth-century print by Stradanus

9 (*top*) The ruins of the famous castle of Krzyztopor, the residence of Christopher
Opalinski the governor of Sandomierz, built between 1631 and 1644
10 (*above*) The Farnese palace at Caprarola, begun in the mid-sixteenth century on
the foundations of an old castle. A magnificent example of an Italian Renaissance
villa, it is particularly noted for the beauty of its gardens which were completed
in 1587

11 (*left*) Longleat, Wiltshire, perhaps the most distinguished example of Elizabethan architecture, completed in about 1580

12 (*below*) The courtyard of the Hotel de Sully, built between 1624 and 1629. This is one of the finest examples of the great town houses that sprang up during the ambitious rebuilding of Paris in the early seventeenth century

13 (*top*) Rembrandt's *Syndics of the Cloth Makers of Amsterdam* allows us a revealing look at the confident faces of the burghers of the most successful trading city in Europe

14 (*above*) *The Provost of the Guilds and the Aldermen of Paris*, an official portrait by Philippe Champaigne (1602-74). This grouping represents not so much the bourgeoisie as the *noblesse de robe*, men whose commercial origins lay well behind them and who were established members of the great civic corporations

15 (*right*) The Ständebaum or Tree of Ranks, late medieval in concept, was a commonplace of sixteenth-century literature. Peasants, as the roots of the tree, form the basis of society, and all other ranks are founded on them

16 (*below*) N. Guérard's engraving of the French peasant 'born to labour' shows him with his working implements, his one aim being (*centre right*) to pay off his taxes

17 (*below right*) A sixteenth-century German view of the peasant as a factor of production, composed entirely of agricultural implements. In pre-industrial Europe the health of the economy depended wholly on the output of the farm labourer and the peasant

18 The interior of a witch's house, from a print of 1579. The witches are preparing to transport themselves to the Sabbath on broomsticks

19 Joan Prentis, shown with her familiars, was one of the accused at the witch trial held in Chelmsford, Essex in 1589

20 The most notorious of the English witch-hunters was Matthew Hopkins, self-styled 'Witchfinder General', who operated at the height of the English Civil War. The witches in this illustration relate the names of the demon familiars, and show the shapes they take

21 (*top*) A sixteenth-century printer in an engraving by Stradanus
22 (*above left*) and 23 (*above right*) In these engravings of 1568 the activities of typographers and bookbinders are shown in detail. With a higher literacy rate and a better sense of organisation than other artisans, printing workers tended to take the lead in agitation for better working conditions

WICHAEL SERVETVS HISP... VS DE ARAGOVIE

Jordanus Brunus Nolanus

24 (*above left*) The execution of Michael Servetus at Geneva in 1553 gave rise to the most important of the controversies over toleration in the Reformation era, and impelled many adherents of the Reformed Churches to adopt a more liberal attitude to religious liberty than that held by Calvin

25 (*above right*) Guy Patin (1601-72) the distinguished French surgeon, was a firm defender of traditional medicine, yet at the same time a lively and independent thinker

26 (*left*) Giordano Bruno (1548-1600) entered the priesthood in Naples in 1572 but left it shortly after and spent most of his life wandering through Europe, adopting new beliefs and then rejecting them. Returning to Italy in 1591 he was arrested by the Inquisition and burnt at the stake at Rome in 1600

27 (*above*) *Interior of the Grote Kerk at Haarlem* by Gerrit Berckheyde, illustrating the austere face of Dutch Calvinism. The pulpit, instead of the altar, has become the centre of divine service

28 (*right*) The Synod of Dort (1618-19) was of profound importance in Calvinist history. In Holland it raised vital theological and political issues, while abroad it led to a split in the world of Reformed theology, creating for the first time a school of liberal Calvinism

29 (*above left*) The peasantry ridden by soldiery, depicted in a fly-sheet of the Thirty Years' War. In the majority of recorded cases, the excesses of soldiers were one of the chief causes driving the rural classes to revolt

30 (*above right*) The Mediterranean countries were heavily afflicted by banditry. Rural poverty drove men to theft and brigandage, and the nobility encouraged them for their own purposes. Catalan bandits, illustrated in this sixteenth-century woodcut, were the most notorious of those operating in the Iberian peninsula

31 Episodes from the revolt of Masaniello in Naples are vividly captured in this turbulent canvas by Micco Spadara (1647). The rebels were soon divided and crushed. The real inspirer of the rising, the priest Genoino, ended his days in prison in Spain

32 (*above left*) 'Brave messengerss, they that go wandering in strange countries!' A Callot engraving of seventeenth-century French gypsies. First observed in western Europe in the late fifteenth century, the gypsies seem to have come from Asia Minor through eastern Europe. Iberian gypsies, on the other hand, are presumed to have come originally from the African continent

33 (*above right*) The Counter Reformation saw the growth of a great refugee problem. The most notorious expulsion of a minority occurred in Spain, where from 1609 onwards the Moriscos were forcibly expelled in their thousands. This sketch of the expulsion, by Carducho, fails to present the Moriscos in their proper national dress

34 A late sixteenth-century engraving of Italian gypsies. Still preserving some traces of Oriental dress, as this print shows, the gypsies swelled the ranks of the wandering beggars in western Europe

35 (*top*) At the battle of the White Mountain in 1620 the Czech nation lost its independence to invading German troops. In subsequent months, as religious repression increased, thousands of Czechs emigrated from their country. Leading rebel noblemen were executed in the main square of Prague in June 1621, as this print shows

36 (*above*) A fly-sheet showing the declaration of one of the peace treaties that brought an end to the Thirty Years' War in 1648. The weapons of war lie broken, flags of rejoicing emerge. The peace marked the end of an era, but it also provoked problems that led to the strengthening of governmental power in the late seventeenth century

tensive expenses against me, for my late father also considered it to be adequate income, since he held it fitting and honourable to keep a good table. I am my father's son, and cannot live the way others do.' With regard to technical innovation, it can be argued that apart from the institution of serfdom itself, no fundamental change in the method of exploitation of the soil occurred.

There were no doubt several progressive developments in some areas. It has been claimed for Bohemia, for instance, that the decline of the urban economy and the rise of rural production led to a transference of enterprise from the towns to the countryside, so that a rural domestic industry grew up precisely in the years after 1648 when the worst effects of the Thirty Years War and of agrarian depression were being felt. It is unlikely, however, that arguments like this can prove the contribution of serfdom to economic growth unless they are supported by extensive statistical research. For it is undeniable that in the long run the serf economy was one that harmed the internal market by undue emphasis on export; hindered the expansion of urban enterprise; depressed the labour force; and concentrated wealth in the hands of a feudal aristocracy. Eastern Europe and its peasantry developed in a direction opposite to that of the west. In the west the bourgeoisie and commercial capital developed hand in hand; in the east they did not merge until the nineteenth century. In the west the peasants were developing towards greater freedom and mobility; in the east it was the reverse.

III

FAITH AND REASON

7 NEW DIMENSIONS OF THE SPIRIT

Il faut premièrement regarder Dieu et non pas soi-même.
CARDINAL PIERRE DE BERULLE

There were neither witches nor bewitched until they were talked and written about.
The inquisitor ALONSO SALAZAR DE FRIAS (1612)

The period 1550-1660 coincides with what historians call the Counter Reformation, a term which, when originally employed in the mid-nineteenth century, conveyed the idea of a conservative and defensive movement against the Protestant Reformation. Subsequent historians, many of them Catholic, soon began to point out that the movement was not merely a reactionary response, and that many of the reforms associated with it had their roots in the pre-Reformation period; so that it was in some measure just to speak also of a Catholic Reformation which was analogous to and an extension of, but clearly also a reaction against, the growth of Protestantism. Seen from this point of view the Counter Reformation turns out to be a vast and diverse concept with its origins in the late fifteenth century — in, for example, the Netherlands spiritual school of the *devotio moderna* — and its final manifestations in the work of late seventeenth-century reformers like the Abbé de Rancé, founder of the Trappists. Over this time span the movement took its main impetus from the Latin countries, with the result that the structure and practice of the Catholic Church became heavily Latinised, as indeed it remained up to the major reforms of the Second Vatican Council.

The Catholic Church was re-born, with the active aid of three midwives — Spain, Italy and France. Only by appreciating the role of these three countries can we begin to understand the immense flowering of the religious life that gave back to the Roman Church the initiative it lost at the Reformation.

SPIRITUAL RENEWAL

The principal key to the spiritual achievement of the Counter Reformation is the Council of Trent (1545-63). There the debates which led finally to the decrees on Justification (1547) gave ample evidence of the differing theological attitudes of the Church fathers. Some of those who spoke up for a definition that would arrive at a compromise with the Lutheran doctrine were representative of a liberal Catholic tradition that had arrived at its position independent of the Reformation. This key relevance of Justification needs re-emphasis, in view of the minor part it has been assigned by some historians, for Justification involved the whole commitment of the individual Christian and as such was rightly seen as the central spiritual issue. The startling agreement reached between Contarini and the Lutherans at the Colloquy of Regensburg in 1541 on this one doctrine, was testimony to the common spiritual roots of the participants. Trent, however, changed all this: it was not that the Council rejected altogether the spiritual experience involved in Justification, or the various forms in which grace could be received; what it rejected was the private mystical certainty which ruled out the efficacy of the Church and the sacraments. The Council thus defined Justification in an active, not a passive, sense. It was to be attained not merely through the acceptance of God's imputation of grace: it was to be won actively, through participation in his mystical body, the Church. This, in a sense, was to be the tone of all Counter Reformation spiritually. The whole direction of the movement was to turn away from the incessant struggle for personal salvation towards the achievement of the salvation of all men; to turn, in short, from prayer to activity, from contemplation to apostolate.

If mysticism or reflection played a part in this, it was to be directed away from self towards the service of this larger purpose. This activist and outward-looking spirituality was to be the great hallmark of the Catholic Reformation and perhaps the principal reason for its success. For all its apparent hostility to the fathers of Christian Humanism, orthodox Catholicism produced a humanism of its own that was to strike more profound roots in the laity than the intellectual brilliance of the Erasmians.

In order not to misinterpret this emphasis on activity, we need only look at the writings of three prominent saints whose work was fundamental to the Counter Reformation. In St Teresa of Avila's spiritual works (*The Interior Castle, The Ladder of*

Perfection), in the *Spiritual Exercises* of St Ignatius Loyola, and in St Francis de Sales' *Introduction to the Devout Life*, the one concern of the authors was the individual soul and its relationship with God. St Teresa's *Autobiography* is no more than the story of a soul's search for perfection. The Christian's prime concern was his interior life, and all his duty lay in the service of God. Was there then a contradiction between the internal and the external emphasis in Catholic spirituality?

The answer is supplied by the *Spiritual Exercises* (published 1548). Essentially a work on spiritual perfection, the Exercises were a manual of practice rather than meditation. Ignatius did not exhort, he guided. The soul was to be subjected, bullied, trained. The *Exercises* were not directed to clergy alone: they were drawn up for both clergy and laity. They were not aimed at the spiritual direction of a monastic order, they were a weapon to enable all manner of men to reach spiritual perfection. Each man was to fulfil himself, in accordance with the teachings of the Church. The founding of the Jesuits was itself an expression of this humanism, for activity in the world rather than contemplation was Ignatius' primary objective. Absolute devotion to the Church became a necessary complement of interior rejuvenation. In this way the apparent dichotomy between individual spirituality and external activity was resolved.

The real backbone of this activity was to be mental prayer, and here again the whole practice and technique of prayer was taken out of the cloister and put into the midst of the world. Prayer was to be the great means of ascent to God, but it did not need clerical guidance: each individual, with the help of innumerable manuals, was to be enabled to fight his own way. The work that most perfectly represented this spirituality was the great product of the *devotio moderna*, the *Imitation of Christ* (*ca* 1418), which went through innumerable editions in the course of the sixteenth century and in France alone from 1550 to 1610 was issued in thirty editions. But more genuinely typical of Counter Reformation humanism was the *Introduction to the Devout Life*. Francis de Sales had originally sent a series of letters of spiritual guidance to a noble lady in Paris. He was prevailed upon to issue these as a book, and in 1609 the *Introduction* was published in Paris. It immediately became a phenomenal success. The second edition was issued in 1609, the third in the following year. By 1620 there were already over forty French editions, and by 1656 the book had been published in seventeen different languages.

Like the *Imitation*, the *Introduction* was non-theological. Far more than the *Imitation*, it was directed to the perfection of ordinary laymen in their ordinary daily and secular activities. 'It is heresy', was St Francis' view, 'to wish to exclude the devout life from the company of soldiers, from the artisan's shop, the prince's court, the married household. Wherever we may be, we must and can aspire to the perfect life.' For the bishop of Annecy-Geneva, the Catholic's work and prayer were both part of one task, his perfection as an individual in the service of God.

Complementing the Christian's private prayer was his prayer through the channels of the Church. The Counter Reformation and Trent brought about a virtual revolution in sacramental worship: the old forms remained, but both theory and practice were radically altered. The Christian was reminded that the primary aim of prayer was worship. All the sacraments were reaffirmed, re-defined and reinforced. Confession was to be more habitual, communion more regular, weekly Mass obligatory. New devotions centring around the consecrated Host came into being, and the Mass became once more the central fact of the spiritual life of both clergy and laity. The effect of these changes was, however, still to be far from ideal: for a priest to say Mass daily was still infrequent after Trent, and monthly or even weekly communion remained a daring innovation well into the seventeenth century.

INSTITUTIONAL REFORM

The success of the Counter Reformation would be incomprehensible if we were to consider only the success of its literature. The major part of the Christian population was illiterate, cut off from spiritual manuals and even more from the official Latin of the Church. Ignorant of theology and of Trent, the faithful could only rely on their pastors. It was because of this that the most important Catholic leaders concentrated not on a direct mission to the people so much as on a reform of the institutions through which the clergy worked. The obsession with clerical reform, common to the great pre-Reformation changes brought about by Cisneros in Spain and to the work of Bellarmine and other officials of the Roman Curia during the Reformation, was to dominate the practical deliberations of the fathers at Trent. Reform of bishops and of priests (Trent was not permitted to discuss reform of the Curia) was their prime concern. This emphasis on the clergy did not occur merely because of Protestant denunciation of abuses: the Catholic authorities had already been aware of the need for change. They had moreover been regularly reminded of it by the witty invective of Erasmus, and the work of Cisneros heralded the way to a wider cleansing of the Augean stables. But pressure for change soon came under suspicion when some of the reformers neglected caution. In Spain St Teresa struggled against powerful opposition, and at one stage her writings were denounced to the Inquisition. In Italy the Capuchins came near to being abolished after the sensational defection to Protestantism of their General, Ochino. Fortunately the momentum for change survived. Ignatius managed to obtain papal approval in 1540 for his new Society, and so the greatest, and in many ways most typical, of the Counter Reformation orders came into existence.

Like the Jesuits, new orders were almost without exception directed towards the apostolate, in the full spirit of the Counter Reformation. But all the clergy, both regular and secular, were alike subjected to the primary demand that they should be properly educated, trained and prepared for service. The undeniably correct emphasis on the great external achievements of the new orders — in social service and in education above all — is unfortunately liable to make us underestimate the enormous internal reforms they carried out. The Society of Jesus was an outstanding example of internal change. In its emphasis on discipline and obedience it recalled the most rigorous features of the classic mediaeval rules; yet because it was not a monastic order but an active participant in the world, its members were each encouraged to develop their own gifts in the service of the Church. The Society achieved a virtually unique combination of rigidity and flexibility. From the very first it therefore produced some of the most outstanding figures of the Counter Reformation.

The Church relied ultimately for its strength on the ordinary priest rather than on roving missionaries. Oddly enough, this basic factor was very much neglected until the very end of the sixteenth century. The spectacular gains made by the Catholic party in Counter Reformation Europe were made on the level of political and military aggrandisement, on the level of university and secondary education and of public preaching (perhaps the greatest of the preachers was the Dutch Jesuit St Peter Canisius, whose labours helped to hold central Germany and Austria for Rome). The foundation of new orders, important as this was, still did little to cure the fundamental weaknesses of the secular clergy. St Philip Neri in Rome was one of the first to devote his efforts primarily to the rehabilitation of the priesthood. In 1575 he founded the Congregation of the Oratory, which was at first meant to be not a new order but rather an association devoted to prayer and discussion, to helping the poor and educating the young. The example of St Philip found its most notable emulators in the leaders of the French Counter Reformation. It was Cardinal Pierre de Bérulle, the principal inspirer of the Catholic revival in France, who in 1611 established an Oratory modelled on that of St Philip.

The French Counter Reformation came later than any other, thanks to the half century of civil war in the country. As the last major Catholic country to reform itself, France offers a strikingly clear example of the various influences that combined to produce the movement for reform in Catholic Europe. The political impetus to reform; introduction of change at an aristocratic, courtly level; seizure of initiative by the Jesuits; emphasis on the foundation of new orders; education of the young; inculcation of a new piety, with an emphasis on Mariolatry; the spread of Spanish and Italian influences; greater attention to the role of the priesthood: these were practised in France with an energy scarcely paralleled elsewhere. It is often said that the decrees of the Council of Trent were not received in France. This is only a half-truth. The Parlement of Paris refused to register the Tridentine decrees, but they were adopted without hesitation in 1615 by the general assembly of the French Church.

The political impetus to reform came from the *dévot* party centred round the Marillac family and Cardinal Bérulle, who stood for a policy of alliance with Spain against Protestant Europe. It was at this aristocratic level (particularly with the mystical circle of Paris, meeting at the residence of Madame Acarie) that the inspiration for reform in the French Church originated, and the movement never quite shook off its noble origins: even St Vincent de Paul relied for his success largely on court favour. The success of the Jesuits, who returned to France in 1603 and were warmly encouraged by Henry IV, was perhaps the most emphatic illustration of what the Counter Reformation could achieve. In 1617 they received permission to teach children and within a few years had arrogated to themselves the major part of public education in France. By 1626 in the Paris region alone they had twelve colleges and over thirteen thousand pupils.

Bérulle's Oratory also in time came to take part in education (rivalry over this helps to explain Jesuit unpopularity among many Counter Reformation leaders) and founded a total of forty-three colleges within twenty years. The foundation of new orders and the establishment of new convents went on at a remarkable pace. In the first half of the seventeenth century alone, something like seven thousand five hundred religious houses were established. Old religious orders were refounded (renovation of the Benedictine rule led, for instance, to the foundation of the Congregation of Saint-Maur and to Angélique Arnauld's reform at Port Royal), and new ones established (by Olier, Eudes and Jeanne de Chantal, among others). The introduction of the reformed Carmelite order into France in 1605 by Madame Acarie and Bérulle was particularly significant, for it made clear how much France was benefiting from the reform movement in the other Latin countries. The French Carmel drew directly on Bérulle's own experiences during a visit to Spain in 1604, and the Bérullian Oratory was directly modelled on St Philip's Roman one. Saint Teresa's writings entered France along with her reformed Carmelites, and her books went through numerous French editions from 1601 onwards.

In St Vincent de Paul (1581-1660), the greatest saint of Catholicism's great century, the Counter Reformation successfully fused piety and practice. The religion which Bérulle represented was above all mystical, a mysticism centred on the person of Christ. Bérulle valued holiness above reform. A reformer, as Henri Bremond once pointed out, tries to bring the clergy to a minimum of religious observance and good behaviour, but Bérulle sought to bring them to a maximum of virtue. The sole aim of the Oratory, an aim it never lost even after it felt compelled to enter the world of education, was to improve the priesthood and make it more holy. This became the guiding principle of Bérulle's protégé, Vincent de Paul. Vincent's immense labours on behalf of the poor, the hungry and the abandoned are described later on briefly in this book. There is no space to discuss his deeply personal commitment to work among prisoners and galley slaves (he had himself been enslaved in Tunis in 1606). But though his fame rests on these works of external charity, his primary purpose was to serve his fellow priests. 'Christianity depends on the priests': that was the theme of his whole programme. The point was to change the Christian people by changing their ministers. From 1628 onwards Vincent drew up regular retreat programmes for ordinands; their popularity caused them to be adopted in diocese after diocese throughout France. These seminary courses were perhaps his most profound and lasting achievement, for the priests who were trained by Vincent helped to rescue France for the Church at the level where it most mattered, in the urban and rural parishes. Nor was this action programme an exclusively male one. To add to the numerous female orders established by the French Counter Reformation, under women as notable as St Jeanne Chantal and Angélique Arnauld, St Vincent contributed his own Ladies of Charity and Daughters of Charity.

In so bureaucratic a body as the Catholic Church, a reform of the clergy on this scale was appropriate and essential if the channels of grace, long muddied and blocked, were to be freed again. The concern of the Council of Trent with organisation of the clergy and the enormous effort made by Vincent de Paul to reform the seminaries were based on this premise. The Church and Christian people must be purified through the ministers of the gospel. That the programme was largely successful cannot be doubted. There occurred, however, an important loss of balance which did not get righted until the twentieth century. The justifiable concern with the role of the clergy served eventually to inflate the clergy at the expense of the laity, an ironical result when we consider the truly humanist aspirations of the leaders of the Counter Reformation. Trent never came round to considering the role of the laity in the Church. What transpired, then, was not merely an inevitable increase in papal power, but also a reversion to that clericalism which the reformers, both Catholic and Protestant, had consistently tried to avoid.

MISSION AND CONVERSION

It is traditional to ascribe the great missionary endeavours of the sixteenth century to the Counter Reformation. This claim is correct if we are referring to the internal reconversion of Europe to the Catholic faith, but less tenable if we mean to refer to the work of men like St Francis Xavier. On the contrary, the truly inspired and apostolic missions outside Europe commenced before the great age of the Counter Reformation and died away at its height. The idealistic missionary period in America and Asia lasted from about 1520 to about 1570, a half century of genuine Christian evangelisation. Rome took no part in it nor, with the outstanding exception of Xavier, did the Society of Jesus. The great work of the Jesuits in Japan, Canada and Paraguay belongs mainly to the early seventeenth century, when the heavy hand of imperial control had begun to disrupt the pure missionary ideal; and the high aims of the Paraguayan Utopia were the exception rather than the rule to the kind of missionary policy then being pursued in America.

The great achievements of Counter Reformation missionary enterprise were in Europe rather than overseas. How successfully were the people brought back to the Faith? What evidence there is points to a phenomenal movement back to Catholicism. All sections of society were affected. In Languedoc the change was from a heresy-infected, anti-tithe peasantry in the mid-sixteenth century, to a predominantly Catholic tithe-paying peasantry in the early seventeenth. The sect-ridden Poland of the 1570s became the Jesuit-dominated Poland of the 1640s. Even in Protestant England, the Reformation court of Elizabeth became, under the early Stuarts, a court of Catholic queens, recusant lords and the occasional Jesuit. Where the reaction was instigated by secular authorities, the people were evangelised in such a way that they had become believing Catholics in little more than a generation. There is little need to repeat that much of the 'conversion' of this period was carried out at sword-point. The case of Bohemia illustrates only too clearly the propensity of the Counter Reformation to rely on military force. But this was still an age of state religion, and Protestants were no less ready than Catholics to rely on the secular arm. Important as the role of the state may have been, undue attention to its activity is likely to distort the historical image. For no matter how significant the forces of coercion may have been, whether with Alba in the Netherlands or Tilly in the Thirty Years War, the Counter Reformation was not about them. In the words of a recent historian, 'what is conventionally called the Counter Reformation was fundamentally a powerful revival of religion and should be studied as such'.

The reverse side of this picture must not be forgotten. If true religion flourished, so too did disbelief and irreligion, so too did irrationality and witchcraft.

THE KINGDOM OF DARKNESS: WITCHCRAFT IN EUROPE

The practice of 'witchcraft', which to modern ears suggests no more than an antiquated exercise of obscure rites long since exposed by centuries of rationalism, was so fundamental an issue in the lives of sixteenth- and seventeenth-century Europeans that hundreds of thousands of them were executed for it. This great persecution, which has only recently begun to receive the attention it deserves, can be said to have arisen from a conjunction between popular superstition and theological fantasy.

The popular superstition was nothing more complex than folk magic, the white and black magic of rural communities. We may define white magic as the sort that was supposed to provide cures and solutions that could not ordinarily be obtained. Fortune-telling, love-potions, healing by charms, divination for lost goods, come under this category. What religion and medicine could not provide was provided by white magic. Black magic was the obverse side of the coin, and referred in general to two things: the obtaining by diabolic means of the sort of service white magic usually provided, and the deliberate doing of evil (maleficium, evil-doing) through magic. A maleficium might involve, for example, putting a curse on people or making their cattle sick. Both white and black magic had a recognisable social function in the early modern period: both were, in a sense, rational activities.

The stage at which ordinary European folk magic became irrational was the stage at which the devil entered history. It was when the doctrine of the witches' Sabbath began to be taken seriously in the fourteenth and fifteenth centuries that the witch-craft problem really materialised. There were two principal components of the Sabbath which gave an entirely new twist to witchcraft and brought down on it the wrath of the authorities. Firstly, the meeting together of witches at the so-called Sabbath implied that here was a fraternity, an evil fraternity which by its nature could only be international; secondly, since the purpose of the meeting was allegedly to worship the devil, all witches had by definition bound themselves to Satan and renounced Christ. The old folk magic had now been expanded into a vast diabolic menace, and because it was diabolic the theologians stepped in with their observations. Thanks to the fertile theological mind, the *Malleus Maleficarum* (Hammer of Witches) (1486) became the first in a long line of printed manuals that claimed to analyse witchcraft.

The distinction between black and white magic now became suddenly very urgent. The crime that both lawyers and theologians agreed to be punishable by death was that of *maleficium,* or sorcery. It was sorcery that involved sexual congress with the devil, transportations (often scores of miles) to the Sabbath, the keeping of familiars, the withering of crops, the murder of children and the cursing unto death of their elders. Those who wished to detect sorcery could read about the symptoms in any one of several manuals written by men of the very highest intelligence: those for instance by the great jurist Jean Bodin (1580), by the coadjutor bishop of Trier, Peter Binsfield (1589), by the chief justice of Burgundy, Henri Boguet (1591), by the procurator-general of Lorraine, Nicolas Rémy (1595), or by the distinguished Belgian Jesuit Martín del Rio (1599). These writers drew on witch trials of the sixteenth century for their evidence, and were themselves used as authorities by subsequent witch finders. Thanks partly to them, the public learnt about the Sabbath and the great diabolic conspiracy it involved. The one exception to this picture was England. There for the entire period up to the mid-seventeenth century no witch or sorcerer was ever condemned for the Sabbath or diabolism. In England a witch was charged on her own account, as a causer of *maleficia,* never (save perhaps after 1645) as one of a sect of demonolaters.

What sort of people were prosecuted for witchcraft? In an attempt to explain a mania that gripped a continent for well over a century, some historians have attempted to identify witchcraft with mountainous or remote areas. The German historian Hansen, for instance, emphasised that the superstition arose mainly in the mountains of the Alps and Pyrenees. He pointed to the fact that the name applied to one group of Alpine heretics — the Vaudois — was by the fifteenth century being applied also to witches in France, as though in confirmation not only of their common heterodoxy but also of their mountainous origins. The theory is an appealing one. The biggest Spanish outbreak, in 1610, was in the Pyrenees; the biggest French one, as recorded by Pierre Delancre, was in Toulouse and the French Pyrenees. The great witchhunter Henri Boguet operated in the mountainous regions of Franche Comté in the late sixteenth century. An analysis of some of the regions afflicted by witch mania shows that for the most part the victims came from remote and relatively inaccessible regions with a low cultural level and a poor record of practising Christianity. Where Christ had not reached, the old folk superstitions were still strong. Perhaps the most intensively affected area was central Europe, both by the borders of Switzerland and within Switzerland. The Valtelline was a hotbed of witchcraft, and so too was Geneva in the time of Calvin. We might assume, then, that the victims of witchcraft prosecutions were mainly unlettered mountaineers out of reach of civilisation. This is disproved, however, by lowland areas such as Essex and the Netherlands where the mania flourished within easy reach of large urban centres. Indeed in several German city-states the process could not avoid being anything other than an urban phenomenon. These contradictions suggest that it is not easy to be exact about the milieu in which witchcraft prosecutions arose, and that it may be more valuable to look at the social setting of a witch-ridden community than at its geographical location.

It is easier to describe the class and character of the victims of witchhunts. All the detailed studies point to the fact that they came from the lower levels of society. It was in these levels that superstition flourished. 'It is amazing', commented the Italian humanist Galateo when the witch fear first began seeping through southern Italy in the early sixteenth century, 'how this fantasy has seized on everyone through being spread by the poorer classes'. There is every reason for believing that a time of economic depression could lead to spiritual despair, to a heightening of superstition, to an open resort to demonianism. The evidence available for sixteenth-century Essex is not very definite about the economic or other circumstances of victims. But an analysis of three hundred and sixty-six cases in the county of Namur between 1509 and 1646 makes it clear that for the most part they came from the less privileged sectors, and included cowherds, prostitutes, servants and priests' concubines. In Namur the majority of those prosecuted were in the general category of social outcasts. This was not surprising, since in a small commutiny it was the exceptional poeple — the old, the weak-minded, the ugly, and sometimes even the exceptionally beautiful — who drew upon themselves the victimisation of the rest of society. A study of witchcraft in the Jura region has shown that the aged and the senile, the sick, hysterical and deformed made up the majority of victims in the period we are considering. It was the Italian friar Samuele de Cassinis, the first person anywhere in Europe to denounce the persecution, who pointed out in the early sixteenth century that so-called witches were invariably '*quaedam ignobiles vetulae, aut personae idiotae atque simplices, grossae et rurales*'; in short, they were the old and weak-minded. It would appear, as with all persecutions, that it was the people who were least able to defend themselves who were singled out for punishment. This is certainly true of those who were mentally disturbed and suffered from various pathological afflictions. Doctors and clergy would repeatedly pronounce such people to be sane, whereupon they immediately became liable to prosecution. The cases of 'diabolic possession' at the convent of Notre-Dame du Verger at Oisy (Artois) in 1613-15, and at the convent of the Ursulines at Loudun in France, suggest that enclosed and isolated communities were liable to suffer from this form of visitation. The phenomenon also occurred on a grander scale, however, as Delancre testified during his mission to the Labourd region (Bayonne) in 1609. There in one village he discovered 'over forty persons afflicted with epilepsy by the sorcerers, and a countless number of others barking like dogs'.

It was these people, poor, outcast, maimed and afflicted, who were accused of conjurations and crimes so terrible that judges, bishops and even kings bestirred themselves to take part in the work of extermination. The attitude to the crimes varied according to the court. If the victims were accused of intercourse with the devil, of resorting to the Sabbath and of renouncing their baptism in favour of Satan, the Church courts would be inclined to severity, since all these acts savoured of heresy. If, on the other hand, the main accusation was one of harming and killing through *maleficia*, secular courts might be more involved. In practice, people were usually prosecuted on both counts, and there was no general pattern to the behaviour of courts. Accusations of *maleficia* inevitably predominated: all but eleven of a group of five hundred and three people prosecuted in the courts of Essex from 1560 to 1680 were accused of injuring or killing humans or their property. Even a brief reading of the evidence at witch trials makes it plain that the crimes were usually impossible and the prisoners invariably innocent. What then of the great number of voluntary confessions obtained in England and elsewhere without the benefit of torture? Of the many possible answers to this question, the following, supplied by a Scottish judge in 1678, is one example:

> I went when I was a Justice-depute to examine some Women who had confest judicially, and one of them, who was a silly creature, told me under secresie that she had not confest because she was guilty, but being a poor creature who wrought for her meat and being defam'd for a Witch, she knew she would starve, for no person thereafter would either give her meat or lodging; and that all men would beat her, and hound Dogs at her, therefore she desir'd to be out of the World.

It was this victimisation by society that precipitated witchcraft accusations, as contemporaries were well aware. The observations of Reginald Scot, an Englishman whose *Discoverie of Witchcraft* (1584) was one of the most influential books to be written against the mania, show clearly how petty suspicions, jealousies and gossip eventually ended in a criminal prosecution.

> May it please you to waie what accusations and crimes they laie to their charge, namelie: She was at my house of late, she would have had a pot of milke, she departed in a chafe bicause she had it not, she railed, she curssed, she mumbled and whispered, and finallie she said she would be even with me: and soon after my child, my cow, my sow or my pullet died, or was strangelie taken. Naie (if it please your Worship) I have further proofe: I was with a wise woman, and she told me I had an ill neighbour, and that she would come to my house yer it were long, and so did she; and that she had a marke above hir waste, and so had she: and God forgive me, my stomach hath gone against hir a great while. Hir mother before hir was counted a witch, she hath beene beaten and scratched by the face till bloud was drawne upon hir, bicause she hath beene suspected, and afterwards some of these persons were said to amend. These are the certeinties that I heare in their evidences.

The overwhelming majority of alleged witches were women, usually old women. By the logic of this, a large proportion were widows, though married women were also common. Young witches were uncommon. Very many of these women really believed in their own magical powers, and many were totally convinced that they had been transported to Sabbaths and had had sexual intercourse with the devil. At the level of folk superstition, there was nothing unusual about this. The Italian peasants of this period who believed in the cult of the *benandanti* were convinced that they had the power to leave their bodies at night and go out and battle against the powers of darkness. The beliefs of the *benandanti*, however, were a purely local, tribal cult with no associations of *maleficia*. What staggered the courts trying witchcraft was that in case after case the accused came up with virtually identical stories, and that these stories varied very little from country to country, so that right across Europe there emerged the terrifying vision of hundreds of thousands of formerly Christian souls dedicated to the service of Satan. Early suspicions that the Sabbaths were merely meetings at which sexual orgies took place were soon dispelled. Sex played little or no part in witchcraft, whose whole spirit was against sex and fertility. The alleged orgies of the Sabbath, far from being fertility rites, were in fact infertility rites: congress with the devil, it was well known, froze the womb.

Since prosecution and condemnation were only the last stages of the procedure against witchcraft, it is obvious that it was the first stage — denunciation — which was the critical one. Had there not been repeated and regular denunciations the authorities would have shown scant interest in the esoteric habits of a minority of the population. A recent study of witchcraft in Essex attempts to give a wholly rational explanation of the social setting which produced denunciations. 'Witchcraft accusations', the author argues, 'occurred when a traditional ethic of neighbourly charity was being undermined.' In other words, the situation was very similar to that outlined by Reginald Scot. Neighbours in a community were ceasing to practise mutual help; resentment, jealousy and suspicion gave rise to accusations. Proceeding from this interesting explanation, it is possible to argue that the victimisation of the lower classes, of the poor and unfortunate, was also the result of a change in the structure of community relations. But if the explanation is valid for Essex it is extremely difficult to accept it as equally valid for the greater part of Europe in the two centuries, 1500 to 1700, which saw the rise and fall of the witch mania. The openly irrational and pathological character of many witchcraft outbreaks suggests that sociological explanations alone are not sufficient, and need to be supplemented by research into medical and psychological aspects as well.

One curious feature of many outbreaks was the leading part played by children. Several of the cases in the city of Valenciennes consisted of children denouncing their own parents: in 1590 Jeanne Cuvelier was accused by her own son, in 1662 eight-year-old Catherine Polus accused her father. An outbreak at Chelmsford (Essex) in 1579 appears to have started with a sick child's accusations, and in the famous Warboys case the evidence for the prosecution rested principally on the evidence of three children, who were accused by their victim of 'wantonness' or malice. The important outbreak in Sweden in 1669 revolved entirely round a group of children accused of witchcraft. One of the best-known cases initiated by the accusations of children was that of 1692 in Salem (Massachusetts), which ultimately cost twenty-two lives. Perhaps the most bizarre of all cases involving children occurred in Spain, when the inquisitor Salazar in 1611-

12 visited Navarre to reconcile self-confessed witches to the Church. According to his own report, 1802 people came forward and confessed themselves to be witches, and of these a total of 1384 consisted of children under the age of fourteen. Fortunately for these children, the Spanish Inquisition had decided not to accept the veracity of their statements. In other parts of Europe children were often executed without mercy: at Valenciennes fifteen-year-old Marie Carlier was executed secretly in prison at dawn to avoid public reaction; and at Quingey (Franche Comté) in 1657, as two boys of thirteen and eleven were being taken out to execution one of them, dimly aware of the horror into which his statements had led him, cried out to the examining officer, 'You made me say things I didn't understand!' The problems involved in the investigation of such cases go far beyond the merely sociological.

To understand why the century 1550-1660 was so important that it can be taken without question as the peak period for the witch mania, we need only look at some figures. Some of the statistics for deaths are certainly inflated. Nicholas Rémy of Lorraine is said to have gathered the materials for his study of the worship of demons, published in 1595, from the trials of about nine hundred persons he had sentenced to death in the preceding fifteen years. An examination of the court records does not support this suggestion: for the period 1550 to 1660 what we do have is a minimum total (minimum, because of possible gaps in the records) of one hundred and twenty death sentences and a total of eight hundred and thirty-two prosecutions. The chief justice of Burgundy from 1598-1616, Henri Boguet, has been credited with six hundred executions, but close scrutiny of the records has apparently so far produced only twenty-five or twenty-six actual executions for this period. It seems likely, then, that the six hundred deaths attributed to Delancre in 1609, the six hundred attributed to the bishop of Bamberg from 1622 to 1633, and the nine hundred attributed to the bishop of Würzburg in about the same period, may all be gross exaggerations. But there are many figures of comparable dimensions that cannot be revised.

In Würzburg a total of one hundred and fifty-seven persons were executed in twenty-nine separate burnings between 1627 and 1629. The victims included three canons, fourteen assistant clergy, the widow of the chancellor of the diocese, several city councillors, the most beautiful girl in Würzburg, several children aged from nine to twelve years, four inn-keepers, several old women, and so on. In England, at Essex Assizes alone, between 1560 and 1680 some one hundred and ten people are known to have died accused of witchcraft; many other deaths were unrecorded. In Geneva between February and May 1545 as many as thirty-four people were executed, or about one every three days. The records of the High Court of Justiciary in Edinburgh for the sixteenth and seventeenth centuries list about one thousand eight hundred witchcraft cases. On a more local scale, let us look at the village of Winningen (pop. three hundred) in the archbishopric of Trier. Between 1631 and 1661 in this small village, at least thirty-four people are known to have been prosecuted for witchcraft, and of these at least twenty-eight are definitely known to have been executed. In all but one of the thirty-four cases, torture was used. Winningen was an ordinary town, with no exceptional history of diabolism. Other towns in the area were equally subject to the mania. In eight other local villages, between 1629 and 1652 a total of twenty-six people were burnt for witchcraft. The highest incidence for persecution in Trier was in 1587-93 when in twenty-seven villages in the archbishopric a total of three hundred and sixty-eight people were burnt alive for sorcery.

Over a broad time-span, the total of cases comes to a derisory annual average. But to calculate in averages is totally misleading, for the outbreaks of witch mania were spasmodic, almost irrationally so. It is consequently impossible to trace any general pattern or rhythm in the persecution. In the archbishopric of Trier, cases did not really start before 1591. In Essex the peak year was 1584. In Lorraine and in Namur the number of known cases tried by the courts, in five-year totals, is plotted as a curve in Figure 18. Though the curves show no pattern they emphasise the fact that the most intensive period for prosecutions was in the late sixteenth and early seventeenth centuries.

At this stage it becomes essential to define what we mean by a 'witch mania'. Do we mean that suddenly thousands of em- bittered old women started consorting with the devil, or believed that they were consorting? Or do we mean that suddenly thousands of fanatical clergy and lawyers started inventing stories about innocent people and started executing them? Put another way, the problem comes to this: was there actually an increase in the practice of black magic, or was there merely and solely an increase in the *prosecution* of this alleged crime?

271

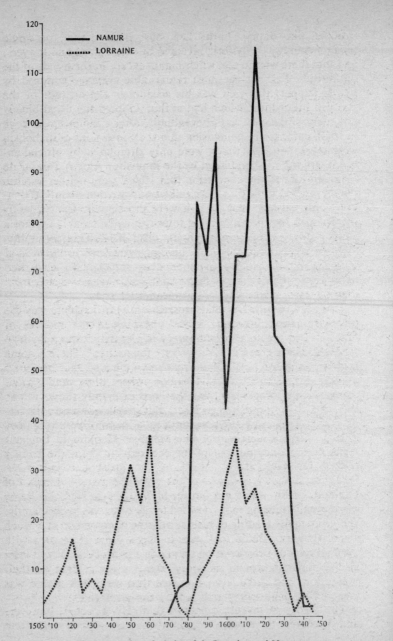

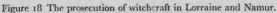
Figure 18 The prosecution of witchcraft in Lorraine and Namur.

Some, like Henry Charles Lea, have insisted that the whole phenomenon was a hysteria invented by theologians and lawyers, and that there was no real witch mania except in the minds of the authorities. Perhaps the most remarkable evidence adduced by Lea to support this view was his account of the attitude of the Spanish Inquisition, which had at first adopted the usual bloody and repressive measures but eventually, after a famous *auto de fe* in 1610, came to the conclusion that the confessions of diabolism were mere fantasies which were only stimulated by official interest. An inquiry conducted by the inquisitor Alonso Salazar de Frias led him to the conclusion that 'there were neither witches nor bewitched until they were talked and written about'. Witchcraft only existed, that is, if it were prosecuted. Consequently the Spanish Inquisition refused to prosecute 'witches', and not a single witch was executed in Spain after 1610. This possibility, that the whole mania was the unhappy result of inventive and scholarly minds piecing together stray information and then initiating a prosecution of alleged sorcerers, emerges clearly from even a cursory reading of the European witch trials.

To maintain with Lea that prosecution by officialdom was the principal cause, however, leaves unexplained the motives of officials. Did the great witchhunters deliberately foster a myth to serve their own greed or their private fanaticism? There is some evidence of greed: in 1626 a Frenchman claimed that he found himself in a certain town in Lorraine 'where there were a great many accused of sorcery, and they executed only those, it was said, who had something to lose'. But greed was never an important motive, since the vast majority of victims were very poor indeed. Corrupt mercenaries like Matthew Hopkins in England made their money not out of the accused but from the bounty offered for each arrest. None of the great persecutors — Delancre, Bouguet, Remy — or the great theorists — James I of England, Bodin — had any but the highest ideals. Nicholas Remy was a kindly, retiring man, devoted to his large and loving family, and given to the reading of history and the composition of French and Latin verse. Bodin took care to check some of his data with the trial records before setting them down in his book. For at least all the major figures in the story, there is not a stain on their reputation, and there is no evidence that the witch mania was invented or deliberately fostered by the authorities.

The theory of invention cannot be totally rejected, however, and there were three main ways in which a concept as impossible as the Sabbath could have gained acceptance as reality. The interrogators, in the first place, could have put words into the mouths of their prisoners. The aged and simple-minded could easily have been led astray by skilful questioning. Secondly, torture may have created the Sabbath. Lea shows convincingly that witchcraft and the Sabbath seemed to proliferate wherever torture was used, and that the rise and fall of the mania appear to coincide with the use of torture for cases of 'sorcery'. England, in his view, escaped the Sabbath because torture was not used, and the first real appearance of the Sabbath was in 1645, when Hopkins used a form of torture. The third possibility of invention is simply that of self-deception: hysteria and auto-suggestion. Short of actually believing in the visible personal intervention of the devil in human affairs, we must treat this category seriously, for it was a large and important one, But even a psychiatric explanation of auto-suggestion leaves us with the difficulty of explaining why it took the form of belief in witchcraft.

The widespread nature of 'court' sorcery may be identified with the theory that witchcraft was 'invented' or 'imposed' from above. Sorcery in high places seemed to experience a distinct and suspicious increase whenever political crises occurred. The principal outbreaks in Scotland and England fall into this category. The first serious nation-wide outbreak of witchcraft in Scotland was in the years 1590-7, a period when the Earl of Bothwell was accused of 'consulting with witches . . . to conspire the King's death'. After Bothwell's escape from Edinburgh Castle in 1591 the proclamation issued against him claimed that he had had 'consultation with necromancers, witches and other wicked and ungodly persons'. Needless to say, several political opponents were executed as sorcerers during this crisis. The two other great witchcraft crises in Scottish history, in 1640-50 and in 1660-3, were both deeply involved with internal politics. In England the principal period for witchcraft prosecution was the reign of Queen Elizabeth, and fears for the queen's life governed the whole attitude of the Privy Council. Any rumours of witchcraft occurring in the country were immediately reported to the Council and sifted for signs of plots against the queen. In 1568-71 plots involving Mary Queen of Scots had important witchcraft complications. Eventually the Council transferred all jurisdiction over this crime from Church courts to state courts. In France Richelieu denounced his political opponent Luynes as a sorcerer. 'It is extremely likely', the cardinal reported, 'that Luynes made use of charms, through his connection with two well-known magicians who gave him herbs to put in the king's slippers, and powder to put in his clothing.' The king's judges were no less concerned for His Majesty's safety: in 1631 we find them condemning perpetually to the galleys, for the crime of *lèse-majesté*, men 'who had made prognostications and horoscopes against the life of the king'. In the Russia of Ivan the Terrible witchcraft was rampant. Prince Kurbsky, the contemporary opponent of the Tsar, atributed the great persecution by Ivan of his enemies in the 1560s, to a real or alleged fear of sorcery. 'There had never before been such unheard-of persecution', reports Kurbsky. Unfortunately we have no figures for the witch scare in Muscovy. It is known that tsars such as Ivan III and Basil Shuisky resorted to witches, and Kurbsky himself believed in sorcery. A contemporary Russian source admitted that 'Russians are attracted by and given to witchcraft'.

The alternative to the theory of an imposed belief, is that there was a real increase in practice and belief. 'Whence comes the witch?' asked Michelet in his study of *La Sorcière*. 'I say unhesitatingly: from times of despair.' Sorcery, Michelet argued, took its origin in times of depression, both economic and personal. Sorcery would come in times of war, of famine, of economic and social crisis, of loss of faith, certainty and orientation. Hence the great witchhunts during the civil wars in France, during the Thirty Years War in Germany, and during the *oprichnina* in Russia. Brouette, whose work on the county of Namur is one of the few scientific studies we possess of witchcraft, argues likewise that 'the appearance and development of Satanism are connected with the misfortunes suffered by a country's inhabitants'. If this is understood in the sense of material misfortune, there are countless examples to support the contention. Galateo's evidence for sixteenth-century Italy, that it was the 'poorer classes' among whom the fantasies spread, can be borne out by cases elsewhere. In rural areas ravaged by war and shortage of food the population readily put their hopes in extraordinary methods, and victimised those in whom they saw their ills personified. One of the most illustrative and horrifying examples can be found in the war-torn Dijonnais of 1644. A madman from the village of Arcée made a tour as witch-finder through the Flavigny region. Wherever he went, reported a local parish priest, the villagers assembled for him, and 'he would look over them and point out such and such a one as a witch or sorcerer, and these would immediately be taken off and immersed (i.e. the water ordeal), and they eventually died in the process. Others would light ovens and throw in all those he said were sorcerers.' It was this ready and despairing acceptance of the reality of witchcraft that gave Matthew Hopkins a field day in the south of England in 1645-7. It was not that the masses literally turned to diabolism, but that in their sufferings they saw the workings of the devil more clearly than ever before, and out of this realisation was born the savagery with which they annihilated the servants of Satan. In every European country the most intensive outbreaks of witch persecution were in times of disaster. Taking the long view, the equation of crisis and witchcraft becomes even more striking. It was the very period of the greatest price rise—the late sixteenth and early seventeenth century—that saw the most numerous cases of accusation and persecution of witches.

Developing Michelet's viewpoint in non-material terms, at least two distinct approaches to an explanation of the persecution are possible. Witchcraft can be identified on one hand with the advent of Reformation heresies, on the other with the advent of the irrational. It was the German Dominican, Sprenger, co-author of the *Malleus Maleficarum*, who argued in the fifteenth century that sorcery was quite simply heresy. In a brilliantly grotesque piece of textual scholarship, he claimed that the word *maleficium* 'comes from *maleficiendo*, which significes *male de fide sentiendo* ', or, in other words, heresy. Subsequent historians, including all the leading German scholars of the witch mania, agreed that the coincidence of the persecution of witches with that of heretics was of some significance. Many so-called witch trials were in fact, if we look at the proceedings, heresy trials: the accused were tried principally for renouncing baptism, refusing the sacraments and so on. This helps to explain, the argument goes, the role played by Jesuits and other religious leaders, such as Calvin, in the destruction of witches. The special role assigned to the devil (Luther, we must remember, threw an ink-pot at him) was an essential part of this age of intense religious conflict. Only when the Age of Faith gave way to the Age of Reason did the persecution die away. The argument is an important one, but not always convincing. Spain, for instance, suffered large outbreaks of witchcraft persecution, at Calahorra and in Catalonia, a full generation before the beginning of the heresy hunts. While the argument does little to explain the persecution in general, it certainly helps to explain its intensity at certain epochs.

The advent of the irrational can be felt throughout the culture of the age. As a method of explaining the mania it is totally inadequate, for it takes no account of the social conflicts inherent in the witchcraft phenomenon. But it suggests powerfully that the acceptance of belief in sorcery made persecution acceptable even to the learned. To the learned, moreover, there was no contradiction between witchcraft and reason. The great search for knowledge was still no more than a continuation of the search for the philosopher's stone. We are back with Napier, up in Edinburgh, using logarithms in order to compute the number of the beast in the Apocalypse. The outburst of intellectual activity that distinguished the age was permeated, perhaps more than ever, by magic, by the resort to sources beyond empiricism. Why else did doctors of science resort to alchemy, astrology and magic with a passion unknown to the Middle Ages? Why do Bosch and Brueghel the Elder assume so important a place in the art of the period, and the iconography of the age pullulate with monsters and demons? It was no accident that now, in 1587, the Faust tradition broke into print in Germany, to be translated into Dutch in 1592, English the same year, and French in 1598. Faust was no reactionary scholastic. It was his very hatred of the schools and love of reason that drove him to extend the frontiers of knowledge. Similarly it was his love of reason that drove the English scientist Joseph Glanvil in his *Sadducismus triumphatus* (1666) to argue in favour of the reality of witchcraft, which he felt to be as valid a subject for enquiry as any other. This strange intellectual world, it can be argued, is proof that the irrationality of witchcraft was no fringe activity but an integral part of the mental climate.

To accept irrationality as the norm, however, makes it all the more difficult to categorise the views of the leading opponents of the persecution. Both the Spanish and Roman Inquisitions were known to oppose the death penalty. The Russian Orthodox Church likewise refused to allow execution. Were these institutions therefore enlightened? In Milan in 1611 two women who confessed to commerce with Satan, homicide and other unspeakable crimes, were given a short prison sentence by the inquisitors. In many countries not under the yoke of the Inquisition they would have suffered death. Was there, moreover, any significance in the fact that some of the most influential opponents of the persecution were Catholics? — men like de Cassinis (*Questione de la strie* (The problem of witches), 1505), Adam Tanner and Friedrich von Spee *(Cautio criminalis,* 1631). The most famous of all opponents was the Calvinist doctor of the Duke of Cleve, Johann Weyer, a Netherlander who in 1563 published at Basel his *De praestigiis daemonum* (The deceptions of demons). In the preface to his work Weyer explained that 'I fight with natural reason against the deceptions which proceed from Satan and the crazed imagination of the so-called witches. My object is also medical, in that I show that illnesses which are attributed to witches come from natural causes.' Neither Catholics nor Calvinists were necessarily obscurantist.

The historical study of witchcraft continues to raise problems to which no clear answers are available. The internal analysis of witchcraft is no major problem. Its pathological nature was recognised already in the sixteenth century, and has been exhaustively studied in the case of Lorraine by Delcambre. The problem that persists is the external one: why should the rise and decline of the persecution coincide with the beginnings of the modern age? What social forces, what collective mentalities, made this age of crisis also one of unreason?

THE PRACTICE OF RELIGION AND THE GROWTH OF UNBELIEF

The breakdown of the mediaeval Church and the success of sectarianism in the sixteenth century lead one to question whether the changes reflect an increase or a decrease in the actual practice of religion. Was the age of the Counter Reformation really an age of faith? Or were changes possible rather because men had ceased to feel intensely about religion?

In approaching a century when ideological change was widespread, any definition of 'irreligion' cannot be too narrowly cast, particularly since all the Churches insisted on accusing each other of atheism and idolatry. In the Middle Ages anticlericalism may have been one pointer to irreligion, but by the sixteenth century it had become the stock-in-trade of religions radicals and is consequently very difficult to identify with lack of faith. In Puritan England, for instance, anticlericalism was rampant among those very people who believed in their direct personal relationship with God. Attendance at church and communion in Catholic countries is equally unreliable as a basis, not merely because figures for these are scarce but also because it was only after the Council of Trent that Sunday attendance became obligatory and regular communion was encouraged. Figures for Easter communion give no real indication of the state of religious belief or practice, since the moral and social pressure to conform, particularly in country areas, was very strong. In any case, nearly every single adult in a Catholic parish communicated at Easter.

It can hardly be doubted that there was a high degree of indifference to established religion. How else could the profound confessional changes of the sixteenth century, involving in some regions a rapid alternation between the major Christian faiths, have been carried through so successfully? How else could magical superstition—assuming that it actually existed and was not foisted on to the masses—have gained the upper hand among so many communities of the time? It is usually held that both the changes and the superstition were products of an age of intense belief and credulity: but could they not equally have been the fruit of incredulity?

The religion of the mass of the people is almost inaccessible to the historian. Those who lived settled lives in both town and country appear to have practised their faith regularly, attending church and using the public devotions of their religion. In Catholic countries the norm of regularity in the Christian life was attendance at Mass, in Protestant countries the church and the pulpit combined to induce conformity for, as Charles I of England once remarked to his son, 'people are governed by the pulpit more than the sword in times of peace'. It was the unsettled classes, notably the poor and homeless, who had little or no contact with religion. Since they constituted over one-fifth of the population of the towns, there is every possibility that irreligion was a significant feature of daily life. Even in the country the rural poor were seldom in regular contact with the Church. One extraordinary case is reported by a Jesuit writing from Périgord in 1553. 'Near Bordeaux', he wrote, 'stretch about thirty leagues of forest, whose inhabitants live like rude beasts, without any concern for heavenly things. You can find persons fifty years old who have never heard a Mass or learnt one word of religion.' A parish priest in the Rouen area reported in 1698 (a period when there was no lack of clergy) that 'there are many poor and suchlike who come from outside the parish, who are very disordered and remain several years without going to confession'. It may be thought that their 'disorder' was a pure accident of circumstance and not a conscious defection from religion. But the attitude of the urban poor suggests just such a defection. The seventeenth-century historian Henri Sauval, who knew his Paris in every minor detail, testified of the beggars of Paris that they neither practised marriage nor resorted to the sacraments. They had a statue in the Cour des Miracles before which they prayed, but this was their only concession to superstition; and when they entered a church it was only to cut purses. In 1595 when the police arrested a young beggar in Rome he informed them that they (the beggars) were not well-disposed to the Faith: 'among us few practise it, because most of us are worse than Lutherans'. The Spanish writer Pedro Ordóñez, writing in 1672, observed of the urban vagabonds that 'they live like barbarians, for they are not known to, nor have they been seen to, go to Mass or confession or communion'.

In some respects the area of unbelief was far vaster than these observations suggest. Certain racial minorities, such as the gypsies, were not normally committed to the Christian religion. Pagan superstitions still lingered in the woods and mountains of central Europe and in the remote regions of Scandinavia. Even in the citadel of conformity, Spain, there was enough resistance to the official religion for the Inquisition to be kept at work. The descendants of converted Jews, the *conversos,* were openly hostile to the Faith they formally professed. The numerous recorded cases of sacrilege and blasphemy, examples like that of the man who urinated against the walls of the church or another who spat on the floor at the elevation of the Host, prove a tradition of undying hatred of Catholicism. In regions where the Moriscos lived, the traveller could pause and wonder as, on the eve of a Muslim fast, every dwelling in sight remained shuttered and closed and no living man could be seen: this among a people nominally Christian. But the religion of Castilians themselves was questioned by contemporaries. When Guicciardini came as Florentine ambassador in the early sixteenth century he concluded that Spaniards were 'very religious in externals and outward show, but not so in fact'. Almost the same words were used by the Venetian envoy Tiepolo in 1563. These were hostile witnesses, and cannot easily be trusted. Yet Spain did not lack its own free-thinkers, among them a native pharmacist arrested by the Inquisition at Laguna (Tenerife) in 1707. He is reported to have said 'that one could live in France because there there did not exist the poverty and subjection that today exists in Spain and Portugal, since in France they do not try to find out nor do they make a point of knowing who everyone is and what religion he has and professes. And so he who lives properly and is of good character may become what he wishes.'

The pharmacist's view of France was not wholly correct. Open unbelievers were prosecuted there as readily as in Spain, particularly if they came from the lower classes or the lesser bourgeoisie. But it was true that considerable licence was given to doubters among the upper classes, of whom there were very many indeed. The seventeenth century in France was one of saints, but also one of unbelievers. La Noue observed at the time that 'it was our wars of religion that made us forget religion'. The ruling circles in the early seventeenth century were riddled with unbelief or 'libertinism' as it has been called. Many factors contributed to this attitude: the late wars, anticlericalism, the new co-existence between Catholics and Protestants that followed the Edict of Nantes, the epicurean court of Henry IV, among others. Some made a profit out of their irreligion, like Jérémie Ferrier, a Huguenot pastor, who abjured his faith in 1613, drew large pensions as a priest till his death in 1626, and claimed that for fourteen years he had preached Christ without believing in him. Most unbelievers kept their attitude concealed. This was advisable particularly after the enormous shock in 1623, when the poet Théophile de Viau was arrested for blasphemy and later condemned to death, a sentence which was subsequently commuted to banishment. The result was that, as Pierre Bayle claimed, many 'die like everyone else, after confession and communion'. 'Unbelief', the Sieur de Rochemont wrote in 1665, 'has its laws of prudence'. Hypocrisy and dissimulation became the necessary accompaniments to a loss of faith.

The most famous French unbelievers were drawn from the ranks of intellectuals who frequented the literary academies of the period, such as the Rambouillet; or the philosophic academies, of which the most outstanding was that of the humanist brothers Dupuy, which met for twenty-eight years from 1617 to 1645 in the mansion of the President de Thou. Unfortunately the word 'unbeliever' is as inadequate as any other to describe the general attitude of these intellectuals, whose 'libertinism' was in fact no more than a restrained scepticism or Pyrrhonism. Two of the most distinguished of the sceptics, Gabriel Naudé (1600-53) and Guy Patin (1601-72), were doctors; neither was an atheist. Patin did not reject faith; rather, he distinguished between the realms of faith and of reason, giving each appropriate limits. Pierre

Gassendi (1592-1655) was perhaps the most paradoxical of the sceptics, since he was a priest who said Mass regularly but was also one of the most prominent libertines. The difficulty in categorising these and other leading thinkers as part of the process of growing unbelief arises from the fact that few of them rejected Christianity as a system. They usually accepted the legitimacy of faith, for this was above knowledge; but all knowledge, they felt, must be subjected to the iron laws of doubt.

The chief intellectual influence on France throughout this period was Italy, and it was there — in Venice, Padua, Rome and Florence — that the humanist sources were drawn upon. Harsh judgments were passed by the French upon Italy. 'It is a country of knavery and superstition; some don't believe enough, others believe too much', was Naude's verdict. He also claimed that 'Italy is full of libertines and atheists and people who don't believe anything'. This surprising observation, though clearly an exaggeration, is a salutary reminder that in Italy the humanist emphasis of the Renaissance was still alive among the elite. Giordano Bruno offered his readers the vision of a totally non-Christian universe. Man, in the person of Bruno, had attained a new horizon:

> Behold now, standing before you, the man who has pierced the air and penetrated the sky, wended his way amongst the stars and overpassed the margins of the world. . . . By the light of sense and of reason, with the key of most diligent enquiry, he has thrown wide those doors of truth which it is within our power to open, and stripped the veils and coverings from the face of nature.

In this scheme of things the Christian faith and the Christian God were irrelevant. Among the Italian libertines, we are informed by Naude, was

> Girolamo Borri, professor of philosophy at Pisa, who was favoured by the Grand Duke. He was a total atheist, but wasn't burnt, though he deserved it. One day he stated that there was nothing in heaven beyond the eighth sphere. The inquisitor wished him to recant. The next day he got up and said to his audience, 'Gentlemen, I have proved to you that there is nothing beyond the eighth sphere. I am required to recant, but I assure you that if there is anything else, it can only be a plate of macaroni for the inquisitor.' Having said this he fled to safety. He would have been burnt several times over if the Grand Duke had not protected him.

Some were in fact burnt. Bruno perished at the stake in Rome in February 1600; Giulio Cesare Vanini (1585-1619), a Neapolitan priest and once doctor to Clement VIII, was burnt outside his country, at Toulouse. Thomas Campanella (1568-1639) only just escaped execution, but was imprisoned for twenty-seven years and tortured seven times. Despite their apparent appeal to reason as the basis for their new approach to Christianity, these thinkers and others like them — such as Cesare Cremonini, a professor at Padua who was denounced to the Holy Office in 1604 — really drew their inspiration from pre-Christian, pagan sources. Their outlook was not necessarily directed towards the Age of Reason; it was based firmly in the traditions, myths and esoteric philosophy of a past age. To break out of the dogmatic circle created by Christian philosophy and by St Thomas Aquinas, they conjured up the ancient gods, the lost arts and the secret rites. To escape one religion they created another, notably the magical cult of the sun to which Bruno and Campanella gave credence. Unbelief began in mystification.

It was in this age of questioning and growing doubt that the mystifiers, who always claimed that they were men of reason, resorted to superstitions older than the Faith they hoped to supersede. Freemasonry, which became historically significant only in the early seventeenth century, attracted many because of its implied access to long-hidden knowledge. It was this that led the English antiquarian Dr William Stukeley to join the movement and 'to be initiated into the mysteries of Masonry, suspecting it to be the remains of the mysteries of the ancients'. In some sense this spirit could be described as a rationalist one, for it involved the search for human truths that were independent of revelation. The widespread resort to magic and cabbalism which accompanied the departure from Christian tradition, was a feature of the Renaissance and permeated the thought and practice of many late-Renaissance savants. The trend was not thought of as conflicting with Christianity in any formal way. But the belief in secret knowledge and the resort to secret associations of the adept and initiated was clearly at variance with official discipline. Perhaps the most remarkable of the 'societies' that practised the new mystification were the Rosicrucians.

The Rosicrucians seem not to have actually existed, in the sense of a society with members. The first publication announcing their existence, the *Fama Fraternitatis* (1614), was followed by other works, but no clue was ever given to the authors of these writings or to the activity of their society. When the *Fama* appeared it created widespread excitement among intellectuals. In Germany, its place of origin, it was avidly read and soon taken up in other countries. Within three years it ran into nine different editions, as well as several foreign translations. Many seekers after knowledge tried to join the order, but failed to contact any known members. Descartes, who was living at Frankfurt in 1619, was one of these seekers; after vain attempts, he decided that the order did not exist. Leibniz at the end of the century openly proclaimed it to be a 'fiction'. The real significance of the Rosicrucians, however, is not in their reality but in the response they aroused. The hunger for esoteric knowledge, the rage for the unknown and unknowable, was further inflamed by the myth that a secret society had inherited from a fifteenth-century German nobleman, Christian Rosenkreuz ('Rosy Cross'), the ancient lore of the Middle East. Much of the myth had been in fact created by the Lutheran thinker Johann Valentin Andreae (1586-1654), probable co-author of the *Fama,* and the man who more than anyone else can be called the founder of Rosicrucianism. Many nevertheless continued to believe in the Rosicrucian claims. In Germany the philosopher Michael Maier expounded the doctrine that the brethren of the Rosy Cross had access to the ancient truths of Persia and India; in England the physician Robert Fludd looked on Rosicrucianism as a new system of natural philosophy.

Although this distortion of belief cannot be looked upon as unbelief, it was certainly a prelude to it, for it sought knowledge outside the framework of dogmatic certainty. The search for esoteric knowledge was, if we may so term it, a right-wing deviation from religion; on the left, the deviation consisted in by-passing religion without contradicting its truths. This latter, secularist, spirit was most clearly represented in the democratic tenets of the Levellers and Diggers, whose whole social philosophy was non-theistic. Gerrard Winstanley, the Digger leader, went so far as to define religion only in terms of social justice: 'True religion and undefiled is thus: to make restitution of the Earth which hath been taken and held from the common people by the power of Conquests formerly and so set the oppressed free.'

Two centuries before Marx, Winstanley described religion as the opium of the people: 'This divining spiritual Doctrine is a cheat; for while men are gazing up to Heaven imagining after a happiness, or fearing a Hell after they are dead, their eyes are put out; that they see not what is their birthrights, and what is to be done by them here on Earth, while they are living.'

In rather a different way, the certainty of dogma was being undermined by another humanist impulse: toleration.

TOLERATION: THE CASE HISTORY OF BASEL

One of the most notorious events of the Reformation period was the burning for heresy at Geneva in 1553 of Michael Servetus, the Aragonese anti-Trinitarian. Blame for the execution must correctly be put on John Calvin. This and other burnings have frequently been explained away on the grounds that it was an intolerant age. Approval of Servetus' execution was virtually universal among the Protestant churches. But the contrary response of a minority was sufficient proof that many convinced Christians, schooled in the humanist tradition, had begun to accept the necessity of respect for conscience. Perhaps the most significant centre of liberalism in this age of religious strife was the Swiss city of Basel.

Contemporary testimony to the connection between Servetus and Basel came from Pier Paolo Vergerio, once a papal nuncio, now a minister of the gospel in Switzerland. Vergerio was unhappy about the execution of Servetus. This resort to Catholic methods, he wrote to Bullinger at Zurich, would make the papists 'scoff that under the guise of reformation the churches were being deformed and the fundamentals shaken'. Shortly after he wrote: 'a friend has written to me from Basel that Servetus has supporters there'. The chief threat to Calvin from Basel came in the form of a little book entitled *De haereticis, an sint persequendi* (On whether heretics should be persecuted), purporting to be written by one Martin Bellius at Magdeburg, but in fact issued (in 1554) by Sebastian Castellio from Basel. Castellio, a native of French Savoy, had formerly been a colleague of Calvin's in Geneva, and had moved to Basel in 1544 after a disagreement. In 1553 he became a professor of Greek at Basel University and lived peacefully in the city till his death in 1563. By his writings he was to prove himself one of the foremost apostles of liberty of belief. But Castellio was no innovator in this matter. Already before him Basel had established itself as a humanist centre. From 1522 to 1529 it had been the city of Erasmus. There the Reformation overtook him: in 1529 the Mass was abolished, the city was taken over by the reformer Oecolampadius and his party, and Erasmus felt obliged to leave. Despite this development,

Basel under Oecolampadius still remained liberal. The reformer himself was a great admirer of Erasmus, and like him was a seeker after the *pax ecclesiarum* of the humanists. Not surprisingly, Erasmus decided to return to Basel in 1535. He died there in the following year and lies buried in the city's cathedral.

Calvin soon recognised Basel as the focal point of liberalism. 'At Basel', reports a manscript we have from Castellio's own hand,

> there are three professors whom the Calvinists treat openly as Servetists: they are Martin Borrhaus, principal professor of theology; Celio Secundo and Sebastian Castellio, both professors of letters. These last two have written against the persecution. As for Borrhaus, Servetus sent him his book (his *Errors on the Trinity,* for which he was burnt) before publishing it. Borrhaus sent a friendly reply, saying that he approved certain parts, disliked others and that there were some he didn't understand. On the persecution, he has told several people that in his view nobody should be persecuted for his beliefs.

It was clear that Castellio and his colleagues maintained a tradition alien to the concepts held in Geneva. At Basel the spirit of humanism was kept defiantly alive throughout the late sixteenth century.

In 1540, as Calvin was preparing to go to Switzerland and to undertake the reform of Geneva, the very year that Pope Paul III approved the Society of Jesus and the Roman Inquisition began its work in Italy, the Basel publishers Froben and Episcopius brought out an edition of the works of Erasmus. The friend and executor of Erasmus, Boniface Amerbach, was at this time professor of law at the university: later he was its rector. Long after the Reformation had split the humanists, Amerbach continued to keep in touch with his friends throughout Europe. He maintained his friendship with the Italian humanist Jacopo Sadoleto even after the latter became a cardinal of the Roman Church. Whenever Sadoleto sent letters to Germany he would make the messenger pass through Basel with one for Amerbach. '*Utinam vero D. Jacobus Sadoletus cardinalis viveret!*' ran one of Amerbach's letters in 1556. It was an echo from an age undivided by ideology. Yet Amerbach's vision was not fixed exclusively on the past. Though well aware of Castellio's very radical opinions, his esteem for him was so great that he made him tutor to his only son Basil, himself destined to become a distinguished scholar. Basil's whole upbringing was a humanist programme: a Swiss

Protestant, he was educated successively at Tübingen, Padua, Bologna and Bourges.

In September 1557, three years after the controversy over *De haereticis,* the reformers Beza and Guillaume Farel came to Basel to confront those who had supported Servetus in his heresy. Falling into a heated discussion with the intellectual leaders of Basel, they made the mistake of insulting Erasmus. 'The worst of troublemakers', Farel called him, and Beza exclaimed, 'Erasmus, why, basically he was an Arian!' A public protest was thereupon drawn up and signed by Amerbach, Froben and Episcopius. It said: 'We the undersigned declare your action dishonest and your assertion a pure calumny. We believe that the name of Erasmus deserves to be respected by all honest men.'

The continuity of humanism in Basel proves adequately that the traditions of intellectual freedom were to some degree kept alive in spite of the international divisions created by dogma. The period 1530-80 in Basel was not only one of great activity at the university: it was also one that was distinguished by the great editions of Renaissance classics. No sectarian bias was shown in the selection of books to be printed. Catholics, reformers and sectarians were all equally represented. A new edition of Petrarch, editions of Ficino, Pico della Mirandola, the lesser works of Boccaccio and Dante, the histories of Guicciardini and Machiavelli, works by Bruni, Bembo and Aeneas Sylvius: all these issued from the presses of Basel over a period of years. Sadoleto was not forgotten. Nor were the works of the Italian exiles, such as Curione, Vergerio and Peter Martyr Vermigli. Nor were radicals such as Ochino and Socinus denied the liberty of appearing in Basel. It was as though a new era had opened up in the life of letters. Pierre de la Ramée, the Huguenot refugee who came to Basel and who later in 1572 was to become one of the victims of the massacre of Saint Bartholomew, was moved to say of Aeneas Sylvius, with whom the city had special links because he had founded the university in 1460: *'hic nostrae Romae Romulus fuit',* he was the Romulus of our Rome. In this phrase two ages of humanism, one native to Italy and one to France, stretched out to meet at Basel.

Basel was one of the principal refuges in Europe for fugitives from persecution. The great Erasmus, Hans Denck the Anabaptist leader, Sebastian Franck the free-thinker, John Calvin himself (the first edition of his *Institutes* was published there in 1536), were among the eminent refugees of the early sixteenth century who found shelter. But it was the Italians who were the most significant in the history of religious toleration. Curione came to Basel in 1546, Jacobus Acontius in 1557, Faustus Socinus in 1576. More important than their presence was the fact that they and their friends found it possible to publish their writings freely in Basel. Curione in 1554 wrote an *Apologia pro M. Serveto* under a pseudonym, and published it in Basel. The humanist Mino Celsi, who had fled to Basel in 1571, wrote a work which was published in 1577, two years after his death, called *In haereticis coercendis* (On punishing heretics). With the Basel circle he shared not only a rejection of the death penalty in matters of faith, but also a firm reliance on the tradition of the greatest of the humanists: '*magnus ille, nec umquam satis laudatus Erasmus*' ('the great Erasmus, who can never be praised enough').

Three men in particular had a special part to play in Basel's liberal influence. These were the distinguished former head of the Capuchin Order, Bernardino Ochino, who published his *Thirty Dialogues* at Basel in 1563; Acontius, who in 1565 published one of the most fruitful works ever written on religious liberty, *Satan's Stratagems;* and Socinus who in July 1578, while at Basel, completed his principal work, *De Jesu Christo servatore* (Jesus Christ the servant).

Ochino's story is well known. After his escape from Italy in 1542 he eventually settled down in Zurich. The stern discipline there obliged him to publish his *Dialogues* in Basel. The book attacked the physical repression of heresy, but it was for his apparent justification of polygamy that the magistrates of Zurich decided to proceed against the illustrious convert. Now an old man of seventy-six, he was expelled from the city and forced to set out in a wintry December with his four small orphaned children. He eventually found refuge in Poland among the Anabaptists, but not before the plague had carried off three of the children. Ochino's story overlaps with that of Castellio, who had been a close friend, and had translated Ochino's Italian text into Latin for its publication in Basel. On hearing of his friend's expulsion, Castellio made preparations to go into voluntary exile with him. Poor health frustrated his intentions, and he died in December 1563. His body, which was at first interred in the cathedral cloister, was later moved by three young Polish nobles to a family tomb in the city.

Another Italian who chose Poland as his home, with far-reaching results, had come into contact with Castellio only posthumously. Faustus Socinus, the father of Socinianism, stayed at Basel from 1576. In the course of his work he came across some manuscript writings of Castellio, which impressed him so greatly that he arranged to publish them. In 1578 he completed his principal work, *De Jesu Christo servatore,* in Basel, though it was published only in 1594. Shortly after this he went to Poland to help the anti-Trinitarian movement. The Socinians were to become the most logical and consistent supporters of intellectual freedom.

The link between Poland (the first European country to establish religious toleration, in 1573) and Basel is even more striking than the incidental examples of Ochino and Socinus might suggest. Basel was the principal Swiss university frequented by Polish students: the peak period for attendance was 1555-71, but the numbers continued at a high level up to the Thirty Years War. The Erasmian tradition was preserved through the work of the irenicist Andrew Frycz Modrzewski, whose *De republica emendanda* (on reforming the state), after being confiscated in Cracow, was published in Basel in 1554. Here a German translation appeared in 1557 and in 1559 the printer Oporin brought out an edition of Modrzewski's collected works.

The example of Socinus shows how Basel had become a seed-ground for liberalism, which radiated outwards from the city. While Socinus was establishing religious harmony at Rakow in Poland, another Italian exile, Acontius, was developing his own work on the theory of toleration in England. Fleeing from Italy to Basel in 1557, he had entered the circle of Castellio and Curione. Though resident in England after 1559, he chose to publish his major work, *Satan's Stratagems,* at Basel in 1565. This became one of the most influential works on toleration written in the sixteenth century, and was translated into all the major languages of Europe.

Needless to say, Basel had its own falls from grace. In May 1559, in precisely the same month and year that the Spanish Inquisition was burning its first Protestant heretics in the city of Valladolid, the Protestant city of Basel held its own *auto de fe*. The victim was the Anabaptist leader David Joris, who had lived under a pseudonym in the city from 1544 till his death in 1556, and whose mortal remains were now exhumed and consigned to the flames. Among the Catholic cantons of Switzerland a saying soon arose that 'Basel burns dead heretics but not the living'.

Intended as a slight, the phrase was really a commendation. Basel never became a city of blood. Its record in the darkest days of the witch mania, when helpless victims were being executed in cities throughout Europe, was almost impeccable: only one victim was ever condemned for sorcery in Basel.

After the controversy over Servetus, Calvin's teaching triumphed and became the dominant form of Protestantism in western Europe. Ironically however the seeds of dissolution were sown by Castellio. It took a generation for Bellianism (as the doctrine of *De haereticis* was called) to mature, but when it did it threatened to undermine the structure Calvin had established. As early as 1555 the leading Calvinist pastor in Württemburg was being accused by Farel of attempting to 'Castellionise the country', that is, to introduce toleration. In France among the Calvinists a small group arose who called themselves the 'disciples of Castellio'. They were insignificant in numbers and influence, but provided the beginnings of a liberal party in the Reformed Church. When the religious wars broke out in his native country, Castellio in the autumn of 1562 penned his *Conseil à la France désolée*. He appealed to his countrymen to forgo violence as a solution to religious quarrels, and to respect the consciences of their opponents: 'support both religions and leave them free, so that everyone may follow without hindrance whichever he chooses'. His appeal was directed to both sides. 'To those who force another's conscience it suffices to say: would you like your consciences to be compelled by others?' The appeal was neglected, but it formed one of the bases on which the *politique* party in France constructed its programme of national reconciliation. It became, moreover, a text utilised by the Huguenot leader and publicist Du Plessis Mornay, in his work both in France and in the war-ravaged Netherlands.

In the Netherlands, which were occupied after 1566 with the rebellion against Spain, Castellio's writings became one of the fundamental texts of liberty. In 1578, under the auspices of Du Plessis Mornay, the *Conseil* was translated into Dutch and distributed. In subsequent years several other works were translated by Dirck Coornhert, perhaps the most important of all protagonists of toleration in the period after Castellio's death. From the beginning of the struggle for independence there thus existed a strong (mainly Calvinist) minority for whom intellectual freedom and civil liberty were inextricable goals. As this party grew, it turned for support to the Basel writers. In 1611 Acontius'

Satan's Stratagems appeared in Dutch. In 1612 the unpublished treatise by Castellio, *Contra libellum Calvini,* was at last put into print; and in the following year this and other works composing the *Opera Castellionis* were issued in Dutch. Both Castellio and Coornhert were inevitably enlisted in support of the Arminian (Remonstrant) struggle for freedom. The ideological split within Dutch and international Calvinism between the liberals and the rigorists was confirmed at the Synod of Dort in 1619.

While the controversy at Dort was a profound one involving many far-reaching issues, it is not entirely fanciful to view it in some sense as the final act of the drama that began with the burning of Servetus at Geneva in 1553. Here in the Netherlands, in the country of Erasmus, the heirs of liberal humanism were confronting the proponents of dogmatic theology. The ghost of Erasmus had come home. The Remonstrants lost at Dort, but their ideology eventually won: through the Independent tradition in England and the Saumur tradition in France, they produced a liberal school that undermined the dogmatic structure of Calvinism, and led eventually to the Enlightenment. This ancestry is unmistakable. It may be expressed in one sense by emphasising the way in which the Erasmianism which Castellio represented became subsumed in Calvinism and eventually superseded the old orthodoxy of Geneva. In another sense, we can point to the influence which the philosophy of doubt and of *docta ignorantia* (learned ignorance) exercised on and through Castellio. Implicit in his early writings, it does not become explicit until his *De arte dubitandi* (The art of doubting), which remained unpublished until 1937. Here Castellio claimed that 'if Christians doubted themselves a little, they would not commit all those murders'. The criterion of truth which he proposed was 'before all Scriptures and ceremonies': it was the voice of reason. With him, then, as with Bayle — the greatest product of liberal Calvinism — freedom was based on conscience and reason. Small wonder that the historian Lecky considered Castellio one of 'the most eminent forerunners of the Enlightenment'. The rise of rationalism may well have been the last thing Castellio desired, but it was a movement to which he, and Basel, contributed in no small measure.

THE CRISIS OF AUGUSTINIANISM
Despite its leading role in the struggle of the Dutch people against Spain, Calvinism by the early seventeenth century was still no

more than a minority religion in the United Provinces. Most of the population was nominally Catholic. But the real threat to Calvinist ascendancy was from the ghost of Erasmus, that ghost we have already seen returning from Basel to the Netherlands. With the appointment in 1602 of Arminius (1560-1609) to the second chair of theology at Leiden University, the Erasmian tradition won a public platform which enabled it to mount an attack on official Calvinism.

Arminianism in the United Provinces was both a religious and a political problem. The views expressed in the Arminian-inspired Remonstrance which was presented to the States of Holland in 1610, were broadly speaking representative of liberal humanism. The issue which eventually came to symbolise the differences between Remonstrants and their opponents the Counter-Remonstrants (led by the professor of theology at Leiden, Gomarus), was that of predestination. The conflict became political when the Remonstrants won support, and toleration for their views, from the patrician oligarchy. The Counter-Remonstrants gravitated to the party of the House of Orange. It was the political conflict between these parties that led to the temporary victory of Prince Maurice of Orange-Nassau and the execution of the republican leader Oldenbarnevelt in 1619. At approximately the same time a national synod of the Dutch Church was held at Dort (Dordrecht), from November 1618 to May 1619. At this synod the Remonstrants were condemned as heretics and expelled from the official Church.

Dort was nothing less than a general council of the Calvinist churches. Of the more than one hundred representatives at-tending, about one-fourth came from Calvinist churches outside the United Provinces. Though orthodoxy triumphed at the synod, a seed had been sown which was to disrupt the dogmas of the Reformed churches. In the words of the orthodox party, the doctrines of the Arminians were semi-Pelagian. In this phrase the long-disputed question of the part played by grace and free will in man's salvation was once more brought into issue.

Saint Augustine had been pre-eminent among those Catholic theologians who emphasised the supreme role of God in the scheme of man's salvation. Both Catholic and Protestant thinkers were to draw generously on his formulations in the attempt to explain anew the relationship between God and man. It was through him that Calvin was influenced to develop the theory of predestination that was reaffirmed at Dort. The Arminians

292

objected not simply to predestination but to the many consequences which followed from the acceptance of the doctrine. The official stress on God's omnipotence and man's helplessness led, they felt, to the abhorrent conclusion that it was God who willed man's sins and even his damnation. They held that far from being a mere passive recipient of God's grace, man was on the contrary endowed with enough free will to resist God's grace. It followed that no man was securely saved (as predestination affirmed) but that even the saints might backslide. There was no elect securely saved through omnipotent grace. God's grace was the same for all men, Christ had died for all and not merely for the chosen few. In the excited atmosphere at Dort, these propositions were quite rightly taken to be subversive of the whole structure of Calvinist theology. The Arminians had in fact departed from the essentials and, as their future history would show, were to travel even farther from received doctrine than their early leaders would have allowed.

Their part in undermining Calvinist orthodoxy lay not only in their own beliefs but also in the impulse they gave for a general reassessment of fundamentals by the delegates at Dort. The delegates from England and Bremen in particular were representative of a section of Calvinists who wished to meet some of the criticisms made by the Arminians. They conceded that Christ had died for all men, an important concession in the circumstances; but they also preserved the belief that only an elect would be saved. It was this liberal position, adapted and extended by Calvinists in France, that became one of the sources of the movement to rationalism.

The canons of the synod of Dort were framed in such a way that they accommodated the liberal point of view. The orthodoxy of the canons thus allowed some latitude in their actual interpretation. This was not enough for the Arminians, who vigorously condemned the orthodox position in all its nuances; but it was enough for an important minority among the Calvinists who did not share the rigid views of the Genevan theologians. It was in France, with the most numerous Calvinist community in Europe, that the debates at Dort had the most serious repercussions.

The year 1618, which witnessed the opening of the synod, was doubly significant for French Calvinism, for it was the year of the installation as professor of theology at the Academy of Saumur of the Scotsman John Cameron. Saumur, founded in

1604 by the Huguenot leader Du Plessis Mornay, grew to become the most outstanding theological college of the French Protestants. Cameron did not shrink from re-thinking basic beliefs in the light of Dort, and it was he who proposed the doctrine of 'hypothetical universalism', an extension of the liberal position at the synod. Cameron shared the liberal and fully orthodox view that Christ had died for all men but that only a few (the elect) would be saved. It was, however, in the manner of saving that Cameron's novelty emerged. God does not overwhelm the sinner with grace and so make it impossible for him to reject salvation; instead, he illumines the intellect with such force that the will necessarily assents, so that it is the understanding and reason that produce faith. The faith that justifies is therefore the faith of reason. There were other corollaries that followed from Cameron's writings, but it is clear that he had already progressed beyond the limits of the conservative theologians. At Saumur his closest collaborator was Moïse Amyraut, who later became rector, and whose writings on grace and predestination were to emphasise the rationalist trend that theology at the Protestant Academy would take. For Amyraut and his followers, reason became the central criterion of faith: all doctrines contrary to reason were false. The Academy at Saumur had a profound influence on Huguenot theologians, and infused into many of them a religious liberalism that made the acceptance of religious toleration easier. In 1664 a Cartesian professor named Chouet was appointed to the chair of philosophy at the Academy. In 1669 he moved to Geneva at the invitation of a former pupil of Amyraut at Saumur, Louis Tronchin, now professor of theology in the Calvinist capital. Both Chouet and Tronchin taught the philosophy of Descartes, and among the pupils who came to them in 1670 in Geneva was Pierre Bayle.

The evolution from universalism through Descartes to rationalism and Bayle was particularly significant because it occurred within a framework not of irreligion but of total belief. The aim of those committed Calvinists who questioned predestination was to reclaim for man some part in the acceptance of his own salvation. That acceptance could only be through the free exercise of man's reason, and it was reason that the Arminians and liberals introduced into the structure of Calvinism. Out of this intensely Calvinistic background, out of the controversies associated with erudite theology, there developed a profound crisis which for Bayle could be solved in only one way: by insisting that 'every dogma which is not verified and registered in the supreme court of Reason and natural light, can have only shaky authority', and that reason therefore is the arbiter of all belief.

While the disputes on grace and predestination in the Calvinist churches developed towards rationalism, within the Catholic Church the crisis of Augustinianism produced a move in the other direction. As before, the controversy originated in the Netherlands, this time in the southern provinces, at the Catholic University of Louvain. Conflict between the faculty of theology, which was Augustinian in its outlook, and the Jesuits, who were hostile to Augustinianism, led in 1567 to a papal condemnation of the teachings of a professor of theology, Michel de Bay (Baius). The victory of the Jesuits on this occasion led them to continue their vigilance against their opponents. Their alarm seemed justified, for in 1640 a large posthumous volume by Cornelis Jansen, bishop of Ypres from 1636 to his death in 1638, was published under the title of *Augustinus*.

The *Augustinus*, far from being the product of only one man's reflections, was in some ways a work of collaboration, had taken ten years of mature thought, and drew consciously on a wealth of patristic teaching. Perhaps the strongest direct personal influence on the author was his friend and one-time fellow student, the Abbé de Saint-Cyran. Their interest in St Augustine, explicit in the title of Jansen's book, was common not only to many Belgian theologians but also to the most prominent leaders of the French Counter Reformation. Cardinal Bérulle was an ardent disciple of St Augustine, and his own friendship with Saint-Cyran was based on a regard for the Augustinian view of God's supreme grandeur. The close links between Saint-Cyran and Bérulle are worth emphasising, for they illustrate clearly the common origins of both French Jansenism and the French Counter Reformation. There was no inherent contradiction between the two; both emphasised man's dependence on the saving grace of God. It was only as political issues intruded into the picture and as the Jesuits, enemies both of Bérulle and of Saint-Cyran, warmed to the controversy, that the crisis erupted in the heart of French Catholicism and 'Jansenism' began to be identified as a heresy.

In 1638 Jansen died; three years later his *Augustinus* was condemned by the pope, and in 1643 Saint-Cyran too died. Their passing might have signalled the end of controversy. It was at this stage, however, that the Arnauld family intervened, for without the Arnaulds there would have been no Jansenism. Saint-Cyran had been a close friend of the family since the 1620s; in the 1630s he became spiritual director of Angélique's convent of Port-Royal; and it was under his aegis that young Antoine — the twentieth and youngest child of prolific parents — obtained his doctorate at the Sorbonne in 1635 with a thesis on St Augustine. It was Antoine, *le grand Arnauld* as he came to be called, who in 1643, a few months after his master's demise, published his work on *Frequent Communion* and so kindled again a dispute that was to endure for another thirty years.

The core of the Jansenist controversy lay in the Five Propositions on grace which Innocent X condemned in 1653 in the bull *Cum occasione* and which were allegedly contained in the *Augustinus*. Behind the great debate over the propositions lay a fundamental divergence between Jesuit and Jansenist (and their respective partisans) over the means of salvation and the part played by man in it. Standing firmly by their interpretation of Augustinianism and the omnipotence of God's grace, the Jansenists rejected their opponents' views as semi-Pelagian. The problem may have been no more than academic in normal times. But this was the high tide of the French Counter Reformation, and the task of evangelisation might have been gravely compromised by a doctrine which belittled man's efforts and set so much store by God's predestination. At first strongly attracted by the energy that radiated from Port-Royal, the French missioners were rapidly disenchanted. 'My daughter', St Francis de Sales asked reprovingly of Mère Angélique, 'would it not be better to cast your net wider and to bring in more fish?' The conviction of being the elect, of being more accessible to God's grace than others, of being among the few predestined to salvation in a world of the damned, soon seized on Port-Royal and explains why Jansenism never became a proselytising movement. St Vincent de Paul, in his earlier days a friend of Saint-Cyran and a collaborator with Port-Royal's extensive charitable activity, ended by calling on Catholics to crush 'this little monster which is beginning to ravage the Church, and which will finally lay it waste if it is not strangled at birth'.

The internal history of Jansenism came to an end, for all practical purposes, in 1669 when Pope Clement IX imposed the truce known as the 'peace of the Church'. Later developments, culminating in the physical destruction of Port-Royal des Champs in 1711, and the bull *Unigenitus* in 1713, were almost exclusively political. Jansenism as a purely religious deviation perished, and surfaced briefly only in the bizarre episode of the Convulsionaries of Saint-Médard. In this way an obsession with grace, nurtured and defended by the most eminent intellects of the day, degenerated into irrational ecstasy.

The Jansenists came to be known as the Calvinists of the Catholic Church; the Arminians, in their turn, were suspected of being secret papists (a few did actually become Catholics). Despite their common basis in the controversy over grace and salvation, the two heterodox movements had little in common ideologically and were directed towards different destinations. The Arminians were outstanding believers in religious toleration and gave a remarkable impetus to the growth of rational thought; the Jansenists were notoriously intolerant, not only of their fellow Catholics and the Jesuits but in particular of the Protestants. To think only in terms of dogma, however, is to fail to grasp the entire perspective of the crisis, which was social no less than religious.

It may plausibly be argued that, notwithstanding their essential differences, the two heterodoxies were expressions of bourgeois ideology. In the United Provinces it was the burgher class, independent, well-educated, hostile to theocratic control and passionately concerned to defend freedom of trade, that espoused the Remonstrant cause. Freedom of conscience was essential to them if the trade of the nation, in which people of all nations and faiths participated, was to flourish. Amsterdam was a liberal stronghold, and it was the burgomaster there, Cornelis Hooft, who in 1598, during a celebrated blasphemy trial, declared that 'it is very strange that those who so strenuously maintain the doctrine of predestination should insist upon persecution or forcing of conscience, for if their doctrine be true no man can avoid that to which he is ordained'. Rigid Calvinism, far from being the ideology of progress, was the very doctrine that the commercial classes of Holland rejected. The bourgeois content of Jansenism is less easy to define. What is undeniable is that the core of Jansenist support came from the *noblesse de robe*, the middle-class bureaucracy. A small group of the upper nobility (principally from the Condé family, and including Madame de Longueville and the Prince de Conti) patronised Port-Royal, but none ever took an intimate part in its religious life. One group among the bourgeoisie, on the other hand, committed themselves wholly to Jansenism: in this number were the Caulet, Pavillon,

Pascal and, most notable of all, the Arnauld families. It has recently been argued by the Marxist critic Lucien Goldmann that these bourgeois represented the vanguard of the struggle of the *officier* class against the onset of royal absolutism, and that the failure of their protest led them to withdraw from the world into the mysticism of Port-Royal. Unfortunately, no real evidence exists for this thesis.

If the Augustinian controversies that racked the Netherlands and France point to anything, it is to the common inheritance of both Catholic and Protestant in Counter Reformation Europe. Both the Catholic and Reformed Churches were confronted by deviations that sprang from a common source. It was this realisation that made men like Hugo Grotius, a distinguished refugee from Calvinist persecution, emphasise how much all the dissenting parties really possessed in common. 'All my life', wrote Grotius in 1641, 'I have burned with the desire to bring reconciliation to the Christian world.' Quoting St Augustine, in one of his works he reminded his readers how difficult it was to cure people of deep-seated errors by the use of force. The way to religious peace was through tolerance, through the doctrine of Erasmus. Strife elsewhere in Europe, particularly in the Thirty Years War, also made men yearn for that unanimity that had once existed in Christendom. Religious controversy, far from leading to further splits, led to a renewed desire for unity. The Jansenists fought bitterly for their right to remain within the structure of the Catholic Church; the Remonstrants desired nothing more than peaceful activity and the right to differ, within the official fold, in the spirit of the 'mutual tolerance' demanded by Episcopius, one of their leaders.

8 COMMUNICATION AND IMAGINATION

The art of Printing will so spread knowledge that the common people, knowing their own rights and liberties, will not be governed by way of oppression.

SAMUEL HARTLIB. A description of the famous kingdom of Macaria. (1641)

To have all men alike, tis but a Utopian fiction, the Scripture holds forth no such thing.

JOHN COOKE. Unum Necessarium or the Poor Man's Case.   (1648)

This was in many ways an age of unbounded optimism. Gómara, as we have seen, was already in 1552 so rash as to proclaim that 'all has now been traversed and all is known'. Renaissance humanism, in its unquenchable thirst for knowledge, did nothing to dampen this supreme confidence. As the frontiers of experience, science, artistic creation and geographical exploration were extended, there seemed to be every reason for believing in the amazing capacity of man to master the known world. Any historical textbook will list the extraordinary scientific achievements of the age, the new perspectives in thought and philosophy. The spread of knowledge was so remarkable that it has now become accepted to speak of it in terms of a revolution: the educational revolution, the scientific revolution, are landmarks in the evolution of some European societies. But to speak in such terms without qualification is to risk some distortion, for if there were revolutions they occurred without materially affecting in any way the lives of the vast majority of Europeans. This chapter is concerned with some of the implications of the extension of human knowledge, and with some of its internal contradictions.

LITERACY AND THE PEOPLE

Although a knowledge of reading and writing was considered desirable in mediaeval Europe, it was still looked upon largely as a practical skill, a qualification rather than a cultural necessity. Many mediaeval monarchs and even prelates of the Church were illiterate: they were not however uncultured, for they had readers who read to them and scribes who wrote for them. The importance of literacy as a practical qualification is reflected in the statutes drawn up by an archbishop of York for a college he founded in 1483, in which one of the purposes of the foundation was said to be that 'youths may be rendered more capable for the mechanic arts and other worldly affairs'. This technical importance of literacy would always be important. The supreme technical use was of course in the service of the Church, for only a literate clergy could be the arbiters of religious (no less than social) life. In a very special sense, too, literacy was the preserve of the Church, which had a monopoly control over education.

The invention of printing, involving quicker and cheaper methods of book production, revolutionised the problem of illiteracy. Living in the century immediately after the development of the printing press by Gutenberg, Francis Bacon described it as one of the three great inventions (the others were gunpowder and the compass) which had 'changed the appearance and state of the whole world'. The immense possibilities and perspectives opened up by the invention are not our immediate concern here. Did printing bring about any change in the cultural level of the common people? In at least three distinct respects — in the promotion of education, in (mainly religious) propaganda, and in the development of popular taste—literacy and the printed book had an important part to play.

The advent of the printed book did not by itself promote literacy. Books were still relatively expensive, and editors devoted their efforts to works that the ordinary man in the street could not always hope to understand. The greater accessibility of books nevertheless helped to inspire an upsurge of interest in education. The theory of communicating knowledge became profoundly modified, and pedagogy became a science in itself, the most distinguished of all educational thinkers during this period being Comenius. It became widely accepted that it was natural to acquire a literate education, not solely because literacy had certain practical uses but because it was morally right and proper for a human being to gain knowledge. No data are available for changes in literacy rates that may have resulted from this approach, but for England at least there is evidence that the essentials of reading and writing were being communicated to a high proportion of the common people. In the country areas the village school (as at Wigston, Leicestershire, in the 1580s) brought both privileged and poor children together to the common task of learning. In the city of Norwich there was free elementary education for the children of the poor. Thanks to religious motivation and to the availability of the printed word, primary education expanded both in England and on the continent. There is no way of telling whether this brought about any change in popular literacy. In the first place, even though the number of schools may have increased (particularly in England) it seems that the poorer classes were not obtaining the opportunity of attending them. Secondly, we have no continuous samples to allow us to test the development of literacy over a given period. At most, we have random examples, from which it is very unsafe to generalise.

Even in the relatively remote north of Europe, in central Sweden, a writer of 1631 could report that the people were 'so fond of letters, that although public schools are very few, nevertheless the literate instruct the others with such enthusiasm that the greatest part of the common people and even the peasants are literate'. What, however, did it mean to be literate ? The usual criterion is the ability to read and to write. But when judging literacy through the documents, historians have been obliged to rely on little more than a single test—the ability to sign one's own name. Though this leaves the way open to many objections, the fact is that evidence based on signatures has usually been very plausible. Just the sort of people we should expect to be literate (the middle class, artisans) signed their names; labourers and soldiers made a mark. Of the one thousand two hundred and sixty-five people in rural Surrey in 1642 who protested their loyalty to the government on paper, one third signed their names and the rest made a mark. The variation in literacy according to social class was quite notable. In the English village of Limpsfield only twenty per cent of the servants but sixty-two per cent of the householders signed their names. In the Narbonne area in late sixteenth-century France, literacy among the bourgeoisie went up to about ninety per cent, among the urban artisans it was about sixty-five per cent, and among the rural population it varied from ten to thirty per cent.

We are so accustomed to the desirability of universal literacy that it requires some effort to realise how dangerous and revolutionary (in ideological and political terms) the ability to read and write could be. With the widespread dissemination of new ideas through the mass medium of the printing press, new and subversive ideas could all too readily be put within the grasp of the lower orders. The ideological strife of the Reformation era consequently led to a curious ambivalence in official attitudes to education. On the one hand both Catholics and Protestants were concerned to educate their followers to read their own manuals of religious instruction; on the other, both sides were equally concerned not to allow undesirable literature to fall into the hands of untutored believers. On the social level, likewise, every effort was made not to allow so much education to the lower orders that they might get ideas above their station. This dilemma — whether or not to educate the people — was a serious one that all cultural and political leaders, humanist and liberal alike, had to face.

Was it a coincidence that it was the Netherlands, breeding ground of heresies and revolution, that had probably the highest rate of literacy in Europe? 'Nowhere else', wrote Erasmus in 1525, 'does one find a greater number of people of average education.' In the late sixteenth century Guicciardini reported that 'the greatest part of the people of the Low Countries master the rudiments of grammar; almost all, and even peasants, know how to read and write'. It seems that what impressed Guicciardini was rather the contrast with Italy than the extraordinary literacy of the Netherlanders, for even by 1630 the rate of literacy in progressive Amsterdam was somewhat less than fifty per cent.

Elementary education was not necessarily a step towards greater literacy. In many countries the 'grammar' taught at schools as an adjunct to reading and writing was Latin grammar. The use of Latin was deliberately fostered by writers who believed that knowledge was the preserve of the few, and even innovators like Copernicus preferred to use Latin in the belief that the mysteries of science should not be communicated to the common public. Latin became a symbol of obscurantism to the Protestant reformers, and they fought against it bitterly on the grounds that it prevented the mass of the people gaining access to the truth. There can be no doubt that Latin had long ceased to be an adequate method of communicating with the people. Wherever the reformers went, whether in England where illiterate Catholic priests had reduced the canon of the Mass to a nonsensical mumbo-jumbo, or in France where St Vincent de Paul found unlettered clergy unable to remember the text of the rites, the need for the vernacular became obvious. Vernacular sermons and books assumed a greater importance than ever before, for they could change the minds and hearts of the population.

When Sir Thomas More in 1533 claimed that nearly three-fifths of the English people could read English, and hence could read a vernacular translation of the Bible, his purpose was to express alarm at the evil that could be done by unlicensed literature. More's figures were certainly wrong, but the fear of literacy in the native tongue persisted. Henry VIII in his later years regretted that he had allowed the Bible to be circulated in English. 'I am very sorry to know how that most precious jewel the Word of God is disputed, rhymed, sung and jangled in every alehouse. I am equally sorry that the readers of the same follow it so faintly and coldly in living. For this I am sure, that charity was never so faint among you and virtuous and godly living was never less used, and God Himself among Christians was never less reverenced, honoured and served.' This was the established view, shared more by Catholics than by Protestants, for they were more on the defensive. It is not surprising then that Catholics were perhaps the most distrustful of anything more than the most elementary literacy. Though Catholics in this period were by no means hostile to education, they took care to define its limits and to subject all higher education to the most rigorous control. Spanish policy was perhaps the most extreme. Within the peninsula a firm control over methods of education was exercised, and Philip II in 1559 forbade Spaniards from studying outside the peninsula at any but four specifically named colleges. In the American colonies the government adopted an openly restrictive attitude. It was a sixteenth-century viceroy of New Spain, Gil de Lemos, who said curtly to a deputation of settlers: 'Learn to read, write and say your prayers, for this is as much as any American ought to know.'

The promotion of literacy among the common people was undertaken with any seriousness only by Protestant countries. The reason was simply an ideological one: the Bible was the basis for faith, and the Bible must be read. 'The Scripture', Luther had argued passionately, 'cannot be understood without the languages, and the languages can be learned only in school. If parents cannot spare their children for a full day, let them send them for a part. I would wager that in half of Germany there are not over four thousand pupils in school. I would like to know where we are going to get pastors and teachers three years from

303

now.' The indoctrination of Protestant people and children could only come about through a rise in the level of literacy. After the Reformation it was the Protestants above all who achieved the greatest successes in popular education. Much of the success of the Reformed movement in France was based on efforts at promoting literacy. Elementary textbooks and alphabet manuals were distributed among the population. In 1562, for example, the Parlement of Paris was asked to prosecute a butcher who had distributed an heretical alphabet book to about two hundred children aged under ten years. Once the people had learned to read, they were encouraged to consult for themselves, in their own tongue, the sacred text that the Church hesitated to put into their hands.

Although the role of Protestantism as a spur to literacy should not be exaggerated (progress was slow, schools and teachers were inadequate in number, the poorer classes benefited very little), it is difficult to avoid the impression that by the end of the seventeenth century it was the Protestant countries, England and the United Provinces above all, that were the most literate in Europe. For England it has been estimated that by the mid-seventeenth century there was a school for every four thousand four hundred of the population and one approximately every twelve miles. In the Puritan section of the population, where piety presupposed literacy because of the heavy reliance on inspirational reading, there was a remarkably high concentration of culture. Cromwell's army must certainly have been the most literate army ever known till that time, if we may judge by documents and petitions drawn up by the men, which suggest that the vast majority of non-commissioned officers and men could sign their names.

THE DEVELOPMENT OF PROPAGANDA

The whole purpose of getting the population to read was to convince them of the correctness of your own views. The Counter Reformation period can therefore be looked at as a prolonged exercise in the development of techniques of persuasion. The pulpit was used as perhaps never before, but by its nature its effectiveness was restricted to the four walls of a building. It was the printed word, disseminated through books, fly-sheets and newspapers, that ultimately emerged as the most convincing method of propaganda.

In mediaeval times the pulpit had been the chief moderator of public opinion, and this function continued throughout the seventeenth century. Unprecedented success was achieved by the preachers of the Counter Reformation, who in this way stemmed the great advances made by Lutherans through use of the pulpit. St Peter Canisius, perhaps the most noteworthy of all the Catholic preachers in Europe, is said to have preserved Vienna for the Faith by his oratory. In France at a later epoch Bourdaloue reaped a harvest of conversions through his sermons. Significantly, both these priests were Jesuits, for it was the Jesuits who, on the Catholic side, made the most intelligent use of new techniques in order to win over the mass of the population. Sermons achieved a dual success, moreover. They were delivered by word of mouth; subsequently, they were printed and distributed so as to reach an even wider audience. In this way both the literate and illiterate would be served.

So great was the power of the pulpit that ecclesiastical authority was required in order to obtain a licence to preach. The continental Reformation liberated the pulpit from Catholic episcopal control, but in episcopal England the bishops still kept a tight rein on the public expression of dissentient views. It was this that encouraged Puritan communities in the Anglican Church to appoint to their parishes unofficial 'lecturers' who, because they were not formally parish clergy, did not require a licence to preach. The lecturers might often put forward theological views that differed from those of the official Church. They were appointed by Puritan parishes, peers and city corporations. As a result Puritan attitudes were disseminated with impunity from hundreds of pulpits throughout the country and threatened to subvert the established order. Lecturers, stormed Archbishop Laud in 1629, 'are the people's creatures and blow the bellows of their sedition'. The struggle for the pulpit was thus, in a very real sense, a struggle for men's minds. Lord Falkland in 1641 claimed that the bishops had 'cried down lectures, either because other men's industry in that duty appeared a reproof of their neglect of it, or with intention to have brought in darkness that they may the easier sow their tares while it was night'.

The spoken word was powerful, but transient: it was the permanency of the printed word that alarmed the authorities. Repression and control of information was for the most part directed against printed works. Since it was the Catholic establishment that was on the defensive against new ideas, the printing industry tended to fall under suspicion in Catholic areas, and presses operated (at first) with greater freedom in Protestant territories. The post-Reformation era consequently witnessed a large-scale emigration of printers from Catholic to Protestant Europe. In Germany the printing industry gravitated from the southern principalities towards the north; printers were the one outstanding component of the emigration from sixteenth-century France to Geneva; prominent among exiles who left Antwerp for the northern Netherlands were the Elsevier family. This movement did not by any means denude Catholic Europe of the means of propaganda, but it certainly deprived it of much initiative.

The battle of the books continued throughout this period to be a religious one. The Reformation gave an impetus to the Protestant presses; the Counter Reformation did the same, from about 1570, for the Catholic presses. Though the appearance of the printed book opened endless opportunities for works on literature, travel, law and so on, the religious book (devotional or controversial) was never displaced from its leading position in this period. Of a total of one hundred and sixty-nine books published in Paris in 1598, forty-nine were on religion, up to fifty-four on belles-lettres, seventeen on law, twenty-seven on history and twenty-two on the arts and sciences. In 1645 of a total of four hundred and fifty-six books published during the year, one hundred and seventy-two were on religion, one hundred and ten on belles-lettres, eighty-three on history, thirty-two on law, thirty-four on science, and twenty-five on other matters. About a third of the books published in the half-century between these dates were on religion. To some extent, as we have already seen, this was because the Catholic Reformation occurred in France during those years. But even outside France the preoccupations of the printers show that by the mid-seventeenth century religious disputation (in Holland it was Arminianism, in Belgium Jansenism) continued to dominate the market. The age of reason and science was not yet in sight.

Books were not necessarily the ideal vehicle for propaganda: they were still comparatively expensive and tended to be published in small editions (about 1,250 to 1,500 copies). The Bible was always a best-seller, of course, as were some other books we have noted in the previous chapter. But books in the vernacular were still in a minority, if the catalogues of the international book fair at Frankfurt are anything to go by. From 1564 to 1600 this fair, the largest in Europe, displayed nearly fifteen thousand books of German origin. On the average, no more than a third of these were in the German language. In 1601-5, of 1,334 books at the fair, 813 were in Latin and 422 in German. Only after about 1680 did books in German come to be in the majority. In England the vernacular had a stronger hold on publishing, but despite this there was no notable attempt to use books in the moulding of opinion. The principal difficulty was the censorship, to which books were particularly vulnerable.

The literate public were less likely to read books than short, well-phrased tracts with a clear argument and simple language. Tracts of this nature fell roughly into two categories: printed pamphlets, and fly-sheets in which a block or copper-plate illustration was accompanied by a text. From the pamphlet war of the Reformation to the often cruel propaganda of the Fronde and the Thirty Years War, it was this category that came closest to providing some sort of propaganda for the masses. The fly-sheets usually contained satirical illustrations brilliantly calculated to attract a reader's sympathy or at least his attention. In most cases the text was a piece of doggerel verse, often several stanzas long. Though the whole Counter Reformation period was one of strife and controversy, pamphlet propaganda was not a continuous feature of it. On the contrary, the overwhelming majority of surviving pamphlets date from one central epoch only—the middle decades of the seventeenth century. The existence of a general crisis in political life is nowhere better illustrated than in these collections dealing with three key events: the English Revolution, the Fronde, and the Thirty Years War.

The vast majority of German leaflets dealing with the Thirty Years War attempted to present the justice of one cause and the excesses of the opposing side. The volume of literary output this involved, signalled the emergence of a particular kind of writer: the professional publicist. The Germans were to produce many such in the course of the conflict, notably Kaspar Schoppe, who wrote for the Catholics, and Hoë von Hoenëgg, court preacher to the elector of Saxony, for the Lutherans. All the techniques of crude propaganda — distortion, exaggeration, plain falsehood — were employed generously by these writers. Small wonder that to the historian the most interesting of the fly-sheets are not the blatantly partisan ones so much as those which react against all the protagonists and plead wearily for peace and humanity. Typical of these is one of 1642, protesting bitterly against the sufferings endured by the peasants at the hands of the nobles and soldiery:

> The splendour of the land can no longer be seen,
> War, robbery, murder and arson are laying it waste,
> The free Roman Empire is falling to barbarians.

The propaganda of the Thirty Years War seems often to have reflected popular attitudes, but for the most part it was produced by a handful of skilled publicists. The literature associated with the English Revolution and the Fronde was of a wholly different order.

To contemporaries one of the most alarming aspects of the troubles in England and France was that the rebel leaders had, by their propaganda, invited the common people to partake of mysteries forbidden to them. The assumption, clearly, was that publicity which was meant to win the masses over to one's side was permissible; but publicity that exposed all the issues to the people and invited them to make up their own minds was utterly deplorable. From this point of view, the literature of the 1640s was one of the first great exercises in revolutionary propaganda. 'The people entered into the holy of holies', Cardinal de Retz was to say with satisfaction of the Fronde. In England Clement Walker in his *History of Independency* (1661) criticised the proceedings of the Independents: 'They have cast all the mysteries and secrets of government before the vulgar, and taught the soldiery and the people to look into them and ravel back all governments to the first principles of nature.' Another English contemporary denounced 'the tumultuous risings of rude multitudes threatening blood and destruction, the preaching of cobblers, feltmakers, taylors, groomes and women', a list drawn up no doubt in ascending order of outrageousness.

Revolutionary propaganda was more than an exercise in persuasion; it frequently reflected genuine popular attitudes, and was committed not to the support of established parties but to the questioning of all authority. As soon as the floodgates of censorship had been opened, the sentiments of all sections of the people burst through. The number of pamphlets we have on record point to a very significant propaganda output. In Paris the pamphlet war centred on the period from January 1649 to October 1652. Moreau's catalogue of these Mazarinades (so called after the best known pamphlet, *La Mazarinade,* dated 11 March 1651 and directed against Cardinal Mazarin) lists over four thousand items. It seems likely that the actual total was about twice that figure. The circulation of the pamphlets appears to have been fairly wide, and not restricted only to Paris or even to France; the Dresden library, for example, possesses over three thousand items presumably collected within Saxony and Germany. In the English Civil War the output was higher than had yet been known in Europe. The British Museum collection lists nearly two thousand for the year 1642 alone, an average of nearly six pamphlets a day. For the years 1640 to 1661 the total of surviving pamphlets approaches fifteen thousand. In general the pamphlets in both England and France were not sophisticated propaganda nor the handiwork of experienced publicists. A very high proportion were totally irrelevant to the crisis that produced them: these were simply the produce of scribblers of doggerel. Among the rest, despite their ephemeral character, were a great many that reflected the outlook of the common people, pamphlets full of proverbs, slang, vulgarities and outright obscenities. For sheer volume of publicity, the seventeenth century was one of innovation.

This activity meant a very busy time for the presses. As a Paris printer commented in 1649: 'One half of Paris prints or sells pamphlets, the other half writes for them.' As the leaflets rolled off the presses, vendors would be on hand from early morning to take them out on to the streets. After the capital, came distribution to the provinces, carried out with striking efficiency. Mazarin complained in 1649 of one pamphlet that 'they have sent more than six thousand copies of the leaflet against me and d'Hémery (the finance minister) into all the provinces'. Since censorship regulations were theoretically still in force, pamphleteers always needed to be wary. The Levellers were among the most devious and successful publicists of this time. John Lilburne made himself a thorn in the side of authority by his ability to produce unlicensed pamphlets, rolling regularly off the presses for delivery to the several parts of England. His intention was explicitly to create propaganda: 'I am now determined to appeal to the whole kingdom and Army against them (the Presbyterians)', he proclaimed in 1647. From 1648 to 1649 he was assisted by the existence of a newspaper, the *Moderate*, which presented most of the principal Leveller news to the public. This was one of the first instances of a close-knit revolutionary group making extensive use of the press in order to change the climate of opinion. Incomparably the most important propaganda centre in Europe was the Dutch Republic. In

Amsterdam and in Leiden the presses served the demands of nearly every leading European language. Amsterdam had a virtual monopoly in the production of anti-French propaganda, and subversive literature was also smuggled regularly into England, Scotland and other countries. With the freest press in Europe, the Dutch threatened the security of every state practising censorship.

The history of pamphlets overlaps that of the periodical press. The function of both was to appeal to the public forum, and a pamphlet that appeared periodically (the earliest example in England was the series of Marprelate tracts in 1588 and 1589) was already setting a precedent. The real distinction between the two, however, was that the periodical aspired to give news and was, in effect, a news-sheet. We are so accustomed to the daily communication of news that it now appears to us to be a harmless and necessary part of human intercourse. In the sixteenth century, on the other hand, as in some modern authoritarian states, news could be dangerous. A printer could be accused of betraying information to the enemy, or of deliberate distortion and slander, or of inflaming the people by seditious publication. The penalties for sedition could be severe: in England in 1637 William Prynne had his ears cut off, was heavily fined, and then imprisoned. In Rome in 1572 the pope waxed so indignant at the hostile tone of the *avvisi* that he forbade their publication, and his successor passed an edict against the spreaders of false and malicious news. One of the journalists who fell foul of these regulations in 1587, during the pontificate of Sixtus V, had his hand cut off and his tongue torn out, and was then hanged.

The *avvisi* were principally merchants' newsletters, and were the earliest form of Italian journalism. Those sent from Venice to the Fuggers in Augsburg in 1554-65 were among the earliest, but the first regular series were those sent from his agent in Rome to the Duke of Urbino over the years 1554-1605. The information was collected by journalists called *menanti*. The best known of the newsletters patronised by a business firm were the Fugger newsletters, to which correspondents from every part of Europe contributed. They were not limited merely to business news, but gave information about everything that the writer considered worth reporting. It is not easy to define the difference between published newsletters such as the *avvisi*, and the early newspapers. Periodicity is perhaps the most important criterion. The official *Mercure français*, published at the beginning of the seventeenth century, was issued only annually. Other publications appeared more often, but at very irregular intervals. By general agreement the first 'newspaper' is dated to the early seventeenth century. This was the monthly *Relation* first produced by the Strassburg printer Johann Carolus in 1609 and distributed also in Augsburg. It contained news reports from seventeen different European towns. Another contender for the title of being the first newspaper is the *Avisa, Relation oder Zeitung* which appeared at Helmstedt in the same year 1609. A weekly seems not to have existed until the appearance in 1615 of the *Frankfurter Zeitung*, published by Egenolf Emmel. Germany may rightly claim to have been responsible for both the invention of printing and the beginnings of journalism. The first French newspaper was published in 1620, not in France however but in Amsterdam. It was in Amsterdam too that the first English newspaper came out, in the same year 1620. This was the *Corrant out of Italy, Germany etc.*, which gave regular news reports on the Thirty Years War. In 1621 regular English papers appear to have started, but they were no more than translations from Dutch papers sent over from Holland.

Two things in particular gave a great impetus to the growth of proper newspapers and to a rise in press output. In the first place, the state was concerned to publicise its views as widely as possible. Copies of state edicts were printed and distributed (for the years 1598-1643 alone the National Library at Paris possesses a total of over five hundred thousand different printed papers issued by the state). It was the desire to have a regular platform for official views that led Théophraste Renaudot to found in 1631, on the urging of Cardinal Richelieu, the *Gazette de France*. Renaudot himself admitted that the *Gazette* was basically a journal for 'kings and the powers that be'. But it was also to be a straightforward supplier of information, of use to the average citizen, so that 'the merchant will no longer trade in a besieged and ruined town, nor the soldier seek employment in a country where there is no war: not to speak of the comfort for those writing to their friends, who were formerly forced to give news that was either invented or based on hearsay'. The *Gazette* came out weekly, and consisted of four (later eight) quarto pages. This was the beginning of government propaganda through the printed word. Other states followed suit. Florence got a weekly gazette in 1636, Rome in 1640, Genoa in 1642, the States General of the Dutch Republic in 1649, and in Spain the *Gaceta de*

Madrid was first published by royal order in 1661.

The second outstanding reason for the growth of news organs was the desire of political factions to air their views regularly. News became particularly desirable during a political crisis, and any sort of information was seized on with avidity. Parisians during the Fronde were profoundly influenced by what they read. Renaudot's *Gazette* was particularly prized. 'From the great to the small, everyone discusses what is going on only through the *Gazette*. Those who can afford it buy copies and collect them. Others are satisfied to pay in order to borrow and read it, or else they group together so as to buy a copy.' The same tract that tells us this also goes on to claim that even in their worst days of siege, 'the Parisians, cooped up behind their walls, suffered less from the bread famine than from the lack of gazettes', a lack that occurred whenever events forced Renaudot to suspend publication. 'Bread did not sell better', we are told, than the *Courrier français* did when it appeared. Behind these exaggerations lay the reality that a crisis created a demand for news, an ideal situation for propagandists.

The factions in the English crisis took great care to make their views heard. The breakdown of censorship and licensing during the war gave scope to an unprecedented flood of news-sheets. Some idea of what happened may be gained from the pamphlets in the Thomason collection at the British Museum. For 1641 the collection has only four newspapers, for 1642 it has one hundred and sixty-seven. The peak year is 1645, with seven hundred and twenty-two news-sheets. The two most important newspapers were the royalist *Mercurius Aulicus* (edited from Oxford) and the parliamentarian *Mercurius Britanicus*. The circulation of the former in London alone was put at about five hundred copies. This was the average total circulation for most other newspapers. A circulation of five hundred in London was more significant than might appear. If, say, a dozen papers each sold about this much in London, and each copy was read by four or five people, the papers may well (as one historian argues) have reached half the literate males in London. The press undoubtedly played some part in heightening the political consciousness of the people of London, and nobody could have been more active in this task than John Lilburne and his Leveller colleagues.

With a comparatively low level of literacy, and with the press in its infancy, nothing recognisable as public opinion could have made an appearance through the printed word. It is here that the danger of misinterpretation rises. The pens that wrote were largely in the hands of men with received ideas. How important and widely dispersed then were those ideas that only occasionally (as through the Diggers and the Levellers in England) emerged into print? It is possible on the one hand to refer to them as untypical, the product of an unrepresentative, precocious minority. But there is also good reason to view them — particularly in the Fronde and in other uprisings on the continent — as the tip of the iceberg, a small fraction of the great mass of social radicalism that could not be expressed because, thanks to illiteracy and the primitive state of communication, the avenues of expression had been blocked off.

The old and perpetual barrier to the development of the press was censorship. Control of information had been a natural part of the structure of mediaeval Catholic society, and licences to preach had been strictly controlled by the Church. It was the threat of the unlicensed printing press that got the authorities into a state of panic, and provoked, for the first time in European history, a stream of legislation from every European government. Developments in England were to some extent typical. The first list of prohibited books in England was issued in 1529, and in 1530 a system of licensing by the state was introduced. In 1586 the notorious Star Chamber Decree on the control of the press was passed. Controls were also exercised over the printers themselves. Queen Mary in 1557 organised the printers into a trade guild, the Stationers Company, in which monopoly powers were vested. By 1583 London had twenty-three master printers, all members of the Company, operating a total of fifty-three presses. It was the attempt to break down this alliance of state licensing and monopoly printing that occupied the rebels of the Tudor and Stuart period. The system all but collapsed during the civil wars, but was tightened up thereafter. The great calls for freedom of communication were concentrated in the war years, and one of the first powerful opponents of licensing was the Leveller leader Walwyn who demanded in 1644 'that the Press may be free for any man that writes nothing highly scandalous or dangerous to the state'. Though the stand of Walwyn and the Levellers for a free press was certainly the most advanced made in the Europe of their day, their call has perhaps unfortunately been eclipsed by that of Milton's *Areopagitica* (1644) which, for all its stirring prose, took up a decidedly less liberal position.

In the face of censorship, ideas were communicated slowly,

with great difficulty, and often not at all. The quickest way for a learned author to communicate was still to write in Latin, for the academic world could then comprehend more easily. When Acontius published his *Satan's Stratagems* in 1565, he did not do it in England, where he had been resident since 1559, but at Basel, one of the great centres of European printing; and even then it was published neither in Italian (his native tongue) nor in English, but in Latin. His English readership had to wait many more years for it to be available in their language. The usefulness of Latin was as great as ever. Vernacular literature, though it increased the readership within a country, became another barrier to the free exchange of ideas. Indeed, vernacular literature often aided the task of the censor and helped to block the flow of ideas. England, for example, became more isolated from the continent, a development shown at its clearest by the complete inability of any of the principles of the English Revolution of 1640 to strike root elsewhere in Europe. While the revolutionary ferment shook both England and its American colonies, the continent remained impassive. Cromwell's attempt to export a revised and edited French version of the Agreement of the People to Bordeaux in 1653 was a transparently dishonest move, dishonest because Cromwell had personally crushed the Agreement in England, transparent because his objective was clearly no more than to subvert the French state. Language dictated the possibility of exporting revolution. This, after all, had been one of the fatal reasons why Luther's revolution, rooted in the German tongue, became restricted to the German-speaking lands; whereas Calvin's revolution, rooted in the French tongue, found ready acceptance in Switzerland, France and the Netherlands.

Where censorship probably succeeded most completely was in Spain. The paradox of Spain's cultural development in this period was that it had the widest-ranging empire on earth, yet this universal monarchy did little to universalise, to open up, the country's established ideology. The development of human communication through the press and the written word was — on certain basic issues — stifled more effectively in Spain than in any other country that had experienced Renaissance humanism. On two great issues the crown permitted free speech: on the state of the economy (hence the numerous tracts by *arbitristas)*, and on the state of the colonies. But on cultural and intellectual matters a carefully exercised censorship was imposed with the help both of the state and of the Inquisition. In 1558 a rigorous censorship decree was passed, in 1559 travel abroad to foreign universities was restricted and in this same year the first native *Index* of the Spanish Inquisition was published.

On the whole there is no clear evidence of what impact the printed word in the sixteenth and seventeenth centuries made on the common people, whose reading habits remain almost completely unknown to us. As in every age since Gutenberg, it seems likely that the people were interested not so much in propaganda or in cultural reading as in superficial scribblings and escapist literature, in 'lewd Ballads', 'merry bookes of Italie', and 'corrupted tales in Inke and Paper', to cite English critics of the genre. In late seventeenth-century France tales of this sort were hawked about the country by vendors and sold at low prices to the public, so that almost from the very first days of the dissemination of the printed word it was romantic fiction that really dominated the popular market. Lovers of good literature were naturally aghast at this lowering of the standards of taste. Jerónimo de Zurita, chronicler of the history of Aragon and a sixteenth-century secretary of the Spanish Inquisition, felt so strongly about the issue that for him the suppression of superficial literature appeared to be one of the chief reasons for the existence of censorship. Of books of romance and chivalry he felt that 'since they are without imagination or learning and it is a waste of time to read them, it is better to prohibit them'. Fortunately for the public, who would otherwise have had to feast on very dull fare, censors in practice paid far less attention to superficial than to ideologically dangerous literature.

THE EUROPEAN UNIVERSITIES

So many new universities were founded in the age of the Counter Reformation that it was as though a new age of learning were coming into existence. In Germany there were Dillingen (1554), Jena (1558), Helmstedt (1569), Würzburg (1582), Herborn (1584), Graz 1586) and several others; in the United Provinces there were Leiden (1575), Franeker (1585), Groningen (1614), Harderwijk (1600) and Utrecht (1636); in Britain there were Trinity College, Dublin (1591), Edinburgh (1583) and the new Protestant College at Aberdeen (1593). The expansion of universities took place throughout Europe. In the old universities new colleges were founded and the total student membership rose: Cambridge had one thousand two hundred and sixty-seven students on its books in 1564 and three thousand and fifty in 1622.

The notable expansion of universities presents all the appearances of a boom in higher education. Were there any significant characteristics to this boom? The truth is that to some extent the statistics of expansion are misleading. A great number of the new universities were foundations artificially created to serve an immediate religious or political bent, and without any real hope of attracting students. Of the twenty-two new German universities created between 1540 and 1700, only seven survived into the nineteenth century. Some of them never attracted more than a hundred students, and served a purely local demand. The principal reason why so many new foundations came into existence was not primarily an increased demand for education: it was because Catholics and Protestants refused to attend each other's universities, and instead set up rival colleges of their own. The new establishment at Leiden, for example, was created because Louvain and Douai (the latter founded in 1562) were both in the Catholic southern Netherlands. The Lutherans had obviously taken care to fortify themselves in the institutions that passed to them at the Reformation, and the same was true for the Anglicans. Where the need for denominational education was still felt, the gap was filled by establishments such as Strassburg (1538, created a university in 1621). The Catholics in their turn had to create colleges for their refugees. The first great university created by the Counter Reformation was Würzburg (1582), which was under close Jesuit control and was staffed principally by former professors of Louvain. In Germany the two most famous Jesuit-orientated universities were Ingolstadt (a pre-Reformation university) and Dillingen (newly founded).

The coincidence of the rise in the volume of higher education, with the revolutionary changes of the post-Reformation period, might suggest that the educational impulse was breaking new ground. Once again, on the whole, this was not so. The education offered by the many new places of learning was very much a repetition of old methods and syllabuses, though with a new emphasis on theology. That there was a notable increase in the number of schools and universities, and in the number of scholars attending them, is indisputable. But what was the content of this education? There was no corresponding change in the methods of teaching, or in the subjects taught. Hartlib and Comenius were still struggling in the mid-seventeenth century to bring in that 'revolution' in education which had till then occurred in numbers alone. The situation in the universities was universally deplorable.

Part of the reason for the decay of academic learning in the universities was, as we shall see, the rising tide of demand for civil office. Study of the liberal arts was neglected in favour of the two disciplines — civil and canon law — that offered a promising career. In the German universities the cultivation of the philosophical and natural sciences, of mathematics no less than of biology, was neglected. A fleeting stay at college became one's passport to a career. Besides, wealth could purchase degrees. The Wittenberg professor and poet Frederick Taubmann (1565-1613) wrote in 1604 that 'nothing is easier today than to gain a doctorate, if you have money. Anyone can become a *doctor,* without being *doctus'.* There were numerous complaints of the type of education that Oxford and Cambridge offered. Giordano Bruno in 1583 described Oxford as 'the widow of good learning in philosophy and pure mathematics'. Chemistry and experimental science were apparently neglected and, reported William Harrison in 1587, 'arithmetic, geometry and astronomy . . . are now smally regarded'. 'The secrets of the creation', Gerrard Winstanley complained, 'have been locked up under the traditional, parrot-like speaking from the universities.' Aspects of the decay in Spain may be seen from the case of Salamanca university, which ceased teaching Hebrew in 1555, a year when only one student was registered for this subject. In 1578 the chair of mathematics had been vacant over three years. By 1648 the arts faculty there was described as 'totally lost'. This evidence is negative and unsatisfactory, but of one major issue there can be little doubt. If scientific method advanced in this period it was not, for the most part, at the universities. The great pioneers — Copernicus, Brahe, Kepler, Peiresc — were often educated at universities but did not hold chairs, and pursued their researches in a more independent environment. Perhaps the only significant exception was Italy. There the pursuit of knowledge in universities lingered on. Torricelli was professor of mathematics at Florence in the mid-seventeenth century. Padua, thanks mainly to Vesalius, remained the principal medical school in Europe, and it was to Padua that Harvey went as a young man.

Learned disputation and scientific enquiry flourished less in the universities than in the independent colleges and private academies. Literary salons and philosophical circles were commonplace in late sixteenth-century France and Italy. By the early seventeenth century the scientific academies were much in evidence. The two outstanding Italian ones were the *Lincei* in Rome (founded in 1603), which counted Galileo among its members, and the *Cimento* in Florence (founded in 1657), which included Borelli and other scientists. In England 1660 witnessed the formal establishment of the Royal Society, which could trace its origins back well over a decade earlier. Many of the first members of the Society had been professors of Gresham College, an independent institution set up in 1596 to provide an alternative to the education offered by the major English universities.

At the university level, what occurred in Europe at this period was not an 'educational revolution' (to use a phrase often applied to England) but something far less ambitious. We might call it a 'bureaucratic revolution'. In every nation of western and central Europe in the late sixteenth century, the total attendance at universities increased. Hundreds of young men thronged into long-deserted lecture halls. What was their principal motive? 'The love of letters', observed the president of the chancery of Valladolid in 1638, 'brings only a very few to the colleges.' It was not the desire for learning or education that drove them to go through the process of earning a degree. Parents like Sir Thomas Fairfax must have been in a minority. In 1614 he asked the Master of St John's College, Cambridge, to allocate a good tutor to his son, for 'my greatest care hitherto hath bene, and still is, to breed my sonne a scholar'. Most parents were unlike this: they tended to look on the universities as a means whereby their sons could acquire the proper qualifications for a career. In England, Spain, France, Germany and many another country, the possession of a degree increased the opportunities available to a candidate for public office.

Suddenly 'education' became fashionable and desirable, a status symbol without which no advancement was possible. An important proportion of Renaissance literature had emphasised the desirability of a proper education in training those who were to serve the state. The nobility and upper bourgeoisie took this advice very much to heart, so that it soon became impossible to enter public life without some nominal higher education. The English House of Commons, which in 1563 had only sixty-seven members with some university education, by 1583 had one hundred and forty-five. The state did of course value educated administrators. But statesmen were universally hostile to a situation where even a smattering of education made men think themselves gentlemen, no longer suited to manual labour but more worthy of public position. Cardinal Richelieu was particularly strongly opposed to the extension of education. 'The commerce of letters would totally drive out that of merchandise', he claimed in his *Political Testament*. He also said that 'the state has more need of men trained in the mechanic than the liberal arts'.

At the Estates General of 1614 some deputies of the French clergy complained that the extension of education, much of it poor, 'soon burdens the state with too many educated people, weakens the armed forces, destroys trade and the arts, depopulates agriculture, fills the courts with ignorant people, diminishes the *taille*, inflicts simony on the Church, supernumerary officials on the state, wages and pensions on the Exchequer, and in brief overturns all good order'. That the increase in education was not all of the highest order is confirmed by a French writer of 1627 who reported that the schools 'have produced a great number of leterates, but few educated people... . If someone learns three words of Latin, of a sudden he ceases to pay the *taille*.' Education, it was felt, made one a privileged person. Not surprisingly many political commentators blamed political turmoil on the pretensions of the great number of shiftless educated. The Swedish statesman, Magnus de la Gardie, claimed in 1655 that 'there are more *literati* and learned fellows, especially *in politicis*, than means or jobs available to provide for them, and they grow desperate and impatient'. 'It is a hard matter for men', Hobbes was to point out, 'who do all think highly of their own wits, when they have also acquired the learning of the university, to be persuaded that they want any ability requisite for the government of a commonwealth.' His conclusion in respect of 1640 was simple: 'The core of rebellion, as you have seen by this, and read of other rebellions, are the Universities . . . The Universities have been to this nation, as the wooden horse was to the Trojans.

For Hobbes the Trojan horse was the cultivation of subversive ideas among the educated elite. Looking over Europe as a whole, however, the universities can be seen to have performed a distinctly conservative function. It was they that turned out, year after year, the administrative elite of both Church and state; an elite, be it said, on which both these institutions relied successfully for their continuity through the revolutions of the mid-seventeenth century. If there were 'alienated intellectuals', university graduates who saw little hope of preferment to office and whose outlook was sharply opposed to the ruling oligarchy, they formed so small a proportion that their contribution to unrest was insignificant.

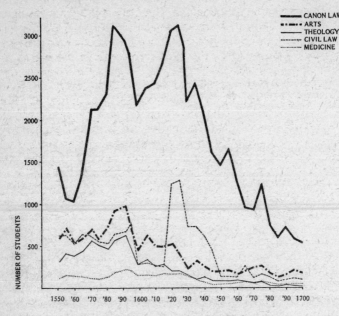

Figure 19 Faculty enrolments at the University of Salamanca.

The universities existed, then, to serve the state. Marburg was the first post-Reformation university to be founded (in 1527, by the Lutheran Philip of Hesse) with the express aim of turning out graduates to serve the established authorities. Whatever the university, anywhere in central and western Europe, two subjects were bound to predominate: canon law (in Catholic countries) and civil law. It is claimed of the sixteenth and seventeenth centuries that they were a pedantic and legal-minded age. The emphasis on law, however, was not simply in the mind; it was the fundamental bias of all education for the upper classes. In England those who did not go to Oxford or Cambridge went to the Inns of Court; many (about fifty per cent of entrants to the Inns) went to both university and Inns. In German universities canon and civil law were the unrivalled leading subjects. The faculty enrolments for Salamanca, illustrated below in Figure 19 confirm the importance of canon law (followed by civil law in the seventeenth century) in Spain.

The expansion of higher education shows a surprisingly consistent pattern in several countries, as we may see from Figure 20, which gives data for England, Germany and Spain. The curve for England represents the estimated number of entrants to Oxford and Cambridge from 1560 to 1699, in ten-year averages; that for Germany gives the average annual enrolment at the universities of Heidelberg, Frankfurt, Leipzig and Jena, in five-year periods between 1546 and 1660; and the curve for Spain gives the numerical totals for matriculations at Salamanca over the period 1550-1780. All three curves illustrate the great boom in university education that occurred in the late sixteenth century. Then from the year 1620 an era of depression commenced as the curve for attendance plummeted. The general crisis of the seventeenth century was felt no less severely in education.

University education served strictly defined social and political needs. For the noble class it was a method of improving the cultural level of the elite, for the bourgeoisie it was the necessary means to acquire qualifications that fitted one for office. Among the most remarkable features of higher education in these years was the extent to which it became dominated not by the rising bourgeoisie, the class we tend to identify with the bureaucratic state, but by the noble and gentry class. It was reported of the Inns of Court by the Venetian ambassador in 1612, for example, that they contained 'five hundred of the wealthiest gentlemen of this kingdom', and the records of the Inns certainly confirm that between 1570 and 1639 gentry made up well over eighty per cent of the entrants. It was in the late sixteenth and early seventeenth centuries that the gentry strengthened their hold on higher education, came thereby to dominate the administrative apparatus of the state, and so prepared the way for the age of aristocratic absolutism in the century after 1660.

The failure of the bourgeoisie was apparent. This is not to say that their educational standards were poorer: on the contrary, the great expansion in school education owed more to the middle classes than anyone else, as we can see by the Puritan effort in England, and literacy must have improved more in the bourgeoisie than in any other social grouping. But their showing in the universities, which were the recruiting ground for public life, was minimal. In Germany and Spain the middle classes were

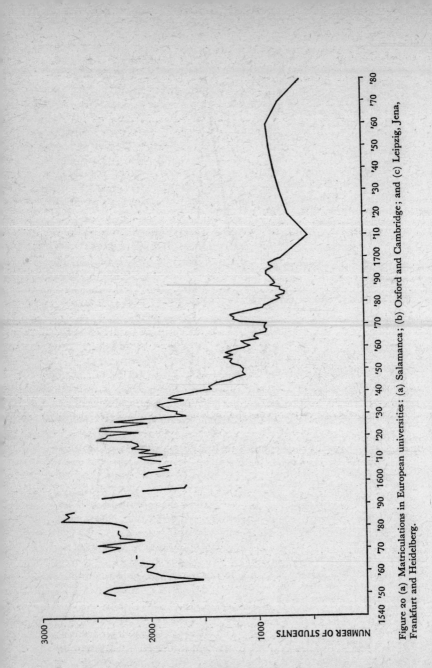

Figure 20 (a) Matriculations in European universities: (a) Salamanca; (b) Oxford and Cambridge; and (c) Leipzig, Jena, Frankfurt and Heidelberg.

322

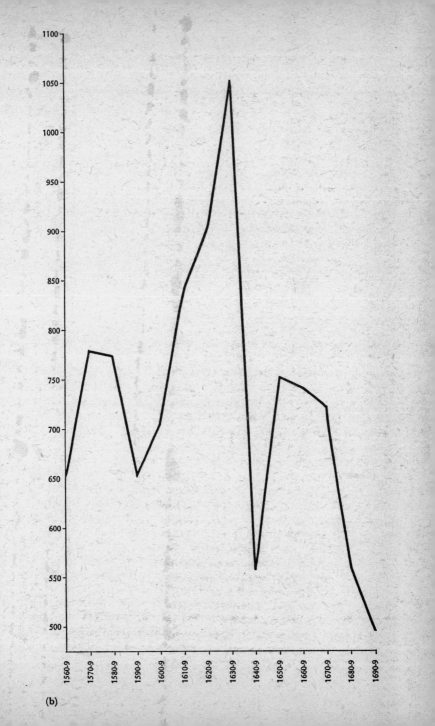

(b)

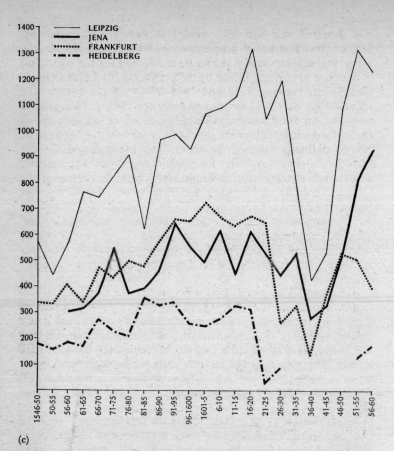

(c)

conspicuous by their virtual absence from the places of higher learning. In England there was a substantial improvement, if imprecise admission figures are anything to go by. Evidence for two colleges at Cambridge suggests that on the eve of the civil war the gentry formed about a third of the intake, the clergy and professional classes about a quarter, artisans and shopkeepers about a sixth. Even these English figures nevertheless mask a trend towards gentry predominance.

At Oxford in 1571 a total of thirty-five gentlemen matriculated, as against fifty-four commoners and twenty-two of unknown origin; by 1594 the proportion was two hundred and twenty-five gentry to one hundred and seventy commoners; and in 1600 it was one hundred and forty-two gentry to one hundred and ten commoners. The social proportions had been reversed. At the same time scholarships that had been reserved for the education of the poor were being seized by the privileged. At Caius College, Cambridge, between 1622 and 1624 fifteen of the twenty-nine scholarships were held by sons of gentry or nobles. This process went on even more demonstrably in Spain, where in the course of the late sixteenth century the sons of the poor were crowded out of places originally reserved for them. The university at Geneva (that is, Calvin's Academy, founded in 1559) had by the early seventeenth century become firmly aristocratic, the resort of the Calvinist nobility of Germany and France, and of the premier families of Britain (Beauchamps, Cavendishes, Cecils, Douglases and Drummonds). Leipzig became dominated by the gentry and the urban patriciates of central Europe and Poland: in the period 1559-1634 its students included six dukes of Saxony, four princes Radziwill, one crown prince (of Denmark) and numerous other higher nobles.

Nobles and gentry each, on the whole, made a distinctive use of higher education. The former tended to use it as a means of 'finishing' themselves, the latter more often than not used it as a stepping stone to an administrative post. In neither case did they feel it necessary to obtain a degree. In Heidelberg between 1550 and 1620 the proportion of matriculands taking their final degree never exceeded five per cent. Of the thirty-five government officials in the 1584 English Parliament, only four of the thirteen who had been to university possessed a degree.

Nobles usually had private tutors for the formative years of their education. Universities — particularly foreign universities— were fitted in at the end in order to 'finish off'. Hence the Grand Tour, a product of the Renaissance which flourished no less in this period of confessional strife. When Sir Philip Sidney undertook it in 1572, the main component of the tour was travel. 'Your purpose is, being a gentleman born', he was later to advise a younger brother, 'to furnish yourself with the knowledge of such things as may be serviceable to your country.' Leaving England at the age of nineteen in the company of a tutor and three servants, Sidney travelled to Paris, Frankfurt, Heidelberg, Strassburg, Vienna, Hungary, Padua, Germany, Poland, Prague and Antwerp, an absence of three years, only some of it spent in study. The whole of noble Europe practised the Tour, the *nobilis et erudita peregrinatio*, as Justus Lipsius described it. Manuals

325

were written for it, such as Jerome Turler's *De peregrinatione* (The Tour) (1574), and another by Thomas Palmer in 1606 which was prepared expressly 'for the youngest sort of such noble gentlemen as intend so recommendable a course'. Public service no less than personal edification was the purpose, if we judge by Sidney's remark above as well as by Sir Thomas Bodley's comment in 1647: 'I waxed desirous to travel beyond the seas for attaining to the knowledge of some special modern tongues and for the increase of my experience in the managing of affairs, being then wholly addicted to employ myself and all my cares into the public of the state.'

In the late sixteenth century Italy was far and away the most popular country of resort. It was the principal foreign country visited by the nobility of England, Germany, France and Spain. Each nation had its peculiar prejudices. John Evelyn gave the English point of view in 1645: 'From the reports of divers curious and expert persons I've been assured there was little more to be seen in the rest of the civil world after Italy, France and the Low Countries but plain and prodigious barbarism.' Sir William Temple reported Dutch habits in the mid-seventeenth century as follows:

> Where these (regent class) families are rich, their youths, after the course of their studies at home, travel for some years, as the sons of our gentry use to do; but their journeys are chiefly into England and France, not much into Italy, seldomer into Spain, nor often into the more northern countrys. The chief end of their breeding is to make them fit for the service of their country.

The tour of foreign parts and universities could often be rapid (one German noble journeying abroad in 1578-80 spent, during his visit to Italy, a few days at Bologna, a few weeks in Perugia, three months in Siena and then one year in Padua, having probably inscribed himself at all these universities without necessarily studying anything). Some definite benefits seem all the same to have been gained by the nobility, despite the frequently superficial nature of the Grand Tour. The Austrian nobility were one group to broaden their cultural horizons. The Austrian Protestants journeyed abroad to Wittenberg, Jena and Marburg universities, the Catholics to Vienna, Ingoldstadt and Louvain; those of either faith who wished to study law went to Padua, Bologna and Siena. Through these travels they extended their knowledge of the romance languages (Spanish was in any case a requisite at the court of Vienna), and contacts with Italy brought them into the sphere of Renaissance literature. In private libraries of the Austrian nobility, three books — all Latin in culture — took pride of place: Cicero's *De officiis*, Petrarch's *Canzionere* and Ariosto's *Orlando furioso*.

The cultural value of the tour emphasises a fact that is easily forgotten, namely that even in the age of ideological conflict the universities had not lost their international character. The rise of state barriers, of *cuius regio eius religio*, did not peremptorily destroy the international republic of letters. Protestants still went to Italy. Calvinism itself contributed to the internationalisation of academic study, by opening the doors of its universities to all nations. Of the one hundred and sixty-one names enrolled in the *Livre du Recteur* of Calvin's Academy at Geneva in 1559, nearly all were foreign to Switzerland. Of the one hundred and ten who matriculated at the Academy from December 1584 to early 1585, nine were Genevan, ten Polish, twenty Netherlandish, three Bohemian, three British, and nearly all the rest from France or Germany. As late as 1653 a Genevan pastor could complain that 'there come to this city a great number of foreign nobility, who live in great licence'. Attendance in the late sixteenth century at Heidelberg, perhaps the most important of the Calvinist universities, included about thirty-nine per cent foreigners. Twelve per cent came from France, nine per cent from Holland and Switzerland, the rest from Austria, eastern Europe and Italy.

Two cases can serve to illustrate the continuing internationalism of the universities. Leiden University, founded in 1575, remained open to both Catholics and Protestants, but it was chiefly as a centre of Calvinism that it flourished. The three main subjects sought and studied were, in order, jurisprudence, medicine and theology. Students came from all over Europe. In the first twenty-six years 1575-1600, of the 2,725 students registered, forty-one per cent came from outside the United Provinces; in the twenty-five years 1601-25 just over forty-three per cent of the 6,326 registered students were foreigners; and from 1626 to 1650 over fifty-two per cent of the 11,076 students were from outside the country. By the seventeenth century students were coming from Spain, Turkey, Ireland and Persia. The German contingent at Leiden was the most significant of all. In the university's first one hundred and seventy-five years, nearly eleven thousand Germans matriculated. In the period 1625-50 over half the foreign students were Germans: in 1639, to take one

327

year, there were more Germans matriculating at Leiden than at nearly every German university. The second case concerns those Germans, both Protestant and Catholic, who went to Italy. Padua was the most popular resort: of Germans studying there between 1546 and 1630, eighteen per cent took arts courses, eighty-two per cent did law. German attendance at the five most popular universities was as follows:

	1570-9	1580-9	1590-9	1600-9
Bologna	498 (7 years)	958	893	242 (2 years)
Perugia	41	39	34	52
Pisa	21	29	45	28
Siena	559 (7 years)	1151	1280	1275
Padua	1194	1608	1678	1467
Total:	2313	3785	3930	3064
Annual Average:	276	379	393	403

Despite this free movement in the academic world, the universities were ineluctably undermined by the two factors we have already emphasised: the study of law, and the grasp of the gentry and noble classes. The vast majority of all students at Dutch universities, and particularly at Leiden, read civil law. It was to study law that most foreigners went to Padua (Harvey, who went to read medicine, was in a minority). The result was not only the unleashing of innumerable superfluous lawyers on to society, but an alteration in the function of universities themselves. Many of them served only to produce officials to fill the courts, the city council or the council of state. University and bureaucracy became closely intertwined, notably in the German principalities and city states. But it was in the most bureaucratic of early modern states, the Spanish monarchy, that the trend reached its most extreme form. There the *hidalgo* (gentry) class virtually monopolised the administrative civil service, and young men went to university solely because a degree was required for employment in the service. Graduates aspired to be professors because these were guaranteed senior administrative positions if they left university for the professions. The incredible turnover in university chairs (one chair of canon law at Salamanca was filled sixty-one times in the course of the seventeenth century) underlines the extent to which the university had become little more than a stepping-stone to office.

Socially, too, the privileged position of the gentry in the universities was a threat. It came to be accepted as right that only the ruling classes required education. 'The gentry require that such as would have the liberall arts and sciences should pay for them', wrote an English observer in 1678, 'without censure (to) keep their blood unmixt with mean conversation.' Correspondingly, only those courses were emphasised that seemed suited to the upbringing of a gentleman. By the mid-seventeenth century, the universities were in the grip of an elitist social philosophy.

THE DISCOVERY AND LOSS OF UTOPIA

An age of crisis will invent its own remedies, fantastic or otherwise. Where one vision has been lost, another will be sought to take its place. The early seventeenth century, in a Europe racked by economic, political and ideological tensions, tried to re-create the conditions for a stable existence, in dreams of visionary communities where internal tension had vanished.

The Europeans had come close to achieving Utopia. Early accounts sent back from America by Columbus and the first *conquistadores* suggested that the natives of the New World had that primal innocence which was lacking on this side of the Atlantic. Long after the Indian populations had been annihilated through slavery and disease, their society shattered and their culture uprooted, the Spanish conquerors continued to harbour dreams of finding a terrestrial paradise in the lands of which they had made a hell. Only the missionaries faced the reality. The pagan paradise had gone, to be replaced by the strife of a Europeanised, Christianised society. It was precisely because the native Indians had lost their own environment that the missionaries attempted to recreate it for them, under ideal conditions. Schooled in the humanists and in Erasmus, hopeful clergy such as Juan de Zumárraga, first bishop of Mexico (1527), attempted to win back the past for the Indians. Zumárraga founded the first American college to educate the natives, the Colegio de Santa Cruz de Tlatelolco. His colleague Vasco de Quiroga, first bishop of Michoacán, had spent some time in reading and annotating More's *Utopia* (which first appeared in 1516). As a result he set up at Santa Fe an entire community based on the practicable principles of *Utopia*; all property and land was held in common, labour was communal, government was through elected representatives. For the first time in history, Utopia was actually put into practice. Similar programmes were attempted by Las Casas in his Utopian community of Vera Paz (True Peace) in Guatemala in the late 1530s. But one by one these

329

schemes collapsed. Santa Cruz, Santa Fe and Vera Paz turned out to be impressive failures. By the 1550s Utopia was seen to be unrealisable.

The period from 1550 to 1600 saw little emergence of Utopian theory and no practice of Utopian schemes. Perhaps the most promising writings of these years came from Italy, with the tract by Francesco Patrizi (1529-97) entitled *La città felice,* published in 1553, and the *Dialogo dell'Infinito,* written between 1583 and 1591 but not published in his lifetime, of Ludovico Agostini (1536-1612). The relative obscurity of these works was a sign of the times. The humanist vision of More and Quiroga had been crushed by the grim hand of imperialism and Counter-Reformation politics. Then after this half-century of dearth, in which the vision had been all but lost, gradually an era of rediscovery emerged. The period from 1600 to 1660 was unprecedentedly rich in Utopian schemes. It is difficult to find an explanation for this astonishing contrast between the periods. Some clue may be got from the late sixteenth-century scholar Jean Bodin, a man of an impressively practical turn of mind, who, when writing his own study of statecraft, *The Republic,* disavowed any intention of writing about some ideal state, 'a republic in the imagination and without effect, such as those which Plato and Thomas More have imagined'. It was this same 'practical' attitude which allowed the Spanish colonists in America to foretell (sneeringly and, of course, accurately) that the little communities set up by Las Casas would fail.

By the seventeenth century it had nevertheless become clear that practical politics was no effective substitute for idealism. The times were too critical to entrust policy to men without vision. The truly great statesmen of the age were those who refused to be limited by what was merely 'practical' and who reached out towards the ideal: men like Sully with his Grand Design of a council of nations to assure universal peace, and Olivares with his plan for a united and just participation of states within the Spanish monarchy. This is not to say that all the schemes of this time were impracticable. In America, Utopia was brought into existence on a hitherto unsurpassed scale.

In Paraguay in the early seventeenth century the Jesuit missionaries found that conversion of the natives would be possible only if they were freed from the harsh labour obligations imposed by the colonial regime. The Jesuits therefore made it their task to liberate the Guaraní tribes from the *encomienda* labour system. They succeeded in prevailing on the colonial legislators in the Audiencia of Charcas to issue in 1611 a number of Ordinances prohibiting Indian slavery and sanctioning the establishment of *reducciones* (Indian settlements). There was considerable opposition to this from the Spanish settlers, who stood to be deprived of cheap labour; but in 1613 the Jesuits declared that failure to observe the Ordinances would amount to mortal sin, and in 1618 their position was substantially endorsed by the government. The way was now clear for the expansion of the Jesuit missions. By 1676 the Society had twenty-two *reducciones* in Paraguay, with a total of 58,118 Indians in them. The Indians held their land in common, were given arms to defend themselves against marauding settlers, and had the most onerous tasks done for them by negro slaves. In these communities the Guaraní population, against the trend of the natives everywhere else in America, actually increased their numbers, a clear sign of success. This experiment in communal Christian living continued until the expulsion of the Jesuits from Paraguay. In one way it may be incorrect to call it a Utopia, for the Jesuits were doing no more than fulfilling the normal requirements for justice laid down by Spanish colonial law. But what distinguished it was that it worked. Despite the ill success of Quiroga and Las Casas, despite the hostility of the settler class, the Jesuits brought a New World Utopia into existence, for only in conditions of freedom could the law of Christ be truly observed.

The Christian nature of the Paraguayan settlements can be paralleled only by the Moravian communities of central Europe, which continued their quiet existence through the turbulence of the Thirty Years War. Contemporaries were critical of the sectarian and authoritarian nature of these Anabaptist groups, but to many they still represented the best that Europe could offer in the way of a Christian community founded on equality and mutual respect. One of those who took this Utopian view was the author of *Simplicissimus*. In total contrast to the horrors of the war in Germany was an Anabaptist community Grimmelshausen's hero visited in Hungary. There he found a community living at peace and supporting itself by its own labour. It practised communal help, gave social security, and had medical, nursery and educational services. 'In short, there was total and loving harmony, which seemed to spring from nothing else but from propagating the human race and the kingdom of God in all integrity.'

The gap between Utopian practice and theory was not as large

331

as we might expect. It was no accident that the Anabaptists chose the mountains of Moravia or the Jesuits the upper reaches of the forested Parana river. Communities of this sort could only exist if planted outside the normal world of men. They must be isolated and self-sufficient: no Utopia could exist without these two fundamentals. Literary Utopias therefore tended to be either walled cities or mysterious islands. The ideal society could be maintained only if protected from invasion by a high wall or a broad sea. Commerce in ideas or commodities could be held with the outside world, but the community must in no way be dependent on it, for that would be to destroy self-sufficiency.

Uniformity was absolutely necessary in Utopia. Among all the population there must be total uniformity of thought and action. Dissidence and minority rights could not be allowed, and freedom of choice must not exist. Only through such uniformity could order and equality be achieved. The consequences could be far-reaching. In order to make as many people as possible act identically, collectivism was essential. The public interest must be put before private interest, and the traditional unit of the family would have to be merged into a larger social organism. At the same time the enforcement of uniformity would lead to asceticism, to the abolition of wealth, luxury, privilege and all divergent and divisive influences. In order to bring about this greater equality, education would play a far greater part than was ever practised in any existing society in seventeenth-century Europe.

The new ideal society would be authoritarian. The Jesuit regime was totally patriarchal, and so was the Anabaptist. It was the dictatorial nature of the Moravian Brethren that repelled the Polish Arians when in the 1560s they held discussions about union with each other. For all its pretensions to freedom from the world's oppression, Utopia could function properly only if all countervailing forces in society were checked, all activity regulated and all aspects of life carefully planned by authority. Moreover movement into and out of the state had to be regulated, so that no unhealthy influences seeped in. The Jesuits would not allow the corrupting influence of other white men into their settlements, a policy followed before them by the Franciscans in Mexico.

These general observations, while common to most Utopian theory, also happened to be true of most of the communities that were actually set up by Europeans. The one major discrepancy between theory and practice was in ideology. The ideal communities of this period were all set up by believing Christians, for expressly Christian reasons. Yet not a single theoretical Utopia of the early seventeenth century was explicity Christian, and the Christian scheme for salvation was in nearly all cases subordinated to the purely secular aim of the temporal good.

Some literary constructions of the period were no more than idealist romances, such as Samuel Gott's *Novae Solymae,* which appeared in London in 1648. The most systematic of the Utopian writers were Campanella, Andreae, Bacon, Hartlib and Winstanley. Their works were produced between about 1610 and 1648, precisely in the years of gathering crisis.

Tommaso Campanella (1568-1639), a native of Calabria, was a man of contradictions. A priest of the Roman Church, his fundamental commitment was to astrology and magic; a protagonist of Spain's universal dominion, he spent over twenty years in a Spanish prison in Naples; defender of Rome's supremacy, he was imprisoned by the pope and fled to France after three years in a Roman gaol. These contradictions emerge in his *City of the Sun,* which he wrote during his imprisonment from 1602 to 1626. Presented as a dialogue between a Grand Master of the Knights Hospitaller and a Genoese sea-captain, the work describes an ideal communistic society free from the corruptions of contemporary societies. Campanella's city has no private property: this is abolished because property encourages acquisitiveness and self-love. 'But when we have taken away self-love, there remains only love for the state.' All things are held in common, all activity done in common. Living, sleeping, eating are mass communal activities. The family is likewise abolished, and procreation is controlled by the state: 'the race is managed for the good of the commonwealth and not of private individuals'. In the city work is held to be noble, and 'they laught at us, who consider our workmen ignoble and hold to be noble those who have learned no trade and live in idleness'. Because everyone works, tasks are completed in a shorter time and the average time worked is four hours a day. Slavery does not exist because it is not necessary. There is universal education from very early youth, and the sciences are encouraged. There is no explicit reference to Christianity, and the city is governed by magistrates who possess the names of the principal virtues. The City of the Sun might easily be interpreted as a secular Utopia but for the fact that it is, as Dr Frances Yates has pointed out, 'a complete reflection of the

333

world as governed by the laws of natural magic in dependence on the stars'. The physical layout of the city is magical and astrological. The chief priest who governs the city represents the sun. Procreation is undertaken at the right astral conjunction, and the careers of inhabitants are decided 'according to their inclination and the star under which they were born'.

When Johann Valentin Andreae (1586-1654) published his *Christianopolis* in 1619 his aim was not to describe an ideal state so much as a tiny community of like-minded people. He conceived of a settlement no larger than a small village: 'about four hundren citizens', he wrote of Christianopolis, 'live here in religious faith and peace of the highest order'. Communism was practised. There was no private property, and 'no one has any money, nor is there any use for any private money'. Manual labour was honourable: everyone took part, and the working hours were short. After what we have already seen of Andreae's Rosicrucianism, it is clear that Christianopolis was really an exclusive society, and the citizens were an elite of savants. Education was universal, and even 'their artisans are almost entirely educated men'. Despite the name of the city, Andreae's concern was with learning rather than religion.

It was the service of learning that also influenced Francis Bacon to describe the mysterious island of *New Atlantis* (written in about 1624, published 1627). The work was left unfinished, and is not strictly Utopian. New Atlantis was a monarchy which still possessed all the standard features of property, wealth and rank, and Bacon showed no interest in discussing improvements in society. The main interest of *New Atlantis* lies in the secret scientific society (the members of Salomon's House) that enjoyed a privileged position in the state. Its members could withhold scientific secrets from the state, and they periodically sent agents out into other countries to learn their secrets. Most commentators have seen this as a pre-figuration of the Royal Society of London, founded in 1660.

Samuel Hartlib (1600-62), of Baltic origin but resident in England after about 1628, was interested more in education than scientific learning. His brief work, *A description of the famous kingdome of Macaria,* published in London in 1641, took the form of a dialogue between a scholar and a traveller, and returned to the more normal outline of an ideal society. Macaria was a monarchy, with a Great Council that sat annually for a short period. Below this Council were five lesser councils, dealing

334

respectively with husbandry, fishing, trade by land, trade by sea, and overseas plantations. One-twentieth of the income from husbandry was taken by the state to finance improvements. Nobody in Macaria held more land than he could exploit. The kingdom was armed, in order to secure peace through strength. The health of its inhabitants was looked after by a college of medicine, and medicaments were distributed free. In many respects all this seems more modern than Utopian. We are also told, however, that there were neither Papists nor Protestants in Macaria, all were non-sectarian Christians. 'There are no diversitie of opinions among them', and a divine who comes up with novel opinions 'shall be accounted a disturber of the publick peace, and shall suffer death for it'. New opinions could not be published but had first to be debated before the Great Council, which decided whether to sanction them.

The four authors we have noted were men of great learning, experience and liberal views, but their Utopias were less a reflection of society's shortcomings than of their own private vision. Andreae and Bacon were frankly elitist, Campanella openly exotic. Hartlib's *Macaria* was by far the most sober blueprint for society, but it was clear that his own concern for reunion among the churches was perhaps the chief rationale for the work. The only writer to base his scheme for the future squarely on the errors of the present, and to locate his ideal state not in some distant island but in his own native country, was Gerrard Winstanley, whose last and most important work, *The Law of Freedom*, was published in 1652.

Winstanley's career with the Diggers had been spent in trying to persuade the authorities to bring freedom and equality to England. Now in 1652, after the collapse of the Digger cause, he presented to Cromwell in book form a summary of his ideas for the new society. 'I have set the candle at your door', he addressed Cromwell, 'you have power in your hand to act for Common Freedom, if you will.' *The Law of Freedom* lacked some of the fire of his earlier published tracts, but in outline it presented most of Winstanley's essential ideas. All land and resources would be held in common by all the people. The economy would be mainly agricultural, practising barter and exchange, but there would be no commerce and no money. The family unit would remain sacred, and so would family property. Government would be under a parliament, elected annually. Knowledge would be made available to all, and education would be free and compulsory.

Information would be circulated throughout the country, and general (rather than just religious) instruction would be given through the pulpit. Law would be codified and not depend on man's interpretation.

For all the confusion and insufficiency of these visionary structures, the Utopias of the early seventeenth century reflected a genuine crisis in ideas. Underlying the dreams was an urgent desire to advance beyond contemporary illusions to the achievement of a true solution, a perfect science, a just society. The crisis lay in the fact that the old structures had already collapsed—the Ptolemaic universe had been shattered, the English monarchy and its institutions had been overthrown — but that little seemed to have altered all the same. Utopia therefore advanced the revolution. To Campanella the Copernican heliocentric universe was fulfilled in microcosm in his City of the Sun; for Andreae and Bacon the scientific republic of letters, threatened by sectarian divisions, was safely preserved in some remote fastness. Winstanley, who had seen deliverance from the Iron Age and from 'the great red Dragon' within the people's grasp, had most cause to hope still for the achievement of his vision: 'that we may work in Righteousness and lay the foundation of making the Earth a Common Treasury for all, both rich and poor'.

IV

A GENERAL CRISIS?

9 THE REVOLUTIONS OF STATE

These days are days of shaking, and this shaking is universal.
JEREMIAH WHITTAKER. sermon before the House of Commons
(1643)

This year can undoubtedly be considered the most unfortunate that
this Monarchy has ever experienced.
THE COUNT-DUKE OF OLIVARES (1640)

Because several political upheavals and revolutions occurred all
over Europe in the decade 1640-50, historians have depicted the
phenomenon as a 'General Crisis'. They have described it in
political, social and economic terms, and some have argued that
it was not merely European but also affected nations as far
distant as Mexico and Japan. Their exposition has naturally not
been limited to the decade in question. 'We must look', writes
Professor Trevor-Roper, 'at the whole regime which produced the
crisis.' The explanations, consequently, have traced the evolution
of the situation back to 1500 and even farther. Historians have
fertile minds: they readily find reason and order in events that
appear not to possess any order. It is therefore now assumed by
many of the most distinguished contemporary historians that the
'Crisis' is an established fact. Is this conclusion warranted?
'History', Tolstoy once observed, 'would be an excellent thing if
only it were true.' The same may be said for the 'General Crisis'.

WAS THERE A CRISIS AND HOW GENERAL WAS IT?

Virtually all periods in history can be described as periods of
crisis, even when the word is employed to mean, as here, a
turning point rather than a mere malaise. This in itself is no
argument against the existence of an important crisis in the
seventeenth century. Doubts may arise rather about the duration
of the crisis and about its component factors.

How long did the crisis (assuming that there was one) last?
When R. B. Merriman first delivered his lectures on the political
revolts of the mid-century, which he later published as *Six
Contemporaneous Revolutions*, the emphasis was on the close

interaction between a number of events that occurred within a few years of each other. It is these few rebellions that are the subject of the present chapter. To explain them it is undoubtedly necessary to go back in time in search of origins, but the essential point is that the political crisis was conceived of as being limited to a decade, no more. Since Merriman, many historians have broadened the perspective of the subject to such an extent that most of the seventeenth century and a large part of the sixteenth have been looked upon as being in continuous crisis. This looks very much like an abuse of terminology. One may have many little crises, or even an extended crisis; but one that occupies over a century has obviously suffered from the inventive ingenuity of a zealous historian.

What went to make up this crisis? The central feature is the series of revolutions of state in 1640-50. 'If we look at them together', Professor Trevor-Roper points out, 'they have so many common features that they appear almost as a general revolution.' It is in the *general* character of the rebellions that the true interest of the controversy lies. There had been several contemporaneous revolutions in previous decades — in the 1560s, for instance — but few common factors that could be pointed to as parts of a general crisis. Agreement on the common features of the revolutions of the 1640s has still not been achieved. The account in the present chapter will make no attempt in this direction. On the contrary, it will be argued that while most European governments shared similar problems and often had the same type of organisational difficulties, the revolutionary situation that arose in each case was unique. There was little in common between the events in England, France, Spain and elsewhere. It is helpful to look at what features they had in common, but undue stress on these can only distort the very important differences between them.

There are other aspects of 'crisis' to which the term 'general' can more plausibly be applied, if only because they are indeed more general and long-term than so immediate and concrete an occurrence as a revolution. In the realm of philosophy and science a true turning-point, a parting of the ways, occurred. Economic historians feel they are particularly justified in speaking of a 'General Crisis'. Accounts which survey culture, government and economy in one breath under the mantle of 'crisis' are in effect doing no more than to argue that the seventeenth century was a period of profound change which substantially affected the quality of life in Europe. It may reasonably be asked whether there was anything particularly unique about the degree of change that occurred at this period which obliges us to dignify it with a special name.

The answer appears to be a negative one. No historian can deny the importance of the developments during this century. The preceding chapters have attempted to show that there was both crisis and change in European society. But to subsume all these under the common heading of a 'General Crisis' does not necessarily help us to understand them, and in fact presents us with an artificial schema of interacting events which unduly simplifies the true richness and complexity of the epoch.

While admitting, then, that crisis was present in this century, it is important to reject those historical explanations which generalise it excessively. There are only two, distinct, senses in which the concept of a 'General Crisis' can be manageably discussed. The first of these, which we have touched on before, is the notable recession in the European economy, observable in the decade 1610-20 and pronounced after about 1640. The second of these is the series of gevernmental crises of the decade 1640-50. The latter are the subject of the present chapter.

THE ENGLISH REVOLUTION OF 1640

In England a conflict between crown and Parliament had been a half-century in the making. Elizabeth in her declining years had already found it difficult to control the House of Commons. Under the first two Stuarts, James and Charles, tensions were magnified and confirmed. There were major conflicts about religion, finance and foreign policy; on the first and the last in particular the differences could be traced back well into Elizabeth's reign. Religion alone was so important an issue that it is possible to discuss the whole conflict of the early seventeenth century in terms of Puritanism, and it was once standard practice to refer to the events of mid-century as a Puritan Revolution. But whatever the precise issue may have been, what really lay at stake was the exercise of power and the ability to control government policy. Sooner or later all disputed points came for discussion to Parliament, and all grievances, whether of religion or finance, were debated there as constitutional issues, It was the constitutional struggle, the struggle for sovereignty, that dominated events up to 1640.

The range of questions that obsessed Parliament, from finance in the Petition of Right (1628) to religion in the Grand

Remonstrance (1641), and the successful attempts of the House of Commons to sit in judgment on monopolists as infringers of the constitution and destroyers of freedom of trade, demonstrate how wide-ranging was the front on which the struggle was fought. But there was no coherent revolutionary party or programme. The most prominent members of the opposition in the early 1620s, like Sir John Eliot and Sir Thomas Wentworth (later Earl of Strafford), believed almost as explicitly in the sovereign rights of monarchy as the king himself. It was the Eleven Years Tyranny (1629-40), a period when no Parliament was summoned, that forced the opposition to consider its attitudes, and that turned the doubters into revolutionaries. When the Long Parliament met in 1640 a majority of the five hundred or so members of the Commons had become convinced that what was required was a total dismantling of the apparatus of courtly absolutism. The legislation of 1641—the Triennial Act, the act against dissolution of Parliament without its own consent, the abolition of the prerogative courts — was truly revolutionary in scope.

Once the process of dismantling had taken place, and the hated symbol of royal policy, Strafford, been executed (in 1641; it was not until much later, in 1645, that Laud went to the scaffold), the unity of the opposition broke apart. The Grand Remonstrance in November 1641 was passed by a bare majority of eleven votes. It was a deliberately aggressive document and it drove even long-standing rebels further towards support for the king. But, for the embattled core, it was the one necessary step of defiance. Had it not been passed, said one of the members present, Oliver Cromwell, 'I would have sold all I possess next morning and never seen England more'. The Remonstrance had been framed as an appeal to the country against the king. But was the country really a protagonist in the revolutionary struggle?

Even when the two parties, Royalists and Parliamentarians, went to war in 1642 there was no serious intention of recruiting the country, that is the mass of the people, to either side. As John Hotham, who served with Parliament in 1642 but joined the king in 1643, said: 'No man that hath any reasonable share in the commonwealth can desire that either side should be conqueror.' His fear was lest 'the necessitous people of the whole kingdom will presently rise in mighty numbers and . . . set up for themselves to the utter ruin of all the nobility and gentry'. The quarrel was essentially one that took place within the ruling class, and it is this that has caused considerable problems of interpretation, for there was no tidy division of interests. There was no exclusively bourgeois revolution against feudalists, nor was there a struggle of the rising gentry for their place in the sun, nor was there a neat religious struggle of Puritans against neo-Papists. All these conflicts did of course occur, but only within a framework that comprised them all. To explain the revolution by analysing the taking of sides has not been a very successful task, if only because men did not always take the side they favoured. We know, for example, that some London merchants supported the king only because they hoped thereby to recover his debts to them; it is also true that property counted for much, and about one hundred members of the Commons who had opposed the king up to 1641 fought for him in the war because their estates were in royalist territory.

One division of interests that was clearly marked was that of 'court' against 'country'. Here 'court' refers to the royal system, the private individuals who were part of it, the control of taxation and lucrative sources of income, the monopoly of government offices, titles of rank and commercial privileges. By 'country' we understand those sections of the ruling class, based both in Parliament and in the provinces and the city of London, who were for various reasons excluded from the workings of the system, and who aimed to seize control of it in order to reform it. Seen in these terms it was a conflict of property and power. Stability depended on the cooperation of the propertied classes in the city and in local government (on the cooperation, that is, of the 'country') with the court. But when property was threatened by arbitrary taxation, by wasteful court expenditure, by unpopular foreign policies, by the granting of monopolies in restraint of free trade: then a split severe enough to lead to civil war could occur in the ruling class.

This does not mean that the tension between 'court' and 'country' was a materialistic one, innocent of ideology. The conflict extended to the Church, to the law, and to other disputed areas. It was the 'court' conspiracy, after all, against which the Puritan gentry, peers and preachers fought in their struggle for a purified Church of England. The Puritans were by and large not separatists: they were dissident brethren, in fact the 'country' party within the established religion. As in the secular sphere, they wished to reform the top-heavy structure of ecclesiastical administration, to devolve authority from bishops to local synods, to reform the tithe system. The question of legal reform was much the same: what was required was decentralisation, simplification, economy. In commerce the merchant classes of London were similarly concerned with an end to state interference and state

343

monopolies, and a return to free competition.

Although we have just stressed that the constitutional conflict was primarily conducted by the upper classes, it remains true that the nation as a whole was drawn into the struggle. More than any other country in Europe, England in this decade could be said to have had a revolution that affected not merely the seat of government but nearly every corner of political life in the land. In this sense, as in many others, it was the most important revolution of the seventeenth century. Beginning in the upper strata of society, its effects filtered through to the common people. A pamphleteer of 1642 gave a warning of the populace that 'now they know their strength', and imagined them hatching revolutionary plots against their masters. Few, if any, plots existed; but the fears were reasonable enough. For, once they had set their hands to the wheel, the rebels of 1641 and 1642 were not sure where the tides would take them, and they were reluctant to follow the logic of revolution right through. 'If we beat the King ninety-nine times', said the Earl of Manchester, commander of the parliamentary armies, in 1644, 'yet he is King still.' 'My lord', Cromwell replied, 'if this be so why did we take up arms at first? This is against fighting ever hereafter.' Cromwell was no revolutionary, but he saw the situation through to its necessary conclusion, the execution of Charles I in 1649 and the establishment of a republic of England.

Analysis of the members of the House of Commons, of the royal household, and of other institutions in which sides were taken, shows little or no difference in the social composition of the parties. There were gentry, nobles, merchants and commoners on both sides equally. It would appear that there was little to distinguish the two. As the Latitudinarian bishop Chillingworth was to comment cynically at a later date, 'all the scribes and pharisees were on one side and all the publicans and sinners on the other'. But as soon as we move from Westminster and the court to the countryside, a more significant social pattern emerges. The economically more advanced southeast of England supported Parliament, royal support came from the less developed north and west. The commercial and industrial interests were almost solidly for Parliament: all the ports chose this side, and so did (as we are told by Clarendon in his *History of the Great Rebellions*) 'Leeds, Halifax and Bradford, three very populous and rich towns, depending wholly upon clothiers'. Most important of all, London after 1643 came out for Parliament. The

344

king's support came naturally from traditional interests, from the greater proportion of the nobility and gentry; 'and also', reported Richard Baxter, 'most of the poorest of the people, whom the other call the rabble, did follow the gentry and were for the King'.

This division, with the rich and poor on one side, and the middling sort on the other, suggests that there may be some truth in the old image of a bourgeois revolution. The image is only partially valid. Bourgeois interests were served and defended by the parliamentarians, but the revolution itself was far more extensive in scope than the interests of any one class.

What was revolutionary about the English Revolution? It would be wrong to think of its work principally in terms of the first acts of the Long Parliament, and the revolutionary period should really be thought of as extending from November 1640, when the Long Parliament assembled, to December 1653, when the Barebones Parliament was dissolved. Those thirteen years were probably the most astonishing in all English history. In them every conceivable proposal for the reformation of the country was put forward; a few passed into law, most passed into limbo. The most permanent and important part of the revolution consisted in the acts of the Long Parliament in 1641 abolishing conciliar and prerogative government. Ironically, few members thought these measures revolutionary; they were looked upon as a necessary remedy for abuses. The council of the North, for example, was abolished principally through a clause introduced by the lawyer Sir Edward Hyde (a royalist during the civil war, created Earl of Clarendon at the Restoration).

It had been a simple matter to overthrow the structure of royal government. When it came to reform in matters of religion and property, the revolution dragged its feet. Some of the changes achieved in these fields, such as the abolition of bishops (they were excluded from Parliament in 1642, but not abolished until 1646), were superficial and perfunctory, and easily reversed at the Restoration. None of the religious experiments of these years, forced through by a small number of zealots, made any appreciable impact on the population: England became no more Puritan as a result of Puritan rule. There were important changes in property ownership as a result of penal legislation: crown lands were sold to the value of nearly three and a half million pounds, Church lands were sold to a value of nearly two and a half, and royalists had estates confiscated and sold to a value far exceeding one million pounds. But most royalists appear to have re-purchased their own land through intermediaries, and crown and

345

Church property was returned at the Restoration. There was no social revolution, no passing of wealth from the old nobility to the new gentry. The civil war delayed reforms. By 1647 the only real power in the country — the army — had impatiently begun to draw up its own plans for reform. In that year, as they lay encamped outside London, the officers drafted a reform document known as the Heads of the Proposals, while the Levellers produced their considerably more advanced programme, the Agreement of the People. These documents and others produced at this time are intrinsically interesting for the advanced and sophisticated political thinking which lay behind them. But the most relevant and significant thing was that it was being felt necessary to demand reforms. When Parliament (in effect, the Commons) prevaricated, the army marched on London and in December 1648 purged the members, leaving only a section of the House, to be known as the Rump.

The rule of the Rump Parliament coincided with that of the republican Commonwealth (1649-53). It also coincided with favourable economic circumstances, so that its members could claim with justice that England had not been so prosperous nor so strong abroad within living memory. But the Rump was little more than an oligarchy, unconcerned with reform and dedicated only to its own self-interest. In August 1652 the council of officers presented it with an ultimatum, asking for a number of listed reforms. The Rump instead drew up plans to make itself a self-perpetuating assembly. When he heard of this, Cromwell in April 1653 marched into the Commons with troops and expelled the members by force. In its place the Barebones Parliament was nominated: over one hundred and thirty men of proven religion and virtue, not elected but hand-picked by the officers. Long held in derision by writers, this unique assembly, which sat from July to December 1653, was in fact one of the most promising ever to sit in Westminster. It took up again the tasks that its predecessors had neglected. Far-seeing measures were proposed in the committee for law reform; changes were discussed in education, the poor law, taxation and other matters. When it began discussing tithes, however, the men of property both inside and outside Westminster became alarmed. On 12 December troops marched in and cleared the House.

With the dispersal of the Leveller movement in 1649 and the end of republican rule in 1653 (in 1654 the Protectorate came into existence), the active phase of the revolutionary years came to a close. The trend after 1653 was a backwards one: back to stability and order if possible, back certainly to the Restoration of the monarchy.

THE FRONDE

Potentially the most dangerous period of the English Revolution was 1647-8, years of a food crisis and a hard winter, conditions which the Levellers exploited in their appeals to the public. In France the same conditions served to introduce the Fronde (1648-53).

No single explanation can suffice for the complex and chaotic events known jointly as the Fronde. The whole regime collapsed into near-anarchy; parties and factions arose based both on principle and on self-interest; for some it was a continuous light entertainment, for others a grim struggle for survival. Was the Fronde a revolution or was it a mere series of abortive coups? For one modern historian, Kossmann, it was 'neither a parliamentary revolution nor a revolution of the people nor a feudal revolution ... it was none of these for it was all of these at the same time'. It is certain that it was the gravest political crisis the *ancien régime* suffered before the Revolution of 1789. No amount of emphasis on its lighter aspects can mitigate the severity of the crisis. Large areas of France were laid waste and thousands of lives lost in the struggle. Louis XIV suffered nightmares in after years whenever he thought of the Fronde, and in 1668 he ordered the burning of all public documents connected with that infamous period, and had copies made that omitted all mention of the rebellion. It was in these years that Saint Vincent de Paul carried out his outstanding missions of mercy. Both state and society were shaken by the civil wars.

The protagonists fell roughly into four groupings. First, there was the circle consisting of the Queen Mother and Cardinal Mazarin, and with them the boy King Louis XIV. Secondly there were the higher nobility, including many princes of the blood; it was their factiousness that reduced the Fronde at times to the level of the children's game after which it was named. In this group were Orleans, the king's uncle; Mademoiselle, his daughter; Condé and Turenne; the beautiful Madame de Longueville, sister of Condé, who looked more like an angel than a woman though, as those who knew her asserted, she was neither of the two but in fact a devil, as proved by the occasion when she assured her brother that if he did not create a diversion for her by going to war against the king she would have to return to her bore of a husband who, as everyone knew, had horns on his head; Paul de Gondi, later Cardinal de Retz, Coadjutor Bishop of Paris, one-time pupil of Saint Vincent de Paul and his most illustrious failure, the only really intelligent man among the Frondeurs and therefore the most dangerous. These and the many others of their class were the most irresponsible of the Frondeurs. Thirdly, there were the bourgeoisie of Paris, the high officials in justice and in municipal government, the principal representatives of constitutional authority in the state (particularly through the *parlements*). Fourthly, all-important but seldom in the forefront, there were the people, the populace of Paris, Bordeaux and other towns.

The period from 1648 to 1649, usually known as the bourgeois Fronde, was undoubtedly constitutional in character. The demands made by the members of all the higher judicial bodies, meeting in the Chambre Saint-Louis of the Palais de Justice in July 1648, consisted of twenty-seven articles, among them demands for the abolition of intendants, the reduction of taxes, the suppression of new offices, and reaffirmation of the rights of the Parlement of Paris. The question of offices was crucial, for it was a governmental decision to create a dozen more senior judicial offices that had provoked a crisis in January that year. But the protest was eventually so broadly based that it is difficult to attribute any one motive to the rebels. The repeated request that foreign traders be curtailed in their activities and foreign cloth (i.e. English and Dutch) not be imported, seems to reflect the strong influence of bourgeois manufacturers in the movement. In August the government felt itself strong enough to reject the demands of the bourgeoisie, and to arrest the popular councillor Broussel. This caused the revolutionary day of barricades. But did the Parlement of Paris, core of the resistance, have any intention of creating a revolution? The English example inspired apprehension in royalist circles. Madame de Motteville, a confidante of the Queen Regent, observed in her memoirs that in the early summer of 1648 'the Parlement began to claim for itself so exorbitant a power as gave cause to fear that the bad example the jurists saw in the Parliament of England had made some impression on them'. The Parisian lawyers were certainly anxious to identify themselves with other struggles for freedom. A writer of a 1649 pamphlet claimed that France was not alone in the fight for liberty, and that England, Catalonia and Naples had already shown the way. But at heart the bourgeois Fronde was non-revolutionary, anti-republician and pro-royalist. The execution of Charles I in England in 1649 caused horror everywhere in France and doomed any nascent republican sentiment (though even as late as December 1651 there was a small republican party in Paris). The demands of the rebels were often radical and far-reaching; their attacks on Mazarin were subversive of the existing regime; but their theory in the end tended only to confirm the divine right of absolute monarchy. Their revolt was anti-ministerial and not anti-regal. 'You are, sire', said Omer Talon, advocate-general of the Parlement, in January 1648, 'our sovereign lord; Your Majesty's power comes from on high and is accountable, after God, to none save your conscience.' Unlike the parliamentarians of England, the Paris lawyers entertained no theory whatsoever of popular sovereignty; they claimed to be *supporting* royal power against the minister and his regime. The revolt was also by implication directed against Richelieu who, according to one pamphlet, had 'perverted and reversed the ancient form of government and changed the tenets of legitimate monarchy into those of tyranny'. Legitimate monarchy, for most of the parliamentarians, meant divine right.

The princely Fronde (1650-3) was even less inclined to question divine right, but the grievances of the nobles were no less serious than those of the bourgeoisie. The higher aristocracy had no fundamental quarrel with the government, other than opposition to Mazarin and to Italian influence. Many of them seem to have treated the whole conflict as a light-hearted diversion, an opportunity to fight out their rivalries. Perhaps the only serious protagonist was Condé, resentful of his loss of influence at court, and of the boy-king ('There's no joy in obeying a fool', he said of Louis) and his mother. He was by far the most serious threat, particularly after 1651, when Bordeaux became his base and the civil war, now extended over half of France, reached its bloodiest and most destructive phase.

It was the lower nobility who had some reason to complain of a deterioration in their position. Though no Estates General met in France after 1614, assemblies of the nobility did occasionally convene (as in 1625 and 1626), and it was at these — sometimes no more than local meetings — that they discussed their complaints. When the government in 1649 decided to summon an Estates General, some of the provincial nobility drew up *cahiers* in which they filed their grievances. The Estates never met, but the impatient nobles held a brief assembly at Paris in 1650 and 1651. The *cahiers* drawn up for the projected Estates by the nobles of Angoumois and Troyes reveal a state of serious discontent. The Angoumois nobles, who tended to concentrate on local issues, complained about taxation, foreign traders, the encroachment of royal judges of their jurisdictions, 'the notable prejudice suffered by the nobles from venality of offices . . . to which access is almost impossible because of their excessive cost', the *Paulette*, and the pretensions of the *noblesse de robe*. Whatever the validity of these and other grievances, they emphasise what has been outlined in a previous chapter, the reality of the crisis through which the European nobility were passing, and which in France made them participate actively in the Fronde. Regional disaffection provoked by the nobles cannot then be dismissed merely as an assertion of the feudal principle and of reactionary aspirations. The disturbances often arose out of genuine political discontent, by elements that feared the extension of state authority represented most clearly in the intendants.

The Fronde was undoubtedly a conflict affecting both state and society: social class and the control of power (i.e. offices) were at issue. But structurally it had little in common with the 'court' and 'country' division that obtained in the English Revolution. Too many contradictions were implicit in the French events, notably the singular paradox that the constitutionalist members of the *noblesse de robe* of Paris were absolutist at heart. For it was the crown alone that could guarantee the social ascendancy of the office-holders at the expense of the traditional nobility. The members of the *noblesse de robe* consequently identified themselves consistently with the king and opposed (as in 1651-2) both Mazarin on one side and Condé on the other. When they made lofty claims, as the parlement of Aix did in 1645. *('Nos sumus reges')* it was not on their own account but because *'vicem regis gerimus'*, they represented the king. In this struggle between bourgeois and noble for the control of office, it is impossible to decide who were the 'ins' and who the 'outs', for the issues were not straightforward.

Although the Fronde has been described above as a major political crisis, its positive achievement was insignificant. It solved no problems, gave birth to no reforms, altered nothing in the structure of the old regime. The history of the intendants is significant in this respect. They were suppressed by the government in 1648 on the request of the Parlement, and an undertaking was given not to reintroduce them. Despite this, the frontier military intendants were allowed to continue, and Mazarin brought the other intendants back surreptitiously under the name of *commissaires*. After Mazarin's victory in 1653 they were openly reintroduced under their old name.

Though his enemies claimed that as minister Mazarin had usurped the royal functions, the cardinal's aim all along had been clear. The chosen successor of Richelieu, his task was to prepare both state and king for absolutism, and this he did successfully in his dual capacity as royal tutor and as prime minister.

THE LABYRINTH: SPAIN AND NAPLES

Unlike England and France, states which were both becoming centralised and possessed the beginnings of a bureaucracy, Spain had no political unity. For the sixty years from 1580 to 1640, however, Portugal had been under the Spanish crown, giving the peninsula the superficial appearance of unity. It was this uneasy federation of provinces in Iberia that was not unexpectedly shattered with the revolts of 1640. In nearly every important detail the events of the peninsula differed qualitatively from what was to occur in England and France. The Spanish problem was one of federalism. No other major European state suffered from this to any comparable degree. What remains true is that the actual revolution in Catalonia was touched off by war, and it was war and the needs of war taxation that were the operative causes of crisis in England and France as well.

When Olivares became chief minister of Philip IV at the latter's accession in 1621, there was little danger of any internal constitutional challenge to royal authority. Spain was in practice an absolute monarchy. There was no effective parliament, the office-holding class was quiescent. But two tragic paradoxes lay behind this absolutism. Peninsular Spain was in fact totally disunited, for the king was really absolute ruler only over Castile; and the greatest weakness of this powerful monarchy lay in what appeared to be its strength — the overseas empire. On both counts the government at Madrid was seriously inconvenienced. Within the peninsula the king's writ ran only over the territories of the crown of Castile. If he wished to act in Catalonia, Aragon or Valencia he had first to consult the Estates of those realms. These realms were not only constitutionally autonomous, they also (as a memorandum presented to Philip III in 1618 pointed out) 'contribute nothing to Your Majesty's expenses beyond their own frontiers, and money even has to be sent to them from Castile to pay their garrisons'. Some sort of income was regularly available from the overseas territories, particularly America, to pay for the rising expenses of the crown. But income from

America was invariably diverted directly to the Netherlands and Milan to pay for military costs, and income from other territories (such as Naples) was likely to cause growing resentment on the part of those who had to pay the taxes. The ultimate result was that Castile and America became almost the sole contributors to Spain's war bill. By the early seventeenth century an influential group of royal advisers, among them Olivares, had come to the conclusion that the other member states of the monarchy should pay their fair share of the costs. 'It is quite unreasonable', the *arbitrista* Pedro Navarrete wrote in 1626, 'that the head should be weakened while the other members, which are very rich and populous, should simply stand by and look on while it has to bear all these heavy charges.'

In fiscal terms, Spain was weak internally because Castile alone contributed satisfactorily to finances; it was weak externally because it had actually to spend money on supporting its far-flung empire. These difficulties were multiplied when it came to problems of government and military recruitment, since in both these matters the non-Castilian provinces enjoyed great autonomy. The political crisis precipitated by Olivares originated in an attempt by Castile to assert its control in real terms. As Olivares put it in his famous secret memorandum of 1624.

> The most important thing in Your Majesty's Monarchy is for you to become King of Spain. By this I mean, Sir, that Your Majesty should not be content with being king of Portugal, of Aragon, of Valencia and count of Barcelona, but should secretly plan and work to reduce these kingdoms of which Spain is composed to the style and laws of Castile, with no difference whatsoever. And if Your Majesty achieves this, you will be the most powerful prince in the world.

The events of 1640 in the peninsula — the Catalan rebellion in the spring and the Portuguese revolt in December — were reflections of an essentially Castilian crisis. Castile's inability to govern a peninsular province; its incapability of paying for the troops billeted there; the failure to raise troops in Catalonia; the refusal of the Castilian nobility to render military service; Olivares' own failure to rally support for his policies in the Castilian ruling class; the plot of the Duke of Medina Sidonia in 1641 to set up an independent Andalucia: all these were symptoms of crumbling authority. Set in the context of a decaying Atlantic trade, mounting inflation at home and military expenditure unattended by success abroad, the events of 1640 mark a turning point in Castile's status as a world power. Olivares fell from power in January 1643, but the decline could not be arrested. The defeat of the Spanish infantry at Rocroi in May 1643 confirmed the diminishing returns from Spain's intervention in Germany. In 1647 the government again declared itself bankrupt. In 1647 Naples revolted against the crown. In 1648 a plot to make Aragon independent under the Duke of Híjar was discovered. In October that year the Treaty of Münster gave the United Provinces their independence from Spain.

This catalogue of failure is often expressed only in terms of Castile's difficulties, as though the sole problem were Castile's ability to hold its empire together. But it is now clear that the crisis was no less one that existed within the rebellious provinces themselves. The ruling classes of Catalonia had been generally opposed to the billeting of Castilian troops in their province. 'This province feels so deeply about the billeting', the viceroy warned Madrid in May 1640, 'that the people are in a state of turmoil . . . There is not a man who can be counted on in the entire province'. By June, after the viceroy had been murdered by a mob in Barcelona on Corpus Christi day, it became clear that the Catalans also had grievances against their own rulers. Rebel groups, long repressed by the social regime, formed themselves into a 'Christian army', and began to terrorise the nobles and gentry. Professor Elliott sums up: 'the hatred of the lesser peasantry and the landless for the wealthy peasant and the noble; the bitterness of the rural unemployed; the desire for revenge of the bandit element against those who had repressed it; the old feuds of town against country, of the poorer citizens against the municipal oligarchies . . . all these burst suddenly and explosively to life in Catalonia'. In the town of Manresa, a typical case, the authorities reported in September 1640 that 'wicked spirits among the worst sort of people . . . turned against certain rich and powerful citizens, calling them traitors to the land, and said that . . . they would burn down their houses'. If Catalonia was in rebellion against Castile, it was also in rebellion against itself. The political crisis had allowed the social crisis to emerge.

Exactly the same turn of events occurred in the Neapolitan revolt of 1647 (which is discussed below in Chapter 10). The rebellion in Naples threatened Spain's authority and the flow of supplies from that city to the troops in Germany and on the French frontier. Fiscal demands from Spain played a leading part in the history of Neapolitan discontent. Nobles who resented Spanish rule gave their support to the French plot to detach

Naples from the Spanish empire. Ironically, some of the leaders of the anti-aristocratic popular revolt, influenced by Genoino, thereupon worked to bring about an alliance with the Spanish authorities. The events in Naples showed clearly that internal tension within the kingdom was the real generator of the convulsions of 1647. The external quarrel, about deference to Spain, was of secondary concern.

Spain's problems were unique, and it is consequently difficult to compare its situation to that of other states. No other nation had so large an empire, nor had its economic and military stability so closely linked to the fate of that empire. No other faced within its frontiers the federal problem that Castile had. Charles I, Mazarin, William II of Orange and Queen Christina were confronted by constitutional and parliamentary opposition; Olivares governed a country where the parliamentary tradition; was moribund. The Stuarts were troubled, we are told, by rising gentry, the Bourbon Regency by rising bourgeois; but the opposition to Olivares was concentrated among the traditional rulers and did not rise out of a new status group.

Like other monarchies, Spain had material problems of war and peace, of diminishing revenue and soaring expenditure. It too suffered from declining trade after the 1620 crisis and from the seventeenth-century depression. Not having yet recovered from the plague of 1599, the country was dealt a further blow by the great mortality of 1647 in Castile and 1651 in Catalonia. If not in politics at least in trade, economy and population, Spain too suffered from a major crisis.

CONFLICT IN NORTHERN EUROPE

In their separate ways the United Provinces and Sweden were thrown into a period of crisis by the coming of a general European peace in 1648. In the Dutch Republic the old split between the republican Hollanders and the House of Orange came to the fore again. Viewed as a struggle between the burgher oligarchy and the Orangist court, or between a peace party and a war party, it had led in 1619 to the victory of the Orangists and the execution of the revered republican leader Oldenbarnevelt. The alignment of parties remained the same on the conclusion of peace in 1648. Immediately after the Treaty of Münster the province of Holland, led by the Amsterdam patriciate, urged a policy of commercial expansion and of peace with England. The first step towards this would have been the disbandment of the large number of troops under their commander-in-chief, William II, and a reduction in military subsidies. Peace with England was not merely a question of trade: the exiled Charles Stuart, brother-in-law of William, was living at The Hague, and a royalist Orange-Stuart alliance was objectionable in every way to Holland's interests. As the chief financial contributor to the Union, Holland seemed about to get its way. The military and William II thereupon decided to force the issue.

William's position was extremely powerful. He was *stadhouder* of six of the seven provinces in the Union (the seventh, Friesland, was governed by his cousin William Frederick), and therefore commanded the support of a majority in the States-General; he had an army of veteran soldiers under him, and all the Dutch fortresses were in the hands of his relatives and followers; the people and preachers supported him wholeheartedly everywhere save in Amsterdam. Although the disbandment of troops was the ostensible issue in dispute, what was obviously involved was control of the Republic. Holland openly kept up diplomatic relations with the regicide Commonwealth in England, and unilaterally began to disband those troops paid by its exchequer: both actions were interpreted as provocations. After failing to make any headway during a visit to the chief towns of Holland, William at the end of July 1650 took direct steps to achieve his ends.

On 30 July, at eight o'clock in the morning, six leading deputies of the States of Holland were arrested in The Hague on William's orders. At the same time an army under William Frederick was sent to seize Amsterdam. The seige failed, but the terms on which the city eventually opened its gates were clearly favourable to the Prince of Orange. Though William had not succeeded fully (Holland still blocked in the States-General a plan by him to help France in the war against Spain), he had been granted extraordinary powers and was poised to assume a dominant role in the Republic. At this juncture, on 6 November 1650, he suddenly died.

His untimely death had momentous consequences: a son and heir, later William III, was born a month afterwards. But the rule of the House of Orange had been decisively cut short, and a whole epoch in Dutch history, that of the rise and consolidation of the Republic, came to an end. The balance of power swung back immediately to the regent class of Holland, whose leadership under the de Witts was to determine the course of Dutch history for the next two decades. In order to bypass the Orangist-inspired States-General, the Hollanders invited all members of the Union to send fresh delegates to a 'Great Assembly' that met in The

355

Hague from January to August 1651. At this meeting the differences of the past were erased, the leading role of the Prince of Orange was eliminated (William III was not appointed as *stadhouder* of Holland, the supreme posts of captain-general and admiral-general were suspended), and Holland seized the initiative in foreign policy.

William II's death interrupted the seemingly irresistible drift of the United Provinces towards absolutist rule. By this historical accident a bourgeois republic was brought into existence and those bourgeois virtues that Sir William Temple was to praise so highly became the norm of life in the state. Even the noble class vied to have their children marry into the regent families.

The Swedish crisis was comparable in some ways. It too was a consequence of the war and the peace; as in the United Provinces, 1650 was a temporary stage and absolutism was not confirmed until well over twenty years thereafter.

By the 1630s Sweden had found its war policy increasingly expensive to finance. Under Gustav Adolf it had been possible to live off subsidies, port-tolls and the countryside. After 1635 some ports ceased to pay tolls, the French were having to finance their own intervention in the war, and campaigns in Germany met greater resistance. It was in this period of the Regency that sales of royal land were multiplied, as an emergency measure. 'We were impelled to use these very necessary means to save the fatherland from danger', a royal official stated in 1638. When Christina (1644-54) came to the throne, such sales were an established expedient for raising money. From about 1648 she indulged in expensive sales not only for fiscal purposes but also in order to gratify favoured individuals. The results were unprecedented. By the end of her reign nearly two-thirds of royal land had passed out of the hands of the crown. The area of noble land in Sweden more than doubled between 1611 (when sales had first commenced) and 1652. Since crown revenue relied a great deal on income from its estates, a financial crisis came into being. Royal revenue dropped from 6.36 million silver dollars in 1644 to 3.79 at the end of Christina's reign.

The balance between social classes was seriously disturbed. The free peasantry on the former crown lands found that they had been transferred to aristocratic control, with a consequent depression in their status. Their grievances remained muted until the harvest failure of 1649-50, the worst in the century; then economic despair made them combine with the clergy and burgher estates to protest to the queen in the Diet of 1650. From the grievances of the people, Christina was told,

> you will see into what an unheard-of state of servitude they have
> declined since private persons took hold of the country; for some treat
> their peasants ill, either by raising their dues, or by imposing in-
> tolerable burdens of day-work upon them, or by imprisonment, or
> threats, or evictions; until the poor peasant is totally ruined.

The parliamentary opposition occurred against a background of
risings elsewhere in Europe and of threats of disaffection within
the country. The Swedish peasants had important political
privileges — notably their own Estate in the Diet — that they felt
to be threatened. But their discontent was directed not so much at
the crown as against the power which the nobility were now accumulating. As an opposition pamphlet of 1649 put it,

> when the privileges of the nobility are increased, extended and im-
> proved to the diminution of the royal revenues and the disadvantage
> of the other Estates; when one Estate is strengthened and exalted,
> and another is oppressed and trampled underfoot until at last it
> becomes an Estate no longer — then this is something which runs
> contrary to a monarchial constitution, and to the crown's intention; it
> is contrary also to the liberties of all the Estates.

The immediate cure demanded at the Diet of 1650, one
calculated to restore revenue to the crown and to diminish the
growth of aristocratic power, was the resumption of all alienated
lands. This call for a *Reduktion* was skilfully exploited by
Christina to enable her to win her main objective, the confirmation of her cousin Charles as hereditary heir to the throne.
Having gained that, she dropped her allies in the lower Estates of
the Diet, refused a *Reduktion* and remained even more firmly in
power. The parliamentary opposition had served only to
strengthen the crown.

The threat of revolt in 1650 was not directed against the crown,
despite the open wastefulness of Christina's court. Nor did the
division of parties represent a class struggle: when the resumption
of crown lands was eventually begun by Charles X in 1655 part of
his support came from the lower nobility. As in the Fronde, the
programme of the non-noble opposition called for serious reforms
in the structure of power, but no serious attempt was made to
touch the royal prerogatives for, as the supplication of the three
lower Estates in the Diet of 1650 put it, 'we esteem Your
Majesty's royal power as the buttress of our liberties, the one
being bound up in the other, and both standing or falling
together'.

357

REVOLUTION IN EASTERN EUROPE

In the mid-sixteenth century the Cossacks in the region of the lower Dniepr obtained from the Polish king permission to settle in the country 'beyond the rapids' *(za porogi)* of the river. From this period the Zaporozhian Cossacks established themselves as a powerful nomadic military community. In time they laid claim to being a nation. The struggle of the Ukrainian Cossacks for their independence from Polish tutelage was of primary importance in east European history. In military terms the Cossacks were a powerful auxiliary of the Polish crown (Cossack regiments were specially recruited by King Stephen Báthory), and were invaluable as a frontier force against the Tatars and Turks. In political terms they were a rising force that held the balance in the east between a decaying Poland and an emergent Muscovy; every revolt against Poland brought closer the day of Muscovite dominance. In religious terms they were the ultimate frontier of Catholicism, in an area where defence of the Orthodox faith (the Cossacks were overwhelmingly Orthodox) was a burning issue. In social terms, they were the protectors of the peasantry, who rallied to them in times of distress: every major peasant revolt in Polish lands took place only with the armed support of the Cossack leaders, as in 1590 with Kosińsky and 1596 with Nalivaiko.

Every move of the Ukrainian Cossacks was likely to have profound repercussions in eastern Europe. The Polish government, which relied constantly on them for help against the Turks, made several efforts to crush the monster it had conjured up, and in 1597, after Nalivaiko's rising, the Sejm actually branded the Cossacks as *hostes patriae* and called for their extermination. But the unusual Cossack way of life — they often lived as nomads, and their military action took the form of banditry and piracy — made it almost impossible to subdue them. In 1645 the Poles once again called on the Cossacks to join them in a campaign against the Tatars. Among the Cossack commanders in 1646 was Bohdan Khmelnitsky. A lesser noble with extensive military experience in Russia and in Flanders, Khmelnitsky at the end of the Tatar campaign turned against his masters and gathered a small force of dissident Cossacks round him. In April 1648 he was acclaimed as Hetman of the Zaporozhians. After a great victory over royalist forces in May (Khmelnitsky was helped by the Crimean Tatars), revolt spread through the Ukraine. The spur to revolt was the Cossack cavalry, but the real source of disaffection was the protest of the peasantry against their Polish landlords. The entire feudal structure of the Polish frontier lands was being uprooted. The peasant fury *(khlopskaya zloba)* was directed at three main enemies: the landlords, the Catholic clergy and the Jews. These were annihilated with a ferocity exceeded only by that used by some royalist leaders, such as the Volhynia nobleman Jerome Wiśnowiecki, against the peasantry.

Khmelnitsky's successes in battle opened both White Russia and Lithuania to him: his marches took him through Lwow and towards the Vistula. By October 1648 he was accepted in Kiev as 'the father and liberator of the country'. All these gains were accepted by the helpless Polish authorities, but the negotiation of agreed terms was more difficult to achieve. As the Poles delayed and spent the spring of 1649 collecting troops, Khmelnitsky was forced to look for external support. In 1649 only the Tatars would help him. Khmelnitsky was therefore obliged to accept an agreement which gave him the provinces of Kiev, Chernigov and Bratslav, but returned three others to Polish hands. No rights were guaranteed to the peasantry. Subsequent military reverses threatened even these gains. By 1653 Khmelnitsky's position was desperate. At this stage, after numerous embassies from the Hetman, the Muscovite Tsar Alexei Mikhailovich announced that he had agreed to help the Zaporozhians. In January 1654 the Agreement of Pereyaslavl united the Ukraine to Great Russia.

This epoch-making Agreement was full of ambiguities and contradictions, but Khmelnitsky had little choice in the matter. Before obtaining any concession from the Tsar, he was obliged to accept for his nation the perpetual authority of Moscow. Only then were terms discussed. The treaty and its far-reaching consequences are not our immediate concern here. There were two direct results: the creation of the Ukraine, and the outbreak of war between Russia and Poland. The storm clouds were about to descend on the Polish state. In 1654 Christina of Sweden had abdicated the throne. Her successor, Charles X, committed himself the following year to an invasion of Poland.

Russia's intervention in the Ukraine and in Polish affairs arose out of a position of strength. The moment of crisis had come, as in France and the Ukraine, in 1648. The urban revolutions of that year (discussed below in Chapter 10) led directly to a conservative reaction in the form of the Law Code of 1649. Representative government also suffered from the reaction. The Zemsky Sobor of 1653, which approved of the incorporation of the Ukraine into

Russia, was the last to meet. Autocratic Russia was poised for expansion.

THE RESPONSE TO POLITICAL CRISIS

We have argued that the general features of the years 1640-50 are most manageably discussed in economic terms. It was a decade of economic difficulty, whose repercussions could be felt throughout the continent from London to Moscow. Bad weather, poor harvests, the consequences of war, depression of trade: all combined to produce high prices and social tension. Looking back at the long-term trend in the economy, historians tend to see these years as a prelude to the depression that occupied the century 1650-1750. The main features of that depression are outside the scope of our theme and will not be discussed here: they included a fall in agricultural and industrial production, a halt to the extension of arable area and of land reclamation, general stagnation in the numbers of the European population, and a generally low price level. In the short term, what made the decade 1640-50 critical was the coincidence of natural disaster and governmental incompetence. The year 1640 may have been revolutionary in Spain and England, but the real flashpoint in most countries came in 1646-8, years of extremely bad living conditions which sparked off major urban and peasant revolts. In England near famine conditions led the Levellers to predict a revolution, in Spain a terrifying epidemic of plague swept through Valencia, Castile and Andalucia.

The incompetence of governments consisted principally in their inability to deal with two things that precipitated all the state crises: war and taxation. Since war was at this time the principal occupation of all European states, it consumed by far the largest proportion of all state revenue, and the demands of war inevitably set up severe strains between governments and the people from whom they demanded taxes. Economic stress and war were such universal causes of crisis that it is little more than a truism to say that they lay at the root of the malaise which afflicted most European states. There were other deep-seated causes of revolution, some that stretched back well over a century, but in nearly all cases war and taxation were the immediate stimulants.

In England it was the need for taxes to finance the war against the Scots that forced Charles I to summon Parliament after a lapse of eleven years. In France it was Richelieu's heavy programme of war taxation that undermined the regime he had set out to strengthen, and Mazarin may have been saved from

360

disaster partly because the Thirty Years War ended in precisely the year that the first Fronde commenced. In Spain the war with France enabled Portugal and Catalonia to break free, and Olivares was not the last minister to be disgraced because of his inability to solve the fiscal problems of the world's biggest imperial power. In Naples it was the excessive tax demands of Spain for the war effort that alienated the propertied classes and drove them to rebellion. In Holland the vital question of control over the military precipitated the coup of 1650. In Sweden all major internal disputes were a backwash of the problems raised by Sweden's intervention in the wars in Germany. In the Slav lands war was the very determinant of politics, and through it the duchy of the Ukraine was born.

Of all social classes, it was the nobility that faced the greatest test. A century of diminishing income and vanishing power bid fair to lead to their destruction in the mid-century crisis. In the face of the anti-aristocratic mood of the English Revolution, Lord Willoughby observed bitterly in 1645, 'I thought it a crime to be a nobleman'. During the siege of royalist Oxford in the civil war a hungry sentry on watch cried down to the parliamentarians: 'Roundhead, fling me up half a mutton and I will fling thee down a Lord.' In Catalonia in 1640 the native nobility were terrorised by the popular insurgents and accused of being traitors to their country; 'and', reported a correspondent from Barcelona, 'they can expect no help from their vassals, who are so tired of them that they will put up with them no longer'. In the Paris of 1649 leaflets began to ask whether the people should any longer tolerate the nobles.

The real threat to the noble class came, however, less from the populace than from the crown. The alliance of intelligent ministers and compliant monarchs was more than the aristocracy cared to suffer. Wentworth's prosecution of the Earl of Cork and the fines levied by the organs of conciliar government under Charles I, Laud's provocative policy in the Court of Wards (Clarendon reported that by it 'all the rich families of England, of noblemen and gentlemen, were exceedingly incensed and even indevoted to the crown'), convinced many English nobles that there was little virtue in supporting the Stuart attempt at absolutism. The regularity of noble plots against Richelieu illustrates clearly enough how the French aristocracy interpreted royal policy. They got their revenge under Mazarin, but even that was a short-lived triumph, for their antics were to be remembered in the sinister words of the young Louis XIV: 'My rebellious subjects, when they took up arms against me, gave me perhaps less cause for indignation than those who stayed by my side and rendered me greater services and attention than all the others, though I was well informed that all the time they were betraying me.' Queen Christina of Sweden threatened the security of her nobility by opening their ranks to scores of parvenus and distributing royal lands indiscriminately. By the mid-seventeenth century it seemed that strong monarchy was, despite all its professions of solicitude, working against the aristocracy. For this reason (among others) the nobles played a leading part in the crisis, and it was they who demanded the resignation of Mazarin and of Olivares. Absolutism was not to their taste.

In England the Lords allied with the Commons to remove Strafford. The defection of the Lords from the crown led inevitably to war. As the political theorist James Harrington was to observe, 'a monarchy divested of its nobility has no refuge under heaven but an army. Wherefore the dissolution of this government caused the war, not the war the dissolution of this government.'

In every European state that suffered a political upheaval the confrontation between the monarch and the ruling class was played out before the representative bodies. The fate of representative government was an issue of the first importance in the crisis. English historians are familiar with the problem, for the English Parliament made it clear throughout the early seventeenth century that it was fighting for what it called its privileges, which it identified with the fundamental rights of the people. As the Commons' Protestation put it in 1621:

> The liberties, franchises, privileges and jurisdictions of Parliament are the ancient and undoubted birthright and inheritance of the subjects of England; . . . the arduous and urgent affairs concerning the king, state and defence of the realm and of the Church of England, and the maintenance and making of laws, redress of mischiefs and grievances . . . are proper subjects and matter of comment and debate in Parliament.

In continental Europe, too, the integrity of constitutional bodies was commonly seen to be the chief protection against tyranny on one hand and anarchy on the other. The Catalans who, like the Aragonese in 1591, refused to cooperate with the Castilian authorities save through their cortes, were well aware of the views of Olivares. The chief minister, writing to the Catalan viceroy in February 1640 when a new meeting of the cortes was being decided upon, remarked that 'nothing is to be discussed in them except the reform of government — we will have none of that usual business of prayers and petitions'. In the event, no cortes were allowed to meet. Mazarin's government showed the same hostility to constitutional bodies. The pretensions of the Parlement of Paris to be the supreme court were firmly rejected, as were its objections to royal prerogatives such as the *lit de justice,* whereby the king sitting in the Parliament could order the passing of measures of which that body disapproved. The government's attempt to call an Estates General in 1649 floundered, for it was clear that Mazarin merely wished to play off the upper Estates against the Third Estate. In practice, rulers assented to a popular assembly only when it served their ends. The Zemsky Sobor of 1648-9 was compliant, the Neapolitan parliament of 1642 was not; the former was given a brief lease of life, the latter was dissolved and did not meet again. In Sweden the struggle was carried out principally at the Diet of 1650. An imaginary conversation published at that time expressed horror at the pretensions of the lower Estates, at their claim for 'a liberty to direct policy, to propose matters for decision, to give advice, to launch a mass of innovations, to peer into *arcana status'.* 'How it has gone in England, since the Estates began upon the same fashion,' continued the same character in the conversation, 'is sufficiently manifest to us from the events of the past few years.'

For a few countries, internal difficulties of government, war taxation and social conflict were aggravated by the arrival of peace in 1648. The great treaties of that year, known collectively as the Peace of Westphalia, involved the shifting of frontiers, withdrawal of armed forces, pensioning-off of mercenary troops, readjustment of financial commitments and the barter of a variety of political and territorial privileges. For many parts of Germany, particularly the Rhineland, it meant an end to thirty years — a whole lifetime — of war. For the Dutch the war had lasted even longer: a full eighty years of struggle for independence. In these circumstances the outbreak of peace could only have been unsettling. In the Swedish Estates in 1635 the Bishop of Västerås had expressed fears of what wartime measures might bring, 'of what befell the Roman Republic, how the constitution was overthrown by the keeping up of great armies, which led to internal dissension, and broke out in dangerous seditions'. But peace brought the greater threat of a monarchy strengthened by habitual obedience in time of war, and this alone made possible the extravagances of Christina's rule. It was the outbreak of peace likewise that precipitated the constitutional crisis in the Dutch Republic and William II's attempted coup d'état; peace that released the French generals to participate in the struggles of the Fronde; peace that brought depression and unrest to the Swiss cantons. Whatever the social and economic causes may have been, it is clear that for some governments the general crisis was provoked by the general peace.

It is when we get beyond straightforward matters of time and circumstance that problems of interpretation arise. Does it further our understanding to try and fit all the political crises into a common mould? The antithesis of court against country is now current among English-speaking historians, yet as a general explanation it adds little to an analysis of events elsewhere, in France and Muscovy for example. The very important emphasis on the role of public office is vital to French history but of little value in Spain and Sweden. It follows that there is a real danger in the whole concept of a 'General Crisis', just as any covering explanation tends to be fallacious in detail. It is misleading to think that the long-term problems of European states were the same, for they quite obviously were not. England and Spain shared little in common in 1640 except for the same date for their revolutions; Moscow and Paris in 1648, Amsterdam and Stockholm in 1650, coincided in time rather than in problem. It is one thing to look at the common difficulties shared by social classes in different countries, quite another to generalise from the very uneven development of European states to the existence of a particularly significant crisis. A turning point did, of course, exist, and the occasion was supplied by the economic difficulties of the decade 1640-50. In those years of fiscal instability and price inflation, of bad harvests and the beginnings of a trade recession, the accumulated problems of governments and the grievances of their subjects exploded in a continent-wide outburst of revolution.

When the crisis had come and passed, all the revolutions proved to be stillborn. They were great attempts at change but none of them, not even the English one, proved itself able to surmount the crisis. The way lay open instead to unchallenged conservatism. There were alterations enough in the century that lay ahead, above all in the spheres of reflection and experiment; in, that is, philosophy and science. These cultural virtues were pursued in an environment of elegant aristocratic leisure. The Iron Age made way for an age of aristocracy.

10 POPULAR REBELLIONS 1550-1660

Steere said that it would only be a month's work to overrun the realm (England); and that the poor once rose in Spain and cut down the gentry, since when they had lived merrily.

Testimony against Bartholomew Steere, carpenter (1597)

Jetzt wöllen wirs gantz Landt aussziehen,
unsere aigne Herrn müssen fliehen. 1

From a song of the rebellious Austrian peasants (1626)

In order to simplify a discussion of the popular risings of the century, we shall assume that the risings fell into three principal groups — town revolts, peasant revolts and social banditry. In addition, we shall assume that it is possible to discuss all the rebellions together, even though the geographical and social conditions of eastern Europe may have meant that rebellions in that area differed greatly in character from those in the west. Finally, though there is no obvious unity about the century we have chosen, we shall argue that the dates are not completely arbitrary; and that for this purpose it is convenient to divide the century thematically in half at about the year 1600.

It is not, of course, entirely satisfactory to generalise in this way. The division between town and peasant revolts is not a very convincing one. It has led in the past to a disproportionate emphasis on peasant revolts, and a consequent neglect of urban discontent. Only in recent years has it been made plain that town and country were often closely connected, that townsmen took a remarkably active and leading part in so-called peasant risings, and that agricultural labourers were a potent force for discontent in towns. The same point can be applied to banditry, which has usually been considered a rural phenomenon. Yet though the bandits invariably operated in the countryside, they very often came from the towns themselves. Town and country cannot easily

1 Now will we sweep throughout the land, and our own lords must flee.

be divided. Those who helped to gather in the harvest in the fields in July were pacing the streets of the city in December: these, the proletariat of seasonal labourers, belonged equally to both town and country, and were the essential component that unified social movements in both.

Division of the revolts into time periods is equally unsatisfactory, for so many common factors can be found in them all that to select fixed periods is in a sense arbitrary. However a certain pattern in the frequency of revolts may be found in the fact that years of hunger were invariably years of discontent. Between 1550 and 1600 the worst food crisis experienced in Europe was in the years 1594-7, a time of great famine which caused severe hardship throughout the continent. Within this half century the peak period for popular rebellions was 1595-7. Between 1600 and 1660 the greatest food crisis was in the years 1647-9. By the same logic of circumstances, the year 1648 witnessed a continent-wide explosion of popular grievances. It is around these peak years of revolution that our survey is woven.

This does not mean that there is necessarily any causal relationship between high prices of food and the incidence of revolt. All too frequently misery simply made it impossible for the population to rise, as in the great crisis of 1660-1, which caused no stir outside Russia. Moreover too many causes intervened in a revolt for the one factor of starvation to be isolated. Sometimes uprisings occurred after the food crisis, when the people had regained their strength to protest. These qualifications, however, do not touch the visible reality of the two crisis periods of 1595-7 and 1648, which coincided with peak price levels in the century 1550-1660.

THE REVOLTS OF THE LATE SIXTEENTH CENTURY
In western Europe the years after 1550 cannot easily be isolated from the years of the *Bundschuh*, the Peasants' Revolt of 1525, the agitation in Alsace, Sweden and elsewhere. The social and religious protest which began in that early period was carried through with increasing vigour after the mid-century.

Perhaps the most significant issue unifying the peasant revolts of the late sixteenth century was that of tithes. In France the Huguenot lords and nobles had to decide whether to discourage their peasant co-religionists from paying these dues to the Catholic Church, or to urge them to pay, so as to preserve political order and social peace. When it became clear that encouragement not to pay meant encouragement to social revolution, the Huguenot leaders meeting at Nîmes in 1562 passed a resolution condemning any refusal to pay dues, and urging the punishment of all who refused as 'sowers of sedition, disturbers of public order'. The noble class closed its ranks. But so long as Protestant ideas played any part among the peasantry, refusal to pay tithes would continue. In the outbreak known as the *Rebeine* of Lyon in 1529, opposition to tithes had been an important issue. By 1560 in Languedoc the movement against tithes had far exceeded the boundaries of the Protestant party. Even Catholics were caught up in what became almost a nonsectarian social grievance. In the *Jacquerie* of Agen in 1560-1 the peasants 'are beginning in some places not to pay their tithes, and also proclaim that they will no longer pay the *tailles* (to the king) or their seigneurial dues'. The junction of an anti-tithe and anti-tax movement in this instance may appear easy to understand, if read as a general protest against all taxes; but it was not common. More frequently it was religion, and anticlericalism, that gave rise to protest against ecclesiastical tithes; so that a purely secular anti-tithe movement, of the kind that happened in Languedoc in the 1560s and 1570s, unaccompanied by any protest against other taxes, is relatively difficult to explain.

The problem of ecclesiastical (as distinct from seigneurial) tithes was universal. Even reformed Sweden suffered from it. The Lutheran clergy in the see of Stavanger complained in 1573 of 'the great hostility and disloyalty shown by the peasants every year over the tithe'. They claimed that if they ever demanded tithes in their sermons 'they were threatened by many and did not feel safe'. It was not surprising that they felt unsafe, since the Norwegian peasants in the 1570s were in revolt. The years 1570 to 1580 saw uprisings in Trondheim province, and from 1573 onwards an organised rebellion led by Rolv de Lynge was in progress. In 1574 the peasants held their own national assembly in Nidaros, at which they aired their grievances. Lynge and other leaders were executed in 1575, but the rebellion went on for several years after.

In these years the peasants of eastern Europe were no less in evidence. Hungary had several peasant rebellions in the late sixteenth century, in 1562, in 1569-70 (led by George Karacsonyi), and that of 1571-3, in Slovenia. One of the largest risings to occur on this eastern frontier of Christendom was the revolt of

the Croat peasantry in 1573. The grievances of the Croats cen-
tered on labour services and tithes. An imperial decree of 1538
had virtually deprived them of freedom of movement; at the same
time their dues were made more heavy. But their principal
complaint was against the taxation levied to support the war
against the Turks, particularly against the *dica*, a war-tax that
was levied on the peasants twenty times between 1543 and 1598.
In April 1572 a local revolt broke out and the peasants sent a
deputation to Vienna to present their grievances. When nothing
came of this, a country-wide uprising burst out in 1573, and
spread throughout Croatia and parts of Styria. At its height the
rebellion involved up to sixty thousand peasants. The basic
demand formulated by the peasants was for the return of their
'ancient rights'. But over and above this simple phrase their
demands were revolutionary: the abolition of the ecclesiastical
tithe, and reduction of seigneurial taxation. The democratic
temper of the rebels is shown by their habitual use of the term
'brotherhood' to describe themselves, and of the word 'brother' as
a form of address within the organisation. By mid-February 1573
the brief uprising had been crushed. The Emperor Maximilian,
who directed its suppression, estimated that about four thousand
Croat and Slovene peasants had been annihilated by his troops.
The leaders, Matthew Gubec and Andrew Pasanec, were tortured
and then executed in Zagreb on 14 February.

The mid-1580s were a time of bad harvests, particularly the
three years 1585-7. They were years of political crisis throughout
western Europe, accompanied by wars in France and the
Netherlands. The social crisis occurred within this framework.
Some of the more savage undertones of popular rebellion came to
the fore in these years of blood. In the town of Romans, in
Dauphiné, in the winter of 1580 a rebellious alliance was formed
between the peasants of the countryside (this was a Protestant
area) and the artisans of the town, led by a certain Jean Serve or
Paulmier. The economic difficulties of the time aggravated
discontent. Encouraged by support from the townsmen, the
peasants refused to pay their tithes and *tailles*. They armed
themselves, broke into châteaux, and threw the *terriers* (court
rolls) into the flames. In Romans the artisans and peasants
danced in the streets, threatening the rich and crying that 'before
three days Christian flesh will be sold at sixpence a pound'. This
symbolic language was directed at the upper classes of the town,
which was now taken over by a popular commune. During the

winter carnival Paulmier sat in the mayor's chair, dressed in a bear's skin, eating delicacies which passed for Christian flesh. When they had their carnival procession, the common people under Paulmier dressed themselves up as prelates and dignitaries, crying 'Christian flesh for sixpence!' Horrified by this cannibalistic disrespect, the richer classes organised their own resources. On the eve of Mardi Gras (Shrove Tuesday: 15 February 1580) they descended on their opponents and massacred them. The slaughter went on for three days. Peasants from the countryside thronged in to save the cause, but it was too late. The resort of the savage symbols of cannibalism signals an interesting development in the morphology of social revolt. The eating of human flesh, here as in other popular revolts, stood for the revolutionary overturning of social values.

In 1585 in Naples a similar but more explicit event occurred. As in Romans, there was a popular uprising, with its heart in the town rather than in the country. The immediate cause of the 1585 rising was a bad harvest and severe shortage of food. Despite famine conditions, the authorities raised the price of bread, and simultaneously authorised the export of several thousand pounds of flour to Spain. An angry mob in May thereupon lynched one of the magistrates responsible, named Starace. His body was mutilated, and pieces of his flesh were offered for sale. His body was then dragged through the streets, and his house and all his belongings were burnt and destroyed. Nothing was stolen. He was killed, and his property sacked, almost as a ritual sacrifice. The mob was concerned 'more with vengeance than with enriching itself', reported the French historian de Thou, a contemporary of these events. The murder precipitated a big revolt, whose cry was *mora il malgoverno, e viva la giustizia*'. The simplest way to measure the extent of this revolt is to see how many were punished in the inevitably brutal repression that followed. Between the middle and the end of July over eight hundred people were brought to trial. Thirty-one were condemned to death after torture, seventy-one were sent to the galleys, and three hundred were banished under pain of death. About twelve thousand people were reported to have fled the city during the repression.

Despite their fundamentally political significance, the events which occurred in Paris in 1588 are interesting as an early example of the way in which the French capital formed itself into a commune in moments of crisis. To the uncertainties and fears caused by war was added the misery of near famine after the bad

harvests of 1586 and 1587. Within Paris a group of plotters allied
to the Catholic League set up a secret council with the aim of
winning the city over to the Duke of Guise. Since the bourgeoisie
and upper classes were royalist, the Leaguers turned to the mass
of the people. When the duke arrived in the capital on 9 May
1588, the seeds of sedition had already been sown. On 12 May,
the famous 'day of barricades', a general uprising of the
population occurred in Guise's favour. 'The spirit of revolt spread
throughout Paris', reports de Thou, who was in the city that day.
'Suddenly all the streets were blocked by barricades . . . In the
evening guards were stationed in all the squares and quarters, but
when the provost wished to issue the orders of the watch in the
king's name, as usual, the rebels refused to accept them from him
and went instead to the Duke of Guise. That was the real
beginning of the revolt.' When the Guises, both duke and cardinal, were subsequently assassinated on the king's orders,
authority in the now anarchic city devolved on to a commune led
by a so-called Council of Sixteen. It was the Sixteen, in alliance
with the common people, who really controlled the city; but their
necessarily harsh methods, which relied on terror and executions,
finally led to a reaction against their rule.

The conditions of the 1590s were catastrophic. The peak year
for revolt, 1595, was also a year of extreme crisis. From 1590 to
1597 harvests were bad, production low, prices crippling. 1595
was a famine year in parts of England, in Languedoc, in Naples.
In Rome prices over the whole period 1590-9 stood at an index of
two hundred, over a base index of one hundred for the years
1570-9. There was no discontinuity with the 1580s as far as the
social crisis was concerned. In 1592, for instance, pamphlets were
being distributed in the streets of Naples, calling on the
population to revolt. These years, from 1585 to 1595, were also
the peak ones for banditry in the Mediterranean lands.

The crisis of 1595-7 was operative throughout Europe, with
repercussions in England, France, Austria, Finland, Hungary,
Lithuania and the Ukraine. Probably never before in European
history had so many popular rebellions coincided in time. The
Finnish peasant revolt occurred in 1596 and 1597. A few English
labourers in the Midlands attempted a rising in 1596, but it came
to nothing. Roger Ibill, a miller of Hampton-Gay, claimed in the
autumn of 1596 to have 'heard divers poor people say that there
must be a rising soon, because of the high price of corn'. He was
joined by Bartholomew Steere, a carpenter, who told him that

'there would be such a rising as had not been seen a great while'. Their hopes were extremely sanguine, and Steere in particular did not find enough popular support to match his revolutionary ardour. He said that 'he would cut off all the gentlemen's heads', and that 'we shall have a merrier world shortly'; he also planned 'to go to London, and be joined by the apprentices'. But though he built up a considerable following the authorities responded swiftly, arrested the leaders, and snuffed out the rising.

The great rising of the *Croquants* in France was concentrated in the years 1593-5. It started in Bas-Limousin, spread throughout Limousin, and at its widest extent covered Périgord, Quercy, Limousin and Languedoc. Originally a peasant rebellion, it became more complex in its social composition and included a large proportion of urban labourers in its ranks. The causes of the rising are easily found: the ravages of war, the depredation of the soldiery, the food crisis of the 1590s, the tax regime. What is interesting about the movement, however, is the fact that Catholics and Protestants marched side by side in a common social protest against the exploiting classes, so that religion immediately assumed a minor place in their programme. The early campaigns of the rebels, who had their own army, were led by commoners, but at a later stage they succeeded in attracting or compelling the upper classes to help them.

The main grievance of the *Croquants* was the fiscal system. They firmly opposed both tithe and *taille*, as well as seigneurial taxes. In a manifesto of March 1594 they also denounced the soldiery, both Catholic and Protestant, 'who had reduced them to starvation, violated their wives and daughters, stolen their cattle and wasted their land'; and reserved for the bourgeoisie the bitter complaint that 'they seek only the ruin of the poor people, for our ruin is their wealth'. The rebel movement was democratically organised. All religious discrimination was prohibited, and they swore 'by faith and oath to love each other and cherish each other, as God commands'. Decisions were made in general assemblies, of which the most important was held in April 1594. It is difficult to believe the accusation made against them by the nobles of Périgord that 'they wished to overthrow the monarchy and establish a democracy on the pattern of the Swiss', though a few leaders may have been as radical as this.

The programme of social justice and religious unity was one that appealed strongly to the king, Henry IV, and in the early stages of the rebellion he had not disguised his sympathy for the

Croquants; but as the rising progressed he and the authorities adopted a harsher attitude. The religious unity of the rebels proved to be their weakest point, and government agents worked to undermine this. The main assembly consisted two-thirds of Catholics and one-third of Protestants. Thanks to the diligent agents, the rebels finally in 1594 voted to split up into confessional armies. This led immediately to a disastrous defeat by government forces at Limoges. By 1594 and 1595 the movement became centred on Périgord, but military engagements were few and invariably disastrous. The famine of 1595 marked the end of the *Croquant* uprising.

None of the major aims of the rebellion was achieved, but there were a few marginal gains of some importance. The movement had been so widespread and popular that the government decided not to undertake the usual bloody repression that followed such uprisings. The reality of popular support is shown by the reaction of Limousin, where all the towns, with the notable exception of the city of Limoges, supported the rising. It had therefore been not simply a peasant rising, but a major outburst of multiple grievances, both urban and rural. The inter-confessional unity of the struggle, moreover, continued after the rebellion. In Languedoc in 1595, for instance, we have the example of the Catholic village of Caux, which banded together with the Protestant village of Faugères in a federation to protect their economic interests against all others.

Upper Austria, or Austria *ob der Enns* (beyond the River Enns), with Linz as its capital city, was the theatre of almost continuous peasant uprisings from 1525 to 1648. The great Peasant Revolt of the Reformation period was only one stage in the constant movement of discontent in central Europe. The risings throughout these years had a strong religious inspiration, in the sense that the rebels believed they were fighting for divine truth and justice. But any religious motivation that existed was invariably subordinate to secular grievances. The rising in Reichenstein from 1567 to 1572 may serve to illustrate the general pattern of the years prior to 1595. This was a small-scale rebellion, led by a Lutheran pastor and a peasant named Siegmund Gaissrucker. The main reason for the revolt was apparently an excessively heavy burden of labour services (the *Robot*). In June 1571 Gaissrucker killed the seigneur against whom the rising was directed, Christoph von Haim, and a price was put on his head. A few manor houses were burnt down, but in general the peasant leadership forbade all looting, and Gaissrucker pinned an order on Haim's castle door ordering his followers not to 'kill, burn or steal". The Lutheran leadership to the rising reflected no more than the sympathy of the lower clergy, and did not detract from the fundamental role of the *Robot*, taxes and prices as basic causes of discontent. A few other minor outbreaks occurred after this, as in Steyr in 1573, where about a thousand peasants formed themselves into a 'Peasants' Union'.

The Austrian revolt of 1594-7 was a major one, large and important enough for us to describe it, like that of 1525, as a war. It lasted for about three years, from May 1594 to September 1597. The movement was recognisably Lutheran in inspiration, since the population were of this faith, and the pastors urged the people to defend themselves against the Catholic Counter Reformation, promoted by Cardinal Khlesl in Lower Austria and by Bishop Passauski in Upper Austria from the 1580s onwards. Some of the circumstances of the rising can be seen most clearly in the contemporary reports made of it. According to de Thou, who used these reports, in 1595

> the peasants, who at the beginning of their revolt observed perfect discipline in their ranks, said that they had taken up arms only to free themselves from the unjust taxes with which the nobles oppressed them; that they were willing to submit themselves, and were not unwilling to pay the contributions levied on them for the war against the Turks.

The matter of the Turkish war was only a half-truth, for it was the imposition of war-taxation that had provoked discontent; yet it is true that the peasants objected not so much to the war-tax itself (it does not feature among their chief grievances) as to the other taxes that had made this latest one insupportable. Negotiations with the authorities were leading to a settlement, says de Thou, when

> the mutiny of the troops being used against the peasants, caused by failure to pay them, disturbed the emperor yet more. They tried to satisfy themselves by pillaging neighbouring towns, despite the efforts of General Rotenau to pacify them. The soldiers at Pressburg sacked four villages in the vicinity. The troops of the Marquis of Burgau ravaged the entire countryside. Eventually the mutineers marched on Vienna, snatched the flags from the hands of their officers, planted them on the city gate and threatened to set the suburbs on fire.

373

The excesses of the army, as well as its indiscipline, strengthened the ranks of the disaffected peasants and enabled them to continue their campaign. Urgent appeals for more troops were sent from Linz to Vienna. The Vienna correspondent of the Fuggers reported on 13 November 1595:

> There be posted up everywhere notices for the levying of troops, for the peasants are waxing ever stronger. They are said to be encamped not far from here, 40,000 strong, near the Danube. They have most stately and experienced leaders who keep strict discipline, so that much might be learned by us from them. Since all the towns in the country must needs send troops, those of Wels were but a short time ago attacked by the peasants and soundly trounced, but not killed. Only their armour and weapons were taken from them, and they were sent back.

At a later stage of the war, the Fugger correspondent in Linz, writing on 1 December 1596, remarked on the still essentially peaceful disposition of the peasants to all except government troops. Most strange of all, he reported, was the fact that 'they seem bewitched, for as soon as the word is given, even in this cold, they leave their wives and children, hasten from their houses and farms, yet attacking neither towns, castles nor even villages'.

On 8 May 1597 the emperor attempted to conciliate the rebels by issuing an Interim, in which the only real concession was that the *Robot* was officially limited to no more than fourteen days in the year. Though such was the law, and though it was officially observed even after the defeat of the peasants in September, substantial infringements soon became commonplace. In the lordship of Schwertberg, owned by Count Heinrich von Starhemberg, the *Robot* in 1660 actually amounted to over seventy-one days in the year.

Despite the Lutheran faith of both peasants and leaders in these risings, religion was not necessarily the prime driving force. The Reichenstein rebels had a pastor as leader; so too did the rebels in the bishopric of Salzburg in 1564, where Pastor Schlafheuser was the head. But in these and other risings it is difficult to consider religion as a main grievance. In 1588, to take one example, we have a popular movement which commenced in the town of Steyr, involving the lower classes from both town and country. The rebellion soon spread as far afield as Styria and Salzburg. Most of the leaders were Protestant, but in fact the movement was directed against all seigneurs irrespective of religion. It was this that led the town council of the very Protestant city of Speyer to comment: 'Many, if not most, of them use religion only as a cover. In reality they are rebelling against the authorities in order to have their burdens lightened.'

The peasant war of 1594-7 must be seen in the same light. The Catholic authorities made much of the fact that the leaders were Lutheran, but the unreality of the religious issue was shown by the firmly repressive attitude of the partly Lutheran government of Upper Austria. Moreover, an examination of the rebels' grievances, as set down in a pamphlet of 1595, shows that for them it was taxation that was the main issue. 'First', they said, 'there is the *Freigeld*.' This was a feudal tax levied when any of a dependent peasant's property was transferred, by sale, or death, or in any other way. It had not been collected, the peasants claimed, 'within human memory', but now it was being imposed and it consumed between one-third and one-half of a peasant's income. All other taxes were simultaneously being increased: 'where a peasant used to pay sixty pence, he now pays several *gulden*'. The first three complaints of the rebels were all against taxation. The fourth concerned the *Robot*: 'Many have to labour for twenty, thirty or more days, and particularly at times when they should be tilling their own soil.'

The rising in Upper Austria had repercussions in Lower Austria too. There the rebels appear to have been more aggressive than in the Linz area, and the Fuggers correspondent could report from Vienna on 15 April 1597 that 'the rebellious peasants have not as yet been pacified, and lie a few thousand strong near Melk. But many of them are being killed, hanged and made prisoners by the cavalry.' At the same time, and in the shadow of the peasants' revolt, as the correspondent informs us,

> the vintagers of Mödling, Petersdorf, Baden, Inzersdorf, Gumpoldskirchen and other places have refused to work any longer for their old wages, (and) have become rebellious. They collected about 2,000 strong, and the nobility and all landowners were commanded to gather with their horses in as great numbers as was possible. They fell upon the rebellious vintagers before daybreak and immediately hanged a drummer and six ringleaders.

The fever of social revolt in these years extended to eastern Europe as well. In 1591-3 there was a large uprising in the Ukraine under the leadership of Christopher Kosiński. It spread through the governorships of Kiev and Bratslav, and had repercussions as far as Mstislav and Minsk. Then in 1596 there was another rising in the Ukraine, led by Severin Nalivaiko; the most important achievement of this movement was that it kept the flame of disaffection alive among the peasants and disturbed the tranquillity of the three realms of Poland, Russia and the Grand Duchy of Lithuania.

To end our look at the revolutionary years 1595-7 we may make use of de Thou's account of the peasant rebellion of 1597 in Hungary:

> The peasants, oppressed by the constant passage of troops and reduced to despair by the garrisons which, on the excuse that they had not been paid, were pillaging everywhere, had already risen in Austria and suddenly revolted this year, adopting as their leader George Brunner, a man of humble origin. They were at first very restrained, and shed no blood whatsoever. They split up into three bands, to forage in houses and villages. People they met were forced to join them, and the booty they obtained in forts and other places was equally divided. Those who were found guilty of having stolen or taken something by force, were severely punished. They took the precaution of making inventories of everything, in order to reimburse the owners, if events ended in another way than that of war.
>
> Among their grievances, they complained of being crushed by taxes and reduced to slavery by the nobility, so that they were unable to meet the demands made of them, and that they could not till or sow their lands when they were claimed for other tasks. They were, above all, obliged to give to their lords one-third of all their produce. They were also, they said, exposed to pillaging by the soldiery. They added that they did not refuse to pay the taxes for the war against the Turks, and that they were ready to follow their seigneurs to the war. These grievances, which appeared to be just ones, so long as the peasants employed nothing more than petitions, became a crime against the state when they took up arms. They passed from threats to disobedience, and from revolt to violence. They forced their seigneurs to leave their homes, and put in chains men of dignity.

An army was sent against them by the emperor, and as a result some of the peasants, from southern Bohemia, deserted the cause. But the main body, drawn from the Danube lands, remained, only to suffer serious defeats, first in a battle near Gravenek and then in the village of Strassen, which the imperial commander burnt about their heads, while women and children perished in the flames. After a short lull, the peasants grouped together again, but were finally routed at Sampelka, and their leaders executed.

BANDITRY AND SOCIAL REVOLT

Popular discontent might erupt into uprisings; but it also expressed itself on a smaller scale in a resort to crime. The frequency of banditry, above all in the late sixteenth and early seventeenth centuries, was another symptom of those very conditions which could cause mass rebellions: heavy taxation, agrarian distress, class resentment. In general all banditry, both aristocratic and popular, was criminal; but it was a form of crime that rose out of political and social crisis, and out of economic disorder. Banditry did not cause crises: it was itself the result of a crisis. Viewed as crime, aristocratic and popular banditry also shared the common factor of thriving in areas usually inaccessible to the government, above all in mountainous regions and in woods.

Beyond this common ground, the two sorts of banditry differed widely. Aristocrats who operated robber bands were reverting to a purely feudal defiance of the state. This was certainly the case with the great bandit-lords of central Italy in the late sixteenth century, most notable of whom was the Duke of Montemarciano, Alfonso Piccolomini, who for thirteen years from 1578 to 1591 was the supreme head of the brigands in the Romagna. Several other distinguished nobles followed Piccolomini's precedent, not always with success: in 1587, as we have seen, when the Grand-Duke Ramberto Malatesta began to operate as a bandit the pope had him seized and executed. Piccolomini himself was hanged in Florence in 1591. So severe were the pope's measures against the bandits that 'this year', reported a Roman newsletter of September 1585, 'we have seen more heads on the Sant Angelo bridge than melons in the market'. The weakness of central authority, then, might give scope to noble criminals, who also benefited from times of war. We can find an example of this in the brigands who operated in Burgundy and Franche-Comté after the Thirty Years War. The seigneurs, reported a local curé, Macheret, in his journal, either paid the bandits money not to touch their lands, or actively allied with them: 'thus the nobility of this countryside always operates through cowardice or through treachery, and does nothing but bring us a great deal of evil'.

Popular banditry, on the other hand, tended to originate as a protest against misery, and seems to have thrived most in periods of economic crisis. Unlike rebellions, which aimed to secure nation-wide support, banditry was at its strongest when its support was purely local. The men who fled to the mountains to join the bands were usually those whose crimes, although culpable in the eyes of the state, had not received general disapprobation in the locality. It was this regional sympathy which defeated all the efforts of governments to annihilate banditry, for denunciations were almost unheard of.

Clearly the nature of banditry could differ greatly according to time and place. In the Reformation period, there were Protestant brigands operating in the Pyrenees; in Catalonia, the activities of the bands might reflect their sympathy with one of the principality's political factions. Despite variations in religion and politics, however, the social significance of the bandits was generally the same. They were localised popular movements which were often the vehicle of social protest. Because of their local nature, however, and because of their primarily criminal activities, they were never significant as a socially revolutionary force.

In western Europe the mountainous regions of central France and the Pyrenees were prominent in the sixteenth century as centres of banditry. When Charles Estienne published his *Guide des Chemins de France* in the mid-sixteenth century, he took care to list some of the roads that were infested by brigands, but no information on their activity has come down to us. Catalan banditry south of the Pyrenees is better known, and has a considerable literature. The peak period for activity here was in the reign of Philip III (1598-1621). It was under this king that the most famous of all the Catalan bandits, Perot Rocaguinarda, began his career in 1602. Much of his fame derives from the appearance he makes in Cervantes' *Don Quixote*. Some guide to his support, at least in ecclesiastical circles, is given by a diarist of his day who reported that 'Rocaguinarda was the most courteous bandit to have been in that region for many years: never did he dishonour or touch the churches, and God aided him'. He ended his career in what became a traditional way, accepting the pardon of the viceroy in 1611 and going overseas to Italy to serve with the troops.

As in Catalonia, the Italian bandits emerged from an agrarian background, and periods of agrarian crisis seemed to provoke further bandit activity. The critical years of the 1580s, followed by a harvest crisis in 1590-1, initiated widespread disturbances. The year 1590 witnessed peasant agitation, with the peasants refusing to make deliveries of produce because there was only enough food for themselves. This led to clashes with the civil

378

authorities. At the same time there was a refusal to pay tithes, which caused trouble with the Church. A Roman newsletter that year reported incidents in the Romagna, where 'numerous peasants have joined the bandits, and commit murders publicly in the streets'. The resurgence of banditry was obviously part and parcel of an agrarian revolt. And one of the most prominent bandit leaders to reflect this revolt was Marco Sciarra.

Sciarra, a native of Castiglione, had been a bandit since 1584-5, when he emerged as the leader of a group which had its headquarters in the Abruzzi. For nearly seven years this group operated in the Marches, Romagna and contiguous regions. His activities were viewed as an anti-Spanish revolt, which helped to bring him popularity. More significant, however, was the fact that he really practised that redistribution of wealth which is the classic hallmark of the 'Robin Hood' type of bandit. He was loved by the poor of Naples 'who used to say', reports a contemporary, 'that he would soon come to occupy Naples, and make himself king'. Even respectable citizens came to look on him as a sort of national hero. Around Rome the countryside was virtually under his control, as the bandits held courts, created magistrates and carried out marriages. Sciarra's decline began in 1592 when he offered his services to the Republic of Venice. Strong papal protests led Venice to betray him to the troops. He escaped but was eventually murdered, by a former friend and companion, in 1593. Sciarra's career exhibits most of the essential characteristics of popular banditry: strong popular support, the cult of the hero, some redistribution of stolen wealth to the poor, the choice of mercenary service as an alternative to punishment, and the final betrayal by former friends.

After 1595 and 1596 the luck of the bandits in Italy began to turn. Capture and assassination robbed them of many of their leaders, and the outbreak of wars in Hungary and elsewhere gave them more gainful employment. Most important of all, necessity forced them to begin robbing the peasants. This alienated the peasantry, whose return to peaceful ways was assured by good harvests in 1597 and 1598. If banditry had at one time seemed likely to emerge as the vanguard of rural agitation, it lost the initiative after the mid-1590s. The cost in lives seems to have been high, if we accept the report of the Venetian ambassador to Rome in 1595 that 'since the death of Sixtus V (1590) up till now, more than five thousand people have died violent deaths in the states of the Church, including those condemned to death as well as those killed by the bandits'.

The combination of peasant agitation and banditry can be seen again in early seventeenth-century France, where the regularity of popular uprisings, particularly under the regime of Cardinal Richelieu, gave ample scope to rebels. In Périgord at this period, the principal bandit was Pierre Grellety. After the collapse of the big uprising led by La Mothe La Forêt, some of the Périgord peasants in the area known as the Paréage continued their agitation and offered the leadership of their movement to Grellety. He accepted the role, and continued the struggle from a base in the woods of Périgord. Their main victims were rich merchants travelling through the forest. This combination of social revolt and banditry was extremely successful. Grellety was never caught and eventually in 1642, in the now accepted way, took up a military commission to serve in Italy, which Richelieu had offered him.

The Spanish bandits of this period operated not only in Catalonia but also in Valencia, Murcia and Castile. Their lives displayed a curious mixture of crime and charity, religion and impiety, the very combination of opposites that made social banditry a unique phenomenon. One bandit of the time of Philip II, for instance, was called *el caballero de la Cruz,* because he always left a crucifix on the graves of his victims. Most bandits wore medals and scapulars around their neck, and practised the official religion; but they also drew on a wealth of superstition, and were known to recite prayers to make themselves invisible to their pursuers. Women were sometimes leaders of the bandit groups, as happened in Granada.

The mountainous areas of the kingdoms of Andalucia, Murcia and Valencia were a favourite area for brigandage, and continued to be so throughout the seventeenth century. One of the more curious groups active in the early half of the century in Andalucia chose to operate in the sierra de Cabrilla. They dressed in every way as gentlemen, were always kind and courteous to their victims, and robbed them of only half their goods: this charitable form of property redistribution earned them the title of *los beatos de Cabrilla*—the holy ones of Cabrilla. But Castile also had its share of bandits. The contemporary diarist Pellicer refers in 1644 to two popular brigands of the time, one named Salgado, who was eventually executed in Valladolid, and one named Pedro Andreu (after another bandit of the same name who had operated in Murcia). This pseudo-Andreu, reported Pellicer at the date 2 April 1644, roams across La Mancha and around Ocaña. Some say he has thirty horsemen, others put it at eighty. There are curious stories about him, such as that he never kills anyone but only takes part of their money, leaving them with enough to continue their journey; that he borrows money from villages and from individuals, giving his word as a pledge, and is punctual in payment.

In Spain, Italy, and France, the countries we have touched upon briefly, banditry and brigandage was a permanent phenomenon only in the mountainous areas where the outlaws could defend themselves and draw almost uninterruptedly on their support in the villages and towns. In the open country of La Mancha it was no more than a temporary, passing phase, a reflection of bad times which soon passed. In eastern Europe, however, banditry was far less dependent on geography, and became a wholly permanent feature of the social troubles of the period.

It was the Russian state and its frontiers that were the principal victims of brigandage in the east. There were two main reasons for this. In the first place, many of the bands were tribal and racial groups which were actively at war against the Tsar of Muscovy. The Tatars sustained themselves partly by attacks on the Russians, and this was even more true of the Cossacks. All the major peasants' revolts in the Russian lands, in Lithuania and in the Ukraine in this period were made possible only because of the active help of the Cossacks. With the military aid given by the remarkably effective forces of the brigands, the peasants were able to exploit successfully the strength that their numbers gave them. In this way banditry became an essential arm of agrarian revolt, and the bandits in turn were accepted as defenders of the people, heroes of a popular tradition that persisted down through Russian history. The second reason for the strength of banditry was the chaos caused in Muscovy by the growth of feudalism and the bitter internal struggles of the period. The breakdown of order during the Time of Troubles, for instance was particularly fruitful in promoting brigandage; the schism in the Russian Church likewise drove many clergy and others to the same occupation. Peasants fleeing from heavier feudal obligations were perhaps the largest single group of people to swell the growth of banditry. Serfs attempted to escape entirely from their seigneurs by going southwards or eastwards: when this exile appeared unappealing, they stayed close enough to Russian civilisation to be able to live off it by plunder. Others who, like the serfs, were also victims of society, helped to make up the robber bands.

In the popular estimation, the work of the bandits was a form of social justice, since their principal victims were merchants and other rich travellers, government officials and tax-collectors. Often secure in their forests, the bandits would emerge in groups that were sometimes over a hundred strong, marauding on the estates of local landowners. In the songs, the *bylini*, that were devoted to their deeds, they emerged as folk heroes whose work to redress the evils of the time earned them legendary status. In these songs the bandit leaders are presented as invincible servants of justice, with miraculous powers such as the ability to hurl back bullets.

> Once, many years ago, brothers, long ages since, ages ago
> under the ancient tsars, evil times came upon us . . .
> Then was Russia given over to evil hands,
> To evil hands, to the boyar lords.

In this recital of the Time of Troubles, it was the noble class who were looked upon as the bringers of evil. The one hero of this epoch, on the other hand, was the famous mid-sixteenth century bandit leader Yermak, whose exploits were so famous that he was eventually pardoned by the Tsar and allowed to go and lead an ill-fated Russian expedition into Siberia. In Russian, as in the Mediterranean lands, an essentially criminal class thus assumed the task of social protest; a protest that was never intended to be revolutionary but which in occasional instances, as in the Bolotnikov rising, considerably furthered the aims of the leaders of popular revolt.

THE REVOLTS OF THE EARLY SEVENTEENTH CENTURY

The transition from the sixteenth to the seventeenth century was not a peaceful one. Upper Austria was, as usual, in a continuous ferment: in Pyhrn there were commotions from 1598 to 1616, in Steyr there was an incident in 1601, in Wildeneck there was a state of emergency that lasted from 1601 right through to 1662. In German territory, Allgäu from 1596 onwards saw a minor peasant struggle, and from 1605-7 the bishopric of Augsburg suffered several peasant uprisings. The first years of the century also brought the spectre of famine. In Russia there was an unimaginable famine from 1601 to 1603, and continuous misery in the couple of years after this. From 1603 to 1605 there were risings of the bonded serfs on a widespread rather than a numerically large scale. The civil disturbances were so significant that a wide area of townships had to be visited by the tsar's *voevodes* in an effort at pacification. They were sent out specifically 'against robbers' rather than rebels, which emphasises the interaction betweeen banditry and peasant discontent. For the year 1604 de Thou had this report in his *Historiae sui temporis:* 'At that time there was a horrible famine that raged in Transylvania and forced the people to eat what was not meant as human food. When even that had been consumed, they ate human flesh. . . . This year was sterile everywhere. . . . Sicily was threatened by famine. . . . In France there was also a great grain shortage in Languedoc and in Provence.'

There was some improvement in the years after this, but particular conditions in several countries still combined to make 1607 a year of rebellion. In England it was the year of the Midlands revolt. Stow's *Annals* (1631) gives the following account:

> About the middle of this month of May 1607 a great number of common persons suddenly assembled themselves in Northamptonshire, and then others of like nature assembled themselves in Warwickshire, and some in Leicestershire. They violently cut and brake down hedges, filled up ditches, and laid open all such enclosures of commons and other grounds as they found enclosed. . . . These tumultuous persons grew very strong, being in some places of men, women and children a thousand together, and at Hill Norton in Warwickshire there were 3,000, and at Cottebich there assembled of men, women and children to the number of full 5,000.

We have the cause of the rising stated specifically by rioters who assured Justices of the Peace that their revolt was not against the king, 'but only for reformation of those late inclosures, which made them of ye porest sorte reddy to pyne for want'. The leader was named John Reynolds, but called Captain Pouch 'because of a great leather pouch which he wore by his side'. Enclosures seem to have been the principal grievance, and now for the first time the terms 'leveller' and 'digger' appeared in England, in this agrarian context. The 'levellers' were simply those who levelled down enclosures, without any hint at a radical social doctrine. They were none the less ferociously repressed. The Earl of Shrewsbury reported at the time that 'one thousand of these fellowes who term themselves levellers were busily digging, but were furnished with many half-pikes, pyked staves, long bills, and bowes and arrows and stones . . . there were slaine some 40 or

50 of them and a verie great number hurt'. The 'diggers' appeared in a well-known petition addressed in this year from *The Diggers of Warwickshire to all other Diggers*. Contemporary opinion was notably unsympathetic to these agitators. Preaching at Northampton in June 1607, after the suppression of the revolt, a parson claimed that 'they professe nothing, but to throwe downe enclosures, though that were indeed no part of common powre; but afterward they will reckon for other matters. They will acompt with Clergiemen, and counsell is given to kill up Gentlemen, and they will levell all states as they levelled bankes and ditches, and some of them boasted, that now they hoped to worke no more.'

In the late spring of 1607 a large revolt broke out in eastern Hungary. This was composed principally of the Haiducks (renegade peasant bandits), who by November numbered about twenty thousand and were joined by large forces of serfs. The Haiduck uprising, though interesting in itself (it had a definite anti-seigneur motivation, and one prelate complained that the rebels 'wished to drive all the nobles into slavery'), was merely part of a wider struggle being undertaken by all sections of the Hungarian nation against the Habsburgs and against German influence. The years 1604 to 1608 in Hungary witnessed a vast tide of revolt, led chiefly by Stephen Bocskay. Popular rebellion became a useful adjunct to the national struggle.

It was in Russia that the most important rebellion of these years occurred. The Bolotnikov uprising of 1606-7 was the biggest ever to occur in Russian history before modern times. It was the biggest because, both in terms of the territory involved and the number of men participating, it exceeded in size the risings of Stenka Razin and of Pugachev; and, even more than these two famous rebellions, it threatened to overturn the Russian state. Of the many burdens that drove the Russian peasant to revolt the most important was the steadily growing weight of labour services and the corresponding economic depression of the rural classes. The legislation of personal servitude seemed imminent, particularly with the decrees of 1581 and 1597, which forbade peasants to move from their lord's land. Though the government periodically restored the right to move, the trend was towards a great limitation of freedom. The economic woes of the peasants were aggravated further by the ruin caused initially by the *oprichnina* and then by the notorious Time of Troubles. But the decisive factor was the great famine of 1601-3, one of the worst in

384

Russian history. 'They were many who died of hunger', reported a contemporary, 'some ate carrion and cats, and people ate people; and there were many dead along the roads and streets.' Despite a decree of 1601 issued by Tsar Boris Godunov against speculators, the price of bread rose tenfold in Moscow. A report drawn up during the famine claimed (with undoubted exaggeration) that in Moscow's three main cemeteries 127,000 people had been buried within the space of twenty-eight months. During these years of disaster mass flights of the peasants occurred. But many soon realised that in a stricken country there was nowhere they could flee. Those who remained accepted new terms of service which involved even more onerous servitude and actual slavery (*kholopstvo*). The famine gave rise to one rebellion, that led by the peasant Khlopko in 1603; he was defeated and executed.

The Bolotnikov uprising of 1606-7 occurred after the beginning of another struggle, a dynastic one, between Tsar Boris Godunov and the pretender, the pseudo-Dmitri. From 1604 a young man claiming to be the true heir to the throne (the real Dmitri had in fact died in mysterious circumstances in 1591) led a vast rebellion supported by Cossacks, boyars and Poles against Godunov. After Godunov's death in 1605 the pseudo-Dmitri succeeded in obtaining the throne, but managed to alienate the boyars of Moscow to such an extent that in May 1606 he was assassinated and his place taken by the boyar prince Basil Ivanovich Shuisky. Shuisky's election in its turn provoked widespread opposition in Muscovy. Boyar armies prepared to march on Moscow. The core of their support was the peasant movement led by Bolotnikov.

Bolotnikov was a former slave *(kholop)* who had fled from his master to the Cossacks. He was captured from them by the Turks, made a galley-slave, was freed by German sailors, taken to Venice, then returned through Germany and Poland to Russia. A man of this calibre was clearly no ordinary slave. Identifying himself with the opposition to the tsar, he became allied to the noble party and made it his task to unite the popular masses.

The main body of the rebel peasants came from the area to the south-west of Moscow: they were drawn from all the estates, monastic and noble, and included both free peasants and *kholopy*. The lower classes from the towns also contributed to the movement. This mass rising of thousands of peasants was made possible to some extent by the political chaos in Muscovy, but there was another factor which strengthened it, and this was the support of the Cossacks from the south of Russia. The military forces of the rebels were in three sections: there was the main peasant rebellion under Bolotnikov, a largely Cossack army from Astrakhan with a new pretender to the throne, the 'tsarevich Peter', and the principal noble army under a member of the gentry, Pashkov. The main purpose of these forces was to occupy Moscow. This could not fail to be the peasant aim, since their hope for freedom was seen to lie only in the will of the father of the people, the tsar. By October 1606 the rebels were under the walls of Moscow. It was then that the profound differences in the policies of the rebels came out into the open. Terrified by the implications of the social struggle for which Bolotnikov was calling, Pashkov went over to Shuisky, and Bolotnikov was forced to withdraw from Moscow after an initial defeat. In the spring of 1607 Bolotnikov and his forces found themselves trapped in the fortress town of Tula. After a lengthy and cruel siege, Tula capitulated in October. Bolotnikov was captured and executed.

The defection of Pashkov had been proof that Bolotnikov's movement was not part of another quarrel among the lords, but a dangerous popular rebellion in its own right. As the historian of the rising, Smirnov, points out, 'the central point of the Bolotnikov uprising, its principal slogan, with which the uprising proceeded, was the annihilation of peasant relationships and the liquidation of feudal oppression'. The complete devotion of the peasants to their tsar, and their constant demand for the restoration of ancient rights, were in complete accord with their revolutionary aims. By appealing direct to the tsar they rejected the system of ranks and personal servitude which gave complete power over a peasant to his seigneur and to none other. By demanding ancient rights they in effect demanded the abolition of all the onerous burdens imposed on them within living memory. The redistribution of the landed estates among the peasantry was one essential feature of Bolotnikov's programme. Moreover there was no doubt that for his followers the enemy was the nobility. When Bolotnikov was besieging Moscow, he 'writt letters to the slaves within the towne, to take armes against their masters and to possesse themselves of their goodes and substance, the feare of whome was almost as great, as it was of the enimie abroad'. In this contemporary English account the threat of social revolution was grimly posed by Bolotnikov.

The next decade in Europe was comparatively peaceful, but the agrarian crisis of the early 1620s provoked a new wave of risings.

In central Europe the rural classes were in addition cursed by the visitation of war, a war that was to last, with few interruptions, for thirty years. Already in 1620 there were scattered revolts; in Naples 'the city witnessed numerous and continuous riots and risings among the populace'. In Austria the peasants rose but Tilly, at the head of an imperialist army of thirty thousand troops, crossed over and suppressed it.

It was not until 1626 that there occurred in Upper Austria what was to be the biggest uprising of the entire war period. It was certainly the largest to have occurred anywhere in central Europe since 1525, and deserves to be described as a 'war' rather than a mere revolt.

The noble class played an important part in the rebellion. Nearly all the nobility of Upper Austria were Lutheran, and their religion was guaranteed by the emperor. But precisely in the early seventeenth century the *Land ob der Enns* was put under Bavarian administration, and a Catholic reaction took place. In 1624 the exercise of the Protestant religion in Upper Austria was prohibited by decree, a perfectly permissible procedure in view of the commonly accepted rule of *cuius regio eius religio*. The introduction of the old faith was inevitably put through by force, with the result that several of the bourgeoisie and nobility of the region, including the Count of Ortenburg and the Freiherr von Zinzendorf, began to plot rebellion. In 1626 the Catholic authorities in Linz began a house to house collection of Protestant books, and in four days managed to fill twenty wagons full. Protestant piety, which relied entirely on books such as the Bible, was outraged.

This religious background to the events of 1626 is essential to any survey of the rising, since the first and most important demand of the peasants was for freedom of religion. As the Emperor Ferdinand was to observe after the rising of 1632: 'this and all preceding rebellions have been caused by the non-Catholic peasants on account of their so-called Confession'. The order of priority of the rebels' demands is shown in the letter they sent to the emperor in July 1626: here religion came first; then the peasants protested against death duties and other taxes and services, and finally against the excesses of the soldiery. The rebels also expressed a great deal of hostility to foreigners, whom they accused of entering the country to occupy lands vacated by refugees who had fled abroad because of religion. Peasants and nobles were not the only participants in the movement, which numbered thousands of urban workers and artisans and even included sailors from the ships that plied the Danube. In such a mass uprising all parties and opinions took part, and despite the Lutheran character of the leaders there were thousands of Catholic peasants in their ranks, and both Catholics and Protestants entered into formal leagues. The Evangelical Union, not surprisingly, condemned the rebellion.

The revolt began in May 1626 when the peasants along the Danube were rallied together by their two principal leaders, Stefan Fadinger and Christoph Zeller. As the movement grew, the dissident nobility came forward to volunteer their services, and in fact the many successes of the rebel armies can be attributed to nothing else but this noble leadership of the military campaigns. The peasants waged a full-scale war against the imperial armies, laying siege to several towns and at one stage besieging Linz itself. It was during this siege that Fadinger was killed. He was the true inspiration of the rising, a folk hero whose memory remained for centuries among the people of Upper Austria. His place as leader was taken by a nobleman, Achaz Willinger. By spring 1627 the rebellion was over: on 26 March Willinger and nine other leaders were executed. After Easter another twenty were also executed. Despite the participation of several nobles in the rising only one, Willinger, was hanged. No such mercy was shown to the common people. By the end of the war over twelve thousand peasants had been killed, and numberless others crippled or driven into exile.

The 1626 peasant war was widely publicised throughout the German lands. News-sheets and pamphlets about it (and against it) were issued in Linz, Augsburg, Frankfurt, Vienna and other cities. From a Vienna news-sheet of 8 July 1626, for instance, we learn that 'the peasants have written to the seigneurs, knights and nobles who have their estates in the *Land ob der Enns*, warning them to come to their support, or they will sack and burn their estates'. The peasants themselves had their own publicity, in the form of songs which they sang when they marched or when they rested, songs which expressed more clearly than anything else what they were fighting for. The most famous of these songs was their theme song, the *Baurenlied* or *Fadingerlied*. It consisted of fifty-five stanzas, each stanza with fourteen lines. Verse after verse celebrated the end of the old order, the destruction of lords and priests, and the emergence of the peasant as master:

> *Das gantz Landt muss sich bekehren,*
> *weil wir Bawrn jetzt werdn Herrn,*
> *können wol sitzen im Schatten.* 1

The day of clerical tyranny was over:

> *Die Pfaffen sollen ihre Clöster lassen,*
> *die Bawrn seyndt jetzundt Herrn.* 2

The land had passed from the seigneurs to the peasants:

> *Jetz wöllen wirs gantz Landt aussziehen,*
> *unsere aigne Herrn müssen fliehen.* 3

Among the peasants at this time was a Lutheran preacher known as the Student Casparus. In November 1626 he composed and sent out from the rebel camp a set of verses which sums up in eight lines what the struggle was about:

> *Der Jesuiter Gleissnerei*
> *Und des Statthalters Tyrannei,*
> *Des Vicedomes Dieberei*
> *Und der Amtleut Finanzerei*
> *Darzu der schwere G'wissenszwang,*
> *Der Auflagn unerschwinglich Drang:*
> *Die habn gemacht in diesem Land*
> *Unter der Baurschaft den Aufstand.* 4

The end of the rising led to Catholicisation of the territory. On 20 May 1627 an imperial patent gave the ruling classes a choice between conforming within three months, or exile. Many thousands of Austrians left their homeland, but the vast majority conformed. Among the exiles were many of the leaders of the 1626 rising, such as pastor Jacob Greimbl, who fled to Prague, and the miller Caspar Weinbuch, who fled to Bavaria.

The years 1628 to 1631 in the western provinces of England witnessed what has been described as the 'largest single outbreak of popular discontent in the thirty-five years preceding the civil war'. These revolts occurred in scattered areas in Gillingham forest (Dorset), Braydon forest (Wiltshire) and in the forest of Dean. What gave the various outbreaks their unity was the leadership of the mysterious 'Lady Skimmington', a pseudonym which seems to have been used by distinct individual leaders but in particular by a certain John Williams. The chief complaint was

1 The whole country must be overturned, for we peasants are now to be the lords, it is we who will sit in the shade.

2 The priests must quit their cloisters, for the peasants are now the masters.

3 Now will we sweep throughout the land, and our own lords must flee.

4 The duplicity of the Jesuits, the tyranny of the regent, thieving by the governor and swindling by officials, severe oppression of conscience and the excessive weight of taxation: it is these that have brought about in this country the uprising of the peasantry.

directed against enclosures, which the rioters pulled down by force. The number of rebels was not negligible: we are told that eighteen townships of the area entered into a confederation and the strength of the rebels was put at over a thousand armed men. What worried the authorities even more were reports that the rioters had 'received private encouragement from some gentleman of quality', and that one clergyman, the curate of Newland, Peter Simon, had encouraged them with words 'constructed as if spoken in maintenance of the doctrine of the equality of all Mankind'.

In Hungary this period is notable for a rising of the peasantry in 1631 and 1632. It is to Upper Austria, however, that we must turn again for the next large rebellion. There in August 1632 a revolt broke out under Jacob Greimbl, who came back under the Protestant banner with several other anti-Catholic zealots, and with the promise of support from Gustav Adolf himself. The rising collapsed and Greimbl was executed in the main square of Linz in February 1633. Another rising in Machland from 1634 to 1636 under a religious enthusiast called Martin Laimbauer led to the execution of nine leaders at Linz in June 1636. The spirit of 1626 was still not crushed, and in the winter of 1633-4 the biggest uprising to take place on German territory during the Thirty Years War occurred in Upper Bavaria, in the Benediktbeuren area, between the rivers Isar and Inn. The leader was the 1626 refugee, Weinbuch. About ten thousand peasants were supposed to have participated, and the rising was eventually put down by the troops of both sides, imperialist and Spanish as well as Swedish.

Of all the areas that suffered popular rebellions during the critical years of the early seventeenth century, we know most about France. The period of the most important rebellions was that which began in about 1630 and led up to the Fronde. The date is not an arbitrary one, for it marks the beginning of Richelieu's harsh fiscal policy, by which he hoped to finance France's foreign commitments, both diplomatic and military, through heavier internal taxation. In all the uprisings of this period, the first and most important grievance of the disaffected was against taxes. This was the one issue that united the various forces — peasantry, townspeople, sometimes the bourgeois and nobility — within the rebel movements.

Between the beginning of the reign of Louis XIII and the outbreak of the Fronde there were four main waves of revolt: in the Quercy region in 1624, in several provinces of the southwest in 1636-7, in Normandy in 1639, and in areas of the south, west and north in 1643-5. By their nature urban revolts were more frequent (and briefer) than rural revolts; they can be found in many large towns and cities for every year from 1623 to 1647. The confined space of a town, where people lived in close contact with each other, enabled relatively minor incidents to reach flashpoint more readily than in the open atmosphere of a rural community. There could not be any clear distinction between urban and rural revolts, since the two invariably overlapped, and uprisings that ended as peasant revolts began in the towns.

The nature of the French risings can be illustrated by looking at the two largest outbreaks, that of the *Croquants* in 1636, and the Norman revolt of 1639. The date 1636 helps to explain popular discontent, for this was the year after the entry of France into the Thirty Years War, and the correspondence of government officials in the provinces (above all in Burgundy and Picardy) reported widespread misery and anger caused by the plague, by poor harvests and by the passage of troops. The authorities were concerned about the possibility of revolt. Already in 1635 there had been a series of uprisings in the cities of the south, notably in Agen. The peasant revolt broke out in May 1636 and was crushed only in November 1637. It came to cover so wide an area—most of the territory between the Garonne and the Loire, an area approximating to one-fourth of France — that it may well be regarded as the biggest peasant rising in French history. It was not a unified, organised revolt, but consisted of the sporadic activity of numbers of wandering bands. The first explosion was in the city of Angoulême and its region, where a massacre of royal tax-agents occurred. In one town, twelve tax officials were murdered, and one (in Saintonge) was cut to pieces while alive. The uprising became so great and widespread that only a royal army could have crushed it, as one of the intendants reported to Richelieu. But the army was occupied elsewhere, in defending France's frontiers, so the government was obliged to arrive at a compromise. In August 1636 the governor and the intendant of Angoulême opened talks with the rebels. Several tax concessions were made, which pacified the rising for the winter. In spring it broke out again, largely provoked by the fact that the intendant had used troops to help him collect taxes. The new centre of the rising became Périgord. There nearly sixty thousand peasants had in 1636 taken up arms, killed the tax-collectors and cried,

' *Vive le Roi sans la gabelle! Vive le Roi sans la taille!* ' The leader of the movement and ultimately of the greater part of the *Croquants*, was a nobleman named La Mothe La Forêt. In the summer of 1637 the movement of military repression started. The Duke of La Valette, son of the governor-general of Guyenne, caught the peasants in the town of Eymet and left over a thousand dead on the ground. By November further action had crushed all but isolated groups of *Croquants*.

Normandy, where the *Nu-Pieds* rebellion broke out, was one of the most heavily taxed provinces in France. Sully once boasted to the English ambassador that the king drew as many taxes from Normandy as from all the other provinces together. Under Richelieu's fiscal regime, the complaints of the estates of Normandy against the burden of *tailles* and *gabelles* went unrelieved. In 1638 the estates were told that circumstances made relief impossible. A rumour in 1639 that the tax on salt, one of Normandy's chief products, was to be raised, proved to be the last straw. In July 1639 an officer named Poupinel arriving in the town of Avranches on some other business was mistaken for a *gabeleur*, and gravely wounded during a riot created by the salt-producers. A few days after Poupinel's death a sheet of verse was found fixed to his tomb. The last stanza ran:

> *Si quelque partisan s'arreste*
> *Pour s'en informer plus avant*
> *Di luy que* Jean Nuds piedz *s'appreste*
> *Pour luy en faire tout autant.*[1]

The personage behind the verse, and the brains behind the subsequent revolt, was a priest named Jean Morel. One of the reasons given for the choice of the pseudonym *Jean Nu-Pieds* was that the taxes of the government had reduced the people to barefoot beggary. Unlike the *Croquants*, the rebellious Normans were well organised. The peasants were formed into an army, called the Army of Suffering — *armee de souffrance*, and at their head went General *Nu-Pieds*. Other leaders gave themselves appropriate officer ranks within the army. The growth of the movement is described as follows in one of the papers of the Chancellor of France, Seguier:

At first they were only a few people of no consequence, and easy to disperse. Bit by bit, however, they grew through the connivance of the

1 If any tax-collector *(partisan)* should stop in order to find out more, tell him that Jean Nu-Pieds is ready to do as much to him.

392

upper classes and the great mobs of common people, till finally they formed a body of five to six thousand well-armed men, and from this they spread throughout the province. Pontorson was the first town to welcome them, Coutance supplied them with men and money. Vire strengthened their numbers, Bayeux aided them and Caen put up with them. The entire countryside subsidised them cheerfully.

The rebels did not act as mere rebels. They set themselves up as an alternative authority to the central government. They took over the whole region, and taxes had to be paid to them in order to support the army. Decrees that ended with a royal or noble style ('given in our camp, the calends of August, and sealed with the seal of our arms, by my lord, (signed) *Nu-Pieds'*) were issued by the army leaders. At the same time, extensive propaganda was carried on to persuade the people that *Nu-Pieds* had come to restore them their liberties.

The above quotation from Séguier shows the close alliance between town and country in the revolt, and the peasants would have been isolated without urban support. Both Caen and Rouen had popular riots which put them for a while under rebel control. The agitation extended much farther than Normandy. There were echoes as far as Poitou, Provence and Languedoc. In Poitiers the leader of the revolt titled himself *Va-nu-jambes.* The Norman uprising was ended in 1640 by bringing over troops from Picardy. The first step was to isolate and crush the revolt in Caen, where the leader, known as *Bras-nu,* was executed and quartered along with his comrades. Next the royal troops met the central force of the *Nu-Pieds* by Avranches and annihilated them, killing most of the leaders. There were not many executions, for there was a shortage of labour for the galleys, to which the prisoners were duly sent.

The urban revolts of the period possess some interesting features. That in Agen occurred as a reaction against the royal victory over a previous revolt in Bordeaux. Public hatred of the *gabelle,* and in general of all taxes, led in June 1635 to a riot which the few troops in the town were unable to repress. Women played a peculiarly outstanding part in the events. An officer of the guard who clashed with the people and was about to be murdered, begged permission to confess himself first, fled into the church and out by the back, was seized again, had both his hands cut off and was dragged through the streets by his legs. The crowd shouted, *'Vive le Roi sans la gabelle!'* Ceremonial mutilation of the crudest sort was practised by women on other

393

victims. In one case a man, already dead, had his eyes torn out by a woman, 'who put them in a handkerchief and took them home'. In another, a woman cut off the private parts of a victim and fed them to a dog: she was later hanged for this crime, together with her innocent son; blood for blood, the ancient pattern of justice. The revolt in Montpellier in 1645, to take another urban rising, was also led by women, allegedly protecting their children against starvation. On this occasion riots were provoked by the killing of an old man by musket fire. The subsequent riots grew into an anti-tax movement, helped by the local peasantry. Though taxes were the main grievance, rioters did not limit their activity to this, but vented their hatred also on the upper classes. In Narbonne the common people in their disrespect of the nobility referred to them as *jean-fesses*, jack-arses.

One of the most controversial aspects of the French revolts is the part played by upper-class leaders, who often fomented and even led the risings. In so far as the rebels were objecting principally to taxation, it is easy to understand why they should have been so encouraged by their betters. The extensive revolt in Languedoc in 1632 was led expressly by the great nobles and bishops. Nobles were in any case the natural leaders, and it took a nobleman, Antoine du Puy de la Mothe, seigneur of La Foret, to mould the *Croquants* of 1636 into a well-organised army. If the nobles objected strongly to heavier royal taxation of the peasants, it was for one reason: peasants who paid their royal taxes in full would have little left to pay for seigneurial dues. The presence of noble leaders, in any case, often helps to explain the limited social aims of the peasantry. La Mothe La Forêt was accused of betraying the cause by a large proportion of his followers, and it is true that he expressly excluded from the list of peasant grievances any which were not purely fiscal. This was the price the rebels had to pay for efficient leadership.

In England one of the most interesting by-products of the civil war was the rise of a widespread popular movement whose only aim was to resist the excesses of the soldiery. The Clubmen, as they were called, consisted for the most part of peasantry who, because of the division of parties in the country, could identify themselves with no one side but opposed either or both vigorously, depending on whose army proved the more unpopular. The great year of their activity was 1645, when they first made an appearance in the West Country. In March the governor of Poole (Dorset) reported that 'there are in our country near one thousand countrymen gotten into a body with guns and clubs to resist the French and Irish among the Cavaliers'. Later that month the contemporary Whitelock reported that 'divers Clubmen were up in several counties, and four thousand of them armed in Dorsetshire threatened to plunder all who did not join with them to extirpate the Cavaliers'. When the parliamentary troops came that way, however, they received the same welcome. A report of July 1645 states that:

> Some officers and others of the (Fairfax's parliamentary) army who went out of the way through Salisbury, found the townsmen very peremptory, being confident of their own strength, by their association with other counties in their meetings of Clubmen, wearing white ribands in their hats (as it were in affront of the army) not sparing to declare themselves absolute neuters.

When not neutral, they could be anti-Parliament. Whitelock reported on 3 July that 'between four and five thousand Clubmen being up in Dorsetshire and Wilts carried themselves very tumultuously and forced the Parliament's quarters at Sturminster; divers slain and wounded on both sides'. Not surprisingly both royalists and parliamentarians were opposed to the Clubmen. An engagement round Sherborne Castle on 2 August 1645 led to the capture by Fairfax of all the principal leaders of the Clubmen. When the Clubmen in return planned a massive rendezvous to rescue their leaders Cromwell intervened with force and routed their forces, which numbered about two thousand. Despite sporadic appearances later, in 1647, this was the end of the movement.

The Clubmen were not an insignificant group. The grand rendezvous of Wilts and Dorset farmers and yeomen at Gorehedge Corner on 25 May 1645 numbered over four thousand people. Moreover, at this meeting the Clubmen planned a system of community protection which was to operate in both towns and countryside. 'We know our strength to be such,' one of their leaders claimed, 'that we are able both against king and parliament to defend ourselves, and to do more if need require.' All their recorded meetings included several thousands: in Somerset in June that year, for example, nearly six thousand assembled to approve a petition against the 'oppression, rapine and violence exercised by Lord Goring's horse'. Movements in other parts of the country copied their methods and borrowed their name: in Cardiff in August there was a meeting of about two thousand, in Chichester in September one of about a thousand, but in both cases the Clubmen were largely pro-royalist. The name 'Clubmen' appears to have derived from the fact that members were usually armed with clubs and pitchforks, and the aggressive intent of their title is confirmed by the couplet which appeared on Clubmen banners and which sums up effectively their very limited social philosophy:

> If you offer to plunder, or take our cattle,
> Rest assured we will give you battle.

1648: THE YEAR OF REVOLUTION

In the history of modern Europe before the twentieth century, two years above all others stand out in their revolutionary importance. One of these is 1848. The other, whose importance has so far been neglected, is 1648. These dates are associated with each other not only in the coincidence that they are precisely two centuries apart, but also in the fact that the reaction aroused by the events of 1648 led to a stranglehold that in some countries was not broken until 1848.

The significance of 1648 as a crisis year is indisputable. It was a peak year for prices, a year of universal agrarian crisis. In England there were bad harvests from 1646 to 1649; the winter 1647-8 was a particularly wet one, and in London 1647-9 saw the highest level for wheat prices in the seventeenth century before 1661. In Andalucia thanks to the rains of 1647 there was a severe bread shortage in 1647 and 1648. In southern Italy and Sicily the heavy rains of February 1647 were followed by a drought and therefore by famine conditions in 1647 and 1648. In Russia too the years leading to 1648 were ones of bad harvest. For many of these countries the worst year in terms of weather, harvest and prices was 1647: the popular explosion was often delayed by a few months.

Though no armed insurrection of the people occurred in England, what did occur was certainly more significant than events anywhere else in Europe. England had overthrown its king, and was shortly to proclaim a republic. Not content with this, a small group of middle-class intellectuals made use of all the most advanced methods of propaganda and subversion in an attempt to bring complete freedom and democracy to the people. The Leveller movement, under the leadership of John Lilburne and of his colleagues, including Richard Overton and William Walwyn, made its first effective appearance in July 1646 when it published a *Remonstrance of many thousand citizens* which called for the establishment of a republican democracy and of religious toleration in England. From this time, the Levellers published several successive policy programmes, drawn up in the form of a national constitution: each of these statements, of which the first appeared in 1647, was called the Agreement of the People.

Because the Levellers failed to create an insurrection, it is often easily forgotten how close they came to creating a revolution. In the critical year 1647, when the army quarrelled with Parliament both over policy and because it had not been paid, the Levellers succeeded in infiltrating the army and in dominating all its proceedings. In October the General Council of the army was obliged to sit down at Putney, near London, and discuss plans to adopt the Agreement of the People as the basis of future policy. Only the ruthless hand of Cromwell succeeded in breaking the Leveller threat. Facing an attempted mutiny by some regiments in November, he arrested the ringleaders and had one shot. It was Cromwell again who in April 1649 arrested a group of Leveller mutineers and had one, Robert Lockyer, executed; a month later, at Burford, he captured another group by treachery and executed three soldiers. But for these actions the Levellers might easily have taken over the army, which alone held power in England, and through the army England might have been given a constitution whose essential demands had in fact to wait for two centuries to be resurrected, by the Chartists.

Cromwell wisely did not underrate the strength of the Levellers, whose popular support in London could be seen clearly by the great crowds that turned out for Lockyer's funeral on 29 April 1649, and by the thousands who greeted Lilburne's release from arrest by the magistrates. From 1647 to 1649 the Levellers' support could be seen in the volume of protest they managed to stir up not only in London but also in the provinces. They made ample use of the presses, and dispatched thousands of leaflets throughout the country. They had their own newspaper, the *Moderate,* for which Overton wrote leaders. Lilburne and his friends resorted regularly to the habit of petitioning Parliament, which was the only sovereign the Levellers recognised. Their petitions give valuable evidence of their support. Four days after the arrest in March 1649 of Lilburne and other Levellers, a petition bearing the signatures of ten thousand Londoners was presented to Parliament; proof not only of support but of the remarkable speed of Leveller organisation. In September 1649 the Levellers produced their most revolutionary pamphlet, *The Remonstrance of many thousands of the free people of England,* which was signed by nearly a hundred thousand people. A postscript to the manifesto stated: 'This is already signed with 98,064 hands, and more to be added daily, so soon as we can give notice hereof to our afflicted brethren in all the counties of England and Wales.'

Recent evaluations of the political philosophy of the Levellers do nothing to diminish the fact that both in language and in intention they were revolutionaries. When the poor harvest of 1647 and the harsh winter that followed began to take effect, Lilburne observed that 'merciless famine is entered into our gates', and warned members of Parliament that 'the tears of the oppressed will wash away the foundations of their houses'. In the spring of 1648 some of the Levellers contemplated the possibility of armed insurrection, 'seeing all present authorities to be perverted from their natural end'; but a second civil war diverted their energies. The failure of the Levellers to rise in 1648 led that winter to the emergence of an even more radical, but far less activist, group known as the Diggers.

The opportunity missed by the Levellers during the crisis of 1647-9 was not to recur; Cromwell's strategy and the return of better times in the 1650s saw to that. Despite their failure, the Levellers were the most advanced thinkers of their time. They questioned every established institution and every received opinion, not as religious sectaries but as wholly secular reformers; and in time nearly every one of their reform proposals was to be accepted by the Parliament of England.

In these years the Spanish monarchy was shaken by disaster both within and without the peninsula. In its Italian possessions the crisis led to major revolts in two of the largest cities of the south—Naples and Palermo. Discontent in the south had multiple causes: resentment of Spanish rule, hatred of the nobles and clergy, opposition to taxes. But it was the bad harvests that precipitated conflict. The 1646 crop was a disaster, that of 1647 virtually non-existent.

To combat the appalling famine conditions of spring 1647, the Archbishop of Palermo ordered public penance to be done for the sins of the people. The view the people took of the famine was rather different. In May a procession which was by no means religious marched into the cathedral and stuck a pole crowned with a loaf of bread on the high altar. At the same time there were shouts of 'Long live the king and down with taxes and bad government'. Mobs thereupon set fire to the town hall, opened the prisons and demolished the tax offices. This protest of the common people, led at this stage by an escaped convict named La Pilosa, alarmed the noble class who fled out of the city to their estates. The archbishop's response was to distribute arms to his clergy. There were risings in other parts of Sicily as well, especially in the villages round Messina: at Sciacca the rioters attacked the town hall and destroyed the archives, at Catania where a shoemaker raised the cry of 'Down with the food taxes and long live the King of Spain', some of the nobility barely managed to escape, and the mob led a procession round the town with the heads of their victims transfixed on sticks.

In Palermo, where the Spanish viceroy, the Marquis of los Vélez, had fled the city, order was restored with the help of the guilds. In August a new popular leader emerged in the form of a goldsmith named d'Alesi. Convinced that law and order were essential, d'Alesi soon won the co-operation of the nobles, the inquisitor, and the established authorities. Some reforms were agreed to in principle, such as the reduction of food taxes and increased guild representation in the government of the city. Finally the viceroy was persuaded to return. By then the revolution had lost its momentum. D'Alesi himself had been flattered, feasted and honoured by the upper classes to such an extent that he lost contact with the popular movement: he rode through the streets in a costume of silk and silver, and the most extravagant titles were bestowed on him. When the quarrels within the popular movement broke out in fighting at the end of August, the authorities seized their opportunity. D'Alesi was caught hiding in a sewer and was promptly killed and decapitated. The inquisitor and others then urged the people to slaughter their former leaders. The opposition, including the guilds, was hopelessly divided. In September, Spanish troops entered the city and set about restoring order in their own way.

The Palermo revolt exhibited the three main features of the urban revolts of 1647-8: the cause of the uprising was a food shortage, the main grievance was against taxes, and the main enemies of the people were the nobility. Almost without exception, the rebels were firm royalists, trusting naïvely in the

399

power of the King of Spain to control the excesses of the aristocracy.

The events of 1647 and 1648 in the city and kingdom of Naples were so complex that a detailed attention to events is necessary. The problems of Naples were very much those of Spain, its overlord. The viceroys of the early seventeenth century, notably Monterey, Medina, the Admiral of Castile, and Arcos (all four following each other in office over the years 1620-47) were troubled by two principal problems: weak administration and an inadequate fiscal regime. Administratively the crown had only limited control over the kingdom of Naples, since the major part was in the hands of feudal lords, petty monarchs like the Count of Conversano or the Duke of Maddaloni. It was the oppression of nobles like these that was to spark off popular revolt. Already in 1638 a Spanish official had noted that 'the tyranny and injustice in that kingdom are worthy of severe punishment'. The nobles were principally responsible for tax evasion: 'powerful persons claim to have less property than they do have, and they force the poor to pay more than is their due'. It was the extreme polarisation between rich and poor in Naples that had given rise to the banditry we have already touched upon.

Taxation likewise was a serious problem for the authorities. The Thirty Years War was causing a severe drain on the resources of the Spanish possessions in Italy. In 1639 alone Naples was obliged to send out armaments, soldiers, and money to the total of two million ducats, for the war effort in Genoa, Milan and Germany. The viceroy of that time, the Count of Medina de las Torres, observed that all parts of the monarchy were suffering extreme economic difficulties but that the worst were 'the crown of Castile, the kingdom of Naples, and Sicily, whose expenses exceed all those of the French crown, the estates of Holland, and their adherents'. The internal and external difficulties of the viceroy explain the uproar that greeted the imposition of new taxation in 1647 by the Duke of Arcos.

The main fury of the people of Naples on 7 July 1647, the day that a riot in the market-place exploded into a major revolt, was directed against the *gabelle*, the salt-tax. Tommaso Aniello (known as Masaniello), the illiterate fisherman who led the rioters, took this as the main point of his protest. 'Now is the time to free ourselves from so many unbearable taxes on salt', went one of his speeches. The shouts of the crowds were of a similar strain — *'Fora le Gabelle!'* Though Masaniello emerged as the popular leader, the real power behind the rising was his adviser, an elderly (he was eighty-six years old) priest named Giulio Genoino. It was Genoino alone who formulated a coherent policy for the popular movement. Masaniello had no real sense of direction: on the one hand he directed a systematic burning of tax-farmers' houses and the execution of several enemies of the uprising, on the other he came to a working agreement with the viceroy, dressed himself up in finery and lost much mass sympathy. His murder on 16 July did not check the revolt.

On the contrary, rebellion now spread rapidly into the countryside. The whole of southern Italy was affected. There was an anti-feudal rising in Calabria, and in Basilicata the various anti-feudal movements united themselves under a single leader. Risings occurred also in Puglia and in the Abruzzi. In Bari, reported a contemporary, there was a 'plot to sack all the houses of the wealthy', so that 'many merchants carried their goods to the citadel for greater security'. In Salerno the houses of the rich were sacked. In Ostium the rising was directed against the landlord Giovanni Zevallos and others.

Genoino's main aim was to lighten the tax burden and to limit the excesses of the noble landowners. In so far as the viceroy was also concerned to strengthen royal power at the expense of the feudal nobility, this provided the basis for a temporary alliance between Arcos and Genoino. The alliance was never firmly based, and subject to pressures on both sides: the Spanish government would never have approved any negotiations with a rebel, and the populace distrusted overtures of this sort.

In October 1647 a Spanish fleet sailed into the bay of Naples, but though some troops were disembarked they failed miserably in their attempt to recover the city. The rebels, under a new popular leader Gennaro Annese, then celebrated their victory by declaring a republic on 24 October. In order to protect the republic some sort of alliance with France was achieved, but unlike its efforts in Catalonia and Portugal, France did not take intervention in Naples seriously, and by April 1648 the Spaniards were back in control. In any case by then the direction of the popular movement had split, with Annese committing himself firmly to the French alliance, and Genoino holding fast by his loyalty to the King of Spain. Genoino's loyalty was poorly rewarded. When the suppression began he was arrested, shipped to Spain, and ended his days in a prison in Málaga.

Within Spain itself, the Spanish authorities were faced by

disaffection. The peninsula was torn apart by separatism: both Catalonia and Portugal had proclaimed their independence, and a plot to declare Andalucia independent had been discovered in good time to avoid disaster. Then in 1648 another plot was discovered, this time to make the kingdom of Aragon independent. Popular participation in these events was limited. It was only in Andalucia that the government had cause to fear the common people. Discontent in the south was general in the 1640s. In 1645 the prime minister, Luis de Haro, visited several towns in the province of Córdoba in search of extra taxes for the war: he found none obtainable, because the province was in a state of rebellion. In 1647 there was a wave of discontent through the south. In the towns of Lucena, Alcalá la Real, Alhama, and elsewhere there were serious uprisings. The near-famine conditions of 1647 were the direct stimulant to rebellion, and it was over bread and taxes that the population rioted. In the town of Albunuelas del Valle they attacked and wounded the tax-collectors. The rebellious town of Theva was occupied by the military governor of Granada after a brief resistance, and eleven of the rebels were hanged on gallows in full view of the villagers.

It was in Granada in May 1648 that the potentially most dangerous uprising took place, for more than any other city in Spain Granada was working class in composition. Though the winter of 1647-8 saw a severe food shortage no riots occurred. It was in 1648 when the food prices fell because of better supplies, that trouble arose, for food distribution remained as bad as before and it was the rich alone who managed to obtain bread. On 18 May the poorer people of the city, chanting 'Long live the king and death to the bad government', began a peaceful agitation that swelled the crowds in the streets. Clamouring for a change of administration, they managed to obtain the appointment of their own nominee as *corregidor* (civil governor). The incident of 1648 was only a presage of things to come, for there were further harvest difficulties in 1650 and 1651, leading once again to uprisings in Andalucia. The year 1652 was notable for it saw rebellions in Seville and Córdoba, as well as another rising in Granada. The continuity of these years is shown by the fact that one of those involved in the Granada plot of 1652 was a priest from Alhama who had been involved in that town's rebellion in 1647. A short discussion of the events of 1652 is not out of place here.

The Córdoba rising began early in the morning of Monday, 6

May 1652 when a poor woman went weeping through the streets of the poor quarter, holding the body of her son who had died of hunger. As other women responded to this scene of misery, they persuaded their men to join them in protest. The riot began in earnest when an armed body of about six hundred men entered and sacked the house of the *corregidor,* who took refuge in a convent. By late morning a crowd of about two thousand had virtually taken over the city. The women appear to have taken the lead in exhorting the rebels, who declaimed against the officials, the nobility and the bishop, and when the latter came out to speak to them they insulted him to his face. Meanwhile they broke into all the houses which they suspected of hoarding grain. On the Tuesday they elected their own *corregidor,* a member of the town's nobility. Despite the fury of the rioters, and the sacking of several houses, not a single person appears to have been killed by them. The king eventually sent extra food supplies to the city and on 16 May issued a general pardon. The Seville rising followed much the same pattern. It began on 22 May and lasted about a week. Here too not a single person appears to have been murdered by the mob. When, instead, an official killed two peaceful citizens and then fled, the rebels seized and killed his horse, and sacked and destroyed his house without robbing a single object. As in Córdoba the people of Seville set up a sort of commune, chose their own *corregidor* (a nobleman) and set up a popular militia to keep peace in the city. They also — very significantly — set free all prisoners in the city, then collected all the documentation of the criminal courts in the main square and set fire to it in full view of the judges of Seville. The Seville rebellion was overcome by treachery. The archbishop and the *corregidor* published a declaration of royal pardon, and when the fears of the rebels were assuaged a troop of cavalry marched in at 3.00 am on Sunday, 25 May. The royal troops were not as sparing of life as the rebels. Marching through the city before dawn, they shot a young boy and an old man who were in their way, then went straight to the home of the popular leader Juan Portillo, took him out and shot him without trial. In the days that followed, several others were hanged and the prisions were repopulated.

The Frondes in France were the most important of all the urban revolutions of the year 1648. To what extent, if at all, can they be discussed in the context of popular rebellion? There can be no doubt that both in Paris and in Bordeaux the Fronde was bourgeois in inspiration. Despite the extensive use which members of the Parlement made of the Parisian crowds, they never at any time accorded the populace constitutional importance. For Omer Talon and his friends popular sovereignty did not exist and the only conceivable political doctrine was that of divine royal sovereignty. 'Your Majesty's authority comes from on high', Talon said in January 1648, 'and is accountable to no one, after God, save to your conscience.' This was hardly the sort of theory on which to base opposition to the crown, and it was not surprising that in the streets republicanism was more common than in bourgeois circles. From 1648 to 1650 there was a small and vocal republican group in Paris, whose ideas occasionally filtered through into the Mazarinades of those years. Frondeurs of this group appear to have been chiefly responsible for the several pamphlets which looked on the French rebellion not as an isolated fight but as part of an international struggle against oppression, in which the peoples of England, Naples and Catalonia had taken the lead. Republicanism as such never became a serious issue, and was probably doomed after the execution of Charles I in 1649. So great was the shock of this event that the Frondeurs outdid each other in dissociating themselves from the English rebels.

The popular struggle, then, never assumed significant proportions. Even the famous barricades, which went up on Wednesday, 26 August 1648 and stayed up until Friday, were not a purely proletarian phenomenon, and were firmly under the control of the bourgeoisie. According to a contemporary account, the 'bourgeois, on the pretext that vagabonds were roaming around and threatening to rob those who were not armed', themselves took up arms in order to control the situation. The speed with which the barricades disappeared as soon as the chief demand of the Parlement, the release of Broussel, had been granted is adequate proof of this control. Though the populace turned against the bourgeoisie in later years, particularly in 1652, in 1648 they were still hopeful of some gains from the alliance. The English royalist representative in Paris, Sir Richard Browne, writing in August 1648, expressed alarm at the trust which the members of the Parlement were putting in the people. The Parisian mob, he said, would only go farther if encouraged, 'so dangerous a thing it is to let that many-headed monster know its own strength'. The little speech which Matthieu Molé, first president of the Parlement, made to the Queen Regent on 27

August when the parliamentary delegation went to demand Broussel's release, showed clearly how the 'monster' could be used as a political threat:

> We have come here, Madame, to ask you for the prisoners. It is not we alone, but a hundred thousand armed men, who ask for them. We have had to cross a hundred barricades to come and bring you our grievances. And we have heard the people crying, 'Long live the king', and many other things that we would not dare repeat to Your Majesty. There is no time, Madame, for you to consider what your policy should be, the people are impatient.

The Fronde in Bordeaux was more popular in inspiration. The first serious disturbances, in August 1648, were precipitated by the export of wheat from the city at a time when, as in the rest of France, starvation was beating on the doors. The Parlement of Bordeaux joined the rebellion and outlawed the governor, the Duke of Epernon, as a public enemy. This first stage of the Bordeaux Fronde ended with a peace in January 1650. The city was next caught up in the Parisian struggle when the Princess of Condé won the leaders of Bordeaux over to her party. From 1651, a new force entered the struggle. The Ormée, a mass movement named after its initial meeting place near some elm trees, was based on popular support but had very divergent aims. It absorbed the Condé party and by June 1652 had set up a commune in the city. The Ormée had a membership of thousands. At the top it was run by a council of five hundred. Merchants, bourgeois and lawyers were (not always voluntarily) members, but the petits bourgeois and the lower classes were more typical participants. The movement appears to have had genuinely radical views. 'It is equality that makes for perfection', claimed one of their pamphlets. 'The real cause of sedition and political strife is the excessive wealth of the few.' Views favouring democracy and a republic were expressed. Cromwell exploited this by sending the ex-Leveller Sexby to Bordeaux with a specially revised edition of the Agreement of the People.

Huguenots and Catholics were jointly members of the Ormée. But the unity of the movement was threatened by economic chaos and the cessation of trade. Some richer Ormistes plotted against the more radical wing. The leaders of the radicals, Villars and Dureteste, joined Condé in supporting an alliance with Spain. The royalists besieged Bordeaux by land and sea, cutting off aid from Spain. By July 1653 it was reported that 'the people are howling for bread and peace'. After a coup in the city, royalist troops marched in on 2 August. About three hundred people were expelled from Bordeaux. Dureteste and a few other leaders were executed.

The risings of 1648 in Muscovy were, in their political effect, more important than those which occurred anywhere else in Europe. The Russian state was suffering a general crisis of major dimensions in which the peasant problem, which we have already mentioned, played an important part. In the towns the crisis was if anything even more severe. Over the whole area of the Moscow governmental region, from 1630 to 1650, we can count about thirty uprisings in the towns. In the city of Moscow itself they occurred in 1633-4, 1637, 1641, 1645 and 1648. The year 1648 saw the greatest concentration of outbursts, most of them in June and July. There were risings in May in Tomsk, in June in Voronezh, in July in Kursk, and in ten other towns from June through September. The current of disaffection continued through to 1650, with risings that year in Pskov, Novgorod the Great and other towns.

From 1645 Russia had been ruled nominally by sixteen-year-old Tsar Alexis Romanov, but the actual power was wielded by the boyar Boris Ivanovich Morozov, a man of serious political purpose, whose priorities were in favour of strengthening the town economy against the already powerful influence of the rural areas and their feudal economy. Only the emancipation of the towns from dependence on the country, and greater freedom for the townspeople in controlling their own trade and in their search for pasture and for fuel, would set the towns on their feet again. To carry out this policy Morozov sought the support of the bourgeoisie and the lesser nobility. He was also supported by those great boyars who, being of recent extraction, had few rights in the towns and could not lose by an increase in urban autonomy. Morozov himself, a new boyar, had only 0.08 per cent of his vast territorial holdings located in towns. He was supported by others like the Trubetskoy and Dolgoruky families who likewise had few town holdings. Against Morozov's party, however, there were powerful forces. To maintain his power he had pushed the Sheremetev and Cherkassky families out of office. Both had extensive holdings in the towns, which would have been threatened if landowner rights there were restricted. The importance of this issue is shown by the fact that though the average holdings of the secular nobility in the towns amounted to about four per cent of their property, Nikita Romanov, one of Morozov's opponents, drew no less than 22·9 per cent of his labour force from the same source. Perhaps Morozov's most powerful opponent was the Church. The patriarch had fourteen per cent of his estates in urban areas, and the Russian episcopate as a whole had about eight per cent in towns. Had Morozov succeeded, *votchina* rights in the towns would have been confiscated. As it was, he taxed urban estates heavily, and managed to restore financial stability to the government, so much so that by 1647 a Swedish commentator praised the 'unprecedented wealth' of the state.

In the process, Morozov managed to alienate the very basis of his support. Taxes rose steeply under his regime, and the burgher class was the first to protest. It was the new salt tax, first raised in 1646 on the suggestion of a merchant named Nazarei Chisti, round which opposition crystallised. When it was levied in the hard conditions of the winter of 1647-8 it aroused universal discontent. In Spring 1648, on top of taxes and food shortages, came news of military reverses in the south and of a junction of Turkish and Tatar forces against Russia. General mobilisation was ordered in April. Discontent of the soldiery was now added to that of the populace of Moscow. On 17 May the tsar left the capital to visit a monastery. When he returned to Moscow on 1 June he was greeted by crowds who pressed petitions against the government into his hand. On the next day, when the tsar ventured out into public the reins of his horse were seized by the crowds, who demanded that he accept their petitions. When he refused to do so, a riot broke out. The tsar returned safely to the Kremlin, but the boyars of his entourage merely fanned the crowd's anger by tearing up the petitions in their faces, and laying about them with knouts. When the royal musketeers *(Streltsy)* were ordered to break up the crowds, a section proclaimed that they 'did not wish to fight for the boyars against the common people'. The crowds therefore obtained complete freedom to attack and burn the houses of Morozov and other members of the government.

There are several interesting aspects of the 1648 uprising. An eye-witness account by a Dutchman, translated soon after into English, tells us that

the Streltsies or life guard, consisting of some thousand Men, whose pay being lessened and diminished in so much that they were

407

not able to live by, took the Commons part, and thereupon in the afternoone they seized on the Court of Morozov . . . The sayd Court they plundred totally, all the stately and pretious things they found they hewed in pieces . . . the plate of gold and silver they did beate flat, the pretious pearles and other jewells they have bruised into powder, they stamped and trampled them under feet, they flung them out of the windowes, and they suffered not the least thing to bee carryed away, crying alowd : *To Naasi Kroof,* that is to say, this is our blood.

The uprising was not exclusively popular in composition. The city garrison also joined the rioters, and without garrison and *streltsy* the populace would not have been able to stir. 'The whole community and all classes', reports a contemporary, took part in the events. It cannot be doubted that the Romanovs and other opposition boyars encouraged the rebels. Those boyars who suffered the sacking of their houses were in the government party, and about thirty-six prominent merchants of the same party suffered likewise. Two leading ministers, Chisti (he of the tax) and Pleshcheev were murdered, and Trakhaniotov, brother-in-law of Morozov and his chief minister, was executed without trial. Morozov was exiled by the tsar on 11 June and sent to a monastery. Meanwhile Moscow had suffered grievously from the uprising: a fire, caused by the violence of 2 June, raged through the city, destroying several thousand houses and reducing 'halfe Moscow in ashes', according to the Dutch source.

In the months following the rising nearly all the leaders of the Russian administration, in both town and country, were changed by the tsar: in the governorship of Vladimir, for instance, a Golitsyn was replaced by a Sheremetev. As a gesture to the popular basis of the risings in Moscow and other cities, the government agreed to a summoning of the Zemsky Sobor. This met in 1648-9. It was one of the last moments of Russian constitutionalism. Already the victory of the anti-Morozov landed magnates was signalled by the issue in 1649 of a new code of laws, the *Ulozhenie,* which confirmed in every respect the wishes of the feudal landowners. Unwittingly, the populace which had rebelled against a hated government in 1648 had succeeded in subjecting Russia yet more firmly to the yoke of feudalism.

The year 1648 saw the gradual snuffing out of popular revolt elsewhere in Europe as well. In Austria the century-long series of peasant uprisings came to an abrupt end in that year. To some extent this was because of the end of the Thirty Years War, for foreign generals (especially the Swedes, with Banér in 1641 and Torstensson in 1645) had periodically tried to encourage the peasants to rise against their masters the Habsburgs. It was also a Swede, General Wittenberg, who encouraged the Upper Austrian uprising of September 1648 under a noble called Wenger. The coming of peace destroyed all hopes of success for this rising. The eastern European peasants too were dependent on military support for their rebellions, as we have already seen, and everywhere it was the Cossacks upon whom they relied. Of these Cossacks the most important figure was that of Bohdan Khmelnitsky.

Khmelnitsky, national hero of the Ukraine, for whose freedom he fought against both Poland and Russia, was Hetman of the Cossacks. It was largely with his support that the peasant risings of the mid-century in Lithuania and in Poland managed to take place. To Khmelnitsky, concerned above all for the Ukraine's independence, encouragement of peasant disaffection had the effect of keeping the Polish authorities busy. In the Grand-Duchy of Lithuania, a part of the crown of Poland, the peasant rising of 1648-9 was entirely dependent on him. 'Not only do the Cossacks support the rebels', complained the Chancellor of Lithuania, Prince Albrecht Radziwill, 'but all our peasants in Rus flock to swell the Cossack forces. It is the serfs above all who join them.' For a time the 1648 risings were successful. The *szlachta,* reported a contemporary, bolted 'from their internal enemies— the Cossacks and the serfs—as though from their greatest foe, the Turk'. Wherever they could the rebellious peasants sacked noble and Church property. However, a lull in the military campaign, for talks between Khmelnitsky and the Poles in August 1649, robbed the peasants temporarily of their protection. The *szlachta* descended on them and slaughtered thousands. By spring 1650 the rising was over.

In the context of Cossack support some mention should be made of the Polish rebellion of 1651 in Podhale province. The leader of the rebellion, known variously as Alexander the Lion or Alexander Napierski or simply Kostka, spent the year 1650 in Khmelnitsky's army in order to learn the techniques of armed struggle. Though the actual rising, which lasted from June to July 1651, never obtained direct armed help from the Ukrainian leader, it is doubtful if Napierski would have proceeded with his plans without the inspiration and possibly the encouragement of Khmelnitsky. The Polish peasants' grievances were standard ones, against labour services and exploitation, against 'the *szlachta* and Jews', to quote their own complaint. Their situation was certainly unenviable, if we may believe the distinguished Polish Jesuit, Peter Skarga, who wrote at the time that 'there is no country in the world where the peasants, subjects of the lords, would be oppressed as they are in our country, under the unlimited authority of the *szlachta*'. The aims of Napierski's rebellions were frankly libertarian: feudal dues and financiers would be eliminated. Napierski himself was also anti-clerical but did not force his views on his Catholic following. Inspired by hopes of help from Khmelnitsky and from Rákóczi in Hungary, he declared that 'we shall go farther through all Poland'. In fact the rebellion never exceeded the boundaries of the governorship of Cracow, and Napierski was executed on 18 July 1651.

There were a few popular movements in southern Germany and Austria towards the end of the Thirty Years War. The most notable was the peasant rising of 1645-7 in the Zillertal, in the Salzburg diocese, where the grievances of the rebels were reflected in one of their songs:

> *Act Gott! ach Gott! lass dich erbarmn!*
> *Das Zillertal ist worden arm*
> *Durch Leibsteuer und Geldaufschlag . . .*[1]

The end of the war, 1648, witnessed no popular repercussions. If the reason for this in the German lands was exhaustion, outside Germany at least some activity could be seen in France, in Spain and in the east of Europe. Of these later risings the most important was the Swiss peasant war of 1653, which is discussed in this section not only for reasons of convenience but also because it was directly precipitated by the peace of 1648.

The Swiss cantons were not free from agitation during the Thirty Years War. There were minor risings in Emmental and Oberland in 1641, and in Zurich in 1645 six peasants were executed. Direct and indirect taxation was the main complaint. In some respects, however, the peasantry benefited from the war. The large influx of refugees from Germany during the war years raised demand, improved the market for agrarian produce, and brought wealth to the northern cantons. This inflationary boom was reversed at the peace. After 1648, as the Germans returned home, 'so also', reported a contemporary, 'does money leave Switzerland'. Prices fell. In the town of Sursee wine prices

1 God have compassion on us! The Zillertal has become impoverished through taxes and impositions . . .

410

between 1642 and 1651 fell by 72·5 per cent. In the town of Zofingen grain prices between 1635 and 1648 fell by the same proportion. To add to the public confusion came devaluation of coinage. On 8 December 1652 the Bern authorities devalued their currency by fifty per cent. This began a nation-wide crisis. On 17 December Lucerne also devalued. Then in January 1653 all the Swiss cantons followed suit. Unfamiliar with the economics of devaluation, peasants saw their savings reduced in value, wage-earners saw their wages halved. The agrarian classes, whether producers who had suffered from deflation or wage-labourers who suffered from devaluation, rose in revolt.

The protest movement was led by Johannes Emmenegger, a wealthy peasant who owned nearly a hundred head of cattle and drank out of a silver goblet. His friends called him the *Edelstein der Bauern*—the jewel of the peasants. The other early leaders included Niklaus Leuenberger, also a wealthy peasant, who was later to become supreme leader of the whole movement; Christian Schibi, an ex-mercenary soldier, military commander of the Lucerne peasants, who was looked upon as a magician and sorcerer, a belief he did his best to cultivate; and Caspar Unternahrer, known as Caspi den Tell, in whose home in December 1652 the first meeting of the discontented peasant leaders took place. A few days after this meeting the peasants sent a message to the city council of Lucerne asking for the revocation of the devaluation and for other reforms. When this was refused all the peasant leaders met on 26 January 1653 in the town of Entlebuch, and took an oath to struggle together for the cause of freedom. It was at this meeting too that a song of protest was drawn up, invoking the name and cause of the nation's hero. This Tell-song, known as the *Entlebucher Tellenlied*, was to become the anthem of the rebellious peasants as they marched to war. Three of its many stanzas went as follows:

> *Ich sing es niemand z'tratzen,*
> *Man soll mich recht verstohn:*
> *Von wegen ganzen Batzen*
> *Ist dieser Krieg herkon . . .*
>
> *Ach Tell! ich wollt dich fragen,*
> *Wach auf von deinem Schlaf!*
> *Die Landvögt wend alls haben,*
> *Ross, Rinder, Kälber, Schaf! . . .*
>
> *Thüend s'usem Land verjagen*
> *Alsbald mit gewehrter Hand,*

The main peasant rising occurred in Lucerne. On 16 March three thousand of them, under the command of Schibi, marched on Lucerne. Both Catholic and Protestant peasants were united in the common cause, and agreements were reached between Protestant and Catholic parties. The Lucerne rebellion led to a virtual surrender by the authorities, who in April agreed to all the main demands of the peasants (except revaluation): the price of salt was lowered, a free trade in livestock was permitted, the *Trattengeld* (a tax on livestock) was revoked, troops were to be financed by the authorities and not by direct taxation, and so on. In Solothurn and Basel the peasants did not even need to put on a show of force. On 3 April the council of Solothurn agreed to abolish the *Trattengeld* and to permit free trade in salt. In Basel, which had already had experience of peasant disorders in the so-called *Rappenkrieg* (1591-4), the government on 9 April made all the concessions agreed upon by Solothurn.

This easy victory was clearly only temporary, and the peasants realised it. On 23 April they called together a mass meeting of several thousand Swiss rebels in Sumiswald. There all the different forces agreed on a joint policy and a common leadership. Taking an oath in the name of the Trinity, they swore to aid each other, and to renew the oath every ten years. The agreement was sworn to by Bern, by ten districts of Lucerne, eleven districts of Solothurn and five of Basel. At this period the rebel camp was estimated to number about two hundred and fifty thousand men. Two more mass meetings of this sort were held, both at Huttwil on 30 April and on 14 May. The latter was apparently the biggest and most ambitious of them all. Secure in the justice of their cause and the strength of their numbers, the peasants took the offensive in a war campaign that covered several weeks in May and June. Their forces were immense. The main body of the rebel army, led by Leuenberger, now supreme leader and uncrowned king of the peasants, exceeded twenty-four thousand men. This strength only delayed the inevitable defeat. By the third week of June 1653 the peasants were defeated and in disarray. It was then

---

[1] I sing this not in defiance, but that men may understand: it was through the coinage, that this war came to our land. . . .
Ah, Tell! I request you, wake up from your sleep! The governors wish to seize all—horses, cattle, calves and sheep! . . .
Drive them away from our country at once, with your armed hand, and bring back peace and quiet into your fatherland.

that the executions commenced. Schibi was executed on 9 July, Leuenberger in Bern on 6 September.

This was the last of the great popular rebellions in the Iron Century. At the years 1648-60 there is a watershed which affects both eastern and western Europe. This is not to say that no rebellions occurred after these dates. On the contrary there were major uprisings in both France and Russia in the late seventeenth century, and so continuously through to 1848. The difference is that whereas the revolts before 1648-60 were struggles against the onset of landlordism and absolutism, by the late seventeenth century the struggle was over, and the people rose up in rebellion within a structure that had already engulfed them. Landlordism and absolutism had triumphed in the west by 1660, in the east serfdom was firmly entrenched by the same date. All the rebellions had been inconsequential: it had not been a century of revolution, but a century of defeat. 'Alas', lamented Gerrard Winstanley in 1650, 'Oppression is a great tree still, and keeps off the sun of freedom from the poor commons still.'

THE STRUCTURE OF POPULAR REVOLT

Apart from the fundamental social and economic problems which lay at the root of popular disaffection, there were a number of factors that made disaffection and discontent flame up into actual rebellion. Our evidence has shown that they can be reduced basically to three: bad harvests, extraordinary taxation and the soldiery.

The coincidence in this period between bad harvests and popular revolt is so striking that it is almost a general rule that the price curve reflects the incidence of popular agitation. There are clearly several exceptions to this. The Swiss peasant war of 1653, for instance, was precipitated by a fall rather than a rise in prices. In the vast majority of cases, nevertheless, it was grain shortage that first aroused the people. It is important to note, however, that a simple food shortage, or a famine, did not by itself cause discontent. So long as the common people could see that everyone was starving like themselves, they were invariably long-suffering. Only when they learned that not everyone was starving, that someone had hoarded grain, that rations were being distributed in favour of the privileged, and that grain was actually being exported despite the famine—only then did they rise. In the Naples of 1585 Starace was murdered because he exported grain, in Bordeaux in 1648 it was the export of wheat that began the

413

Fronde, in Córdoba in 1653 the only looting that occurred was caused by the populace breaking into houses to hunt for hoarded grain. Famine was never a direct reason for rebellion: it always had to be supported by a burning sense of social injustice. Moreover, there was often a time-lag between the peak of the famine and the actual revolt. Agitation on an empty stomach was not always possible. The result was that, as in 1566 in Antwerp, riots broke out when in fact conditions seemed to be improving. It has puzzled historians that the Antwerp populace rioted when food-ships had brought grain to the city and when prices were almost back to normal. The price level, however, is no reliable guide, as the 1648 rising in Granada shows us. According to a citizen writing four days after the outbreak of this rising, wheat prices had fallen 'from 72 *reales* to 44 *reales* more or less, but while the supply and price of grain improved, disorder in the quality and supply of bread increased'. Working only with price data, the historian can conclude that conditions were improving; in actual fact, defrauding and hoarding made the populace even more aware that they were being deprived of the benefits of the fall in prices. Social conflict became far more likely in these circumstances than at a time when there was no obvious relief for popular misery.

Extraordinary taxation appears as a cause for grievance in nearly every rising in this period. All the major peasant revolts and a great number of the urban rebellions were directed against fiscal exactions, against taxes on property, food salt, cattle and other items. The main enemy of the rebels was therefore in most cases the central government. Second only to the central government as a fiscal enemy was the Church. The late sixteenth century in particular saw numerous revolts, in France and Norway for example, against tithes. In Upper Austria and in Bavaria attacks on monasteries were common. Protestant peasants usually tended to object in principle to the tithe. Catholic peasants, as in seventeenth-century Poitou, often took a different view; they objected to the tithe if it were misappropriated to some other purpose, and demanded instead that it be used within the district of payment, to support the local parish clergy. Hatred of seigneurial taxation was, needless to say, universal; but rebels often muted their criticism in this respect, partly because of the military help which some sections of the nobility could offer them.

More than any other social class, the peasants suffered the

brunt of war, and in this period, when war was perpetually present, they suffered particularly badly. The coming of the soldiery usually led to a multiplicity of horrors. Grimmelshausen's *Simplicissimus* has as its major theme the sufferings of the peasants at the hands of the soldiers:

> Ja der Soldaten böser Brauch
> Dient gleichwohl dir zum besten auch;
> Das Hochmut dich nicht nehme ein
> Sagt er: Dein Hab und Gut ist mein.[1]

'They lay waste' says this author, 'everything they come across, whether in front of, in the path of or in the rear of the army, and what they cannot make use of they destroy.' Since the line of march was most often across country, it was the property of the peasants that was destroyed. The billetting of troops in peasant households, in country villages; the seizure of their supplies for food; the trampling of ripening crops by thousands of soldiers; the frequent attacks on their womenfolk; the trail of disaster and not least of disease left by the armies: all these were so commonplace in the century of the Thirty Years War that they hardly need repetition. Yet the significance of the ruin must be kept in mind. War was an instrument of social change. If the soldiery annihilated holdings and livelihood and reduced the peasants to economic dependence and serfdom, they were also the direct cause of numerous uprisings in which the peasants protested against such conditions.

'The seventh of September', wrote the Curé of Boissy-Saint-Léger in 1652, 'I and my poor parishioners were forced to leave our parish because of the violence of the rebel troops, and we took refuge, each where he could, during this miserable war, and the eighteenth of October we returned to our homes.' After tolerating this sort of disruption for years during the Fronde, some peasants began to evolve their own attempts at restoring order. In Milon-la-Chapelle a *laboureur* (peasant farmer) 'collected a company of peasants, all well-armed and resolute, who elected him their captain . . . He took the name of Sauvegrain, signifying by this name that he had no other aim than to save the corn and other grain of the fields.' The fame of the group became so great that the Duchesse of Chevreuse (the Duke was their seigneur) even visited them in the woods to share a meal with them. After the wars, Sauvegrain returned to his plough.

---

[1] The evil practices of the soldiery nevertheless do you some good, for to save you from pride the soldier says: 'Your goods and belongings are mine.'

Other peasants, however, were driven by their experiences in a different direction. A complaint to the French authorities in 1645, at a time when the border provinces had suffered severely because of the Thirty Years War, claimed that for the past ten years 'the administration of justice has stopped and been interrupted, through the passage and lodging of armies which have caused such disorder in the country that the peasants refuse to allow any judicial action to be taken, and instead rebel even against the judges'. For these peasants the disruption caused by the soldiers became a catalyst for revolt, a revolt that was directed not against the immediate cause of their misery but against those who had for so long exploited them.

Was there any geographical pattern to the rebellions? Though this may appear to be a pointless question, since revolts were governed by socio-economic rather than geographical causes, there is good reason for asking it. We have already observed that banditry tended to thrive in mountainous or otherwise inaccessible areas. In seventeenth-century Poland the most important centre for bandits was the mountainous Tatr region, bordering the Carpathians. There they built up a following that thrived for several years, with the help of the local population, and played an active part in the 1651 rising in Podhale. Where the terrain facilitated revolt, risings could develop into large-scale movements. This was almost certainly one reason why the northern Alpine region seems to have been the scene of frequent rebellions. In this area, however—Austria, Hungary, Styria—an even more important reason for popular discontent was the need to raise taxes for the war against the Turks, a reason which always featured as a grievance in the demands of the peasantry.

How important were town and country in the revolts? Here a basic problem that differentiated eastern Europe from western must be noted. In eastern Europe the rural economy dominated the life of the people and of the towns, whereas in the west the towns and the bourgeoisie or nobility controlling them had begun to dominate the rural areas. In the east, therefore, the conditions of social conflict were radically different. In general the revolutionary impetus had to come not from the towns but from the countryside. The urban revolts in Russia in 1648 are no exception to this rule, for in fact one of the issues at stake under Morozov was the excessive predominance of the countryside, and the mobs of urban Moscow consisted largely of peasants. When the common people rose in the east it was under Bolotnikov,

Napierski, Khmelnitsky, men who had lived all their lives outside the towns. In the west, the radical movements tended to originate in and emerge from the towns, and as a rule they had a considerable bourgeois component. It was, of course, no less true for the west that town and country were often difficult to distinguish; nor can it be denied that in all the major uprisings the peasants made up the vast majority of the rebels. Yet a brief look at the French revolts of the early seventeenth century is enough to establish that every significant outbreak began in a town, expanded its support from the town, and maintained its strength so long as it had urban help. The fact that class tension was greater within the confines of urban society will help to explain this. But the fact remains that by the 1640s nearly all the major risings in the west had become urbanised—in Naples, in Paris, in Granada, in Bordeaux. The townspeople, the proletariat, were beginning to take the revolutionary initiative. In eastern Europe, in Russia, no such trend was forthcoming. After the explosion of 1648 in Moscow, and the bloody rising (it was the suppression that was bloody) of July 1662 in the same city, the initiative returned to the countryside, to the Cossacks, to Stenka Razin and his successors.

Nearly every revolt of which we have details shows that both urban and rural elements took part. The followers of Bolotnikov in 1607 included serfs, peasants, urban tradespeople *(posadskie lyudi)* and lesser gentry. The *Croquants* in 1594 were solidly supported by all the towns in Limousin, with the exception of Limoges. The backbone of the *Nu-pieds* revolt consisted not only of peasants but also of rural labourers. The 1626 Upper Austrian rising included peasants, artisans from the towns, and even sailors from the ships on the Danube.

Past neglect of popular agitation has often sprung from a belief that the revolts were small, limited in extent and brief in duration. It is true that few revolts maintained their momentum for any lengthy period. Russian and Polish risings were worst in this respect. When not supported by the Cossacks they degenerated into minor skirmishes, without plan or leadership. Minor revolts had the habit of fading away repeatedly and flaring up just as repeatedly. One example of this sort of endemic rebellion occurred near Linz where the peasants of Wildeneck maintained a ceaseless struggle from 1601 to 1662 against the monastery of Mondsee. This protracted rebellion ended in December 1662 with a trial and the execution of two peasant ringleaders. Purely urban revolts, those contained within the walls of a city, were lucky if they lasted more than a week. But major revolts, those which we can rightly term 'wars', such as occurred in France and in Upper Austria, managed to survive for a surprisingly long time. The Austrian peasant war of 1594-7 lasted for three entire years; the *Croquant* rebellion of 1594 for nearly two. The volume of support for the revolts is likewise not to be belittled. Although no available figures are in any way reliable, it is not easy to dismiss as exaggerations the estimate of a peasant army of forty thousand in Austria in 1595, or one of twenty-four thousand in Switzerland in 1653. These are only figures for armies: estimates for followings are very much higher. The fact that Tilly had to use an army of thirty thousand to put down a rising in Austria in 1620 shows that the authorities seldom underestimated the strength of popular revolts.

Another common misapprehension about popular risings is that they were sanguinary. For Luther and others both before and after him, the peasants were 'murderous'. No other item of upper-class propaganda against the rebels has been so successful as this image of bloodthirsty marauders destroying both life and property. The reality was totally different. Almost without exception, popular rebellions respected human life and property. A typical case was that of Reichenstein in 1571, where Gaissrucker forbade his followers to 'kill, burn or steal'. The Austrian rebels of 1595, far from resorting to an orgy of looting, maintained 'perfect discipline'; and in one remarkable incident that year they did not kill the soldiers who were sent to attack them, but merely disarmed and beat them. De Thou's description of the rebels in 1597 in Hungary has the same picture: 'they were at first very restrained, and shed no blood whatsoever. Those who were found guilty of having stolen were severely punished.' During the Spanish risings in Granada, Córdoba and Seville not a single death was caused directly by the revolutionary populace.

The deaths that did occur as a result of rebel action were so exceptional that they call for some attention. If murders occurred, it was often because the populace had been attacked first. In Moscow in 1648 the people reacted because the boyars had flogged them with knouts. In Granada the first victim to be sought (unsuccessfully) by the rioters was a man who had killed three of their number in a quarrel. The executions attributed to Masaniello's rule in Naples (some two hundred and fifty persons, by one contemporary account) were the result of the discovery of a counter-revolutionary plot inspired by the viceroy. The rebels, in other words, did not usually kill without reason. They might breathe hatred against the nobility, for instance, but the few nobles they killed were those who had the blood of the people on their hands. To this picture of moderation there was one major exception. Confirmed enemies of the people were annihilated without mercy, and usually barbarically, in times of unrest.

In France, Italy, Spain and in other countries no doubt, the tax collector fell into this exceptional category. In Spain the officials collecting the *millones* (food taxes) had a very uncertain expectation of life and were the most hated of all government representatives. In France several of the major revolts began with the murder of tax collectors. It was poor Poupinel's fate in Normandy to be mistaken for one. In Agen in 1635 as we have seen, the murder of tax-men was carried out with the barbarism of a primitive sacrifice. Some victims had their hands and feet cut off, one had his eyes torn out by a woman, another was castrated and his testicles were fed to dogs. On occasions like this the murder itself was less significant than the manner of it. The mutilation, both bodily and sexual, was symbolic of the people's hatred, and all the most extreme actions of the populace must be approached with this symbolism in mind. The ritual of cannibalism practised by Paulmier and his friends at Romans in 1580 was terrifying to his enemies not because it was meant seriously but because it threatened the reversal of all established values, both Christian and secular. Perhaps the most hated of French tax collectors was the *gabeleur* and it was one of these who, in 1636 at Saintonge, 'was cut up into little pieces while still alive, and people took pieces to fix to the doors of their houses, where they can still be seen', as a contemporary tells us. This murder can be described as cannibalistic as well as ritualistic. Much the same fate, as we have seen, was suffered by Starace in Naples in 1585. The rioters on that occasion went so far as to offer pieces of his flesh for sale, an extreme way of demonstrating their total contempt for a man who had, as it were, sold *their* flesh for profit. Not only tax collectors, then, but all profiteers, usurers, all those vultures who fed upon the people, all those who drank their blood: these were the extraordinary victims of what might appear to have been the brutal savagery of the people, but was in reality no more than their resort to a form of justice that was older than civilisation.

Property was treated in precisely the same way. The picture conjured up by our eyewitness in Moscow in 1648, of thousands of people raging through Morozov's mansion, destroying every single precious object in sight and throwing powdered pearls out of the windows to cries of 'this is our blood!', is totally representative. All the wealth that had been squeezed out of the people and reduced to useless gold, silver, crystal and jewels, was now to be destroyed. Since it was not what the people understood by wealth, it was contemptuously reduced to dust. The same thing occurred in Seville in 1652, when the populace sacked an official's house (valued at over ten thousand ducats) with all its belongings, and refused to steal a single one of the valuable objects it contained. The Starace murder was almost identical, except that some of his furniture was taken away and donated to several monasteries in the city of Naples; but no robbery occurred. This refusal of outraged rioters to touch tainted property was one of the most striking aspects of the psychology of popular revolt. The ritualistic destruction of the goods of those whom the people had declared to be anathema, untouchable, sacrificial victims, was carried out wholly intuitively, with no apparent direction and no formal prohibition of robbery. Further striking examples to illustrate this aspect of popular vengeance can be found in the 1647 revolts in Naples. The quotations that follow are taken from contemporary accounts by the eyewitness Alessandro Giraffi and by the English writer James Howell. When the tax commissioner Moschetola became too pressing in his efforts to extract the salt tax from one town,

> the people of that Town being transported with fury, came to Naples and colleaguing with that people they ran about dinner time to the Market-place, where the said Moschetola had a house, and gave him such a hot Alarm that like a Cat he was forced to flee over the tops of the houses to save himself. The women were permitted to go out of the said house, and afterwards they took out all the household-stuff, and carrying it to the open street in a kind of solemnity all was burnt to ashes; besides rich Tapistry and exquisite Pictures there were two cupboards of silver Vessels and a great Library of Books exposed to the fury of the fire; all of which was computed to the value of thirty thousand Crowns, all which was reduced to Cinders.

The account lists the several houses destroyed by the Neapolitan populace, and goes on to observe:

> It was admirable what a regular method they observed in their fiery executions; for they used first to take all the goods out into the Market place to be burnt, crying out *it was the blood of the people* of

Naples, and 'twas death to embeazle the least thing; insomuch that one who had stolen but a peep of Sausage was like to be hang'd by Masaniello; nor did they spare either gold, silver or jewels, but all was thrown into the flames, as also coaches and horses were burnt alive, most rich Tapistries and Pictures; but they saved books and pieces of Piety, which they sent to several Churches.

The ritualistic significance of these burnings comes through clearly in the emphasis on blood. When the house of another farmer of the salt tax was being burnt, for instance, the people cried: 'These goods are our blood!' According to Giraffi, there were cases where 'one taking but a little Towel was kill'd', and 'divers others for stealing but small trivial things, were hang'd by the public Executioner'.

This prevalence of rite and symbolism also occurred in the ideology of rebel movements. Lacking any basis of authority for their rebellion, they appealed to history, to myth, to legend and to God. Side by side with this pseudo-ideology went a formal belief and trust in the king. Nearly all popular movements appealed over the heads of their immediate superiors to the monarchy, as in the case of the Neapolitan revolt of 1647-8, which supported both king and Spain against the nobility. Very rarely indeed did rebels show themselves so radical as to question the existence of monarchy, hence the universal shock felt throughout Europe when the English in 1649 got rid of theirs. It is exceptional to meet cases such as that recorded by Marshal Monluc in his *Commentaires*, of peasant rebels in the late sixteenth century who reacted to a mention of the king by saying, 'What king? It is we who are the kings; the one you speak of is just a little turd.' Despite the almost universal confidence in the king, it is possible to look on this as yet another myth, if only because all rebels took great care to have alternative myths to which to appeal should the king fail them — as he always did. The Swiss rebels of 1653, for instance, appealed directly to the national hero, as the *Entlebucher Tellenlied* makes plain:

> *Ach Tell! ich wollt dich fragen,*
> *Wach auf von deinem Schlaf!*

There were others for whom a national hero such as Tell was not enough. For these God could be the only sanction to rebellion. He was moreover, an interconfessional God or, to put it in rebel terms, a God who championed the poor, of whatever faith, against the rich. Hence the amazing unity, unprecedented at any other level in the history of the time, between Catholics and Protestants in the *Croquant* rebellion, and in the peasant wars in Upper Austria and in Switzerland. On an individual plane, the leaders tended to be sent from God. The bandit Marco Sciarra actually entitled himself *'Marcus Sciarra flagellum Dei, et commissarius missus a Deo contra usurarios et detinentes pecunias otiosas'* — the scourge of God, sent against usurers and hoarders. The same goes for Captain Pouch in the Midlands revolt of 1607. 'He told them that hee had Authorite from his majestie to throwe downe enclosures, and that he was sent of God to satisfie all degrees whatsoever, and that in this present worke hee was directed by the lord of Heaven.' The important point, in this pre-democratic age, was that authority devolved upon one, it came from above, and ultimately from God; almost never did it come from below, from the people.

But authority itself was often not enough. It must be proved by deeds, by miracles. The rebel leaders consequently became invested with supernatural powers in the eyes of their followers, and on occasion deliberately fostered this sense of magic and mystery. Who was the *'Jean Nu-Pieds'* who signed the proclamations of the Normandy rebels? There was not just one: there were at least two. A leader who was known yet unknown, who was one yet many, who was here yet also everywhere: this was the image, probably consciously cultivated by the various rebel leaders, that made the supreme leader appear ubiquitous, elusive, immune to all danger, even immortal. In the songs about Stenka Razin, Stenka hurls back the bullets fired by his enemies. Often the leader promised this immunity to his followers. A typical case is that of Captain Pouch. Wherever the 1607 rising broke out, in the south, in the Forest of Dean, it was reported that Captain Pouch was there. In addition to this ubiquity Pouch had a reputation for being able to grant immunity. He was called Pouch 'because of a great leather pouch which he wore by his side in which purse hee affirmed to his company, yt there was sufficient matter to defend them against all commers, but afterward when hee was apprehended, his Powch was seearched and therein was onely a peece of greene cheese'.

Certain names had a hold on the popular imagination, and sometimes had roots in local folklore. It was these that were used time and again, thus reinforcing the illusion of deathlessness. The Castilian bandit who called himself Pedro Andreu in 1644 was clearly appealing to the reputation of the original holder of this name. Both in 1627 and in 1631 in the Forest of Dean the (male) leader of the revolts against enclosures adopted the name Lady Skimmington, a name with undoubted folk roots. The magic of the appellation '*Nu-pieds*' wielded such influence that in Caen the leader of the rebels called himself '*Bras-nu*', and in Poitiers the leader used the name '*Va-nu-jambes*'. Terms like *Croquants*, Levellers, *Germanías*, played a vital role in the history of popular unrest; they were rallying calls, names with a history, which announced past achievements and future aspirations. The whole literature of popular movements, from peasant revolts to illicit trade unionism, is strewn with hundreds of exotic names like these.

Names and myths were like magic incantations, part of the necessary apparatus of discipline and obedience. The military leader of the Lucerne peasants in 1653, Christian Schibi, was famed as a magician and warlock. His superior, Niklaus Leuenberger, maintained his authority by an outward symbol. He had been given a red cloak by the peasants of Entlebuch, and this he wore wherever he rode throughout the country. Cloaks and pouches were in these cases the visible signs of an authority which seems to have commanded remarkable, even fantastic, obedience. 'He had only to beckon with his hand', reported a contemporary Solothurn chronicler of Leuenberger, 'or scribble a word, and men, women and children would go by day or night, through rain, wind and snow, to deliver his message.' In the same way Catherine de Medici could observe in 1579 of Paulmier, leader of the commune at Romans, that 'he has such great influence and authority that at his slightest word all the people of the town and round about will bestir themselves'. To the Fugger correspondent in Linz in 1596 the absolute dedication of the Austrian rebels could be explained only in terms of witchery. The peasants, he wrote,

> collect in all four quarters and it is believed that the day before yesterday there were 18,000 of them in Kremsmünster. They did no violence, for food and drink were proffered to them at their first demand. Of this, however, they refused to partake. They seem bewitched, for as soon as the word is given, even in this cold, they leave their wives and children, hasten from their houses and farms, yet attacking neither towns, castles nor even villages. They tell the populace, whom they drag along with them, that for all they care, horses, oxen and cows, even the women may perish, and they pawn their cattle with the inn-keepers and drink away their gold.

How revolutionary were the rebels of this period? It is sometimes argued that the social revolt of the time could not have been radical, and was usually little more than reformist. Many historians maintain that the class struggle did not exist, if only because there were no 'classes' in the post-industrial sense. It is true that many insurgents, particularly the peasantry, tended to be conservative. Some risings appear to have had limited aims. The Croat rising of 1573, for example, demanded little more than the restoration of 'ancient rights', by which was usually meant the abolition of increased feudal demands in taxes and services. One of the lords concerned in the events reported how his peasants came to him and asked him 'not to ally with anyone against them, since they had not risen against their lords, but only that their ancient rights be restored to them'. However limited their aims, they none the less, and despite themselves, threatened the social order; and it is accordingly important not to assess an uprising only according to its professed aims. The Croat rebels demanded a reduction of taxes, and the abolition of tithes: had either been granted the structure of authority would have been shaken. Moreover, the cry of 'ancient rights' was, against all appearances, a fundamentally revolutionary one. Like the declamations of English revolutionaries against the 'Norman yoke', it appealed to a near-mythical age of freedom, and in so doing called for the abolition of the existing order. The protest against tithes, which took various forms, threatened the official Christian ideology of the state, for in effect it was a demand for the disestablishment of the Church. This was clearly the intention of Protestant opponents in a Catholic state. At times, however, the protest involved the purest anticlericalism. The Norwegian peasants, according to a nobleman in 1606, had the express intention of doing away with their clergy: 'In several estates the authorities were offered a lot of money so that the people could be without ministers of religion for several years. In places the clergy were paid off, in others chased out.' This was a very exceptional situation, not paralleled in countries with a firm Christian background.

Most popular risings that we know of were directed against the nobles and against the state: a few were also led by nobles. There should be no difficulty therefore in conceding that some revolts were wholly radical while others may even have been conservative. There could also be variations within a single movement: the *Nupieds* revolt was radical in its rank and file, but conservative in its leadership. Noble or gentry leadership of uprisings was so universal a phenomenon that only a wilful dogmatism can deny its existence. In Normandy in 1643, for instance, it was reported that 'the gentry and seigneurs of the villages support and protect the revolt of their vassals'. The lords had their own good reasons for this support, chief among them being the wish to rescue their dependents from the authority and taxation of the state. If the populace chose noble leaders, as they did in Austria in 1626, in Naples in 1647 with the Prince of Bisignano, in Seville in 1652, in France in 1636 with La Mothe La Forêt, there was one simple reason: military leadership. Only the nobles had the professional military guidance required by rebels, and only they had the status to make any negotiations between the parties take place as between equals.

But even with gentry as their leaders the people never ceased to question the whole rationale of the existing order. The anthems of the peasant armies supply ample evidence that they desired an end to class differences. We find the following stanza being sung in the 1626 Upper Austrian revolt:

> *Grosse Fürsten und Herren*
> *müssen drob gehen zu Grund*
> *gleich wider ihr Begehren,*
> *wo sie davon nicht Kehren,*
> *das sey ihn allen Kund.* [1]

And so it was that in 1679 we encounter in Germany the couplet which John Ball preached through England in the fourteenth century:

> *Was bildet sich der Hofmann ein,*
> *Dass er als ich will besser seyn?*
> *Da Adam ackert und Eva spann,*
> *Wer war damals ein Edelmann?* [2]

Egalitarianism was not new, but in many seventeenth-century risings it became commonplace. Its most noble expression was in the writings of the Levellers and the Diggers, who placed the belief in universal rights on a firm philosophical basis. But what the Diggers taught in England was already an article of faith in other countries. 'Trust not the nobility', proclaimed Masaniello in 1647, 'for they are traitors, and our enemies.' 'We bear the

[1] Great princes and lords must fall in the dust, much against their wishes; let it be known to them all that they cannot return therefrom.

[2] Why does the courtier imagine that he is better than I am? When Adam delved and Eva span, who was then a nobleman?

nobility on our shoulders', observed a pamphleteer in Paris in 1649, 'but we have only to shrug our shoulders to throw them on to the ground.' In 1654 the governor of the Lithuanian lands wrote to the King of Poland, 'The whole rabble is aroused, hoping for freedom from labour services and taxes. They wish to be free for ever from lords.' It was this wish that Bolotnikov attempted to exploit in 1607 when he called upon the slaves in Moscow to rise against their masters. The aim of overthrowing the 'evil boyars' is a theme that recurs in Russian ballads and emphasises their popular flavour. The same hatred of the upper classes influenced the rioters of Cordoba in 1652 when they threatened to 'cut off the heads' of the nobles and rich. This antagonism was not solely negative. It also expressed itself in democratic terminology, in the use of the words 'brother' and 'brotherhood' to describe the rebels and their organisation, as though to stress universal equality and the solidarity of the underprivileged. The same hope for solidarity led an Essex labourer to ask in 1594, 'What can rich men do against poor men if poor men rise and hold together?' Very occasionally too a sense of internationalism could be found, a consciousness that the cause of freedom had to be fought for in all countries and not just in one. The English were certainly the most international in this respect, as we can see from the agitation created by the Levellers in favour of the Irish people. In 1649, indeed, an opponent accused William Walwyn, the Leveller ideologist, of 'arguing that the cause of the Irish natives in seeking their just freedoms, immunities and liberties, was the very same with our cause here in endeavouring our own rescue and freedom from the power of oppressors'.

The oppressors were not shaken off, and the optimism of the rebels never bore fruit. Bartholomew Steere in 1596 informed a friend that 'he need not work for his living this dear year, for there would be a merry world shortly'. Despite all millennaristic hopes, this merry world receded farther and farther into the future, until overtaken by the gaunt realities of the Industrial Revolution.

11 THE VOICE OF THE DISPOSSESSED

> Hark! hark! the dogs do bark,
> The beggars are coming to town.
> Old nursery rhyme

> Though the number of the poore do dailie encrease, all things yet
> worketh for the worst in their behalfe.
> THOMAS DEKKER. Greevous Grones for the Poore (1622)

The economic and social movements that we have been considering produced their inevitable toll of victims, and it is with these, the dispossessed of Europe, that we are now concerned. The difficulty in making any adequate survey of the dispossessed is that there are few surviving records of their fate save where the state had a direct material interest in them. Apart from these, who nevertheless remain poorly documented, little is known of the lower orders in Europe, and few historians have had the patience to plough through the criminal records where they perhaps inevitably made their dismal appearance. The 'dispossessed' were quite literally what the word conveys: they were a section of the population that had been deprived of homes and property, where this was relevant, or of the mere means of subsistence, and were condemned to join the floating population in search of a home and a living, wandering from region to region in an often fruitless quest. The most obvious category of dispossessed were the poor.

POVERTY AND THE POOR

No century had ever been so conscious of the poor as the sixteenth. In every major European town and city they were there in their thousands, a comfort to the soul of the casual almsgiver but a curse to the civic authorities, the propertied classes, and the maintainers of the public peace. It was from them that the criminal classes were primarily recruited, which gave as good an excuse as any for the drastic control measures decreed against them.

Contemporary commentators appear to have been unanimous that the numbers of poor and the problem of poverty were both of unprecedented dimensions. From the late fifteenth century onwards the laws against vagabonds and begging multiplied in volume. The problem can most easily be explained by the demographic expansion of the period. But there were also other relevant factors, as we can see by the quickening pace of internal migration. The drift from the land to the towns, which was aggravated by the enclosure of commons, conversion of arable to pasture, and reimposition of old seigneurial dues, created a drifting and workless proletariat. Soon after the beginning of the sixteenth century we get the first quantitative estimates of their numbers. It was then that the first steps were taken by municipalities to control begging and to supply poor relief. At the same period there appeared the first few writings devoted exclusively to the practical problems of mass poverty.

In numbers alone, the poor were a major problem. Chronic vagrancy was almost exclusively an urban phenomenon, thanks to the fact that relief was most easily obtainable in towns: so much so that the distressed rural population invariably moved townwards, while the hungry poor moved from smaller towns to bigger, more wealthy ones. The chief cities of Europe were consequently inundated with beggars, many of whom were not native to the region. The situation in Rome was so serious that it led Sixtus V in a Bull of 1587 to complain bitterly of 'these vagrants wandering through all the streets and squares of the city in search of bread; they fill with their groans and cries not only public places and private houses, but the churches themselves; they provoke alarms and incidents; they roam like brute beasts with no other care than the search for food to appease their hunger and replenish their bellies'. Despite the language used here the pope was not being unsympathetic to the poor; he was merely denouncing the importunate methods of the beggars, whose numbers were so immense that they aroused hostility instead of understanding. Even Juan Luis Vives, whose writings on the subject we shall encounter presently, was led to denounce those poor who 'shamelessly and inopportunely' begged their way round inside the churches; 'they push through the congregation, deformed by sores, exuding an unbearable smell from their bodies', and disturbed the faithful at Mass. There was no quick solution to this situation. Twenty years after the pope's bull, in 1607, a traveller could still report that 'in Rome one sees only beggars'. Pierre de l'Estoile reported of the Paris of 1596 that 'the crowds of poor in the street were so great that one could not pass through', while another contemporary claimed to find in the poor of the city's streets 'only masks and images of death, naked and terrible or clad in a ragged, torn robe, as if every one were deliberately aping the person of Job or of a skeleton or corpse'. Every major city suffered likewise, though it is difficult to translate the evocative descriptions of contemporaries into numerical terms.

In western Europe, it is probable that at least one-fifth of a town's population would consist of the wholly poor. In the city of Troyes in 1551, out of a recorded total of twenty-two thousand five hundred and forty-two inhabitants as many as three thousand seven hundred and fifty-seven fell into the category of beggars and vagabonds, a classification which did not take account of those who were merely in economic distress. The proportion of poor in the population of the city of Louvain towards the mid-sixteenth century has been estimated at 21·7 per cent. The figure for Brussels at the same period was twenty-one per cent, and in the duchy of Brabant as a whole it was 28·5 per cent. A census of Segovia in 1561 (pop. twenty-three thousand) tells us that one-sixth (sixteen per cent) of the population was poor, but since the census covered only the sedentary poor it failed to take account of the very large numbers of vagrants in this industrial city. In Seville in 1594 when the authorities ordered the poor to report to the welfare hospital over two thousand turned up on a single occasion, and made organisation of relief impossible. The purely physical difficulty of controlling such large numbers must have caused extreme alarm to the authorities.

Even discounting some vagrants, and looking only at standards of living, the level of poverty was extremely high. An estimate for eighteen towns in Lower Saxony in the sixteenth century suggests that the number of poor were close to thirty per cent of the population. In the town of Uelzen in the same region as many as thirty-five per cent could have been described as a proletariat in the modern sense of the word. Omer Talon in 1634 claimed that Paris had sixty-five thousand beggars, a figure that presumably covered the vagrant rather than the resident population. While poverty was an undeniable feature in the towns, with their large numbers of unemployed it would be incorrect to say that poverty was exclusively an urban phenomenon. On the contrary, rural pauperism was so common in the European countryside that it often overshadowed urban ills, and we must remember too that many of the beggars in the towns had come originally from the countryside. Early sixteenth-century Normandy is a case in point. A study of forty-five small rural parishes shows that about fifteen per cent of the families were poor or beggars. A contemporary census of forty-six parishes described twenty-four per cent of the families as 'poor and beggars'. In another individual parish the proportion of poor was as high as forty-six per cent.

In the villages around sixteenth-century Valladolid, up to one-fifth of the rural population fell into the category of poor. It was thanks to this degree of poverty that many European villages declined and lost their population. The villagers hung on until the stage was reached at which four-fifths or more of their number were paupers (as in Boecillo and Castronuevo, near Valladolid), and it was then that the drift away from the land to the cities became irresistible. The situation could not have been much better in England, where only a very high rate of poverty in both town and countryside can explain Gregory King's estimate that in 1688 about one quarter of the total population consisted of paupers. This proportion is agreed by a pamphleteer of 1641 who estimated that 'the fourth part of the inhabitants of most of the parishes of England are miserable poor people and (harvest-time excepted) without any subsistence'. English towns too had an inordinate level of pauperism. In Lichfield in the late seventeenth century about 16.8 per cent of the city's total population were paupers. In Exeter, we are informed by a modern historian, 'grinding poverty was the lot of more than half the population'. Of Elizabethan Leicester we are also told that 'fully one half of the population lived below or very near the poverty line'.

The distribution of the poor in the towns followed a common pattern. In Exeter there was a nucleus of wealthy parishes in the centre of the city, around the parish of St Petrock, surrounded by a ring of poorer districts, some outside the city walls. In sixteenth-century Valladolid and seventeenth-century Amiens, too, the centre was largely held by the propertied classes and the poor tended to live in the outer parishes of the city. What we know of urban poverty suggests that it was women and children who made up the bulk of the poor. Of the 765 poor qualifying for relief in the parish of St Gertrude in Louvain in 1541, over half were children. During a food crisis in Amiens in the winter of 1621-2, 1,300 adults and 2,050 children were given aid. The preponderance of children is borne out by figures for Norwich, which in the year 1570 had over 3,300 poor in the city. Of this total, 1,007 were children, 831 women and only 504 men. In Huddersfield in 1622, 419 (or fifty-four per cent) of a registered total of 770 poor were children. In Segovia in 1561 only adults appear to have been counted, giving a percentage of sixty for the number of women among the poor. In Medina del Campo at the same date the women totalled eighty-three per cent of the poor.

Though large-scale poverty was nothing new, it was only in the early sixteenth century that the attention of contemporaries became focussed on it. It is probably correct to assume therefore that there were novel and disturbing features to it in this period. What seems to have concerned people most was the *mobility* of the poor, the rising tide of beggary and vagrancy, which threatened to make poverty spill out of its old restricted channels and flood over so as to threaten the security of the upper classes. The appearance of the *Liber Vagatorum* (the Beggars' Book) in Germany, the order of the Parlement of Paris in 1516 ordering all vagabonds out of the city, the institution of poor relief in 1522 by the cities of Augsburg and Nuremberg and in 1525 by Ypres, were all pointers to the existence of the problem. Harrison in his *Description of England* (1577) pinned the beginnings down specifically when he claimed of organised beggary that 'it is not yet full threescore yeares since this trade began'. In the course of the sixteenth century the problem grew to dangerous proportions.

What contributed to the growth of poverty in Europe? There were two main causes that should be considered distinctly. Firstly, there was the actual economic depression of the lower classes. It is possible to say that their lot was growing worse, but it is difficult to point to specific factors. English writers of the early sixteenth century tended to blame enclosures and exploitation by employers. John Hales reported of the cloth industry, for instance, that 'a few men had in their hands a great many men's livings'. Speaking of 'the poverty of the realm', and particularly of the northern counties, Robert Aske, leader of the Pilgrimage of Grace, claimed in 1536 that 'in the north parts much of the relief of the commons was by succour of abbeys', succour that vanished at the dissolution of the monasteries. There can be little doubt that the many profound changes of the Reformation period, both in England and on the continent, were seldom favourable to the common people. The worsening of the economic position of the labouring classes can be measured by the widening gap between wages and prices, but this kind of evidence is of limited value. A more solid indication is the depreciating value of the coinage,

431

debased periodically in several countries in the sixteenth and early seventeenth centuries, which automatically decreased the purchasing power of the lower classes. Here again however, caution is necessary, since a money economy was still not so widely prevalent as to affect the conditions of the common people.

It was the increase in numbers, the second of our two causes, that was most notable. In a sense the increase was illusory, and can be explained merely by the overcrowding of urban areas by the rural poor, or else by the greater mobility of the poor, who in their search for sustenance made their presence felt everywhere. Population mobility helped to crowd urban centres and to depress the wages of an ever-expanding labour force. But there was also a real increase of numbers, in births, which the figures bear out firmly. Economic difficulties and rising numbers therefore combined to produce an intensification of poverty.

VAGRANCY

The growth of vagrancy as a social problem presupposed a large-scale migration of the poor, and this is precisely what the authorities were concerned to stop, since they were heavily burdened with their own poor without having to take in outsiders as well. A casual reader of the literature might gain the impression that excessive fuss was being made over vagrants, but all the indications are that it was an extremely serious problem. In numbers the wandering poor formed a small army. Distribution of poor relief to some extent aggravated the problem, for beggars naturally went to the sources of supply. An account for 1569 claimed that relief measures in London had 'drawn into this citie great numbers of vagabondes, roges, masterless men and Idle persons as also poore, lame and sick persons dwellyng in the most partes of the realme'. Out-of-doors relief thus fell into rapid disrepute in this period in both Catholic and Protestant countries, as it became clear that it merely encouraged (or at least appeared to encourage) vagabondage. But the hostility to vagrants went deeper than mere resentment of their idleness. Vagrancy threatened every aspect of the ordered society. It betokened unsettled social relationships, broken homes, unemployment, rootlessness; it introduced the unstable stranger into allegedly stable communities; it brought new and alien ways into traditional environments. Thus whether for reasons of security or because of the increased charge on public charity, towns tended to deal mercilessly with apprehended vagrants. As we shall see when we come to look at poor relief, government statutes sometimes even ordered that vagrants be enslaved.

We have no evidence at all about the social origin of vagrants, so that it is almost impossible to say whether they were deliberately idle vagabonds or unemployed people in search of a job. The only discernible category were the ex-soldiers, back from the wars and far from inclined to settle down to steady employment. They brought their habits of violence with them, and contributed greatly to the general fear that the population felt of beggars. Typical is the French complaint in 1537, of ex-soldiers 'in company with other vagabonds, people of slothful and evil life, who are to be found in groups and companies in various places and spots in the Kingdom'. The apparent novelty of the scourge of beggars is emphasised by a decree issued by Charles V in 1531 claiming that 'at present the poor abound in this country in far greater numbers than they used to formerly'. To protect themselves against vagrants the cities of Franconia in 1559 bound themselves together in a league against their 'outrages, murders and robberies'. The plague was a universal one. All strangers of the lower classes who were found to be without fixed residence or employment were commonly treated as idle vagrants. This inevitably meant a wide sweep, as we can see by some orders issued against vagrants in London in 1569; which, we are told, were intended 'to apprehend all vagabonds, sturdy beggars, commonly called rogues or Egyptians, and also all idle, vagrant persons, having no master, nor no certainty how and whereby to live'. If people were idle, it was felt, they were so by choice. This assumption permeated all the legislation of the time. A 1554 decree of Queen Mary of Hungary, governor of the Netherlands, ordered to the galleys all

> brigands and vagabonds who do nothing but oppress poor people going from village to village, and from one farmhouse to another demanding alms and often using threats, and at night retiring secretly to taverns, barns and other similar places, without their poverty resulting from the mischance of war, or other honest causes, but solely from waywardness and pure sloth, through not wishing to work or toil to earn their bread and living.

Whatever the reasons that set vagrants on the road, their mobility was quite astonishing. It is true that the great majority did not venture much farther than their own country or province. But a considerable proportion travelled beyond these ordinary limits in

an effort to find succour. In critical times, sixteen-century
Valladolid received poor from as far away as Galicia and
Asturias. In a group of vagrants seized in Exeter in March 1565,
there were representatives from Cornwall, Somerset, Wor-
cestershire, Berkshire and London. Of three hundred and two
vagrants who came from outside the city to Amiens during eleven
specific years in the early seventeenth century, 19.5 per cent came
from Normandy, 15.2 per cent from Picardy, 8.6 from Brittany,
and four per cent from Franche-Comté. All such intruders,
having no rights of residence nor any claims to charity, were
invariably chastised and expelled without delay.

The traffic was, however, also international. In England the
most troublesome group were the Irish who, fleeing from a land
the English had wasted, found temporary refuge among their
oppressors. Of the Dublin poor a contemporary historian
reported in 1575 that 'our town, that gaineth excessively and
whineth at every farthing to be spent on the poor, is yet oppressed
with scarcity and beggary'. Finding little relief at home, they
crossed the sea, where they met draconian poor laws which
threatened them with expulsion. 'Philip Maicroft and his wife',
says a record from Kent, 'were whipped the 8th March 1602, and
had granted unto them six dayes to be conveyed from officer to
officer out of the country of Kent, and then to be conveyed to
Bristol, the place (as they say) wher they landed, from thence to
be conveyed to Dungarvan in Munster in Ireland, the place (as
they say) of their birth.' In times of severe famine in Ireland, the
emigration increased. The western counties of England suffered a
large influx of Irish poor in 1628-9. There was a complaint in
October 1628 of the 'great concourse of Irish people transported
into this country. The owners of barks make much gain by
transporting them at three shillings a piece for young and old.' In
January 1629, the mayor of Bristol reported that 'the scarcity of
corn in Ireland is such that the poor people of that realm are
enforced . . . to come over into this kingdom'. Again in 1633 the
Somerset justices complained of a 'troop of Irish, that begin again
to swarm out of that country'.

In western Europe the direction of movement seems to have
been north-south, towards the Mediterranean. Even here the
unhappy Irish were not absent. Between France and Spain the
movement was almost exclusively southwards, dominated by the
host of seasonal workers who for all practical purposes were
looked upon as vagrants. Spanish commentators lamented the

descent of this flood on Spain. Navarrete in the early seventeenth century claimed that 'all the scum of Europe have come to Spain, so that there is hardly a deaf, dumb, lame or blind man in France, Germany, Italy or Flanders, who has not been to Castile'. When work could not be obtained, the immigrants became a burden on the welfare services. It was reported of the hospital in Burgos that 'every year, in conformity with its rules of institution, it takes in, cares for and feeds for two or three days, from eight to ten thousand people from France, Gascony and other places'. When soup rations were distributed to the poor in Madrid under Philip IV, the process was known as *andar a la sopa francesa*, so much did Frenchmen predominate among the beggars.

On a more European scale, the vagrant problem was a gypsy problem. It is generally agreed that the gypsies originated in the Indian sub-continent. They appeared in eastern Europe in the fourteenth century and in central and western Europe in the early fifteenth. Their coming coincided with the rise of organised begging and with the intensification of the persecution of witches. There is good reason for thinking that they had some connection with these two phenomena. The organisation into which beggars were banded in Europe closely resembled the gypsies' own organisation; and the cant language of the beggars was often closely related to the speech of the gypsies. Though this identification with the beggars did not help the gypsy cause, even more harm was done by the possible witchcraft connection. Gypsies were repeatedly arrested and accused of sorcery because of the way in which they dabbled in magical cures, in juggling and in fortune-telling. 'It was good to hunt down our comedians and minstrels', observed Henri Boguet, 'considering that most of them are wizards and magicians, having no other objective than to empty our purses and corrupt us.' Gatherings of gypsies in their forest encampments could be mistaken for sabbaths, their performing animals for familiars, their dances for Satanic orgies. Whichever way they turned, the gypsies found themselves hunted.

In Hungary and in Transylvania, they were actually enslaved from the fifteenth century onwards. In Moldavia they were sold at slave markets. In Germany in 1540, Agrippa denounced them because they 'lead a vagabond existence everywhere on earth, they camp outside towns, in fields and at crossroads, and there set up their huts and tents, depending for a living on highway robbery, stealing, deceiving and barter, amusing people with fortune-telling, and other impostures'. Nearly every European

435

state and country appears to have passed resolutions expelling them. In 1560, for example, the Estates General at Orléans called on 'all those impostors known by the name of Bohemians or Egyptians to leave the kingdom under penalty of the galleys'. In Spain the *gitanos* (most of whom appear to have come from north Africa rather than through eastern Europe), fell foul of a Castilian regime which had through the centuries successfully suppressed the cultural identity of its minorities. In 1633 Philip IV ordered them 'no longer to dress as they do, and to forget their language; and that they be taken from their places of habitation, separated from one another, with express prohibition to come together publicly or in secret, forbidden to remember either their name or their apparel, or their ways in dances or otherwise, under penalty of three years imprisonment'. These harsh demands were supported by the official explanation that the gypsies were 'not *gitanos* either by origin or by nature, but Spaniards'.

THE DANGEROUS CLASSES

Two widely differing views of the poor were held by Christians in this period. One, of an old humanist and Christian ancestry, was that the poor deserved well of society since society had not done them well: we shall look at this view in detail when discussing poor relief. The other, held by some Catholics but principally by Protestants, was that the poor deserved only retribution, since their own incapacity had put them where they were.

This second view was popularised by the Reformers, motivated the more outspoken writings of thinkers in England and Scotland, and in general led to a strong disciplinarian attitude in which the poor were regarded constantly as potential criminals. We have Martin Bucer's declaration that 'such as give themselves wilfully to the trade of begging be given and bent to all mischief'. It followed that to give relief to beggars encouraged 'the greatest pestilences and destructions of a commonwealth'. This argument against charity, based on concern for social order, was elsewhere reflected in a strong belief (common of course to most Catholics) that class distinctions had been created by God, and that the poor must stay in their place because they deserved no better. 'God hath made the pore', observed Sir John Cheke to the rebels in Kett's rebellion, 'and hath made them to be pore that he myght shew his might, and set them aloft when he listeth, for such cause as to hym seemeth, and plucke down the riche to hys state of povertie, to shew his power.' Like Sir John Cheke, the upper classes dreaded the poor because of their participation in uprisings. Some felt that their rebelliousness was further proof of their unwillingness to turn their hands to any useful thing. In England some Puritans, notably William Perkins, felt strongly that to be poor was to be wicked, in conformity with a general belief that idleness was evil and bred further evils. For Perkins vagrants were 'a cursed generation'; and begging was a very seminarie of vagabonds, rogues, and stragly persons that have no calling, nor are of any Corporation, Church or Commonwealth'. Others in this tradition expressed themselves even more harshly, notably Cotton Mather in New England at the end of the seventeenth century, who asserted that 'for those who indulge themselves in idleness, the express command of God unto us is that we should let them starve'.

This hostility to idleness expressed itself at a political level by a concern at the threat to public peace posed by vagrants. The concern was of course common to both Catholic and Protestant countries, which explains the frequent legislation against vagabonds. The Elizabethan annalist Strype condemned them as 'lewd idle fellows . . . (who) run from Place to Place, from County to County, from Town to Town, to stir up Rumours, raise up Tales, imagin News whereby to stir and gather together the Kings Subjects, of simplicity and ignorance deceived; . . . devising slanderous Tales and divulging to the People such kind of News as they thought might most readily move them to Uproars and Tumults'. The fear of rumour, so common to Elizabethan England and so discernible in Shakespeare's plays, was exaggerated even further by the knowledge that there were great numbers throughout the realm who could expand false news. But it was not merely the power of the seditious word that struck such terror: more directly, it was the ever-present possibility of riot. As the Bishop of Vance, in France, said in 1657 when proposing that beggars be banned from the streets: 'in the recent disturbances in Paris, they were the people most inclined to sedition and pillage of the houses of the rich'. Any commotion was liable to bring the mob out into the streets, in what appeared to the upper classes to be simple class warfare. Archbishop Whitgift observed under Elizabeth that 'the people are commonly bent to novelties and to factions, and most ready to receive that doctrine that seemeth to be contrary to the present state and that inclineth to liberty'. What evidence is there for this? We have already seen the constant resurgence of popular class sentiment during the European revolutions. It seems that in the English Civil War as well, to quote the evidence of the diarist D'Ewes, 'the rude multitude in divers counties took advantage of those civil and intestine broils to plunder and pillage the houses of the nobility, gentry and others'.

Despite this picture of a constantly rebellious populace, there seems to be little evidence of an endemic state of insurrection. A 'serious threat existeᵤ only in the larger industrial towns, where unemployment among the proletariat provided good reason for revolt, Amiens in 1578, a city of perhaps thirty thousand people, was stated to have had as many as six thousand workers 'supported by the alms of the well-to-do'. In these circumstances charity was no more than an attempt to stave off social unrest. In Troyes in 1574, poor who came from outside the city were, according to a common practice, given leave to stay no more than twenty-four hours. The reason given was illuminating. It was said that 'the richest citizens began to live in fear of a disturbance and of a popular riot by the said poor against them'. Unemployment and poverty explains what happened in the city of Tours at Pentecost in May 1640. About eight to nine hundred silkworkers who were dissatisfied with their wages staged an uprising. Soldiers were called in, and when these were found to be inadequate some royal troops were called in. To penalise the people a tax was imposed on them. This led to another uprising in September, when several tax-officials had their throats cut, and the rioters threatened to put the city to the torch, a threat which eventually brought a temporary compromise solution. The situation in Lyon, probably the biggest industrial city in Europe, must have been extremely worrying. Of its population of one hundred thousand, as many as two-thirds consisted of workers; a large proportion of them lived in extreme poverty, many were regularly unemployed. In 1619 about six thousand of the workers were in receipt of poor relief of some sort; in 1642 the figure was ten thousand. The lesson that unemployment bred insurrection was not forgotten in Spain. In 1679, the authorities in Granada, Spain's largest industrial centre, which had a population of over one hundred thousand, estimated that the number of poor who depended on labour in the silk industry for their daily wage exceeded twenty thousand. Mindful of the 1648 uprising, steps were taken to relieve the distress occasioned this time by the plague. At a later date, 1699, when unemployment in Toledo threatened their livelihood, the silkworkers of that city protested that although over three thousand were out of work no steps had been taken to come to their aid. If this situation were to continue, they threatened,

> it would not be surprising if in order to obtain bread they were to resort to all the means permitted by natural law, and even to those not so permitted. The people have no wish to be angered nor to cause riots or a scandal; all they desire is that, since God has brought better weather, their lot should also be bettered.

The social tension brought about by unemployment was well described by an English writer in 1619: 'The poor hate the rich because they will not set them on work; and the rich hate the poor, because they seem burdenous'. Across the channel, Holland also shared the same problem. A pamphleteer of 1623 wrote, 'Our land teems with people, and the inhabitants run each other's shoes off in looking for work. Wherever there is a penny to be earned, ten hands are at once extended to get it.' It is possible that both these quotations should be related to the 1620 depression, and to the sort of conditions that might have tended to prevail in the two most promising economies of Europe. But there can be little doubt that, in whatever part of Europe, workpeople found it extremely difficult to gain a living wage. In Milan in the year 1620 nearly half the twenty thousand textile workers were unemployed, and one-third of the silkworkers. It was not only urban workers who ran a danger of being laid off. Agricultural workers were part of a system which did not require hands for nearly half the year: they were required only at ploughing, sowing- and harvest-time, and at other periods they were unemployed. The early modern economy was one of regular underemployment: it was, consequently, one in which the greater mass of the working population found it difficult to survive on wages alone, since all too often a half-year's earned wages might have to suffice for a full year.

If the common people were looked upon as the source of all disaffection they were also looked upon as the source of crime. Surviving records give the impression that violence, moral and civil disorder, and outrages on property originated above all among the lower classes. But it requires only a little thought to realise that the records are highly misleading. As we have already seen, the nobility were responsible for a very important part of both urban and rural crime. Their encouragement of factional rivalries in the capital cities and their oppression of subjects in the countryside, involving violation of both property and life, were standard causes for complaint. But they were seldom brought to trial. The judicial system was weighted so as to protect them and the honour of their class. Its repressive activities were directed systematically only against the unprivileged. This point emerges very clearly in Grimmelshausen's *Simplicissimus* (1668) where the bandit Oliver defends his trade by arguing that all great kingdoms have become so by robbery (an echo no doubt of St Augustine's famous phrase), and that robbery is essentially the profession of nobles, poor men being victimised merely for joining in. 'You will see no one but poor and humble thieves being hanged', says Oliver. 'Where have you ever seen a person of high quality punished by the courts?'

There is no doubt that ordinary people were aware of this bias in the law and were unhappy about it. In the English system of justice, where local courts, local justices of the peace and local juries were the dispensers of punishment, popular feeling could make itself felt more strongly and the law was accordingly attenuated. For most of the late sixteenth and early seventeenth centuries in England the law seems not to have been applied in all its rigour. Out of nearly one thousand documented cases that came before the Maidstone Quarter Sessions in this period, in not one case where the result is known were criminals punished with the death penalty to which they were subject if found guilty. Juries and justices conspired to make the harsh laws inoperative. The result was that many prisoners accused of theft (the most common crime coming before the courts) were either found not guilty or successfully claimed benefit of clergy or benefit of the womb. What the situation in Somerset was like is revealed by a letter from Edward Hext, a justice of the peace in that county, in 1596:

> Most commonly the simple Countryman and woman, lokynge no farther then ynto the losse of ther owne goods, are of opynyon that they wold not procure a mans death for all the goods yn the world, others uppon promyse to have ther goods agayne wyll gyve faynt evidence yf they be not stryctly loked ynto by the Justyce.

In some other countries where there was little chance of popular attitudes influencing the courts, hatred of the harsh laws was bound to intensify class hostility. This alone explains the actions of the people of Seville in 1648, as we are informed by a witness:

> They went to the offices of the secretaries of the criminal courts, broke them open, seized all the papers and burned them in the middle of the square, in full view of all the judges. They did the same

with the gallows and ladder in the same square, and with the torture-rack and all the instruments of the executioner. They also burned at the same time the committal records which contain the names of all those imprisoned in all the gaols. But great care was taken not to burn the civil records.

A clear distinction should be made between crime in country and in urban areas. Violence was not usual in the countryside. In the Kentish countryside, most of the crimes (principally theft) appear to have been committed not by local people but by outsiders and travellers, by soldiers in transit to and from Dover, and by people from London. The more serious crimes, such as organised robbery, were committed by gangs operating from London. Rural misdemeanours were seldom of a major sort. A study of four hundred criminal cases that came up for consideration in 1643-4 before the courts in rural Angoulême show that the largest category of complaints (nearly twenty-three per cent) concerned nothing more alarming than trespass and similar property offences. A further twenty-two per cent covered personal wrongs, such as marital infidelity, drunkenness and sorcery. Thefts were as high as sixteen per cent, probably because of grain shortage caused by bad harvests in 1642 and 1643. Violence seems to have featured prominently only in those eighteen per cent of all the cases where attempts to collect debts were the issue. The little evidence that we have for rural areas in other countries tends to confirm the relative scarcity of what we would call today 'crime', that is attacks against property and society, among the mass of the countryside population.

The picture in the towns and big cities was quite different. Problems of housing, health, employment and food supply were aggravated in an urban environment. As the poor multiplied, their grievances grew. Faced by biased and repressive laws, their protest took the form of crime. Ample precedent for their occasional resort to violence was provided by the illegal activities of the privileged classes: noble households whose retainers quarrelled by day and killed by night, clergy who abused their freedom from taxes in order to defraud the government's tax officials by holding open market within their monastery walls. Although it is certain that the incidence of crime was higher in towns, it is difficult to give an analysis of the criminal element, simply because here again the law was not impartial. Of those condemned to corporal punishment by the municipal court at Bordeaux from 1600 to 1650, for instance, nearly fifty-two per cent were vagabonds, travellers, outsiders to the city. This figure does not necessarily mean that the vagabonds were the principal criminal element, but only that the court chose to treat them as such. All European courts acted in this way. In Exeter in the late sixteenth century, as shown by court sentences, the mere fact of leading a 'runagate and vagrant life' was enough to warrant condemnation.

Violence was only too common a feature of urban crime. In 1578 the municipality of Valladolid issued a complaint about the thefts and murders which proliferated in the city to such an extent that two more law officers had to be appointed in addition to the three in existence. Most citizens of substance went about armed, not for ostentation but simply in order to defend themselves against robbery and violence. The situation in Madrid in the following century was even worse. 'Not a day passes but people are found killed or wounded by brigands or soldiers; houses burgled; young girls and widows weeping because they have been assaulted and robbed.' So ran a contemporary report in 1639. 'From Christmas till now,' wrote Jerónimo de Barrionuevo in June 1658, 'there have been over 150 deaths and no one has been punished.' The situation could have been paralleled in Milan, Rome, Paris and London. Though a proportion of these crimes involved clergy and nobility (of one hundred and fifty criminals arrested in Valladolid between 1570 and 1572 two were clergy and ten were *hidalgos*), there is no doubt that the greater mass of them were committed by the 'criminal classes', the under-privileged and unpropertied. Hence the great preponderance of petty theft and robbery with violence among urban crimes.

It was the criminal class of whom the propertied were most afraid, and there is no doubt that such a 'class' existed. Within it there were two main groupings. On the one hand there was a large sector of vagabonds and *pícaros*, men who lived outside the restraints of the social order and whose freedom and activities were always looked upon as a threat by that order. On the other — we shall discuss them presently — there were the beggars.

The *pícaro* was a literary type rather than an historical figure. He emerges as one of the preponderant themes in the literature of Spain's Golden Age. Mateo Alemán's *Guzmán de Alfarache* (1599) is commonly regarded as the earliest novel to describe the amoral vagabond life of the *pícaro*, but already in the *Lazarillo de Tormes*, which appeared half a century early in 1554, the main features of the picaresque life were described, though without the actual use of the word *pícaro*. Perhaps the next famous work of this genre, after these two novels, was Quevedo's *Buscón* (1626). The picaresque world of thieves, vagabonds, prostitutes and swindlers, was not confined exclusively to Spanish society, even though it was the Spanish genius that first transmuted it into print. Italy, Germany and France were no less afflicted by the same social type, and foreign translations of the Spanish novels found a ready market in these countries. The *Lazarillo*, for instance, was translated into German in 1617, *Guzmán* two years earlier in 1615. To say that the *pícaro* was essentially a literary type is not to deny that *pícaros*, social delinquents, actually existed. But in literature the features of the delinquent were romanticised, and his basic criminality glossed over. 'There is no profession more widespread, or more glorified by so many', commented Guzmán de Alfarache. Among the glorifiers was Cervantes, tracing in his *Illustrious Kitchen Maid* the career of Diego de Carriazo, who ended up finally at the Mecca of *pícaros*, the little Andalusian port of Zahara:

> He (Carriazo) learnt to play knuckle-bones in Madrid, baseball in the suburbs of Toledo and cards in the barbicans of Seville, passing through all the grades of *pícaro* to the summit where he found his mastership in the tunny-nets of Zahara, the end of the rainbow for all *pícaros*. O *pícaros* of the kitchen, dirty, fat and shiny; bogus beggars and cripples, counterfeiters, cutpurses from Zocodover or other places in Madrid, braying prayer-mongers, street-porters of Seville, pimps of the lowest order, and all the teeming horde rejoicing in the name — *pícaro!*

Pícaros were often in Spain identified with impoverished *hidalgos* who had taken to vagabondage but still kept up the appearance of gentility. Other countries experienced this phenomenon of the noble beggar, but less markedly. For them the main problem was simply beggary. There came into existence in the late fifteenth century a strange and mysterious fraternity called the Beggars' Brotherhood, which held under its sway vagabonds and professional criminals, and which gave them a degree of organisation hardly suspected outside their ranks. The Brotherhood was an archetypal anti-society, most probably modelled on the gypsy organisation. We know of its structure through various contemporary accounts ranging from the anonymous *Liber Vagatorum* (1455) in Germany, to the *Vie généreuse des Mercelots, Gueuz et Boesmiens* (1596) of Pechon de Ruby in France and *Il Vagabondo* (1627) by the Italian Dominican Giacinto Nobili. Numerous other writings, including many in English and Spanish, were published in the late sixteenth and early seventeenth century on its customs and language.

The principal material function of the Brotherhood was to organise beggary. Beggar vagabonds specialised in imposture of innumerable kinds, each one calculated to attract sympathy and a donation. Disguises, which sometimes extended to actual bodily mutilation where unavoidable, tended to concentrate on emphasising personal misfortune (hence a show of being lame or blind or having a stricken infant), or illness (thus epilepsy could be feigned), or on attracting the sympathy of the devout. The vast majority of these disguised beggars were in fact able-bodied; some were so able-bodied as to be able to adopt several disguises consecutively. The art of imposture became so specialised that beggars would complain when others adopted their particular disguise. It was the task of the Brotherhood to solve these demarcation disputes. The result was the evolution in each country of a specific number of set disguises. In Rome in 1595, when a youth was arrested for begging, he informed the papal police that 'among us poor beggars there are many secret companies, and they are different because each has a distinctive activity'. His statement went on to name nineteen different societies, each with differing membership, clothes and functions: the *famigotti*, for example, pretended to be invalid soldiers, the *bistolfi* wore cassocks, and the *gonsi* pretended to be rustic idiots. By 1627, when Nobili was writing his book, the Italians had twenty-three categories of beggar. The French in the sixteenth century had fourteen, the Germans twenty-eight. It was in this world of false beggars that the great *pícaro* novels such as *Guzmán de Alfarache* were set.

Since the beggars lived off two main sources, imposture and theft, the Brotherhood can to some extent be looked upon as a form of organised crime, a sixteenth-century underworld. But in fact it was the begging alone that was in any way regulated. The cutting of purses, picking of pockets, and street robbery, were left entirely to the initiative of each vagabond, for the essence of the vagabond's life was freedom ond the absence of controls. Their society had its ruler, the king of the beggars, the *grand Coesre* 1 as he was known in France, but he was not a king as others were. It had its rules and code of honour, but it was the honour of

1 Pronounced Couère.

thieves, and the rule was to exploit others just as they, the poor, were exploited by the upper classes. Their morality was not that of society. The seventeenth-century historian Henri Sauval, as we have seen, testified that they did not practise marriage, nor did they frequent the sacraments, and they only entered a church if it was to cut purses. The young man from Rome in 1595, whom we have encountered above, likewise testified that 'among us few practise the faith'. Neither the norms nor the conduct of society, then, were to be their guide. They were an anti-society, organised against it, disbelieving in its ethics, dedicated to cheating and robbing it. They were separated from it by their own jargon, called cant in English, *Rotwälsch* in German, *argot* in French, *jerga de germanía* (jargon of the Brotherhood) in Spanish. Cant had a virtually international vocabulary, many of the essential words being common to all the brotherhoods. It is no coincidence that a high proportion of cant derived immediately from the gypsy language. The first comprehensive account of it in English was Harman's *Caveat for common Cursetors* (1567). In France a 1628 book, *Le Jargon de l'Argot reformé*, summarised both the language and the usages of the French brotherhood. Yet despite this conscious separation from society the beggars were not an organised society of their own, for they were essentially vagabonds, tied to no locale, with their home in any nation they chose to reside in, true citizens of the world.

In each big city, and notably the international ones — Rome, Paris, London, Seville, Medina del Campo in its prime — they had their regular place of assembly, the Court of Miracles. Most frequently it was in the heart of the slum quarter. In Paris, Sauval tells us, it was 'in a very large square at the end of a large, stinking, noisome, unpaved cul de sac. At one time it used to be next to the outer extremity of Paris, but now it is situated in one of the worst built, filthiest and darkest quarters of the city'. There, according to one legend from which the name of the Court apparently derived, all the poor and maimed who entered in would emerge healthy and upright. But according to another, referring to the Court at Rouen, the true miracle was that there 'the poorest among them is deemed the richest', a total reversal of the values of the outside world. The truth, of course, was that wealth also had some status among them. 'The beggars have their magnificences and their fleshpots, like the rich', as Montaigne observed. In Germany there was said to be a noble class among the beggars, who apparently never had to go on the streets themselves in order to beg. But even this, the supreme irony of beggars, with their own alleged kings and underworld courts, was no more than a form of vengeance on a cruel society, As Robert Greene explained, when he came to write his *Defence of Conny Catching* (1592) in justification of the criminal poor: 'This is the Iron Age, wherein iniquitie hath the upper hande, and all conditions and estates of men seeke to live by their wittes, and he is counted the wisest that hath the deepest insight into the getting of gaines.'

There can be no doubt that the beggars were feared. The savagery of legislation against them reflected not so much a paternal concern for corrective punishment as a genuine alarm that the security of society was threatened. It was not without reason that the dissentient nobility of the Netherlands in 1566 gladly took to themselves a title — beggars, *gueux* — that was to strike terror into their opponents. Save in industrial cities like Lyon and Granada, the vagabond beggars seemed more dangerous than the labouring classes, and were in a real sense the proletariat of their time.

POOR RELIEF

Feared and despised by their betters, the poor were still essential to their spiritual welfare for, as Catholic tradition proclaimed, to succour them was a major act of charity. It was this that made Guzmán de Alfarache cynically defend the impostures of false beggars. Since charity was given, he argued, less for the material welfare of the recipient than for the spiritual welfare of the donor, it might as well be given to the false poor as to the real. This perverse view is a good reflection of the weaknesses in the old mediaeval attitude to poverty. Since poverty could never be eradicated ('the poor you have always with you', Christ had said) it was seldom seriously attacked, and was merely exploited as a source for conferring spiritual graces on oneself. Thus outdoor relief, which later writers were to attack as a positive encouragement of mendicancy, became a corporal work of mercy. Rich men, who in their own lives had shown no solicitude for the needy, prepared their way to heaven by leaving sums to the poor in their wills. In Valladolid the consciences of the dying were further eased by the unusual practice whereby rich men arranged to have an entourage of paupers to bear the candles at the funeral; and some even had themselves interred as paupers.

Only in the sixteenth century, with the extraordinary increase in the scale of poverty and vagabondage, did writers, both

Catholic and Protestant, adopt a more constructive attitude towards the problem. Luis Vives quite rightly has the honour of being the first to outline a methodical approach to poor relief, in his *De subventione pauperum* (On the relief of the poor) (1526). Vives' concept of charity was the classic Christian one: the poor have a right to aid, and the propertied have an absolute moral obligation to help them. Where Vives went beyond the facile poor relief of mediaeval times was in his firm opposition to begging and in his rejection of the view that charity was mere material relief. Hospitals must be set up to take the poor off the streets, and relief must consist 'not in mere almsgiving, but in all the ways by which a poor man can be uplifted'. Implicit in this approach was the conviction that the Christian state had a duty to maintain its less fortunate citizens and that the task should not be left to private charity. Other Spanish writers besides Vives were among the most prominent students of the task of poor relief. Juan de Medina in his *Plan of poor relief practised in some Spanish towns* (1545) outlined a scheme to abolish begging and to hospitalise the sick and needy. His plans were apparently already being practised in Valladolid, and seem to have been partially successful, for 'the police testify that, in contrast to former times, they find hardly anyone now to hang or flog for robbery'. Domingo de Soto in the same year produced his *Considerations on the poor,* and in 1598 came Cristóbal Pérez de Herrera's *Discourse on the assistance of the poor.* It was Juan de Mariana in his *De rege et regis institutione* (1599) who confirmed the new emphasis on state intervention by urging that 'piety and justice necessitate relieving the poverty of invalids and the needy, caring for orphans and aiding those in want. Among all the duties of the Sovereign, this is the chief and most sublime. This too is the true purpose of riches, which should not be directed to the enjoyment of one person only, but to that of many; not to the satisfaction of our personal and transient interests, but to the attainment of justice, which is eternal.' Mariana goes on to say: 'the state is bound to compel us to this, by organising poor relief in each locality as one of the public tasks'.

This evolution of Spanish thought towards secular relief is interesting for it contradicts a common assumption that it was the Reformation that was responsible for the laicisation of charity and for the substitution of municipal for clerical relief. Secularisation was in fact common to Catholic and Protestant alike, and was a logical response to the need for control. Already by the 1520s several German cities had seen this. Augsburg began in 1522 with a ban on begging in the street, and appointed six poor-guardians to supervise relief. Nuremburg followed suit, so did Strassburg and Breslau in 1523, Regensburg and Magdeburg in 1524. Vives was the direct inspiration for a scheme put into practice at Ypres in 1525. From this period onwards it was the state, which alone had the police powers required to control vagrancy, that took over care of the poor.

Control of charity in this fashion meant an end to much of the indiscriminate almsgiving of earlier times. Not without reason, then, did many contemporaries, both Catholic and Protestant, protest that the roots of charity had dried up and men's hearts became hardened. The Elizabethan annalist John Stow, looking back to the early sixteenth century, recalled that

> I myself in that declining time of charity have oft seen at the Lord Cromwell's gate in London more than two hundred persons served twice every day with bread, meat and drink sufficient; for he observed that ancient and charitable custom, as all prelates, noblemen, or men of honour and worship, his predecessors, had done before him.

It is hardly necessary to emphasise that the authorities were concerned less with poverty than with the poor, less with charity than with the preservation of social order. At the roots of the new concern over poor relief lay a profound fear of the proletariat. In every case without exception, therefore, the initial steps taken by the authorities were disciplinary rather than ameliorative. As viewed by the Company of the Blessed Sacrament in seventeenth-century France, for example, poverty was a social disorder which involved within it the indiscipline and possible violence of the lower classes. The various measures that came to be adopted in the sixteenth and seventeenth centuries as solutions to the problem — prohibition of begging, hospitalisation and so on — were all in essence repressive measures. None went any way towards abolishing poverty at its roots. The poor relief systems of the period were, in short, punitive.

The earliest control measures consisted in granting beggars a licence to beg within a certain area only, usually the place of their origin. In London in the 1520s genuine native paupers were given licences and identification discs allowing them to beg: all others were to be whipped out of town. The purpose of this was to dissociate begging from vagrancy. As the poor realised they could only beg in their own localities they would cease to drift, and vagrancy would soon cease. Charles V in Spain restricted beggars to an area within six leagues' radius from their home towns. Under Philip II this method of control was centred on the parish: it was the parish priest alone who issued begging licences, each parish created officials to superintend the poor, and an attempt was made to register all vagrants. The licence system failed completely, partly because it was so easy to counterfeit licences. In Scotland the laws restricting beggars to their native parishes were passed in 1535, 1551 and 1555 and not renewed thereafter. In 1556 the Cambridgeshire authorities banned all begging whatsoever and suspended the licence system. Norwich followed this example. By mid-century, then, the licence system was being discarded.

At about the same time the local authorities resorted to the dual system of institutional care and outdoor relief. Institutional care was provided through hospitals: in 1544 the great pre-Reformation London hospital of Saint Bartholomew's was re-founded, and by 1557 there were four 'royal' hospitals in the city — Saint Bartholomew's, Christ's, Bridewell and Saint Thomas'. In order to help pay for such institutions, a compulsory tax for poor relief was decreed in London. Other local authorities followed suit. In order to maintain its workhouses or 'houses of correction', Norwich in 1557 issued regulations for compulsory taxation. In France a similar procedure was followed. The Paris authorities in 1554 set up their first poor hospital, at Saint-Germain; this was subsequently called the Hôpital des Petites Maisons and lasted till the end of the *ancien régime*. Hospitals were meant almost exclusively for the invalid poor; for the able-bodied poor, workhouses were set up. There were workhouses in all the major towns in England and France. They offered refuge and employment, neither in a very appealing form, to those who had no other way of earning their living. Like England, France delegated control of poor relief to the localities. The ordinances of Moulins (1566) and Blois (1579) stipulated that local authorities should raise money through parish collections and tax levies. Lyon was perhaps the earliest of all French cities to provide for the unemployed, and seems to have been the first to set up workhouses. Its hospital, the Aumône Générale, was in existence as early as 1533, and was replaced only in 1614 by the much larger Hôpital Général de la Charité.

The whole purpose of hospitalisation and workhouses was to take poverty off the streets, a purpose that was to be followed even more rigorously in subsequent decades. The trend suggests that open-handed, direct charity had become outdated, and that the predominant problem now was the fear of social disorder.

The English poor relief system, which alone of the European systems has been adequately studied, deserves some detailed attention here, particularly since its development mirrors what little we know of others. The belief that vagrants and beggars were idle by choice rather than circumstance seems to have been uppermost in the minds of the authorities. 'That loathsome monster idleness', is how a pamphleteer of 1580 referred to mass unemployment. Harsh legislation was consequently employed against vagrants. In 1547 a statute actually specified slavery as a penalty for vagrancy. This was normally for two years, but could be for life if the slave tried to escape. Two years later these slavery clauses were repealed. In 1572, however, there was another harsh proposal that became law. A vagrant by this act could be whipped and bored through the ear on the first occasion, adjudged a felon on the second, and be punishable by death on the third. All these penalties were repealed in 1593. The resort to legislation brings out one important feature of the English system — the steady move away from local, voluntary, methods towards centralised and publicly enforced measures. The piecemeal and varying solutions adopted by municipal authorities were seen to be insufficient.

The shift of emphasis from private charity as a spiritually beneficial act to the public control and institutionalisation of charity in the interests of social order, is reflected in the new demand that the poor be forced to work. 'This is the best charity', wrote an English Puritan in the seventeenth century, 'so to relieve the poor as we keep them in labour. It benefits the giver to have them labour; it benefits the commonweal to suffer no drones, nor to nourish any in idleness; it benefits the poor themselves.' At the end of the reign of Queen Elizabeth a comprehensive act to regulate poor relief was passed. This, the act of 1597-8, was amended and re-enacted in 1601. Together, the legislation of these years formed the basis of poor relief in England for the next two centuries. Poor relief was localised: it was placed in the control of churchwardens of the parish and four overseers of the poor appointed every Easter by the justices of the peace. The poor were divided into categories, each of which was to receive particular treatment. The ablebodied poor were either to be put to work or confined in houses of correction; children were likewise either to be set to work or apprenticed; and the sick and maimed poor were to be housed and cared for 'at the general charges of the parish, or otherwise of the hundred or the county'. Begging and vagrancy were prohibited. To finance the work of the Act, a compulsory poor rate was to be raised in each locality. This legislation was devised to meet a severe emergency, for these were years of great economic distress throughout Europe. Predictably, the success was only partial. The harsh regime of the workhouses or houses of correction resembled prison life, and were hated more than prison: their purpose clearly was to make life so unbearable that inmates would prefer to seek work outside. A Somerset justice of the peace, Edward Hext, cited some vagrants in 1596 who 'confessed felony unto me; by which they hazarded their lives; to the end they would not be sent to the House of Correction, where they should be forced to work'. The machinery to run the Poor Law was not adequate over most of the country and soon there were areas where no improvement, and even a deterioration, was visible. Thus an observer of the situation in southeast England in 1622, Thomas Dekker, reported that through the number of the Poore do dailie increase, all things worketh for the worst in their behalfe. For there hath beene no collection for them, no not these seven yeares in many parishes of this land especiallie in countrie townes.'

A clear distinction must be made between the existence of the law and its enforcement. If the law had intended to tidy away the problem of mass unemployment, it failed; and other measures had to be adopted to maintain social peace. It is in this context that the attempt of governments to control wages and prices must be viewed. When all else failed, and when crises such as famine threatened, a free distribution of supplies to the poor was undertaken. In 1623 the bailiffs of Derby reported that 'wee have at the charge of the cheife and ablest inhabitants of this Burrowe (borough) provided 140 quarters of corne which wee weekely afford to the poore as their necessities require under the common price of the markett'. Occasionally the very drastic solution of forced emigration was adopted. In 1617 one London parish contributed 'towards the transportation of a hundred children to Virginia by the Lord Mayor's appointment'. Vagrants were also transported and on one occasion, during the Protectorate, it was proposed to send all the prostitutes in England to the New World. By this date the problem had grown in intensity once more, because of the civil war.

In France the process of attempting to take vagrants off the streets and put them into houses followed roughly the same course, but for one important detail. In England the constant activity of the Privy Council and Parliament gave some sort of national direction to policy. In France (as in most other countries) the initiative remained very much with the local authorities, who found themselves incapable of keeping up with the ruin caused among the people by the civil wars of the late sixteenth century. The measures of this period, such as the setting up of workhouses and alms houses, were temporary ones. It was not until after the wars that more solid policies were followed, at the instance of ministers like Barthélemy Laffemas. In 1611 a decree ordered the compulsory hospitalisation of the poor. Three specified buildings in Paris were set apart for these 'pauvres enfermez'. The measure was hateful to the poor, who prized their liberty, and it failed. (There were the rare cases when poor vagrants, once ensconced in a hospital, refused to leave. This happened at Troyes in 1653 where, as a prison official complained, 'there are a great number of vagabonds, idlers and layabouts who, on the pretext of passing through, settle down and often have a long stay, without there being any way of making them leave'.) After 1616 compulsory hospitalisation was discontinued. The big general hospitals set up at this time did however continue their existence. The chief Paris hospital, the Pitié, was set up in 1612; the Lyon hospital, the Charité, in 1614. They were particularly active during the Frondes, which were another peak period of poverty and vagrancy in France. In 1657 it was estimated that Paris alone harboured forty thousand beggars.

The poor relief work done in the 1650s is forever associated with the name of St Vincent de Paul, whose labours must be identified with the highest Christian ideals of devotion to the poor. 'God loves the poor', St Vincent stressed, 'and he loves those who love them . . . Let us seek out the poorest, the most helpless, and recognise before God that they are our lords and masters.' Though the sentiments were mediaeval, Vincent worked within the framework of the new attitude to poor relief. Ironically, this framework was profoundly hostile to the poor. The Company of the Blessed Sacrament, which devoted much of its time to charitable work, was committed to a policy of hospitalisation, which meant that the poor were to be shut away. Outdoor relief was to be avoided. Hospitals were accordingly set up by the Company at Marseille in 1639, Orléans in 1642,

Grenoble in 1661, and in several other major cities. The plan for the Company's Aumône at Toulouse revealed its hostility to traditional almsgiving, which was regarded as useless to protect 'the poor, who by birth should serve the rich'. In 1656 the Company founded the Hôpital Général des Pauvres at Paris. The institution was made deliberately unpleasant. The inmates could be punished by the directors of the hospital, all their activities were time-tabled, and they were to be 'clothed in grey robes and caps and have each on their robes a general mark and a particular number'.

St Vincent supported the idea of a hospital but opposed the deliberate introduction of a harsh regime; he also favoured outdoor relief for beggars. His own hospital for beggars, the Nom-de-Jésus (1653), provided both shelter and obligatory labour for the inmates. It was through his work in distributing relief of various kinds that he won universal love and respect. Throughout the north of France in the worst years of the Thirty Years War and of the Fronde, in the Ile de France, Picardy, Champagne and Lorraine, he and his helpers were everywhere present to save lives as well as souls. 'At the last distribution of bread we made,' runs a typical report from a helper in one of the towns of Lorraine in 1641, 'there were 1132 poor, without counting the sick, who are numerous and whom we are helping with food and in other ways.' 'For the last two years', states a letter of 1653 from one town in northern France to Vincent, 'the whole of Champagne and this town in particular have lived only from your charity. All the countryside would have been deserted and all the inhabitants dead from hunger if you had not sent someone to relieve them from poverty and give them life.' The work of St Vincent, which was the greatest exercise of practical Christian charity in early modern times, did not long survive the Fronde. In 1656, when better times had returned, the government prohibited any outdoor relief or distribution of alms, and reiterated the order that the poor be gathered into hospitals.

Hospitalisation meant the end of personal Christian charity and the beginning of a soulless dispensation, in which the actual givers of charity were separated from the recipients by a third person: the hospital through which the charity was funnelled. In this way charity too entered the Iron Age. Outdoor relief was still widely practised, especially in Catholic countries. Estimates made in Milan in 1603 indicate that the amount of food distributed annually to the poor at that period totalled 2,192 bushels (*moggia*) of wheat, 4,344 of mixed grain, 890 of rice, various quantities of meat, vegetables and salt, 1,370 kegs of wine and 4,822 long loaves of coarse bread; in addition, 18,690 *lire* was distributed in cash. But the growing trend of private charitable donations, in Italy as in England and France, was towards controlled, institutional giving. The situation in France illustrates the character of the new dispensation. The Paris hospital set up in 1612, the Pitié, which was soon to become the main Parisian one, succeeded in accumulating as many as one thousand and ninety poor by 1661; of these eight hundred and ninety-seven were girls and ninety-five were old women. Another of the Paris hospitals, the Salpétrière, had 1,900 inmates in 1666: of these, one hundred and ten were blind or paralysed, eighty-five were imbeciles, ninety were infirm aged, sixty were epileptics, and three hundred and eighty were sexagenarians or older. The hospitals tended to house women and children only. Men were put to work in the workhouses. Neither hospitals nor workhouses eradicated beggary. Since the former were a form of assistance they encouraged begging; and the latter were so repellent that they obliged the poor to make every effort to keep at large.

The new charity was supported principally by the bourgeoisie. In both Catholic and Protestant countries it was the merchant class that gave generously. In seventeenth-century Holland, where the problem of the poor was considerable, an English traveller could note (in 1685) that 'there is nothing shows more the charitable inclination of the Hollanders than their great care in relieving, maintaining and educating their poor, for there are no beggars to be seen anywhere in the streets'. That the Dutch had to some extent succeeded in incarcerating poverty is suggested by the clearly exaggerated report that there were in Amsterdam 'above eighteen tons of gold distributed every year to poor families, which proves as well the great riches of the town as the good and charitable disposition of the inhabitants'.

It has been suggested by Professor W. K. Jordan for England that it was the Puritan ethic that determined the new willingness to leave large legacies for the poor. It may be more correct to lay the emphasis on the social class rather than on the religion of the donor. In Catholic countries it was no less the bourgeoisie who took the lead in charitable donations. In seventeenth-century Milan, as in England, private donations were by far the most important source of income for the poor. Milanese merchants gave large sums to the hospitals. Among them was Giulio Cesare Lampugnani who, besides giving ninety thousand *lire* in legacies to two charitable institutions, in his will in 1630 left 196,000 *lire* in goods and 63,500 in capital for supplying the poor with bread, rice, coal and clothing. G. P. Carcano in 1623 left the fabulous sum of five hundred thousand scudi to his infant son, to enter into on his majority; until then, the money was to be available for use by the Ospedale Maggiore of Milan and by other institutions. In England it was the merchants of London above all who distinguished themselves in giving to charity. Both before and after the Reformation the greater merchants gave a substantial part of their personal fortunes to charity: in the century before the Reformation the proportion reached twenty-nine per cent of their estates, in the Elizabethan age about one-quarter. One of the most significant aspects of the gifts made by London burghers was the 'secularisation' of their donations, a trend which may have worked in favour of the poor. Over the period 1480-1540, for

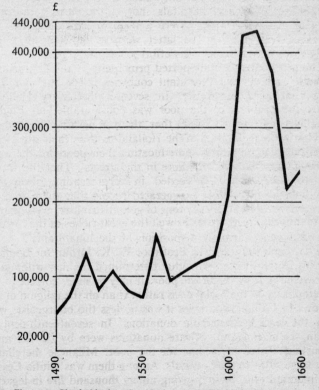

Figure 21 Charitable donations to the poor in England, 1480-1660.

example, the lesser merchants of London gave sixty-one per cent of their gifts to religious purposes and only eighteen per cent directly to the poor. From 1601 to 1640, on the other hand, religion was given no more than 9.8 per cent, while the poor were given 52.4 per cent. The figures may be somewhat misleading (in the earlier period money donated to religion often found its way to the poor, while in the later period the money seldom if ever reached the poor directly and was usually offered to them in the unpalatable form of almshouses), but in absolute terms they reflect a growing concern with a grave social problem. The pattern of poor relief in England from 1480 to 1660 in ten southern countries is illustrated in Figure 21, which shows clearly how the poor came to concern contemporaries. These donations to the poor, moreover, were not given out of piety so much as out of a firmly secular wish to preserve social order by uprooting the vice of poverty.

SLAVERY

The most completely dispossessed of humans, the slaves, are little in evidence in standard accounts of sixteenth century Christian Europe, but they certainly existed in very great numbers. Slavery being principally an economic institution, it supplied labour where it could not be obtained on any other basis, and we must look to a special type of society for its existence. In this period we can find it, broadly speaking, in two principal settings: in the 'colonial' society, and in the 'feudal' society. By adopting these categories, we necessarily exclude from discussion any remnants of classical or mediaeval servitude that may have survived in Europe.

The 'colonial' type of slavery was the predominant one in western Europe, and owed most of its vigour to practice in the Iberian peninsula. There the *Reconquista* — the reconquest of Muslim territory — had since the later Middle Ages led the Christian races to dominate and exploit the defeated Moors. So-called 'Saracen' slaves were a commonplace in central and southern Portugal and Spain in mediaeval times. The struggle between Christian and Muslim extended, of course, beyond the peninsula, and it was through the innumerable battles and piracies at sea that the institution of slavery continued to perpetrate itself. Muslim corsairs were operative throughout the Mediterranean in the sixteenth century, and collected Christian slaves from as far afield as Russia and England. The Christian powers in turn did not scruple to enslave any Moors they could lay their hands upon. With this experience behind them, the Iberian powers accepted slavery as a standard feature of their public life. The mediaeval laws of both Spain and Portugal sanctioned the holding of slaves.

Spanish slavery had been firmly Moorish in character, and continued to be so even after the expulsion of the Moriscos in 1609. When that event took place the only Moriscos not expelled from Spain were those being held as slaves, and these must have numbered several thousand. After each Morisco rebellion in the sixteenth century, and particularly after the rising in the Alpujarra mountains in 1569, large numbers of rebels, reportedly running into thousands, had been sold into slavery. This native source of labour (used mainly for domestic work, but also for the galleys and for forced labour in the mercury mines at Almadén) was supplemented from abroad. The battle of Lepanto brought many Turks into Spanish households; slave raids were also fruitful, as with the expedition made in 1611 by the Marquis of Santa Cruz to the island of Querquenes, when he captured four hundred slaves. On the whole the Muslim slaves in southern Spain tended to be of Turkish or Barbary extraction rather than native Moors, simply because of the extent of piracy in the western Mediterranean.

When the age of discovery began, Iberian slavery took on a new texture. From being a Mediterranean institution it became an Atlantic one. The geographical change also implied a racial one: in the place of Moors, black Africans were traded. In both quantity and quality a new era had commenced, for not only were the negroes enslaved in numbers that exceeded any previous practice but they were employed primarily to serve the needs of the colonial economy in America and elsewhere. The logic of this was that those countries which resorted to slavery in their colonies — Portugal, Spain and, later, France and England — tended to accept the extension of slavery in their own metropolitan territories, thus introducing into Europe the colonial pattern of race relations.

Portugal, the first of European countries to develop the new type of slavery abroad, was the first to be inundated at home. By 1553 a Belgian humanist, writing from Evora, could report that 'there are slaves everywhere here, consisting of negroes and of Moorish captives. Portugal is so full of slaves that I could almost believe Lisbon to have more slaves, of both sexes, than free

Portuguese . . . When I first came to Evora I thought I had entered some city of devils, so many negroes did I meet everywhere.' In 1551 Lisbon was calculated to have one slave for every ten free Portuguese, and in 1573 the total number of slaves (both black and Moor) in Portugal was put at forty thousand. The peak seems to have been reached in 1620, when Lisbon had ten thousand four hundred and seventy slaves. Some of these came from as far afield as India, thanks to the Portuguese incursions into the east. After the early seventeenth century there appears to have been a decline in the number of slaves, owing principally no doubt to the decay of the empire, but also to such factors as manumission, the fear of slave revolts and of the undercutting of wage labourers.

The development of negro slavery in America had a direct effect on Spain. As a Flemish observer was to report in 1655, 'the American trade has given new life to the institution of slavery in this country, so that in Andalucia one sees few servants other than slaves, mostly Moors as well as blacks'. The slave population tended, as elsewhere in the Mediterranean, to concentrate on the seaports. Seville is estimated to have had six thousand three hundred and twenty-seven slaves in 1565, out of a population of eighty-five thousand five hundred and thirty-eight. Most of these were negroes. Cadiz in 1616 had far less, only three hundred Moorish slaves (they were called 'white slaves') and five hundred black. In the north of Spain there were fewer slaves, and in Madrid a law of 1601 forbade their employment. Spanish slaves were employed principally in private households, as domestic servants. A few crown slaves did exist and were used for public works. An important aspect of Spanish slavery that was to be of some significance in the New World was the general lack of a racialist attitude towards blacks. Not only were negroes 'better natured and more loyal' (than other slaves), to quote a writer of 1615; they were also amenable to Christian religion and civilisation. In extremely rare cases they could move right up the social ladder. One such case was Juan Latino, whose parents were both slaves. He began his career as page to the Duke of Sessa, managed to enter the university of Granada, graduated there in 1557, finally obtained a chair in Latin and married the daughter of a noble family.

The two most bitter fruits of the discovery of America were the enslavement of the native American Indians, and the expansion of the trade in blacks from Africa. Though neither of these subjects is our direct concern here, they are important for the light they shed on European attitudes to slavery. European missionaries, conversant with the culture of the Indians and horrified by the barbaric colonising methods of their compatriots, defended the natives of the New World from charges that they were so uncivilised as to be slaves by nature. 'No nation exists today', protested the Dominican missionary Bartolomé de la Casas in 1547, 'nor could exist, no matter how barbarous, fierce or depraved its customs may be, which may not be attracted and converted to all political virtues and to all the humanity of domestic, political and rational men.' Commenting a few years later on the same theme, this great defender of the Indians proclaimed that their natural innocence was such that 'they would be the happiest people in the world, if only they knew God'. A century later, in 1654, the French Dominican Jean-Baptiste Du Tertre could still project the image of the Caribbean Indians as 'the most contented, the happiest, the least corrupt, the most sociable, the least deceitful, the healthiest of all peoples in the world'. Unfortunately in order to protect the Indians most of the missionaries gave their approval to the employment of black slavery. The great Jesuit colony in Paraguay, where the Guaraní Indians lived at liberty, employed hundreds of blacks to do the menial labour. A few prominent individuals (such as Las Casas) objected that the enslavement of the black was as immoral as that of the Indian; but the labour demands of the colonial regime were such that negro slavery became indispensable. Slavery and the Atlantic slave trade thus continued unabated into the nineteenth century. Among those who worked to mitigate its effects were the Jesuits. The Catalan Jesuit, St Peter Claver, the 'apostle of the negroes', devoted his life to the service of the blacks as they disembarked at Cartagena after the long Atlantic crossing. For forty years, from 1614 to his death in 1654, he laboured among them in the most horrifying conditions, and when he died they wept in the streets. From Portugal the outstanding voice was that of Father Antonio Vieira, who in 1653 denounced the practice of negro slavery in Brazil. 'Every man who holds another unjustly in servitude, though able to release him, is certainly in a state of damnation', he thundered. Their voices had no impact on the appalling industry which sent millions of black Africans to their death in a strange continent. 'All ills and toils begin in slavery', commented one Spanish opponent, Father Alonso de Sandoval, in 1627, 'it is one with continuous death . . . and is a combination of all evils'.

Outside the Iberian peninsula, Mediterranean slavery could not rely on the colonial system, and owed its continued existence almost exclusively to piracy. This was certainly true of France, where Marseille and Toulon, as seaports, inevitably had to harbour the booty of slave-hunters. Beyond these Mediterranean ports slavery was very rare in France. There were many recorded cases of slaves in Roussillon (which became French in 1659), but they were nearly all Moorish, an overspill from Spain. The prevailing attitude in France can be summed up in the order issued by the Parlement of Guyenne in 1571 against a slave-trader in Bordeaux. 'France, the mother of liberty', stated the order, 'does not permit slavery.' 'All persons in this realm are free', wrote the jurist Loisel in 1608, 'and if a slave reaches these shores and gets baptised, he becomes free.' The growth of the French overseas empire, however, militated against sentiments like this, and as colonial slavery grew so did its acceptance by metropolitan France, which imported coloured labour mainly through La Rochelle and Nantes.

Piracy made Venice, Genoa and other Italian ports into leading slave centres. The volume of traffic here was evidence of a still flourishing system. The city of Palermo in 1565 is estimated to have had about one thousand five hundred slaves, and other Mediterranean ports must have had comparable numbers. By origin these were almost wholly Muslim. The record we have of the slave cargo brought back from the Levant by four Florentine galleys in June 1574 gives us a total of three hundred humans, made up of two hundred and thirty-eight Turks, thirty-two 'Moors', seven negroes, two Greeks, five Arabs, five Jews, five Russians and six Christians. The market to which they were taken was Messina; there one hundred and sixteen were sold, and most of the Christians freed. Who were the purchasers? There were two main sources of demand. The most obvious buyers were captains who required galley slaves, since this form of labour was commonly in use throughout the sixteenth and seventeenth centuries. The navies of the Italian states and of Spain (many of whose ships were commanded by Italians) were heavily dependent on slaves for rowers. An agent for the Spanish royal galleys shopping for slaves in Genoa in 1573, for instance, bought one hundred slaves from the authorities in February and another thirty-two (these last from Hungary) in April. At this period the cost of such a slave was about one hundred ducats. The places of origin of slaves —

Aleppo, Salonika, Istanbul, Tunis, Algiers — point to the overwhelmingly Muslim character of slavery in the Christian Mediterranean. (In the Arab Mediterranean, of course, it was the Christians who were the slaves. In 1588 it was estimated that over two thousand five hundred Venetian subjects were scattered throughout the Mediterranean *in misera captività*.) The proportion of slave rowers in a ship varied. The command ship of a Spanish squadron at Genoa in 1574 had two hundred and nine rowers, of whom seventy-one were slaves. The rowing complement of four Florentine galleys in 1684 added up to a total of 1,202 men, of whom 586, or nearly fifty per cent, were slaves.

Slaves not used in the galleys were usually employed in private households, since in Italy as in Spain it was domestic slavery that preponderated. They were sometimes put to the usual household tasks, but more often were used merely for display purposes, particularly in noble households. In Rome the papal household itself had slaves on show, and a prince of the Church like Cardinal d'Este was credited in 1584 with having fifty Turkish slaves in his villa in Tivoli. Marcantonio Colonna managed to put two hundred slaves into his triumphal procession after the victory at Lepanto. Domestic slavery, then, was accepted and widely practised. But slavery as a public institution was nowhere formally accepted in Italy, and a fugitive slave (and, even more unquestionably, a baptised slave) was allowed an absolute right to liberty.

The mitigating factor in all this was that the law of Christian Europe did not condemn any class or race of men automatically to slavery. Servitude was looked upon as a temporary condition, the lot of adverse fortune such as being captured in war. Being temporary, it could not be inherited. Moreover it was in those very Mediterranean countries where slavery was most in use — in Spain, France and Italy—that Catholic theology and public law conspired to guarantee the dispossessed their right, both as men and as Christians, to manumission and to social equality. In normal circumstances this would have meant the gradual disappearance of slavery from Europe. But new life was given to the institution by the growth of colonial economies dependent on cheap labour.

Before passing on to discuss 'feudal' slavery, we should note that a degree of servitude equivalent to slavery was common in many parts of Europe. This would happen above all when labourers were forced to work under intolerable conditions. But

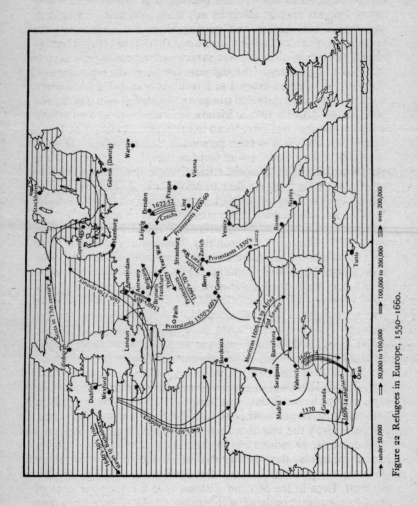

Figure 22 Refugees in Europe, 1550–1660.

→ under 50,000 → 50,000 to 100,000 → 100,000 to 200,000 ⇒ over 200,000

sometimes the laws expressly condoned slavery, as when the English Poor Law of 1547 threatened vagrants with this fate. In Scotland both the poor law and labouring conditions could be savage. A Scottish law of 1605 decreed that 'all masterful and strong beggars may be taken by any man, and being brought to any sheriff (or) baillie and getting them declared masterful beggars, may set his burning iron upon them and retain them as slaves'. Slavery of this sort was sanctioned repeatedly by acts of the Scots parliament throughout the seventeenth century. Scotsmen were even enslaved as a result of war, as in 1650 when some of Montrose's defeated troops were reserved as slaves for the Marquis of Argyll and his friends. Scotland's most capitalised industry, mining, was introduced to the profits of slavery in about this period. Colliers had been personally free up to 1605. Then in July 1606 an act of parliament forbade them moving their labour elsewhere and also in effect froze their wages. The 1606 act applied to coalmines, another in 1607 applied to metal mines, and in 1641 a statute extended these terms to factory workers. The Scottish proletariat were in effect reduced to serfdom.

In eastern Europe, where agrarian serfdom on a large scale was now a basic feature of the economy, sections of the labour force were actual slaves. In Russia slavery was a standard feature of the rural scene. The slaves (*kholopi*) performed essentially the same function as serfs, their distinctive feature being the loss of personal freedom. This freedom could be lost in many ways, and for varying periods of time. One could, for example, become enslaved by contract for a limited or unlimited period; or be enslaved through war; or fall into servitude through indebtedness. On this eastern frontier, slavery through war was fairly common, and Polish slaves rose to positions of responsibility in many noble households. There was in particular a brisk slave trade in Tatars, captured on the south-east frontiers of Muscovy. The distinction between Russian and west European slavery is an important one, emphasised by the fact that in the east slavery was more rural than domestic or industrial. In the steppe, where many estates had no peasants, slave labour was used, and the proportion of slaves to free peasants in some districts here was as high as fifty per cent. Even in the Moscow district, over fourteen per cent of rural homesteads consisted of this category. They were known as *zadvornye lyudi*, 'people who lived away from their master's door', and were expected to perform all the standard feudal obligations. The importance of slavery in the Russian state is shown by the fact that two hundred of the nine hundred and forty articles in the *Ulozhenie* of 1649 were concerned specifically with it. Paradoxically enough, slavery tended to disappear as it intensified. The distinction between a slave and a serf had always been slight, and as both categories became depressed in the course of the seventeenth century they tended to be legally merged into one. The last great distinction between the two was the exemption of slaves from taxation. Laws of 1680 and 1724 made the landless slave as liable to taxation as the landed serf, and with these measures slavery became merged into the larger institution of serfdom.

THE REFUGEES

Relating the sorrows of his people to Don Quixote, the Morisco Ricote lamented: 'Wherever we are we weep for Spain, for we were born there and it is our native land, and nowhere do we find the shelter that our misfortune demands; and it is in Barbary, and in all the parts of Africa where we hoped to be received, cared for and feasted, that we are most abused and maltreated.'

Among the victims of state action, the Moriscos occupy a particularly unhappy place, but if we look over the whole of this period it was by no means a unique place, for the age of the Counter Reformation was, more than any other, the classic age of displaced minorities. Population movements were so extensive, both in the volume of migrants and in the distances they covered, that serious changes in the political and economic complexion of Europe occurred. A glance at Figure 22 shows the magnitude of the problem.

The population movements recorded in the figure were for the most part connected with specific historical events, which we shall examine presently. There were other temporary movements over and beyond these, that give us the impression of a Europe periodically on the move. It was still, despite the Reformation, a Europe of pilgrimages. The picture of Rome in the Holy Year of 1600 illustrates this. In May that year the news-sheets in the papal city reported: 'Never in human memory have so many people come to Rome'. The statement was apparently accurate, for the previous Holy Year, 1575, had brought an estimated four hundred thousand visitors to Rome, whereas 1600 brought five hundred and thirty-six thousand, and this to a city whose resident population in 1600 was about one hundred thousand. Most of the visitors were Italians, but there was always a large proportion of foreigners, particularly from France. Some of the other cosmopolitan towns of Europe could expect a high percentage of foreigners even in normal times. In the main cities the foreign colony averaged between four and eight per cent of the population. One of the more international centres, Antwerp, had over sixteen per cent of its inhabitants in 1568 listed as 'foreigners'. This term probably applied generally to all those not native to the town, which would explain why Zurich in 1637 also had as many as 14.7 per cent of its inhabitants listed as foreigners. A more realistic proportion is given in the figures for London in 1587, when 4.5 per cent of all 'able householders' were foreigners, i.e. non-English.

A substantial number of Europeans, then, were on the move in the cause of religion or for some other reason. To set out on a long journey with the certainty of being able to return home, however, was one thing; to know that return was impossible quite another. For hundreds of thousands, their native land became no more than a memory.

Both the Reformation and the Counter Reformation created refugees, but it is extremely difficult to arrive at a clear indication of their numbers. Refugees from the Catholic states first became numerous in the 1540s, with the creation of the *Chambre Ardente* in France in 1547 and the establishment of the Roman Inquisition in Italy in 1542. The Italian Protestants fled principally, as we have seen, to Switzerland. A few penetrated farther afield, many to England. In 1555 emigration from England began, as a result of the Catholic restoration there. Of the eight hundred or so English refugees who fled to the continent, most went to the Rhineland.

Emigration from France was numerically far more important. Originating in the repression of the 1540s, it reached its peak after the massacre of Saint Bartholomew's. A great many Huguenots went to Germany, particularly to the Palatinate, which was under Calvinist rule for most of the late sixteenth century. But the chief centre of refuge was Switzerland and Geneva. 'The quantity of money being sent secretly from France to help the French in Geneva, is incalculable', claimed the Venetian envoy to France in 1561. 'The city is full of refugees and I have been told that their number is as much as ten thousand.' The exaggeration of numbers was not excessive. From 1549 to 1587 Geneva probably received as many as twelve thousand French refugees, though the real flood was concentrated on 1572. Plans were also made at this period for Protestants to emigrate to America. Admiral Coligny made efforts to set up a Huguenot colony in Brazil, and some groups of emigrants actually left France to go to the New World. In the seventeenth century these efforts continued: in 1627 six hundred Huguenots went to colonise the island of Saint-Christophe. We have already considered the overwhelmingly artisan nature of the French emigration to Geneva. A similar picture is true for the Palatinate, where Huguenot settlements and industrial centres were set up at Frankenthal (1562), Schönau, Saint-Lambert (1577) and Otterberg. Surprisingly few Huguenots went to England.

Perhaps the most important émigrés of this time were the southern Netherlanders, whose contribution to capital enterprise we have touched upon in Chapter 3. Their numbers were so great that they were virtually a nation on the move. The northern Netherlands were overtaken by an enormous flood of immigrants. To the town of Middelburg alone in 1584-5 over one thousand nine hundred southern families came. Southern immigration to Leiden was so heavy that it came to be looked on as a Flemish city, though the Flemings (most came from Bruges) in fact formed only ten per cent of the population. Some indication of the importance of the immigration may be gained by looking at figures for accessions to citizenship (though it must be remembered that only a small proportion of immigrants ever applied for or were eligible for citizenship). In Leiden from 1500 to 1574 only 7.2 per cent of new citizens (*bourgeois*) had come from the south; from 1575 to 1619 the figure rose to 38.4 per cent. In Amsterdam over the period 1575 to 1606 the southerners made up thirty-one per cent of all new citizens. In Middelburg from 1580 to 1591 southerners made up three-fourths of new citizens.

The Netherlanders went abroad to several cities (in London up to the end of the sixteenth century they always formed about five-sixths of the total foreign population), but their chief concentration was in west Germany and notably in Frankfurt-on-Main. Here Walloons predominated over Flemings. From 1554 to 1561 in Frankfurt a total of 38.4 per cent of those obtaining citizenship (*Bürgerrecht*) were Netherlanders. The numbers of immigrants were disturbingly large: in 1561 the refugees totalled two thousand and thirty-six persons, at a time when Frankfurt's population was almost fifteen thousand. From 1585 to 1590 the number of refugees reached a total of five thousand three hundred.

The movement of so large a number of people could not fail to have serious repercussions on the life of the host town. In Frankfurt, for example, the newcomers were opposed both by the artisans and by the upper bourgeoisie. Restrictions were placed on access to citizenship. In 1583 refugees were forbidden to buy houses without the permission of the authorities. In 1586 it was decreed that no foreigner could become a citizen unless he married into the family of a citizen. It was the tension within Frankfurt that caused the Netherlanders to disperse to new centres such as Hanau, which had two thousand immigrants already in 1606. Some cities, notably the oligarchic Swiss ones, began to exclude newcomers almost entirely from citizenship. In Basel the number of accessions to this honour actually fell during these years from an average annual forty-five in the 1550s to no more than about ten in the 1650s.

The decline of the Celtic nations of Britain was emphasised by the great numbers that went overseas to seek employment. Political turmoil and economic depression in Scotland drove its natives abroad, mainly to the Baltic countries. According to an estimate of 1620, there were in Poland alone about thirty thousand Scots. It was the Irish people who, more than any other European nation of this period, suffered agony and crucifixion. Successive onslaughts by English troops, first under Elizabeth and then under Cromwell, dispossessed the majority of the Irish ruling class, transported thousands of inhabitants from fertile to less hospitable regions of the island, forced Ireland's political and cultural elite into exile and condemned the remaining Irish to a secondary status in their own land. Writing in 1596, at the end of the Elizabethan era, the poet Edmund Spenser described the province of Munster as ' a most populous and plentiful country suddenly made void of man and beast', a description which could have applied to other parts of the island. Successive attempts at rebellion failed, and after each attempt the English gave ample encouragement to the dissident Irish to take up service in foreign armies. In September 1610, for example, two ships with six hundred Irish aboard were despatched northwards to serve the Swedish crown. Being Catholics, however, it was to the service of Spain and other enemies of England that the exiles tended to rally.

Irish nobles, soldiers, clergy and scholars were all obliged to emigrate. Every Catholic university on the continent had its contingent of Irishmen, who were offered no education at home.

467

Typical of these wandering scholars was young Christopher Roche of Wexford who in 1583, at the age of twenty-two, took passage to Bordeaux, worked and taught for his living for eighteen months then went on to study in Toulouse, Paris, Lorraine (for three years), Antwerp, Brussels, Douai and St Ouen, a long tour of eight years, during which he both worked for his food and studied when his circumstances allowed. The anguish and yearning of an exiled scholar is reflected in a passage in the writings of Fergal O'Gara, working in Belgium where he made a collection of Irish historical poems: '12th of February at Lisle in the Low Country 1565; here I break off until morning, and I in gloom and grief; and during my life's length unless only that I might have one look at Ireland. Fergal O'Gara of the Augustinian Order.'

During the great Cromwellian repression Sir William Petty was secretary to the English administration and had full access to the state papers. His statistics for the desolation wreaked on Ireland appear if anything to be underestimates. He estimated the whole population of Ireland (including the English) in the mid-century to be about one million, one hundred thousand. These were made up of about two hundred thousand families, of whom one hundred and sixty thousand 'have no fix'd Hearths'. 'The number of young Children under seven years old is one quarter of the whole, *viz*, 275,000.' These figures represented substantially the state of the population *after* the period of wars. During that actual period, 'about 504,000 of the Irish perished, and were wasted by the sword, plague, famine, hardship and banishment, between the 23 of October 1641 and the same day 1652'. Included in this total were the deportees, of whom 'there were transported into Spain, Flanders, France, 34,000 soldiers; and of boys, women, priests etc. no less than 6,000 more, where not half are returned'; and those transported to the Bardadoes and elsewhere as slaves (estimated at about ten thousand).

Somewhat comparable to the fate of the Irish, in that they too were a nation, was that of the Moriscos. These were the only minority in this period to be expelled bodily from their native country on grounds of race alone. The English had been careful to rid Irish soil not of the peasantry who worked it but only of the class that owned it: 'their hands begin to wax hard with labour', wrote the lord deputy of Ireland in the 1580s. The Castilian authorities, on the other hand, were adamant that every Morisco tiller of the soil should leave the peninsula. There was strong opposition to this from the landowners, particularly in Valencia where the nobles relied entirely on Moriscos for the agricultural development of their estates. This was to be the last of the many deportations suffered by Moriscos. In 1569, as the result of a rebellion, they had been expelled from Granada and scattered throughout the peninsula. The subsequent half-century witnessed numerous unsuccessful attempts to pacify and Christianise them. All these attempts were bound to be abortive since they were accompanied by harsh legislation forbidding them any racial or cultural distinctiveness: their language, their clothing, their customs all came under attack. When the expulsion was eventually decided upon it was in the firm conviction that they were an alien minority, a strange view to take of people who knew no home but Spain. Cervantes, a contemporary of these events, made one of his Morisco characters in *Quixote* applaud the heroic act of Philip III, 'to expel poisonous fruit from Spain, now clean and free of the fears in which our numbers held her'. This was the official view, but from the lips of a Morisco it appears totally implausible beside the words of Ricote, quoted above: 'wherever we are we weep for Spain, for we were born there and it is our native land'.

The expulsion was ordered in April 1609 and with various intervals continued up to 1616. The most recent study of the number of those actually expelled, suggests a figure of 272,140 or, rounded off to allow for omissions, 275,000. The breakdown by regions is as follows:

Valencia	117,464
Catalonia	3,716
Aragon	60,818
Castile	90,142

They left the peninsula for various directions of the compass. The great majority went to north Africa, to Tetuan and other Moroccan areas where they could remain in the proximity of their Spain. In some towns, as in Algiers, they were well received; in others, they were hated as foreigners. Perhaps as many as fifty thousand were received in France, but most decided to travel on again to the Levant, for the French government required them to become Catholics. Aragonese and Andalucian Moriscos in this way came to settle in Salonika and Istanbul. It was the biggest racial uprooting in Counter-Reformation Europe.

The most momentous of all the emigrations of this epoch — the emigration to America — cannot properly be described as a movement of refugees. The Spaniards who went to New Spain and Peru, and whose numbers elude all attempts at measurement, often came from the lowest echelons of the population, but they were not dispossessed of their homeland. Nor, despite numerous unfortunates who were transported to the North American colonies, was the movement of English Puritan settlers one of refuge. The English crossed the Atlantic for reasons of conscience (among other reasons), but return to England was never barred to them, and great numbers went home regularly.

The last groups of refugees to concern us here are those who suffered from the Thirty Years War and from its prelude, the rebellion of the Czech people in 1618. The battle of the White Mountain in November 1620 marked the victory of the Habsburgs and the end of Czech independence. The fate of the Czechs, bad enough in itself, was considerably exaggerated by Protestant propaganda. The first refugees were the elite who had served the Winter King, Frederick of the Palatinate. Mainly nobles and bourgeois, they crossed the frontier into Saxony with all the possessions they could gather. Early in 1621 the arrests and expulsions began. Fifty of the Czech leaders were arrested and their estates confiscated: in June twenty-five of them were executed, their number including both Catholics and Protestants. The new governor of Prague, Liechtenstein, offered a pardon to those who would come forward and exculpate themselves for their part in the rebellion. Nearly seven hundred and thirty gentry came forward, were duly pardoned, and then had their estates confiscated in whole or in part. Religious persecution was not immediately put into effect. As late as Easter 1622 communion in both kinds was still being given in Prague, and it was not until 1623 and 1624 that the last Protestant clergy were ordered out of the country. The imposition of Catholic orthodoxy was a lengthy process which took up at least another five years after this. The religious refugees of 1623 (who must be distinguished from the rebel refugees of the earlier period) went initially to Lusatia and Silesia, two of the confederate states of the crown of Bohemia. Thence they were ordered out by an order of the king, Ferdinand, in August 1628. Only the previous year, on 31 July 1627, Ferdinand had decreed the expulsion of all nobles who did not become Catholics.

The religious persecution provoked internal disorder and further emigration. The lands confiscated from Protestant nobility, for example, were handed over to foreigners who had entered Bohemia in the Habsburg service, to Germans, Italians, Spaniards and others. The new landowners introduced a system of harsher feudal services, and thereby provoked risings among the peasantry. Almost without exception the risings appealed back to the Hussite tradition and invoked the name of Zižka. In Moravia there was a revolt of the Vlachs led by Ladislaw Velen of Zerotín; this was not put down for the entire duration of the Thirty Years War. In Bohemia in 1625 the peasants rose under Adam of Hoděiov, and in 1627 the Lutheran preacher Matthias Ulický, supported by Czech gentry, led a peasant uprising in Čáslav.

Both towns and countryside suffered enormously from Habsburg repression and internal dislocation. By 1627, according to a contemporary estimate, about thirty-six thousand families (one hundred and fifty thousand persons) had left Bohemia. Most of the upper-class refugees stayed across the border in Lutheran Saxony, where special churches were put at their disposal. In 1629 the town of Freiberg apparently had five hundred and twenty-eight Czechs, and Pirna (the most popular centre) well over two thousand. Few of the refugees were reconciled to exile. When Ferdinand died in 1637 a plea was sent to his successor by one hundred and twenty-nine Czech nobles and two hundred and sixty-seven leading Czech bourgeois in exile, asking that they be allowed to return. But the request was rejected. In Bohemia the depopulation caused by emigration was aggravated by plague and famine. Whole sections of cities were deprived of their inhabitants. In Prague alone in the 1620s nearly one thousand two hundred householders were ordered to quit their dwellings. Voluntary and involuntary evacuation reduced the population of many towns by as much as one-third. By the end of the Thirty Years War the population of the province of Bohemia had sunk from one million, seven hundred thousand to nine hundred and thirty thousand, and that of Moravia from eight hundred thousand to less than six hundred thousand.

The war years 1618-48 were the most notable of all in creating, perhaps for the first time in modern history, a refugee problem of significant dimensions. Much of the loss in population attributed to Germany at this period can be blamed, as we have observed, on the movement of inhabitants rather than their actual annihilation. Similarly we can attribute much of the refugee situation not so much to the war itself as to circumstances arising out of the war. Bohemia is a case in point. In the same way the flood of refugees from Austria can be explained more by the progress of the Counter Reformation in that country than by the presence of imperialist troops. Already between 1598 and 1605 nearly eleven thousand Austrian Protestants had left their homeland. During the Thirty Years War the collapse of the 1626 peasant revolt led to another great emigration: between that date and 1660 something like thirty thousand Protestants fled from Austria.

Since several factors combined to produce refugees during the war, and since the movement of the refugees was in varying directions, it is difficult to give a simple picture of the situation. One of the more important effects of German population movements was the way in which they succeeded in extending the German-speaking frontier. In Alsace-Lorraine, the frontier of the German language was extended several miles as a result of emigration after the Thirty Years War. Germans spilled over the frontiers into Switzerland and Bohemia, extending their culture likewise into those regions. But for the most part the refugees moved within German territory, leaving their homes because of religious persecution or economic destruction, and attempting to set themselves up elsewhere within the German-speaking lands. Some areas were therefore repopulated by a high proportion of outsiders. In some parts of the region around Magdeburg, as many as forty-four per cent of those who had settled after the end of the war were outsiders. The little town of Frohse, north of Magdeburg, can serve as an example of the turnover in population. Before the war it had one hundred and ten families, by 1649 there were only eight. By 1651 a total of thirty-two families were in residence, but of these twenty were strangers (including four from Silesia, three from Holstein, two each from Switzerland and Italy, and one each from Bohemia, England and Scotland).

It should not be forgotten that a very high proportion of the émigrés in early modern times were propertied people from the upper classes. This was true, for instance, of Ireland and Bohemia, where the new rulers undertook a systematic dispossession of the old ruling circles. In the process, the whole level of civilisation of the country was seriously impaired. Available details for about ten thousand of the Bohemian exiles in Saxony show that among this number were four hundred and twenty-two nobles, one thousand seven hundred and eighty-eight intellectuals and clergy, and eight thousand four hundred and eighty-six peasants and artisans, figures which emphasise the damage suffered in the upper cultural level. Political persecution tended to hit the upper classes first. Where war alone was the cause of emigration, the refugees tended to come from the lower sections of the population, and in Germany during the Thirty Years War, as *Simplicissimus* makes plain, it was the peasants above all who were the victims. There were also indirect victims of war, such as manufacturers and traders whose profits would suffer, and it was people like this who drifted from Antwerp and the cities of the southern Netherlands and south Germany. Thanks to them, capital was transferred to the northwest, to Amsterdam and Hamburg.

Rich and poor refugees alike qualify to be described as dispossessed. Like the Moriscos, few saw their native homes again. 'If I forget thee, Jerusalem, let my tongue cleave to the roof of my mouth . . . How shall we sing the Lord's song in a strange land?'

12 THE TURN OF THE TIDE

All authority belongs to us. We hold it of God alone.
Declaration of Louis XIV (July 1652)

The Soveraign, in every Commonwealth, is the absolute Representative of all the subjects; and therefore no other can be Representative
of any part of them.

HOBBES, Leviathan (1651)

The Europe of 1660 was substantially different from that of 1550.
No previous century perhaps had seen so rapid a rate of change in
the political and social life of the continent. The outside world
had been opened up to exploration and settlement, empires once
at their peak were now on the point of dissolution, the religious
complexion of entire nations had been altered. Of all the ways in
which the change can be measured, the progress of science offers
one of the clearest case studies. In the 1540s we are in the world
of Copernicus and Paracelsus; the one a hesitant, tradition-
bound, secretive ecclesiastic whose 'revolutionary' heliocentric
theory was little more than a re-discovery of the ancients; the
other a fantastical medical practitioner with unorthodox cures
and a profound belief in 'natural philosophy' and magic. By
1660, with the foundation of the Royal Society of London, we are
in the empirical, experimental world of Boyle and Newton, a
world in which God was an external maintenance engineer rather
than an immanent spirit.

It would nevertheless be false to consider this an age of
unequivocal progress. In every century, apparent advance occurs
only at the cost of some worsening of the human condition. The
efforts made to surmount the critical conditions of the early
seventeenth century were met from about mid-century by a
growing tide of reaction.

EBB AND WITHDRAWAL

The trade crisis of 1620, as we have seen, introduced the parting
of the ways between southern and northern Europe. For England

and Holland the slump proved to be only temporary. For the Mediterranean trading area, on the other hand, there was no turning back. Historians have often been in the habit of speaking loosely about 'the decline of Spain' or 'the decline of Italy'. In fact, these countries could not have declined as it were in a vacuum. Economic life was not as fragmented as that. Just as a declaration of bankruptcy by Philip II could cause a chain-reaction of bankruptcies among financiers across Europe, so economic changes in any one country affected other nations with which it traded. The state of the international market affected home industry: thus it seems that after 1620 some Italian manu-facturers, finding shrinking sales abroad, turned to produce for home consumers instead. And there is no doubt that external markets were shrinking, if we take price data as our guide; so that it is possible to build up a general picture of the slow decay of trade over a wide area, in this case southern Europe and the Mediterranean. The most obvious factor in this decay was the stoppage of the outlet for Italian and south German goods to northern Europe through Antwerp. The strangulation of this great port was a major disaster also for the Spanish empire, which saw the riches of the entrepôt trade pass inexorably to Amster-dam, Hamburg and other northern cities.

Given the unfavourable economic conditions then prevailing, we can say that 'decline' occurred in Spain, Italy and part of Germany at roughly the same period. When the cities of northern Italy suffered their recession, the transalpine cities with which they traded (notably Augsburg) likewise decayed. When Spain underwent difficulties, its Italian territories suffered from the backwash. But beyond these interacting factors there were im-portant internal problems.

In the German lands the process of decline was uneven. The Hanseatic towns on the Baltic coastline were in decay by the early sixteenth century, and by mid-century non-German interests (Dutch traders in the west, Polish and East Prussian exporters in the east) had taken the lead in the northern seas. In the late sixteenth century the collapse of Antwerp created a major dis-location in the trading centres of the Rhineland and southern Germany. By the early seventeenth century, three crises had arisen: the trade depression of 1620, the agrarian slump of the same decade, and the monetary inflation of the *Kipperzeit*. By the time that recovery from these had begun, the Thirty Years War, the great plague epidemic of 1635-6, and their attendant horrors, had struck severe blows at Germany's internal strength. The political complexion of the Empire was modified in several ways by this situation. The northwest emerged as the most flourishing region, with Hamburg as its thriving centre. In the east, economic difficulties consolidated the power of the landed classes.

Italy had been one of the most highly industrialised areas in Europe, with big textile manufactures and an assured market in the Levant and in northern Europe. A few figures will illustrate the change that had occurred by the mid-seventeenth century. The export of Genoese silk fell by about eighty per cent between 1565 and 1697. The city and republic had about eighteen thousand silk looms towards the end of the sixteenth century; in 1608 there were only three thousand. Milan had five thousand silk looms in 1628 and two hundred in 1662. At the beginning of the century it had nearly seventy woollen-cloth firms, with a total annual production of fifteen thousand pieces; by 1640 there were only fifteen firms, with an output of some three thousand pieces. Many factors have been adduced to explain this: competition from cheaper English and Dutch cloth, the conservatism of guild regulations, the growth of competitive Anglo-Dutch shipping, crippling taxation, high wage levels, the conservatism of a businesss elite that preferred to invest profits in office and land rather than industry. Natural factors were important: a number of famines afflicted the population in the early seventeenth century, but the most devastating impact of all came from the great plagues of 1630 and 1657. The Thirty Years War did not improve matters: in 1641 one Italian writer blamed the contraction of foreign markets on 'the disastrous effect of the wars in France, Flanders and Germany'.

Spanish decline was to some extent the inevitable consequence of empire. Commitments in Europe were enormously expensive. As an *arbitrista* of 1687 observed, 'the court of Rome, the subsidies to Germany, the upkeep of Flanders, the wars in Milan and Catalonia, drain the blood out of this body through all its veins'. The life-blood was bullion, which for too long had been a source of easy wealth to the country. In relying on American wealth, the peninsula neglected its own resources. Long-term returns from investment in native industry were neglected in favour of the surer profit from exporting raw materials. The promising textile industries of Spain were made to compete with imported foreign goods. Spain, head of the largest empire ever known till then, never became a strong economic power in its own right. Investment in enterprise was in any case rendered less desirable by severe monetary inflation, which wiped out gains almost as soon as they were made. To this economic weakness may be added such factors as population decrease (particularly after the plague of 1599), oppression of racial minorities, the inordinate fiscal burden placed on Castile alone, and the impoverishment of agriculture.

It is now accepted that the concept of 'decline' needs modification. One cannot speak merely of 'the decline of Spain', for the economic development of different regions of the peninsula was not parallel. In the seventeenth century it is more appropriate to speak of the decline of Castile. The same principle applies to Italy and Germany. In Italy many industries, to free themselves from the controls so readily exercised in the cities, transferred to the countryside. Silk production was transferred in this way. External trade declined, but sometimes this was because of a greater attention to the home market. It must be remembered, moreover, that industry does not by itself mean wealth. Those investors who took their profits out of industry to put into the land were also helping the economy. When we look at industrial decline we may merely be observing a re-structuring of the economy in favour of agriculture.

There were two general consequences of this situation. Firstly, the economic difficulties experienced as a result of the seventeenth-century crisis encouraged the state to intervene more actively in order to protect the national interest. Secondly, over large areas of Europe the economic uncertainty encouraged greater investment in the land. On both counts, the power of the state and the ruling classes was reinforced.

THE CONSERVATIVE REACTION

The second of these two factors, namely the land, constituted the basis of the social regime that dominated Europe for over a century. This statement may seem to be equally applicable to periods before and after the one we are considering, but there were particular features which characterised the century after about 1650. These were the increasing commitment of the gentry and bourgeoisie to landed fortunes, as a necessary concomitant to social rank and political office; the important role, in an economic conjuncture not suited to heavy investment, attached to rentals (rather than direct exploitation); and, above all, the

477

privileged position granted to landholders by the state. After the splendid opportunities opened up by trade and finance in the sixteenth century, and carried on well into the seventeenth by men like Louis de Geer, the flight to land can only be looked upon as socially reactionary. Economic conditions were partly responsible for this, but the explanation must be principally political: the revolutions of 1648 made it necessary to stabilise social relationships, and it was through the system of landowner-ship that this was achieved. The century or so that stretched from the assumption of power by Louis XIV to the French Revolution was the age of the landed aristocracy.

We have qualified the emphasis on land as 'socially reac-tionary', but in economic terms a good case can be made out for seeing elements of progress in it. This could take the form of greater investment in the soil or, as in England, a freeing of the land market from feudal restrictions. 'Do not all strive to enjoy the land?' Gerrard Winstanley asked sardonically in 1650. 'The gentry strive for land, the clergy strive for land, the common people strive for land; and buying and selling is an art, whereby people endeavour to cheat one another of the land.' The im-portant changes in landownership that occurred around mid-century strengthened the position of the landed classes. Feudal tenures and the Court of Wards were abolished by Parliament in 1646. This meant that the crown ceased to be the ultimate land-lord in the realm. Landowners now gained full ownership of their estates. In 1647 a law of entail was first brought in. Owners could now settle their land on their eldest son and prevent alienation of the family estate. This prepared the way for the great con-solidations of property in the eighteenth century. When an act was passed in 1660 to confirm the measure of 1646, no additional privileges were extended to lesser landowners, whether copy-holders or free tenant farmers. The smaller men failed to win that security of tenure which the big landowners had obtained. General insecurity was aggravated by the land sales of the inter-regnum. Royalist sympathisers alone (this does not include crown or Church lands) suffered confiscation of estates to the extent of about £1,250,000, and a further £1,500,000 was lost in fines. A number of people lost their lands permanently in this way, but no revolution in ownership occurred. Many bought back their own property, and what was unredeemed often went to members of the same social class. Very few new men moved up the ladder. Perhaps the most important result of the sales was the acceptance of greater mobility in agrarian relationships.

The sum total of this was a situation favourable to the interests of the big, expanding landowner, the English squirearchy and aristocracy. A property franchise made sure that only those with a material interest could vote for the government of England. Game laws came in principally with the Restoration. Yeoman farmers were forbidden to shoot wild fowl even on their own land; the squirearchy, contrariwise, were given rights to chase their fox across everyone else's. The period after the Restoration was not one of great expansion: agricultural prices were generally poor and profits only moderate. But political and economic consolidation laid the basis for conservative rule. As R. H. Tawney put it:

> the revolution (of 1640), which brought constitutional liberty, brought no power to control the aristocracy who, for a century and a half, alone knew how such liberty could be used. . . . Henceforward there was to be no obstacle to enclosure, to evictions, to rack-renting, other than the shadowy protection of the Common Law; and for men who were very poor or easily intimidated, the Common Law, with its expense, its packed juries, its strict rules of procedure, had little help.

The conservative landed regime in the German lands after the Thirty Years War has been discussed in a previous chapter. As elsewhere in the east, aristocratic control led to what we may call, for want of a better term, the feudalisation of the soil. The ascendancy of the noble class was not anything new, for they had long been the natural rulers of the eastern lands. What was new was that this ascendancy was reaffirmed by the state in conditions where one might have expected an extension of state power at the expense of the nobles. But the noble estates were the backbone of the economy, and rulers such as Frederick William (the Great Elector) of Brandenburg chose to ally with them against the towns. In Brandenburg after 1660 excise taxes were levied on the produce of the towns, but the nobility were allowed exemption, so giving them an obvious advantage in their estate economy. In Prussia the Estates granted an excise in 1662, but this likewise was used in favour of the nobles and against the towns. In Russia and other eastern lands the story was the same: serfdom and noble dominance went hand in hand, and the towns were opened up to aristocratic influence.

In Piedmont the late seventeenth century proved to be a period of aristocratic consolidation on the land. The noble class —

recruited both from the old families as well as from successful bourgeois — continued to accumulate estates, and at the same time provided most of the capital for the bonds issued by the state from 1653 onwards. Clergy and aristocracy together provided two-thirds of these loans to the state. It was to preserve the economic power of this class that the rulers of Piedmont introduced legislation to protect noble holdings. The most important step in this direction was Charles Emmanuel II's edict of 1648 encouraging the practice of primogeniture. At the same time the burden of taxation on noble lands was lightened, until by the eighteenth century they were paying virtually no taxes. The power of the aristocracy was strengthened in all walks of life. Only under Victor Amadeus II in the early eighteenth century were any steps taken to reduce their hold on political life, but their economic and landed predominance remained undisturbed.

Sweden never became a country of great estates, but the political crisis of 1650 showed clearly that there was a serious danger of both crown and peasants being eclipsed by the wealthy aristocracy. The great controversies of the seventeenth century revolved round the question of whether alienated royal lands should be given back by the nobility. Both Charles X and Charles XI adopted the policy of resumption of estates as a method of strengthening the crown. The need for a resumption was generally unquestioned, even by many of the nobles themselves. Many of the recently ennobled were particularly resentful of the property concentrated in the hands of the older aristocracy. Conflict within the noble Estate was a clear pointer to a top-heavy ruling class. Where nobles in other countries were by 1660 beginning to accept the need to pursue profitable callings, a section of their class in imperialist Sweden had gravitated to the old concept of nobility. Their viewers are reflected in the speech made by Gustav Bonde, an intelligent and sensible minister of the crown, in June 1661:

> The principal interest of the Nobility consists in their being employed in the service of the state, and in having lands and farms to give them a livelihood, in conjunction with their wages; and these lands are a *sine qua non,* without which a nobleman cannot exist. For it does not become him, like the other three Estates, either to learn a craft, or to walk behind a plough, and sooner than do so he will betake himself to unlawful pursuits.

These examples are sufficient to illustrate the general trend all over Europe. Whether freed from feudalism (as in England) or subjected anew to it (as in the east), the land became the mainstay of an aristocratic regime. Even the prosperous bourgeoisie of Amsterdam had, by the late seventeenth century, joined the same process of evolution. The conservatism of the period should not, of course, be looked at exclusively in terms of the noble ethic. The English squirearchy, for example, felt consciously and proudly that they were not part of the old peerage. The reaction consisted not in titles so much as in a way of life. But, titles or not, the trend was unmistakable. We have already quoted the views of an English visitor on the Dutch in the early eighteenth century: 'their government is aristocratical: so that the so much boasted liberty of the Dutch is not to be understood in the general and absolute sense, but *cum grano salis*'.

THE CONSOLIDATION OF ABSOLUTISM

As mentioned above, the state in the seventeenth century began to intervene directly in the control of the economy. The late seventeenth century has been accepted as the period when mercantilism was most practised, and the statesmen of most European nations of the period, with Colbert at their head, have been credited with mercantilist policies. For the moment, mercantilism may be considered simply as the sort of economic policy practised by an absolutist regime. If we take this to mean a policy based on power, in which trade was viewed as an aspect of power and in which protectionism was accepted, it seems likely that only a strong state authority could have carried the programme out successfully. It would be reasonable to consider Colbert for France and Truchi for Piedmont as mercantilist ministers. But looked at in more detail the identification of absolutism and mercantilism is not wholly convincing, for states with a freer process of decision-making, such as England and Holland, were also capable of pursuing protectionist and power-orientated commercial policies. Moreover absolutist France tended to use its enormous power for territorial rather than mercantile ends, and this ultimately wrecked Colbert's own programme of expansion.

Mercantilism in its broadest sense was practised by most European states, even those with few authoritarian pretensions. It was a policy that made sense in a century of slack markets, agricultural depression and limited industrial growth. The fact that absolutist states adopted mercantilist policies tells us little about mercantilism but a great deal about absolutism. From the mid-seventeenth century the crown began to arrogate more power to itself, both in trade and in other activities.

There are four main aspects of absolutism to be considered: the new concept of royal authority, the end of constitutional government, the indispensable support of a ruling class, and the emergence of a theory of state power.

In Europe as a whole the Third Estate had responded to the seventeenth-century crisis with revolution; their rulers reacted with absolutism. Absolutism was born out of the difficulties experienced by monarchs with their budgets, their administrative machinery and their ruling classes. The failure of the seventeenth-century revolutions, and the reorientation made necessary by war, brought the demand for a firm hand. The result was an attempt at absolutism in Holland in 1650, its imposition on Brandenburg-Prussia and Russia in the 1650s, its introduction into Denmark in 1660 and France in 1661, into Sweden in 1680 and Piedmont at about the same time, and the failure of an attempt to introduce it into England after 1685. The basis for much of this development had been laid well before mid-century, particularly in France, where the deliberate aim of the Bourbons and their advisers had been to strengthen government. Claude Joly, the constitutionalist opponent of Mazarin, wrote during the Fronde that 'France has never been a despotic government, unless it be in the last thirty years, when we have been subject to the mercy of ministers'. It was during those years that Le Bret, in his *De la souveraineté du Roy* (1632), had asserted that 'the king is the only sovereign in his kingdom, and sovereignty is no more divisible than the point in geometry'. 'The sovereign command resides in a single person, and obedience in all others.'

Absolutism, then, meant undisputed royal power. It did not mean arbitrary power. This distinction was a vital one, rooted in the events of the mid-century. The king, in other words, could do without the need to consult a parliament; but he must not threaten the property and security of his subjects. This was all that 'absolutism' signified, and the term cannot in any way be equated with despotism or tyranny. When Le Bret declared the sovereignty to be unlimited, he nevertheless went on to specify that the monarch must respect private property, could not alter the succession to the throne, and could not issue a command contrary to divine law. Bossuet, well known as an exponent of Louis XIV's absolutism, could still specify that the absolute sovereign must abide by the laws of the kingdom.

The distinctions made by Le Bret and others were extremely important in practice. Absolutism might mean the rule of a single person, but that person could only maintain himself with the support of certain social forces. In the Europe of the late seventeenth century, those forces were the propertied classes. The day of the higher aristocracy was over, and every European state (except perhaps Spain) realised this. Louis XIV may have expressly set his face against them, yet there was nothing original about this. The Danish king, the Muscovite tsar, had done it before him. They, like the King of Sweden, preferred to rely on the lower nobility, the squirearchy and the ennobled bourgeoisie. Some insight into Swedish policy is given by the opinion of the Florentine diplomat Count Magalotti during a visit to that country in 1674:

> It is to be feared that the King of Sweden may succeed, with the help of the new nobility, in doing what the King of Denmark did with the help of the burghers, who hated the nobility and therefore lent themselves to his plan of freeing himself from dependence upon the Estates and making himself absolute. The same thing could occur in Sweden, where it might easily happen that the new nobility, which hates the old, would unite with the king to destroy and abolish the power of the Council and liberate the king from its yoke.

Wherever it was established, absolutism relied on the governing class to support it. It could not govern without the aid of that class. England was no exception to continental practice. The Tory gentry, who coexisted with Charles II's regime, would have been even more compliant under James II if he had not seemed to be threatening their property rights.

Finally, absolutism involved an end of representative assemblies, or at least an end to their initiative in government. The Parlement of Paris (not a representative assembly) was silenced in the 1660s, a direct result of the Fronde. The Diet in Brandenburg lost its effective power after 1653, the Estates of Prussia after 1663. The last Zemsky Sobor in Russia met in 1653. Habsburg Castile had no cortes after 1665.

Far from being a century of revolution, this had been a century of reaction. The greatest philosopher of the age after 1650 was not Hobbes, who stands at the head of it with his uncompromising theory of the Leviathan, a theory so realistic that few would accept its validity. It was Locke: the philosopher of intellectual reason and social reaction, whose views of government as the

483

defender of property set the tone for an age of gentry predominance.

It was fitting that the Iron Century should have ended with the victory of authority and property. Like twin pillars they stood, true guarantors of civilisation and progress, at the end of the straits that led out from an inland sea of pre-industrial beginnings into the boundless ocean of material advancement. 'England', wrote an anonymous pamphleteer on the events of 1648-9 (and for England one may equally read Europe), 'hath received many a sudden change, but never such a change as now. Heretofore the poor people toiled themselves, in shifting one tyrant out of the saddle to set up another; but now they have driven out not only the tyrant, but tyranny itself.' 'The baseless fabric of this vision' (to borrow the words of the greatest English poet of that Iron Age) melted away before the eyes of those who had set such store by it.

Bibliography

The following selective bibliography is divided up according to each chapter of the book, and is limited to those secondary works that I have found particularly useful. Since the bias is towards social history, many standard books dealing with political and other aspects have been omitted.

GENERAL WORKS

The best general studies of Europe as a whole have been written by historians working in British and American universities. Perhaps the most interesting broad surveys are those produced by leading French historians, in which problems of interpretation are given pride of place. In this section I have listed some general surveys as well as some urban studies.

T. Aston, *Crisis in Europe 1560-1660*. London 1965.

B. Bennassar, *Valladolid au siècle d'or*. Paris 1967.

C. R. Boxer, *The Dutch seaborne empire 1600-1800*. London 1965.

F. Braudel, *The Mediterranean and the Mediterranean world in the age of Philip II*. 2 vols. London 1972-3.

— *Capitalism and material life, 1400-1800,* London 1973.

The Cambridge Economic History of Europe, vol. IV: The economy of expanding Europe, ed. E. E. Rich and C. H. Wilson. Cambridge 1967.

E. M. Carus-Wilson, ed., *Essays in Economic History*. 3 vols. London 1954, 1962.

C. W. Chalklin, *Seventeenth-century Kent*. London 1965.

P. Chaunu, *La civilisation de l'Europe classique*. Paris 1966.

G. N. Clark, *The seventeenth century*. 2nd edn. Oxford 1947.

J. Delumeau, *Vie économique et sociale de Rome dans la seconde moitié du XVIe siècle,* 2 vols. Paris 1957-9.

P. Deyon, *Amiens, capitale provinciale*. Paris 1967.

H. Drouot, *Mayenne et la Bourgogne*. 2 vols. Paris 1937.

J. H. Elliott, *Europe divided 1559-1598*. London 1968.

L. Febvre, *Philippe II et la Franche-Comté*. Paris 1911.

G. Freytag, *Pictures of German life*. 2 vols. London 1862.

P. Goubert, *Beauvais et le Beauvaisis de 1600 à 1730*. 2 vols. Paris 1960.

B. Haendcke, *Deutsche Kultur im Zeitalter des dreissigjährigen Krieges.* Leipzig 1906.

H. Koenigsberger and G. Mosse, *Europe in the sixteenth century.* London 1968.

E. Le Roy Ladurie, *Les Paysans de Languedoc.* 2 vols. Paris 1966.

W. T. MacCaffrey, *Exeter, 1540-1640.* Harvard 1958.

R. Mandrou, *Introduction à la France moderne. Essai de psychologie historique 1500-1640.* Paris 1961.

Storia di Milano. Fondazione Treccani degli Alfieri. Vols. X and XI.

R. Mousnier, *Les XVIe et XVIIe siècles.* Vol. IV of *Histoire Générale des Civilisations.* 5th edn. Paris 1967.

The New Cambridge Modern History. Vol. III: *The Counter Reformation and Price Revolution (1559-1610).* Cambridge 1968. Vol. IV: *The Decline of Spain and the Thirty Years War (1610-1648/59).* Cambridge 1970.

L. Romier, *Le royaume de Cathérine de Médicis.* 2 vols. Paris 1922.

H. R. Trevor-Roper, *Religion, the Reformation and social change.* London 1967.

E. W. Zeeden, *Deutsche Kultur in der frühen Neuzeit.* Frankfurt 1968.

P. Zumthor, *Daily life in Rembrandt's Holland.* London 1962.

CHAPTER I: THE DIMENSIONS OF LIFE

G. Aleati, *La popolazione di Pavia durante il dominio spagnolo.* Milan 1957.

D. Beltrami, *Storia della popolazione di Venezia.* Padua 1954.

J. Beloch, *Bevölkerungsgeschichte Italiens.* 3 vols. Berlin 1937, 1939, 1961.

B. Bennassar, *Recherches sur les grands épidémies dans le nord de l'Espagne à la fin du XVIe siècle.* Paris 1969.

H. Bergues et al., *La prévention des naissances dans la famille.* Paris 1960.

C. Cipolla, *Clocks and Culture 1300-1700.* London 1967.

C. Creighton, *A history of epidemics in Britain.* 2 vols. Cambridge 1891-4.

L. Dechesne, *Histoire économique et sociale de la Belgique.* Paris-Liège 1932.

M. Devèze, *La vie de la forêt française au XVIe siècle.* 2 vols. Paris 1961.

Y. Durand, *Cahiers de doléances des paroisses du bailliage de Troyes pour les Etats-Généraux de 1614.* Paris 1966.

A. Feillet, *La misère au temps de la Fronde.* Paris 1862.

G. Franz, *Der Dreissigjährige Krieg und das deutsche Volk.* Stuttgart 1961.

R. Gascon, 'Immigration et croissance au XVIe siècle: l'exemple de

Lyon (1529-1563)', *Annales,* vol. XXV (1970).

I. Gieysztorowa, 'Guerre et régression en Masovie aux XVIe et XVIIe siècles', *Annales,* vol. XIII (1958).

D. V. Glass and D. E. C. Eversley, eds., *Population in History.* London 1965.

L. Henry, *Anciennes familles genevoises. Etude démographique XVIe-XXe siècle.* Paris 1956.

T. H. Hollingsworth, *The demography of the British peerage.* Supplement to *Population Studies,* vol. XVIII, no. 2 (1965).

H. Kamen, 'The social and economic consequences of the Thirty Years War', *Past and Present,* vol. XXXIX (1968).

E. Keyser, *Bevölkerungsgeschichte Deutschlands.* Leipzig 1943.

——, 'Neue deutsche Forschungen über die Geschichte der Pest', *Vierteljahrschrift für Sozial- und Wirtschaftsgeschichte,* vol. XLIV (1957).

F. Lebrun, *Les hommes et la mort en Anjou aux XVIIe et XVIIIe siècles.* Paris 1971.

R. Burr Litchfield, 'Demographic characteristics of Florentine patrician families', *Journal of Economic History,* vol. XXIX, no. 2 (1969).

R. Mols, *Introduction á la Démographie Historique des Villes d'Europe du XIVe au XVIIIe siècle.* 3 vols. Louvain 1955.

Anne-Marie Piuz, 'Alimentation populaire et sous-alimentation au XVIIe siècle. Le cas de Genève', *Schweizerische Zeitschrift für Geschichte* vol. XVIII (1968).

O. Placht, *Lidnatost a společenská skladba Českého státu v. 16-18 století* (The population and social structure of Bohemia in the 16th and 17th centuries). Prague 1957. With German summary.

F. Prinzing, *Epidemics resulting from wars.* Oxford 1916.

E. Scholliers, *Loonarbeid en honger. De levenstandaard in de XVe en XVIe eeuw te Antwerpen.* Antwerp 1960. With French summary.

B. Urlanis, *Rost naseleniya v Evrope* (Population growth in Europe). Moscow 1941.

Villages Désertés et Histoire Economique XIe-XVIIIe siècle. Paris 1965.

E. Woehlkens, *Pest und Ruhr im 16. und 17. Jahrhundert.* Hanover 1954.

E. A. Wrigley, *Population and history.* London 1969.

——, 'Family limitation in pre-industrial England', *Economic History Review,* vol. XIX, no. I (1966).

A. Wyczanski, *Studia nad konsumcja zywności w Polsce w XVI i pierwszej polowie XVII w* (Studies on food consumption in Poland in the 16th and early 17th centuries). Warsaw 1969. With French summary.

CHAPTER 2: CHANGE AND DECAY

W. Abel, *Agrarkrisen und Agrarkonjunktur in Mitteleuropa vom*

13. bis zum 19. Jahrhundert. New edn. Hamburg 1966.

——, *Geschichte der deutschen Landwirtschaft vom frühen Mittelalter bis zum 19. Jahrhundert.* Stuttgart 1962.

C. M. Andrews, *The colonial period of American history.* 4 vols. Yale 1964 edn.

Y. S. Brenner, 'The inflation of prices in early sixteenth-century England', *Economic History Review,* vol. XIV, no. 2 (1961).

A. Chabert, 'Encore la révolution des prix au XVIe siècle', *Annales,* vol. XII (1957).

C. Cipolla, 'La prétendue révolution des prix. Reflexions sur l'experience italienne', *Annales,* vol. X (1955).

C. Gibson, *Spain in America.* New York 1966.

J. D. Gould, 'The trade depression of the early 1620s', *Economic History Review,* vol. VII, no. I (1954).

——, 'The price revolution reconsidered', *Economic History Review,* vol. XVII, no. 2 (1964).

E. J. Hamilton, *American treasure and the price revolution in Spain 1501-1650.* Cambridge, Mass. 1934.

I. Hammarstrom, 'The Price Revolution of the sixteenth century: some Swedish evidence', *Scandinavian Economic History Review* (1957).

S. Hoszowski, *Les prix à Lwow (XVIe-XVIIe siècle).* Paris 1954.

——, 'The revolution of prices in Poland in the 16th and 17th centuries', *Acta Poloniae Historica,* vol. II (1959).

P. Laslett and J. Harrison, 'Clayworth and Cogenhoe', in *Historical Essays 1660-1750 presented to David Ogg.* London 1963.

E. Le Roy Ladurie and P. Couperie, 'Le mouvement des loyers parisiens de la fin du Moyen Age au XVIIIe siècle', *Annales,* vol. XXV (1970).

A. Liautey, *La hausse des prix et la lutte contre la cherté en France au XVIe siècle.* Paris 1921.

E. H. Phelps Brown and S. V. Hopkins, 'Wage-rates and prices: evidence for population pressure in the 16th century', *Economica,* vol. XXIV (1957).

——, 'Builders' wage-rates, prices and population: some further evidence', *Economica,* vol. XXVI (1959).

E. E. Rich, 'The population of Elizabethan England', *Economic History Review,* vol. II (1950).

R. Romano, 'Tra XVI e XVII secolo. Una crisi economica: 1619-1622', *Rivista Storica Italiana,* vol. LXXIV (1962).

I. Schoffer, 'Did Holland's golden age coincide with a period of crisis?', *Acta Historiae Neerlandica,* vol I (1966).

L. Stone and A. Everitt, 'Social mobility in England 1500-1700', *Past and Present,* vol. XXXIII (1966).

C. Verlinden et al., 'Mouvements des prix et des salaires en Belgique au XVIe siècle', *Annales,* vol. X (1955).

C. Wilson, *England's apprenticeship 1603-1763.* London 1965.

CHAPTER 3: THE GROWTH OF CAPITALISM

K. R. Andrews, *Elizabethan privateering.* Cambridge 1964.

E. Baasch, *Holländische Wirtschaftsgeschichte.* Jena 1927.

V. Barbour, *Capitalism in Amsterdam.* Michigan 1963 edn.

H. I. Bloom, *The economic activities of the Jews of Amsterdam in the seventeenth and eighteenth centuries.* Williamsport, Pa. 1936.

W. Bodmer, *Der Einfluss der Refugianten-einwanderung von 1550-1700 auf die schweizerische Wirtschaft.* Zurich 1946.

W. Brulez, 'De diaspora der Antwerpse kooplui op het einde van de 16e eeuw', *Bijdragen voor de Geschiedenis der Nederlanden,* vol. XV (1960), 4.

A. Dietz, *Frankfurter Handelsgeschichte.* 2 vols. Frankfurt 1921.

J. L. M. Eggen, *De invloed door Zuid-Nederland op Noord-Nederland uitgeoefend op het einde der XVIe et het begin de XVIIe eeuw.* Ghent 1908.

A. Ernstberger, *Hans de Witte, finanzmann Wallensteins.* Wiesbaden 1954.

G. Fischer, *Aus zwei Jahrhunderten Leipziger Handelsgeschichte 1470-1650 (Die kaufmännische Einwanderung und ihre Auswirkungen).* Leipzig 1929.

R. Froberger, *Die Manufaktur in Sachsen von ende des 16. bis zum Anfang des 19. Jahrhunderts.* Berlin 1958.

T. Geering, *Handel und Industrie der Stadt Basel.* Basel 1886.

H. Hauser, *Travailleurs et marchands dans l'ancienne France.* Paris 1929.

——, *Les débuts du capitalisme.* Paris 1927.

R. W. K. Hinton, 'The Mercantile system in the time of Thomas Mun', *Economic History Review,* vol. VII, no. 3 (1955).

A. Hyma, 'Calvinism and capitalism in the Netherlands, 1555-1700', *Journal of Modern History,* vol. X (1938).

E. Heckscher, *Mercantilism.* 2 vols. London 1962 repr.

H. Kellenbenz, *Sephardim an der unterem Elbe.* Wiesbaden 1958.

H. Lapeyre, *Une famille de marchands: les Ruiz.* Paris 1955.

——, 'La banque, les changes et le crédit au XVIe siècle', *Revue d'histoire moderne et contemporaine,* vol. III (1956).

J. Lejeune, *La formation du capitalisme moderne dans la principauté de Liège au XVIe siècle.* Paris 1939.

R. J. Lemoine, 'Les étrangers et la formation du capitalisme en Belgique', *Revue d'Histoire économique et sociale,* vol. XX (1932).

J. Mathorez, *Les Etrangers en France sous l'Ancien Régime.* 2 vols. Paris 1919-1921.

J. U. Nef, *The Rise of the British Coal Industry.* 2 vols. London 1932.

——, *War and Human Progress.* London 1950.

F. A. Norwood, *The Reformation refugees as an economic force.* Chicago 1942.

A. Paul, 'Les réfugiés huguenots et wallons dans le Palatinat du Rhin du XVIe siècle à la Révolution', *Revue Historique,* vol. CLVII (1928).

H. M. Robertson, *Aspects of the rise of economic individualism*. London 1933.

W. R. Scott, *The constitution and finance of English, Scottish and Irish joint-stock companies to 1720*. 3 vols. repr. New York 1951.

I. Scouloudi, 'Alien immigration into and alien communities in London 1558-1640', *Proceedings of the Huguenot Society of London,* vol. XVI, no. I (1938).

W. C. Scoville, 'Minority migrations and the diffusion of technology', *Journal of Economic History,* vol. XI (1951).

H. Sée, *Modern Capitalism*. London 1928.

E. Silberner, *La guerre dans la pensée économique du XVIe au XVIIIe siècle*. Paris 1939.

W. Sombart, *Der moderne Kapitalismus*. 3 vols. in 5 tomes. Munich-Leipzig 1916-27.

——, *Krieg und Kapitalismus*. Munich-Leipzig 1913.

——, *The Jews and Modern Capitalism*. London 1913.

R. H. Tawney, ed., *Thomas Wilson's Discourse upon Usury*. London 1925.

J. W. Troust, 'Geneva and the first refuge: a study of the social and economic effects of French and Italian refugees in Geneva in the 16th and early 17th century'. Oxford 1968 D. Phil. thesis (unpublished).

H. van der Wee, *The Growth of the Antwerp Market and the European Economy*. 3 vols. Antwerp 1963.

J. G. van Dillen, *Bronnen tot de Geschiedenis van het Bedrijfsleven en het Gildewezen van Amsterdam 1512-1632*. 2 vols. The Hague 1929, 1933.

R. van Roosbroeck, *Emigranten. Nederlandse vluchtlingen in Duitsland (1500-1600)*. Louvain 1968.

G. Unwin, *Industrial organisation in the sixteenth and seventeenth centuries*. Repr. London 1957.

C. Wilson, 'Mercantilism: some vicissitudes of an idea', *Economic History Review,* vol. X, no. 2 (1957).

G. Witzel, 'Gewerbegeschichtliche Studien zur niederländischen Einwanderung in Deutschland im 16. Jahrhundert', *Westdeutsche Zeitschrift für Geschichte und Kunst,* vol. XXIX (1910).

J. Yernaux, *La métallurgie liégeoise et son expansion au XVIIe siècle*. Liège 1939.

CHAPTER 4: NOBLES AND GENTLEMEN

G. d'Avenel, *La noblesse française sous Richelieu*. Paris 1901.

——, 'La fortune de la noblesse sous Louis XIII', *Revue Historique* (1883).

F. E. Baldwin, *Sumptuary legislation and personal regulation in England*. Baltimore 1926.

Y.-M. Bercé, 'De la criminalité aux troubles sociaux: La noblesse rurale du Sud-Ouest de la France sous Louis XIII', *Annales du Midi,* vol. LXXVI (1964).

D. Bitton, *The French nobility in crisis 1560-1640.* Stanford UP 1969.

O. Brunner, *Adeliges Landleben und Europäischer Geist.* Salzburg 1949.

——, *Neue Wege der Sozialgeschichte.* Göttingen 1956.

J. C. Davis, *The decline of the Venetian nobility as a ruling class.* Baltimore 1962.

M. Berengo, *Nobili e mercanti nella Lucca del Cinquecento.* Turin 1965.

P. Deyon, 'A propos des rapports entre la noblesse francaise et la monarchie absolute pendant la première moitié du XVIIe siècle', *Revue Historique,* vol. CCXXXI (1964).

A. Domínguez Ortiz, *La sociedad espanola en el siglo XVII.* Vol. I. Madrid 1963.

H. Kellenbenz, 'German aristocratic entrepreneurship. Economic activities of the Holstein nobility in the 16th and 17th centuries', *Explorations in Entrepreneurial History,* vol. VI (1953-4).

Ruth Kelso, *The doctrine of the English gentleman in the sixteenth century.* Repr. Gloucester, Mass. 1964.

W. Kirchner, 'Entrepreneurial activity in Russian-Western trade relations during the sixteenth century', *Explorations in Entrepreneurial History,* vol. VIII (1955).

J. P. Labatut, *Les ducs et pairs de France aux XVIIe siècle: étude sociale.* Paris 1972.

R. Mousnier et al., eds., *Problèmes de stratification sociale. Deux cahiers de la Noblesse pour les Etats Généraux de 1649-1651.* Paris 1965.

E. L. Petersen, La crise de la noblesse danoise entre 1580 et 1660', *Annales,* vol. XXIII (1968).

H. Rosenberg, 'The rise of the Junkers in Brandenburg-Prussia 1410-1653', *American Historical Review,* vol. XLIX, nos. 1-2 (1943-4).

L. Stone, *The crisis of the aristocracy, 1558-1641.* Oxford 1965.

W. Lee Ustick, 'Changing ideals of aristocratic character and conduct in seventeenth-century England', *Modern Philology,* vol. XXX (1932-3).

P. de Vaissière, *Gentilshommes campagnards de l'Ancienne France.* Paris 1903.

S. J. Woolf, *Studi sulla nobila piemontese nell'epoca dell'assolutismo,* in *Memorie dell'Accademia delle Scienze di Torino,* ser. 4, no. 5 (1963).

L. P. Wright, 'The military orders in 16th and 17th century Spanish society', *Past and Present,* vol. XLIII (1969).

A. Wyczanski, *Studia nad folwarkiem szlacheckim w Polsce w latach 1500-1580* (Studies on the noble estates in Poland, 1500-1580). Warsaw 1960.

G. Zeller, 'La vie aventureuse des classes supérieures en France sous l'Ancien Régime: brigandage et piraterie', *Cahiers internationaux de Sociologie,* vol. XXVIII (1960).

——, 'Une notion de caractère historico-social: la dérogeance', *Cahiers internationaux de Sociologie,* vol. XXII (1957).

CHAPTER 5: THE EUROPEAN BOURGEOISIE

R. Baron, 'La bourgeoisie de Varzy au XVIIe siècle', *Annales de Bourgogne,* vol. XXXVI (1964).

L. Bulferetti, 'L'oro, la terra e la società', *Archivio Storico Lombardo,* ser. 8, vol. IV (1953).

B. Caizzi, *Il Comasco sotto il dominio spagnolo.* Como 1955.

J. Estèbe, 'La bourgeoise marchande et la terre à Toulouse au XVIe siècle', *Annales du Midi,* vol. LXXVI (1964).

J. Kaufmann-Rochard, *Origines d'une bourgeoisie russe.* Paris 1969.

H. P. Liebel, 'The bourgeoisie in southwestern Germany, 1500-1789: a rising class?', *International Review of Social History,* vol. X (1965).

R. Mousnier, *La vénalité des offices sous Henri IV et Louis XIII:* Rouen 1946.

——, 'Le trafic des offices à Venise', *Revue Historique de Droit français et étranger,* no. 4 (1952).

——, 'L'opposition politique bourgeoise à la fin du XVIe siècle et au début du XVIIe siècle., *Revue Historique,* vol. CCXII (1955).

C. Normand, *La bourgeoisie française au XVIIe siècle.* Paris 1908.

R. Pernoud, *Histoire de la bourgeoisie en France.* 2 vols. Paris 1962.

T. K. Rabb, *Enterprise and Empire. Merchant and gentry investment in the expansion of England 1575-1630.* Harvard 1967.

D. J. Roorda, 'The ruling classes in Holland in the 17th century', in *Britain and the Netherlands,* vol. II, Groningen 1962, ed. J. S. Bromley and E. Kossmann.

G. Roupnel, *La Ville et la Campagne au XVIIe siècle.* Paris 1922.

K. W. Swart, *Sale of offices in the seventeenth century.* Hague 1949.

H. R. Trevor-Roper, 'The Gentry', *Economic History Review* supplement (1953).

M. Venard, *Bourgeois et paysans au XVIIe siècle.* Paris 1958.

J. Vogt, 'A propos de la propriété bourgeoise en Alsace (XVIe-XVIIIe siècles), *Revue d'Alsace,* vol. C (1961).

CHAPTER 6: THE PEASANT ECONOMY

K. Blaschke, 'Das Bauernlegen in Sachsen', *Vierteljahrschrift für Sozial- und Wirtschaftsgeschichte,* vol. XLII (1955).

J. Blum, *Lord and peasant in Russia.* Princeton 1961.

F. L. Carsten, *The origins of Prussia.* Oxford 1954.

C. d'Eszlary, 'La situation des serfs en Hongrie de 1514 à 1848'. *Revue d'Historie économique et sociale,* no. 4 (1960).

C. J. Fuchs, *Der Untergang des Bauernstandes und das Aufkommen der Gutsherrschaften in Neuvorpommern und Rügen.* Strassburg 1888.

W. G. Hoskins, *The Midland peasant.* London 1957.

E. Kerridge, *The Agricultural Revolution.* London 1967.

Zs. Kirilly et al., 'Production et productivité agricoles en Hongrie à l'époque du féodalisme tardif (1550-1850)', in *Nouvelles études historiques publiées . . . par la Commission Nationale des Historiens Hongrois.* 2 vols. Budapest 1965.

F. Lütge, *Geschichte der deutschen Agrarverfassung vom frühen Mittelalter bis zum 19. Jahrhundert.* Stuttgart 1963.

A. Mika, 'Feudalni velkostatek v jižnich čechách (XIV-XVII stol.)', *Historicky Shornik* (The great feudal estates in southern Bohemia), vol. I (1973).

A. Miller, *Essai sur l'Histoire des Institutions agraires de la Russie centrale du XVIe au XVIIIe siècles.* Paris 1926.

Zs. P. Pach, *Die ungarische Agrarentwicklung im 16-17 Jahrhundert.* Budapest 1964.

P. Raveau, *L'Agriculture et les classes paysannes dans le Haut Poitou au XVIe siècle.* Paris 1926.

J. Rutkowski, *Histoire économique de la Pologne avant les partages.* Paris 1927.

D. Saalfeld, *Bauernwirtschaft und Gutsbetrieb in der vorindustriellen Zeit.* Stuttgart 1960.

N. Salomon, *La campagne de Nouvelle Castille à la fin du XVIe siècle.* Paris 1964.

S. O. Shmidt, 'K izucheniyu agrarnoy istorii Rossii XVI veka' (Research into the agrarian history of 16th century Russia), *Voprosi Istorii,* 1968 (5).

I. Sinkovics, 'Le servage héréditaire en Hongrie aux 16-17e siècles', in *La Renaissance et la Réformation en Pologne et en Hongrie,* Budapest 1963.

C. D. Skazkin, 'Osnovnie problemi tak nazivaemogo vtorogo izdaniya krepostnichestva v sredney i vostochnoy Evrope' (Basic problems of the so-called second serfdom in central and eastern Europe), *Voprosi Istorii,* 1958 (2).

B. H. Slicher van Bath, *The agrarian history of western Europe A.D. 500-1850.* London 1963.

——, 'The yields of different crops (mainly cereals) in relation to the seed c. 810-1820', *Acta Historiae Neerlandica,* vol. II, 1967.

R. E. F. Smith, *The enserfment of the Russian peasantry.* Cambridge 1968.

A. Soom, *Der Herrenhof in Estland im 17. Jahrhundert.* Lund 1954.

W. Stark, 'Ursprung und Aufstieg des landwirtschaftlichen Grossbetriebs in den Böhmischen Ländern' (no. 7 of Rechts- und

Staatswissenschaftliche Abhandlungen . . . der Deutschen Universität in Prag. 1934).

R. H. Tawney, *The agrarian problem in the sixteenth century.* London 1912.

J. Thirsk, ed., *The agrarian history of England and Wales,* vol. IV: *1500-1640.* Cambridge 1967.

H. H. Wächter, *Ostpreussische Domänenvorwerke im 16. und 17. Jahrhundert.* Würzburg 1958.

K. Winkler, *Landwirtschaft und Agrarverfassung im Fürstentum Osnabrück nach dem Dreissigjährigen Kriege.* Stuttgart 1959.

T. Wittmann, 'Los metales preciosos de América y la estructura agraria de Hungria a los fines del siglo XVI', *Acta Historica Szegediensis,* vol. XXIV (1967).

CHAPTER 7: NEW DIMENSIONS OF THE SPIRIT

It is impossible to select from the vast mass of books about the Counter Reformation. The social history of religion in this period is unfortunately almost totally unexplored. Three recent English discussions, and two older French works, are noted below.

J. Bossy, 'The Counter Reformation and the people of Catholic Europe', *Past and Present,* vol. XLVII (1970).

A. G. Dickens, *The Counter Reformation.* London 1968.

H. O. Evennett, *The Spirit of the Counter Reformation.* Cambridge 1968.

H. Bremond, *Histoire littéraire du sentiment religieux en France.* 11 vols. Paris 1920-36.

P. Coste, *Monsieur Vincent.* 3 vols. Paris 1934.

Witchcraft, a much-neglected subject, has at last begun to attract serious students. Mainly modern studies are mentioned here.

B. Baranowski, *Procesy Czarownic w Polse w XVII i XVIII wieku* (Witch-trials in 17th and 18th century Poland). Lódz 1952.

K. Baschwitz, *Hexen and Hexenprozesse.* Munich 1963.

G. F. Black, *A Calendar of Cases of Witchcraft in Scotland 1510-1727.* New York 1938.

G. Bonomo, *Caccia alle streghe.* Palermo 1959.

E. Brouette, 'La civilisation chrètienne du XVIe siècle devant le problème satanique', *Etudes carmélitaines,* vol. XXVII (1948).

——, 'La sorcellerie dans le comté de Namur au début de l'époque moderne (1509-1646)', *Annales de la Société archéologique de Namur.* vol. XLVII (1954).

L. Duparchy, 'La justice criminelle dans la terre de Saint-Oyend-de-Joux', *Mémoires de la Société d'Emulation du Jura,* 5th series, vol. II, 1891.

C. Ginzburg, *I benandanti. Ricerche sulla stregoneria.* Turin 1966.

W. Krämer, *Kurtrierische Hexenprozesse im. 16 und 17. Jahrhundert.* Munich 1959.

H. C. Lea, *Materials towards a history of witchcraft.* 3 vols. Repr. New York 1957.

G. L. Kittredge, *Witchcraft in Old and New England.* New York 1956.

C. L'Estrange Ewen, *Witch hunting and witch trials.* London 1929.

Théophile Louise, *De la sorcellerie et de la justice criminelle à Valenciennes (XVIe et XVIIe siècles).* Valenciennes 1861.

A. D. J. Macfarlane, *Witchcraft in Tudor and Stuart England.* London 1970.

R. Mandrou, *Magistrats et sorciers en France au XVIIe siècle.* Paris 1968.

R. Mudhembled, 'Sorcellerie, culture populaire et christianisme au XVIe siècle, principalement en Flandre et en Artois', *Annales,* Jan.-Feb. 1973.

W. Notestein, *A History of Witchcraft in England from 1558 to 1718.* Washington 1911.

Soldan-Heppe, *Geschichte der Hexenprozesse.* 2 vols. Ed. by M. Bauer. Munich 1911.

K. Thomas, Religion and the decline of magic. London 1971.

The only books on the decline of belief concern the upper classes of the time, and select individuals who can be judged by their writings.

J.-R. Charbonnel, *La pensée italienne au XVIe siècle et le courant libertin.* Paris 1919.

F. T. Perrens, *Les libertins en France au XVIIe siècle.* Paris 1896.

R. Pintard, *Le libertinage érudit dans la première moitié du XVIIe siècle.* 2 vols. Paris 1943.

R. H. Popkin, *The history of scepticism from Erasmus to Descartes.* Assen 1964.

G. Spini, *Ricerca dei Libertini.* Rome 1950.

F. Yates, *Giordano Bruno and the Hermetic tradition.* London 1964.

——, *The Rosicrucian Enlightenment.* London 1972.

For Basel and the Castellio tradition, some useful books include the following.

Peter Bietenholz, *Der italienische Humanismus und die Blütezeit des Buchdrucks in Basel.* Basel 1959.

F. Buisson, *Sébastien Castéllion, sa vie et son oeuvre (1515-1563).* 2 vols. Paris 1892.

P. Burckhardt, *Geschichte der Stadt Basel von der Zeit der Reformation bis zur Gegenwart.* Basel 1942.

F. Heer, *Die dritte Kraft.* Frankfurt 1960.

W. Kaegi, *Humanistische Kontinuität im konfessionellen Zeitalter.* Basel 1954.

J. Lecler, *Toleration and the Reformation.* 2 vols. London 1960.

The literature on Arminianism and Jansenism is immense. I am noting a couple of books on specific aspects.

G. Brandt, *History of the Reformation in and about the Low Countries.* 4 vols. London 1721.

L. Cognet, *Le Jansénisme.* Paris 1964.

L. Goldmann, *The hidden God*. London 1964.

W. Rex, *Essays on Pierre Bayle and religious controversy*. The Hague 1965.

CHAPTER 8: COMMUNICATION AND IMAGINATION

On literacy, the following works give references to other available material.

C. Cipolla, *Literacy and development in the west*. London 1969.

L. Stone, 'Literacy and education in England, 1640-1900', *Past and Present*, vol. XLII (1969).

On propaganda and journalism there is a large but uneven literature. I have found the following to be among the more relevant for my purposes.

E. A. Beller, *Propaganda in Germany during the Thirty Years War*. Princeton 1940.

D. W. Davies, *The world of the Elseviers 1580-1712*. The Hague 1954.

J. Frank, *The beginnings of the English newspaper 1620-60*. Harvard 1961.

M. N. Grand-Mesnil, *Mazarin, la Fronde et la Presse 1647-1649*. Paris 1967.

E. Hatin, *Histoire politique et littéraire de la Presse en France*. 8 vols. Paris 1859-61.

H.-J. Martin, *L'Apparition du Livre*. Paris 1958.

——,*Livre, pouvoirs et société à Paris au XVIIe siècle (1598-1701)*. 2 vols. Geneva 1969.

K. Schottenloher, *Bücher bewegten die Welt*. 2 vols. Stuttgart 1951-2.

——, *Flugblatt und Zeitung*. Berlin 1922.

F. S. Siebert, *Freedom of the press in England 1476-1776*. Urbana, Illinois 1952.

Scattered information on the social and political role of the European universities may be obtained from the few general studies that exist, but particularly from the invaluable published matriculation lists.

C. Borgeaud, *Histoire de l'Université de Genève*. Vol. I: *L'Académie de Calvin 1559-1798*. Geneva 1900.

K. Charlton, *Education in Renaissance England*. London 1965.

M. H. Curtis, *Oxford and Cambridge in transition 1558-1642*. Oxford 1959.

F. de Dainville, 'Collèges et fréquentation scolaire au XVIIe siècle', *Population (1957)*.

G. Erler, *Die Jüngere Matrikel der Universität Leipzig 1559-1809*. 3 vols. Leipzig 1909.

F. Eulenberg, *Die Frequenz der deutschen Universitäten*. Leipzig 1904.

——, 'Ueber die Frequenz der deutschen Universitäten in früherer Zeit', *Jahrbücher für Nationalökonomie und Statistik*, vol. LXVIII (1897).

S. d'Irsay, *Histoire des Universitiés françaises et étrangères.* 2 vols. Paris 1933-5.

R. L. Kagan, *Students and Society in early modern Spain,* Baltimore 1974.

——, 'Universities in Castile 1500-1700', *Past and Present,* vol., XLIX (1970).

H. F. Kearney, *Scholars and Gentlemen: Universities and Society in Pre-Industrial Britain, 1500-1700.* London 1970.

S. Merkle, *Die Matrikel der Universität Würzburg.* Leipzig 1922.

H. Schneppen, *Niederländische Universitäten und deutsches Geistesleben.* Munster 1960.

J. Simon, *Education and Society in Tudor England.* Cambridge 1966.

——, 'The social origins of Cambridge students 1603-1640', *Past and Present,* vol. XXVI (1963).

S. Stelling-Michaud ed., *Le Livre du Recteur de l'Académie de Genève (1559-1878).* Geneva 1959.

L. Stone, 'The educational revolution in England 1560-1640', *Past and Present,* vol. XXVIII (1964).

The historical context of Utopian schemes in the early modern period has never been adequately investigated. Historians tend to limit themselves to a study of the texts. The Mexican scholar Silvio Zavala, in his various studies on Vasco de Quiroga, is virtually the only one to have studied the social setting of Utopia.

M. L. Berneri, *Journey through Utopia.* London 1950.

L. Firpo, *Lo stato ideale della controriforma.* Bari 1957.

F. E. Held, *Christianopolis, an ideal state of the seventeenth century.* New York 1916.

M. Mörner, *The political and economic activities of the Jesuits in the La Plata region.* Stockholm 1953.

R. Ruyer, *L'Utopie et les Utopies.* Paris 1950.

CHAPTER 9: THE REVOLUTIONS OF STATE

Any standard political history will give a lengthy reading list for this section. I am doing no more than list one work for each area.

W. E. D. Allen, *The Ukraine: a history.* Cambridge 1940.

J. H. Elliott, *The revolt of the Catalans.* Cambridge 1963.

P. Geyl, *The Netherlands in the seventeenth century.* London 1964.

E. H. Kossmann, *La Fronde.* Leiden 1954.

R. B. Merriman, *Six contemporaneous revolutions.* Repr. New York 1963.

M. Roberts, 'Queen Christina and the general crisis of the seventeenth century', *Past and Present,* vol. XXII (1962).

I. Roots, *The Great Rebellion 1642-1660.* London 1966.

CHAPTER 10: POPULAR REBELLIONS 1550-1660

D. G. C. Allan, 'The rising in the West, 1628-31', *Economic History Review,* vol. V, no. 2 (1952).

S. I. Arkhangelsky, *Krestyanskie dvizheniya v Anglii v 40-50kh godakh XVII veka* (Peasant movements in England in the 1640-50s). Moscow 1960.

P. Barbier and F. Vernillat, *Histoire de France par les chansons.* 8 vols. Paris 1956.

A. R. Bayley, *The great civil war in Dorset 1642-1660.* Taunton 1910.

R. Boutruche, ed., *Bordeaux de 1453 à 1715.* Bordeaux 1966.

H. N. Brailsford, *The Levellers and the English Revolution.* London 1961.

Yu.V.Bromley, 'Vosstanie khorvatskikh i slovenskikh krestyan 1573 g.' (The 1573 rising of Croat and Slovene peasants), *Uchenie zapiski instituta Slavyanovedeniya,* vol. XI (1955).

K. V. Chistov, *Russkie narodnie sotsialno-utopicheskie legendy XVII-XIX vv* (Popular socio-utopian legends of 17th-19th century Russia). Moscow 1967.

A. Czerny, *Bilder aus der Zeit der Bauernunruhen in Oberösterreich.* Linz 1876.

——, *Der zweite Bauernaufstand in Oberösterreich 1595-1597.* Linz 1890.

A. Domínguez Oritz, *Alteraciones andaluzas.* Madrid 1973.

A. d'Ambrosio, *Masaniello: rivoluzione e controrivoluzione nel Reame di Napoli (1647-1648).* Milan 1962.

J. Diaz del Moral, *Historia de la agitaciones campesinas andaluzas.* Madrid 1929.

D. Eeckaute, 'Les brigands en Russie du XVIIe au XIXe siècle: mythe et réalité', *Revue d'Histoire moderne et contemporaine,* vol. XII (1965).

J. H. Elliott, 'Revolution and continuity in early modern Europe', *Past and Present,* vol. XLII (1969).

E. F. Gay, 'The Midland revolt and the inquisitions of depopulation of 1607', *Transactions of the Royal Historical Society,* vol. XVIII (1905).

G. Grüll, *Bauer, Herr und Landesfürst.* Linz 1963.

C. Hill, 'The many-headed monster in late Tudor and early Stuart political thinking', in C. H. Carter. ed., *From the Renaissance to the Counter Reformation.* London 1966.

C. Hill and E. Dell, eds., *The Good Old Cause.* London 1949, repr. 1970.

W. G. Hoskins, 'Harvest fluctuations and English economic history 1480-1619', *Agricultural History Review,* vol. II (1953-4).

——, 'Harvest fluctuations and English economic history 1620-1759', *Agricultural History Review,* vol. XVI (1968).

J. Jacquart, 'La Fronde des Princes dans la région parisienne et ses conséquences matérielles', *Revue d'Histoire moderne et contem-*

poraine, vol. VII (1960).

J. L. H. Keep, 'Bandits and the law in Muscovy', *Slavonic and East European Review,* vol. XXXV (1956-7).

E. Kerridge, 'The revolts in Wiltshire against Charles I', *Wiltshire Archaeological Magazine,* vol. LXVII (1958).

H. G. Koenigsberger, 'The revolt of Palermo in 1647', *Cambridge Historical Journal,* vol. VIII, no. 3 (1946).

H. Koht, *Les luttes des paysans en Norvège du XVIe au XIXe siècle.* Paris 1929.

L. Loewenson, 'The Moscow rising of 1648', *Slavonic and East European Review,* vol. XXVII (1948-9).

R. Mandrou, *Classes et luttes de classes en France au début du XVIIe siècle.* Florence 1965.

I. S. Miller, 'Krestyanskoe vosstanie v Podgale v 1651 godu' (The peasant uprising in Podhale in 1651), *Uchienie zapiski instituta Slavyanovedeniya,* vol. II (1950).

R. Mousnier, *Fureurs paysannes.* Paris 1967.

D. L. Pokhilevich, *Krestyane Belorussii i Litvy v XVI-XVII vv* (The peasantry of White Russia and Lithuania, 16th-18th centuries). Lwow 1957.

B. Porchnev, *Les soulèvements populaires en France 1613-1648.* Paris 1963.

J. Reglà and J. Fuster, *El bandolerisme català.* 2 vols. Barcelona 1962-3.

N. N. Samokhina, 'Feodalnaya reaktsiya v Avstrii vo vtoroy polovine XVI v. i krestyanskoe vosstanie 1595-1597 gg' (Feudal reaction in Austria in the late 16th century and the peasant rising of 1595-7). *Srednie Veka,* vol. v (1954).

M. Schipa, 'La cosi detta rivoluzione di Masaniello', *Archivio storico per le province napoletane,* vol. II (1916).

I. I. Smirnov, *Vosstanie Bolotnikova 1606-1607* (The Bolotnikov uprising 1606-7). Leningrad 1951.

P. Smirnov, *Pravitelstvo B. I. Morozova i vosstanie v Moskve 1648 g* (The government of B. Morozov and the Moscow rising of 1648). Tashkent 1929.

——, *Posadskie lyudi i ikh klassovaya borba do seredini XVII veka* (Tradespeople and their class struggle up to the mid-seventeenth century). 2 vols. Moscow 1947-8.

D. Mack Smith, *A history of Sicily.* 2 vols. London 1968.

W. Steinitz, *Deutsche Volkslieder demokratischen Charakters aus sechs Jahrhunderten.* 2 vols. Berlin 1954, 1962.

M. Steinmetz, *Deutschland von 1476 bis 1648.* Berlin 1965.

F. Stieve, *Der oberösterreichische Bauernaufstand des Jahres 1626.* 2 vols. Munich 1891.

R. Villari, *La rivolta antispagnola a Napoli. Le origini (1585-1647).* Bari 1967.

H. Wahlen and E. Jaggi, *Der schweizerische Bauernkrieg 1653.* Bern 1952.

G. Walter, *Histoire des paysans de France*. Paris 1963.

S. A. Westrich, *The Ormée of Bordeaux*. Baltimore 1972.

A. A. Zimin, 'Nekotorie voprosi istorii krestyanskoy voiny v Rossii v nachale XVII v' (Some queries on the history of the peasant war in early 17th century Russia), *Voprosi Istorii,* 1958 (3).

CHAPTER 11: THE VOICE OF THE DISPOSSESSED

W. Abel, *Der Pauperismus in Deutschland am Vorabend der industriellen Revolution*. Dortmund 1966. (This covers only a few pages).

Mr W. Ashley, *An introduction to English economic history and theory*. London 1925.

F. Aydelotte, *Elizabethan rogues and vagabonds*. Oxford 1913.

B. Bennassar, 'Economie et société a Ségovie au milieu du XVIe siècle', *Anuario de Historia Económica y Social,* vol. I, no. 1, 1968.

Y.-M. Bercé, 'Aspects de la criminalité au XVIIe siècle', *Revue Historique* (1968).

P. Boissonnade, *Le socialisme d'Etat. L'industrie et les classes industrielles en France (1453-1661)*. Paris 1927.

P. Bonenfant, *Le problème du pauperisme en Belgique à la fin de l'ancien régime*. Brussels 1934.

Piero Camporesi, ed., *Il Libro dei Vagabondi*. Turin 1973.

E. Chill, 'Religion and mendicity in seventeenth-century France', *International Review of Social History.* vol. VII (1962).

J.-P. Clébert, *The Gypsies*. London 1963.

A. Cormack, *Poor relief in Scotland*. Aberdeen 1923.

J. Cuvelier, 'Documents concernant la réforme de la bienfaisance à Louvain au XVIe siècle', *Bulletin de la Commission Royale d'Histoire,* vol. CV. Brussels 1940.

D. B. Davis, *The problem of slavery in western culture*. Cornell 1966.

J. Deleito y Piñuela, *La mala vida en la España de Felipe IV*. Madrid 1951.

P. Deyon, 'A propos du paupérisme au milieu du XVIIe siècle', *Annales,* 1967.

A. Dominguez Ortiz, 'La esclavitud en Castilla durante la edad moderna', *Estudios de Historia Social de España,* vol. II. Madrid 1952.

B. Geremek, 'La popolazione marginale tra il Medioevo e l'era *Lyon, 1534-1789.* Lyon 1971.

A. S. Green, *The making of Ireland and its undoing 1200-1600*. London 1908.

J. P. Gutton, *La société et les pauvres: l'exemple de la généralité de Lyon' 1534-1789.* Lyon 1971.

E. M. Hampson, *The treatment of poverty in Cambridgeshire 1597-1834*. Cambridge 1934.

R. W. Henderson, 'Sixteenth-century community benevolence: an attempt to resacralize the secular', *Church History,* 38 (1969).

P. Heupgen, *Documents relatifs à la réglementation de l'assistance publique à Mons du XVe au XVIIIe siècle.* Brussels 1929.

K. Hinze, *Die Arbeiterfrage zu Beginn des modernen Kapitalismus in Brandenburg-Preussen.* Berlin 1927.

M. Jiménez Salas, *Historia de la asistencia social en Espana en la edad moderna.* Madrid 1958.

W. K. Jordan, *Philanthropy in England 1480-1660.* London 1959.

Kentish Sources. IV: *The Poor.* Maidstone 1964.

E. von Kraemer, *Le type du faux mendiant dans les littératures romanes depuis le moyen age jusqu'au XVIIe siècle.* Helsinki 1944.

W. Kuhn, *Geschichte der deutschen Ostsiedlung in der Neuzeit.* Vol. I. Cologne 1955.

L. Lallemand, *Histoire de la Charité.* 4 vols. Paris 1910. Vol. IV: XVI-XIX century.

A. Landau, 'Die materiellen Zustände der untern Classen in Deutschland sonst und jetzt', in *Germania,* ed. E. M. Arndt. 2 vols. Vol. I. 1851-2.

H. Lapeyre, *La géographie de l'Espagne morisque.* Paris 1959.

E. M. Leonard, *The early history of English poor relief.* Cambridge 1900.

R. Livi, *La schiavitù domestica nei tempi di mezzo e nei moderni.* Padua 1928.

R. Mandrou, 'Les Français hors de France aux XVIe et XVIIe siècles', *Annales,* 1959.

——, 'Les Protestants français réfugiés à Genève après la Saint-Barthélemy', *Revue suisse d'Histoire,* vol. XVI (1966).

H. Mauersberg, *Wirtschafts- und Sozialgeschichte zentraleuropäischer Städte in neurer Zeit.* Gottingen 1960.

C. Maxwell, *Irish history from contemporary sources (1509-1610).* Dublin 1923.

E. Melling, ed., *Kentish sources.* VI: *Crime and punishment.* Maidstone 1969.

G. Panel, *Documents concernant les pauvres de Rouen.* 3 vols. Rouen 1917.

C. Paultre, *La repression de la mendicité et du vagabondage en France sous l'Ancien Régime.* Paris 1906.

C. A. Pescheck, *Die böhmischen Exulaten in Sachsen.* Leipzig 1857.

Sir W. Petty, *The political anatomy of Ireland.* London 1691.

I. Pinchbeck and M. Hewitt, *Children in English society.* Vol. I: *From Tudor times to the eighteenth century.* London and Toronto 1969.

J. F. Pound, 'An Elizabethan census of the poor', *University of Birmingham Historical Journal,* vol. VIII (1962).

B. Pullan, *Rich and poor in Renaissance Venice. The social institutions of a Catholic state to 1620.* Oxford 1971.

C. J. Ribton-Turner, *A history of vagrants and vagrancy.* London 1887.

A. Rumeu de Armas, *Historia de la prevision social en España.* Madrid 1944.

'Slavery in modern Scotland', *The Edinburgh Review,* vol. CLXXXIX (1899).

E. Scholliers, 'Vrije en onvrije arbeiders voornamelijk te Antwerpen in de 16e eeuw', *Bijdragen voor de Geschiedenis der Nederlanden,* vol. XI, no. 4 (1956).

A. Tenenti, 'Gli schiavi di Venezia alla fine del Cinquecento', *Rivista Storica Italiana* (1955).

I. A. A. Thompson, 'A map of crime in sixteenth-century Spain', *Economic History Review,* vol. XXI, no. 2 (1968). For a note on the basic fallacy in this otherwise useful article, see H. Kamen, 'Galley service and crime in sixteenth-century Spain', *ibid.,* vol. XXII, no. 2 (1969), pp. 304-5.

C. Verlinden, *L'esclavage dans l'Europe mediévale.* Vol. I: *Péninsule Ibérique — France.* Bruges 1955.

A. Vexliard, *Introduction à la sociologie du vagabondage.* Paris 1956.

H. C. White, *Social criticism in popular religious literature of the 16th century.* Repr. New York 1965.

E. Winter, *Die Tschechische und Slowakische Emigration in Deutschland im 17. und 18. Jahrhundert.* Berlin 1955.

A. Yakovlev, *Kholopstvo i kholopi v moskovskom gosudarstve XVII v* (Slavery and slaves in seventeenth-century Muscovy). Vol. I. Moscow 1943.

CHAPTER 12: THE TURN OF THE TIDE

Since this chapter looks forward to the theme of absolutism without developing it fully, I have noted only a few general discussions here.

F. Carsten, *Princes and Parliaments in Germany.* Oxford 1959.

F. Hartung and R. Mousnier, 'Quelques problèmes concernant la monarchie absolue', *Relazioni del X Congresso Internazionale di Scienze Storiche: Storia Moderna.* Vol. IV. Florence 1955.

R. Hatton, *Europe in the Age of Louis XIV.* London 1969.

M. Roberts, *Sweden as a great power.* London 1968.

J. Stoye, *Europe unfolding 1648-1668.* London 1969.

INDEX

banking, 111-16
Barbary Company, 135
Barcelona, 113, 205
Barrionuevo, Jerónimo de, 442
Basel, 17, 314, 412, 466; capitalism, 96, 106, 117; toleration, 285-91
Báthory, Stephen, 357
Bavaria, 27, 54, 237, 242-3, 390
Baxter, Richard, 92, 216, 344
Bay, Michel de, 295
Bayle, Pierre, 281, 294
Beauvais, 15, 17, 88, 165; bourgeoisie, 183, 186, 193; peasantry, 39, 110, 228, 230
Beekow, 53
Beggars Brotherhood. 279-80, 442-5
Behaut, Louis de, 99
Béjar, duke of, 152-3, 154
Belgium, decline in, 41-2; wages in, 75; see also Netherlands
Bellarmine, cardinal, 258
Benavente, count of, 166, 191
Berkeley, Lord Henry, 168
Bern, 411-13
Bernal Diaz, 5, 60
Bernard, Samuel, 105
Bernoully, Jacob, 98
Bérulle, Pierre de, 255, 260-1, 295
Bethlen Miklos, 149
Beza (Théodore de Béze), 287
Bilbao, 32-4
bills of exchange, 113, 120
Binsfeld, Peter, 265
birth control see contraception
birth rate, 14-20
Bisignano, prince of, 166, 424
Blessed Sacrament, Company of the, 448, 452
Blommaert, Abraham, 102
Bodin, Jean, 50, 64, 66-8, 205, 265, 273, 330
Bodley, Sir Thomas, 326
Boguet, Henri, 265, 270, 273, 435
Bohemia, 27, 30, 108, 237, 251, 263, 377, 471-3
Bologna, 287
Bolotnikov, 384-6, 417-18, 426
Bonvisi, firm of, 97
Bordeaux, 146, 279, 314, 441; Fronde in, 348-9, 404-5, 413, 417
Borromeo, family, 209
Bosch, Hieronymus, 277
Bothwell, earl of, 274
Bourdaloue, Louis, 305

bourgeoisie, definition of, 181-3; capitalism, 109, 125, 150, 213-14, 248-9; and nobles, 149, 159-71; economic life, 183-7; as rentiers, 187-91, 191-6, 199, 205-8; land, 189-94; office-holding, 194-8
Bourges, 287
Boyle, Richard, 57
Boyle, Robert, 12, 474
Bradley, Humphrey, 104, 221
Brahe, Tycho, 317
Brandenburg,53,85; nobles, 149, 210-11, 214, 479, 482; peasants, 236-40, 248-9
Brauw, Johan de, 103
Brazil, 103, 106
Bremen, 27, 292
Breun, Dominicus, 99
Brichenteau, Nicolas de, 165
Briers, Daniel de, 99, 101
Bristol, 35
Brueghel the Elder, Pieter, 277
Bruges, 103, 466
Brunel, Olivier, 103
Brunner, George, 376
Brunswick, 224, 229, 232, 245
Bruno, Giordano, 282-3, 317
Brussels, 42, 103, 429
Bucer, Martin, 436
bullion see America; and economic growth, 129-30, 133, 208
Burghley, Lord, 176
Burghley House, 156
Burgos, 33
Burgundy, 41, 182, 270

Caen, 393
cahiers, 176
Caillot, Nicolas, 196
Cajetan, cardinal, 94
Calabria, 166
Calahorra, 276
Callot, Jacques, 40
Calvin, John, 285-6, 287
Calvinism, 327; and capitalism, 89-95; and Castellio, 290-1; and Arminianism, 292-4
Cambridge, 315, 317-18, 324
Cameron, John, 294
Campanella, Tommaso, 283, 333, 335
Camus, Jean, 199
Canisius, St Peter, 259, 305
Cano, Sebastián del, 10
Capdebosc family, 15

capitalism, 89-135; Calvinism, 89-95; money, 109-16; commerce, 116-22; industry, 122-7; bullion, 128-31; war, 132-5; agriculture, 131-2; monopoly, 125, 134

Caprarola, 158

Carafa, 166

Cardoso, Ruy Fernández, 106

Carmelites, 261

Carré, John, 102

Casas, Bartolomé de las, 59-60, 330-1, 459

Casparus, Student, 389

Cassinis, Samuele de, 266, 278

Castellio, Sebastian, 285-91

Castile, 151, 190-1; population, 14, 17-19, 26, 47; inflation, 64-71; rents, 78, 81; decline, 84-8; cortes, 64, 139, 230, 483

Castillo de Bobadilla, 145

Catalonia, 276, 351-3, 378-80

Cateau-Cambrésis, peace of, 82

Cécile, Pierre, 192

Cellórigo, Martín González de, 47, 69, 206-8, 213

Celsi, Mino, 288

censi, 188-9

censorship, 303, 306, 312-15

censos, 188-91, 206-7, 230

Cervantes, 378, 443, 469

Chalais, count of, 176

Champagne, 143, 453

Chantal, St Jeanne de, 262-3

Charles I of England, 178, 340-4, 348, 353, 360-1

Charles II of Spain, 178

Charles V, emperor, 11, 66, 433

Charles X of Sweden, 357-8, 480

Charles Emmanuel II, 180, 480

Chatsworth, 156

Cheke, Sir John, 436

Chevreuse, duke of, 415

Child, Sir Josiah, 121

China, 129

Christian IV of Denmark, 162

Christina of Sweden, 178, 353-7, 359, 361

Cigales, Antonio de, 190

Cimento academy, 318

Cinq-Mars, marquis of, 176

Cisneros, cardinal, 50, 258

Clarendon, earl of, 344, 361

Claver, St Peter, 459

Clayworth, 52

Clement IX, 296

clocks, 11-13

Clubmen, 394-6

Cogenhoe, 52

coinage *see* debasement

Coke, Roger, 121

Colert, 6, 35, 121, 133, 146, 481

Coler, Jacob, 222

Coligny, admiral, 466

Cölmer, 237, 240

Cologne, 16, 44, 55, 98, 101

Colonna, Marcantonio, 153

Columbus, Christopher, 8

Colyton, 17, 46

Comenius, 300, 316

commerce, 116-22; English, 87, 117-22, 130, 133-4, 213; Dutch, 86-7, 117-22, 130, 133; and nobles, 145-51; with America, 128-9

Como, 188, 208, 232

compagnonnage, 127

Comuneros, 173, 205

Condé, prince of, 153, 174, 249, 297, 348, 349, 405

Constantinople, 87

Contarini, cardinal, 259

Conti, prince of, 156, 297

contraception, 19-20

conversos, 107, 206, 280

Coornhert, Dirck, 290-1

Copernicus, 302, 474

copper, 83, 85

Córdoba, 402-3, 414, 418, 426

Corneille, 158

cortes of Castile, 64, 139, 230, 483

Cortés, Hernan, 5, 11, 59

Cossacks, 56, 357-8; and popular revolt, 357, 381, 385, 409, 417

Courtrai, 42

Coventry, 183

Coymans, Balthasar, 103

Cracow, 289, 410

Cramer von Claussbruch, Heinrich, 99-100

Cranfield, 83

credit, 109-16

Cremona, 96

Cremonini, Cesare, 283

crime, 439-45

crisis, general 3, 84-8, 338-40, 364 474-7; population crisis, 24, 26-7, 46-8; *see also* depression

Croatia, 368, 424

Cromwell, Oliver, 108, 135, 142, 147,

Monferrat, 140
monopoly, 125, 134
Montaigne, 445
Montaud, Nicolas de, 199
monti, 188
Montmorency, duke of, 176
Montmorency-Bouteville, 143
Montpellier, 27, 191, 394
Moors, 99, 412-13
Moravian, Brethren, 332-3
More, Sir Thomas, 61, 303, 329-30
Morel, Jean, 390
Moriscos, 280, 457, 464, 468-9, 473
Morocco, 56
Moroni family, 209
Morozov, Boris, 209, 406-8, 416, 420
Moscow, 85, 169, 242, 385-6, 406-7, 416-20
Mothe, Jean de la, 53
Motolinia, Fray Torbio de, 5
Motte, Lucien, 186
Moucheron, Balthasar de, 103
Münchhausen, Stats von, 149, 157
Mun, Thomas, 184-5
Muzio, Girolamo, 93, 130, 202

Nalivaiko, Severin, 358, 376
Namur, 266, 271
Napier, John, 277
Napierski, Alexander, 409, 417
Naples, 23-27, 30, 33, 64, 82, 214, 379; nobility, 160, 166, 178; revolts of, 353, 369, 387-8, 419-21.
Naudé, Gabriel, 281-2
Navarrete, Pedro, 351, 435
Navigation Act, 1651, 121, 132
Nelli, Fabio, 32
Neri, St Philip, 260
Netherlands, 38-9, 55, 82, 126, 134, 306, 433; refugees, 98-105
Nevers, duke of, 159
Newcastle, 35, 123
newspapers, 309-12
Newton, Sir Isaac, 474
Nidaros, 367
Nîmes, 367
Nobili, Giancinto, 444
nobility, 139-80, 349-50, 356; family structure, 14, 17-19; violence 141-5, 173; in business, 134-51, 210; conspicuous consumption, 151-9, 160; as bandits, 142-3, 377; as land-owners, 152, 160-71, 235; and rebuilding, 156-8; and price

revolution, 159-71; and crown, 171-80, 360-1; inflation of honours, 177-80; debts of, 190-4; bourgeois definition of, 217; and serfdom, 239-51; and education, 321-9; hatred of, 360-1, 425; and popular revolts, 387, 392, 393, 425-6; and absolutism, 477-84
noblesse de robe, 192, 197-8, 349; *see also* nobility
Noiron-les-Cîteaux, 249
Norfolk, duke of, 147, 161
Normandy, 197, 199, 392-3, 419, 425, 430, 434
Northampton, 201
Norway, peasants of, 367, 424
Norwich, 101, 183, 301, 430, 449
Noue, Francois de la, 142, 155-6, 158, 281
Nuremburg, 46, 431

Ocampo, Florián de, 70
Ochino, Bernardino, 259, 287-8
Oecolampadius, 286
offices, income from, 152, 161-2, 176, 183-7; sale of, 177-8, 195-8, 349
Oglander, Sir John, 168
Oldenbarnevelt, 292
Olderburg, Anton I von, 149
Olivares, 85, 166, 174, 213, 231, 330, 351-3, 361
Olomouc, 110
Oporin, 289
oprichnina, 160, 169, 275, 384
Ordónez, Pedro, 280
Oropesa, count of, 154
Orsini family, 153, 166
Ortenburg, count of, 387
Ortiz, Luis, 69
Os, Dirck van, 103
Ostorog family, 170
Osuna, duke of, 164, 166
Oudenarde, 42
Ovando, Juan de, 83
Overijssel, 103
Overton, Richard, 397
Oviedo, Ferdández de, 60
Oxenstierna, 135
Oxford, earl of, 156; university of, 317, 320-1, 324-5

Padua, 283; university of, 287, 317,

325-6
Palavicino, Horatio, 97
Palermo, 27, 460; revolt, 398-9
papacy, 153, 155, 158
Paraguay, 59, 331
Paris, 13, 27, 41, 126, 306, 370;
   Parlement of, 13, 125, 193, 217,
   260, 304, 348, 362, 404, 431;
   poverty in, 429, 437, 449, 452; and
   Fronde, 348-50, 405, 414
Parlement, of Bordeaux, 405; of
   Lyon, 147; of Paris see Paris
Parliament, Barebones, 345; Long,
   59, 344-5; Rump, 133, 345
Patin, Guy, 281
Patrizi, Francesco, 330
Paulette, 196
Paulmier, Jean, 368-9, 419, 423
peasantry, 218-51; wages in kind, 110;
   expropriation, 80-1, 226, 235-42,
   247; obligations of, 229, 236-8, 240;
   serfdom, 235-51; revolts, 365-426
Pellicer, José, 380
Pellizzari family, 96
Pembroke, earl of, 154
Percy estates, 161
Pereyaslavl, treaty of, 359
Pérez, Antonio, 174
Pérez. Marcus, 107, 109
Perkins, William, 437
Perrière, Guillaume de la, 140
Pestalozzi, Giulio Cesare, 101
Peter, Hugh, 59
Petre estates, 78
Petty, Sir William, 224, 468
Philip II, 11, 66, 82-4, 115, 145, 175,
   185, 205, 303, 449
Philip III, 66, 82, 154, 351, 378, 469
Philip IV, 159, 166, 174, 177, 436
Picardy, 40
picaro, 442-3
Piccolomini, Alfonso, 144, 377
Piedmont, 161, 180, 479-80
Pigafetta, Antonio, 5
Pignatelli family, 166
piracy, 128-9; in Mediterranean, 87-8,
   134-5, 460-1
Pizarro, 7, 59
plague, *see* epidemics
Plantin, Christophe, 126
Podhale, 409, 416
Poitou, 73, 78, 110, 182, 393, 414
Poland, 47, 155, 263, 289; nobles,
   169-71, 232-4; inflation, 66, 71, 234,

242-3; serfdom, 245, 246, 250; and
   Ukraine, 357-9
politiques, 290
Pomerania, 45, 149, 157, 210, 235,
   237, 239, 247, 249
pomeshchiki, 170, 238, 242
pomestye, 170
poor relief, 432, 446-55
popular revolts, 365-425; noble leadership of, 385, 392, 394, 424;
   population, 14-48; growth, 20-7,
   40-1, 52-3; decay, 27-48; mobility,
   51-61, 431-6, 464; and price
   revolution, 70-1
Port-Royal, 296
Portugal, empire of, 4; merchants
   from, 98, 107-8; slavery in, 456
postal service, 7-8
Pouch, Captain, 383, 422
poverty, 427-56; *see also* poor relief
Prague, 101, 470
price revolution, 61-84; causes, 64-71;
   and nobles, 159-64
printers, 13, 126, 307, 310, 312
printing, 299-307
propaganda, 304-15
Prussia, 157, 210, 237, 239, 243, 246
Prütze, Balthasar, 241
Prynne, William, 310
Pskov, 242
Puritans, 305, 321, 342-6

Quevedo, Francisco de, 442
Quiroga, Vasco de, 61, 330-1

Radziwill family, 170, 409
Rákóczi estates, 245
Ralegh, Sir Walter, 118, 159, 173
Rambouillet, marquis of, 153
Ramée, Pierre de la, 287
Ramillon family, 182
Ramusio, Gian Battista, 4
Rancé, abbé de, 255
Rantzau, Heinrich, 148, 234
Ratzeburg, 53
refugees, 464-73; and capitalism,
   95-109; from Italy, 96-8; from
   Belgium, 98-106, 465; from France,
   106, 465; from Spain, 467-9
Regensburg, colloquy of, 256
Reichenstein, 374-5, 418
Rémy, Nicolas, 265, 270, 273

Viau, Théophile de, 281
Vicenza, 96
Vieira, Antonio, 459
Vienna, 71, 73-6, 233, 374
Vincent de Paul, St, 19, 40, 261, 296, 302, 346, 452
Virginia colony, 57-8
Virginia Company, 214
votchina, 170, 407

wages, 72-6; in kind, 110
Walker, Clement, 308
Walker, Edward, 178
Wallenstein, 101, 148
Walsingham, Sir Francis, 174
Walwyn, William, 313, 397, 426
war, effect on population, 39-46; cost of, 81-4; and capitalism, 133-5
wars of religion in France, 40, 140, 159-60, 290-1
Warboys case, 269
Warsaw, 71, 233
Weber thesis, 89-94
Weinbuch, Caspar, 389
Weissenburg, 54
Welsers, 114
Wemyss, earl of, 148
Wentworth, Thomas, 341, 361
Werth, Johann von, 44
Weyer, Johann, 278
Whitgift, archbishop, 437
Whittington, Dick, 55-6
Wigston Magna, 78, 227
William the Silent, 107
William II of Orange, 354-5, 363
Willinger, Achaz, 388
Wilson, Thomas, 50, 161
Winningen, 271
Winstanley, Gerrard, 284, 317, 333, 335, 413, 478
Winthrop, John, 56
Wiśnowiecki, Jerome, 358
witchcraft, 263-78, 290
Witte, Arnold, 101
Witte, Hans, 101, 109
Wittenberg, 326
Witt, de, 203-4, 355
Wolfenbüttel, 232
Wünschendorf, 239
Württemberg, 45, 212, 290
Würzburg, 270, 315

Xavier, St Francis, 5, 7, 262

yeomen, 81, 225
Yermak, 56, 382
yield ratios, 221-2, 243
Ypres, 448

Zagreb, 368
Zahara, 443
Zametti, banker, 97
Zanino, Evangelista, 96
Zeller, Christoph, 388
Zemsky Sober, 170, 359, 362, 408, 483
Zinzendorf, Freiherr von, 387
Zumárraga, Juan de, 329
Zurich, 24, 54, 96, 410, 465
Zurita, Alonso de, 315